PROGRAM
DERIVATION

INTERNATIONAL COMPUTER SCIENCE SERIES

Consulting editors   **A D McGettrick**   University of Strathclyde

                              J van Leeuwen   University of Utrecht

SELECTED TITLES IN THE SERIES

The UNIX System   *S R Bourne*

Software Specification Techniques   *N Gehani and A D McGettrick (Eds)*

Modula-2: Discipline & Design   *A H J Sale*

Parallel Programming   *R H Perrott*

The Specification of Computer Programs   *W M Turski and T S E Maibaum*

Performance Measurement of Computer Systems   *P McKerrow*

Syntax Analysis and Software Tools   *K J Gough*

Concurrent Programming   *N Gehani and A D McGettrick (Eds)*

Functional Programming   *A J Field and P G Harrison*

Comparative Programming Languages   *L B Wilson and R G Clark*

Distributed Systems: Concepts and Design   *G Coulouris and J Dollimore*

Software Prototyping, Formal Methods and VDM   *S Hekmatpour and D Ince*

C Programming in a UNIX Environment   *J Kay and R Kummerfeld*

Clausal Form Logic: An Introduction to the Logic of Computer Reasoning
T Richards

An Introduction to Functional Programming through Lambda Calculus
G Michaelson

Software Engineering (3rd Edn)   *I Sommerville*

High-Level Languages and their Compilers   *D Watson*

Interactive Computer Graphics: Functional, Procedural and Device-Level
Methods   *P Burger and D Gillies*

Elements of Functional Programming   *C Reade*

Software Development with Modula-2   *D Budgen*

PROGRAM DERIVATION

The Development of Programs From Specifications

Geoff Dromey

Griffith University, Brisbane, Australia

ADDISON-WESLEY
PUBLISHING
COMPANY

Sydney · Wokingham, England · Reading, Massachusetts
Menlo Park, California · New York · Don Mills, Ontario
Amsterdam · Bonn · Singapore · Tokyo · Madrid · San Juan

Cover designed by Crayon Design of Henley-on-Thames
and printed by The Riverside Printing Co. (Reading) Ltd.
Typeset by Quorum Technical Services, Cheltenham UK.
Printed in Singapore.

First printed 1989.

British Library Cataloguing in Publication Data
Dromey, R.G. 1946–
    Program derivation: the development of
    programs from specifications. -
    (International computer science series)
    1. Computer systems. Programs. Design
    I. Title   II. Series
    005.1'2

    ISBN 0-201-41624-7

Library of Congress Cataloging in Publication Data
Dromey, R. G., 1946–
    Program derivation.

    (International computer science series)
    Bibliography: p.
    Includes index
    1. Electronic digital computers--
Programming.   I. Title.   II. Series.
    QA76.6.D77   1989   005.1   88-8055
    ISBN 0-201-41624-7

Programming Courses should teach methods of design and construction, and the selected examples should be such that a gradual development can be nicely demonstrated.

N. Wirth

Preface

The primary aim of this book is to make the principles of program derivation from specifications accessible to undergraduates early in their study of computing science.

The proliferation of personal computers in the home and in schools has meant that there are large numbers of people who have had exposure to using computers and even to 'writing' programs in languages like BASIC. This situation has left many people with the misconception that computing science education is focused upon the coding and debugging of computer programs, whereas this is far from the ideals and objectives of the science. For too long people have tried to learn how to build programs without the support of a rigorous mathematical and logical framework. As a consequence, the cost of developing high-quality software remains at a premium. There is but one chance of overcoming these problems, and that is to recognize computing science for what it really is, a mathematically-based discipline concerned with the application of rigorous methods for the specification, design, and implementation of computer systems.

It is one thing to be able to write down a few pages of program statements but it is an entirely different matter to produce correct programs that provably satisfy their specifications. That anything less is acceptable merely reflects the stage of development of the discipline.

What we have to offer in this book is not something that can cure all these problems. The intent has been to provide an introduction to the level of precision, habits of mind, and modes of reasoning, necessary for producing high-quality verifiable software at a reasonable cost.

There are plenty of computing science academics who have recognized the need for rigour and have introduced the ideas of formal program derivation into their courses. This in itself is not enough. Too often the formal aspects of program derivation are not introduced to students until long after they 'know' how to write programs. The implicit message conveyed by a belated introduction to formal program derivation is that it is not an essential part of the discipline – how could it be when they already know how to write programs! Essential things must always come early in a course if they are to be taken seriously. Introducing program derivation right from the outset is a key challenge facing computing science educators. We have to face this challenge if we are to gain the advantages that formal program derivation can deliver.

There is no question with the argument that it is easier to teach the formal aspects of program derivation later in a course rather than near the beginning, but this sort of reasoning completely misses the point. It has been my repeated experience that very few students respond in the way we would hope to a belated introduction to formal program derivation. They learn the techniques but seldom attempt to apply them beyond the class exercises they are given. This is a sorry state of affairs that can only be rectified by an early exposure to formal program derivation.

The best time to do this is at the start of a university or college course although some will prefer to offer material of this level in the second or third years of a course.

There are two key ideas in this book. The first is a model for the stepwise development of programs. *It is shown that programs can be constructed by a sequence of refinements, each of which establishes the postcondition, or goal, of the computation for progressively weaker preconditions. The model makes a direct link between specifications and the stepwise refinement process.* Each refinement is guided by a transformation that weakens the precondition specification for which the postcondition is established. The state model for computation provides the foundation upon which this model for stepwise refinement is built. Interpreting this model for stepwise refinement directly, a program may be constructed by a sequence of refinements each of which expands the set of initial states for which the postcondition is established. This strategy realizes a limiting form of top-down design.

The second key idea in this book *establishes the connections between data structure, the refinement process, and the program control structure that the refinement process yields.* The reason for trying to make these connections is to ensure that the control structure of derived programs matches the structure of the data to be processed. Programs that possess this characteristic are usually much easier to understand and maintain.

Presenting these key ideas is not by itself enough to make formal program derivation palatable to novice programmers. The real key lies in the nature of the exercises and examples that are considered. Formal program derivation involves considerable notation and several difficult concepts. If these notations and concepts are simply presented to students and then the students are asked to work with and apply them, the chances of success are very small. Students must be eased into formal program derivation. One way of doing this is to start by focusing on *interpretation* rather than application. Only after students have had very considerable practice at interpreting formal specifications are they ready to start writing and using them in program derivation.

The logic and mathematical groundwork provided in Chapters 2, 3 and 4, together with their accompanying exercises, go a long way towards building students' confidence to tackle program derivation. Without paying serious attention to the exercises there is little hope of learning how to derive programs. It would have been easy to write this book and assume the requisite logic and mathematical background. This path has not been taken for several reasons. Firstly, most treatments of mathematics and logic have not been designed to support the writing of specifications and the derivation of programs. What is needed to support program derivation is a treatment of discrete mathematics that presents it as both an abstract reasoning calculus and as a notation suited for formal manipulation. As a consequence, the treatment must be slow and thorough if students are to acquire the level of mathematical maturity needed to apply effectively formal methods to program derivation.

Throughout the book Dijkstra's 'guarded commands' *program design language* has been used to express derived algorithms. The decision to opt for guarded commands rather than use a conventional *program implementation language* like Pascal or Modula-2 is not one that has been taken lightly. There are two principal reasons for making this choice. Firstly, deriving algorithms directly into an implemented programming language provides too much unnecessary distraction. During the derivation process we need to focus only on design considerations and not on implementation details. Subsequent translation from guarded commands to a standard programming language is essentially a mechanical process (automatic or otherwise) that is easy to do after the hard work of derivation is complete. The second important reason for opting to use guarded commands is that it provides a very simple and concise notation for expressing algorithms.

We suggest that there is strong pedagogical merit in the overall stance that we have taken.

There are several ways in which this book can be used to study program derivation:

Programme 1   Abridged introduction to program derivation

To obtain a focused but limited introduction to the main ideas of program derivation the following material would need to be covered along with the accompanying exercises:

Chapter 1   All sections
Chapter 2   Sections 2.3 and 2.4
Chapter 3   Section 3.2
Chapter 4   All sections
Chapter 5   All sections
Chapter 6   A selection of examples from each section

This treatment would be deficient particularly with regard to the background needed for advanced program specification and derivation.

Programme 2   Introduction to program derivation

For those who have previously had a course in discrete mathematics, Chapters 2 and 3 could be omitted from Programme 1 and selected examples from Chapters 7, 8 and 9 could be added.

Programme 3   A second course in program derivation

Those who have previously had an introduction to program specification and derivation would need to cover the following material:

Chapter 5	Sections 5.5, 5.6 and 5.7
Chapter 6	Sections 6.1 to 6.4
Chapters 7–12	All sections

The examples in the later chapters tend to be more advanced. Also, within chapters the later examples are usually more difficult.

Programme 4   Formal program derivation

Programmers, computer science graduates and others wishing to gain an understanding of formal methods of program derivation might be best advised first to read Chapter 1 and then study:

Chapter 4	All sections
Chapter 5	All sections
Chapters 6–12	Selected examples as required

In pursuing this programme it would probably be necessary to refer back to Chapters 2 and 3 from time to time.

As a final word on using this book, proficiency in specifying problems and formally deriving programs only comes with lots and lots of practice – there are no shortcuts.

The time for a more formal and more careful approach to programming has long since arrived! The words of Victor Hugo sum up the present situation:

There is one thing stronger than all the armies of the world,
and that is an idea whose time has come.

Acknowledgements

There have been many friends, colleagues, and students who have helped me with this book. I am particularly indebted to David Gries and Jifeng He for a number of stimulating discussions in the early stages of this work. I would also like to thank Wlad Turski for helpful comments on some of the ideas in Chapter 5. I also appreciate the helpful suggestions for improving the manuscript made by David Billington, Trevor Chorvat, Andrew McGettrick, Tony Hoare, and a number of anonymous referees.

I would like to thank the following eminent Computer Scientists for permission to use their words of wisdom at the beginnings of Chapters:

R. W. Floyd, C. A. R. Hoare, F. P. Brooks, E. W. Dijkstra, W. Turski.

The professionalism of Stephen Troth in bringing this manuscript to publication has been of the highest order. His support and encouragement together with that of editor Andrew McGettrick and production editor Sheila Chatten is deeply appreciated. I would also like to thank Helen Whiter, Olwen Schubert, Kathryn Stanford and Lenore Olsen for their care and patience in preparing the manuscript.

Finally I would like to thank my wife, Aziza, and daughter, Tashen, for their support and understanding throughout this project.

R. Geoff Dromey

Brisbane, Australia
June 1988

Publisher's acknowledgements

The publisher would like to thank the following for giving their permission to reproduce some of their material:

Cambridge University Press for R.G. Dromey, 1987, Derivation of Sorting Algorithms from a Specification, *The Computer Journal,* **30**(6); R.G. Dromey and T. Chorvat, 1989, Structure Clashes – An Alternative to Program Inversion, *The Computer Journal*(in press).

The Institute of Electrical and Electronic Engineers, Inc. for R.G. Dromey, 1988, Systematic Program Development, *Transactions on Software Engineering,* **14**(1). (© 1988 IEEE).

John Wiley and Sons Limited for R.G. Dromey, 1985, Program Development by Inductive Stepwise Refinement *and* Forced Termination of Loops, *Software – Practice and Experience,* **15**(1), pp.1–28 *and* 29–39. Reproduced by permission of John Wiley and Sons Limited.

Macmillan Publishing Company for a quotation from *Aims of Education and Other Essays* by Alfred North Whitehead. Copyright 1929 by Macmillan Publishing Company, renewed 1957 by Evelyn Whitehead. Reprinted with permission.

Contents

Preface   **vii**

Part 1   TOOLS FOR PROGRAM DERIVATION

Chapter 1   Introduction   **3**

1.1	The Problem of Programming	3
1.2	The Role of Mathematics and Logic	5
1.3	How Programs Are Derived	7
1.4	Program Derivation – A First Look	20
	Summary	24
	Bibliography	24

Chapter 2   Logic for Program Design   **27**

2.1	Introduction	27
2.2	Specification Methods	27
2.3	Propositional Calculus	32
2.4	Predicate Calculus	54
2.5	Proof Methods	76
	Summary	81
	Exercises	82
	Bibliography	90

Chapter 3   Mathematics for Specification   **91**

3.1	Introduction	91
3.2	Set Concepts	92
3.3	Relations	112
3.4	Functions	122
3.5	Bags	139
3.6	Sequences and EBNF	144
3.7	Mathematical Induction	158
	Summary	176

| | Exercises | 178 |
| | Bibliography | 185 |

Chapter 4   Specification of Programs   **187**

4.1	Introduction	187
4.2	Preconditions	188
4.3	Postconditions	193
4.4	Loop Invariants	206
4.5	Variant Functions	219
	Summary	226
	Exercises	227
	Bibliography	242

Part 2   MODEL FOR PROGRAM DERIVATION

Chapter 5   Program Derivation   **245**

5.1	Introduction	245
5.2	State Model	247
5.3	The Weakest Precondition	250
5.4	Guarded Commands	265
5.5	Program Derivation – An Example	282
5.6	Model for Program Derivation	293
5.7	Systematic Decomposition	312
	Summary	318
	Exercises	319
	Bibliography	323

Chapter 6   From Specifications to Programs   **325**

6.1	Introduction	325
6.2	Specification Transformations	328
6.3	Generating Sub-problems	330
6.4	Generating Auxiliary Problems	333
6.5	Basic Examples	340
6.6	Simple Loops	345
6.7	Nested Loops	368
	Summary	394
	Exercises	395
	Bibliography	396

Part 3   THE DERIVATION OF PROGRAMS

Chapter 7   Searching   **399**

| 7.1 | Introduction | 399 |

7.2	Linear Search	400
7.3	Binary Search	402
7.4	Two-dimensional Search	407
7.5	Common Element Search	411
7.6	Rubin's Problem	414
7.7	Saddleback Search	418
	Summary	420
	Exercise	420
	Bibliography	421

Chapter 8	**Partitioning**	**423**
8.1	Introduction	423
8.2	Simple Pivot Partitioning	424
8.3	Straight Pivot Partitioning	426
8.4	Pivot Partitioning	428
8.5	Interval Partitioning	431
8.6	Finding the Kth Largest Element	435
8.7	Dutch National Flag	438
	Summary	441
	Exercise	442
	Bibliography	443

Chapter 9	**Sorting**	**445**
9.1	Introduction	445
9.2	Transformations of a Sorting Specification	446
9.3	The Selection Algorithms	451
9.4	The Insertion Algorithms	460
9.5	The Partitioning Algorithms	462
	Summary	466
	Exercise	467
	Bibliography	469

Chapter 10	**Text Processing**	**469**
10.1	Introduction	469
10.2	Simple Pattern Match	470
10.3	Simple Pattern Search	472
10.4	Boyer and Moore Algorithm	475
10.5	Text Editing	483
10.6	Text Formatting	484
10.7	Comment Skipping	491
	Summary	494
	Exercise	495
	Bibliography	495

Chapter 11   Sequential Problems   **497**

    11.1   Introduction   497
    11.2   The Majority-element Problem   498
    11.3   The Maximum Sum-section Problem   501
    11.4   The Stores-movement Problem   506
    11.5   Two-way Merge   511
    11.6   Sequential File Update   513
    11.7   The Telegrams Analysis Problem   520
        Summary   526
        Exercise   527
        Bibliography   528

Part 4   PROGRAM IMPLEMENTATION

Chapter 12   Program Implementation   **531**

    12.1   Introduction   531
    12.2   Programming Style   532
    12.3   Initialization of Loops   554
    12.4   Termination of Loops   571
    12.5   Loop Structuring   581
    12.6   Lookahead Implementation   597
    12.7   Forced Synchronization of Loops   602
        Summary   616
        Exercise   617
        Bibliography   618

Index   **619**

Part 1
TOOLS FOR PROGRAM DERIVATION

A number of tools are needed to derive programs effectively. Logic and discrete mathematics may be used to specify problems adequately and to support the sequences of constructive reasoning steps that must be made in deriving and proving programs correct.

In Chapter 1 of this book we examine the role of logic and mathematics in program derivation. We then go on to introduce a model for formal program derivation. The foundation on which program derivation is built is a precise specification. The predicate calculus, together with set-based notations and formalisms, provide a powerful set of tools for specifying problems. They allow us to write concise specifications that are readily amenable to the sort of transformations that are needed to derive programs.

To derive and characterize programs several specialized forms of specification are required. A precondition is used to describe the input or data that is to be processed, while the output or goal of a computation is described by a postcondition. A third form of specification, an invariant, plays a vital role not only in characterizing computations but also in guiding the derivation of programs. A final form of specification needed to model computations is the variant function. Variant functions characterize the termination properties of programs. All these different forms of specification are discussed in Chapter 4.

Chapter 1
Introduction

There is always a first step in a journey of ten thousand miles
Chinese Proverb

1.1 The Problem of Programming
1.2 The Role of Mathematics and Logic
1.3 How Programs Are Derived
1.4 Program Derivation – A First Look
      Summary
      Bibliography

1.1   The Problem of Programming

The premium quality of a program is its *correctness*. In spite of this, there are very few complex prográms in use today that do not contain some sorts of errors, anomalies, or peculiarities. Fortunately, most of these defects are extremely subtle and become apparent only in very unusual circumstances. The trouble is that very unusual circumstances *do* occur from time to time.

The root cause of the lack of quality in programs lies not simply with the people responsible for producing the software but rather with the inadequate methods that are employed to develop programs. The response of the programming community to this situation has been to develop methods for such things as:

- project management
- requirements analysis
- top-down problem decomposition
- structured programming
- abstract data types

3

- information hiding
- program walkthroughs
- rigorous testing.

These developments have led to considerable improvements in program quality. However, correctness remains a major problem. Programmers still regard it as inevitable that the programs that they write will contain errors (or 'bugs' as they are more usually called). In fact many practitioners claim that as much as one third to one half of all programming effort is expended in 'debugging' programs. Worse still, the act of 'removing a bug' more often than not introduces other bugs.

The present situation is not a happy one particularly because we are increasing our dependency on the use of computers in life-critical applications such as air-traffic control, nuclear reactor control and life-support systems.

The following random sample of program errors that have come to public attention in recent times gives a glimpse of the seriousness of the problem.†

- The space shuttle Discovery flew upside down during a laser-beam missile defence experiment because it expected information in nautical miles and was given it in feet.
- The first version of the F-16 navigation software inverted the aircraft whenever it crossed the equator.
- A version of the Apollo II software had the moon's gravity appearing repulsive rather than attractive.
- A computer error caused a US warship's gun to fire in the opposite direction from its intended target during an exercise off San Francisco in 1982.
- In February 1984, the cash machines of two UK banks had serious compatibility problems because one remembered the leap year and the other did not.
- In 1983 the Vancouver Stock Exchange index was found to be at 725 points rather than 960 points due to a cumulative error in the way the index was calculated.
- A series of accidental radiation overdoses was administered by cancer therapy machines in Georgia, USA in 1986 because of an error in the controlling computer program.

Such errors are just the tip of the iceberg.

How is it that software is so susceptible to errors? Much of the difficulty lies in the sheer complexity of the tasks being programmed. There

---

† Many other examples can be found in the *Software Engineering Notes* reference quoted in the Bibliography.

are usually a huge number of variables and relationships that need to be taken into account when building any substantial software system.

Errors can be introduced into a software system at three distinct stages. There are:

- defects in the requirements that result from the failure of the software to cope with all aspects of the environment in which it is used;
- design errors that result from the failure of the design to match the stated requirements;
- implementation defects that result from the failure of an implementation to satisfy its design details.

Requirements defects and design errors propagate right down to the implementation level. In fact these sorts of errors are usually much more insidious and harder to correct than implementation defects.

The question that needs to be asked is 'given the problems with program correctness, is there a way forward to greater reliability and higher productivity'? The answer at this stage has to be a qualified 'yes' but it will require a substantial change in our approach to programming.

1.2   The Role of Mathematics and Logic

What, above all else, needs to be recognized is that programming is a mathematical activity and programs are complex mathematical expressions. These perceptions, if taken to their logical conclusions, completely change our whole conception of programming.

A mathematical view of programming tells us that

- programs can be *proved* correct in much the same way as theorems in mathematics are proved correct;
- the 'intended meaning' of a program can be described using mathematics and logic;
- the assertion that a program satisfies a specification is a mathematical statement.

Probably the most important aspect of a mathematical view of programming is as follows:

> The development of a proof of correctness and the construction of a correct program that satisfies its specification can proceed hand in hand. A program can literally be derived from its specification.

It is this approach to program development that holds the key to greater reliability and higher productivity.

These facts about programming have been known for some time. Why haven't programmers, and the software industry in general, been rushing to adopt the mathematical approach to programming?

The reason usually given for rejecting the practicality of a mathematical approach to programming is that it can only be used for small programs. What this line of argument overlooks is that formal methods of specification are now being successfully applied to a growing number of quite large software problems. Once there is a formal specification base, a mathematical approach to deriving a program to satisfy the specification becomes much more within the realms of possibility. The problem of size remains daunting if we insist that manual formal program derivation in the large should be handled in exactly the same way as formal program derivation in the small.

There are two ways of confronting the 'size problem'. We can adopt an approach similar to that taken in the applied sciences and engineering where the mathematics applied in the field has been adapted to the size of the problem. Not all variables and relationships that might be considered in a laboratory experiment are taken into account. Instead, the mathematics is used to focus on critical relationships and crucial variables. In making these simplifications the problem is still solved with rigour within a supporting mathematical framework. Enough formal reasoning is retained to allow others to verify their reasoning and if necessary detect errors in correctness. Such an approach to program derivation is possible provided we have a formal specification as our starting point.

The other alternative for dealing with the size problem is to rely upon a semi-automated programming environment that can assist with technical steps such as proof checking, equivalence transformations, weakest precondition calculations, and so on. We may expect, as the discipline matures, that such tools will achieve greater prominence. With their assistance the program designer will be relieved of a lot of tedious detail and the need to perform mechanical tasks.

There is one other essential ingredient needed to support a mathematical approach to program derivation. It will require the support of all concerned in the program development process. This means changes in attitudes and practices on the part of the managers, the programmers, and the customers. Without strong support from all groups the task will be very difficult.

1.3   How Programs Are Derived

The principal steps in deriving a program are **specification, design** and **implementation**.

- First, a specification is constructed. It should be unambiguous, consistent, and complete.†
- Then a sequence of refinements or design decisions is made. Each contributes to the final solution to the problem in some measurable way. Refinements should be guided by the original specification or other specifications that have been derived from it.
- Finally, after completing a detailed description of the design, the necessary additional steps are made to take the design through to an implementation in an executable programming language.

1.3.1   The role of the specification

The first step towards deriving a program involves constructing a suitable specification. The specification is of central importance for the following reasons:

- A program cannot be 'correct' in its own right. It can only be correct with respect to some separate entity – its specification.
- A specification defines the problem and serves as the instrument of communication and contract between the person(s) commissioning the program and those responsible for constructing the program.
- When a specification is in an appropriate form it can be used constructively to guide the development of the program and its accompanying proof of correctness.

The specifications of interest to us are those involving relations on two sets:

- One set describing the allowable initial states or inputs, or data *supplied* to the program.
- A second set describing the corresponding final states, or required output or data *produced* by the program.

The role of the program is to transform one set of data (the input) into another set of data (the output) see Figure 1.1.

What a specification must do is identify or characterize the two sets of data and the relationships between them which define the problem. In some cases the inter-relationship between input and output is important, while in other problems intra-relations in the input or the output are more important.

†Formally a specification consists of a set of statements T. It is *complete* if, for an arbitrary statement t, that statement either is, or is not, a member of T. For a specification T to be *consistent* it should be possible to deduce either a statement t or a statement 'not t' from T, but not both.

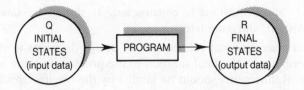

Figure 1.1   The state-model for a program specification.

Most of the problems we will be concerned with can be specified by two predicates:

- a **precondition** Q characterizing the allowable initial states
- a **postcondition** R characterizing the allowable final states.

Together, the pair (Q, R) define a specification. In order to satisfy a specification the input must make Q true and the output must make R true. A **predicate** in this context is a condition that is true or false depending on the values of its variables. For example the relation:

$$N > 0$$

is a predicate that is *true* for N = 1, 2, 3, ... and *false* for N = 0, −1, −2, ...

An example of a specification where it is required to sort N integers is as follows:

Precondition Q :   There is at least one integer to be sorted.

Postcondition R :   The input data is to be rearranged so that the integers form a sequence from the smallest to the largest.

Up to now, we have not considered whether specifications should be formal. For our sorting problem a formal specification could take the form:

$$Q : N \geq 1$$

$$R : (\forall j \ : \ 1 < j \leq N \ : \ a_{j-1} \leq a_j) \qquad \wedge \qquad \text{perm}(a, A)$$

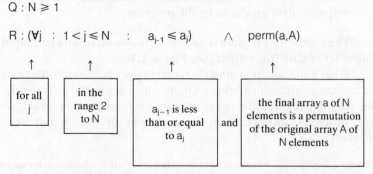

Earlier we suggested that a specification should be unambiguous, consistent, and complete. A formal, mathematically sound mode of expression appears to have the best chance of meeting this list of requirements. Several things, however, need to be put into perspective.

The validity of any specification does not depend on it being expressed formally. Too often validity is equated with a formal mode of expression. It should be remembered that no matter how grand or impressive a formal description is, it ultimately depends on a context which can only be described, at best, informally. Formality should be used in program specifications, but not as an end in itself. Prime objectives in constructing specifications are clarity and economy – they should not be sacrificed for formality. Some things are easier to specify with less formality. By the same token we should not fall into the trap of using an informal mode of expression simply because we have not taken the trouble to discover whether a more formal mode of expression is warranted. Such explorations usually deepen our understanding of problems and place us in a stronger position to make better judgements of the degree of formality appropriate for specifying a given problem. A balance is usually better than a strong bias either towards formality or informality.

Once a suitable specification for a problem has been created a design process which employs the specification can commence.

1.3.2 The design process

Design involves two essential ingredients:

- decomposition of a problem into simpler sub-problems;
- refinement of the strategy for solving a problem (or sub-problem) by introducing additional detail that makes the strategy more explicit.

To provide some insights into the program design process it is useful to review a familiar design problem – that of building a house. There are some interesting parallels between this process and designing programs. The major steps in building a house are as follows:

- The process starts with the client visiting an architect. The architect interviews the client and obtains details of his or her requirements, such as:

   three bedrooms, which should all be in one area,
   two bathrooms,
   a large lounge,
   a kitchen with large bench space,
   a dining room.

- Next, using the client's requirements as a guide, the architect draws up a plan (or specification) for the house. For the above requirements

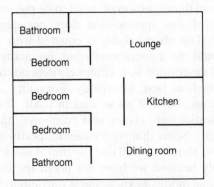

Figure 1.2   Initial schematic floor plan for a house.

the architect might propose a floor plan such as that shown in Figure 1.2. The architect will also provide elevation sketches showing how the house will appear from the front, the back and the sides.

- The architect then consults the client again to check if the basic specification is to the client's satisfaction. Any problems with the specification are settled at this stage, *before* building commences. It would be far too costly, for example, to try to change the size of the kitchen after *all* of the frame of the house had been put up.

- The next step is for the architect to provide detailed specifications that can be used by the builder to construct the house. These detailed specifications will be refinements of the original specification drawn up for the client. They will focus on a lot of detail for individual rooms, for example where the sink is to be put, the sizes of the cupboards, and where the plumbing and electrical wiring are to be located.

- Armed with the detailed specification and design, the builder and the other tradespeople set about the process of constructing the house according to the specifications. The architect has the responsibility of ensuring that the building satisfies its specifications.

There are three important lessons that program designers can learn from the house-building process.

Lesson 1   It would be unthinkable to build a house without a detailed plan and design document. The design document is always the reference point for all subsequent activities.

Lesson 2   The process of creating a plan and developing a design from that plan are clearly separated from the process of building the house. This is highlighted by the fact that the architect and the builder are almost always different people.

Lesson 3   The detailed design is arrived at by a process of refinement. There is a progression from the general to the specific. Detail is gradually factored into the design only after broad general issues have been settled and the problem has been broken down into manageable sub-problems. For example, the dimensions of the bathroom mirror are never at issue when a decision is being made about where the dining room is to be located.

What do these lessons hold for computing scientists? Too often programs are constructed without adequate specification and design considerations. This practice has resulted in the production of much software of very poor quality that is a nightmare to maintain and use. We must recognize that programming, like building houses, is a goal-oriented and specification-driven activity. It requires thorough specification and design phases. These processes need to be separate from the program implementation phase. Implementation should be a largely mechanical phase provided the specification and design phases have been handled properly.

The analogy between program construction and house-building is at its weakest when it comes to comparing the respective decomposition processes. The 'room' concept makes it much easier to decompose and refine the house-design problem. It is true that programs get decomposed into modules (which might be likened to rooms) but these are often not easy to discern.

The design strategy for decomposition and refinement that we will focus upon follows from Polya's well-known problem-solving dictum:

> if you can't solve a problem, then there is an easier problem you can't solve – find it!

When the strategy of finding an easier problem is viewed in terms of formal specifications simpler (or easier) problems correspond directly to systematic transformations that can be applied to specifications. This correspondence holds the key to the systematic derivation of programs from formal specifications.

When considering strategies for finding simpler problems it is important that the solutions to the simpler problems always contribute to the solution of the original problem. The decomposition strategy that we will adopt exhibits this property. It starts by identifying and building a mechanism that will satisfy the postcondition under the most restrictive conditions we can find. Quite often the most restrictive or strongest useful precondition for making a refinement is the postcondition itself ($Q' \equiv R$). The task then is to start by making a refinement that tries to *confirm* whether the postcondition already applies. Confirming a postcondition is frequently the simplest way of establishing it. Furthermore, a mechanism for confirming a postcondition provides a solution to a problem for a very restrictive, but quite feasible, precondition. All subsequent refinements should provide progressively less restrictive solutions to a problem.

The problem decomposition strategy we have alluded to identifies:

(1)   a *simpler mechanism* that can contribute to the solution of the original problem;

(2)   a *condition* under which the simpler mechanism can establish the postcondition.

There are two outcomes that follow from these two identifications:

- when the condition in (2) does not apply we will have identified a separate condition and another simple problem requiring solution;
- the condition established by the mechanism in (2) when the postcondition is not satisfied identifies another simpler problem that will need to be solved in order to establish the postcondition.

We will now examine two problems to clarify this design strategy.

Problem 1

Suppose we have a group of people scattered among several threatened locations A, B and C each of which is progressively further from some safe destination location D.

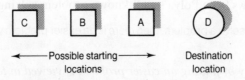

←———— Possible starting ————→   Destination
            locations   location

In order to save the people they must all be transported from where they live (i.e. A, B, or C) to the safety of destination D. Furthermore, we will assume that in order to transport the people to the destination location, it is necessary quickly to build a makeshift road network through to D.

The simplest way to proceed would be to propose the following refinement.

Refinement 1: (precondition Q_1)

1(a)   Build a road from A to D, the destination
1(b)   Transport the population from A to D

The 'mechanism' we have constructed will 'solve the problem' in the very restricted circumstance that:

'the *whole* population lives at location A'

This refinement will also contribute to the general solution to the problem. A refinement such as:

'build a road from C to B'

is rejected because at this stage of the design it could not establish the postcondition (that is, allow any of the population to reach the destination D).

Refinement 2: (precondition Q_2)

Having made the refinement 1, if we then:

2(a) Build a road from B to A

2(b) Transport the population from B to A and then to D

we will have a mechanism that will solve the problem in the restricted circumstance that:

'the whole population lives at either locations A or B'

Our complete mechanism after the two refinements will be:

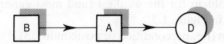

Refinement 3: (precondition Q_3)

In the context of having made refinements 1 and 2, if we then:

3(a) Build a road from C to B

3(b) Transport the population from C to B and then onto A and subsequently D

we will then have a mechanism that will solve the problem in the circumstances that:

'the whole population lives at either locations A, or B, or C'

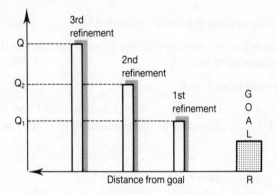

Figure 1.3   Schematic view of establishing a goal by a sequence of refinements each of which establishes the goal for progressively weaker preconditions.

This condition for solving the problem corresponds to the precondition for our original problem.

The strategy that has been used here begins with a refinement for a strong precondition that is as close as possible to the goal (or postcondition) we are seeking to establish. Successive refinements then progressively take us to greater 'distances' from which the postcondition can be reached. In the process, with each additional refinement, a more general solution to the problem is reached. This corresponds to the most straightforward systematic way of using specifications to guide the derivation of a program. There is a progression from solving the problem for the strongest useful precondition to solving the problem for the weakest (and most general) precondition. This is illustrated in Figure 1.3.

A condition (i.e. precondition or postcondition) is said to be stronger if it is true for *fewer* cases. For example the condition

N > 0   which is true for N = 1, 2, 3 ...

but excludes N = 0, is *stronger* than the condition

N ⩾ 0   which is true for N = 0, 1, 2 ...

From the alternative point of view N ⩾ 0 is *weaker* than N > 0.

Problem 2

Suppose the task (or postcondition) is

'to get the person P a drink',

given a bottle B and a glass G. In solving this problem we will assume that P has indicated a preference for what is in bottle B. Furthermore we will also assume that B is not empty and the glass G is either empty or it has been filled from B. These constraints represent the precondition.

First refinement

The simplest way to establish the postcondition of getting P a drink would be first to

'check if the glass G is full'

This test yields two sub-problems:

(1)   if the glass is not full we must solve another problem first, that of 'filling the glass G' before applying step (2);

(2)   if we are lucky, and the glass is full, we can establish the postcondition by simply 'handing the glass to P'.

Summarizing, the two steps are

(1)   **if** glass G is not full **then**
      'make another refinement'
      fi†
(2)   hand glass to person P

Second refinement

To solve problem (1) identified in the first refinement we need to

'check if the bottle B is open'

This test again yields another two sub-problems:

(1)′   if the bottle B is not open then we must first open the bottle, then apply (2)′;

(2)′   if we are lucky, and the bottle is already open, we simply fill the glass G.

Our 'program' after two refinements will therefore take the form:

(1)   **if** glass is not full **then**

    (1)′   **if** bottle is not open **then**
          'make another refinement'
          fi
    (2)′   fill the glass G from the bottle B
    fi
(2)   hand glass to person P

† **'fi'** is used to indicate the end of an **'if'** statement for the corresponding step number ((1), (2), ...)

Third refinement

To solve problem (1)′ all that remains is 'to open the bottle'. Incorporating this our 'complete program' to solve the problem takes the form:

(1)   **if** glass is not full **then**

      (1)′   **if** bottle is not open **then**
              open the bottle B
      fi
      (2)′   fill the glass G from the bottle B
   fi

(2)   hand glass to person P

      This example, although artificial and simplistic, conveys something of the underlying design strategy we will employ. General problems are solved by proceeding from the most restrictive circumstances (the simplest or easiest problem to solve) to the most general solution. What is important to recognize about this design strategy is that the very simple mechanisms for achieving the goal in the restricted circumstances can contribute in a harmonious way to solving the general problem, for example 'hand glass to person P', the mechanism identified first, contributes to solving the general problem.

      What has been neglected in our discussion of the design process is the question 'how can specifications be used constructively to assist with program derivation?' Central to this endeavour is the application of what are called **weakest precondition calculations**. These calculations can help us to identify suitable commands and conditions that will ensure that specifications are satisfied by a computation (in other words they allow constructive proofs of correctness to be created). We will not attempt to provide the technical detail that is needed to understand these calculations here. That will be left to the extensive discussion in Chapter 5.

      What we will do instead is give a simple example that conveys some notion of how program commands may be identified by calculation rather than by guesswork or intuition – their usual method of construction.

      To see how this is done, consider the problem of computing the quotient q and remainder r when a natural number X is divided by a divisor D. This problem can be solved first by assigning to r the value of X and then repeatedly subtracting multiples of D from r until r is less than D. With each subtraction, 1 is added to the quotient q. As an example, suppose $X = 28$ and $D = 5$. Table 1.1 illustrates how the remainder r and quotient q may be computed.

Table 1.1

r	q	X	D
28	0	28	5
23	1	28	5
18	2	28	5
13	3	28	5
8	4	28	5
3	5	28	5

The remainder is $r = 3$ and the quotient $q = 5$. The relation between q, r, X, and D is captured by the equation

$$X = q \times D + r \tag{1}$$

which holds for *all* valid combinations of q, r, X and D, that is for

$r = 3$ $q = 5$ $X = 28$ $D = 5$ we have $28 = 5 \times 5 + 3$
$r = 8$ $q = 4$ $X = 28$ $D = 5$ we have $28 = 4 \times 5 + 8$ and so on

The equation (1) is an **invariant** of the quotient/remainder calculation. In the equation, X and D are constants which are not changed by the computation and q and r are variables which change throughout the computation. The equation holds even when the variables change their values. A simple program to perform this repetitive subtraction process using assignment statements is as follows:

```
r := X ; q := 0 ;          r and q are given initial values
WHILE r ≥ D DO
    r := r – D;⎤          these steps are repeated
    q := q + 1⎦          until r is less than D
END
```

Now let us return to the problem of identifying commands by calculation. If q' and r' represent different values of the q and r variables then the following equation

$$X = q' \times D + r' \tag{2}$$

will also hold. Now suppose we also know that the equation

$$r' = r – D \tag{3}$$

holds (this corresponds to the program command $r := r – D$), but let us assume we do not know what the command involving q should be. Then the two forms of the invariant (equations (1) and (2)) together with (3) could be used to identify the missing command involving q.

What we are interested in is an expression for q′ expressed in terms of the variables and constants in (1). To identify this expression for q′ we need to solve for q′ using the equations (1), (2) and (3).

To do this we first substitute in (2) for X from (1)

$$q \times D + r = q' \times D + r'$$

We can also use (3) to substitute for r′. This yields:

$$q \times D + r = q' \times D + (r - D)$$

which, when simplified, gives:

$$q' = q + 1$$

(from this we may obtain the missing program command q := q + 1).

This symbolic manipulation of equations to identify 'q′ = q + 1' is typical of simple weakest precondition calculations where equations with an *invariant* form (e.g. (1) and (2)) are often used in constructing commands.

Weakest precondition calculations are like completing a jigsaw puzzle in which there is one piece missing – eventually the 'shape' of the missing piece becomes clear.

To illustrate further this mode of calculation suppose we had the same two equations:

$$X = q \times D + r \tag{1}$$
$$X = q' \times D + r' \tag{2}$$

and this time suppose we knew that

$$q' = q + 1 \tag{3}$$

but we did not know what the command involving r was.

Our job would be to find an expression for r′ in terms of the variables and constants in (1). When we do this we get:

$$q \times D + r = q' \times D + r'$$

Including the definition for q′ from (3) we get:

$$q \times D + r = (q + 1) \times D + r'$$

which simplifies to yield:

$$r' = r - D$$

(from this we may obtain the missing program command r := r − D).

In this second calculation a different piece of the 'jigsaw' was missing but still the calculation yielded consistent results. When using weakest precondition calculations constructively there is usually a missing expression or condition that can be discovered by making the calculations.

There is one remaining question that we have overlooked: 'what constitutes a good design?' In any attempt to understand what makes a design good we soon discover that it is an elusive quality. Whitehead in his discussion of it suggested that *'good design is the achievement of a perceived need simply, and without waste'*. Another suggestion made by Pick is that *'good design is intelligence made visible'*. Others have suggested that good design is an achievement of unity, a harmony of all the parts, in proportion, and in the way they are fitted together. The ideal synthesis is an irresistible goal – it is elusive, the marrying of philosophical concept and practical objective.

Good design is intimately linked to the notion of form, and the possession by form of the quality of simplicity.

In the design process there is a constant need to make choices of representation, strategy, structure, and so on. A primary consideration is most often the quality of simplicity. As is often remarked, *'simplicity is the hallmark of truth'*. Simplicity is also the yardstick by which we measure elegance in design. It is very easy to ignore the consideration of simplicity on the grounds that it is at best subjective, vague, variable, and therefore too elusive for serious study. Even if this is the case we cannot afford to ignore the consideration of simplicity. Its impact on design is far too important. When careful consideration is given to the notion of simplicity it soon becomes apparent that we are not dealing with a single, easily ascertained characteristic of designs or systems, but rather with a multiplicity of inter-related and sometimes conflicting characteristics, few of which are easy to measure or pinpoint specifically. What we need to appreciate is that simplicity, however we choose to define it, is the single most important ideal that we strive for to create elegance in design.

1.3.3 The implementation step

Application of the decomposition techniques and the weakest precondition calculations we have alluded to can take the design right through until all we are left with is a relatively straightforward mechanical translation from a design language to a conventional program implementation language. In this context a design language is a very simple notation for expressing how a problem should be solved. It lacks many of the features of program implementation languages which are designed for execution by a computer. It should be emphasized that the objective of the design process is to factor the problem into an explicit design language called **guarded commands**. The advantage of using a design language is that it is free of most of the implementation detail of conventional programming languages. We do not want to be distracted by implementation detail when focusing on a program derivation and its accompanying proof of correctness.

Given the relatively straightforward nature of the implementation step we will not pursue it further here.

1.4   Program Derivation – A First Look

In this section we give an example showing the major steps in the program derivation process. We will do this informally. Later on, in Chapter 5, we will see how formal methods can be used to give the process much needed precision.

The major steps in the program derivation process are:

- first to specify precisely what the problem is that must be solved and to identify any constraints on the data that must be processed to achieve the goal;
- then to use the specification to guide how the problem is solved;
- finally to solve the problem by completing a sequence of small manageable tasks (refinements) each of which ultimately contributes to the final solution.

As an example, suppose that the problem to be solved requires *some numbers to be sorted*.

Stage 1   Specifying the problem

The phrase 'some numbers to be sorted' tells us what the problem is we are required to solve.

However, this statement as a specification is far too imprecise. It leaves open many questions:

(1)   how many numbers are to be sorted?

(2)   what is the smallest number of numbers that may need to be sorted?

(3)   are there any other special characteristics of the data?

(4)   what kinds of numbers are they: integers, reals or natural numbers?

(5)   are they to be arranged from largest to smallest (descending order) or from smallest to largest (ascending order)?

(6)   do any of the numbers occur more than once?

Until these questions are settled there is no point in attempting to derive a program.

These questions need to be resolved either with the person requiring the program (if there is such a person) or, on our own behalf, if we require the program. To do this we will take each of the questions, one at a time:

- To be of general use the program should be able to sort an arbitrary number (say N) of numbers.
- An obvious response is the smallest number of numbers that may need sorting would be two. However what would happen if there is only one number to sort? The program should handle this smaller problem too. It should 'sort' *one or more numbers*. The number of numbers to be sorted, N, is greater than or equal to one, that is

    $N \geq 1$

- Let us assume we have been told that the numbers to be sorted are *integers*.
- Let us also assume we are told that the numbers are to be arranged from *smallest to largest*.
- In the interests of generality our program should cope with numbers that *occur more than once*.

With these questions settled we could complete a formal specification for the problem. At this stage we will simply write down the formal specification for the problem given in Section 1.3.1.

$Q : N \geq 1$
$R : (\forall j : 1 < j \leq N : a_{j-1} \leq a_j) \wedge \mathrm{perm}(a, A)$

It is not important to be able to understand this specification yet. All we wish to do is give a preview of what a formal specification looks like.

What we are now interested in is showing informally how the design process may be applied to solve this problem. Later, in Chapter 5, the formal derivation for the same problem is presented.

First refinement (Q_1 – only one element to sort)

Our first refinement should be one that 'solves' the problem in the most restrictive circumstances we can find. If there were only *one* element to sort this would be the simplest problem to solve. Our first refinement may therefore take the form:†

(1) 'place the data in an array'
(2) **if** there is only one element to sort **then** the task is completed
     elseif there is more than one element **then**
          '*make another refinement*'
     fi

---

† In the algorithm description '**elseif**' can be read as '**else if**' and '**fi**' by itself is used to indicate the end of an '**if**' statement for the corresponding step number (i.e. 1, 2, 3, ...etc.)

Second refinement (Q_2 – all the elements are sorted)

The first refinement tells us that if there is more than one element further refinements are necessary. The next most restrictive precondition we could contemplate would involve two (or more) elements all in 'sorted order'. Making a check to see if the data is already sorted amounts to *confirming the postcondition*. Such a check again divides the problem into two. Either the data is sorted and we are done, or there are one or more elements out of order which require additional processing.

Writing these steps down we get:

(1)   place the data in an array

(2)   **if** there is only one element to sort **then** the task is completed
      elseif there is more than one element **then**

    (3)   test if array is sorted by searching for an element that is out of order

    (4)   **if** the array is sorted **then** the task is complete
        elseif the array is not sorted **then**
          'make another refinement'
        fi

  fi

Third refinement (Q_3 – only the last element out of place)

If, after the second refinement, the array is not sorted, then a precondition has been identified with an element out of order. In the most restrictive circumstances, if we are lucky, only the *last* element will be out of place, that is

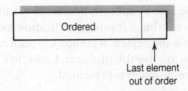

Last element
out of order

The third refinement will need to 'insert' this element that is out of place. To understand this suppose we have:

1	3	4	5	6	2	

where the '2' is out of order. After the insertion we would require the following configuration to be produced:

1	2	3	4	5	6

Making this latest refinement we get:

(1)   place the data in an array
(2)   **if** there is only one element to sort **then** the task is completed
    elseif there is more than one element **then**
      (3)   test if the array is sorted by searching for an element that is out
          of order
      (4)   **if** the array is sorted **then** the task is complete
          elseif the array is not sorted **then**
          (5)   insert the element found to be out of order
          (6)   **if** there are no more elements to sort **then** the task is
              complete
              elseif there are more elements to sort **then**
                  'make another refinement'
              fi
          fi
    fi

Fourth refinement (Q_4 – an arbitrary set of data)

To make the next refinement we employ the mechanisms we have developed in the last two refinements. The complete mechanism to achieve the sort then becomes:

(1)   place the data in an array
(2)   **while** there are more elements to sort **do**
      (3)   test if the remainder of the array is sorted by searching for an
          element that is out of order
      (4)   **if** the array is sorted **then** the task is complete
          elseif the array is not sorted **then**
          (5)   insert the element found to be out of order
          (6)   **if** there are no more elements to sort **then** the task is
              complete
              elseif there are more elements to sort **then** return to step
              (2)
              fi
          fi

The informal derivation of the insertion sort algorithm clearly illustrates the progression from a very restricted solution to the problem to progressively more general solutions. The example also illustrates clearly how different refinements fit together to produce an overall solution to the problem.

With the completion of this informal derivation we should now be ready to embark on the process of studying the necessary logic and mathematics needed for formal program derivation.

SUMMARY

- Designing programs that correctly satisfy their specified requirements is a challenging and difficult task.
- Much of today's software contains subtle undetected errors. Many
  programmers regard it as inevitable that their programs will contain
  errors.
- Fixing an error in a program quite often results in the introduction of
  other errors.
- By taking a mathematically-based approach to programming it is
  possible to develop simultaneously a proof of correctness and a
  corresponding program that satisfies its specification.
- To derive a program it is necessary to progress through specification, design, and implementation phases.
- A specification defines a problem, and, when it is in an appropriate
  form it can be used to guide the derivation of a program and its proof
  of correctness.
- A specification consists of two parts, a precondition and postcondition. The precondition describes the input data and any constraints
  upon it. The postcondition describes the required output or purpose
  of the computation. The role of the program is to consume the input
  and produce the output.
- The design process involves the decomposition of a problem into
  sub-problems, and the refinement of the solution to a problem by the
  progressive introduction of additional detail.
- Programs are often constructed without adequate attention to the
  specification and design phases.
- A powerful design strategy for deriving programs from formal
  specifications involves making a sequence of refinements each of
  which establishes the postcondition for progressively weaker preconditions until a general enough solution is obtained which solves
  the problem for the given precondition.
- Weakest precondition calculations can be used to assist with the
  derivation of programs from formal specifications.
- The program implementation step is a relatively straightforward step
  provided the appropriate emphasis has been placed on the
  specification and design phases.

Bibliography

Alexander, C. (1964), *Notes on the Synthesis of Form*, Harvard University Press,
     Cambridge, Mass.

Courtois, P.J. (1977), *Decomposability*, Academic Press, N.Y.

Dijkstra, E.W. (1984), *The Threats to Computing Science,* EWD-898.

Hesse, M. (1974), *The Structure of Scientific Inference*, Macmillan, London.

Hoare, C.A.R. (1986), Maths adds safety to computer programs, *New Scientist*, **111**(1526), 53–6, (18 September).

Hoare, C.A.R. (1986), The Mathematics of Programming, *Byte* **11**(8), 115–23.

Lister, A.M. (1987), *How Much Should You Trust a Computer*, Inaugural Lecture, University of Queensland.

Mayal, W.H. (1979), *Principles in Design*, Design Council, London.

Naur, P. (1982), Formalization in program development, *BIT*, **22**, 437–53

Santayana, G. (1961), *The Sense of Beauty*, Colher, N.Y.

Shaw, M. (1987), *A Sampler of Systems Problems and Failures Attributable to Software*, Electronics Research Laboratory, April.

Simon, H.A. (1962), The architecture of complexity, *Proc. Am. Phil. Soc.*, **106**(b), 467–82.

Smith, C.S. (1981), *A Search for Structure*, MIT Press, Cambridge, Mass.

Software Engineering Notes (1980–87), Newsletter of the ACM Special Interest Group on Software Engineering, **5–12**.

'Something rotten in the state of software' (1988), *The Economist*, **306** (7582), 81–4, (9 January).

Waddington, C.H. (1977), *Tools for Thought*, Paladin, London.

Chapter 2
Logic for Program Design

What is not fully understood is not possessed

Goethe

2.1 Introduction
2.2 Specification Methods
2.3 Propositional Calculus
2.4 Predicate Calculus
2.5 Proof Methods
Summary
Exercises
Bibliography

2.1 Introduction

Success in the systematic development of programs rests on:

- our ability to specify problems precisely and,
- having specified a problem, to use that specification to guide the development of the program and its accompanying correctness proof.

The discipline of logic can provide substantial help with these tasks.

2.2 Specification Methods

Before a program can be designed we need a description or a characterization of its required properties or behaviour. As we saw earlier the term usually given to such descriptions of requirements is **specification**. There are a number of methods open to us for providing a specification for a problem, including the use of logic. We will now examine several of the better known methods of specification.

2.2.1   Specification using natural language

The most obvious way to describe specifications is to use natural language. The only practical way to do this is by choosing and defining each term carefully so there can be no mistake about its meaning. The designation of a concept by more than one term should always be avoided. If these guidelines are adhered to it is possible, although often quite difficult, to create consistent and accurate natural language specifications. Consistency and accuracy are not enough. Specifications should possess a number of other desirable qualities which natural language specifications often lack. The main weaknesses of natural language specifications are as follows:

- They are often not very concise.
- There is always the risk with problems of meaning and interpretation.
- They can be difficult to structure in a way that makes them easy to comprehend.
- They are not easily manipulated and so they can play no significant constructive role either in the stepwise development of programs or in the stepwise development of a program's correctness proof.
- When decomposition of a problem is carried out on the basis of structure we are limited by the vocabulary used to describe the specification.

These potential problems with natural language specifications suggest that other methods need to be considered. One such approach is to use programming language constructs.

2.2.2   Specification using programming language constructs

Programming languages are formal languages. They can offer a greater precision than natural language when used for writing specifications. However, programming languages are designed to describe algorithms or strategies for computation. They are therefore better suited to describe *how* a problem is solved rather than *what* it is. In choosing to use a programming language to specify a problem the fundamental law of separation of concerns is violated: strategy is mixed with design properties and requirements. This has several negative consequences:

- It can lead to the introduction of unnecessary complication (for example, irrelevant implementation details) into a specification. This happens because such specifications describe more than basic requirements.
- It introduces the risk of making decisions about the form and structure of a solution to a problem too early in the design phase.
- Specifications built from programming constructs, although formal, do not help with formal manipulation for problem decomposition.

There are various other methods that have been used for writing specifications. Most of them suffer to varying degrees from the problems we have identified. Fortunately there is another system for specification open to us that has less problems. It involves the use of a logic-based notation.

2.2.3   Specification using logic notation

Why is logic notation not more widely used for problem specification? The situation for many people is not unlike the situation with typing. There are many who persist with their one-finger–two-finger typing skill rather than make the extra effort to master touch-typing. Clearly with typing once the touch-typing discipline is mastered one quickly learns to appreciate the much greater power and freedom that has been gained. Although analogies like this are often superficial we suggest that the investment of time and effort to master the principles of logic needed for specifying problems is time very well spent. The program designer who has mastered the use and manipulation of symbols has added a powerful aid to his or her reasoning, means of expression, and problem-solving ability.

In the remainder of this section we will touch upon some of the important philosophical and technical issues associated with the use of logic in program derivation. This discussion provides the motivation for much of what follows in the rest of the book. It is however not expected that the novice reader will appreciate the full import of this discussion until after the first seven chapters have been thoroughly digested.

Logic is probably best characterized as a science of order and form. When a logic notation is used to specify problems it provides specifications that are precise, comprehensive, economical, and easy to manipulate either by hand or machine. A further benefit from the use of a refined and precise symbolism is that it can often help us to uncover the underlying structure of problems. Logic brings with it a formalism for attaining conceptual richness and rigorous deductive inference. The use of logic notation should not however be accepted without question. The use of formality does not necessarily guarantee the validity of a specification. We need to use formality intelligently, in a way that serves us best, rather than mechanically, where we can end up being its servant.

A primary concern in creating a specification is to make appropriate classifications of things. The notion of **predicate**, one of the cornerstones of logic, turns out to be probably the most economical and elegant means of classifying things. Predicates allow us to create very simple defining forms. A predicate-based defining form need contain only a single element, the variable whose values characterize the defined class or set. A predicate therefore gives us a means of classifying an element and its generalization delimits the associated set. By using predicates to define sets, we can then use sets to define order, relations, functions and sequences. This gives us a very powerful formal classification system that is well suited for the precise specification of problems.

An advantage of logic notation, in addition to its power of classification, is its support for systematic transformation to other equivalent or related forms (for example, weaker or stronger specifications). This gives the opportunity to explore simpler or perhaps more fertile formulations of a problem.

Langer summed this up nicely with her remark that 'the intelligent use of equivalent forms is the touchstone of logical insight'. In our work on program design a very effective transformation that we will frequently use will involve the introduction of new free variables into a specification. The more variables there are the greater the potential for finding different ways to solve a problem.

There is also another important consequence that follows from using logical structures and notation to specify program-design problems. The precision of a logic specification not only improves the clarity of the design requirements but it can also provide new insights into the very nature of the design process. Formal specifications can also be used as a basis for program development either by automated or semi-automated means. Gains we make in this area are crucial to our objective of building program design into a science of structure and form.

The arguments that have been advanced in favour of using logic in program design do not imply that we can necessarily improve the efficiency of our thinking by use of logic notation or logic operations in some prescribed manner. Rather, to paraphrase Reichenbach, logic can be an effective regulative of thought but not its propelling force. It can help us to focus but not control the creative thought processes needed to design programs. In other words program designers need logic as an instrument of vision, much as biologists need a microscope to reveal the forms that they work with. It is then up to the biologists, and the computing scientists, to interpret and work with the forms that their respective instruments of vision reveal.

A specification provides a description not only of the design goal but also of the constraints imposed by the context or domain. It is a necessary and sufficient starting condition for program development. A worthy goal is to try to find ways to use a specification as an instrument of construction with logic helping to provide the mechanics for the structural decomposition of problems.

In developing programs a primary concern is to factor the associated problem into a sequence of manageable development steps. Ideally each of these development steps should correspond to the progressive manipulation of a specification in some way. The developmental manipulations that we will concentrate upon will be those that correspond to changing a predicate in some way or to the introduction of new variables into a specification. In terms of the state model introduced in the previous chapter, refinements that accompany each change in a specification are intended to extend the set of initial states for which the postcondition is established.

The same predicates which are used to guide the stepwise construction of a program can be used in conjunction with the methods of logical inference to develop a constructive proof of a program's correctness. In this regard we will take the now widely accepted position that the development of the proof should proceed hand-in-hand with the development of the program. We will now examine briefly the ideas associated with the use of logic for correctness proofs.

The early approaches to this problem focused on the use of *a posteriori* analyses of complete programs. The difficulty with these approaches was that the programs were usually written without any regard for how they might subsequently be proved. This often caused proofs to be unnecessarily complicated thereby devaluing the practical use of these techniques.

More recently there has been a trend to use constructive proof methods where the proof is seen as being an integral part of the program development process. The proofs are based on two things, a formal functional specification and a formal model of program semantics. The particular method of constructive program proof that we will be using requires, at each stage of the refinement process, a decision about exactly what assertion must be satisfied next. Then what is called a predicate transformer is applied to identify the corresponding program construct needed to establish the truth of that assertion. The development process reduces to a largely deductive discipline with each refinement being preceded by the formal manipulation of existing assertions. This approach is based upon a set of axioms and a set of inference rules. Beyond this there is little need for extra notation over and above that of the program. Abstract definitions of meaning are given for each programming language construct. This permits us to treat programs as linguistic entities with their own syntax and semantics, and an associated state space. Using this model the notation:

$$\{Q\}\ S\ \{R\} \tag{1}$$

indicates that the execution of a sequence of program statements S, which begins in any state satisfying the predicate Q, is guaranteed to terminate in another state satisfying the predicate R. The predicate Q is an assertion called the **precondition** and R is an assertion called the **postcondition**.

By introducing another predicate, called the weakest precondition, it is possible to express (1) in the more familiar notation of the predicate calculus. We take wp(S,R) to represent the *weakest precondition* of a command S with respect to a postcondition R. The predicate wp(S,R) characterizes the set of all initial states such that if S is begun in any one of them it will terminate with R true. Instead of (1) we can write:

$$Q \Rightarrow wp \ (S,R) \tag{2}$$

which may be read as 'Q implies the weakest precondition for S establishing R'. A program S is said to be totally correct with respect to the precondition Q and postcondition R if the relation (2) holds.

A detailed discussion of weakest preconditions will be given later in Section 5.3. For now the following very simple example will be used to explore the concept. If S is the assignment 'i := i + 1' and R is the condition 'i ⩾ 1' then:

$$wp \ (\text{'i} := \text{i} + 1\text{'}, \text{i} \geqslant 1) \equiv \text{i} \geqslant 0 \tag{3}$$

This means that 'i := i + 1' can terminate with R established only if the condition i ⩾ 0 is true immediately *before* the assignment is executed. On the other hand if the condition i < 0 applies, the command 'i := i + 1' cannot establish R.

The concept of the weakest precondition underpins the use of predicate transformers to construct program statements that are guaranteed to satisfy particular assertions at each stage in the development of the program. We will return to this topic in Section 5.3.4 when program development from specifications is discussed in detail.

The previous discussion underlines the need for a working knowledge of logic in order to be able to carry out the necessary manipulations of specifications and assertions to guide the development and construct proofs of programs. We will therefore now turn to an examination of the propositional calculus and the predicate calculus.

2.3 Propositional Calculus

The modern perspective of logic is that of a diverse and highly formal discipline. In the present treatment of logic we will focus mainly on those aspects of the discipline most relevant for program design. Our concern is to provide sufficient background to enable the reader to be comfortable with the kinds of logical expression and reasoning that are most frequently needed in program design.

Logic as such is a formal language built from a precise syntax and semantics. To explain its syntax and semantics a number of definitions and conventions need to be introduced. Our primary concern is to provide a set of rules that are well defined and free of any of the vagueness or ambiguity that is possible with natural language.

The building blocks for logical constructs are the set of all declarative sentences. Our objective is to be able to construct, symbolize, and reason with various types of logical or declarative sentences. The only declarative sentences of interest to us are those that can be classified as either *true* or *false*, but not both. Such sentences are usually called either **propositions** or **statements** (hence the names propositional calculus or statement calculus). Declarative sentences may be either elementary or compound sentences. Compound sentences may be built from elementary declarative sentences (i.e. elementary propositions) that are combined or modified using a set of well-defined **connectives** or **operators** (these connectives are sometimes referred to as the **sentential** or **propositional** or **logical** connectives). As an example, two elementary declarative sentences are:

'It is lunchtime'
'There is a big queue at the cafeteria'.

They can be combined to make a compound declarative sentence (or proposition or propositional expression) using the connective 'and':

'It is lunchtime *and* there is a big queue at the cafeteria'.

We will now examine the logical connectives.

2.3.1 Connectives

There are five basic connectives used to combine and modify propositions. They are listed in Table 2.1. The two propositions used with the connectives are symbolized by p and q.

Table 2.1

Connective	Usage	Symbolic form	Operation
not	not p	$\neg p$	negation
and	p and q	$p \wedge q$	conjunction
or	p or q	$p \vee q$	disjunction
if p then q	p implies q	$p \Rightarrow q$	implication
p if and only if q	p equivalent to q	$p \equiv q$	equivalence

A number of other symbols are sometimes used to identify the connectives. Some are listed in Table 2.2.

Table 2.2

Operation	Equivalent symbolic form
negation	~p, −p
conjunction	p & q, p . q
disjunction	
implication	p → q, p ⊃ q
equivalence	p ↔ q

In logic a precise set of rules governs the use of these connectives. Conventional and tabular statements of these rules can be given. Both are provided below. A useful property of the tabular (truth-table) representations is that they show at a glance the truth or falsity of a compound sentence or proposition simply from a knowledge of the truth or falsity of its component propositions.

Negation (¬p)

The truth of a proposition is denied by asserting its negation.

> **Rule**
> The negation of a true proposition is false whereas the negation of a false proposition is true.

Truth table (negation)†

p	¬p
T	F
F	T

The second line of this truth table tells us that if a proposition p is true then the proposition ¬p is false.

Conjunction (p ∧ q)

Two propositions may be conjoined to yield a single compound proposition called the conjunction of the two propositions.

> **Rule**
> The conjunction of two propositions is true if and only if both component propositions are true.

†The symbols *T* and *F* are abbreviations for *true* and *false* respectively.

Truth table (conjunction)

p	q	p∧q
T	T	T
T	F	F
F	T	F
F	F	F

The second line of this truth table shows that if two propositions p and q are both true then the compound proposition formed by their conjunction will also be true. The rule of usage for the conjunction connective makes it *truth functional* in that the truth or falsity of the conjunction of two propositions p and q is a function solely of the truth or falsity of these two propositions.

Disjunction (p ∨ q)

Two propositions may be disjoined to yield a single compound proposition called the disjunction of the two propositions.

> **Rule**
> The disjunction of two propositions is true if and only if at least one of the propositions is true.

Truth table (disjunction)

p	q	p∨q
T	T	T
T	F	T
F	T	T
F	F	F

Implication (p ⇒ q)

The construction 'if ... then ...' together with two propositions p and q replacing the dots may be used to form an **implication** or **conditional proposition**. In the construct:

> **if p then q**

or in its equivalent symbolic form:

> p ⇒ q

we refer to the proposition p as the **antecedent** and to the proposition q as the

consequent. Another common idiom in logic for implication is 'p is a sufficient condition for q'.

> **Rule**
> An implication is only false if its antecedent p is true when the consequent q is false. In all other instances the implication is true.

Truth table (implication)

p	q	$p \Rightarrow q$
T	*T*	*T*
T	*F*	*F*
F	*T*	*T*
F	*F*	*T*

There is sometimes confusion about the idea that an implication is true when the antecedent is false. Because the concept of implication is so useful in program design we will try to overcome the confusion. The problem arises in part because of people's experience with conditional sentences in the everyday use of natural language. The following conditional sentence illustrates the difficulty:

if it is raining **then** the roof is wet   (1)

There are four cases that must be considered if we are to fully understand this sentence.

Case 1

If we have

'it is raining' = TRUE

and

'the roof is wet' = TRUE

then everyone will agree that (1) is a true statement.

Case 2

Also if we have

'it is raining' = TRUE

and

'the roof is wet' = FALSE

then we may expect that there will be wide agreement that the implication (1) is false within the bounds of normal interpretation. This accounts for the two straightforward cases for implication.

There are however two other cases that must be dealt with.

Case 3

Where we have

'it is raining' = FALSE

and

'the roof is wet' = TRUE

there is little in our experience with natural language that can usefully guide us into making a judgement as to whether the implication (1) should be true or false.

Case 4

Also where we have

'it is raining' = FALSE

and

'the roof is wet' = FALSE

there is again little to suggest whether the implication (1) should be either true or false.

In logic and mathematics, to overcome this difficulty, the position taken is that whenever the antecedent is false (i.e. 'it is raining' = FALSE) the implication is true *regardless* of whether the consequent (i.e. 'the roof is wet') is true or false.

Having taken this stance, we then have to be prepared to admit implications like:

if 'it is raining' **then** $2 + 3 = 5$ (2)

as a true implication on the grounds that its consequent is true. On intuitive grounds it is easy to argue that this implication is meaningless because the truth of the consequent has no dependence on the truth of the antecedent. This objection however loses its force as soon as we realize that it is probably very difficult to formulate a precise enough characterization of dependence to be of use in formal logic. We will therefore choose to admit implications like (2).

Table 2.3

Handle	Latch	Existence
down (T)	in (T)	can exist (T)
down (T)	out (F)	cannot exist (F)
up (F)	in (T)	can exist (T)
up (F)	out (F)	can exist (T)

Another objection that is sometimes raised against the present definition of implication is that it is counter-intuitive to describe any implication as true when its antecedent is false. Going back to our earlier example:

if 'it is raining', **then** 'the roof is wet'

If both 'it is raining' and 'the roof is wet' are false we would still expect that few would argue against designating the implication (1) as true. If on the other hand we have a situation where the antecedent is false but the consequent is true (e.g. if 'it is raining' is false while 'the roof is wet' is true) then again we would not expect most people to argue strongly against designating the implication (1) as true.

An example that is useful in providing an intuitive understanding of implication is the model illustrated in Table 2.3 for a door-latch. The handle 'implies' the latch.

The implication table completely characterizes the behaviour of a *working* door-latch. When the handle is pressed down the latch is retracted into the locking mechanism (see row 1 of the table). However, if the handle were pressed down and the latch did not retract, it would signify that the door-latch was broken and no longer behaving like a door-latch (see row 2 of the table). It is also possible for the handle to be up and the latch retracted. Pushing the latch in by hand when the door is open would achieve this configuration without destroying the door latch (see row 3 of the table). Finally the 'rest' position for the door-latch is where the handle is up and the latch is extending out from the locking mechanism (see row 4 of the table). For those who remain unconvinced by these sorts of arguments it is simply a matter of regarding $p \Rightarrow q$ as shorthand for both $\neg p \vee q$ and $\neg(p \wedge \neg q)$.

Equivalence ($p \equiv q$)

The construction '... if and only if ...', together with two propositions p and q replacing the dots may be used to form an **equivalence** or **biconditional** proposition. The equivalence 'p **if and only if** q' has the same meaning as '**if** p **then** q, and **if** q **then** p'.

Rule
An equivalence is true if and only if its two members are either both true or both false.

Truth Table (equivalence)

p	q	$p \equiv q$
T	*T*	*T*
T	*F*	*F*
F	*T*	*F*
F	*F*	*T*

Conditional Connectives (cand and cor)

Two other useful connectives that are employed in specifications and some programming languages are:

> **cand**   conditional AND ($\wedge$)
> **cor**   conditional OR ($\vee$)

The rules for evaluation with these connectives are:

> e1 **cand** e2

(1)   e1 is always evaluated
(2)   e2 is only evaluated if e1 is true

> e1 **cor** e2

(1)   e1 is always evaluated
(2)   e2 is only evaluated if e1 is false

Conditional evaluation prevents the consideration of undefined components in specifications, for example, a subscript that is out of range. The connective **cand** behaves like **and** when both e1 and e2 need to be evaluated and **cor** behaves like **or** when both e1 and e2 need to be evaluated.

2.3.2   Formation rules for propositions

Every compound proposition or propositional expression is formed from elementary propositions or propositional variables by use of the logical connectives. If we define an **elementary propositional expression** as a proposition that does not contain any connectives, then the main formation rules for propositional expressions may be as follows:

Rule 1
Every elementary proposition or propositional variable is a propositional expression.

Rule 2
The negation of a propositional expression yields a new propositional expression.

Rule 3
Every combination of two propositional expressions by means of a logical connective is also a propositional expression.

Notice here that the rules are recursive in that propositional expressions are defined in terms of propositional expressions. This is a frequently used definitional device.

These rules require that propositional expressions (or compound propositions, or just propositions) be constructed in a stepwise manner. These expressions assume a structure that reflects this construction. Parentheses may be used to identify the required structure. Some examples are:

$$p \vee (\neg q) \Rightarrow r$$
$$((p \vee q) \wedge (\neg r)) \Rightarrow (q \Rightarrow p)$$

To keep to a minimum the number of parentheses needed to guarantee a desired meaning for a compound proposition a precedence rule for the evaluation of the connectives and the negation operator may be introduced. The order of evaluation that we choose to adopt is:

EVALUATE FIRST $\neg, \wedge, \vee, \Rightarrow, \equiv$ EVALUATE LAST

Apart from this, the conventions for parentheses are the same as those used in algebra and arithmetic. Some equivalent expressions with and without parentheses are given in Table 2.4.

Table 2.4

With parentheses	*Without parentheses*
$p \vee (q \wedge r)$ (cf. $p + (q \times r)$)	$p \vee q \wedge r$ (cf. $p + q \times r$)
$(p \wedge q) \Rightarrow r$	$p \wedge q \Rightarrow r$
$p \wedge (\neg q) \Rightarrow r$	$p \wedge \neg q \Rightarrow r$
$((p \vee q) \wedge (\neg r)) \Rightarrow (q \Rightarrow p)$	$(p \vee q) \wedge \neg r \Rightarrow (q \Rightarrow p)$
$(q \wedge r) \equiv p$	$q \wedge r \equiv p$

In applications we will sometimes retain unnecessary parentheses in order to emphasize particular structure in a formula.

2.3.3 Tautologies

The notion of tautology plays an important role in logical inference and in the manipulation and simplification of propositions. A tautology is a compound proposition which possesses a form that guarantees it will remain true independently of the truth-values of its component elementary propositions. The following is a more formal definition:

Tautology †
A proposition is a tautology if and only if it always remains true when any of its component elementary propositions are replaced in all occurrences by other elementary propositions.

One of the simplest examples of a tautology is $p \vee \neg p$. The following truth table for all truth values of the elementary propositions confirms that it is a tautology.

p	¬p	$p \vee \neg p$
T	*F*	*T*
F	*T*	*T*

As this example suggests truth tables may be used to decide whether compound propositions with a relatively small number of component elementary propositions are indeed tautologies. Unfortunately the number of rows in a truth table grows exponentially with the number of component elementary propositions. A single proposition leads to two rows in the truth

† The opposite of a tautology is a *contradiction*. A contradiction is a proposition which is always false no matter what values are assigned to its elementary propositions; contradictions can be constructed from the negation of tautologies.

table, for two component propositions there are four rows, for three component propositions there are eight rows, and so on. The four combinations for two propositions p and q are:

p	q
T	T
T	F
F	T
F	F

In general, for n distinct component elementary propositions, there are 2^n combinations of truth values (and hence 2^n rows in the truth table) to consider. This underlines the limited use of this method for deciding whether particular expressions are tautologies. We will therefore need to consider other more appropriate ways of addressing this question.

Two useful notions that follow from the idea of the tautology are the concepts of **tautological implication** and **tautological equivalence**. These concepts will now be examined.

Tautological implication
A proposition p is said to tautologically imply a proposition q if and only if the implication p ⇒ q is a tautology.

What this means in terms of truth tables is that for any row of the table in which p is true, then q will also need to be true for p to tautologically imply q. For example, given:

p	q	p ∨ q
T	T	T
T	F	T
F	T	T
F	F	F

it follows that p tautologically implies p ∨ q but p ∨ q does *not* tautologically imply p.

Tautological equivalence
A proposition p is said to be tautologically equivalent to a proposition q if and only if p tautologically implies q, and q tautologically implies p.

What this means in terms of truth tables is that in any row of the table in which p is true, q will also need to be true, and in any row in which p is false, q will also need to be false – in other words their columns must match. For example $\neg(\neg p \vee q)$ is tautologically equivalent to $p \wedge \neg q$ since their truth-table columns are identical.

p	q	$\neg(\neg p \vee q)$	$p \wedge \neg q$
T	T	F	F
T	F	T	T
F	T	F	F
F	F	F	F

a and b can only be tautologically equivalent when $a \equiv b$ is a tautology. Consider $p \Rightarrow q$ and $\neg p \vee q$ for example:

p	q	$\neg p \vee q$	$p \Rightarrow q$	$(p \Rightarrow q) \equiv (\neg p \vee q)$
T	T	T	T	T
T	F	F	F	T
F	T	T	T	T
F	F	T	T	T

Analytic transformations

Tautologies provide a vehicle for making the analytic transformations necessary to manipulate and simplify complex propositions. All propositions may be classified as either **analytic, synthetic**, or **contradictory**. Tautologies are analytic while propositions that are neither tautologies nor contradictions are synthetic. Tautologies are always true for all combinations of truth values of their elementary propositions. In contrast synthetic propositions (also called contingencies) can be false for some combinations of truth values of their elementary propositions. Synthetic formulae carry information about restrictions of the truth-values of their elementary propositions. On the other hand tautologies do not convey similar information. They place *no* restrictions on the truth-values of elementary propositions. It is the structure of a tautological proposition that guarantees its truth. This property of tautologies is essential for them to be able to serve as instruments for analytical transformation. To explore a proposition it is absolutely necessary that any analytic transformations employed do not in any way add anything to the meaning of that proposition.

A considerable number of useful tautologies have been identified. Some of the more well-known ones will be listed below. Those involving equivalences are particularly important. They allow us to replace one propositional form by another that is logically equivalent. For example, given the proposition $(p \wedge p) \wedge q$ and the knowledge that $p \wedge p$ is logically equivalent to p we can replace $p \wedge p$ by p to obtain the simpler but equivalent

Table 2.5

Tautology (T)	Comment or description
(1) $p \equiv p$	law of identity
(2) $p \vee p \equiv p$ $p \wedge p \equiv p$	idempotent laws
(3) $\neg(\neg p) \equiv p$	law of double negation
(4) $p \vee \neg p \equiv T$	law of the excluded middle (*tertium non datur*)
(5) $\neg(p \wedge \neg p) \equiv T$	law of contradiction (also used as $p \wedge \neg p \equiv F$)
(6) $(p \Rightarrow \neg p) \equiv \neg p$	*reductio ad absurdum*
(7) $p \vee q \equiv q \vee p$ $p \wedge q \equiv q \wedge p$ $(p \equiv q) \equiv (q \equiv p)$	commutative laws
(8) $(p \vee q) \vee r \equiv p \vee (q \vee r)$ $(p \wedge q) \wedge r \equiv p \wedge (q \wedge r)$	associative laws
(9) $p \vee (q \wedge r) \equiv (p \vee q) \wedge (p \vee r)$ $p \wedge (q \vee r) \equiv (p \wedge q) \vee (p \wedge r)$	distributive laws
(10) $(p \Rightarrow q) \wedge (q \Rightarrow r) \Rightarrow (p \Rightarrow r)$ $(p \equiv q) \wedge (q \equiv r) \Rightarrow (p \Rightarrow r)$	transitive laws
(11) $\neg(p \vee q) \equiv \neg p \wedge \neg q$ $\neg(p \wedge q) \equiv \neg p \vee \neg q$ $\neg(p \Rightarrow q) \equiv p \wedge \neg q$ $\neg(p \equiv q) \equiv (p \equiv \neg q)$	de Morgan's laws
(12) $p \vee T \equiv T$ $p \vee p \equiv p$ $p \vee (p \wedge q) \equiv p$	*or*-simplification (note $p \vee F \equiv p$ $T \vee T \equiv T$ $T \vee F \equiv T$)
(13) $p \wedge T \equiv p$ $p \wedge p \equiv p$ $p \wedge (p \vee q) \equiv p$	*and*-simplification (note $p \wedge F \equiv F$ $T \wedge F \equiv F$ $T \wedge T \equiv T$)
(14) $(p \Rightarrow q) \wedge (p \Rightarrow r) \equiv (p \Rightarrow q \wedge r)$ $(p \Rightarrow r) \wedge (q \Rightarrow r) \equiv (p \vee q \Rightarrow r)$ $(p \Rightarrow q) \vee (p \Rightarrow r) \equiv (p \Rightarrow q \vee r)$ $(p \Rightarrow r) \vee (q \Rightarrow r) \equiv (p \wedge q \Rightarrow r)$	implication- simplification
(15) $p \Rightarrow q \equiv \neg q \Rightarrow \neg p$ $(p \equiv q) \equiv (\neg p \equiv \neg q)$	contraposition
(16) $p \Rightarrow p \vee q$ $(p \Rightarrow q) \Rightarrow (p \Rightarrow q \vee r)$ $(p \Rightarrow q) \Rightarrow (p \wedge r \Rightarrow q)$ $(p \Rightarrow q) \Rightarrow (p \Rightarrow (p \wedge q))$	law of additition law of absorption

Table 2.5   (*Cont.*)

Tautology (T)	Comment or description
(17) $p \wedge q \Rightarrow p$	law of simplification
(18) $(p \wedge q \Rightarrow r) \Rightarrow (p \Rightarrow (q \Rightarrow r))$ $(p \vee q \Rightarrow r) \Rightarrow (p \Rightarrow r)$	law of exportation
(19) $(p \Rightarrow (q \Rightarrow r)) \Rightarrow (p \wedge q \Rightarrow r)$ $(p \Rightarrow (q \wedge r)) \Rightarrow (p \Rightarrow q)$	law of importation
(20) $p \Rightarrow (q \wedge \neg q) \Rightarrow \neg p$	law of absurdity
(21) $p \wedge (p \Rightarrow q) \Rightarrow q$	law of detachment
(22) $\neg q \wedge (p \Rightarrow q) \Rightarrow \neg p$	
(23) $\neg p \wedge (p \vee q) \Rightarrow q$	

proposition $p \wedge q$. In general if two propositional forms are logically equivalent one may be substituted for the other in one or more places. The resulting proposition will be logically equivalent to the original proposition. Equivalent propositional forms behave like identities. They can be verified using truth tables by case analysis. Because of their obvious use we have listed separately the tautologies that may be used to eliminate connectives.

Tautologies for eliminating connectives (T)

$$p \vee q \equiv (\neg p \Rightarrow q)$$
$$p \vee q \equiv \neg(\neg p \wedge \neg q)$$
$$p \wedge q \equiv \neg(p \Rightarrow \neg q)$$
$$p \wedge q \equiv \neg(\neg p \vee \neg q)$$
$$p \Rightarrow q \equiv \neg p \vee q$$
$$p \Rightarrow q \equiv \neg(p \wedge \neg q)$$
$$(p \equiv q) \equiv (p \Rightarrow q) \wedge (q \Rightarrow p)$$
$$(p \equiv q) \equiv (p \wedge q) \vee (\neg p \wedge \neg q)$$

The more extensive table of tautologies is given in Table 2.5.

2.3.4   Derivations using tautologies

The symbolic nature of logical propositions or formulae means they are open to manipulation much in the same way as mathematical formulae. Compare for example the laws of associativity, commutativity, and distributivity with the equivalent numerical algebraic transformations where

'∨' is interpreted as '+' and '∧' is interpreted as '×'. For the distributive laws we have:

$$p \wedge (q \vee r) \equiv (p \wedge q) \vee (p \wedge r)$$

compared with

$$p \times (q + r) = p \times q + p \times r$$

In making such a comparison it is important to note that in the algebra of logic there is a second distributive law. For example:

$$p \vee (q \wedge r) \equiv (p \vee q) \wedge (p \vee r)$$

whose analogue in the algebra of numbers (for example, $p + (q \times r) = (p + q) \times (p + r)$) does *not* hold. This law together with de Morgan's laws expresses the duality or mutual interchangeability of '∨' and '∧' in certain formulae. For example, if for one of de Morgan's laws, '∨' is substituted for '∧' and vice versa, then the other law of de Morgan is obtained. By means of substitution and replacement it is possible to derive many of the formulae in our tautology table from other formulas listed there. For example:

$$
\begin{aligned}
p \Rightarrow q &\equiv \neg p \vee q && \text{(implication)} \\
&\equiv q \vee \neg p && \text{(commutivity)} \\
&\equiv \neg q \Rightarrow \neg p && \text{(implication)}
\end{aligned}
$$

and

$$
\begin{aligned}
(p \equiv q) &\equiv (p \Rightarrow q) \wedge (q \Rightarrow p) \\
&\equiv (\neg p \vee q) \wedge (\neg q \vee p) \\
&\equiv (\neg p \wedge \neg q) \vee (q \wedge \neg q) \vee (p \wedge \neg p) \vee (p \wedge q) \\
&\equiv (p \wedge q) \vee (\neg p \wedge \neg q)
\end{aligned}
$$

To make the last simplification the rules $a \wedge \neg a \equiv F$ and $b \vee F \equiv b$ have been used.

Our interest in applying derivations is often to reduce a formula to its simplest form where the only connectives are '∧' and '∨' and negation applies only to elementary propositions. There are two such forms. One is called a **disjunctive normal form** in which the major connectives are disjunctions. In general it has the form:

$$(p_1 \wedge p_2 \wedge \ldots) \vee (q_1 \wedge q_2 \wedge \ldots) \vee \ldots$$

The other normal form is **conjunctive normal form** in which the major connectives are conjunctions. In general it has the form:

$$(p_1 \vee p_2 \vee \ldots) \wedge (q_1 \vee q_2 \vee \ldots) \wedge \ldots$$

Both synthetic and analytic formulae can be reduced to these normal forms.

These normal forms provide a means for checking whether a given formula is a tautology and also whether two different propositions are tautologically equivalent. When a formula is in disjunctive normal form, if two of its terms taken together constitute a tautology (for example, $p \vee \neg p$), then it follows that the whole disjunction must be a tautology. For example, it follows that:

$$p \vee (q \wedge \neg p) \vee \neg p$$

is a tautology since it contains '$p \vee \neg p$'. To illustrate how normal forms may be used to determine whether two different expressions are tautologically equivalent consider:

$$\neg((p \Rightarrow \neg q) \wedge (r \Rightarrow p))$$

and

$$(q \Rightarrow \neg p) \Rightarrow \neg(r \Rightarrow p)$$

Reducing both expressions to disjunctive normal form we get:

expression (1):

$$
\begin{aligned}
\neg((p \Rightarrow \neg q) \wedge (r \Rightarrow p)) &\equiv \neg(p \Rightarrow \neg q) \vee \neg(r \Rightarrow p) \\
&\equiv \neg(\neg p \vee \neg q) \vee \neg(\neg r \vee p) \\
&\equiv (p \wedge q) \vee (r \wedge \neg p) \quad \text{(normal form)}
\end{aligned}
$$

expression (2):

$$
\begin{aligned}
(q \Rightarrow \neg p) \Rightarrow \neg(r \Rightarrow p) &\equiv \neg(q \Rightarrow \neg p) \vee \neg(r \Rightarrow p) \\
&\equiv \neg(\neg q \vee \neg p) \vee \neg(\neg r \vee p) \\
&\equiv \neg(\neg p \vee \neg q) \vee \neg(\neg r \vee p) \\
&\equiv (p \wedge q) \vee (r \wedge \neg p) \quad \text{(normal form)}
\end{aligned}
$$

Comparing the normal forms for the two expressions we see they are tautologically equivalent. In making comparisons to test for tautological equivalence it is essential that the simplification is taken as far as possible. For example the formula:

$$(p \wedge q) \vee (p \wedge \neg q) \vee (r \wedge s)$$

which is in disjunctive normal form, can be simplified further by application of the distributive law for example:

$$
\begin{aligned}
(p \wedge q) \vee (p \wedge \neg q) \vee (r \wedge s) &\equiv p \wedge (q \vee \neg q) \vee (r \wedge s) \\
&\equiv p \vee (r \wedge s)
\end{aligned}
$$

Another important form of derivation is that where implications are derived instead of the more substantial equivalent expressions. Implications provide the basis for making inferences. For example if we start out with the expression:

$$\neg(p \vee q) \tag{1}$$

then by applying de Morgan's law we obtain the equivalent expression:

$$\neg p \wedge \neg q \tag{2}$$

Then, by the law of simplification, since

$$\neg p \wedge \neg q \Rightarrow \neg p$$

we derive the conclusion

$$\neg p \tag{3}$$

The expression (3) is reached from (2) by an *inference*. Therefore if (1) is true then (3) must also be true and so we end up with the following tautological implication:

$$\neg(p \vee q) \Rightarrow \neg p \tag{4}$$

Horn clauses

An important disjunctive form is the **horn clause**. Horn clauses are used for derivation by the resolution method (this technique is employed by the logic programming language Prolog). A horn clause is made up of the disjunction of one or more elementary propositions or atoms of which at most one is not negated.

p
p ∨ ¬q
p ∨ ¬q1 ∨ ¬q2

Important implications with the forms:

(1) $p1 \vee p2 \vee ... \vee pN \Rightarrow q$ (equivalent to the conjunction of N horn clauses)

(2) $p1 \wedge p2 \wedge ... \wedge pN \Rightarrow q$

have equivalent horn clause representations, that is,

$$p1 \vee p2 \vee ... \vee pN \Rightarrow q \equiv (q \vee \neg p1) \wedge (q \vee \neg p2) \wedge ... \wedge (q \vee \neg pN)$$

$$p1 \wedge p2 \wedge ... \wedge pN \Rightarrow q \equiv q \vee \neg p1 \vee \neg p2 \vee ... \vee \neg pN$$

The resolution principle

Resolution is a useful simplification strategy that can sometimes be applied to formulae that have been reduced either to conjunctive normal form or disjunctive normal form. It is appropriate to apply resolution either when there are two conjuncts or disjuncts one containing a proposition p and the other containing ¬p.

If p and ¬p occur in a formula in conjunctive normal form then the two conjuncts

$$(p \lor q) \land (\neg p \lor r)$$

can be replaced by the single conjunct

$$q \lor r$$

This represents an application of the **conjunctive resolution rule**

$$(p \lor q) \land (\neg p \lor r) \Rightarrow q \lor r$$

which is a tautology.

If on the other hand p and ¬p occur in a formula in disjunctive normal form, then the two disjuncts

$$(p \land q) \lor (\neg p \land r)$$

can be replaced by the single disjunct

$$q \lor r$$

This represents an application of the disjunctive resolution rule

$$(p \land q) \lor (\neg p \land r) \Rightarrow q \lor r$$

which is also a tautology.

In both of the above simplification steps the replacements do not alter the validity of the resulting formulae. Other simplification rules can be applied when we have two conjuncts or disjuncts that share a proposition p. These rules may be summarized as follows:

$(p \land q) \lor (p \land r)$	can be replaced by	$p \land (q \lor r)$
$(p \lor q) \land (p \lor r)$	can be replaced by	$p \lor (q \land r)$
$p \land (p \lor q)$	can be replaced by	p
$p \lor (p \land q)$	can be replaced by	p

All of these replacements *do not* alter the validity of the formulae they simplify. In applying these rules there are two underlying strategies.

(1)   One approach to establishing the validity of some theorem is to first transform it to its disjunctive normal form, then apply various simplifications in an effort to reduce the formula to a known tautology (e.g. $p \lor \neg p$).

(2)   The other approach is to first negate the formula, then transform it to conjunctive normal form, and finally apply various simplifications in an effort to reduce the formula to a known contradiction (e.g. $p \land \neg p$). If this can be done, the original theorem to be proved must have been true since it has been shown that its negation is false.

Rules of derivation

The method of derivation that we have alluded to may be formalized by a set of rules for substitution, replacement, and inference.

Rule of substitution
A formula resulting from a tautology may be asserted when an arbitrary proposition is substituted for all occurrences of some other arbitrary proposition in the original formula.

In other words if the original formula is a tautology then so will be the resulting formula derived by the substitution.

As an example, given the tautology

$$p \land (p \Rightarrow q) \Rightarrow q$$

if we replace p in *all* instances by the proposition $r \lor s$, the resulting formula

$$(r \lor s) \land ((r \lor s) \Rightarrow q) \Rightarrow q$$

is also a tautology. When a formula is not a tautology, that is

$$(p \land q) \lor (p \land u)$$

and we replace a proposition (e.g. p) by some arbitrary proposition (e.g. $r \lor s$) the resulting formula

$$((r \lor s) \land q) \lor ((r \lor s) \land u)$$

is logically equivalent to the original formula.

Of equal importance in derivation is the notion of **replacement**. Replacement provides a means by which compound expressions and constants may be replaced. The expression introduced must be **equivalent** to the expression it replaces. There is no requirement that the replacement be made in all the available places where the original expression occurs. This is different to substitution.

Rule of replacement

A formula resulting from a true formula may be asserted when an equivalent propositional expression is substituted for one or more occurrences of a particular expression in the original formula.

As an example, given the tautology

$$(r \Rightarrow s) \wedge ((r \Rightarrow s) \Rightarrow q) \Rightarrow q$$

if we replace one occurrence of $r \Rightarrow s$ by the logically equivalent proposition $\neg r \vee s$, that is

$$(r \Rightarrow s) \wedge ((\neg r \vee s) \Rightarrow q) \Rightarrow q$$

the resulting formula is logically equivalent to the original formula.

The remaining rules for derivation concern inference and deduction.

2.3.5   Inference and proof

Truth tables are of only limited use for checking the validity of arguments. The theory of logic has therefore sought to provide a more practical set of tools and principles for reasoning. This aspect of logic is described in terms of a theory of inference. An important practical objective of any theory of inference is to provide a set of criteria that can be used systematically to decide whether a particular line of reasoning may be accepted as correct purely on the basis of its form. The form of such chains of reasoning (or deductions) is just an ordered sequence of propositions which are given to support the contention that the last member of the chain, the conclusion, may be inferred from certain initial propositions called premises. If the premises of an inference are accepted as true on the basis of experience or empirical evidence, along with the derivations made, then the conclusion deduced can be regarded as true.

Consider the following premises:

Premise 1.   **if** 'it is raining' **then** 'the roof is wet' $(p \Rightarrow q)$
Premise 2.   'it is raining' (p)

we may ask what conclusion can be logically inferred from these two premises? Clearly the conclusion that can be logically inferred from these premises is:

Conclusion: 'the roof is wet'

We now need to examine a framework that will put the derivation of conclusions from a set of premises on a sound basis. The theory of inference that we will consider rests on three rules of derivation, one relating to the introduction of premises (P), a second involving the use of tautological implications (TI), and a third rule based on the notion of conditional proof (CP).

The rules are:

Rule of premises (P)
A premise may be used at any point in a derivation.

Rule of tautological implication (TI)
A proposition q may be introduced into a derivation if there is a set of other sentences that precede it which have the property that their conjunction tautologically implies q.

Rule of conditional proof (CP)
If q is derived from p and a set of premises, then the implication $p \Rightarrow q$ may be derived from the premises alone.

These three rules, together with a set of inference rules can be used to make inferencial derivations from a set of premises that have been symbolically expressed using the propositional connectives. The tautological implications given earlier can be used to make inferences. However, we need to distinguish between the concepts of inference and implication. The following example, which introduces the **primary rule of inference**, illustrates the difference.

Rule of Inference (Modus ponendo ponens PP)†			**Tautological implication**
			$(p \wedge (p \Rightarrow q)) \Rightarrow q$
Schema	$p \Rightarrow q$	(*premise*)	
Representation	p	(*premise*)	
	q	(*conclusion*)	

The modus ponendo ponens (PP) (i.e. mood of affirming) is the primary rule of inference. It is the rule most frequently used in formal derivations. What

† Also written sometimes as 'Modus ponens'

this rule says is '*if* it is known that the proposition p ⇒ q is true and that the proposition p is also true, *then* we can conclude that the proposition q is true.' In the interests of making derivations simpler it is convenient to supplement this primary rule with a set of secondary rules of inference which have their origins in traditional logic. The schemas for these rules are listed below.

Modus tollendo tollens (TT)

$$p \Rightarrow q$$
$$\underline{\neg q}$$
$$\neg p$$

Addition (AD)

$$\underline{\quad p \quad}$$
$$p \vee q$$

Modus tollendo ponens (TP)

$$p \vee q$$
$$\underline{\neg p}$$
$$q$$

Adjunction (A)

$$p$$
$$\underline{q}$$
$$p \wedge q$$

Double negation (DN)

$$\underline{\quad p \quad}$$
$$\neg\neg p$$

Hypothetical syllogism (HS)

$$p \Rightarrow q$$
$$\underline{q \Rightarrow r}$$
$$p \Rightarrow r$$

Conjunctive simplification (C)

$$\underline{p \wedge q}$$
$$p$$

Disjunctive syllogism (DS)

$$p \vee q$$
$$p \Rightarrow r$$
$$\underline{q \Rightarrow s}$$
$$r \vee s$$

Disjunctive simplification

$$\underline{p \vee p}$$
$$p$$

Biconditional simplification (B)

$$\underline{p \equiv q}$$
$$p \Rightarrow q$$

This list of inference rules is sufficient for most simple derivations although additional rules are sometimes borrowed from traditional logic.

The process of using a rule of inference to move from one set of propositions to another amounts to *proving* that the latter proposition follows logically from the former. A set of simple conventions are used for presenting such proofs. Each line of a proof consists of a sequence number, and then the symbolized step in the proof, followed by an indication of which lines (if any) and which rule was used to derive the current step. As an example, suppose for some propositions p, q, and r, we are given the premises:

$$p \Rightarrow \neg q \qquad \text{(premise 1)}$$
$$p \qquad\qquad \text{(premise 2)}$$
$$\neg q \Rightarrow r \qquad \text{(premise 3)}$$

and we are required to prove the conclusion r. This may be symbolized as

$$p \Rightarrow \neg q, p, \neg q \Rightarrow r \vdash r\dagger$$

Using the abbreviations for the rules given in this section the proof may be constructed as follows:

Proof

(1)	$p \Rightarrow \neg q$	P
(2)	p	P
(3)	$\neg q \Rightarrow r$	P
(4)	$\neg q$	PP 1, 2
(5)	r	PP 3, 4

Sometimes it is necessary to derive a conclusion that is an implication. A conditional proof is often used for this purpose. For example given the following four premises a conditional proof may be applied to yield:

$$e \Rightarrow c \wedge d$$

Proof

(1)	$a \Rightarrow (b \Rightarrow c \wedge d)$	P	
(2)	$\neg e \vee a$	P	
(3)	b	P	
(4)	e	P	(premise of conditional proof)
(5)	a	TP 2, 4	
(6)	$b \Rightarrow c \wedge d$	PP 1, 5	
(7)	$c \wedge d$	PP 3, 6	
(8)	$e \Rightarrow c \wedge d$	CP 4, 7	

Note that only a line that is a premise can be conditionalized. Conditionalization on line (5), i.e. $a \Rightarrow c \wedge d$, is invalid.

Similar proof techniques may be used to demonstrate that a given set of premises is inconsistent. This is done by making a logical derivation that establishes a contradiction (for example, $p \wedge \neg p$). This is an indirect proof technique.

2.4   Predicate Calculus

The propositional calculus alone does not provide either a rich enough means of expression or an adequate power of reasoning for program design.

---

† '$\vdash$' is a metasymbol that is used in making statements about formulae, but it is not part of a formula. $\vdash$ may be read as 'it is true'.

However, the extensions to logic that belong to the predicate calculus go a considerable way towards providing the power of reasoning and expression necessary for the construction and manipulation of specifications needed in program design. We will begin our introduction to the predicate calculus by an examination of the structure of the simplest possible expressions. This requires precise definitions for **terms** and **predicates** to replace their less precise, but common usage.

2.4.1 Terms

Terms are used to name, label, or identify entities. They may be either constants, variables or functions of terms. Examples of terms are:

constant:	3 and 'a' are terms
variable:	x and y are terms
function of terms:	plus(x,y), which is more often written 'x + y' is a term. Here the function plus of two terms x and y is itself a term.

Whatever would pass as a value parameter used in calling a Pascal procedure would pass the classification test for a term. The most important kind of terms are **variables**. To represent variables we commonly use letters and names like x and y. Variables play a role in predicate calculus similar to that of nouns and pronouns in natural language. They also provide the basis for expressing things much more concisely than other alternatives. For example, instead of writing:

Canberra is the capital of Australia

if we let

c = 'Canberra'

and

a = 'the capital of Australia'

and interpret 'is' as identity we may express the above statement more crisply using the terms c and a as:

c = a

Hence c represents a constant and a represents a description. Both c and a are terms as is c = a. Variables that function as terms do not usually name or designate unique objects. More often they designate sets of objects.

For example, in the expression

x > 0

the variable x characterizes a set of numbers. The expression will only be true for numbers greater than zero. There is however no obligation to restrict x to positive values. The truth-value of such expressions can only be determined when x is replaced by a number. As we saw earlier the notion of a term, as it is used in the predicate calculus, is generalized further to include expressions like 'x + y'. For example, the term 'x + y' in the expression:

x + y > 0

designates the number 3 when x is replaced by 1 and y is replaced by 2. A term is therefore an expression that names or describes an entity, or that results in a name or designation of a unique entity when its component variables are replaced by names or descriptions of unique entities.

A simple formal definition of a term is as follows:

Term
A term is either a constant, or a variable, or a function of other terms.

2.4.2   Predicates

Predicates, like terms, describe things, but in a different way. To understand the notion of predicate consider first its use in natural language. There, it is used to describe the word or words in a sentence or clause which identifies what is said about the subject of the sentence. For example, in the sentence

John is tall

the word John is a term. However the phrase is tall does not satisfy the definition of a term. Clearly the two components of this sentence John and is tall have a fundamentally different logical nature. A distinction is made between an **entity**, and a **property** which may be attached to entities.

The phrase is tall refers to a property of John. It is classified as a predicate because it refers to a property of an entity. This is in direct contrast to terms which serve to uniquely identify entities. In this sense a term completely describes an entity. We can also adopt a relational interpretation of our example. We can say that an **entity-property** relation holds between an entity denoted by the word John and a property denoted by the word tall.

Other examples of predicates (underlined) that ascribe a property to an entity are:

John is a man
John runs
John is running

From these examples we see that a predicate can denote a property or quality or aspect that an individual can possess. In logic predicates are given a broader role. As well as ascribing properties to entities, predicates are also used to denote relations that hold among two or more entities, for example

> John is taller than Mary

is an example of a **two-place predicate**. It (i.e. the is-taller-than relation) is a relation between two terms. To emphasize that it is a two-place predicate it could be written as follows:

> is-taller-than (John, Mary)

or symbolically:

> I(j,m)

Another two-place predicate is 'x < y' which could be written as:

> less-than (x,y)

All such relational statements may be either true or false and so we might describe such predicates as relations in truth-value form.

An example of a three-place predicate would be:

> John ran the marathon with Mary

which could be expressed as:

> ran ... with (John, the marathon, Mary)

There is no restriction on the number of places a predicate may involve although the most commonly encountered relational predicates are two-place predicates.

We now have enough background to be able to provide a suitable working definition for predicates. Predicates, as they are used in logic, assume a much broader role than the one they play in natural language. In particular, they are not distinguished according to their grammatical function. A suitable definition for our purposes is:

Predicate
A predicate is a formula that may be used either to ascribe a property to an entity or to assert that certain entities stand in some relationship.

It is now necessary to extend the use of predicates by the introduction of quantifiers.

2.4.3 Quantifiers

It is often necessary to ascribe properties to *some* or *all* of a set of elements. We also need to be able to characterize relations that hold among some or all members of a set of elements. To do this it is necessary to extend the notation that we have introduced by including quantifiers and a set of rules and conventions that govern their use.

Earlier, in our discussion of expressions, we found that it was not always possible to assign a truth-value until the variables were replaced by particular values. For example, it is not possible to say whether the expression

$$x + y > 0$$

is true or false until both x and y have been given particular values (for example, if x was replaced by 1 and y was replaced by 0 the expression would evaluate to *true*).

Quantification provides a means for writing certain expressions that may be true or false without requiring that their variables all be replaced by specific values.

Universal quantification

A common form of expression that is often used in logic, mathematics, and program design is

> For all x, x has property P

In some treatments of the predicate calculus the phrase 'for all x' is referred to as a **universal quantifier**, while in other treatments 'for all' is regarded as **the universal quantifier**. We will adopt the latter convention. There are a number of different conventions that are used to symbolize this. The most common notation is probably

> (∀x) (Px)   this says that for all x, in the given universe of discourse, the predicate Px is true. Here '∀' symbolizes 'for all', and Px is a formula that possibly contains x.

Sometimes the '∀' is omitted and the universal quantifier is expressed simply as (x) and so we get (x)(Px). In still other cases, (Ax)(Px) is used.

Some examples are:

$(\forall x) (x > 0)$ is satisfied by all positive numbers

$(\forall x) (\forall y) (x + y > 0)$ is satisfied by all pairs of numbers whose sum is positive

$(\forall x) (\forall y) (x > 0 \wedge y > 0 \wedge x + y = 10)$ is satisfied by all pairs of positive numbers that add up to 10.

Simply adding a quantifier to a formula does not necessarily guarantee to make it true or false, for example

$(\forall x) (x + y > 0)$

is neither true nor false until y is bound to some value.

Existential quantification

Another form of expression commonly used is

For some x , x has property P

Other ways of saying 'for some x', are 'there exists an x such that', or 'there is at least one x such that'. As with universal quantification there are two conventions. In some treatments 'for some x' is treated as **an existential quantifier** whereas in other treatments 'for some' is regarded as **the existential quantifier**. We will adopt the latter convention. All these phrases are described as **existential quantifiers**. The most common symbolization:

$(\exists x) (Px)$ which is satisfied if for some x in the given universe of discourse the formula Px is true.

Sometimes existential quantification is represented by $(Ex) (Px)$.
Examples are:

$(\exists x) (x > 0)$ which is satisfied if there is some number or numbers such that $x > 0$ is true.

$(\exists x) (\exists y) (x > 0 \wedge y > 0 \wedge x + y = 10)$ is satisfied if there exists some pair or pairs of numbers (x,y) such that $x + y = 10$.

Care should be taken in using the following form for existential quantification:

$(\exists x) (Px \Rightarrow Qx)$

Consider the false statement

> Some primes are divisible by 10

If Px symbolizes 'prime' and Qx symbolizes 'divisible by 10' then we might be tempted to symbolize the above statement as:

$$(\exists x)\,(Px \Rightarrow Qx)$$

To see that this is not a correct symbolization consider the logically equivalent statement:

$$(\exists x)\,(\neg Px \vee Qx)$$

which means that we would be affirming that some numbers are not prime or they are divisible by 10. The appropriate symbolization for this problem is:

$$(\exists x)\,(Px \wedge Qx)$$

This expression, unlike the previous one, is false because no prime is divisible by 10.

2.4.4 Well-formed formulae

Previously we provided formation rules for constructing properly formed propositional expressions from propositions and the logical connectives. These rules need to be extended to accommodate the use of predicates and quantifiers. To do this we introduce the notions of **well-formed formula** (some texts refer to them as logical formulas or as just formulae) and **atomic formula** (in some texts the terms **elementary formula** or **atomic expression** are used).

Atomic formula
An atomic formula consists of a predicate followed or flanked by the terms which are its arguments.

For example:

$$x + y = z \quad \text{(which may be written as equals}(x + y, z))$$

satisfies the definition of an atomic formula. It consists of two terms, $x + y$ and z which flank the predicate symbol '='. Other examples are:

x is prime   (which may be symbolized as is-prime (x))
Px   (where P is a predicate and x a variable)

The latter expression may also be written as P(x). The syntax for terms and atomic formulae follows conventional notation used for writing expressions and formulae in mathematics. To achieve complete formality a recursive definition of 'term' is needed. We will not pursue that line here. Having sufficiently established the notion of atomic formula it is possible to give a recursive definition of the formation rules for more general formulae that admit predicates and quantifiers.

A well-formed formula must conform to the following rules:

Rule 1

Every atomic formula is a well-formed formula.

Rule 2

The negation of a well-formed formula P is a well-formed formula ¬P

Rule 3

Combination of two well-formed formulae by means of a logical connective (i.e. ∧, ∨, ⇒, and ≡) yields another well-formed formula.

Rule 4

If Px is a well-formed formula, and x is a free variable in P, then (∀x) (Px) and (∃x) (Px) are also well-formed formulae.

These rules are sufficient to define the syntax of well-formed formulae. They do not however provide any guarantees about the semantics of such formulae.

Several other conventions relating to the scope of quantifiers and the use of variables are needed to supplement the formation rules for well-formed formulae.

Quantifier scope

In the formula

   (∀x) Px ∧ Qx

there may be uncertainty about whether the quantifier, with its quantified variable x, is applied to Qx as well as Px. A scope rule convention may be used to overcome this problem.

Scope rule
The scope of a quantifier in a well-formed formula extends only to the smallest well-formed formula that follows the quantifier.

In our previous example applying this rule we find that the quantifier only applies to Px. Using underscores to indicate scope we have:

(∀x) P̲x̲ ∧ Qx

Parentheses may be used to extend the scope of a quantifier. For example,

(∀x) (P̲x̲ ∧̲ Q̲x̲)

In this last example the quantifier applies to both Px and Qx. The extension to the application of more than one quantifier is straightforward:

(∃x) (∃y) $\underline{(x > 0 \land y > 0 \land x + y = 10)}$†

2.4.5 Bound and free variables

There are two types of variables in well-formed formulae that involve quantifiers. Those that are controlled by a quantifier and those that are independent of any quantifier. The following definitions provide the necessary distinction between these two types of variable occurrences.

Bound variable
An instance of a variable in a well-formed formula is said to be *bound* only when it is inside the scope of the quantifier that applies it to the formula.

Free variable
An instance of a variable in a well-formed formula is said to be *free* only when that occurrence is not bound by any quantifier whose scope it is within.

---

† For notational brevity this formula may be expressed as:
∃ x,y $(x > 0 \land y > 0 \land x + y = 10)$

In the example we gave earlier, that is

$(\forall x)\, Px \wedge Qx$

the variable x used by '$\forall$' is both free and bound. Most treatments of predicate calculus permit variables to be both free and bound within one formula. However, because of the way we need to manipulate formulae in program design it is clearer and more convenient to adopt the convention of allowing only formulae where variables are either free or bound but not both. This restriction is stated in the following rule.

Variable restriction rule †
All variables in a formula should be either free or bound but not both, and a given variable in a formula, if bound, should be bound, only to one quantifier.

Applying the restriction rule, the most recent formula given should have been written:

$(\forall x)\, Px \wedge Qy$

where the variable x is bound and the variable y is free. Note that

$(\forall x)\, Px \wedge Qx$ is equivalent to $(\forall y)\, Py \wedge Qx$

but

$(\forall x)\, Px \wedge Qx$ is not equivalent to $(\forall y)\, Px \wedge Qy$

In the formula

$(\exists x)\, (x < y)$

the variable y, although it is within the scope of the quantifier, remains free because it is not bound by the quantifier. Another way of defining the scope of a quantifier is to say that it is that part of a predicate in which variables are bound by the quantifier.

The well-formed formulae that we use in program design almost invariably contain free variables. In fact in program design it is useful to distinguish further between what are called *fixed* free-variables and *non-fixed* free variables. These two types of variables loosely correspond respectively to the 'input data' and the 'output data' of a program.

---

† Formulae of the following form are permitted (see Section 2.4.6)
$\quad (\forall i)\, (1 \le i \le m \Rightarrow (\forall j)(1 \le j \le n \Rightarrow x \ne B_{i,j}))$
where i is bound to the quantifier of greater scope, and free with respect to a subordinate quantified expression.

For example, consider the problem of reading in two numbers and writing out the value of the larger of these numbers:

INPUT :   X, Y   (fixed free variables)
OUTPUT: z   (non-fixed free variable)

The specification for this problem is

$$(z = X \land X \geq Y) \lor (z = Y \land Y \geq X)$$

Convention
In writing specifications we will use the convention that fixed free variables are written using capitals and non-fixed free variables (those set by the program) are written using lower-case letters.

2.4.6   Quantification over ranges

In program design we deal with problems that involve computations over finite restricted domains and ranges. We therefore frequently want to use expressions like:

For all values i in the range R, the predicate P_i is true

There are several ways specifying such quantified expressions. Consider an example where it is necessary to specify that a fixed sequence of N elements is in non-descending order. This can be expressed as:

$$(\forall i)(1 \leq i < N \Rightarrow a_i \leq a_{i+1})\dagger \tag{1}$$

In formula (1) the range for the bound variable i is used as an antecedent of the implication and the relation which is quantified is used as the consequent of the implication.

Another convention for representing quantified expressions has been introduced by Dijkstra and adopted by a number of other computing scientists. It is slightly more concise and structured to isolate the range descriptors for bound variables. In this notation 'A' is used instead of '∀' and 'E' is used instead of '∃'. The example above would be expressed as:

$$(Ai : 1 \leq i < N : a_i \leq a_{i+1})$$

---

† The following abbreviation may be used $\forall i \in [1 .. N\text{-}1] (a_i \leq a_{i+1})$

As another example to express the fact that m is equal to the maximum value in a fixed array A[1..N] we could write:

$$(\forall i)\,(1 \leq i \leq N \Rightarrow m \geq A_i) \wedge (\exists i)\,(1 \leq i \leq N : m = A_i)$$

The second conjunct expresses the fact that m is a value in the array.

We will choose to interpret quantification over a finite range, that is

$$(\forall i)\,(1 \leq i \leq N \Rightarrow P_i) \qquad \text{as shorthand for} \qquad P_1 \wedge P_2 \wedge \ldots \wedge P_N$$

where each P_i is a predicate. The whole expression is only true if all the predicates are true.

It is also possible to give a recursive definition for universal quantification over a range in the following way:

$$(\forall i)\,(m \leq i < j \Rightarrow P_i) \equiv T \qquad\qquad\qquad \text{for } j = m - \text{empty range}$$

and

$$(\forall i)\,(m \leq i < j + 1 \Rightarrow P_i) \equiv (\forall i)\,(m \leq i < j \Rightarrow P_i) \wedge P_j \qquad \text{for } j > m$$

Convention

Universal quantification over an empty range (for example, $m \leq i < j$ for $j = m$) is by definition always *true*.

This convention is not unlike the one adopted for summation over an empty range, where the identity element is zero. For universal quantification T (or *true*) serves as its identity element.

Existential quantification† over a range is handled similarly. We use

$$(\exists i)\,(1 \leq i \leq N \wedge P_i)$$

which we choose to interpret as shorthand for

$$P_1 \vee P_2 \vee \ldots \vee P_N$$

where each P_i is a predicate. The whole expression is true if at least one P_i is true. It is only false if each P_i is false. A recursive definition of existential quantification over a range may be given as:

$$(\exists i)\,(m \leq i < j \wedge P_i) \equiv F \qquad\qquad\qquad \text{for } j = m - \text{empty range}$$

†Dijkstra's notation for existential quantification is $(Ei : 1 \leq i \leq N : P_i)$

and

$$(\exists i)\, (m \le i < j + 1 \land P_i) \equiv (\exists i)\, (m \le i < j \land P_i) \lor P_j \qquad \text{for } j > m$$

Convention
Existential quantification over an empty range is *false*.

The relationship between universal quantification over a range m .. n and existential quantification over the same range for the same predicates P_m, P_{m+1}, ..., P_n may be established in the following way:

$$\begin{aligned}
P_m \land P_{m+1} \land \ldots \land P_n &\equiv \lnot\lnot(P_m \land P_{m+1} \land \ldots \land P_n) && \text{for } m \le n \\
&\equiv \lnot(\lnot P_m \lor \lnot P_{m+1} \lor \ldots \lor \lnot P_n) && \text{by de} \\
&\equiv \lnot(\exists i)\, (m \le i \le n \land \lnot P_i) && \text{Morgan}
\end{aligned}$$

and so we have in general:

$$(\forall i)\, (m \le i \le n \Rightarrow P_i) \equiv \lnot(\exists i)\, (m \le i \le n \land \lnot P_i)$$

Even though in computations we can deal with finite ranges it is often necessary to use infinite ranges in definitions. For example, to define that a natural number n is prime amounts to saying that 'no natural number in the range 2 to n − 1 exactly divides into n. Using the familiar **mod** operator this can be expressed as

$$\text{prime}\,(n) \equiv n > 1 \land (\forall i)\, (2 \le i < n \Rightarrow n \bmod i \ne 0)$$

Here there is no upper limit on the value of n.

2.4.7   Other specifiers

To simplify some specifications we introduce several other more specialized quantifiers or operators. The new operators do not all quantify logical expressions, and are therefore not part of logic.

Summation specifier (Σ)

In program specifications it is often necessary to characterize the sum of a set of quantities. Mathematics provides the operator Σ for this purpose. To specify the sum S of a sequence of entities:

$$(a_1, a_2, \ldots, a_N)$$

we could write

$$S = \sum_{i=1}^{N} a_i$$

To obtain a linear notation similar to other quantifiers we may use

$$S = \Sigma \, (a_i : 1 \leqslant i \leqslant N)$$

which is shorthand for

$$S = a_1 + a_2 + ... + a_{N-1} + a_N$$

It is sometimes necessary to refer to the sum over an empty range (i.e. where N = 0). The value of the sum S over zero terms is 0, the **identity-element** for addition, that is

$$\Sigma \, (a_i : 0 < i \leqslant 0) = 0$$

Product specifier (Π)

To specify the product P of a sequence of terms:

$$(a_1, a_2, ..., a_N)$$

we will again adopt a linearized version of the notation used in mathematics. The mathematical specification for the product of N terms is:

$$P = \prod_{i=1}^{N} a_i$$

We will write this specification as:

$$P = \Pi(a_i : 1 \leqslant i \leqslant N)$$

which is shorthand for:

$$P = a_1 \times a_2 \times ... \times a_{N-1} \times a_N$$

The identity element for the product of zero terms, like the value of 0!, is defined as 1, that is

$$\Pi(\, a_i : 0 < i \leqslant 0) = 1$$

Counting specifier (#)

It is sometimes necessary to specify the count of the number of indices in a given range for which a certain property or condition holds. To handle these situations the **counting specifier**, #, may be used. Given a property P, then:

$$\#(i : 0 < i \leq N : P_i)$$

denotes the number of different values of i in the range $1 \leq i \leq N$ for which P_i is true.

For example, to specify the count of the elements in the sequence:

$$(a_1, a_2, ..., a_N)$$

that have the value zero we could write:

$$c = \#(i : 0 < i \leq N : a_i = 0)$$

The count over an empty range is always zero, that is

$$\#(i : 0 < i \leq 0 : P_i) = 0$$

Maximizing specifier (MAX)

To specify the largest index in a given range for which a particular property P holds the maximizing specifier may be used. For a property P

$$\textbf{MAX} \ (i : 0 < i \leq N : P_i)$$

denotes the maximum value for the index i in the range $0 < i \leq N$ for which P_i is true. If there were no value for which P_i was true, then **MAX** (i : ...) would have the value 0, that is

$$\textbf{MAX} (i : 0 < i \leq 0 : P_i) = 0$$

The specifier **MAX** is sometimes used in conjunction with a quantifier. For example to specify the value p of the largest index in an array a[1..N] such that all the elements in the segment a[1..p] are not equal to x we could write:

$$p = \textbf{MAX} (i : 0 < i \leq N : (\forall j : 0 < j \leq i : a_j \neq x))$$

If p were less than N this would imply that $a_{p+1} = x$. Simply writing:

$$(\forall j : 0 < j \leq i : a_j \neq x)$$

without maximizing i would not achieve the desired specification. In this example, if all the elements were equal to x, the value of **MAX** (i : ...), would be zero.

Minimizing specifier (MIN)

The minimizing specifier complements the maximizing specifier. It may be used to specify the smallest index in a given range for which a particular property P holds. Given the property P

$$\textbf{MIN } (i : 1 \leqslant i \leqslant N : P_i)$$

denotes the minimum value of the index i in the range $1 \leqslant i \leqslant N$ for which P_i is true. In the case where there was no value in the range $1 \leqslant i \leqslant N$ for which P_i was true, then **MIN** (i : ...) would yield the value $N + 1$. For example, consider the following problem which is closely related to the problem we specified using the **MAX** specifier. Suppose we wish to identify the smallest index q, in the range $1 \leqslant i \leqslant N$ for which an element in the array a[1..N] was equal to x then we could write

$$q = \textbf{MIN } (i : 1 \leqslant i \leqslant N : a_i = x)$$

If x were not present, the q would receive the value $N + 1$.

2.4.8 Inference rules for quantifiers

The rules of inference discussed earlier for the connectives need to be extended to handle proofs involving quantified predicates. To handle such proofs we apply rules that allow us to drop any quantifiers. We then conduct the derivations using the inference rules for the connectives. Sometimes we need to add a quantifier at the end of a derivation to obtain the final conclusion.

Before introducing rules for removing and inserting quantifiers we need some notation for symbolizing the replacement of a variable by a term in a formula. If P is a formula, x is a variable, and a is a term, then P_a^x is the formula that results when each free occurrence of x in P is replaced by a. Given P is $(\forall y) (y > x)$:

$$P_2^x : (\forall y) (y > 2)$$
$$P_{x+z}^x : (\forall y) (y > x + z)$$

Universal specification

The first and most useful of the additional inference rules expresses the fact that whatever is true for all entities with a particular property is also true for any given entity which has that property. This is usually referred to as the rule of **universal specification** (some texts also use the term **universal instantiation** or the **rule of specialization**). This rule may be stated more formally as follows:

Rule of universal specification (US)
An instance of a universal quantification with bound variable x is that well-formed formula which results from deleting the quantifier and replacing all of the remaining occurrences of the bound variable x by some particular value a from the range over which x is quantified and the formula is true.

The schema for this inference rule is

$$\frac{(\forall x)(Px)}{P_a^x} \quad (\forall\text{-elimination})$$

This rule tells us that if we can establish $(\forall x)(Px)$ then we can conclude P_a^x. For example, if x is restricted to humans and Socrates is a human, and $P(x)$ denotes 'x is mortal' provided we can establish or we are prepared to assume 'all men are mortal' (i.e. $(\forall x)(P_a^x)$) then universal specification allows us to conclude 'Socrates is mortal'.

As an example, from the formula:

$$(\forall x)(Px \Rightarrow Qx)$$

we may infer by universal specification both

$$Pa \Rightarrow Qa$$

and

$$Pb \Rightarrow Qb$$

provided P and Q admit the terms a and b for x. Other examples of this rule using the schema representation are:

$$\frac{(\forall x)(x \geq 0)}{x \geq 0} \qquad \frac{(\forall x)(x \geq 0)}{y \geq 0}$$

$$\frac{(\forall x)(x \geq 0)}{4 \geq 0} \qquad \frac{(\forall x)(x \geq 0)}{y + z \geq 0}$$

The universal specification rule enables the derivation of formulae which can be dealt with by the inference rules of propositional logic. Consider the application of this rule.

Suppose we are given the two premises:

$(\forall x)\,(Px \Rightarrow \neg Qx)$ P
Qa P

and we are required to prove $\neg Pa$.

In other words we have:

$(\forall x)\,(Px \Rightarrow \neg Qx)\,,\,Qa \vdash \neg Pa$

Applying universal specification the proof may be given as follows:

Proof

(1) $(\forall x)\,(Px \Rightarrow \neg Qx)$ P
(2) Qa P
(3) $Pa \Rightarrow \neg Qa$ US 1
(4) $\neg Pa \vee \neg Qa$ T 3
(5) $\neg Pa$ TP 2,4

Existential specification

In addition to the rule for $\forall$-elimination there is also a rule for **existential specification** which provides a means for $\exists$-elimination. The idea embodied in this rule is that if P is true for some x then we can choose some object a for which P is true. The rule may be stated as follows:

Rule of existential specification (ES)

An instance of an existential quantification with bound variable x is that well-formed-formula which results from deleting the quantifier and replacing all of the remaining occurrences of the bound variable x by some particular value a from the range over which x is quantified for which the formula is true.

The schema for this inference rule is:

$$\frac{(\exists x)(Px)}{P^x_a} \qquad (\exists\text{-elimination})$$

In applying this rule a must be restricted to x's universe of discourse. Here, a is not arbitrary (as it was for universal specialization). It must correspond to P^x_a being true.

This rule tells us that if $(\exists x)\,(Px)$ is established then there must exist at least one element as such that P^x_a is true. For example if x is restricted to humans and P(x) denotes 'x is a millionaire' provided we can establish or we are prepared to assume 'there exists a man who is a millionaire' (i.e. (∃x) (Px)) then by existential specification there must be at least one particular man who is a millionaire.

Universal generalization (UG)

This inference rule indicates that if P is true for x, and x is not restricted (that is, it represents an arbitrary element of the domain) then it can be inferred that P is true for every element of the domain.

The schema for this rule is:

$$\frac{Px}{(\forall x)(Px)} \qquad (\forall\text{-introduction})$$

Existential generalization (EG)

This inference rule handles the situation where if P is true for a particular element a from the domain then it can be inferred that there is an x for which P is true.

The schema for the rule is:

$$\frac{P_a^x}{(\exists x)(Px)} \qquad (\exists\text{-introduction})$$

examples are:

$$\frac{x > 0}{(\exists x)(x > 0)} \qquad \frac{y > 0}{(\exists x)(x > 0)} \qquad \frac{1 > 0}{(\exists x)(x > 0)} \qquad \frac{y + 1 > 0}{(\exists x)(x > 0)}$$

We will now use of some of these rules in a proof. Given

$$(\forall x)\,(Px \Rightarrow Qx)\;,\;(\exists x)\,(Px) \vdash (\exists x)\,(Qx)$$

and using both existential specification and universal specification, we get:

Proof

(1)	(∀x) (Px ⇒ Qx)	P
(2)	(∃x) (Px)	P
(3)	Pa	ES 2
(4)	Pa ⇒ Qa	US 1
(5)	Qa	PP 3,4
(6)	(∃x) (Qx)	EG 5

Interchange of quantifiers (E)

Frequently in the use of quantified formulae it is useful to be able to make transformations that require the replacement of a universally quantified formula by a logically equivalent existentially quantified formula and vice versa. With a set of rules for interchanging quantifiers it becomes easy to do things like moving from an assertion that x has some property to an equivalent assertion that not every x is without this property. Rules that permit such interchanges are given in Table 2.6.

Table 2.6

Formula			Derived rule
E.1	$(\forall x)\,(Px)$	$\equiv$	$\neg(\exists x)(\neg Px)$
E.2	$(\exists x)\,(Px)$	$\equiv$	$\neg(\forall x)\,(\neg Px)$
E.3	$\neg(\forall x)\,(Px)$	$\equiv$	$(\exists x)\,(\neg Px)$
E.4	$\neg(\exists x)\,(Px)$	$\equiv$	$(\forall x)\,(\neg Px)$

Denials (D)

Another useful transformation of an expression is to construct its **denial**. A denial of an expression P has the same meaning as $\neg$P. Clearly, $\neg$P is the simplest denial of P but it is not always the most useful. For example, when there is a negation in front of an expression it is usually desirable to transfer that sign as far as possible into the expression. The following rules may be used to construct useful denials of expressions and formulae in the predicate calculus.

D.1 $\neg(P \vee Q) \equiv \neg P \wedge \neg Q$
D.2 $\neg(P \wedge Q) \equiv \neg P \vee \neg Q$
D.3 $\neg(P \Rightarrow Q) \equiv P \wedge \neg Q$
D.4 $\neg(P \equiv Q) \equiv (P \equiv \neg Q)$
D.5 $\neg(\forall x)\,(Px) \equiv (\exists x)\,(\neg Px)$
D.6 $\neg(\exists x)\,(Px) \equiv (\forall x)\,(\neg Px)$

Some examples of transforming denials to equivalent forms are:

(1)	$\neg(\forall x)\,(Px \vee Qx)$	$\equiv$	$(\exists x)\,\neg(\,Px \vee Qx)$	(D.5)
		$\equiv$	$(\exists x)\,(\neg Px \wedge \neg Qx)$	(D.1)
(2)	$\neg(\exists x)\,(Px \Rightarrow Qx)$	$\equiv$	$(\forall x)\,\neg(\,Px \Rightarrow Qx)$	(D.6)
		$\equiv$	$(\forall x)\,(Px \wedge \neg Qx)$	(D.3)
(3)	$\neg(\forall x)\,(\forall y)\,(\exists z)\,(x+y=z)$	$\equiv$	$(\exists x)\,\neg(\forall y)\,(\exists z)\,(x+y=z)$	(D.5)
		$\equiv$	$(\exists x)\,(\exists y)\,\neg(\exists z)\,(x+y=z)$	(D.5)
		$\equiv$	$(\exists x)\,(\exists y)\,(\forall z)\,\neg(x+y=z)$	(D.6)

Derived inference rules (Q)

Two formulae are said to be **logically equivalent** if and only if each is derivable from the other by the rules of inference. There are many such derived rules, and although they are dispensable, a small subset of them that are frequently used in derivations is provided in Table 2.7.

Table 2.7

Formula				Derived formula
Q.1	From	$(\forall x)\,(\forall y)\,P$	it can be inferred that	$(\forall y)\,(\forall x)\,P$
Q.2	From	$(\exists x)\,(\exists y)\,P$	it can be inferred that	$(\exists y)\,(\exists x)\,P$
Q.3	From	$(\exists x)\,(\forall y)\,P$	it can be inferred that	$(\forall y)\,(\exists x)\,P$
Q.4	From	$(\forall x)\,(P \vee Q)$	it can be inferred that	$(\forall x)\,P \vee (\forall x)\,Q$
Q.5	From	$(\exists x)\,(P \vee Q)$	it can be inferred that	$(\exists x)\,P \vee (\exists x)\,Q$
Q.6	From	$(\forall x)\,(P \Rightarrow Q)$	it can be inferred that	$(\exists x)\,P \Rightarrow (\exists x)\,Q$
Q.7	From	$(\exists x)\,(P \wedge Q)$	it can be inferred that	$(\exists x)\,P \wedge (\exists x)\,Q$

2.4.9 Identity

The identity relation plays a significant role in applications of logic. It is a concept that is often regarded as so simple that it may be overlooked without penalty. However, if it is not properly understood it may be misused. The need for it in logic arises because there are frequently situations where two or more variables may refer to the same or different objects. Identity is used to resolve questions of *sameness* or *difference of reference* for such variables.

In natural language also, because there is redundancy in naming things, there is a need for the concept of identity. As an example, it is clear that '7' and 'the largest prime less than 10' refer to the same entity. In other words, 7 is *identical with* or *equal to* the largest prime less than 10. This may be symbolized using:

largest prime less than 10 = 7

On the other hand, for the isosceles triangle ABC

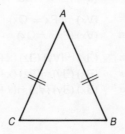

while we may say

$$\text{length } (AB) = \text{length } (AC)$$

it is not appropriate to say AB 'is equal to' AC, as this would imply identity, which is clearly not the case.

Several important properties of identity are embodied in the following rules.

Law of identity
Every entity x, is always identical with itself. In symbolic form
x = x.

The identity relation is *symmetric*, that is

$$x = y \Rightarrow y = x$$

and *transitive*, that is

$$x = y \land y = z \Rightarrow x = z.$$

Principle of extensionality
This principle provides a basis for important manipulations of program specifications. Stated informally it tells us that if x = y then whatever is true of x is also true of y and whatever is true of y is also true of x. The principle of extensionality may be stated formally as:

$$(\forall x)\,(\forall y)\,(x = y \Rightarrow Px \equiv Py)$$

Leibnitz's law†
If every property of x is also a property of y, then x = y

Inference and identity

The principle of extensionality can be converted into a rule of inference.

† This is also called the **principle of identity of indiscernibles**.

Such a conversion is needed to allow term substitutions to be made in derivations. For example if we have

x + 2y = 11

and we know that

y = x + 1

then a rule is needed to permit us to substitute (x + 1) for y. This inference rule may be stated as follows:

Inference rule for identity (ID)
From the formula P and the identity t = s, a new formula Q may be derived by replacing one or more occurrences of the term t in P by s. Then from P, and the identity t = s, we can conclude Q.

A simple application of this rule in a derivation is:

(1)   2 > 0   P
(2)   2 = 1 + 1   P
(3)   1 + 1 > 0   ID 1, 2

We now have at our disposal most of the basic tools from propositional and predicate logic that are likely to be needed to work with, and manipulate, the specifications encountered in program design.

2.5   Proof Methods

In program design a primary concern is proving programs correct. Constructive proof methods are best suited to this task. Also, we sometimes have to prove the validity of certain formulae and results. A variety of proof methods may be used for such tasks. We will discuss here only some of the most common and most useful proof techniques.

Direct proofs

Previously we have given several examples of direct formal proofs. This method of proof has the form:

> If P and Q are two propositions, and if P ⇒ Q, then when P is true it should be possible to show by a sequence of valid logical deductions and manipulations, that Q is also true.

The truth of the conclusion depends on the truth of the premises and the validity of the proof. Rules of inference provide the framework for such proofs.

In practice, constructing direct proofs can be difficult. The greatest stumbling block is deciding which known facts should be used in constructing a chain of reasoning that leads to the desired conclusion.

As an example, suppose that we wish to show by a direct proof that the following relation holds for any natural number n.

$$\left(\frac{n+1}{n}\right)^n \geq 2$$

Proof

This relation can be rewritten as:

$$\left(1 + \frac{1}{n}\right)^n \geq 2$$

At this point we may ask what other known results would be useful in establishing this relation? In trying to develop this proof here our job becomes much easier if we remember that the Bernoulli inequality has a similar form, that is

$$(1 + x)^n \geq 1 + nx \qquad \text{for } x \geq -1 \qquad \text{(Bernoulli inequality)}$$

Using this result we get:

$$\left(1 + \frac{1}{n}\right)^n \geq 1 + n\left(\frac{1}{n}\right) \qquad \text{where } x = \left(\frac{1}{n}\right)$$

and so

$$\left(1 + \frac{1}{n}\right)^n \geq 2$$

which leaves the proof complete.

Less formal direct proofs like this one are made easy or difficult depending upon what facts we are able to bring to bear. Without a knowledge of Bernoulli's inequality the proof would be much more difficult. Unfortunately, there are no recipes for success in constructing proofs apart from lots of practice and experience.

Another application of a direct proof involves showing that:

$$\sum_{i=1}^{n} i = \frac{n}{2}(n+1)$$

As we will see later, this result is easily proved by mathematical induction. Direct proofs of this result are also straightforward.

Proof (1)

Expanding the summation we get:

$$\sum_{i=1}^{n} i = 1 + 2 + 3 + ... + (n-2) + (n-1) + n$$

Now if we add the first and last terms their sum is $(n+1)$. Also if we add the second and second last terms their sum is again $(n+1)$ and so on. There are $n/2$ such terms in a sum of this form and so we have:

$$\sum_{i=1}^{n} i = \frac{n}{2}(n+1)\dagger$$

When n is odd, and all pairwise sums have been formed, there is effectively 'half' a term left over. This is accommodated directly in the fraction $n/2$. This result may also be proved in a slightly different way:

Proof (2)

There are two ways in which the sum of the first n positive integers can be written:

$$\sum_{i=1}^{n} i = 1 + 2 + 3 + ... + (n-1) + n$$

$$\sum_{i=1}^{n} i = n + (n-1) + ... + 2 + 1$$

Summing the terms pairwise we get:

$$2\sum_{i=1}^{n} i = (n+1) + (n+1) + ... + (n+1) + (n+1)$$

which after collecting terms becomes

$$2\sum_{i=1}^{n} i = n(n+1)$$

which may be rearranged to give:

$$\sum_{i=1}^{n} i = \frac{n}{2}(n+1)$$

† This formula is often referred to as Gauss' formula.

Indirect proofs†

For some applications, indirect proofs provide an efficient alternative to the direct proof method. The underlying strategy for an indirect proof is to start with the assumption that the statement P which is to be proved is false (i.e. $\neg P$ is true). Then prove by valid deductions that this leads to a contradiction or logically false conclusion (for example, $q \wedge \neg q$ or $1 = 2$ etc.). Because only valid steps have been made in constructing the proof the origin of the contradiction points to an incorrect initial proposition (i.e., the assumption of $\neg P$ has been false). The more formal basis of the indirect proof method follows from fact that the implications $P \Rightarrow Q$ and $\neg Q \Rightarrow \neg P$ are equivalent. Therefore $\neg Q \Rightarrow \neg P$ is a tautology only when $P \Rightarrow Q$ is a tautology. To prove P $\Rightarrow Q$ it is sufficient to prove $\neg Q \Rightarrow \neg P$.

EXAMPLE

A well-known example of an indirect proof is Euclid's demonstration that there are infinitely many primes.

Theorem P: There is no largest prime number.

Proof

The proof is begun by assuming $\neg P$, that is that a largest prime p_n does exist. The finite set of primes would then be:

$$\{p_1, p_2, ..., p_n\}$$

This assumption allows the construction of another number with the form:

$$N = (p_1 \times p_2 \times ... \times p_n) + 1$$

None of the primes in the assumed set $\{p_1, p_2, ..., p_n\}$ is a factor of N since the following relation holds:

$$(\forall i) \, (1 \leq i \leq n \Rightarrow N \textbf{ mod } p_i = 1)$$

Therefore either N is a prime number not in the assumed set, or it is a product of primes not in the assumed set. This conclusion is a direct contradiction of the assumption that there are finitely many primes. It follows that the original assumption was incorrect and therefore that there are infinitely many primes.

† Also called **proof by contradiction** or **reductio ad absurdum**.

EXAMPLE

Another result that can be proved indirectly is the observation that all pairs of consecutive Fibonacci numbers are relatively prime, that is, they share no common divisor other than one.

The Fibonacci sequence is a sequence in which all members, other than the first two, are generated by the sum of their two predecessors, that is

$$\left. \begin{array}{l} f_1 = 1, f_2 = 1 \\ f_{n+2} = f_{n+1} + f_n \end{array} \right\} \tag{1}$$

where f_n is the nth Fibonacci number and the sequence is:

1, 1, 2, 3, 5, 8, 13, ...

Proof

To prove the result we assume f_{n+1} and f_{n+2} are both divisible by some natural number n which is greater than one, that is

$$f_{n+2} = n \times g_{n+2} \tag{2}$$
$$f_{n+1} = n \times g_{n+1}$$

for some g_{n+2} and g_{n+1}. Now from (1) and (2) it follows that

$$f_n = f_{n+2} - f_{n+1} = n \times (g_{n+2} - g_{n+1})$$

and so f_n must also be divisible by n. Also for the Fibonacci number preceding the nth we know that:

$$f_{n-1} = f_{n+1} - f_n$$

And since f_{n+1}, and f_n are divisible by n it follows that f_{n-1} must also be divisible by n. This line of reasoning can be continued right down to the first Fibonacci number. It follows that since $f_1 = 1$, and each of its successors is divisible by n, the only possible value of n is 1. This contradicts the original assumption that adjacent Fibonacci numbers are not relatively prime. This can only mean that the original assumption must have been incorrect and therefore that adjacent Fibonacci numbers *are* relatively prime.

Other proof techniques

Apart from the methods of proof discussed in the previous section probably the most widely used proof technique involves the application of mathematical induction. Because mathematical induction has other applications, particularly in relation to sequences, we will reserve our discussion of it until after sequences have been treated in the next chapter.

Another class of problems requires proofs involving quantified assertions such as (∀x) Px and (∃x) Px. To prove (∀x) Px it is necessary to show that Px is true for an arbitrary x and then apply the rule of universal generalization to conclude (∀x) Px.

What is called an **existence proof** may be applied to establish (∃x) Px. Such proofs are either **constructive** or **non-constructive**. The objective in a constructive proof is to find an a such that Pa is true. Then by the rule of existential generalization it is possible to conclude (∃x) Px. A non-constructive proof of (∃x) Px is usually made by showing that ¬(∃x) Px implies a statement that is logically false.

SUMMARY

- The use of logic allows the creation of specifications that are precise, comprehensive, economical, and easy to manipulate.

- Logic is a formal language with precise syntax and semantics and therefore free of any of the ambiguity or vagueness found in natural language.

- Logical constructs are built from declarative sentences that are either true or false. Such sentences are called propositions.

- The connectives, 'not', 'and', 'or', 'implies', and 'is equivalent to' are used to build compound declarative sentences from simple declarative sentences. Truth tables are used to define the connectives. A precise set of rules governs the use of the connectives.

- Tautologies are important logical constructs. They remain true for all combinations of truth values of their elementary propositions. Tautologies are used to simplify and manipulate complex propositions.

- Logic provides a practical set of tools and principles for reasoning. These tools and principles are embodied in a theory of inference. The theory of inference allows a line of reasoning to be accepted purely on the basis of its form. Schemas are used to describe the rules of inference.

- The propositional calculus by itself is not powerful enough to satisfy all the needs for program derivation.

- The extensions to logic that belong to the predicate calculus go a long way to overcoming the limits of the propositional calculus for program derivation.

- A predicate is used either to ascribe a property to an entity or to assert that certain entities stand in some relationship.

- Quantifiers play an important role in the predicate calculus, ascribing properties to *some* or *all* of a set of elements.

- To make the writing of some specifications more convenient a number of other specialized quantifiers are also employed which are useful for counting, and for minimizing or maximizing on indices.

- Direct and indirect proof methods are sometimes needed in program design for the purpose of establishing the validity of certain formulae and results.

■ *EXERCISE 2.1   Truth tables*

Truth tables allow us to determine the truth or falsity of a compound proposition simply from a knowledge of the truth or falsity of its component propositions. This means that we can use truth tables to determine whether or not a compound proposition is a tautology. We can also use truth tables to determine whether two different propositions are equivalent. In order to carry out these operations we need to employ the truth table definitions for the propositional connectives.

Example (showing a proposition is a tautology)

It is required to show

$$p \land (p \lor q) \Rightarrow (p \lor q)$$

is a tautology. To do this all possible pairs of truth values for p and q must be considered under the influence of the various connectives. In our example the order in which the columns are evaluated is indicated by the accompanying numbering scheme.

Solution

p	∧	(p	∨	q)	⇒	(p	∨	q)
T	T	T	T	T	T	T	T	T
T	T	T	T	F	T	T	T	F
F	F	F	T	T	T	F	T	T
F	F	F	F	F	T	F	F	F
4	5	1	3	2	9	6	8	7

Column 9 is all true which indicates that implication is satisfied by the proposition, and so the proposition is a tautology since it is true regardless of the values of its elementary propositions.

Problems

1. For two propositions p and q, state the truth table definitions of disjunction, conjunction, negation, implication, and equivalence.

2. Using truth tables and the definitions for the propositional connectives verify the following tautologies:

   (a) $p \land p \equiv p$

   (b) $p \lor p \equiv p$

   (c) $p \lor \neg p$

   (d) $p \lor F \equiv p$

   (e) $p \lor T \equiv T$

   (f) $p \land T \equiv p$

   (g) $p \land F \equiv F$

   (h) $p \land \neg p$ (show is a contradiction)

3. Using truth tables and the definitions of the propositional connectives verify
    the following tautologies:

    (a) $p \land q \Rightarrow p$
    (b) $(\neg p \Rightarrow (p \land q)) \equiv p$
    (c) $p \land (p \Rightarrow q) \Rightarrow q$
    (d) $(p \land q) \lor (\neg p \land r) \Rightarrow q \lor r$
    (e) $(p \lor q) \land (\neg p \lor r) \Rightarrow q \lor r$

■ **EXERCISE 2.2**   *Range specifications*

The precise characterization of ranges for variables plays an important part in
writing specifications that can be used in program derivation. To formally specify
ranges the following notational conventions may be employed.

Notation Used	Meaning
$a < b$	a 'is less than' b
$a \leqslant b$	a 'is less than or equal to' b
$a = b$	a 'is equal to' b
$a \neq b$	a 'is not equal to' b
$a \geqslant b$	a 'is greater than or equal to' b
$a > b$	a 'is greater than' b
$a \land b$	a 'and' b
$a \lor b$	a 'or' b
$a < i < b$	i 'is greater than' a 'and less than' b
$i \in [a..b]$	i is a member of the range from a to b

The following problems are intended to test comprehension of range
specifications.

Example

Give the complete list of integer values of i that satisfy the following range
relations:

    Range relation: $1 < i < 5$
    Integer list: (2,3,4)

Problems

1. (a) $0 < i \leqslant 4$ (f) $0 < i \land i < 4$

    (b) $0 < i < 4$ (g) $0 \leqslant i \land i < 4$

    (c) $0 \leqslant i < 4$ (h) $0 \leqslant i \land i \leqslant 4$

    (d) $0 \leqslant i \leqslant 4$ (i) $i \in [0..4]$

    (e) $0 < i \land i \leqslant 4$ (j) $i \in [1..4]$

2. For each of the following range specifications identify:
    (i)   the smallest integer value of i that satisfies the relation
    (ii) the largest integer value of i that satisfies the relation

(iii) the smallest integer value of N that satisfies the relation

(iv) the largest integer value of N that would make the range empty and the relation false.

(a) $0 < i < N$	(g) $N \geqslant i \geqslant 0$
(b) $0 \leqslant i < N$	(h) $1 < i < N+1$
(c) $0 \leqslant i \leqslant N$	(i) $i > 0 \wedge i < N$
(d) $N \geqslant i > 0$	(j) $0 < i \wedge i < N$
(e) $N > i > 0$	(k) $0 > i \wedge i > 0$
(f) $N > i \geqslant 0$	

3.   Given the range specification

$$0 \leqslant i < j \leqslant N$$

(a) What is the smallest integer value that i can assume?
(b) What is the largest integer value that i can assume?
(c) What is the smallest integer value that j can assume?
(d) What is the largest integer value that j can assume?
(e) What is the smallest integer value that N can assume?

4.   Provide range specifications that indicate that i is present within each of the following ranges:

(a) 0, 1, 2, ..., N	(e) N, N−1, ..., 0
(b) 1, 2, 3, ..., N	(f) N, N−1, ..., 1
(c) 0, 1, 2, ..., N−1	(g) N−1, N−2, ..., 0
(d) 1, 2, 3, ..., N−1	(h) N−1, N−2, ..., 1

5.   Write down predicates for the ranges in Problem 1. In your answer use only the '=' relation and the logical connectives (do not use $<, \leqslant, >, \geqslant$).

■ *EXERCISE 2.3   Propositional simplification I*

In carrying out program derivation transformations and proofs of correctness it is necessary to be able to apply the laws of equivalence to simplify propositions.

Notation used	*Meaning*
p, q	are propositions
T	symbolizes 'True'
F	symbolizes 'False'
$\wedge$	symbolizes 'and'
$\vee$	symbolizes 'or'
$\Rightarrow$	symbolizes 'implies'
$\neg$	symbolizes 'not'
$\equiv$	symbolizes 'equivalence'

The following problem sets are ordered approximately according to their degree of difficulty.

1. Simplify the following propositions as far as possible using the laws of equivalence:

    (a) $p \lor T$ (h) $(p \land q) \lor T$
    (b) $T \lor p$ (i) $(p \land T) \land q$
    (c) $p \land T$ (j) $(p \lor T) \lor q$
    (d) $T \land p$ (k) $p \lor (T \land q)$
    (e) $p \Rightarrow T$ (l) $p \land (T \lor q)$
    (f) $T \Rightarrow p$ (m) $p \lor (T \lor q)$
    (g) $(p \land q) \land T$ (n) $p \equiv T$

2. Simplify the following propositions as far as possible using the laws of equivalence:

    (a) $p \lor F$ (h) $(p \land q) \lor F$
    (b) $F \lor p$ (i) $(p \land F) \land q$
    (c) $p \land F$ (j) $(p \lor F) \lor q$
    (d) $F \land p$ (k) $p \lor (F \land q)$
    (e) $p \Rightarrow F$ (l) $p \land (F \lor q)$
    (f) $F \Rightarrow p$ (m) $p \lor (F \lor q)$
    (g) $(p \land q) \land F$

3. Simplify the following propositions as far as possible using the laws of equivalence:

    (a) $p \lor p$ (hint use distributive law first)
    (b) $p \land p$ (hint use distributive law first)
    (c) $p \Rightarrow p$
    (d) $p \equiv p$
    (e) $p \lor \neg p$
    (f) $p \land \neg p$
    (g) $p \Rightarrow \neg p$
    (h) $\neg p \Rightarrow p$
    (i) $p \equiv \neg p$
    (j) $\neg p \Rightarrow \neg p$

4. Simplify the following propositions as far as possible using the laws of equivalence:

    (a) $(p \lor F) \lor (p \lor q)$ (e) $(\neg p \lor q) \lor (p \lor \neg p)$
    (b) $(p \lor F) \land (p \lor q)$ (f) $(\neg p \lor q) \land (p \land \neg p)$
    (c) $(p \land T) \lor (p \land q)$ (g) $(\neg p \lor q) \lor (p \land \neg p)$
    (d) $(p \land T) \land (p \land q)$ (h) $(\neg p \lor q) \land (p \lor \neg p)$

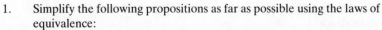

■ *EXERCISE 2.4 Propositional simplification II*

The following problem sets are also ordered approximately according to their degree of difficulty.

1. State the following laws of equivalence

    (a) the distributive laws
    (b) the law of implication
    (c) de Morgan's laws

2. Simplify the following propositions as far as possible using the laws of equivalence:

(a) $\neg p \vee (p \vee q)$

(b) $\neg p \wedge (p \vee q)$

(c) $\neg p \vee (p \wedge q)$

(d) $\neg p \wedge (p \wedge q)$

(e) $p \vee (\neg p \vee \neg q)$

(f) $p \vee (p \wedge q)$

(g) $(\neg p \wedge q) \vee p$

(h) $\neg p \Rightarrow (p \wedge q)$

(i) $p \Rightarrow p \vee q$

(j) $p \Rightarrow p \wedge q$

(k) $p \vee (p \vee q)$

(l) $(p \wedge q) \vee p$

(m) $p \wedge (p \vee q)$

(n) $p \wedge (p \wedge q)$

3. Using the laws of equivalence verify the following equivalences:

(a) $p \vee (p \wedge q) \equiv p$

(b) $(\neg p \wedge q) \vee p \equiv p \vee q$

(c) $\neg p \Rightarrow p \wedge q \equiv p$

(d) $(p \vee q) \wedge (p \vee \neg q) \equiv p$

(e) $(p \Rightarrow q) \equiv (\neg q \Rightarrow \neg p)$

4. Simplify the following propositions as far as possible using the laws of equivalence. Also indicate which of these propositions are tautologies:

(a) $p \vee \neg (p \wedge q)$

(b) $p \vee \neg (p \vee q)$

(c) $p \wedge q \Rightarrow \neg p$

(d) $p \vee q \Rightarrow \neg p$

(e) $p \wedge q \Rightarrow p$

(f) $\neg p \wedge (p \vee q) \Rightarrow q$

(g) $\neg p \Rightarrow (p \wedge q)$

(h) $p \wedge (p \Rightarrow q) \Rightarrow q$

(i) $p \Rightarrow (q \Rightarrow (p \wedge q))$

(j) $(p \vee q \Rightarrow r) \Rightarrow (p \Rightarrow r)$

(k) $\neg q \wedge (p \Rightarrow q) \Rightarrow \neg p$

(l) $(p \Rightarrow q) \wedge (q \Rightarrow r) \Rightarrow (p \Rightarrow r)$

■ *EXERCISE 2.5* *Introduction to specification*

In writing specifications for use in program design it is necessary to be able to define certain relations symbolically using the familiar operators (for example, $<$, $=$, $\leqslant$, $>$, and so on). For example we may symbolize the relation 'x is less than y' by $x < y$.

We also need to be able to form complex statements by combining other statements using the logical connectives (for example, and ($\wedge$), or ($\vee$), not ($\neg$), equivalence ($\equiv$), and implies ($\Rightarrow$)).

For example to symbolize 'x is less than y and x is greater than zero' we may write:

$$(x < y) \wedge (x > 0)$$

In writing statements like these we also need to employ the conventions for writing algebraic expressions.

To gain familiarity with the use of these tools, give symbolic specifications for the following statements:

1. (a) x is a natural number that is at least one and at most ten.

(b) x is a natural number greater than one and less than ten.

(c) x is greater than or equal to one and less than or equal to ten.

(d) x is at most ten.

2. (a) s is the sum of the fixed integers A and B.
   (b) z is equal to the average of x and y.
   (c) x is a multiple of k.
   (d) f is a factor of N.
   (e) x is a natural number that is a power of 2.
   (f) D is an exact divisor of two natural numbers X and Y.
   (g) r is the remainder of X divided by D, and q is the quotient.

3. (a) z is set to the smaller of X and Y.
   (b) z is less than the minimum of X and Y.
   (c) k is the largest power of 2 that is less than or equal to the natural number N.
   (d) k is the smallest power of 2 that exceeds the natural number N.
   (e) a is the largest natural number whose square is less than or equal to the natural number N.
   (f) x is a natural number between one and a hundred, that is exactly divisible by another natural number y.

4. (a) a and b are set such that a is equal to the smaller of A and B, and b is equal to the larger of A and B.
   (b) a, b, c is a sequence in non-descending order, formed by setting a, b, and c to X, Y and Z, three arbitrary integers.
   (c) p is equal to 1, 2 or 3 depending on whether X is the smallest of X, Y, Z or Y is the smallest, or Z is the smallest, respectively.

■ *EXERCISE 2.6 Logical inference and proof*

Using the rules of inference, modus ponendo ponens (PP), modus tollendo ponens (TP), and double negation (DN) where necessary complete the following direct proofs given the following premises (P) in each case.

1. $P \Rightarrow \neg Q, \quad \neg Q \Rightarrow R, \quad P \vdash R$

2. $P, \quad P \Rightarrow Q, \quad Q \Rightarrow \neg R \vdash \neg R$

3. Prove S given the premises
$$P \Rightarrow \neg Q, \quad \neg Q \Rightarrow R, \quad P, \quad R \Rightarrow S \vdash S$$

4. Prove Q given the premises
$$P \Rightarrow \neg R, \quad \neg R \Rightarrow Q, \quad P \vdash Q$$

■ *EXERCISE 2.7 Relations on arrays*

Arrays are one of the principle data structures that we must work with in program design. In writing specifications for problems it is often convenient to view data as if it were stored in an abstract array. An array describes a collection of elements which are distinguished and referenced by their subscript values. The elements in an array may satisfy certain relations, for example, they may be arranged in ascending order, or they may all be greater than zero.

Notation used	Meaning
A_1	refers to the value stored in index position 1 of the array A
A_2	refers to the value stored in index position 2 of the array A
A_i	refers to the value stored in index position i of the array A
$A_i < X$	the element at index position i in the array A is less than X.

Problems

The following problems all make use of the array:

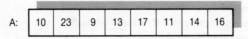

A: | 10 | 23 | 9 | 13 | 17 | 11 | 14 | 16 |

where $A_1 = 10$, $A_2 = 23$, $A_3 = 9$, $A_4 = 13$, $A_5 = 17$, $A_6 = 11$, $A_7 = 14$, $A_8 = 16$.

1. What integer value of X would satisfy the relation

    $$X \leq A_1 \wedge X \leq A_2 \wedge X \leq A_3 \wedge X \leq A_4 \wedge X \leq A_5 \wedge X \leq A_6 \wedge X \leq A_7 \wedge X \leq A_8$$

    if X were present in the array A?

2. What is the smallest integer value of X that would satisfy the relation

    $$X \geq A_1 \wedge X \geq A_2 \wedge X \geq A_3 \wedge X \geq A_4 \wedge X \geq A_5 \wedge X \geq A_6 \wedge X \geq A_7 \wedge X \geq A_8$$

3. Give a value of X which satisfies the relation

    $$X = A_1 \vee X = A_2 \vee X = A_3 \vee X = A_4 \vee X = A_5 \vee X = A_6 \vee X = A_7 \vee X = A_8$$

4. Give a value of X which satisfies the relation

    $$X \neq A_1 \wedge X \neq A_2 \wedge X \neq A_3 \wedge X \neq A_4 \wedge X \neq A_5 \wedge X \neq A_6 \wedge X \neq A_7 \wedge X \neq A_8$$

5. Given the relation

    $$X \neq A_1 \vee X \neq A_2 \vee X \neq A_3 \vee X \neq A_4 \vee X \neq A_5 \vee X \neq A_6 \vee X \neq A_7 \vee X \neq A_8$$

    (a) Could X be present in the array? (If so, supply a suitable value).
    (b) Could X not be present in the array? (If so, supply a suitable value).

6. Suggest what changes to the array would be needed for its given elements to satisfy the relation

    $$A_1 \leq A_2 \wedge A_2 \leq A_3 \wedge A_3 \leq A_4 \wedge A_4 \leq A_5 \wedge A_5 \leq A_6 \wedge A_6 \leq A_7 \wedge A_7 \leq A_8$$

7. Do the elements in the array A satisfy the relation

    $$A_1 \leq A_2 \vee A_2 \leq A_3 \vee A_3 \leq A_4 \vee A_4 \leq A_5 \vee A_5 \leq A_6 \vee A_6 \leq A_7 \vee A_7 \leq A_8$$

■ EXERCISE 2.8   Interpreting relations

The following propositions expressed in extensional form express some useful relations on an array of elements. Subsequently we will see how to express these relations using quantifiers. To complete the current exercise provide values for X, N, p, i and the array elements A[1..N], B[1..N] which satisfy each of the relations below:

1. $X = A_1 \vee X = A_2 \vee X = A_3 \vee ... \vee X = A_N$

2. $(X \geqslant A_1 \wedge X \geqslant A_2 \wedge X \geqslant A_3 \wedge ... \wedge X \geqslant A_N) \wedge (X = A_1 \vee X = A_2 \vee X = A_3 \vee ... \vee X = A_N)$

3. $X \leqslant A_1 \wedge X \leqslant A_2 \wedge X \leqslant A_3 \wedge ... \wedge X \leqslant A_N$

4. $A_1 \neq A_2 \wedge A_2 \neq A_3 \wedge ... \wedge A_{N-2} \neq A_{N-1}$

5. $A_1 \neq A_2 \wedge A_3 \neq A_4 \wedge A_5 \neq A_6 \wedge ... \wedge A_{N-1} \neq A_N$

6. $A_1 \geqslant A_2 \wedge A_2 \geqslant A_3 \wedge A_3 \geqslant A_4 \wedge ... \wedge A_{N-1} \geqslant A_N$

7. $1 \leqslant p \leqslant N \wedge A_1 \leqslant A_p \wedge A_2 \leqslant A_p \wedge ... \wedge A_N \leqslant A_p$

8. $A_1 \leqslant X \wedge A_2 \leqslant X \wedge ... \wedge A_i \leqslant X \wedge A_{i+1} \geqslant X \wedge A_{i+2} \geqslant X \wedge ... \wedge A_N \geqslant X$

9. $B_1 = A_N \wedge B_2 = A_{N-1} \wedge B_3 = A_{N-2} \wedge ... \wedge B_N = A_1$

10. $A_1 = A_2 \vee A_2 = A_3 \wedge A_3 = A_4 \wedge ... \wedge A_{N-1} = A_N$

11. $X = A_1 \wedge X = A_2 \wedge X = A_3 \wedge ... \wedge X = A_N$

12. $A_1 = A_2 \wedge A_2 = A_3 \wedge A_3 = A_4 \wedge ... A_{N-1} = A_N$

13. $A_1 = A_N \wedge A_2 = A_{N-1} \wedge A_3 = A_{N-2} \wedge ... A_{N/2} = A_{(N/2 + 1)}$

14. $a_1 = A_2 \wedge a_2 = A_3 \wedge a_3 = A_4 \wedge ... \wedge a_{N-1} = A_N \wedge a_N = A_1$

■ EXERCISE 2.9   Quantification and specification

1. Write down the extensional form for the following quantified expressions:

    (a) $(\forall j : 1 \leqslant j \leqslant 4 : P_j)$ (c) $(\forall j : 0 < j \leqslant 4 : P_j)$
    (b) $(\forall j : 1 \leqslant j < 4 : P_j)$ (d) $(\forall j : 0 \leqslant j \leqslant 4 : P_j)$

2. Write out the extensional form for the following quantified expressions:

    (a) $(\forall j : 1 \leqslant j < 4 : a_j \leqslant a_{j+1})$ (g) $(\forall j : 1 \leqslant j \leqslant 1 : x \neq a_j)$
    (b) $(\forall j : 0 < j \leqslant 4 : a_{j-1} \leqslant a_j)$ (h) $(\forall j : 0 < j \leqslant 1 : x \neq a_j)$
    (c) $(\forall j : 1 \leqslant j < 2 : a_j \leqslant a_{j+1})$ (i) $(\forall j : 1 \leqslant j < N : a_j \leqslant a_{j+1})$
    (d) $(\forall j : 1 \leqslant j < 1 : a_j \leqslant a_{j+1})$ (j) $(\forall j : 0 < j \leqslant N : a_{j-1} \leqslant a_j)$
    (e) $(\forall j : 0 < j \leqslant 0 : a_{j-1} \leqslant a_j)$ (k) $(\forall j : 1 \leqslant j < N : x \neq a_j)$
    (f) $(\forall j : 1 \leqslant j \leqslant 4 : x \neq a_j)$

3. Write out the extensional form for the following quantified expressions:

    (a) $(\exists j : 1 \leqslant j < 4 : a_j \leqslant a_{j+1})$ (g) $(\exists j : 1 \leqslant j \leqslant 1 : x \neq a_j)$
    (b) $(\exists j : 0 < j \leqslant 4 : a_{j-1} \leqslant a_j)$ (h) $(\exists j : 0 < j \leqslant 1 : x \neq a_j)$
    (c) $(\exists j : 1 \leqslant j < 2 : a_j \leqslant a_{j+1})$ (i) $(\exists j : 1 \leqslant j < N : a_j \leqslant a_{j+1})$
    (d) $(\exists j : 1 \leqslant j < 1 : a_j \leqslant a_{j+1})$ (j) $(\exists j : 0 < j \leqslant N : a_{j-1} \leqslant a_j)$
    (e) $(\exists j : 0 < j \leqslant 0 : a_{j-1} \leqslant a_j)$ (k) $(\exists j : 1 \leqslant j < N : x \neq a_j)$
    (f) $(\exists j : 1 \leqslant j \leqslant 4 : x \neq a_j)$

4. What is wrong with the following expressions given the array is a[1..4]:

    (a) $(\forall j : 1 \leqslant j \leqslant 4 : a_j \leqslant a_{j+1})$
    (b) $(\forall j : 1 \leqslant j \leqslant 4 : a_{j-1} \leqslant a_j)$

5. Write out the extensional form for the following expressions:

    (a) $s = \Sigma(A_j : 1 \leqslant j < 4)$ (f) $s = \Sigma(A_j : 1 \leqslant j \leqslant 4)$
    (b) $s = \Sigma(A_j : 0 < j \leqslant 4)$ (g) $s = \Sigma(A_j : 1 \leqslant j \leqslant 1)$
    (c) $s = \Sigma(A_j : 1 \leqslant j < 2)$ (h) $s = \Sigma(A_j : 0 < j \leqslant 1)$
    (d) $s = \Sigma(A_j : 1 \leqslant j < 1)$ (i) $s = \Sigma(A_j : 1 \leqslant j < N)$
    (e) $s = \Sigma(A_j : 0 < j \leqslant 0)$ (j) $s = \Sigma(A_j : 0 < j \leqslant N)$

6.   Write out the extensional form for the following expressions:

(a) $p = \Pi(A_j : 1 \leqslant j < 4)$ (f) $p = \Pi(A_j : 1 \leqslant j \leqslant 4)$
(b) $p = \Pi(A_j : 0 < j \leqslant 4)$ (g) $p = \Pi(A_j : 1 \leqslant j \leqslant 1)$
(c) $p = \Pi(A_j : 1 \leqslant j < 2)$ (h) $p = \Pi(A_j : 0 < j \leqslant 1)$
(d) $p = \Pi(A_j : 1 \leqslant j < 1)$ (i) $p = \Pi(A_j : 1 \leqslant j < N)$
(e) $p = \Pi(Aj : 0 < j \leqslant 0)$ (j) $p = \Pi(Aj : 0 < j \leqslant N)$

■ *EXERCISE 2.10   Using quantifiers*

Quantifiers often allow us to express complex propositions more simply and
succinctly. The following propositions expressed in extensional form fall into this
category. Re-express the propositions using quantifiers:

1. $X = A_1 \vee X = A_2 \vee X = A_3 \vee \ldots \vee X = A_N$

2. $(X \geqslant A_1 \wedge X \geqslant A_2 \wedge X \geqslant A_3 \wedge \ldots \wedge X \geqslant A_N) \wedge (X = A_1 \vee X = A_2 \vee X = A_3 \vee \ldots \vee X = A_N)$

3.   Express your answer to (2) without using an existential quantifier.

4. $X \leqslant A_1 \wedge X \leqslant X_2 \wedge X \leqslant A_3 \wedge \ldots \wedge X \leqslant A_N$

5. $A_1 \neq A_2 \wedge A_2 \neq A_3 \wedge \ldots \wedge A_{N-1} \neq A_N$

6. $A_1 \neq A_2 \vee A_3 \neq A_4 \vee A_5 \neq A_6 \vee \ldots \vee A_{N-1} \neq A_N$

7. $A_1 \geqslant A_2 \wedge A_2 \geqslant A_3 \wedge A_3 \geqslant A_4 \wedge \ldots \wedge A_{N-1} \geqslant A_N$

8. $1 \leqslant p \leqslant N \wedge A_1 \leqslant A_p \wedge A_2 \leqslant A_p \wedge \ldots \wedge A_N \leqslant A_p$

9. $A_1 \leqslant X \wedge A_2 \leqslant X \wedge \ldots \wedge A_i \leqslant X \wedge A_{i+1} \geqslant X \wedge A_{i+2} \geqslant X \wedge \ldots \wedge A_N \geqslant X$

10. $a_1 = A_N \wedge a_2 = A_{N-1} \wedge a_3 = A_{N-2} \wedge \ldots \wedge a_N = A_1$

11. $A_1 = A_2 \vee A_2 = A_3 \vee A_3 = A_4 \vee \ldots \vee A_{N-1} = A_N$

12. $X = A_1 \wedge X = A_2 \wedge X = A_3 \wedge \ldots \wedge X = A_N$

13. $A_1 = A_2 \wedge A_2 = A_3 \wedge A_3 = A_4 \wedge \ldots A_{N-1} = A_N$

14. $A_1 = A_N \wedge A_2 = A_{N-1} \wedge A_3 = A_{N-2} \wedge \ldots A_{N/2} = A_{(N/2 + 1)}$

15. $a_1 = A_2 \wedge a_2 = A_3 \wedge a_3 = A_4 \wedge \ldots \wedge a_{N-1} = A_N \wedge a_N = A_1$

Bibliography

Blumberg, A.E. (1976), *Logic : A First Course*, Knopf, N.Y.

Hamilton, A.G. (1978), *Logic for Mathematicians*, Cambridge University Press,
        London.

Norris, F.R. (1985), *Discrete Structures : An Introduction to Mathematics for
        Computer Science*, Prentice-Hall, Englewood Cliffs, N.J.

Pospesel, W., (1976), 'Predicate Logic', Prentice-Hall, Englewood Cliffs, N.J.
        (1976)

Reichenbach, H. (1980), *Elements of Symbolic Logic*, Dover, N.Y.

Stanat, D.F. and D.F. McAllister (1977), *Discrete Mathematics in Computer
        Science*, Prentice-Hall, Englewood Cliffs, N.J.

Suppes, P. (1957), *Introduction to Logic*, Van Nostrand, Princeton, N.Y.

Chapter 3
Mathematics for Specification

Invention or discovery, be it in mathematics or anywhere else, takes place by combining ideas.

J. Hadamard

3.1 Introduction
3.2 Set Concepts
3.3 Relations
3.4 Functions
3.5 Bags
3.6 Sequences and EBNF
3.7 Mathematical Induction
Summary
Exercises
Bibliography

3.1 Introduction

Programs operate on data that belong to sets and produce results that also belong to sets. Specifications are needed to characterize such sets. Set theory, together with logic, provides an important set of tools for program specification. It also provides the basis for a theory of relations, functions and sequences. In combination with sets, these tools provide a powerful armament for specification.

In the previous chapter we saw how predicates were used to characterize the properties of things. This means of characterization provides a very powerful tool for defining all sorts of collections or sets of things. And since, in writing specifications, we are almost always interested in describing data with certain properties, a study of the underlying theory governing such descriptions is important. We will begin an introduction to this theory by considering sets.

Set theory has evolved into a formal axiomatic theory and is often presented in such terms (Suppes, 1957). Here, our primary interest is only in identifying some of the more important set tools that are useful for program specification. We therefore treat the topic somewhat less formally.

3.2   Set Concepts

Rather than attempt to provide a precise definition of 'set' it is easier to start by exploring informally what a set is, and what can be done with sets. From this viewpoint *a set is any collection of entities*. Here the use of the word 'collection' is not intended to imply that such collections are necessarily finite (e.g. the primes form a perfectly good set, as do the set of people who have lived more than 1000 years) or even that there is any uniformity in the type of entities that make up sets (e.g. a car, a cat, and the moon form a perfectly respectable, albeit whimsical set).

Of course, the sets of primary interest to us in program design are usually uniform in type and often finite. Examples are the set of all natural numbers, the set of all prime divisors of a given natural number, the set of all transactions for a particular product, and so on. The power of set theory stems from the fact that it helps us formulate general properties of collections that apply to all their instances.

Sets therefore provide an important vehicle for attaining generality in specifications. It is hoped that this generality is subsequently reflected in program implementations designed to meet the specifications. Of central importance in describing sets are the notions of membership and identity.

Membership and identity

The entities which make up a set are called the **members** or **elements** of the set. Members of a set are said to *belong* to that set. To symbolize that the element x belongs to, or is a member of the set A, we use

$$x \in A$$

where '$\in$' may be interpreted as a two-place predicate. This means '$x \in A$' is true if x is in A, and it is false otherwise. The symbolization $x \notin A$ describes the fact that x does not belong to the set A. Here we have used the convention of employing capital letters for sets and small letters for elements of sets.

A knowledge of *all* the members of a set is sufficient to completely define that set. Small sets are often designated by enclosing the symbols representing their elements in braces. For example, the set of vowels can be specified as:

{a,e,i,o,u}

and the set of decimal digits is:

{0,1,2,3,4,5,6,7,8,9}

It follows that if two sets have exactly the same members then they are identical. The equality between two sets A and B is symbolized by:

A = B

The concept of identity that we saw earlier applied to individuals extends to sets, and leads to a corresponding axiom of extensionality.

Axiom of extensionality
Two sets are equal if and only if they contain the same elements.

This axiom may be stated formally as follows:

$(\forall x)(x \in A \equiv x \in B) \equiv A = B$

The order of the elements in the *representation* of a set plays no part in determining the identity of that set. The following are all representations of the same set:

A = {red, orange, green}
B = {orange, red, green}
C = {red, red, orange, green}

Repetition of elements in the representation of a set, as in C, *does not* change the identity of the set. Such set representations are called bags.

The notion of a set also generalizes to admit sets whose elements are themselves sets. For example the set A below:

A = {{1,2}, {1,3}, {2,3}}

is a set with three members {1,2}, {1,3} and {2,3} which are themselves sets. A set with a member is *not* considered identical with that member, (the symbol '≠' indicates non-identity of two sets), that is

{{1,2}} ≠ {1,2}

These two sets are different because {{1,2}} has only *one* element whereas

{1,2} has *two* elements. A similar situation occurs where the member is not itself a set, for example

$$\{1\} \neq 1$$

However,

$$x \in \{x\}$$

which tells us that x belongs to the set whose only member is x.

Subsets and inclusion

The idea of individual membership of sets is not powerful enough for many applications. A generalization is needed to accommodate a relation which denotes **group membership** of sets. This generalization is handled in the following way. For sets A and B, if every member of the set A also belongs to the set B, then A is a **subset** of B, or we may say A is **included in** B (another mode of expressing this is to say B is a **superset** of A). It is convenient to regard '⊆' as a two-place predicate. This means $A \subseteq B$ is true if A is included in B and it is false otherwise. A more formal definition for set inclusion is:

$$A \subseteq B \equiv (\forall x)(x \in A \Rightarrow x \in B)$$

examples are:

$$\{1,2\} \subseteq \{1,2,3\}$$
$$\{\{1,2\}\} \subseteq \{\{1,2\}, \{1,3\}\}$$

Note that {1,2} is a member of but *not* a subset of {{1,2},{1,3}}. This definition admits the property that every set is a subset of itself, that is

$$A \subseteq A \quad \text{and} \quad \{1,2\} \subseteq \{1,2\} \quad \text{are both true}$$

Where $A \subseteq B$ it is possible that $A = B$ or $A \neq B$. In the latter case A is a **proper subset** of B. The symbol '⊂' is used as an abbreviation for '**is a proper subset of**'. Symbolically the definition is:

$$A \subset B \equiv A \subseteq B \wedge A \neq B$$

An example is:

$$\{1,2\} \subset \{1,2,3\}$$

Set inclusion is **transitive**, that is for sets A, B and C we have that:

$$A \subseteq B \wedge B \subseteq C \Rightarrow A \subseteq C$$

However, unlike identity, set inclusion is not **symmetric**. The notions of membership ($\in$) and inclusion ($\subseteq$) are also quite distinct. This difference is shown up in that set inclusion is always **reflexive** (that is A $\subseteq$ A is always true) while membership is not reflexive (that is A $\in$ A is false) for all meaningful sets.

Specification of sets

So far, in our discussion of sets, we have focused only on constructing sets by enumerating all their members. This technique is referred to as an **extensional** method of specification. In specifying some sets, it is not convenient or even possible to write down all the members of the set. For example, specifying the set of primes:

$\{2,3,5,7,11,...\}$

by adopting the practice of only writing down the first few terms can easily lead to misinterpretation. To overcome this difficulty, a second, more powerful and economical means of set specification is employed. It involves specifying subsets of a particular set by describing characteristic properties of the members of the subset, that is:

Principle of comprehensive specification†
For every set A and every well-formed formula Px there is another set B whose elements are those elements x of A for which the property Px holds.

It follows from the axiom of extensionality for sets that the principle of comprehensive specification uniquely determines the set B, which is defined using the notation:

B = $\{x \in A \mid Px\}$††

and we may also write:

$\{x \mid x = a\} = \{a\}$

For many applications the Px are simple predicates. For example, the set of all odd primes may be specified comprehensively in the following way:

$\{x \in \mathbb{N} \mid (\forall j)(2 \leqslant j < x \Rightarrow x \textbf{ mod } j \neq 0)\}$

---

† In axiomatic set theory this principle is usually called the axiom of specification.
†† Some computing science texts use the notation B = $\{x:A \mid Px\}$ where the set A from which the subset B is constructed is looked upon simply as a type.

That is, the set of all odd primes is just a subset of the natural numbers $\mathbb{N}$. Each member x of the prime subset has no exact factor in the range 2 to $x - 1$.

Empty set

The principle of comprehensive specification does not forbid us from writing the following set specification.

$$\{x \in A \mid x \neq x\} \tag{1}$$

The resulting set clearly has no elements. It is convenient to allow empty sets. The **empty set** has several interesting properties. For two sets A and B, if A is an empty set then the statement:

$$(\forall x)(x \in A \Rightarrow x \in B) \tag{2}$$

must be true simply because its antecedent is always false. And, if B is also an empty set, then

$$(\forall x)(x \in B \Rightarrow x \in A) \tag{3}$$

will also be true. Then from (2) and (3), and the axiom of extensionality, it follows that if two sets A and B are empty then

$$A = B$$

In other words there is *only one* empty set. The empty set is usually symbolized by either $\varnothing$ or $\{\}$ although some texts favour Λ (we use the latter symbol for the empty string). We may write:

$$\{x \mid x \neq x\} = \varnothing$$

The empty set is a subset of *every* set. Therefore for every set A the following relation holds:

$$\varnothing \subseteq A$$

We can prove this by showing that it cannot be false. The only way $\varnothing \subseteq A$ could be false, would be if $\varnothing$ contained an element that did not belong to A. However since $\varnothing$ has no elements at all this is absurd. We therefore conclude that $\varnothing \subseteq A$ is true for all A.

The empty set appears when we wish to refer to all subsets of a particular set. For example the set of all subsets of the set $\{a, b\}$ has four members, that is:

$$\{\{a,b\}, \{a\}, \{b\}, \varnothing\}$$

This leads to the notion of what is called a powerset.

Powersets

The set of all subsets of a set A is referred to as the **powerset** of A. It is denoted by $\mathbb{P}$(A). We have:

$\mathbb{P}(\{a,b\}) = \{\{a,b\}, \{a\}, \{b\}, \varnothing\}$
$\mathbb{P}(\{a,b,c\}) = \{\{a,b,c\}, \{a,b\}, \{a,c\}, \{b,c\}, \{a\}, \{b\}, \{c\}, \varnothing\}$

If a set A has n elements then its powerset $\mathbb{P}$(A) has 2^n elements.

Set cardinality

The cardinality of a set is the count of the number of members in the set. It is symbolized by #A (some texts use |A| or **card**(A)). For example

A = {2,3,4}	and	#A = 3
B = {{1,2}, {3,4,5}, {6}}	and	#B = 3

3.2.1   Set operations

There are several important ways in which sets may be combined to form other sets. These operations will now be discussed.

Union

The **union** of two sets A and B (symbolized by A ∪ B) is that set formed from all the elements that belong to A, or to B, or to both.
Symbolically we have:

$A \cup B = \{x \mid x \in A \vee x \in B\}$

and in the predicate calculus:

$(\forall x)(x \in A \cup B) \equiv x \in A \vee x \in B$

Graphically the union of sets A and B is represented by the shaded area in Figure 3.1. Such diagrams as this are called Venn diagrams. U defines the universe with respect to which the operation is carried out. Examples of universes are the set of natural numbers, the set of integers, and the set of alphabetic characters. A universe must always contain at least one member. Often in practice when discussing such operations the universe is left implicit. As an example, given the sets

A = {2,3,4}
B = {3,4,5,6}

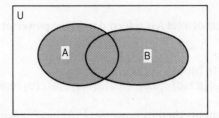

Figure 3.1   The union A ∪ B of two sets A and B.

their union takes the form

A ∪ B = {2,3,4,5,6}

Intersection

The **intersection** of two sets A and B (symbolized A ∩ B) is that set formed from all the elements that belong to *both* A and B. Symbolically we have:

A ∩ B = {x | x ∈ A ∧ x ∈ B}

We can also express the intersection of A and B as:

A ∩ B = {x ∈ A | x ∈ B}

Graphically the intersection of sets A and B is represented by the shaded area in Figure 3.2. The intersection of the two sets

A = {2,3,4}
B = {3,4,5,6}

is given by

A ∩ B = {3,4}

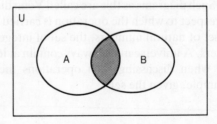

Figure 3.2   The intersection of A ∩ B of two sets A and B.

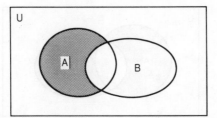

Figure 3.3   The difference A – B of two sets A and B.

When

$$A \cap B = \varnothing$$

the two sets A and B are said to be **disjoint** or **mutually exclusive** since they have no members in common.

Complementation

There is an operation in set theory referred to as **complementation** which is similar to the operation of subtraction in arithmetic. (It is sometimes referred to as a **difference** operation). The **relative complement** of the set B in the set A, is that set (symbolized by A – B) formed from all the elements of A that are not contained in the set B. Symbolically we have:

$$A - B = \{x \in A \mid x \notin B\}$$

In this definition there is no assumption that B is a subset of A. It follows that the two sets A – B and A – (A ∩ B) are identical because the relative complement operation A – B amounts to deletion of those elements of B that happen to be in A.

Graphically the relative complement of the set B in the set A is represented by the shaded area in Figure 3.3. For the two sets

A = {2,3,4}
B = {3,4,5,6}

their difference is given by

A – B = {2}

There is also another form of set difference that must sometimes be employed; it is called the symmetric difference.

Symmetric difference

The **symmetric difference** (or **absolute complement**) of two sets A and B (symbolized by A + B) is that set formed from elements that belong to only A

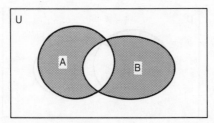

Figure 3.4   The symmetric difference A + B of two sets A and B.

or only B but not to both. It is defined in terms of the difference operation as follows:

$$A + B = (A - B) \cup (B - A)$$

Graphically the symmetric difference of the sets A and B is represented by the shaded area in Figure 3.4. For the two sets

$$A = \{2,3,4\}$$
$$B = \{3,4,5,6\}$$

their symmetric difference is given by:

$$A + B = \{2,5,6\}$$

It is frequently convenient to work with the **complement** of a set A. This set is denoted by A′ and defined with respect to some superset U. In defining such a superset it should be noted that there is no set of all sets (this is demonstrated very convincingly by Russell's paradox (Lin, 1974). In other words there is no universal set. It is, however, possible to assume the existence of a fixed set U in a given discourse and that other sets that will be considered are all subsets of this set U.

The complement of a set A may then be defined as:

$$A' = U - A$$

It also follows that:

$$A - B = A \cap B'$$

Some important properties of set complements are captured in the set-theoretic analogues of De Morgan's laws encountered earlier in the discussion of the propositional calculus.

For any two sets A and B, De Morgan's laws assume the form:

(1) $(A \cup B)' = A' \cap B'$
(2) $(A \cap B)' = A' \cup B'$

This encounter with De Morgan's laws again raises the question about possible relationships between the set operators and the logical connectives discussed earlier.

3.2.2   Analytic set transformations

Set theory, like the propositional calculus, has its own list of useful laws and identities (most of which have their analogues in the propositional calculus) which may be employed for the manipulation and simplification of complex set specifications. It is convenient to divide these laws up into two lists. If we let U be a set in the given domain of discourse and A, B, and C be subsets of U then the primary list of set laws are:

Primary set laws

(1)	$A \cup \emptyset = A$	} Identity
(2)	$A \cap U = A$	} laws
(3)	$A \cup B = B \cup A$	} Commutative
(4)	$A \cap B = B \cap A$	} laws
(5)	$A \cup (B \cap C) = (A \cup B) \cap (A \cup C)$	} Distributive
(6)	$A \cap (B \cup C) = (A \cap B) \cup (A \cap C)$	} laws
(7)	$A \cup A' = U$	Law of the excluded middle
(8)	$A \cap A' = \emptyset$	Law of contradiction

Secondary set laws

(9)	$A \cup A = A$	} Idempotent
(10)	$A \cap A = A$	
(11)	$A \cup U = U$	Identity
(12)	$A \cap \emptyset = \emptyset$	Dominance
(13)	$\emptyset \neq U$	Universe inequality
(14)	$(A')' = A$	Involution
(15)	$A \cup (B \cup C) = (A \cup B) \cup C$	} Associativity
(16)	$A \cap (B \cap C) = (A \cap B) \cap C$	
(17)	$A \cup (A \cap B) = A$	} Absorption
(18)	$A \cap (A \cup B) = A$	
(19)	$(A \cup B)' = A' \cap B'$	} De Morgan's laws
(20)	$(A \cap B)' = A' \cup B'$	
(21)	$A - A = \emptyset$	} Laws of set difference
(22)	$A - (A \cap B) = A - B$	
(23)	$A \cap (A - B) = A - B$	

(24) $(A - B) - B = A - B$

(25) $(A - B) - A = \emptyset$

(26) $(A - B) \cup B = A \cup B$

(27) $(A \cup B) - B = A - B$

$\left.\right\}$ Laws of set difference (cont.)

3.2.3 Specification of set operations

Set operations are often implemented in programs using the array data structure. It is interesting to study how such operations are specified for arrays.

Union of two arrays

Given two arrays of unique elements A[1..M] and B[1..N] (however, there may be elements in A that are also in B and vice versa), we want a specification for a new array that is effectively the **union** of the elements in the two arrays.

We start by specifying a new array C[1..M + N]

$$(\forall i)\, (1 \leqslant i \leqslant M : C_i = A_i) \wedge (\forall j)\, (1 \leqslant j \leqslant N : C_{M+j} = B_j)$$

We then specify a new array D[1..M + N] which is the ordered permutation of C[1..M + N], that is

$$(\forall i)\, (1 \leqslant i < M + N : D_i \leqslant D_{i+1}) \wedge \mathrm{perm}(D,C)$$

Now to get the number of elements in the union we do a count on the ordered array:

$$p = \#(i : 1 \leqslant i < M + N : D_i < D_{i+1}) + 1$$

The union of the elements in A[1..M] and B[1..N] may then be defined by the following two predicates:

$$(\forall i)\, (1 \leqslant i \leqslant p : \mathrm{union}_i \in A[1..M] \vee \mathrm{union}_i \in B[1..N])$$

$$(\forall i)\, (1 \leqslant i < M + N : D_i < D_{i+1} \Rightarrow D_i \in \mathrm{union}[1..p]) \wedge D_{M+N} \in \mathrm{union}[1..p]$$

Intersection of two arrays

Again assume we are given two arrays A[1..M] and B[1..N] each consisting of unique elements. There may however be elements in A that are also in B and vice versa.

Starting with the ordered permutation used in the union specification we have:

$$(\forall i)\ (1 \leq i < M + N : D_i \leq D_{i+1}) \wedge perm(D,C)$$

We can use the following formula to count the number of elements in the **intersection** of the two arrays, q:

$$q = \#(i : 1 \leq i < M + N : D_i = D_{i+1})$$

The intersection of the elements in A[1..M] and B[1..N] may then be defined by the following two predicates:

$$(\forall i)\ (1 \leq i \leq q : intersection_i \in A[1..M] \wedge intersection_i \in B[1..N])$$
$$(\forall i)\ (1 \leq i < M + N : D_i = D_{i+1} \Rightarrow D_i \in intersection[1..q])$$

Symmetric difference of two arrays

Given two arrays A[1..M] and B[1..N] a specification for their symmetric difference may be given as follows.

Taking up our specification again at the point where we had defined the ordered permutation used in the union specification we get:

$$(\forall i)\ (1 \leq i < M + N : D_i \leq D_{i+1}) \wedge perm(D,C)$$
$$d = M + N - 2.q$$

The symmetric difference of the two arrays A[1..M] and B[1..N] may then be defined by the following predicates:

$$(\forall i)\ (1 \leq i \leq d : disjoint_i \in A[1..M]\ \textbf{XOR}\ disjoint_i \in B[1..N])$$

where x **XOR** y is defined as $(x \wedge \neg y) \vee (y \wedge \neg x)$

$$((\forall i)(1 \leq i \leq M + N : \#(j : 1 \leq j \leq M + N : D_i = D_j) = 1) \Rightarrow D_i \in disjoint[1..d])$$

3.2.4   Pairing

Sets provide the basic foundations for defining relations and functions. However, before we begin to discuss relations and functions we need to consider some set construction principles exemplified in the notions of unordered and ordered pairs.

Unordered pairs

To introduce this idea we will begin by stating what is known as the principle of pairing.

> ### Principle of pairing
> If a and b are elements then there is a set C such that a ∈ C and b ∈ C.

The principle of comprehensive specification together with the principle of pairing allows us to conclude that for any two elements a and b there is a set C that contains both of them and nothing else. Since x = a ∨ x = b is a valid set-defining predicate we have:

$$\{x \in C \mid x = a \vee x = b\}$$

or, by the axiom of extensionality, the equivalent set

$$\{a,b\}$$

This set is called an **unordered pair** formed from a and b.

Ordered pairs

It is often convenient to arrange the elements of a set in some order. We are all familiar with alphabetical order but set representations like:

$$\{b,a,c,d\} \quad \text{and} \quad \{a,b,c,d\}$$

whose elements are ordered differently are not distinguished. A convention, based on the use of subsets, may be used to capture the notion of order.

To describe the order in the set:

$$A = \{b,a,c,d\}$$

we could form a set of subsets with the following property.

> ### Ordering rule
> For each position in the order a subset is created which includes only the element that occurs at that position in the order together with all the elements that occur before the current element in the order.

Applying this rule to the set A above we get:

$$O = \{\{b\}, \{a,b\}, \{a,b,c\}, \{a,b,c,d\}\}$$

From this set O, irrespective of how the elements are arranged either in the set or in the subsets, it is possible to retrieve the order of the elements in the original set A.

The ordered sets of primary interest to us are those involving just two elements. They are referred to as **ordered pairs**.

Ordered pair †
An ordered pair of two elements, with a the first element and b the second element is the set (a, b) defined according to the ordering rule as:

$$(a,b) = \{\{a\}, \{a,b\}\}$$

In the set (a, b), a is referred to as the **first coordinate** and b is the **second coordinate**. It can be shown that if (a,b) and (x, y) are ordered pairs and if (a, b) = (x, y), then a = x and b = y. However, for $a \neq b$:

$$(a, b) \neq (b, a)$$

and

$$(a, b) \neq \{a, b\}$$

even if a = b. However, the equality holds for the following pairs of set representations:

$$\{a,b\} = \{b,a\}$$
$$\{a,b,b\} = \{a,b\}$$

The ideas for ordered pairs may be extended to ordered n-tuples based on the ordered pairs. An ordered triple (a, b, c) is an ordered pair whose first coordinate is also an ordered pair, that is:

$$(a, b, c) = ((a, b), c) = \{\{a\}, \{a,b\}, \{a,b,c\}\}$$

In general for an ordered n-tuple we have

$$(a_1, a_2, a_3, ..., a_n) = ((a_1, a_2, a_3, ..., a_{n-1}), a_n)$$

Finite sequences, important tools for writing specifications, are defined in terms of ordered n-tuples.

3.2.5   Cartesian products ††

The concept of the ordered n-tuple provides a powerful means for

---

† Sometimes angle brackets, i.e. <a, b> are used to identify ordered pairs.
†† The term 'cross-product' is also used to denote this operation.

constructing sets with interesting and useful properties. In the jargon of computing scientists it can provide a means for constructing new and more complex types from simpler types. It is then possible to construct sets defined by predicates using these more complex types. A starting point for this is the Cartesian product of two sets.

Cartesian product
If A and B are sets then the Cartesian product of these two sets, symbolized by A × B is the set of all ordered pairs (a, b) such that a ∈ A and b ∈ B.

Symbolically we have:

$$A \times B = \{(a,b) \mid a \in A \wedge b \in B\}$$

As an example of a Cartesian product if:

A = {a, b, c}
B = {1, 2}

then

$$A \times B = \{(a, 1), (a, 2), (b, 1), (b, 2), (c, 1), (c, 2)\}$$

Note that in general A × B ≠ B × A. For example we have:

$$B \times A = \{(1, a), (1, b), (1, c), (2, a), (2, b), (2, c)\}$$

In forming Cartesian products there is no restriction that the *two* sets used to form the product are of the same cardinality.

It is possible to construct product sets from more than two sets. For example, from a set of days, a set of months, and a set of years, a product set of dates may be constructed. The Cartesian product

date = DAY × MONTH × YEAR

denotes the set of ordered triples

$$\{(d, m, y) \mid d \in DAY \wedge m \in MONTH \wedge y \in YEAR\}$$

Each element of this set of ordered triples is of the form:

(day, month, year).

One member of the product set might be

(21, november, 1946)

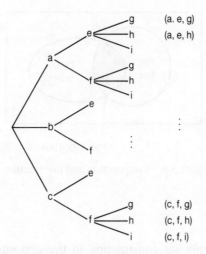

Figure 3.5   Construction of Cartesian product for A × B × C.

As another example consider the sets A = {a, b, c}, B = {e, f} and C = {g, h, i),
and their Cartesian product A × B × C. Figure 3.5 shows how all the *triples*
may be systematically identified.

Cartesian products may be used with other set operations. For sets A, B, C
and D the following relations hold:

$$A \times (B \cup C) = (A \times B) \cup (A \times C)$$
$$A \times (B \cap C) = (A \times B) \cap (A \times C)$$
$$A \times (B - C) = (A \times B) - (A \times C)$$

In other words, the Cartesian product distributes over union, intersection,
and set difference. Also we have:

$$(A \cap B) \times (C \cap D) = (A \times C) \cap (B \times D)$$

To illustrate how relations like this are proved, consider the first relation:

$$A \times (B \cup C) = (A \times B) \cup (A \times C)$$

To prove this relation let (a, d) be an arbitrary element of the set A × (B ∪ C).
Therefore

$$
\begin{aligned}
(a, d) \in A \times (B \cup C) &\equiv a \in A \wedge d \in (B \cup C) \\
&\equiv a \in A \wedge (d \in B \vee d \in C) \\
&\equiv (a \in A \wedge d \in B) \vee (a \in A \wedge d \in C) \\
&\equiv (a, d) \in (A \times B) \vee (a, d) \in (A \times C) \\
&\equiv (a, d) \in (A \times B) \cup (A \times C)
\end{aligned}
$$

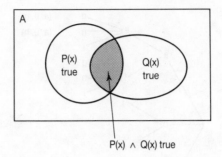

Figure 3.6   Conjunction and intersection.

Projection

It is possible to apply set construction in the opposite direction to the Cartesian product. We know that every set of ordered pairs is a subset of the Cartesian product of two sets. That is, if every element of a set C is an ordered pair, then there exists two sets A and B such that:

$$C \subseteq A \times B$$

where

$$A = \{a \mid (\exists b) \, ((a, b) \in C)\}$$
$$B = \{b \mid (\exists a) \, ((a, b) \in C)\}$$

A is called the **projection** of C onto the first coordinate, and B is called the projection of C onto the second coordinate.

3.2.6   Logical connectives and set operations

A simple relationship exists between the set operators and the propositional connectives. It is most easily described in set-theoretic terms. To illustrate the relationships we will assume that P(x) and Q(x) are predicates of the members which are true on some set A.

Conjunction and intersection

The relationship between conjunction and intersection is given by the set equality which defines a subset of A:

$$\{x \in A \mid P(x) \wedge Q(x)\} = \{x \in A \mid P(x)\} \cap \{x \in A \mid Q(x)\}$$

This may be represented graphically by a Venn diagram (Figure 3.6).

The subset corresponding to the intersection of the two sets defined by P(x) and Q(x) is identical to the set defined by the predicate P(x) ∧ Q(x).

Disjunction and union

The relationship between these two operators indicates that the subset of A corresponding to the union of the two sets defined by P(x) and Q(x) is identical to the set defined by the predicate P(x) ∨ Q(x), that is:

$$\{x \in A \mid P(x) \lor Q(x)\} = \{x \in A \mid P(x)\} \cup \{x \in A \mid Q(x)\}$$

This set is represented graphically in Figure 3.7.

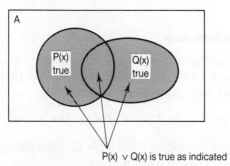

P(x) ∨ Q(x) is true as indicated

Figure 3.7   Disjunction and union.

Negation and difference

In this case, for a predicate P(x) on a set A the set defined by the predicate ¬P(x) is equal to the set of those elements in A not in the set defined by P(x), that is:

$$\{x \in A \mid \neg P(x)\} = A - \{x \in A \mid P(x)\}$$

This is shown in Figure 3.8.

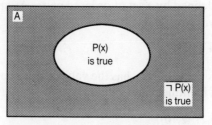

Figure 3.8   Negation and difference.

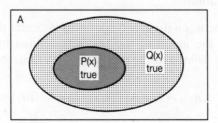

Figure 3.9   Implication and inclusion.

Implication and inclusion

When considering implication we are only interested in the situation where $P(x) \Rightarrow Q(x)$ is true for all x. In this case, if $P(x)$ is true, then $Q(x)$ must also be true. Formally we have (as shown in Figure 3.9):

$$(\forall x \in A)(P(x) \Rightarrow Q(x)) \text{ iff } \{x \in A \mid P(x)\} \subseteq \{x \in A \mid Q(x)\}$$

The truth of the implication $P(x) \Rightarrow Q(x)$ therefore corresponds to set inclusion and $P(x) \Rightarrow Q(x)$ is true for all $x \in A$.

Similarly for equivalence $P(x) \equiv Q(x)$ is true for all $x \in A$ if and only if

$$\{x \in A \mid P(x)\} = \{x \in A \mid Q(x)\}$$

3.2.7   Predicates and sets of states

Both simple and complex predicates can be used to specify sets. In program design we want to specify sets of states. To understand this idea we need to describe the term 'state' in the programming context. A state corresponds to a configuration of a computer's memory at a particular point in time. A state is defined by the association of each identifier in a program with a value. It consists of a set of ordered pairs of the form (identifier, value) where all the identifiers are distinct. This suggests that a state is really a function from a set of identifiers to a set of values (see the discussion of functions later in this chapter) which is defined by a set of ordered pairs. As an example consider the predicate $P(x, y, z)$ expressed in terms of x, y and z:

$$P(x, y, z) : x + y < z$$

Now suppose x has the value 3, y has the value 2 and z has the value 10. The state for this set of identifiers and values is:

$$S = \{(x,3), (y,2), (z,10)\}$$

It is possible to evaluate the predicate $P(x, y, z)$ in the state S by replacing all identifiers by their respective values in the state. The resulting expression is then simplified and evaluated. For our example we have:

$$x + y < z \equiv 3 + 2 < 10$$
$$\equiv 5 < 10$$
$$\equiv \text{TRUE}$$

It follows that the predicate P(x, y, z) is true in the state S. In computing science it has become common pactice, for reasons of shorthand, not to distinguish between a predicate and the set of states it characterizes. When this convention is adopted, rather than referring to the set of states in which the predicate P(x, y, z) is true, we refer to the states P(x, y, z) or the states in P(x, y, z). This leads to another convention that is used when describing predicates, the notion of strength.

Strength of predicates

It is convenient to be able to refer to the **relative strength** of predicates, strength being a measure of the size of the state space that the predicates characterize. A *stronger* predicate places more restrictions on the combinations of values of its identifiers for which it is true. If P and Q are two predicates on the same state-space (e.g. (x, y, z)) and P is *stronger* than Q (or equivalently Q is *weaker* than P) then P will describe only a subset of the states described by Q.

More formally, if $P(x_1, \ldots, x_N)$ and $Q(x_1, \ldots, x_N)$ are predicates on the variable state space $(x_1, \ldots, x_N)$ such that:

$$\{(x_1, \ldots, x_N) \mid P(x_1, \ldots, x_N)\} \subset \{(x_1, \ldots, x_N) \mid Q(x_1, \ldots, x_N)\}$$

then P is *stronger* (more restrictive) than Q and consequently Q is *weaker* (less restrictive) than P. It also follows that P is stronger than, or the same strength as, Q if and only if $P \Rightarrow Q$.

The weakest predicate of all is T (i.e. true) or any other tautology, because it characterizes the set of *all states*. It follows also that the strongest predicate is F (i.e. false), or any other contradiction, because it characterizes the set of *no states*.

An important instance of strength arises with implications. If we have that $P \Rightarrow Q$ then the predicate Q is at least as weak if not weaker than the predicate P, that is Q characterizes all those states characterized by P and possibly more. Also, with respect to conjunction and disjunction, for the predicates P and Q the following limiting cases obtain when we take into account overlap:

P ∧ Q is *stronger than,* or the same strength as P
P ∧ Q is *stronger than,* or the same strength as Q
P ∨ Q is *weaker than,* or the same strength as P

Some examples are:

$x > 0 \wedge x < 10$	is stronger than	$x > 0$
$x > 0 \wedge y > 0 \wedge (x + y = z)$	is stronger than	$x > 0 \wedge y > 0$
$N > 0$	is stronger than	$N \geqslant 0$
$(\forall j : 1 \leqslant j < N : a_j < a_{j+1})$	is stronger than	$(\forall j : 1 \leqslant j < N : a_j \leqslant a_{j+1})$

3.3   Relations

Relations are important in program specification. Even if we are not familiar with the mathematical concept of a relation, we certainly are familiar with its informal counterpart used in natural language. Some examples are:

> Philip is the father of Charles.
> 3 is less than 7.
> Jack loves Jill.

In the linguistic use of relations there is usually an underlying notion of connectedness. However, this notion is, in general, too vague to submit to precise definition and therefore cannot be part of any useful mathematical definition. Informally, a relation between two mathematical entities a and b is some condition that is either true or false when a and b are bound to particular values. As an example 'less than' symbolized by '$<$' is a relation between pairs of natural numbers, for example:

> $1 < 2$ is *true*
> $2 < 1$ is *false*

It is convenient to define the mathematical concept of relation in terms of the notions of ordered pairs and sets. In fact a **relation** may be considered as a set of ordered pairs. We are mostly interested in relations that stand between two entities. Such relations are referred to as binary relations. They may be defined as follows:

Binary relation
For two sets A and B that are not necessarily distinct, if an element a of A is related to an element of b of B by a binary relation R, then the ordered pair (a, b) from the Cartesian product A × B will belong to the subset of ordered pairs from A × B which completely define R.

For a binary relation R defined by a set of ordered pairs the following predicate holds:

$(a, b) \in R$

where

$a \in A$ and $b \in B$

This is often written in the form:

$a \, R \, b$

where $a \, R \, b$ is read as 'a is R-related to b'. Taking $a \, R \, b$ to mean $(a, b) \in R$ allows some notational convenience which may be demonstrated by the following example. If the relation 'less than' is symbolized by '$<$' and we let R be '$<$' then we end up with:

$a < b$

which corresponds to the standard notation. This correspondence extends to other binary relations which serve as infix operators.

Another notation sometimes used to designate ordered pairs of a relation is:

$a \mapsto b$

There are also other expressions used to define relationships e.g. 'a maps to b under R', and 'R maps a to b'. It is important to understand that an ordered pair, say (a, b), is *not* a relation, but the set consisting of that ordered pair i.e. $\{(a, b)\}$ *is* a relation.

To illustrate the use of these tools consider the relation 'less than' on the set of natural numbers N. It is the set of all ordered pairs (x, y) of natural numbers such that for some positive natural number z, the equality $x + z = y$ holds. This set (or relation) may be described formally by:

$\{(x, y) \mid (\exists z \in \mathbb{N})(x + z = y \land z \neq 0)\}$

Sometimes it is necessary to consider relations that hold among three or more things. An example of a *ternary* relation is that of parenthood (for example, *Zeus* and *Hera* are the parents of *Diana*). The following conventions may be used for constructing such order relations. First a letter or name identifying the relation is written down followed by an ordered n-tuple for the names of the things among which the relation holds. Our ternary relation for parenthood could be expressed by:

$P(a, b, c)$

We say that P is a relation such that for all a, b, and c, $P(a, b, c)$ holds if and only if a and b are the parents of c.

3.3.1 Properties of binary relations

Binary relations have several relevant fundamental properties. When a relation R is included in A × B we may say that R is a relation *from* A to B. A relation in A × A is described as a relation *on* A. The properties of relations that we will consider are:

(1)   A relation R on a set A is reflexive if

$$(\forall x \in A)\, x\, R\, x$$

For example, the relation '≤' on the set of natural numbers N is reflexive. It is also reflexive on subsets of N. Suppose

$$A = \{1, 2, 3\};\ \text{then}$$
$$R = \{(1, 1), (1, 2), (1, 3), (2, 2), (2, 3), (3, 3)\}$$

As another example consider that

$$A = \{a, b\} \qquad B = \{a, b, c\}$$

then the relation

$$R = \{(a, a), (b, b)\}$$

on the set A is reflexive, but the relation R on B is not reflexive because (c,c) is not a member of R.

(2)   A relation R on the set A is symmetric if

$$(\forall x, y \in A)(x\, R\, y \Rightarrow y\, R\, x)$$

For example the relation '≠' is symmetric on any subset of the natural numbers. Suppose

$$A = \{1, 2, 3\};\ \text{then R on A is}$$
$$R = \{(1, 2), (1, 3), (2, 3), (2, 1), (3, 1), (3, 2)\}$$

For the set A = {a, b, c} the relation R_1 on A

$$R_1 = \{(a,c), (b,c), (b,b), (c,a), (c,b)\}$$

is also symmetric but the relation

$$R_2 = \{(a,c), (b,c), (c,b)\}$$

is not symmetric (because (c,a) ∉ R_2).

(3)   A relation R on a set A is transitive if

$$(\forall x, y, z \in A)(x\, R\, y \wedge y\, R\, z \Rightarrow x\, R\, z)$$

The relation '≤' on any subset of the natural numbers is transitive. Suppose we consider '≤' on the set A = {1, 2, 3}; then

$$R = \{(1, 1), (1, 2), (1, 3), (2, 2)\ (2, 3), (3, 3)\}$$

is transitive. The relation

$$R = \{(a,b), (b,c), (a,c)\}$$

on the set A = {a,b,c} is also transitive.

Domain, range, and co-domain of a relation

A relation R from A to B is defined by $R \subseteq A \times B$. The set of all left co-ordinates of the ordered pairs in R is referred to as the **domain** of R. It is written:

dom R

and defined formally by

dom R = {a $\in$ A | ($\exists$b $\in$ B) (a R b)}   hence dom R $\subseteq$ A.

The set of all right coordinates of the ordered pairs in R is referred to as the **range** of R. It is written:

ran R

and defined formally by

ran R = {b $\in$ B | ($\exists$a $\in$ A) (a R b)}   hence ran R $\subseteq$ B.

The set B is called the **co-domain** of R. Unfortunately the set A is not usually given a name. It is really the **parent-domain** of R.

These concepts are illustrated by the following example. The relation of marriage R is defined by the set of all ordered pairs of males m and females f that are married. We may then interpret:

m R f   as man m is married to woman f

where

dom R	is the set of married men
ran R	is the set of married women
parent-domain of R	is the set of *all* men
co-domain of R	is the set of *all* women.

The union of the domain and range of a binary relation is known as its *field*.

Power relation

Earlier we saw how the powerset of a set was constructed from all its subsets. There is also a corresponding concept in the theory of relations. Given two sets A and B their Cartesian product $A \times B$ yields the set of all ordered pairs that may be used as elements for relations formed from A and B. The powerset of this Cartesian product, that is P ($A \times B$) is the set of all possible relations that can be formed from A and B. It is described as the **power-relation** of A and B and is symbolized by $A \leftrightarrow B$ where

$$A \leftrightarrow B = P(A \times B)$$

For our purposes in specification $A \leftrightarrow B$ may be viewed as a new *type*, much as we view the set of natural numbers as a type. Our interpretation of this type is as the set of all possible values that elements of the type may assume. $A \leftrightarrow B$ fulfills the role of characterizing all possible relations that can be constructed from A and B.

Identity relation

The **identity** or **equality** relation I_A on a set A is the set of all ordered pairs in $A \times A$ with equal coordinates, that is

$$I_A = \{(a, a) \mid a \in A\}$$

For example, given $A = \{1,2,3\}$

$$I_A = \{(1,1), (2,2), (3,3)\}$$

Inverse relation

The **inverse** R^{-1} of a relation R from A to B is that relation from B to A that consists of all the ordered pairs which, when reversed, belong to R. Symbolically we have:

$$R^{-1} = \{(b, a) \mid (a, b) \in R\}$$

For example if R is a relation on A where

$$A = \{1,2,3,4\} \quad \text{and} \quad R = \{(1,2), (2,3), (3,4)\}$$

then the inverse of R is

$$R^{-1} = \{(2,1), (3,2), (4,3)\}$$

3.3.2 Equivalence relations and partitions

A relation R is an **equivalence relation** on a set A if it is reflexive, symmetric, and transitive. The relation of identity is an equivalence relation. For the set

$$A = \{a,b,c\}$$

the relation

R = {(a,a), (b,b), (c,c)}

is an equivalence relation on A. Another (the largest) equivalence relation on A is the Cartesian product A × A. Before further discussion of equivalence relations we need to introduce the concept of a partition.

> **Partition**
> A partition of a set A consists of a set of disjoint subsets (called blocks) of A whose union is the set A.

As we shall see below partitions have a connection with equivalence relations. Two partitions P_1 and P_2 of the set

A = {a,b,c,d,e,f}

are

P_1 = {{a, b}, {c, d}, {e, f}}
P_2 = {{a}, {b,c,d}, {e,f}}

but the following set

P_3 = {{b,c,d}, {e,f}}

is not a partition of A since a is not an element of the union of the subsets of P_3.

We may now consider an equivalence relation in between the two extremes of identity and the Cartesian product for the set

A = {a,b,c,d,e,f}

In this case we choose to use a tabular form for the equivalence relation on the set A = {a,b,c,d,e,f}. In the table below the ticks identify ordered pairs present in the equivalence relation. For example, the tick in the bottom right hand corner indicates the presence of (f,f). The need to be reflexive, symmetric and transitive means that partitions always define square blocks in a table. When an element is related only to itself (e.g. f) it defines a square of unit size.

	a	b	c	d	e	f
a	✔	✔				
b	✔	✔				
c			✔	✔	✔	
d			✔	✔	✔	
e			✔	✔	✔	
f						✔

This example brings out the connection between an equivalence relation on a set A and a partition of the set A. From an equivalence relation on a set A we can define a partition of A where any pair of elements in the same block are related while any two elements in different blocks are not related. In this example a partition is:

P = {{a,b}, {c,d,e},{f}}

This partition is induced by the equivalence relation (and vice versa) and the blocks in the partition define equivalence classes, the next topic for discussion.

Equivalence classes

The concept of equivalence class is an important extension to the notion of equivalence relations. Associated with an equivalence relation R on A is another set [a] called the R-equivalence class of a on A (for a ∈ A) whose elements $\propto$, are characterized by:

$\propto$ ∈ [a] iff ($\propto$ ∈ A ∧ a R $\propto$)

that is

[a] = {b ∈ A | a R b}

For a in A, the equivalence class of a, with respect to the equivalence relation R, is the set of all those elements $\propto$ in A for which a R $\propto$ holds. As an example, if R = A × A (that is the *universal relation*) then A is the only associated equivalence class, whereas if R is equality on A then each equivalence class consists of a single element from A. Each element in A is a member of only one R-equivalence class in A. Objects that are in some way equivalent generate identical classes.

The equivalence classes of the elements of A for our equivalence relation in tabular form are:

[a] = [b] = {a, b}
[c] = [d] = [e] = {c, d, e}
[f] = {f}

A consequence of this principle of abstraction is that it can often provide a means for significantly reducing the number of objects that need to be considered. We can deal with equivalence classes of objects rather than a much larger original set of objects (for example, a typical reduction might involve consideration of the order of $\log_2 N$ equivalence classes as opposed to say N original ordered n-tuples. For N = 1024 this may mean considering 10 equivalence classes rather than 1024 ordered n-tuples).

3.3.3   Ordering relations

We frequently need to recognize precedence in computing science. Ordering relations can help us to do this. The definition of the order concept for relations rests on the notion of **antisymmetry** (not to be confused with **asymmetry**).

Here we will define both asymmetry and antisymmetry as they are applied to relations. A relation R on a set A is *asymmetric* if we have:

$$(\forall x, y \in A) (x\,R\,y \Rightarrow \neg\,y\,R\,x)$$

When $x\,R\,y$ is present $y\,R\,x$ must not be present for the asymmetry property to apply. A relation R on a set A is *antisymmetric* if:

$$(\forall x, y \in A) (x\,R\,y \wedge y\,R\,x \Rightarrow x = y)$$

The relations 'less than or equal to ($\leq$)' and set inclusion $\subseteq$ are both antisymmetric. We can now define a *partial ordering* of a set.

Partial ordering
A relation R is a partial ordering on the set A if and only if R is reflexive, transitive, and antisymmetric.

The relations $\leq$ and $\subseteq$ are both partial orderings. The word 'partial' is used in the definition because not every pair of elements of the set must be related. As an example, given the set A, and the relation R

A = {1,2,3,4}
R = {(1,1),(2,2),(3,3),(4,4),(1,2),(2,3),(1,3)}

We see that R is a partial ordering on the set A. In this case 4 is not related to the other elements in A.

3.3.4   Graph and tree relations

The theory of relations has a strong association with graphs and trees, both important data structures in computing science. A relation R from A to B is just a subset of the Cartesian product A × B. A graph of such a relation may be constructed by writing down the elements of A in one column and the elements of B in a second column, and then, for each pair (a, b) ∈ R, drawing an arrow between the two columns that represents the pair. A graph of this form is called a **bipartite graph**. The bipartite graph for the relation:

R = {(a,1), (a,3), (b,1), (b,2), (c,4)}

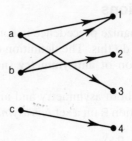

Figure 3.10   Bipartite graph for relation R.

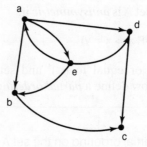

Figure 3.11   Directed graph for relation R.

could take the form shown in Figure 3.10.

In many applications the pairs in a relation are formed between elements of the *same* set. In such cases the relation R is described by:

$$R \subseteq A \times A$$

A bipartite graph could also be used to represent such a relation. An alternative representation for such cases involves the construction of what is called a **directed graph**. Such a representation is built by drawing a point (called a **node** or **vertex** of the graph) for each element of the set A and then drawing an arrow from a to a' for each pair (a,a') in the relation R. The arrows are called **edges** or **arcs**.

For the set A = {a,b,c,d,e} and the relation

$$R = \{(a,b), (a,d), (a,e), (b,c), (d,c), (e,a), (e,b), (e,d)\}$$

the corresponding directed graph could be represented by Figure 3.11.

For a given node, the number of arrows eminating from it is referred to as its **out-degree** and the number of arrows pointing to a node is referred to as its **in-degree**. In the example the node a has an out-degree of 3 and an in-degree of 1.

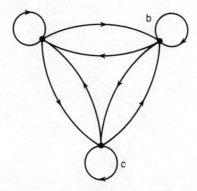

Figure 3.12   Directed graph of an equivalence relation R.

In directed graphs of equivalence relations the properties of reflexivity, transitivity, and being symmetric show up very clearly. This can be seen in the graph of the equivalence relation R given in Figure 3.12.

R = {(a,a), (a,b), (a,c), (b,b), (b,a), (b,c), (c,c), (c,a), (c,b)}

Another important class of graphs are those that obey the rule that there is at most only one way to get from one node to another by following the arrow directions. These structures are referred to as **trees**.

A **tree** on a set A is a directed graph which is again described by a relation of the form:

R ⊆ A × A

The number of edges going *into* a node is called its **in-degree**, and the number of edges going *out of* a node is called its **out-degree.** One node of a tree, called the **root**, has an in-degree of zero, while all other nodes of the tree have an in-degree of one which means there is only one path of edges from the root to any other node. A **leaf** node is one with an out-degree of zero.

More formally we can define a tree as a directed graph with a non-empty set of nodes such that:

- one node called the root of the tree has an in-degree of zero,
- every other node has an in-degree of one, and
- for every node in the tree there is a directed path from the root to that node.

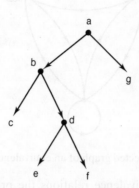

Figure 3.13   Directed graph representation of a binary tree relation R.

As an example a **binary tree** (where all nodes other than leaf nodes have an out-degree of two) may take the form shown in Figure 3.13.

The relation for this tree is:

R = {(a,b), (a,g), (b,c), (b,d), (d,e), (d,f)}

The root of the tree is a and c, e, f, and g are leaf nodes.

In some applications we have to deal with graphs and trees where no importance is placed on the direction of the connection between pairs of elements. Such structures are referred to as **undirected graphs** and **trees**. From a relational viewpoint this means that the pair (b,a) is always present whenever the pair (a,b) is present. Such structures are symmetric and the convention of drawing a line between pairs of elements rather than using arrows is adopted. Having introduced the most useful of the relations we can now turn to the discussion of functions.

3.4 Functions

A function is a special kind of relation. Like relations, functions have a role to play in program design. A rich theory of functions has been developed because of their central importance in mathematics. In the present discussion we will try to focus only on those aspects of the subject most pertinent to program design.

The concept of function is often introduced informally with a definition something along the following lines.

> **Function**
> A function is a rule which associates with each element of a given set a single element of some other not necessarily distinct set.

As with the treatment of relations, set theory provides a vehicle for a precise definition of functions. It avoids the need to involve the semantics of the term 'rule' used in the preceding definition.

For two sets X and Y a function or total-function (see later) from X to Y is a relation f (where dom f = X) such that for each x in X there is a unique element y that satisfies $(x,y) \in f$.

For each x the unique element y is denoted by f(x). Convention has it that for functions f(x) = y is used in preference to the relational notations x f y and $(x,y) \in f$.

The common notation

$f : X \rightarrow Y$

is interpreted as 'f is a function from X to Y'. The term **mapping** is sometimes used in place of the word 'function'. When the domain and co-domain of a function are clearly understood it may be denoted simply by f. The notation

$x \mapsto f(x)$

is used to indicate that f(x) in Y is the value associated with x.

Domain, range, and co-domain of a function

Three important properties employed in characterizing a function are its **domain, co-domain,** and **range**. There is some variation in the literature in the definition of these terms. Some care in their application is therefore needed. We will adopt the conventions introduced for relations.

In general a function $f : X \rightarrow Y$ is a subset of $X \times Y$ where members x of X appear *exactly once* as the first component of ordered pairs of the form (x, y). X is the *parent domain* of f and the set Y is the *co-domain* of f.

In dealing with functions in general it is necessary to accommodate situations where a function f is not defined for all values in its domain X. Also there may be values in its co-domain Y for which there are no corresponding values in its domain. Some additional terminology is needed to handle these variations.

For a function $f : X \rightarrow Y$ if y = f(x) then y is referred to as the **image** of x under f and x is a **pre-image** of y under f. Schematically this is shown in Figure 3.14.

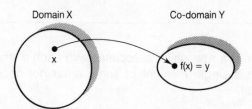

Figure 3.14   Schematic representation of a function.

The subset of X for which f is defined (symbolized by dom f) is referred to as the *domain* of f and dom f ⊆ X. Formally we have

$$\text{dom } f = \{x \in X \mid (\exists y \in Y)(y = f(x))\}$$

In some cases the domain of a function f is a Cartesian product of sets. A function with a domain

$$X_1 \times X_2 \times ... \times X_n$$

is a function of n variables. The value of f at $(x_1, x_2, x_3, ..., x_n)$ for each $x_i \in X_i$ is

$$f(x_1, x_2, ..., x_n)$$

The subset of Y for which f is defined (symbolized by ran f) is referred to as the *range* of f, and ran f ⊆ Y

$$\text{ran } f = \{y \in Y \mid (\exists x \in X)(f(x) = y)\}^\dagger$$

In other words, the range of f is the subset of the co-domain Y that is made up of the image of the elements of X. It is that part of Y that f actually 'ranges over'.

Using these definitions we may formally describe a function f from X to Y as a relation from X to Y for which

(1)   dom f = X
(2) $(\forall x \in X)(\forall y, z \in Y)((x,y) \in f \wedge (x,z) \in f \Rightarrow y = z)$

An example illustrating these ideas for a function $f : X \rightarrow Y$ is as follows:

X = {1,2,3,4}	parent domain of f
Y = {a,b,c,d,e}	co-domain of f
f = {(1,a), (2,b), (3,c), (4,d)}	the function f
dom f = {1,2,3,4}	the domain of f
ran f = {a,b,c,d}	the range of f

---

† Some texts refer to ran f as the image of f but this can be confusing as it refers to a subset rather than a single value.

3.4.1   Partial and total functions

As mentioned earlier some functions are not defined for all elements of their parent domain. Such functions are referred to as **partial functions**. They are often encountered in computing science. Their ability to accommodate undefined values makes partial functions well-suited for expressing possible functional relationships that may be encountered in program execution. A partial function f, from a set X to a set Y, may be denoted by:

$f : X \nrightarrow Y$

This partial function associates with each element x of a subset of X (called the *domain* of f) a single element y in Y, called the *image* of x.

When we say that $f : X \nrightarrow Y$ is a partial function we mean that there is a subset dom(f) of X (i.e. dom(f) $\subseteq$ X) for which $f : \text{dom}(f) \rightarrow Y$ is a function according to the usual mathematical convention. If dom(f) = X then f is a **total function**. The function

$f = \{(1,a), (2,b), (3,c), (4,d)\}$

is clearly a total function†.

For the sets

$X = \{1,2,3,4\}$
$Y = \{a,b,c,d,e\}$

and the function

$f = \{(1,a), (2,b), (3,c)\}$

we have that

dom f = $\{1,2,3\}$
ran f = $\{a,b,c\}$

Therefore, f is a partial function since dom f $\subset$ X (i.e. $\{1,2,3\} \subset \{1,2,3,4\}$).

As another example consider the following partial function on the natural numbers $\mathbb{N}$:

$f : \mathbb{N} \times \nrightarrow \mathbb{N}$

where

$f(x,y) = \{x \textbf{ div } y \quad\quad \text{for } y > 0 \quad\quad$ (we could also write $z = f(x,y)$)
$\{undefined \quad\quad \text{for } y = 0$

---

† To distinguish partial functions from ordinary functions, the latter are referred to as total functions.

This function f is a partial function since for all pairs where y = 0 (that is where we have (x,0)), the image value f(x,y) or z is undefined.

We can now explore various types of functions and their properties.

3.4.2   Classification of functions

Some additional terminology is needed to characterize and classify the various types of functions that we may encounter.

Injective or one-to-one functions

A function f : X → Y is described as **injective** or **one-to-one** provided all elements in its domain have distinct images, that is

$$f(x_1) = f(x_2) \quad \text{implies } x_1 = x_2$$

A function

$$f_1 = \{(a, 1), (b,2), (c, 3)\} \quad \text{is injective}$$

while

$$f_2 = \{(a, 1), (b, 1), (c,3)\} \quad \text{is not injective}$$

Surjective or onto functions

A function f : X → Y is said to be **surjective** (or f is a function from X **onto** Y) provided *every* y ∈ Y is the image of some x ∈ X.

Bijective or one-to-one correspondence functions

A function f : X → Y is said to be **bijective** if it is both injective and surjective. That is, all elements in its domain have distinct images and every y ∈ Y is the image of some x ∈ X. In other words, there is a one-to-one correspondence between the sets X and Y.

The bipartite graphs shown in Figure 3.15 make a clear distinction among these three classes of function.

X = {a,b}	X = {a,b,c}	X = {a,b,c}
Y = {1,2,3}	Y = {1,2}	Y = {1,2,3}
f₁ = {(a,1), (b,3)}	f₂ = {(a,1), (b,1), (c,2)}	f₃ = {(a,2), (b,1), (c,3)}
is injective	is surjective	is bijective

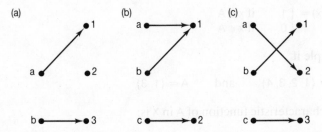

Figure 3.15 Biparte graphs showing injective, surjective and bijective functions.

With the terminology that has been introduced there are now a number of other functions that can be identified.

Identity function

A function $f : X \to X$ defined by $f(x) = x$ (or $y = x$) which associates each element in X with itself is called the **identity function**. It is denoted $Id(X)$ or 1_X.

We have

$$Id(X) = \{(x,x) \mid x \in X\}$$

For example if $X = \{1,2,3\}$ then

$$Id(X) = \{(1,1), (2,2), (3,3)\}$$

is the identity function on X. The identity function is a bijection.

Constant function

A function $f : X \to Y$ is said to be a **constant function** if there is some $b \in Y$ such that $f(x) = b$ (or $y = b$) for every $x \in X$.

For a constant function we have

$$c_b = \{(x,b) \mid x \in X\} \qquad \text{for a fixed b in Y.}$$

Characteristic function

Consider a subset A where $A \subseteq X$ and X is non-empty. The relation

$$\{(x,y) \in X \times \{0,1\} \mid (x \in A \Rightarrow y = 1) \wedge (x \notin A \Rightarrow y = 0)\}$$

defines a function from X to $\{0,1\}$ called the **characteristic function** of A in X, which is denoted by $\chi_A : X \to \{0,1\}$ where:

$$\chi_A(x) = \begin{cases} 1 & \text{if } x \in A \\ 0 & \text{if } x \notin A \end{cases}$$

For example if

$$X = \{1, 2, 3, 4\} \quad \text{and} \quad A = \{1, 3\}$$

then the characteristic function of A in X is:

$$\chi_A = \{(1,1), (2,0), (3,1), (4,0)\}$$

Inverse function

Earlier we saw how a relation R from X to Y had an inverse defined by:

$$R^{-1} = \{(y,x) \mid (x,y) \in R\}$$

It follows that since a function $f : X \rightarrow Y$ is also a relation from X to Y, its inverse f^{-1}, must be a relation from Y to X. When $f : X \rightarrow Y$ is bijective then $f^{-1} : Y \rightarrow X$ is a function called the **inverse function of** f.

For example, if $X = \{a, b, c\}$ and $Y = \{1, 2, 3\}$ and f is a function from X to Y defined by:

$f = \{(a,1), (b,3)(c,2)\}$ or

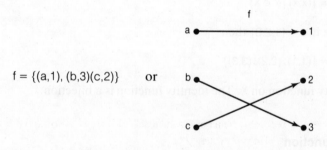

then the inverse function f^{-1} from B to A is

$f^{-1} = \{ (1,a), (3,b)(2,c)\}$ or

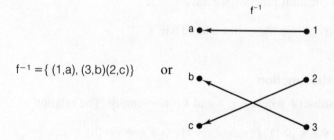

Reversing the arrows of the bipartite graph for f yields the inverse function f^{-1}. When the inverse function of f exists, the following identities hold:

(1) $f^{-1}(f(x)) = x$ for all x in the domain of f
(2) $f(f^{-1}(y)) = y$ for all y in the range of f.

The problem of computing the inverse of a function is more complicated when the function is defined by an equation. The following example illustrates how we might proceed in such circumstances.

Given

$$f(x) = ax + b$$

we first replace all occurrences of x by $f^{-1}(y)$ which yields

$$f(f^{-1}(y)) = a f^{-1}(y) + b$$

We then simplify this using (2) which yields

$$y = a f^{-1}(y) + b$$

Finally we solve the resulting equation for $f^{-1}(y)$. This leads to

$$f^{-1}(y) = \frac{y}{a} - \frac{b}{a}$$

Unfortunately this technique can yield an 'inverse' even when one does not exist.

Permutation functions

A bijection, $f : A \to A$, from a finite set A onto itself is called a **permutation** of A. For the set $A = \{1,2,3,4\}$ a permutation of A is

$$f = \{(1,3), (2,4), (3,2), (4,1)\}$$

Permutation functions are sometimes needed in specifications. For example, whenever we sort the representation of a set A in an array a, it is necessary to include in the specification the restriction that the sorted result should be a permutation of the original data A. This is usually written as perm(a,A). It is expressed in the predicate calculus as:

$$perm(a,A) \equiv (\forall k : 1 \leqslant k \leqslant N : \#(j : 1 \leqslant j \leqslant N : a_k = a_j) = \#(j : 1 \leqslant j \leqslant N : a_k = A_j))$$

where

$$A = (A_1, A_2, ..., A_N) \quad \text{and} \quad a = (a_1, a_2, ..., a_N)$$

Order notation

We will now briefly examine another important role of functions in computing science.

A notation based on the use of functions has been adopted for making quantitative measures of the relative performance of different algorithms. The notation is an **order notation**. It is commonly referred to as the **O-notation.** The O-notation depends on a computational model that allows the essence or dominant aspect of a computation to be characterized independently of any considerations that relate to a particular programming language. What we are interested in doing is characterizing an algorithm's performance in terms of the size (e.g. n) of the problem being solved. The relative cost of multiplying two n × n matrices and searching a list of length n will obviously be quite different. It is this dependence on the problem-size which the O-notation is able to measure.

Suppose we have an algorithm in which the dominant mechanism (the statements executed most) is executed cn^2 times, where n is the problem size and c is a constant. This algorithm is said to have an 'order n^2' complexity. To describe this situation we usually write $O(n^2)$. The reason for describing this algorithm's performance as $O(n^2)$ is set out below.

A function f(n) is said to be $O(g(n))$ if there is a constant c such that:

$$f(n) \leqslant c.g(n)$$

holds for all values of $n \geqslant 1$. This relationship can also be written in limit form, that is

$$\lim_{n \to \infty} \frac{f(n)}{g(n)} = c \qquad \text{where } c > 0$$

Clearly g(n) is proportional to f(n). We say that the two functions f(n) and g(n) are of the **same order.**

As an example suppose we have an algorithm whose dominant instruction is executed the following number of times:

$$4n^2 + 12n + 9$$

for a problem-size of n. We have

$$f(n) = 4n^2 + 12n + 9$$

and

$$\lim_{n \to \infty} \frac{4n^2 + 12n + 9}{n^2} = 4$$

It follows that the asymptotic complexity of this algorithm is $O(n^2)$.

3.4.3   Functional composition

A familiar task in computing science, and in other disciplines, is to carry out some action or computation and then follow it with another computation

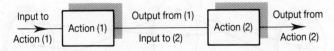

Figure 3.16   Schematic representation of a composite action.

that depends on the outcome of the first. A simple schematic representation of such a composite action might be as shown in Figure 3.16.

There are many instances where Action (1) and Action (2) may be conveniently modelled by functions. In such cases, functional composition may be used to model the composite action, which is, itself, a function. For two functions f : X → Y, and g : Y → Z to be composable the range of the first function should be a subset of the domain of the second function. The resulting function formed from the two functions is h : X → Z. It converts an x in X into h(x) = g(f(x)) in Z where h denotes g ∘ f and '∘' indicates function composition.

More formally the **composition** of the functions f : X → Y and g : Y → Z is the new function g ∘ f : X → Z which satisfies (g ∘ f) x = g(f(x)), for all x in X.

Symbolically we have:

$$g \circ f = \{(x,z) \in X \times Z \mid (\exists y \in Y)\,((x,y) \in f \wedge (y,z) \in g)\}$$

The composition of g ∘ f is applied right to left, that is the function f is applied first followed by the function g. Schematically this is shown in Figure 3.17.

Composition of functions is conveniently illustrated by diagrams when it is necessary to deal with sets. For example, given

$$X = \{1,2,3\}, \qquad Y = \{4,5,6\} \qquad \text{and} \qquad Z = \{7,8,9\}$$

and the functions

f = {(1,5), (2,4), (3,4)}	where	ran f = {4,5}
g = {(4,9), (5,7), (6,8)}	where	ran g = {9,7,8}

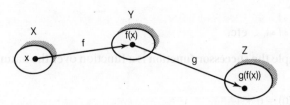

Figure 3.17   Schematic representation of function composition.

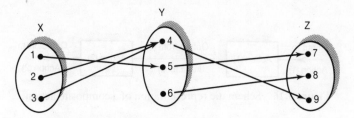

Figure 3.18   An example of function composition.

then we have the situation depicted in Figure 3.18 and the composition function $g \circ f : X \to Z$ is given by

$$g \circ f = \{(1,7),(2,9),(3,9)\} \qquad \text{where} \qquad ran(g \circ f) = \{7,9\}$$

The following example illustrates how composition may be carried out when functions are represented by equations. Suppose we have

$$f(x) = x + 1$$
$$g(x) = x^2$$

then

$$(g \circ f)(x) = g(f(x))$$
$$= g(x + 1)$$
$$= (x + 1)^2$$

It is interesting to compare the above result with $f \circ g$,

$$(f \circ g)(x) = f(g(x))$$
$$= f(x^2)$$
$$= x^2 + 1$$

A comparison of these two examples tells us that functional composition is *not* commutative. It is, however, associative. That is, if we have $f : X \to Y$, $g : Y \to Z$, and $h : Z \to A$, then

$$h \circ (g \circ f) = (h \circ g) \circ f$$

A function composed with itself a number of times may be represented by:

$$f^1 = f,$$
$$f^2 = f \circ f,$$
$$f^3 = f \circ f \circ f, \dots \text{etc.}$$

As an example the **successor function** is a function over the natural numbers $\mathbb{N}$ such that

$$succ(n) = n + 1$$

and the successor function composed with itself k times yields:

$$\text{succ}^k(n) = n + k$$

Repeated composition of a function f with itself can be defined inductively, (see Section 3.7) as:

(1) $f_0(x) = x$ (base clause)

(2) $f^{n+1}(x) = f(f^n(x))$ for $n \in \mathbb{N}$ (inductive clause)

We now need to consider a means for distinguishing a function from its values.

3.4.4 Lambda notation for functions

The **lambda notation** provides a means of referring to functions without 'naming' them. For example, if f is a function so that for all real numbers x:

$$f(x) = x^2$$

then

$$f = \{(x, x^2) \mid x \in \mathbb{R}\}†$$

However, it is incorrect to refer to either x^2 or $f(x)$ as functions. What the lambda notation provides is a means for obtaining an expression that designates a function. This is accomplished by prefixing expressions like 'x^2' with the abstraction operation '(λx)' which has the job of binding the variable x. In this respect λx behaves somewhat like a quantifier. For example:

$$(\lambda x)(x^2)$$

is a function whose value for the argument 2 is:

$$[(\lambda x)(x^2)](2) = 4$$

From another viewpoint, an expression such as '$x - y$' can provide the basis for defining a function f of x, or a function g of y. A convenient way to distinguish between these two functions is to introduce the 'λ' symbol and define the two functions as:

$f = (\lambda x)(x-y)$ sometimes written $f = \lambda x.x-y$
$g = (\lambda y)(x-y)$

Hence

$$f = \{(x, x-y) \mid x \in X\}$$

and

† $\mathbb{R}$ designates the real numbers.

$$g = \{(y, x-y) \mid y \in Y\}$$

Prefixing the expression $(x-y)$ with the operator 'λx' serves to *abstract* the function $(\lambda x)(x-y)$ from the expression. Application of the operator λx provides a systematic way of taking an expression that includes x, and producing a notation for the corresponding function of x. The lambda notation for abstraction may be defined more formally in the following way.

Lambda abstraction

For distinct variables x and z and a term t that does not contain z the following identity holds:

$$(\lambda x)(t) = \{(x,z) \mid z = t\}$$

These conventions permit us to do λ-**conversion**. Consider for example the evaluation of f above at $x = 1$. We get:

$$(\lambda x)(x-y)(1) = 1-y \qquad \text{(cf. other notation } f(1) = 1-y)$$

In the expression

$$(\lambda x)(x-y)$$

the variable 'y' is a free variable. A new function can be abstracted from the term $(\lambda x)(x-y)$ by prefixing it with (λy). We get:

$$(\lambda y)(\lambda x)(x-y)$$

This expression does *not* designate a function of two variables in the usual sense. Instead it designates a function whose range is a set of functions $(\lambda x)(x-y)$. If the domain of the original function is the natural numbers, then we have:

$$(\lambda y)(\lambda x)(x-y) = \{(0, \lambda x\,(x-0)), (1, \lambda x\,(x-1)), (2, \lambda x\,(x-2)), \ldots\}$$

This is in contrast to a function f of two variables x, and y where we have:

$$f(x,y) = x-y$$

and

$$f = \{((0,0), 0), ((0,1), -1), ((0,2), -2), \ldots\}$$

The lambda notation can be extended to functions of more than one variable. For example, suppose

$$f(x,y) = x-y$$

then in lambda notation

$$f = (\lambda x \, y)(x-y)$$

and

$$f(3,2) = (\lambda x \, y)(x-y)(3,2) = 3-2 = 1$$

The arguments of the function (i.e. 3,2) are listed in the same order as the corresponding variables (i.e. x,y) are listed after the lambda.

A λ-notation for functions of more than one variable is not absolutely necessary since $f = (\lambda \, x \, y) \, (x-y)$ can be rewritten as

$$f = (\lambda x)((\lambda y)(x-y))$$

This process is known as **currying**. For $x = 3$ and $y = 2$ we get:

$$\begin{aligned} f &= (\lambda x)((\lambda y)(x-y)(2))(3) \\ &= (\lambda x)(x-2)(3) \\ &= 1 \end{aligned}$$

Another way of viewing the lambda notation is as a means for giving a default name to a function that has not been named otherwise. As an example, the function that returns the absolute value of its argument, abs, is given the definition

$$abs(x) = (\text{if } x \geqslant 0 \text{ then } x \text{ else } -x)$$

Applying λ-abstraction to this definition yields the default name

$$abs = (\lambda x)(\text{if } x \geqslant 0 \text{ then } x \text{ else } -x)$$

Some complications arise in applying λ-abstraction to recursive definitions. This topic is beyond the scope of the present work.

A property of lambda expressions not covered previously is that they are not changed by a change in the name of the parameters, provided they are distinct, that is

$$(\lambda x)(x + 1)$$

and

$$(\lambda y)(y + 1)$$

denote the *same* function and are interchangeable.

3.4.5 Operators on functions

There are a number of useful operators on functions that can be applied in specifications. Some of these are discussed below.

Domain restriction operator ($\lhd$)

Given a function $f : X \to Y$ over a domain X, the **domain restriction operator** $\lhd$, when applied with a set S, constructs a partial function whose elements are those members of f with domain $X \cap S$ or $\text{dom}(f) \cap S$. More formally we have:

$$S \lhd f = \{(x,y) \in f \mid x \in S\}$$

The function $S \lhd f$ *may* be partial on X but is total on $X \cap S$.

As an example, if we have a function f where

$$f = \{(1,1), (2,4), (3,9), (4,16), (5,25)\}$$

and

$$S = \{2,3,4,6,7\}$$

and

$$X = \{1,2,3,4,5\}$$

then

$$S \lhd f = \{(x,y) \in f \mid x \in S\} = \{(2,4), (3,9), (4,16)\}$$

Range restriction operator ($\rhd$)

Given a function f over a domain X, then the **range restriction operator** $\rhd$, when applied with a set T related to its range Y, yields a partial function $f \rhd T$ whose elements are those members of f whose second coordinate fall within T. Therefore we have:

$$f \rhd T = \{(x,y) \in f \mid y \in T\}$$

As an example, if we have a function f where

$$f = \{(1,1), (2,4), (3,9), (4,16), (5,25)\}$$

and

$$T = \{3,4,5,6,7,8,9,10\}$$

and

$$X = \{1,2,3,4,5\}$$

then

$$f \triangleright T = \{(2,4), (3,9)\}$$

and

$$\text{dom}(f \triangleright T) = \{2,3\}$$

Domain subtraction operator ($\triangleleft$)

Given a function $S \triangleleft f$ over a domain X, the **domain subtraction operator** , when applied with a set S, yields a partial function $S \triangleleft f$ whose elements are those members of f with first coordinates not in S.

This function may be described by:

$$S \triangleleft f = \{(x,y) \in f \mid x \in X - S\}$$

where $X - S$ involves a set difference. An alternative definition is:

$$S \triangleleft f = (X - S) \triangleleft f$$

As an example, if we have a function f where

$$f = \{(1,1), (2,4), (3,9), (4,16), (5,25)\}$$

and

$$S = \{2,3,4,6,7\}$$

and

$$X = \{1,2,3,4,5\}$$

then

$$S \triangleleft f = \{(1,1), (5,25)\}$$

Range subtraction operator ($\triangleright$)

Given a function f with a range Y, then the **range subtraction operator** '$\triangleright$', when applied with a set T, yields a partial function f $\triangleright$ T whose elements are those members of f with second coordinates that are not in T. Formally we have:

$$f \triangleright T = \{(x,y) \in f \mid y \in Y-T\}$$

An alternative definition is:

$$f \triangleright T = f \triangleright (Y-T)$$

For example, if

$$f = \{(1,1), (2,4), (3,9), (4,16), (5,25)\}$$

and

$$T = \{1, 25\}$$

and

$$Y = \{1,4,9,16,25\}$$

then

$$f \triangleright T = \{(2,4), (3,9), (4,16)\}$$

Override operator ($\oplus$)

The functional override operator '$\oplus$' handles the situation where a function f $\oplus$ g is identical with another function f except for that part of its domain which is common to another function g. Functional override may be defined in the following way:

$$f \oplus g = (dom(g) \triangleleft f) \cup g$$

that is

$$(\forall x \in dom(g)) ((f \oplus g)(x) = g(x))$$

and

$$(\forall x \in (dom(f) - dom(g)))((f \oplus g)(x) = f(x))$$

Also

$$dom(f \oplus g) = dom(f) \cup dom(g)$$

The following example illustrates the use of functional override. If we have two functions f and g

$$f = \{(1,1), (2,4), (3,9), (4,16), (5,25)\}$$
$$g = \{(4,5), (5,6), (6,7), (7,8), (8,9)\}$$

and

$$dom(f) = \{1,2,3,4,5\}$$
$$dom(g) = \{4,5,6,7,8\}$$

then

$$f \oplus g = \{(1,1), \quad (2,4), \quad (3,9), \quad (4,5), (5,6), (6,7), (7,8), (8,9)\}$$
$$\leftarrow\text{like original 'f'} \rightarrow \quad \longleftarrow \text{like original 'g'} \longrightarrow$$

3.5 Bags

Some collections of data that we wish to specify in program design contain repeating elements. Such collections are called **bags** or **multisets**. A bag may be defined as a total function from a set S to the natural numbers $\mathbb{N}$, that is

$$B : S \rightarrow \mathbb{N}$$

This function specifies the number of occurrences of each element in the bag. What distinguishes bag theory from set theory is that the number of occurrences of an element in a bag is significant. In contrast, in set theory, it is the membership relation which characterizes a set.

The notation $B(x)$ denotes the number of occurrences of the element x in the bag B (some authors use $\#(x,B)$ to represent the number of x in B).

To construct a theory of bags it is possible to borrow most of the concepts and notation that is employed in set theory.

3.5.1 Bag concepts

We will now look at some useful properties, concepts, and operations, associated with bags.

Bag membership

For a bag B, with the base set S as its domain, we have

$$B : S \rightarrow \mathbb{N}$$

and the notation

$$x \in B$$

is used to indicate that x is *a member of* the bag B. An *empty* bag is a bag with no members.

It follows that

$$x \in B \qquad \text{means} \qquad B(x) > 0$$

and

$$x \notin B \qquad \text{means} \qquad B(x) = 0$$

Two bags A and B are equal if $A(x) = B(x)$ for all x. This is symbolized by $A = B$. For example

$$\{a,b,c\} \;=\; \{b,a,c\}$$

but

$$\{a,a,b,c\} \;\neq\; \{a,b,c\}$$

Bag representation

There are two useful representations for bags. The simplest and most obvious is to use an extensional form where we write down each element x of the bag B, $B(x)$ times. This corresponds closely to set notation. We choose to enclose the elements of a bag in the outlined set braces $\{\,\}$ to obtain the necessary differentiation from sets. As an example a bag of letters B might be represented by

$$\{a,b,a,c,a,c,d\}$$

where

$$B(a) = 3, B(b) = 1, B(c) = 2, B(d) = 1 \qquad \text{and} \qquad B(e) = 0$$

In this representation, the order of the elements in the bag is not important but the number of occurrences of each element defines the bag.

A second way to represent bags is to use a functional representation which defines a bag as a set of ordered pairs. For the 'bag of characters' example, the representation would be:

B = {(a,3),(b,1),(c,2),(d,1),(e,0)}

where the base set or member set S is:

S = {a,b,c,d,e}

To specify the bag of prime factors of the natural number N the following expression may be used:

$$f = \{(x,k) \in \text{Prime} \times \mathbb{Z}^+ \mid k = \textbf{MAX} \, (j \in \mathbb{N} : N \bmod x^j = 0)\}†$$

Bag cardinality

The **cardinality** of a bag B, written $|B|$, (or card(B)) is simply the sum of all the occurrences of each element in the bag:

$$|B| = \Sigma \, (B(x) : x \in S)$$

For our character bag above we have:

$$|B| = 3 + 1 + 2 + 1$$
$$= 7$$

Subbags and inclusion

A bag A is a subbag of a bag B if $A(x) \leq B(x)$ for all x. This is symbolized by:

$$A \subseteq B$$

If A satisfies this relationship, then we may say A is included in B. Given the bags:

$$A = \left\{ 7, 6, 9, 7, 9, 5 \right\}$$
$$B = \left\{ 7, 6, 9, 9, 5, 7, 5 \right\}$$

we may describe A as a subbag of B.

† Where $\mathbb{Z}^+$ denotes the positive integers.

3.5.2 Bag operations

There are several ways bags may be combined to yield other bags. As with set theory, we may define the operations of bag union, and bag intersection.

Bag union

The **union** of two bags A and B (symbolized by A $\cup$ B) is that bag formed by including for each element in the two bags, the maximum number of times it occurs in either (but not both) bag.

For C = A $\cup$ B we have:

$$C(x) = \textbf{max}(A(x), B(x)) \quad \text{for all } x \text{ in A and B}$$

For example, given:

$$A = \{a,a,b,c,c,c,d\}$$
$$B = \{b,b,c,c\}$$

then

$$A \cup B = \{a,a,b,b,c,c,c,d\}$$

Bag intersection

The **intersection** of two bags A and B (symbolized by A $\cap$ B) is that bag formed by including for each element in the two bags, the minimum number of times it occurs in either (but not both) bag.

For C = A $\cap$ B we have:

$$C(x) = \textbf{min}(A(x), B(x)) \quad \text{for all } x \text{ in A and B}$$

Using the bags A and B defined in the union example, the intersection A $\cap$ B is:

$$A \cap B = \{b,c,c\}$$

Bag sum

The sum of two bags A and B (symbolized by A + B) is that bag formed by including, for each element in the two bags, the sum of the occurrences in the two bags.

For C = A + B we have:

$$C(x) = A(x) + B(x) \quad \text{for all } x \text{ in A and B}$$

Using the bags A and B defined in the union example, the sum A + B is:

$$A + B = \{a, a,b,b,b,c,c,c,c,c,d\}$$

Bag difference

The difference of two bags A and B (symbolized by A – B) is defined by:

$$C(x) = A(x) - D(x) \qquad \text{for all } x \text{ in A or B}$$

where

$$C = A - B \qquad \text{and} \qquad D = A \cap B$$

Using the same bags A and B defined in the union example again we get:

$$A - B = \{a,a,c,d\}$$

Bag insertion

In specifying programs we often need to model the operation of adding an element a to a bag B which results in the creation of a new bag B'. The simplest way to do this is to define a function into(a,B) which yields a new bag B' where:

$$B' = B \oplus \{(a, B(a) + 1)\}$$

Given

$$B = \{(b,4),(c,2),(d,1)\}$$

then

$$\text{into}(c,B) = \{(b,4),(c,3),(d,1)\}$$

As an alternative, bag insertion can be defined using bag sum, $B + \{a\}$.

Bag deletion

It is also necessary in specifying programs to be able to model the operation of deleting an element from a bag B. This also results in the creation of a new bag B'. This can be done by defining a function outof(a,B) which yields a new bag B' where:

$$B' = B \oplus \{(a, B(a) \dot{-} 1)\}$$

and $\dot{-}$ is the **monus function**, that is

$$\dot{-} : \mathbb{N} \times \mathbb{N} \to \mathbb{N}$$
$$(x,y) \mapsto x \dot{-} y$$

with

$$x \dot{-} y = x - y \quad \text{if } x \geqslant y$$
$$= 0 \quad \quad \text{if } x < y$$

Alternatively, bag deletion could also be defined using bag difference, that is $B - \{a\}$. Given

$$B = \{(b,4),(c,2),(d,1)\}$$

then

$$outof(c,B) = \{(b,4),(c,1),(d,1)\}$$
$$outof(e,B) = \{(b,4),(c,2),(d,1)\}$$

3.6   Sequences and EBNF

A **sequence** is just a special type of function whose domain is a subset of the natural numbers $\mathbb{N}$. For the most part we are interested only in finite sequences. They are well suited for characterizing arrays, files and lists. For a set S, a finite sequence of S is defined by a finite partial function from the natural numbers to S, that is

$$Seq : \mathbb{N} \nrightarrow S$$

As an example, the first N members of the odd sequence:

$$1,3,5,7, \dots$$

may be formally characterized by the following set of ordered pairs:

$$Oddseq = \{(i, 2i-1) : 1 \leqslant i \leqslant N\}$$

A slightly shorter notation is:

Oddseq = (2i−1 : 1 ⩽ i ⩽ N)

The first five members of the odd sequence could be indicated in the following three ways:

(1,3,5,7,9)

or

{(i, 2i−1) : 1 ⩽ i ⩽ 5}

or

(2i−1 : 1 ⩽ i ⩽ 5)

The sequence of squares

1,4,9,16, ...

may be represented by

Squares = (i² : 1 ⩽ i)

Unlike for sets, the two sequences

(1, 3, 5, 7, 9)

and

(1, 7, 3, 9, 5)

are *not* equal. For sequences *order* is a distinguishing feature.

The parentheses '(' and ')' are used to indicate a sequence. The empty sequence is denoted by ( ), compared with the empty set, which is sometimes characterized by { } and we have ( ) = { }.

Sometimes it is convenient to be able to designate a sequence S without knowing in advance how many members are to be included. In such cases the convention of applying the counting operator # to the name of the sequence may be employed. For example to specify a sequence of squares we may use

f = (i² : 1 ⩽ i ⩽ #f)

3.6.1   Extended Backus-Naur Form

The Backus-Naur Form (BNF) is a notation originally invented to describe important parts of the syntax of the Algol-60 programming language. It can also provide a very useful alternative for characterizing some sequences (particularly textual) that we are likely to encounter when writing specifications for programs.

In its application to programming languages BNF is used to define a grammar which in turn specifies sequences of lexical terms that form valid programs in the language. A BNF grammar, whether it is used for defining the syntax of a programming language or some other application, consists of a finite set of formal definitions which define a language (i.e. a data description language). The restrictions on the language are that each string in the language be finite in length and contain only characters chosen from a fixed finite alphabet of symbols.

The simplest type of grammar rule is one which identifies elements of a finite language, for example

<letter> ::= "a"|"b"|"c"|...|"x"|"y"|"z"

This rule may be read as 'a letter is defined as either an "a" or a "b" or a "c" ... etc.' The term <letter> is called a **syntactic category** , and "a" and "b" etc.; are referred to as **terminal symbols**. BNF is used to define context-free grammars. Such grammars require no account of context to be taken when applying the grammar rules. BNF functions as a meta-language or language for defining languages.

Much of the power of BNF comes from the use of recursively defined grammar rules. In such rules a syntactic category is defined in terms of itself. For example, a <word> which consists of a finite sequence of letters, may be defined by:

<word> ::= <letter> | <word><letter>

Left-recursion was used in the original applications of BNF. We will use both left- and right- recursion here. For example <word> could have been defined equally well by right-recursion:

<word> ::= <letter> | <letter><word>

Concatenation is achieved simply by juxtaposition of symbols. Definitions like that for <word> are sometimes expressed by a set of **production rules** rather than by a single composite rule, for example

<word> ::= <letter>
<word> ::= <word><letter>

A more familiar application of BNF is for the specification for an identifier, for example

<identifier> ::= <letter> | <identifier><letter> | <identifier><digit>

A characterization to this level of detail is needed when attempting to design an appropriate recognizer for identifiers.

Some extensions have been made to the original BNF to make it more flexible. The extended notation is referred to as EBNF. One important extension has been to allow repetition. If we were to define a word as consisting of zero or more letters concatenated together this could be expressed using the iterative notation by:

$$< word2 > ::= \{< letter >\}$$

A word consisting of *exactly* n letters would be represented by:

$$< word3 > ::= \{< letter >\}^n$$

A variable length word consisting of at most n letters would have the representation:

$$< word4 > ::= \{< letter >\}^n_0$$

A word that is either empty, or contains at most a single letter, is given the notation

$$< word5 > ::= [< letter >]$$

To redefine our original word as a sequence of *one or more* letters, a notation similar to that employed in formal language theory may be used, that is

$$< word > ::= \{< letter >\}^+$$

An alternative to the iterative version is

$$< word > ::= < letter > \{< letter >\}$$

To handle *alternatives*, a convention which employs parentheses and "|", may be used

$$< signedinteger > ::= ("+" \mid "-") < unsignedinteger >$$

For an integer that may be signed or unsigned we may use:

$$< integer > ::= ["+" \mid "-"] < unsignedinteger >$$
$$< word3 > ::= \{< letter >_i \mid 0 \leqslant i \leqslant n \}$$

To illustrate how these conventions might be employed, consider the problem of specifying a line of text consisting of zero or more finite words, with possibly leading and trailing blanks and one or more blanks between words. A typical line of this form would be:

__ line __ __ __ of __text __ __   where '__'denotes a space

A suitable specification for such a text line is

> < line > ::= {<space>} |
> {<space>}<word>{{<space>}+<word>}{<space>}

A typical application with text is to remove leading and trailing spaces and multiple spaces between words. Such a form-line, consisting of one or more words, could be specified by

> <formline> ::= <word> {<space><word>}

The use of a grammar notation like EBNF can serve two useful functions as a specification tool. Firstly, it can completely and unambiguously define allowable forms for the data specified. Secondly it can serve to emphasize underlying structure in data that may subsequently need to be exploited in the development of a program.

A related development for syntax definition in more recent times has been the introduction of syntax diagrams. They can also be used to represent certain types of program specifications. They do not, however, lend themselves to the sort of manipulations and transformations that may be needed in the course of the development of a program.

3.6.2   EBNF and the definition of a programming notation

As was remarked earlier, the BNF notation was originally invented to describe important parts of the syntax of programming notations. We will use it to describe the syntax of the simple programming notation called **guarded commands** used in this book. Guarded commands was originally defined by Dijkstra using weakest preconditions. Here we will show how EBNF may be used to define the principal components of the guarded commands syntax. Subsequently, in Chapter 5, we will characterize the semantics of guarded commands in terms of weakest preconditions.

The guarded commands notation is a simple, concise, formal language designed for use in program derivation. It is not intended to be an implementation language like Pascal, Modula-2, or C. Conversion of derived programs is a straightforward matter; in fact a translator to accomplish it is easy to implement. The advantage of this notation is that it allows the expression of algorithms with the minimum of extraneous detail.

Being a formal language it consists of an infinite set of sequences of symbols. Each member of the set is called a **sentence**, which corresponds to a **program**. Obviously the set of all programs is infinite. This set can be defined comprehensively only by the rules for composing syntactically correct programs. These rules correspond to the **syntax** of the programming language. In what follows we will use EBNF to define important elements of the guarded commands syntax. We will also introduce the semantics of the language. Later, in Chapter 5, the semantics of the language will be treated in more detail.

A guarded commands program is constructed from members of the following symbol classes:

identifiers, numbers, delimiters, operators, strings and comments

An **identifier** consists of a sequence of letters and digits in which the first character must be a letter. Using EBNF:

identifier ::= letter {letter|digit}

Typical identifiers are:

i, N, max, d2

Numbers may be either integer or real. An integer may be formally defined by:

integer ::= ["+"|"−"]digit{digit}

where we define a digit as:

digit ::= "0"|"1"|"2"|"3"|"4"|"5"|"6"|"7"|"8"|"9"

The **delimiters** and **operators** are made up of a list of keywords and special symbols. The keywords (excluding declarations) are:

do, **od**, **if**, **fi**, **then**

Other important operators and delimiters are:

+, −, *	addition, subtraction and multiplication
/, div	real division, integer division
:=	assignment
=, ≠	equal, not equal
<, ≤	less than, less than or equal to
>, ≥	greater than, greater than or equal to
∧, ∨, ¬	and, or, not
cand, cor	conditional AND, conditional OR
[]	guarded command separator
;	statement separator
, " '	punctuation
( ), [ ]	expression brackets, index brackets
→	guard-statement separator

Strings consist of a sequence of characters enclosed in either single or double quotes:

'single quote string'
"double quote string"

Comments are enclosed in braces:

{this is a comment}

The text of a program is composed of **statements**. There are three principal types of statements:

assignment statements, conditional statements (**IF**), repetitive statements (**DO**),

and statements formed from sequences of these statements. Formally we have:

statement ::= assignment | **IF** | **DO** | statement { ; statement }

Assignment

Assignment statements are the simplest type of statement. An assignment statement when executed changes the value of a variable, and in so doing changes the state of a computation. It has the form:

assignment ::= identifier ':=' expression

An assignment executes by evaluation of the expression and then replacement of the identifier's value with that of the expression. Examples are:

s := s + i
i := i + 1

Evaluation of expressions with operators and parentheses follows closely the conventions for evaluation of arithmetic and algebraic expressions.

A special kind of assignment, called a **multiple assignment**, is used to assign the values of a sequence of expressions $(e_1, e_2, ..., e_N)$ to a sequence of identifiers or variables $(x_1, x_2, ..., x_N)$. It is written as:

$$x_1, x_2, ..., x_N := e_1, e_2, ..., e_N$$

where x_1 is assigned the value of e_1, x_2 is assigned the value of e_2, and so on.

The rule of computation for multiple assignment states that all expressions are evaluated *before* any assignments are made. As an example, to swap the values of two variables x and y, we may use:

x, y := y, x

This multiple assignment succeeds whereas the sequentially executed statements

x := y;
y := x

do not achieve a swap of the x and y values.

IF statement

An **IF** statement allows the selection and execution of just one of a number of possible commands S_1, S_2, ..., S_N. To define an **IF** statement it is necessary to introduce the concept of a **guarded command**†. A guarded command is of the form:

guard → statement

The guard is a predicate which evaluates to either true or false. The statement to the right of the arrow is executed only if the guard evaluates to true. In other words, the guard protects or guards the statement. Formally we have

guarded-command ::= guard "→" statement

An **IF** statement can now be formally defined as:

IF ::= "**if**" guarded-command {"**[]**" guarded-command} "**fi**"

Where only a single guarded command is needed we will use the form:

IF ::= "**if**" guarded-command "**then**" statement "**fi**"

For a set of guards B_1, B_2, ..., B_N and a set of statements S_1, S_2, ..., S_N we have

if $B_1 \rightarrow S_1$
[] $B_2 \rightarrow S_2$

.
.
.

[] $B_N \rightarrow S_N$
fi

† There is a semantic inconsistency here. It would have been better to use 'command' instead of 'guarded command'. However the terminology seems to have stuck.

Examples are:

```
if x ≥ y → m := x
[] x ≤ y → m := y
fi

if x > 0 then m := x fi
```

For purposes of translation, a Modula-2 **IF** statement that has a similar intent may take the form:

```
IF B₁ THEN S₁
ELSIF B₂ THEN S₂
        .
        .
        .
ELSIF Bₙ THEN Sₙ
ELSE WriteString("IF-error")
END
```

It is important to note that with guarded commands, the condition of all guards being false is an error condition, unlike standard Modula-2 and Pascal implementations. The reason for this is made clear in Chapter 5.

The single guarded command form is used as a shorthand. Instead of writing

```
if B → S
[] ¬B → skip
fi
```

we write as equivalent

```
if B then S fi
```

Here there will be no error condition when B is false.

DO statement

The repetitive **DO** statement, like the **IF** statement, is built from guarded commands. The EBNF specification is:

```
DO ::= "do" guarded-command {"[]" guarded-command} "od"
```

For guards B_1, B_2, ...,B_N and statements S_1, S_2, ...,S_N we have:

```
do B₁ → S₁
[] B₂ → S₂
        .
        .
        .
[] Bₙ → Sₙ
od
```

A single iteration of the **DO** statement takes place by arbitrarily selecting the guards one at a time until one (i.e. B_i) is found that is true, the corresponding statement S_i is then executed. This selection and execution process continues until all the guards B_1, B_2, ..., B_N are false.

Where there is only a single guarded command we have:

do B → S **od**

The following command 'sorts' the values attached to a, b, c, and d.

do a > b → a, b := b, a
[] b > c → b, c := c, b
[] c > d → c, d := d, c
od

This **DO** statement terminates when $\neg(a > b) \wedge \neg(b > c) \wedge \neg(c > d)$ is true which is equivalent to the 'sorted' condition:

a ≤ b ≤ c ≤ d

For the purpose of translation a Modula-2 **WHILE** statement with a similar intent to the **DO** statement is

WHILE B_1 **or** B_2 **or** ... **or** B_N **DO**
   IF B_1 **THEN** S_1
   ELSIF B_2 **THEN** S_2
        .
        .
   ELSIF B_N **THEN** S_N
   END
END

Where there is a single guarded command, that is

do B →
   S
od

the corresponding Modula-2 implementation below is directly equivalent:

WHILE B **DO**
   S
END

For reasons of composition and efficiency, (see Section 12.5) it is convenient in certain contexts to employ an unguarded repetitive statement that is equivalent to the repeat-loop employed in Modula-2. The guarded commands version has the form

repeat
  S
until ¬B

Procedures

A procedure is used in a program to identify and describe a sequence of statements that perform some well-defined task (for example sort a sequence of numbers, swap the values of a pair of numbers, search a list for some number, and so on). Any statements that appear in a program may be used in a procedure. Before a procedure can be used it must be declared or defined. Here we will provide a limited form of procedure declaration. For a more detailed discussion of procedures consult language manuals on either Pascal or Modula-2.

PROCEDURE ::= identifier "(" parameter-list")"; body END

where

identifier — is the name of the procedure
parameter-list ::= [["var"] identifier ":" type {";" ["var"] identifier ":" type}]
type ::= "integer"|"real"|"char"
variable-list ::= identifier {"," identifier}":" type {";" identifier{"," identifier}":" type}
body ::= ["var" variable-list ";"] statement

Parameters are used to pass information into procedures and return results from a procedure to the program or procedure which called the procedure.

A procedure command appears in a program in the following form:

procedure-command ::= identifier "("identifier-list")"

where

identifier — is the name of the procedure
identifier-list ::= identifier {"," identifier}

The actual parameters used by the procedure are identified in identifier-list. They must have types that match those in the parameter-list sequence of the corresponding procedure declaration.

This completes our description of the main elements of the guarded commands notation that we will use in this book. In some instances, where input/output, declarations and procedures are needed, the conventions employed in either Pascal or Modula-2 will be borrowed. Tail recursion is also employed in some cases. It is defined in Chapter 5.

3.6.3   Top-down sequence description (TDSD)

There are a number of well-known problems involving sequences that are not easily specified by EBNF. Such problems are usually handled by two-level grammars. Rather than take that approach here, we will introduce a simple set of conventions powerful enough to meet our needs for sequence description.

The notation is designed to conveniently describe structure present in sequential data. It provides a weak specification of input and output data that enables a top-down description of structure in sequential data.

As an example, consider the following transaction data:

Product	Quantity	
product1	23	↑
product1	29	
product1	48	all transactions for product1
product1	10	
product1	4	↓
product2	33	↑
product2	17	all transactions for product2
.	.	
.	.	
.	.	

which represents a sequence of stores movement transactions for a product set, {product1, product2, ...}. Taking a top-down view of this data it may be considered as:

a sequence of transactions for product1   followed by
a sequence of transactions for product 2   followed by
.   .
.   .
.   .

The transactions for each individual product also form a sequence. To describe this data at the top level we can write:

transactions_file = **Seq**(product_group)   (1)

where

product_group = **Seq**(PRODUCT_IDENTIFIER, quantity)   (2)

and

$$\text{product\_identifier} \in \{\text{product1, product2, ..., productn}\} \qquad (3)$$

and

$$\text{quantity} \in \mathbb{Z} \qquad (4)$$

Statement (1) tells us that the transaction_file consists of a sequence of product_groups

$$(\text{product\_group}_1, \text{product\_group}_2, ...)$$

Statement (2) tells us that each product_group consists of a sequence of (product_identifier, quantity) pairs in which the product_identifier is *fixed* for a given product_group. To indicate that the product_identifier is held constant for each product_group, it is written in all capitals. The other member of the pair, quantity, is written in lowercase indicating it is a *variable* which may or may not vary from one member of the sequence to the next. With this description, PRODUCT_IDENTIFIER is fixed for one group although it will change with the change in the product_group.

For the ith product_group the transactions belonging to its sequence are the pairs:

$$((\text{PRODUCT\_IDENTIFIER}_i, \text{quantity}_{i1}), (\text{PRODUCT\_IDENTIFIER}_i, \text{quantity}_{i2}), ...)$$

A sequence s with N members

$$(m_1, m_2, ..., m_N)$$

is denoted by

$$s = \textbf{Seq}^N(m)$$

A sequence may contain zero or more members. If the sequence s is followed by the sequence t the resulting concatenated sequence is described by:

$$s @ t$$

A sequence s which is followed by a string constant "ZZZZ" is represented by:

$$s @ \text{"ZZZZ"}$$

To describe the situation where an identifier remains fixed at a higher level of description than where it is primarily used, a parameter mechanism is used. For example, if the product_identifier above remained fixed at the product_group level as well, we would write:

transaction_file = **Seq**(product_group[PRODUCT_IDENTIFIER])

This parameterization makes product_identifier 'visible' at the product_ group level. These conventions are all that are needed at this stage.

Many sequences have order properties associated with them. To handle ordered sequences the associated relations are attached. For example to describe the sequence

$a_1, a_2, a_3, ...$

where

$a_1 < a_2 \wedge a_2 < a_3 \wedge a_3 < a_4 \wedge ...$

we would write

Seq(a : <)

A sequence consisting of pairs

$(a_1, b_1), (a_2, b_2), ...$

that is ordered on both its components may be written:

Seq(a : <, b : ≤)

In this case all the $a_1, a_2, ...$ are unique and in ascending order whereas all the $b_1, b_2, ...$ are in non-descending order with the possibility of duplication. The sequence

Seq(a : <, b)

is ordered on the a-sequence but not on the b-sequence.

A sequence of elements $a_1, a_2, ...$ with no adjacent duplicates is described by:

Seq(a : ≠)

A transactions file transfile, ordered by a component key, in which there are multiple transactions for a given key value (this happens for the sequential file update problem – see Chapter 11) could be represented as follows:

transfile = **Seq**(transgroup[key : <])
transgroup = **Seq**(KEY, action, data)
key ∈ {PRODUCT1, PRODUCT2, ...}
data ∈ $\mathbb{Z}$
action ∈ {INSERT, DELETE, UPDATE}

This description indicates that the keys within a group are constant but that the keys within successive groups are in ascending order. Making 'key : <' visible achieves this ordering.

To reference components of a tuple, for example, (KEY, action, data) we use the following dot (.) notation:

    transgroup.KEY
    transgroup.action
    transgroup.data

These conventions are sufficient to meet most of our needs for specifying sequences.

3.7   Mathematical Induction

The notion of mathematical induction occupies a position of importance both in mathematics and in computing science. It is well suited for reasoning about sequences, and for proving assertions about programs. It also provides powerful inference rules for the natural numbers and the positive integers. The latter is the most prominent application of mathematical induction and so it will be considered first.

What is known as the *first principle of mathematical induction* underpins many of the applications of this tool. This principle is captured in the following theorem.

First principle of mathematical induction†
If P_n is a predicate concerning the natural numbers†† and it is assumed

(1)   that P_0 is a true statement, and

(2)   for all natural numbers, $k \geqslant 0$, if P_k is true then P_{k+1} is true

then it may be concluded that P_n is a true statement for all natural numbers.

Some statements of this principle are based on the positive integers 1, 2, 3, ... rather than on the natural numbers but this only means we start with P_1 rather than P_0.

† Also called the 'principle of weak induction'.
†† $\mathbb{N}$ denotes the set of natural numbers 0, 1, 2, ...

The first principle of mathematical induction is a rule of inference for the natural numbers and therefore it may be represented formally by the schema:

$$\frac{P_0 \quad (\forall k)(P_k \Rightarrow P_{k+1})}{(\forall n)(P_n)}$$

A proof by induction over the natural numbers involves showing:

(1)   Firstly, that P_0 is true – *the base step*
(2)   and then showing $(\forall k)\ (P_k \Rightarrow P_{k+1})$ – *the induction step*

The following example illustrates the proof technique.

EXAMPLE 1

It is well known that the sum of the first $n+1$ natural numbers is given by $n(n+1)/2$, that is

$$0 \qquad\qquad = \frac{0(0+1)}{2} = 0$$

$$0+1 \qquad\quad = \frac{1(1+1)}{2} = 1$$

$$0+1+2 \qquad = \frac{2(2+1)}{2} = 3$$

$$0+1+2+3 = \frac{3(3+1)}{2} = 6$$

And so in general

$$\vdash (\forall n \in \mathbb{N}) \quad \left(\sum_{i=0}^{n} i = \frac{n(n+1)}{2} \right)$$

where

$$P_n: \quad \left(\sum_{i=0}^{n} i = \frac{n(n+1)}{2} \right)$$

A proof of this result may take the form

Proof

(1)
   Base step – establish P_n for $n = 0$
   For the LHS we have

$$\sum_{i=0}^{n} i = \sum_{i=0}^{0} i$$
$$= 0$$

and for the RHS we have

$$\frac{n(n + 1)}{2} = \frac{0(0 + 1)}{2}$$
$$= 0$$

and so P_0 is established.

(2) *Induction step* – establish $(\forall n)(P_n \Rightarrow P_{n+1})$
First assume the induction hypothesis P_n is true, that is

$$P_N: \sum_{i=0}^{n} i = \frac{n(n + 1)}{2}$$

We need to show P_{n+1} also holds. Replacing n by $n + 1$ directly in P_n yields

$$\sum_{i=0}^{n+1} i = \frac{(n + 1)(n + 2)}{2}$$

Now for the LHS we have:

$$\sum_{i=0}^{n+1} i = \sum_{i=0}^{n} i + (n + 1)$$

$$= \frac{n(n + 1)}{2} + (n + 1) \qquad \text{(by the induction hypothesis)}$$

$$= \frac{(n + 1)(n + 2)}{2}$$

Since the LHS of (1) is the same as the RHS and the n chosen was arbitrary, it follows that $(\forall n)(P_n \Rightarrow P_{n+1})$ holds.

Therefore by the inference rule for the first principle of mathematical induction we may conclude $(\forall n)(P_n)$.

The next example illustrates the use of mathematical induction over the positive integers.

EXAMPLE 2

Another well-known result in mathematics is that the sum of odd integer sequences starting at 1 always yields a perfect square.

$$
\begin{array}{ll}
1 & = 1 \\
1 + 3 & = 4 \\
1 + 3 + 5 & = 9 \\
1 + 3 + 5 + 7 & = 16
\end{array}
$$

And so in general for a positive integer n we have:

$$1 + 3 + 5 + ... + (2n - 1) = n^2$$

or

$$(\forall n \in \mathbb{Z}^+) \left(\sum_{i=1}^{n} (2i - 1) = n^2 \right)^\dagger$$

where

$$P_n: \quad \sum_{i=1}^{n} (2i - 1) = n^2$$

A proof using mathematical induction over the positive integers is as follows.

Proof

(1) · *Base step* – establish P_n for n = 1
For the LHS we have

$$\sum_{i=1}^{n} (2i - 1) = \sum_{i=1}^{1} (2i - 1)$$
$$= 1$$

and for the RHS we have:

$$n^2 = 1^2$$
$$= 1$$

It follows that P_1 is established.

(2) *Induction step* – establish $(\forall n)(P_n \Rightarrow P_{n+1})$
First assume the induction hypothesis P_n is true, that is

$$P_n: \quad \sum_{i=1}^{n} (2i - 1) = n^2$$

We need to show that P_{n+1} holds. Replacing n by n + 1 directly in P_n yields:

$$\sum_{i=1}^{n+1} (2i - 1) = (n + 1)^2$$

† $\mathbb{Z}^+$ denotes the set of positive integers 1, 2, 3, ...

Now for the LHS we have:

$$\sum_{i=1}^{n+1} (2i - 1) = \sum_{i=1}^{n} (2i - 1) + 2(n + 1) - 1$$

$$= n^2 + 2(n + 1) - 1 \qquad \text{(by the induction}$$
$$= n^2 + 2n + 1 \qquad\qquad \text{hypothesis)}$$
$$= (n + 1)^2$$

Since the LHS of (1) is the same as the RHS and the n chosen was arbitrary it follows that $(\forall n)(P_n \Rightarrow P_{n+1})$ holds. Therefore, by the inference rule for the first principle of mathematical induction, we may conclude $(\forall n)(P_n)$.

EXAMPLE 3

The sum of the squares of the first n positive integers has the following simple closed form:

$$1 + 4 + 9 + 16 + ... + n^2 = \frac{n(n + 1)(2n + 1)}{6}$$

or

$$(\forall n \in \mathbb{Z}^+)\,(P_n) = \frac{n(n + 1)(2n + 1)}{6}$$

where

$$P_n: \quad \sum_{i=1}^{n} i^2 = \frac{n(n+1)(2n+1)}{6}$$

As with our previous two examples, this formula may be proved by mathematical induction.

Proof

(1) *Base step* – establish P_n for $n = 1$
     For the LHS we have

$$\sum_{i=1}^{n} i^2 = \sum_{i=1}^{1} i^2$$
$$= 1$$

and for the RHS we have

$$\frac{n(n+1)(2n+1)}{6} = \frac{1(1+1)(2 \times 1 + 1)}{6}$$

$$= 1$$

and so P_1 is established.

(2) *Induction step* – establish $(\forall n)(P_n \Rightarrow P_{n+1})$
First assume the induction hypothesis P_n is true, that is

$$P_n: \quad \sum_{i=1}^{n} i^2 = \frac{n(n+1)(2n+1)}{6}$$

We need to show that P_{n+1} holds. Replacing n by n+1 directly in P_n yields:

$$\sum_{i=1}^{n+1} i^2 = \frac{(n+1)(n+2)[2(n+1)+1]}{6}$$

Now for the LHS of this equality we have

$$\sum_{i=1}^{n+1} i^2 = \sum_{i=1}^{n} i^2 + (n+1)^2$$

$$= \frac{n(n+1)(2n+1) + 6(n+1)^2}{6} \text{ (by the induction hypothesis)}$$

$$= \frac{n(n+1)(2n+1) + 6(n+1)^2}{6}$$

$$= \frac{(n+1)(2n^2 + 7n + 6)}{6}$$

$$= \frac{(n+1)(n+2)(2n+3)}{6}$$

$$= \frac{(n+1)(n+2)[2(n+1)+1]}{6}$$

Since the LHS of (1) is the same as the RHS and the n chosen was arbitrary, it follows that $(\forall n)(P_n \Rightarrow P_{n+1})$ holds.

EXAMPLE 4

Mathematical induction may also be used to prove properties of data structures. For example, it can be used to prove that the number of

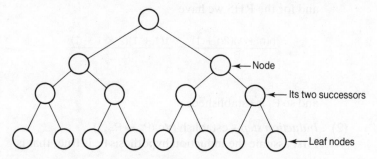

Figure 3.19 Schematic representation of a complete binary tree.

nodes at the ith level of a binary tree is less than or equal to 2^2 by induction on the number of levels i. A binary tree is of the form shown in Figure 3.19. Each node of a binary tree (apart from the leaf nodes) has two successors.

Proof

(1) *Base step*
    If i=0, the binary tree has only one node at this level and the total number of nodes is

$$2^0 = 1$$

(2) *Induction step*
    Assume the result is true for an arbitrary natural number i. We will then try to prove it holds for (i + 1). Consider a binary tree T with k nodes at the ith level. By the induction hypothesis it follows that

$$k \leq 2^i$$

Each of these k nodes can have at most two children so that the number of nodes at level (i + 1) is at most

$$2 \times k \leq 2 \times 2^i = 2^{i+1}$$

as required. And so we may conclude that the number of nodes at the ith level of a binary tree is less than or equal to 2^i.

EXAMPLE 5

We can also use mathematical induction to prove that a finite set A_n with n elements has 2^n distinct subsets. The set of all subsets of a set is in fact the powersets $\mathbb{P}(A_n)$. We therefore need to prove

$$P_n : \#\mathbb{P}(A_n) = 2^n \qquad \text{for} \qquad n \geq 0$$

where

$$A_n = \{a_1, a_2, \ldots, a_n\}$$

Proof

(1) *Base step* – establish P_n for $n = 0$
For the LHS we have

$$A_0 = \varnothing \quad \text{and so} \quad \mathbb{P}(A_0) = \{\varnothing\}, \text{ therefore}$$
$$\# \mathbb{P}(A_0) = 1$$

and for the RHS we have

$$2^n = 2^0$$
$$= 1$$

It follows that P_0 is established.

(2) *Induction step* – establish $(\forall n)\, P_n \Rightarrow P_{n+1}$
First assume the induction hypothesis P_n is true, that is

$$P_n : \# \mathbb{P}(A_n) = 2^n$$

We need to show that P_{n+1} holds. Replacing n by $n + 1$ directly in P_n yields

$$\# \mathbb{P}(A_{n+1}) = 2^{n+1} \tag{1}$$

Now for the LHS we have:

$$A_{n+1} = A_n \cup \{a_{n+1}\} \quad \text{where} \quad a_{n+1} \notin A_n$$

and every subset of A_{n+1} is either a subset of A_n or it is formed by adding a_{n+1} to a subset of A_n, that is

$$\mathbb{P}(A_{n+1}) = \mathbb{P}(A_n) \cup \{X \cup \{a_{n+1}\} \mid X \in \mathbb{P}(A_n)\}$$

Now

$$\# \mathbb{P}(A_n) = 2^n \qquad \text{(by the induction hypothesis)}$$

and

$$\# \{X \cup \{a_{n+1}\} \mid X \in \mathbb{P}(A_n)\} = 2^n \qquad \text{(by the induction hypothesis)}$$

and so it follows that

$$\#\mathbb{P}(A_{n+1}) = 2^n + 2^n$$
$$= 2.2^n$$
$$= 2^{n+1}$$

Since the LHS of (1) is the same as the RHS and the n chosen was arbitrary it follows that $(\forall n)\,(P_n \Rightarrow P_{n+1})$ holds. Therefore by the inference rule for the first principle of mathematical induction we may conclude $(\forall n)\,P_n$.

Generalized first principle of mathematical induction

In the previous applications of mathematical induction we have worked either with induction over the natural numbers or over the positive integers. Some problems are of a form where a statement P_n is false for the first $b - 1$ natural numbers, but is true for all natural numbers greater than or equal to b.

The corresponding inference rule, which involves simply changing the base case takes the form:

$$\frac{P_b \quad (\forall k)(k \geqslant b \Rightarrow (P_k \Rightarrow P_{k+1}))}{(\forall n)(n \geqslant b \Rightarrow P_n)} \qquad \text{where } b \geqslant 0$$

To establish that P_n holds for all natural numbers greater than or equal to b, it is first necessary to show as the base step that P_b holds, and then that $P_k \Rightarrow P_{k+1}$ holds for an arbitrary k such that $k > b$. As an example, for values of $n \geqslant 1$ we have:

n	2^n	n!	$2^n < n!$ (P_n)
1	2	1	false
2	4	2	false
3	8	6	false
4	16	24	true
5	32	120	true
.	.	.	.
.	.	.	.
.	.	.	.

Proof

(1)   *Base step* – establish P_4

$$2^n < n! \equiv 2^4 < 4!$$
$$\equiv 16 < 24$$
$$\equiv \text{True} \qquad \text{and so } P_4 \text{ is established.}$$

(2) *Induction step* – establish $(\forall k)(k \geqslant b \Rightarrow (P_k \Rightarrow P_{k+1}))$
Assume the induction hypothesis P_k is true, that is

$$P_k : 2^k < k!$$

Now we need to show that P_{k+1} holds. Replacing k by $k + 1$ directly in P_k yields

$$2^{k+1} < (k + 1)!$$
$$2 \cdot 2^k < (k + 1)k!$$

Assuming P_k is true then this relation is also true provided

$$2 < k + 1$$

Now since we are only concerned with k values that are greater than or equal to 4 this last relation will hold. We may therefore conclude by the generalized first principle of mathematical induction that

$$(\forall n)\,(n \geqslant 4 \Rightarrow P_n)$$

An alternative way of proving P_n involves considering Q_m where

$$Q_m : 2^{m+3} < (m + 3)!$$

If it can be shown that Q_m is true for every positive integer, then it will follow the P_n is true for values of $n \geqslant 4$. A proof for Q_m may proceed as follows.

Proof

(1) *Base step* – establish Q_1

$$2^{1+3} < (1+3)!$$

Simplifying we get

$16 < 24$ and so Q_1 is established.

(2) *Induction step* – establish $(\forall m)(Q_m \Rightarrow Q_{m+1})$
To prove this assertion a proof of $Q_m \Rightarrow Q_{m+1}$ for an arbitrary positive integer is needed. For this we assume the induction hypothesis Q_m is true. We then have the assertion

$$Q_m : 2^{m+3} < (m + 3)!$$

and we need to show that Q_{m+1} holds. Replacing m by $m + 1$ yields

$$2^{(m+1)+3} < ((m + 1) + 3)!$$

that is

$$2^{m+4} < (m + 4)!$$

Now assuming Q_m is true it follows that

$$2 \times 2^{m+3} < 2 \times (m+3)!$$

And since $2 < (m+4)$ is true for all positive integers m it follows that Q_{m+1} holds. Since the m chosen was arbitrary it follows that $(\forall m)(Q_m \Rightarrow Q_{m+1})$.

Therefore we may conclude $(\forall m)Q_m$, and that P_n is true for all values of n where $n \geqslant 4$. In the proof for this example we have chosen to use an indirect approach.

Second principle of mathematical induction

Some problems involving sequences are not accommodated by the first principle of mathematical induction or its generalization. Other variations of the method have therefore been proposed. The most important of these is the *second principle of mathematical induction*.

Second principle of mathematical induction†
If P_n is a predicate concerning the natural numbers and

(1) P_0 is a true statement, and,
(2)   for any natural number k, if P_j is true for every natural number $j < k$, then P_k is true

then P_n is a true statement for all natural numbers.

The second principle of mathematical induction, being a rule of inference, may be represented formally by the schema:

$$\frac{(\forall k)((\forall j)(j < k \Rightarrow P_j) \Rightarrow P_k)}{(\forall n)P_n}$$

The induction hypothesis needed in a proof that employs this rule of inference is

$$(\forall k)(k < n \Rightarrow P_k)$$

If, by assuming that the induction hypothesis holds, P_n can be shown to be true, then it follows that $(\forall n)P_n$ holds. Applications of the second principle of mathematical induction assume a stronger induction hypothesis than that employed in proofs that use the first principle of mathematical induction. The base step P_0, of the first principle of mathematical induction is implied

† Also called the 'principle of strong induction' or the 'principle of complete induction'.

by the hypothesis of the second principle of mathematical induction. That is, if $n = 0$ then $k < 0$ is false for all natural numbers k. Therefore

$$(\forall k)(k < 0 \Rightarrow P_k) \qquad \text{is true}$$

and

$$(\forall k)(k < 0 \Rightarrow P_k) \Rightarrow P_0 \qquad \text{is equivalent to } P_0.$$

The second principle of mathematical induction is most often used in proofs where the properties of an element generated in a given step depend on the properties of elements generated in several previous steps. That is, $P_0, P_1, ..., P_k$ are assumed and then used to establish P_{k+1}. The derivation of P_{k+1} is usually made easier when more than a single assumption is in hand. The stronger second principle of mathematical induction is often used in applications where it would otherwise be difficult to apply the first principle.

EXAMPLE 6

It is known that for the nth element of the Fibonacci sequence f_n, the following relation holds:

$$P_n : f_n < \left(\frac{5}{3}\right)^n \qquad \text{for } n \geq 1$$

The second principle of mathematical induction may be used to prove this result. Terms in the Fibonacci sequence

$$1, 1, 2, 3, 5, 8, 13, ...$$

may be defined in the following way:

$$f_1 = 1, \qquad f_2 = 1$$
$$f_n = f_{n-1} + f_{n-2} \qquad \text{for } n > 2.$$

Proof:

(1) Establish P_1:

$$1 = f_1 < \left(\frac{5}{3}\right)^1 \qquad \text{for } n = 1$$

Simplifying

$$1 < \frac{5}{3}$$

(2) Establish P_2:

$$1 = f_2 < \left(\frac{5}{3}\right)^2$$

Simplifying yields

$$1 < \frac{25}{9}$$

Now assume for a natural number $k \geq 2$ that P_j is true for every natural number $j < k$. It is then necessary to show that this assumption implies P_k is true, that is

$$f_k < \left(\frac{5}{3}\right)^k$$

By the assumption made P_{k-1} and P_{k-2} are true statements, that is the relations

$$f_{k-1} < \left(\frac{5}{3}\right)^{k-1}$$

$$f_{k-2} < \left(\frac{5}{3}\right)^{k-2}$$

both hold.
Now using the fact that

$$f_k = f_{k-1} + f_{k-2} < \left(\frac{5}{3}\right)^{k-1} + \left(\frac{5}{3}\right)^{k-2} = \left(\frac{5}{3}\right)^{k-2} \left(\frac{8}{3}\right)$$

and

$$\left(\frac{5}{3}\right)^{k-2} \left(\frac{8}{3}\right) < \left(\frac{5}{3}\right)^k = \left(\frac{5}{3}\right)^{k-2} \left(\frac{5}{3}\right)^2$$

therefore

$$f_k < \left(\frac{5}{3}\right)^k$$

and it follows by the second principle of mathematical induction that since:

$$\frac{8}{3} < \frac{25}{9}$$

P_n is true for every natural number, and so the proof is complete.

In some applications of the second principle of mathematical induction it is necessary to do a proof by cases. Consider the problem of proving the following result.

EXAMPLE 7

P_n: All natural numbers greater than one can be written as a product of one or more prime numbers.

Now assume as the induction hypothesis that for an arbitrary natural number $k > 1$ that P_j is true for every natural number $j < k$ (that is for all j in the range of $1 < j < k$ it is assumed that j can be written as a product of primes). To proceed with the proof it is necessary to show that this assumption implies P_k is true.

Proof (by cases)

The natural number k is either a prime or not a prime. Proceeding by case analysis:

Case I   If k is prime, it consists of the product of one prime.

Case II   If k is not prime, it can be written as a product of the form:

$$k = x \times y \qquad \text{where} \quad 1 < x \leqslant y < k$$

It follows from the assertion of the induction hypothesis that x and y may be written as products of primes and consequently so can their product.

Therefore since k can be written as a product of primes it follows by the second principle of mathematical induction that P_n is true for every natural number greater than one.

Inductive proofs of programs

The application of mathematical induction to provide a proof of partial correctness (excluding termination considerations) for a given program segment follows a similar pattern to applications requiring the proof of formulae.

EXAMPLE 8

Prove that the following program segment raises the number 2 to the power n, and assigns the result to s. Assume $n \in \mathbb{N}$. We have

$$P_i : s = 2^i$$

as our induction hypothesis.

The program segment is

```
i := 0; s := 1;
do i < n → {Pᵢ}
    i := i + 1;
    s := s + s
od
```

After the ith time through the loop $s = 2^i$.

Proof

(1) *Base step* – establish P_i for $i = 0$
     For the LHS we have

$$s = 1$$

and for the RHS we have

$$2^i = 2^0$$
$$= 1$$

It follows that P_0 is established.

(2) *Induction step*
     First assume that the induction hypothesis

$$s = 2^i$$

We need to show P_{i+1} holds. Replacing i by $i + 1$ directly yields:

$$P_{i+1} : s' = 2^{i+1} \tag{1}$$

Now for the LHS we have:

$$s' = s + s \quad \text{(s' is introduced to model the assignment)}$$
$$s' = 2^i + 2^i \quad \text{(by the induction hyothesis)}$$
$$= 2^{i+1}$$

Since the LHS of (1) is the same as the RHS and the i chosen was arbitrary it follows that the induction hypothesis holds.

Inductive specification of sets

Earlier we discussed the use of predicates with free variables to specify sets. However, predicates are not always the most appropriate tools for specifying some sets. In particular, sets that are infinite or associated with formal languages are usually difficult to specify using predicates. In such cases, a recursive or inductive specification is often the most appropriate.

The inductive method of specification for sets always requires the use of three clauses; a **basis clause**, an **inductive clause**, and an **extremal clause**. We will use this method of specification to characterize two important set closures used in computing science. The following conventions are needed. Σ is defined as a finite set of symbols called an **alphabet.** A string S over the alphabet Σ is formed by concatenation of symbols from Σ. The string ab represents the concatenation of the string b with the symbol a. For $S = a_1 a_2 a_3 \ldots a_n$ with $n \in \mathbb{N}$ and, for all a_i in S, $a_i \in \Sigma$ the length of S is n. The empty string, which has a length of zero, is denoted by Λ.

Specification of the positive closure (Σ^+)

The set Σ^+ of all non-empty strings over an alphabet Σ may be defined inductively as follows:

(1) $a \in \Sigma \Rightarrow a \in \Sigma^+$ (basis clause)
(2) $b \in \Sigma^+ \land a \in \Sigma \Rightarrow ab \in \Sigma^+$ (inductive clause)
(3)   The set Σ^+ contains only elements formed by a finite number of applications of (1) and (2).   (extremal clause)

Σ^+ consists of an infinite set of strings of finite length.

If, for example:

$\Sigma = \{0,1\}$

then

$\Sigma^+ = \{0, 1, 00, 01, 10, 11, 000, \ldots\}$

The set of all finite strings of symbols from the alphabet Σ is called the **Kleene closure** and is denoted by the Σ^*. The set includes the empty string Λ. It can be specified similarly to the positive closure, or even more simply as

$\Sigma^* = \Sigma^+ \cdot \{\Lambda\}$

If $\Sigma = \{0, 1\}$ then Σ^* represents the set of all finite binary sequences including the empty sequence.

Inductively defined functions

We have just seen how induction was used to define certain sets. When the domain of a function is an inductively defined set the function is also often defined conveniently by induction.

For example, factorial can be inductively defined as a function f on the natural numbers $\mathbb{N}$ in the following way:

(1) f(0) = 1   (basis clause)
(2) f(n + 1) = (n + 1) × f(n)   for all n ∈ $\mathbb{N}$ (inductive clause)

The well known Fibonacci sequence

1, 1, 2, 3, 5, 8, 13, ...

may also be inductively defined as a function f on $\mathbb{N}$ for example,

(1)   f(0) = 1, f(1) = 1
(2)   f(n + 2) = f(n + 1) + f(n)   for all   n ∈ $\mathbb{N}$

Structural induction

The application of induction is not limited solely to the natural numbers. In computing science it is frequently necessary to consider induction over recursively defined data structures such as lists and trees. The technique used to reason inductively about these sorts of unbounded structures is referred to as **structural induction**.

Such structures consist of **basic** and **composite** elements. Making this distinction, the induction rule takes the following form:

Principle of structural induction
If P_n is a property of the data structure and it is assumed

(1) P_e, the required property for the basic elements is true, and

(2) for all composite elements if the required property P_{ce} is true, then the required property is true for objects P_{ob} which contain P_{ce}

then it may be concluded that P_n holds for all allowed realizations of the data structure.

A proof by structural induction involves showing

(1)   firstly, that the required property for the base elements P_e is true
(2)   and then showing for all composite elements ($\forall$ce) (P_{ce} ⇒ P_{ob}) – *induction step*.

To illustrate this technique suppose we have the following recursively defined binary tree structure with pointers LEFT and RIGHT:

node = leaf
node = tree

tree = (LEFT (node), RIGHT (node))

Now consider a recursive function count applied to a binary tree t which satisfies this definition, that is

```
count (t: node) : int;
    if leaf (t) → return 1
    []¬leaf (t) → return plus(count (LEFT (t)), count (RIGHT (t)))
    fi
end
```

A specification for this function might be given in terms of the cardinality of the set of leaf nodes, that is

c = card (leafset (t))   ... *specification*

where

```
leafset (t: node) : set;
    if leaf (t) → return {t}
    [] ¬leaf (t) → return leafset (LEFT (t)) ∪ leafset (RIGHT (t))
    fi
end
```

A proof that count satisfies this specification requires that a result is proved about all binary trees that satisfy our definition. This requires structural induction over the tree structure.

Proof
Base step
Assume for the basis that

leaf (t)

is true. It then follows that

count (t) = card (leafset (t))
          = card ({t})
          = 1

and so count holds for the base element.

Inductive step
Now assume

¬leaf(t)

is true. It then follows that

count(t) = plus (count (LEFT (t)), count (RIGHT (t)))   **(1)**

Now using the inductive hypothesis

count (LEFT (t)) = card (leafset (LEFT (t)))   **(2)**
count (RIGHT (t)) = card (leafset (RIGHT (t)))   **(3)**

Substituting for (2) and (3) in (1) we get

count (t) = plus (card(leafset (LEFT (t)), card (leafset (RIGHT (t)))
= card (leafset (LEFT (t)) $\cup$ leafset (RIGHT (t)))

but this is just

card (leafset (t))

and so count holds for an arbitrary composite element. The proof is therefore complete.

SUMMARY

- A study of discrete mathematics which includes sets, relations, functions, and sequences is necessary to provide a powerful armament for program specification and program derivation.
- Set theory is important because it helps us to formulate general properties of collections that apply to all their instances.
- The central concepts of set theory are built around the notion of individual and group membership of sets. A knowledge of all members of a set is sufficient to define that set. The idea of group membership is an extension of the idea of individual membership. Repeating elements and the order of the elements are of no consequence in defining sets.
- As well as defining sets simply by their members, a powerful alternative is to define sets using a predicate which is true for all members of the set. This idea is embodied in the principle of comprehensive specification.
- Important operations that may be used to build other sets from existing sets are union, intersection, complementation and symmetric difference.
- Basic set theory, together with notions of ordered sets (the most important of which are ordered pairs and Cartesian products), provides the necessary tools for defining the important mathematical constructs – functions and relations.
- Another interesting aspect of set theory is that it can be used to describe the relationship between set operators and the propositional connectives.
- A further important link between logic and set theory appears in the use of predicates to describe sets of states. A state in this context is

just a set of ordered pairs, each consisting of a variable with its associated value.

- Relations are used in specifications to express the notion of connectedness between members of sets. In simplest terms a relation is just a set of ordered pairs or ordered sets.

- Probably the most important relations are those that involve the relationship between members of two sets A and B. Such relations are called binary relations. The important sets associated with binary relations are the Cartesian product set, the domain set, the co-domain set and the range set. The relation itself is defined as a subset of the ordered pairs in the Cartesian product of A and B.

- A function is just a special kind of relation which associates with each element of a given set a single element of some other not necessarily distinct set. Functions are important in program specification for defining operations on sets of data. A function, like a relation, may be described formally as a set of ordered pairs.

- In computing science we often need to model the notion of one action after another. The concept of functional composition may be used for this purpose.

- As with sets, there are a number of important operators on functions that can be used in specifications. These operators are used to restrict and contract the range and domain sets that belong to functions. The resulting operations on functions yield new functions.

- Some problems in program design involve collections of data with repeating elements. The theory of bags or multisets is used to specify such data.

- What distinguishes bag theory from set theory is that the number of occurrences of an element in a bag is significant. This contrasts with set theory where it is the membership relation which characterizes a set. A bag may be defined formally as a function from a set to the natural numbers.

- Another important class of data that we need to be able to characterize in program design is the sequence. A sequence, like a bag, is just another special type of function whose domain is a subset of the natural numbers. With sequences order is important.

- There are two important ways of specifying a sequence, as a set of ordered pairs, or using a grammar. The Extended Backus-Naur Form (EBNF) notation is employed for the grammar.

- To reason about sequences and prove assertions about programs the notion of mathematical induction may be employed.

■ *EXERCISE 3.1   Sets*

1. Which of the following statements involving set equality and set membership are true?

    (a) $1 \in \{1,2,3,4\}$
    (b) $1 \in \{2,3,1,4\}$
    (c) $1 \in \{2,3,4\}$
    (d) $2 \in \{1,3\}$
    (e) $\{1\} \in \{1,2,3,4\}$
    (f) $\{2\} \in \{1,3\}$
    (g) $\emptyset \in \{1,2,3\}$
    (h) $\{1,3\} \in \{\{1,3\},\{2,3,4\}\}$
    (i) $\{1\} \in \{\{1,2,3\},\{4,5\}\}$
    (j) $\{1\} \in \{\{2\},\{1\},\{3,4\}\}$
    (k) $\{1\} \in \{2,3,\{1\},4\}$
    (l) $\{1,2\} \in \{\{1,2,3\}, 4\}$
    (m) $\{\emptyset\} \in \{1,2,3\}$

    (n) $\{1,2,3\} \in \{1,2,3\}$
    (o) $\{1,2,3\} \in \{\{1,2,3\}\}$
    (p) $\{1\} \in 1$
    (q) $1 \in 1$
    (r) $1 \in \{1\}$
    (s) $\{1\} \in \{1\}$
    (t) $\{1,2,3\} = \{1,3,2\}$
    (u) $\{1,2,2\} = \{2,1\}$
    (v) $\{1,1,1\} = 1$
    (w) $\{1\} = 1$
    (x) $\{1,1,1\} = \{1\}$
    (y) $\{\{1,2\},3\} = \{3,\{2,1\}\}$
    (z) $\{\{1\}\} = \{1\}$

2. Which of the following statements involving set inclusion are true?

    (a) $1 \subseteq \{1,2,3,4\}$
    (b) $1 \subseteq \{2,3,1,4\}$
    (c) $1 \subseteq \{2,3,4\}$
    (d) $2 \subseteq \{1,3\}$
    (e) $\{1\} \subseteq \{1,2,3,4\}$
    (f) $\{2\} \subseteq \{1,3\}$
    (g) $\emptyset \subseteq \{1,2,3\}$
    (h) $\{1,3\} \subseteq \{\{1,3\},\{2,3,4\}\}$
    (i) $\{1\} \subseteq \{\{1,2,3\},\{4,5\}\}$
    (j) $\{1\} \subseteq \{\{2\},\{1\},\{3,4\}\}$
    (k) $\{1\} \subseteq \{2,3,\{1\},4\}$
    (l) $\{1,2\} \subseteq \{\{1,2,3\},4\}$

    (m) $\{\emptyset\} \subseteq \{1,2,3\}$
    (n) $\{1,2,3\} \subseteq \{1,2,3\}$
    (o) $\{1,2,3\} \subseteq \{\{1,2,3\}\}$
    (p) $\{1\} \subseteq 1$
    (q) $1 \subseteq 1$
    (r) $1 \subseteq \{1\}$
    (s) $\{1\} \subseteq \{1\}$
    (t) $\{1,1,2,2\} \subseteq \{1,2\}$
    (u) $\{1,2\} \subseteq \{1,1,2,2\}$
    (v) $\{1,2\} \subseteq \{1,1,2,2\}$
    (w) $\{1,2\} \subseteq \{1,3,2\}$
    (x) $\{\{1,3\}\} \subseteq \{\{1,3\},\{2,3,4\}\}$

3. Express the results of the following *set union* operations in extensional form:

    (a) $\{1,2,3\} \cup \{4\}$
    (b) $\{1,2,3\} \cup \{4,5\}$
    (c) $\{1,2,3\} \cup \{2,3,4\}$
    (d) $\{1,2,3\} \cup \{1,2,3\}$
    (e) $\{1,2,3\} \cup \{2,3,1\}$

    (f) $\{1,2,3\} \cup \{1,\{2\},3\}$
    (g) $\{1,\{2,3\}\} \cup \{\{2,3\}\}$
    (h) $\{1,2\} \cup \{\emptyset\}$
    (i) $\{1,2\} \cup \emptyset$
    (j) $\{1,2,3\} \cup \{1,2,3,4\}$

4. Express the results of the following *set intersection* operations in extensional form:

    (a) $\{1,2,3\} \cap \{4\}$
    (b) $\{1,2,3\} \cap \{4,5\}$
    (c) $\{1,2,3\} \cap \{2,3,4\}$
    (d) $\{1,2,3\} \cap \{1,2,3\}$
    (e) $\{1,2,3\} \cap \{2,3,1\}$

    (f) $\{1,2,3\} \cap \{1,\{2\},3\}$
    (g) $\{1,\{2,3\}\} \cap \{\{2,3\}\}$
    (h) $\{1,2\} \cap \{\emptyset\}$
    (i) $\{1,2\} \cap \emptyset$
    (j) $\{1,2,3\} \cap \{1,2,3,4\}$

5. Express the results of the following *set difference* operations in extensional form:

(a) $\{1,2,3\} - \{4\}$

(b) $\{1,2,3\} - \{4,5\}$

(c) $\{1,2,3\} - \{2,3,4\}$

(d) $\{1,2,3\} - \{1,2,3\}$

(e) $\{1,2,3\} - \{2,3,1\}$

(f) $\{1,2,3\} - \{1,\{2\},3\}$

(g) $\{1,\{2,3\}\} - \{\{2,3\}\}$

(h) $\{1,2\} - \{\emptyset\}$

(i) $\{1,2\} - \emptyset$

(j) $\{1,2,3\} - \{1,2,3,4\}$

6. Express the results of the following *Cartesian product* operations in extensional form:

(a) $\{1\} \times \{2\}$

(b) $\{1,2\} \times \{3\}$

(c) $\{1,2\} \times \{2,3\}$

(d) $\{1,2,3\} \times \{1,2\}$

(e) $\{1,2\} \times \{1,2,3\}$

(f) $\{1,2,3\} \times \{3,4,5\}$

7. Given $A = \{1,2,3,4\}$ and $B = \{2,4,6\}$ express the results of the following set operations in extensional form:

(a) $A \cap (A \cup B)$

(b) $A \cup (A \cup B)$

(c) $A \cup (A \cap B)$

(d) $(A \cup B) - B$

(e) $(A \cup B) - (A \cap B)$

(f) $A \cap (A - B)$

(g) $(A - B) \cup B$

(h) $(A - B) \cap B$

8. Write out the powersets $\mathbb{P}(A)$ in extensional form corresponding to each of the following sets A:

(a) $\emptyset$

(b) $\{1\}$

(c) $\{1,2\}$

(d) $\{1,2,3\}$

9. Write out the five smallest members of each of the following comprehensively specified sets ($\mathbb{Q}$ refers to the rational numbers):

(a) $\{n : n \in \mathbb{N}\}$

(b) $\{2n : n \in \mathbb{N}\}$

(c) $\{2n+1 : n \in \mathbb{N}\}$

(d) $\{n \bmod 2 : n \in \mathbb{N}\}$

(e) $\{n \bmod 3 : n \in \mathbb{N}\}$

(f) $\{n^2 : n \in \mathbb{N}\}$

(g) $\{n(n+1) : n \in \mathbb{N}\}$

(h) $\{2^n - 1 : n \in \mathbb{N}\}$

(i) $\{n \in \mathbb{Q} : 2n+1 \in \mathbb{N}\}$

(j) $\{n \in \mathbb{N} : n/2 \in \mathbb{N}\}$

(k) $\{n \in \mathbb{N} : n/3 \in \mathbb{N}\}$

(l) $\{n \in \mathbb{N} : n/2 \notin \mathbb{N}\}$

10. Write comprehensive specifications for the following sets:

(a) $\{1,3,5,7,\dots\}$

(b) $\{1,4,9,16,\dots\}$

(c) $\{0,3,8,15,\dots\}$

(d) $\{0,4,8,12,16,\dots\}$

(e) $\{2,5,10,17,\dots\}$

(f) $\{0, 1/2, 2/3, 3/4, \dots\}$

(g) $\{1,2,4,8,16,\dots\}$

(h) $\{2, 3/2, 4/3, 5/4, \dots\}$

11. Given an array A[1.. N] write a comprehensive specification for the set of elements in A[1..N]

(a) that are less than their right-adjacent neighbours

(b) that occur more than once

(c) that are greater than x

(d) that are even

(e) that are odd

(f) that are also elements of an array B[1..N]

(g) that occur only once in A[1..N]

(h) that are divisible by 5

(i) that are prime numbers

(j) that are composite numbers.

■ *EXERCISE 3.2   Relations*

1. Write down suitable relations formed from sets of ordered pairs which describe the following graphs.

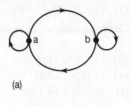

(a)

(b)

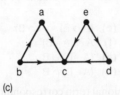

(c)

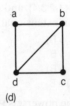

(d)

2. Draw graphs for each of the following relations.

(a) R = {(a,1),(b,2),(2,b),(2,a)}
(b) R = {(0,1),(0,0),(1,0),(1,1)}
(c) R = {(0,0),(0,1),(1,0),(−1,0),(0,−1),(−1,−1),(1,1),(−1,1),(1,−1)}

3. For each of the relations in Question 2 indicate dom R, ran R, and R⁻¹.

4. (a) Define the relation 'less than' (<) on the set A = {1,2,3,4}
    (b) Define the relation 'less than or equal to' (≤) on the set A = {1,2,3,4}
    (c) Define the relation 'not equal' (≠) on the set A = {1,2,3,4}
    (d) Define the relation ⊆ on the set $\mathbb{P}$(A) given A = {a,b,c}
    (e) Define the inverse of < on the set A = {1,2,3,4}
    (f) Define the inverse of ≤ on the set A = {1,2,3,4}
    (g) Define the inverse of ≠ on the set A = {1,2,3,4}
    (h) Define the inverse of = on the set A = {1,2,3,4}

5. For each of the following relations, state whether it is reflexive, transitive, symmetric, or an equivalence relation.

    (a) {(1,2),(2,1),(1,3),(3,1)}
    (b) {(1,2),(2,1),(1,3),(3,1),(2,3),(3,2)}
    (c) {(1,1),(1,2),(2,1),(2,2),(1,3),(3,1),(3,3)}
    (d) {(1,1),(1,2),(2,2),(2,3),(3,3),(3,4),(4,4)}
    (e) {(1,1),(3,1),(2,2),(1,2),(3,3),(3,2)}
    (f) {(1,1),(2,2),(3,3)}
    (g) {(1,2),(1,1),(2,1),(2,2)}
    (h) {(2,3),(2,1),(3,1)}
    (i) {(1,2),(2,3),(3,4),(1,3)}

6. For the set A = {a, b, c} give an example of:

    (a) a relation that is reflexive
    (b) a relation that is transitive
    (c) a relation that is symmetric

(d) a relation that is reflexive and transitive
(e) a relation that is reflexive and symmetric
(f) a relation that is transitive and symmetric
(g) a relation that is reflexive, transitive and symmetric.

7. For each of the following relations state whether it is reflexive, transitive, symmetric or an equivalence relation.

(a) the relation 'greater than' ($>$) on the natural numbers $\mathbb{N}$
(b) the relation 'greater than or equal to' ($\geq$) on the natural numbers $\mathbb{N}$
(c) the relation 'equal to' ($=$) on the natural numbers $\mathbb{N}$
(d) the relation 'not equal to' ($\neq$) on the natural numbers $\mathbb{N}$.

8. For $R \subseteq \{0,1...,5\} \times \{0,1,...,5\}$ where a R b if a **MOD** 3 = b **MOD** 3

(a) write the ordered pairs in the equivalence relation R
(b) identify each of the equivalence classes.

■ EXERCISE 3.3   Functions

1. Which of the following relations are functions given dom R = {a, b, c} and that the codomain is {1, 2, 3}:

(a) R = {(a, 1), (b, 1), (c, 1)}
(b) R = {(a, 1), (b, 1), (c, 2)}
(c) R = {(a, 1), (a, 2), (a, 3)}
(d) R = {(a, 1), (b, 2), (c, 3)}
(e) R = {(a, 1), (c, 2)}

2. Given x and y are real numbers which of the following relations are functions?

(a) $R = \{(x, y) \in \mathbb{R} \times \mathbb{R} \mid y = x\}$
(b) $R = \{(x, y) \in \mathbb{R} \times \mathbb{R} \mid y = x^2\}$
(c) $R = \{(x, y) \in \mathbb{R} \times \mathbb{R} \mid y^2 = x\}$
(d) $R = \{(x, y) \in \mathbb{R} \times \mathbb{R} \mid y < x\}$

3. Give an example using ordered pairs of a function that is:

(a) injective
(b) surjective
(c) bijective
(d) injective but not surjective
(e) surjective but not injective

4. Indicate whether each of the following functions is injective, surjective, or bijective:

(a) $f : \mathbb{Z} \to \mathbb{Z}$ where $f(x) = x$
(b) $f : \mathbb{Z} \to \mathbb{Z}$ where $f(x) = x + 1$
(c) $f : \{a, b, c\} \to \{1\}$
(d) $f : \mathbb{Z} \to \mathbb{Z}$ where $f(x) = x^2$
(e) $f = \{(2, 4), (4, 1), (1, 3), (3, 2)\}$

5. (a) What is the inverse of the function:

   f = {(a,1), (b,4), (c,9), (d,16)}

   (b) What is the characteristic funcion of A on X given:

   X = {1, 3, 5, 7, 9}   and   A = {3, 5, 9}

6.   (a) Consider the functions $f : X \to X$ and $g : X \to X$ where $X = \{1,2,3,4\}$. Compute
      $f \circ g$ and $g \circ f$ given:
$$f = \{(1,2), (2,3), (3,4), (4,1)\}$$
$$g = \{(1,2), (2,3), (3,4), (4,4)\}$$

      (b) Given the functions $f : \mathbb{R} \to \mathbb{R}$ and $g : \mathbb{R} \to \mathbb{R}$ defined by:
$$f(x) = x^2 \qquad g(x) = x+1$$
      determine $f \circ g$ and $g \circ f$.

7.   Describe the following functions using lambda notation:

      (a) $f : \mathbb{R} \to \mathbb{R}$ such that for every $x \in \mathbb{R}$ $f(x) = 0$
      (b) $f : \mathbb{R} \to \mathbb{R}$ such that for every $x \in \mathbb{R}$ $f(x) = x + 1$
      (c) $f : \mathbb{R} \to \mathbb{R}$ such that for every $x \in \mathbb{R}$ $f(x) = x^2 + 2x + 1$
      (d) $f : \mathbb{R} \times \mathbb{R} \to \mathbb{R}$ such that for every $x,y \in \mathbb{R}$ $f(x,y) = x^2 + 2xy + 2x + 2y + 1$

8.   Evaluate the following functions expressed in lambda notation:

      (a) $(\lambda x)(x^2 + 2x + 1)(3)$
      (b) $(\lambda x)(x^2 + 2x + 1)(x^2)$
      (c) $(\lambda x)((\lambda y) (x^2 + y))(2,5)$
      (d) $(\lambda y)((\lambda x) (x^2 + y))(2,5)$
      (e) $(\lambda xy)(x^2 + y)(2,5)$
      (f) $(\lambda yx)(x^2 + y)(2,5)$

9.   Given a function f over a domain X and range Y and another function g over
      domain Z where:
$$f = \{(1, 2), (2, 4), (3, 6), (4, 9), (5, 11)\}$$
$$g = \{(2, 8), (4, 27), (6, 64)\}$$
      and
$$S = \{1, 3, 5\}$$
$$T = \{2, 4, 6, 8, 10, 12\}$$
$$X = \{1, 2, 3, 4, 5\}$$
$$Y = \{2, 4, 6, 9, 11\}$$
$$Z = \{2, 4, 6\}$$
      determine each of the following functions:

      (a) $f \lhd S$ (f) $f \rhd T$
      (b) $f \lhd T$ (g) $f \rhd (Y-T)$
      (c) $f \rhd T$ (h) $f \oplus g$
      (d) $f \unlhd S$ (i) $g \oplus f$
      (e) $f \lhd (X-S)$

10.   Let a function $f : \mathbb{N} \to \mathbb{N}$ be defined by $f(n) = 3n + 2$ and let $g : T \to \mathbb{N}$ be defined by
      $g(n) = n$, and given
$$S = \{2n+1 : n \in \mathbb{N}\} \qquad T = \{2n : n \in \mathbb{N}\}$$
      describe each of the following functions:

      (a) $f \lhd S$ (f) $f \rhd T$
      (b) $f \lhd T$ (g) $f \rhd (Y-T)$
      (c) $f \rhd T$ (h) $f \oplus g$
      (d) $f \unlhd S$ (i) $g \oplus f$
      (e) $f \lhd (X-S)$

■ EXERCISE 3.4   Specification using EBNF

1.   Give an EBNF specification for integers in the range -999 to 999.

2. Use EBNF to specify possible days of the month with their appropriate endings, for example

    1ST, 2ND, 3RD, 4TH, 5TH, ... 31ST

3. Give an EBNF specification for the times indicated by a 24 hour clock (a typical time is 14:57).

4. Use EBNF to specify car number plates in your state or country.

5. Write a specification for a paragraph of text given that it is made up of one or more sentences each consisting of one or more words. Note the first word in a sentence starts with a capital letter. In this specification assume there are only single spaces between words and the only punctuation mark is a full stop.

6. Use EBNF to specify valid dates in the 20th century. An example of the form required is:

    26th January 1988

7. Use EBNF to specify the private entries in your city's telephone directory. Give only sample terminal symbols for suburbs and street names or alternatively specify these in more general terms.

■ EXERCISE 3.5   Bags

1. Given the following bags represented in extensional form, provide the corresponding functional representations:

    (a) ⟨1, 2, 1, 1, 3, 5, 2⟩
    (b) ⟨1, 1, 1, 2, 2, 3, 5⟩
    (c) ⟨1, 2, 3, 5⟩

2. Given the following bags represented in functional form, provide the corresponding extensional representation:

    (a) {(a, 1), (b, 2), (c, 3), (d, 4)}
    (b) {(d, 4), (c, 3), (b, 2), (a, 1)}
    (c) {(a, 4), (b, 3), (c, 2), (d, 1), (e, 0)}

3. Given the bags

    $B1 = ⟨1, 2, 2, 2, 3, 3, 3, 4, 4, 5⟩$
    $B2 = ⟨2, 2, 4, 4, 4, 6, 6, 8, 8⟩$
    $B3 = ⟨1, 2, 2, 3, 3, 4⟩$

    determine each of the following

(a) $|B1|$	(g) $B1 \cap B2$	(m) $B1 + B2$
(b) card(B2)	(h) $B1 \cap B3$	(n) $B1 + B3$
(c) $B3 \subseteq B2$	(i) $B1 - B2$	(o) into(5, B1)
(d) $B3 \subseteq B1$	(j) $B1 - B3$	(p) into(5, B2)
(e) $B1 \cup B2$	(k) $B2 - B1$	(q) outof(5, B1)
(f) $B1 \cup B3$	(l) $B3 - B1$	(r) outof(5, B2)

4. Let $B1 : \mathbb{N} \to \mathbb{N}$ be the bag defined by $B1(n) = n \text{ mod } 2$ and $B2 : \mathbb{N} \to \mathbb{N}$ be the bag defined by $B2(n) = n \text{ mod } 3$. Describe the bags

    (a) $B1 \cup B2$ (b) $B1 \cap B2$

(c) B1 – B2   (e) B1 + B2

(d) B2 – B1   (f) B2 + B1

■ *EXERCISE 3.6   Mathematical induction*

1. Using mathematical induction prove

(a) $\displaystyle\sum_{i=1}^{n} 2i = n(n + 1)$

(b) $\displaystyle\sum_{i=0}^{n} (2i + 1) = (n + 1)^2$

(c) $\displaystyle\sum_{i=1}^{n} i^2 = \frac{n(n + 1)(2n + 1)}{6}$

(d) $\displaystyle\sum_{i=1}^{n} i(i + 1) = \frac{n(n + 1)(n + 2)}{3}$

(e) $\displaystyle\sum_{i=1}^{n} i^3 = \frac{n^2(n + 1)^2}{4}$

(f) $\displaystyle\left(\sum_{i=1}^{n} i\right)^2 = \sum_{i=1}^{n} i^3$

(g) for all $n \in \mathbb{N}$ prove

$\displaystyle\sum_{i=1}^{n} 2^i = 2^{n+1} - 1$

2. Using mathematical induction prove

$\displaystyle\sum_{i=1}^{n} ar^{i-1} = \frac{a(r^n - 1)}{r - 1}$

for $n \in \mathbb{N}$ and $a, r \in \mathbb{R}$ and $r \neq 1$.

3. Using mathematical induction prove

$\displaystyle\sum_{i=1}^{n} (a_{i+1} - a_i) = a_{n+1} - a_1$

for all $n \in \mathbb{Z}^+$.

4. Using mathematical induction prove

$\displaystyle\sum_{i=1}^{n} (a_i + b_i) = \sum_{i=1}^{n} a_i = \sum_{i=1}^{n} b_i$

for all $n \in \mathbb{Z}^+$.

5. For all $n \in \mathbb{Z}^+$, the expression $n^2 + n$ always has 2 as a factor.

6. Given

$n! = 1$ for $n = 0$

$$n! = n \times (n-1)! \qquad \text{for } n > 0$$

prove

$$n! = \prod_{i=1}^{n} i$$

7. For all $n \in \mathbb{Z}^+$ prove
$$2^n > n$$

8. Use mathematical induction to prove a set A with n elements has 2^n possible subsets (its powerset $\mathbb{P}(A)$).

Bibliography

Arbib, M.A., A.J. Kfoury, and R.N. Moll (1981), *A Basis for Theoretical Computer Science*, Springer-Verlag, N.Y.

Berg, H.K. and W.K.L. Giloi (1979), *The Use of Formal Specification of Software*, Lecture Notes in Comp. Sci., Vol.36, Berlin.

Bobrow, L.S. and, M.A. Arbib (1974), *Discrete Mathematics*, Saunders, Washington D.C.

Gersting, J.L. (1982), *Mathematical Structures for Computer Science*, Freeman, San Fransisco.

Halmos, P. (1960), *Naive Set Theory*, Van Nostrand, Princeton, N.J.

Hayes, I. (ed.) (1987), *Specification Case Studies*, Prentice-Hall, London.

Hickman, J.L. (1980), A note on the concept of multiset, *Bull. Aust. Math. Soc.*, **22**, 211.

Lew, A. (1985), *Computer Mathematics*, Prentice Hall, London.

Lin, S.T. and Y. Yin (1974), *Set Theory: An Intuitive Approach*, Houghton Mifflin, Boston, Mass.

Lipschutz, S. (1966), *Finite Mathematics*, McGraw-Hill, N.Y.

Liu, C.L. (1977), *Elements of Discrete Mathematics*, McGraw-Hill, N.Y.

Neel, D.(ed.) (1982), *Tools for Program Construction*, CUP, Cambridge.

Peterson, J.L. (1981), *Petri Net Theory and the Modelling of Systems*, Prentice-Hall, Englewood Cliffs, N.J.

Prather, R.E. (1976), *Discrete Mathematical Structures for Computer Science*, Houghton Mifflin.

Preparata, F.P. and T.E. Yeh (1973), *Introduction to Discrete Structures*, Addison-Wesley, Reading, Mass.

Solow, D. (1982), *How to Read and Do Proofs*, Wiley, N.Y.

Stanat, D.F., and D.F. McAllister (1977), *Discrete Mathematics in Computer Science*, Prentice-Hall, Englewood Cliffs, N.J.

Staunstrup, J. (1981), *Program Specification*, Lecture Notes in Computer Science, Vol. 134, Springer-Verlag, Berlin.

Stoll, R.R. (1961), *Set Theory and Logic*, Freeman, San Fransisco.

Suppes, P. (1957), *Introduction to Logic*, Van Nostrand, Princeton, N.J.

Suppes, P. (1957), *Axiomatic Set Theory*, Van Nostrand, Princeton, N.J.

Tremblay, J.P. and R. Manchair (1975), *Discrete Mathematical Structures with Applications to Computer Science*, McGraw-Hill, N.Y.

Youse, B.K. (1963), *Mathematical Induction*, Prentice-Hall, Englewood Cliffs, N.J.

Chapter 4
Specification of Programs

A problem well-defined is half solved

C. Kettering

4.1 Introduction
4.2 Preconditions
4.3 Postconditions
4.4 Loop Invariants
4.5 Variant Functions
    Summary
    Exercises
    Bibliography

4.1 Introduction

The primary specification for a program consists of a precondition Q, and a postcondition R. A program S satisfies its specification (Q, R) if, when executed in a state satisfying Q, it terminates in a state satisfying R. A specification describes *what* the program should do and the implementation determines *how* the task is actually accomplished. A good program specification should not contain information about the implementation.

Specifications play a central role in program design. They provide a precise definition of a problem, identify limitations of a program, and provide a constructive framework for the development of programs. They also serve a documenting role by identifying certain critical states or sub-goals that a program passes through before establishing the postcondition.

The precondition defines constraints on the input or data that the program is required to handle. It should include bounds on the size of a problem, assumptions about the input data, bounds on variables, and

187

descriptions of structure in the input data. The role of the postcondition in defining a problem is to precisely characterize what the program must achieve. It employs a set of variables and a set of constraints that characterize the goal.

Preconditions and postconditions play a central role not only in problem definition but also in guiding the development of the program and its constructive proof of correctness. The basic strategy is to make transformations on the **primary specifications** (i.e. Q and R) to derive **secondary specifications** called **invariants**. Invariants are specifications which indirectly describe how a computation may be accomplished. They do this by identifying conditions that must be maintained (or kept invariant) while certain program variables are changed.

In simplest terms, the strategy for developing a program involves changing certain program variables while maintaining an invariant (or invariants) until some additional constraint is satisfied. Together, the invariant plus the constraint should imply the postcondition. A formal correctness proof for programs follows from this model.

What has been described is an oversimplification of the process. For other than very simple problems, a number of invariants and sub-goals must be identified in the course of the development.

There is one other type of specification needed to guide the development of a program and establish its total proof of correctness. This specification is called a **variant function** or **bound function.** The variant function is closely linked to the constraints that must be satisfied along with the invariant in order for the postcondition to be implied. More explicitly it is a function of the program variables that measures progress towards establishing the postcondition.

How the various specifications are derived and employed in designing programs is the subject of the chapters which follow. For the present we will return to a more detailed examination of the various elements of a complete program specification.

4.2 Preconditions

The precondition is an important part of a program specification. It defines the interface between a mechanism for a computation and the data or parameters that are supplied to that mechanism. It should also identify and make explicit conditions or constraints that the input data for a computation must satisfy if it is to be used correctly by the mechanism. For this reason the precondition is sometimes called an **input assertion.**

More formally a precondition is a predicate which characterizes the set of initial states for which a problem must be solved. It specifies the subset of all possible states that the mechanism should be able to handle correctly. Data-type information is usually taken as implicit in these specifications.

Preconditions for problems have no fixed structure. There is no unique set of ingredients for specifying constraints on input data. The form assumed by a precondition is determined by the nature of the problem being specified and by the variables used to describe it. Precondition constraints used in a particular specification usually come from one or more of the following categories.

4.2.1 Problem size

Programs must frequently handle problems of varying size. The strategy employed by the mechanism should be independent of the problem size. For example, the *same* strategy may be used to find the maximum among 10, 100, or 1000 given numbers. For problems that share this characteristic there is a lower bound on the problem size. The precondition used to specify this type of problem should identify this lower bound. This can require careful examination of definitions associated with the problem.

As an example, consider the task of writing a precondition for the problem of identifying the maximum in a fixed array of N arbitrary integers A[1..N]. An index i can be used used to identify the maximum in the array. The postcondition is therefore:

$$1 \leq i \leq N \wedge (\forall j : 1 \leq j \leq N : A_i \geq A_j)$$

Throughout this book we will employ the convention of using upper case to denote fixed free variables (that is data not changed by the implementation) and lower case for variables assigned by programs. This allows consistency with specifications to be upheld. The fixed integer N defines the problem size. The definition suggests that the smallest problem size for which a maximum is defined is N = 1. The other, perhaps likely choice for the smallest problem size, is N = 0. However, the maximum is undefined for an empty array. The precondition for this problem is therefore

$$Q_{max} : N \geq 1$$

As a second example, consider a specification for the sum of an array of N fixed integers. Here, the sum is defined for a problem size of N = 0. The appropriate precondition is

$$Q_{sum} : N \geq 0$$

In identifying preconditions based on problem size we are usually only interested in the lower bounds. Placing an upper bound on problem size is relevant only if a problem may exceed the limits of the computer's memory or if a computation may take an inordinate amount of time to complete (for example it is easy to write a permutation generation algorithm that will generate all permutations of N elements where N has the value 20. This computation would, however, not complete in the lifetime of the universe).

4.2.2   Bounds for variables

The importance of correctly specifying preconditions is shown clearly by the greatest common divisor (gcd) problem. The following specification defines the greatest common divisor of two positive integers X and Y:

$Q_{gcd} : X > 0 \wedge Y > 0$
$R : \quad y = gcd(x,y) \wedge gcd(x,y) = gcd(X,Y) \wedge x=y$

An implementation that can be derived to compute the gcd is

```
x, y := X, Y;
do x < y → y := y − x
[] y < x → x := x − y
od
```

With this implementation, if either X or Y is negative, the mechanism will not terminate. Also, if both X and Y have the value zero, the result produced by the mechanism will be incorrect.

To make the implementation completely safe, a guard is needed to ensure that the precondition is satisfied in the first place. This example shows that if preconditions are not identified, and the accompanying implementation guarded accordingly, an erroneous result or a termination problem may arise. It is at the boundary values for variables, and at problem-size limits, where mechanisms are most vulnerable to error or failure.

Another example, the problem of computing quotient q and the remainder r from dividing the natural number X by D requires the specification

$Q_{rem} : X \geqslant 0 \wedge D > 0$
$R : \quad X = q \times D + r \wedge 0 \leqslant r < D$

The accompanying mechanism is

```
q, r := 0, X;
do r ≥ D →
   r := r − D;
   q := q + 1
od
```

Again, this mechanism will not terminate if the precondition Q_{rem} is not satisfied.

The problem of computing the integer square root is another problem that is valid only for positive integers. It requires the precondition

$$Q_{sqrt} : N \geqslant 0$$

4.2.3 Properties and assumptions about input data

The simplest precondition is that required for a mechanism which functions correctly for all inputs that satisfy the type constraints of its variables. Such mechanisms or functions are defined as total. Their precondition is true. For example, the mechanism

if X > Y **then** max := X **else** max := Y **fi**

which selects the larger of two integers, functions correctly for all integer values and has the precondition specification:

$$Q_{gtr} : true$$

In some programming applications the data has certain properties or structure which is assumed and exploited in implementations. For example, in searching an ordered array A[1..N] for a particular value X we may exploit the order in the data and thereby complete the search with at most $\log_2 N$ comparisons. A precondition and binary search implementation for achieving this are

$$Q_{bs} : 1 \leqslant N \wedge (\forall j : 1 \leqslant j < N : A_j \leqslant A_{j+1}) \wedge X \leqslant A_N$$

```
i, j := 0, N + 1;
do i ≠ j − 1 →
    m := (i + j) div 2;
    if A_m < X → i := m
    [] A_m ⩾ X → j := m
    fi
od;
present := (A_i = X)
```

It functions correctly only if the data satisfies the precondition. If an empty array (i.e. N = 0) or X > A_N is encountered, present is not well-defined. A binary search that handles this case directly will be given later.

In some applications, mechanisms are constructed which rely on some property of the data to guarantee termination. For example, to search an array A[1..N] for the location of an element equal to X, known to be present, the following precondition Q_{sch} and implementation may be used:

$$Q_{sch} : N \geqslant 1 \wedge (\exists j : 1 \leqslant j \leqslant N : X = A_j)$$

```
i := 1;
do A_i ≠ X → i := i + 1 od
```

If an element equal to X is not present, the mechanism will reference an array location that is out of bounds. This last example underlines the risk of designing mechanisms with preconditions that are not sufficiently general to accommodate the range of data that could be encountered in practice.

In seeking to make preconditions more general (i.e. weaker) programs become less vulnerable and less dependent on their input.

As an example of generalizing a precondition, consider again the problem of 'binary-searching' an ordered array A[1..N] for some element X. Assume that the array may be empty (i.e. N = 0 is possible) or $X > A_N$. Our previous precondition was

$$Q_{bs} : 1 \leqslant N \wedge (\forall j : 1 \leqslant j < N : A_j \leqslant A_{j+1}) \wedge X \leqslant A_N$$

A new more general precondition is

$$Q : 0 \leqslant N \wedge (\forall j : 1 \leqslant j < N : A_j \leqslant A_{j+1})$$

An implementation that accommodates this case directly is

```
i , j := 0, N + 1;
do i < j – 1 →
    m := (i + j) div 2;
    if Aₘ < X → i := m
    [] Aₘ = X → i , j := m, m
    [] Aₘ > X → j := m
    fi
od;
present := (i = j)
```

This implementation, unlike the earlier one, returns present = false when N = 0, as we would expect for an empty array. The assignment to present introduces no risk of a reference outside the array bounds because of the simpler index test. This 'symmetric' binary search also has the interesting characteristic of terminating as soon as an element equal to X is found.

For the linear search described earlier, there may be no way of guaranteeing the presence of X in A[1..N]. Instead there is the risk of referencing an element outside the array bounds. One way to overcome this sort of problem is to change the data (and hence the precondition) by adding an element equal to X (called a sentinel) onto the end of the array, that is

$$A_{N+1} := X$$

This guarantees the precondition

$$Q : (\exists i : 1 \leqslant i \leqslant N + 1 : A_i = X)$$

which is sufficient to ensure termination of the linear search algorithm, that is

```
i, A_{N+1} := 1 , X;
do Aᵢ ≠ X → i := i + 1 od
```

Unfortunately, it is not always possible or desirable to use sentinels. A more general solution to the linear search problem is to use a guard on the subscript, that is

```
i , n := 0 , N;
do i ≠ n →
    if A_{i+1} ≠ X → i := i + 1
    [] A_{i+1} = X → n := i
    fi
od
```

This algorithm can terminate with $A_{i+1} = X$, not $A_i = X$, as in the previous implementation.

We cannot always generalize a mechanism to accommodate all possible cases. When this happens, guards that follow from the precondition should be included to guarantee the precondition. For the gcd implementation given earlier, the protected mechanism would take the form:

```
if X > 0 ∧ Y > 0 then
    x , y := X , Y;
    do x > y → x := x − y
    [] y > x → y := y − x
    od
fi
```

4.3   Postconditions

The postcondition is usually the most important part of a program specification. It defines the **range** of a computation. There are three central roles that the postcondition can play in program development.

- It can provide a precise and preferably formal statement of what a program or function should accomplish.
- It can assist the constructive development of programs.
- It can be used in the development of a constructive proof of correctness for a program.

In this chapter we will focus on the role of postconditions as specifications. In this context a postcondition should identify and make explicit all conditions and constraints that apply to final states of a mechanism which follow from initial states satisfying the precondition.

There are often a number of different ways of expressing the postcondition for a particular problem. This variability can cause problems because the usefulness of a specification is dependent on the form that it takes. Accepting that it is prudent to separate the specification process from the implementation process, the postcondition should assume a form that makes it an *implicit* specification.

Principle

A postcondition should provide a description of what a mechanism is required to accomplish without any consideration of how the task is to be accomplished.

4.3.1   Guidelines on the form of postconditions

The detailed nature of any postcondition is strongly influenced by the particular problem being specified. There are, however, certain qualities and attributes that postconditions should have that are not directly dependent on the problem being specified. These qualities and attributes can mostly be traced back to the strength or weakness of the specification (that is as measured by the number of states that it describes). As a general rule, programs should be developed for the strongest specification of a problem. In what follows this advice will be elaborated upon.

As with preconditions, the aim is to make postconditions as general as possible. It is hoped that the more general the postcondition the more widely applicable is a program that establishes it. While our underlying goal is generality, at the same time it is highly desirable that we constrain the most general postcondition. To do this it is necessary to make the ranges and bounds on any free variables as tight as possible and to include as many constraints (implicit or otherwise) as are known to apply to the state space of the variables associated with the problem.

The richer the constraints in a specification the more avenues there are to assist the development of the program. On the other hand, a poorly constrained postcondition may give little or no clues for developing a program. Tight constraints on the ranges and/or bounds of free variables assist us in making appropriate choices for the initialization of free variables. Here, our overall goal is to make specifications logically precise. *Precision is the hallmark of a specification*.

These guidelines give us a better chance of creating specifications that are directly useful in the derivation of the corresponding programs. In the next chapter, we will see the advantages of starting out with a strong but general specification. Even so, it may still be necessary to make a variety of transformations on a postcondition in search of a form that can best assist us with the development of a program.

4.3.2 Some comparisons of postcondition specifications

To demonstrate the application of the guidelines for writing specifications it is instructive to compare some different specifications for a selection of simple problems.

EXAMPLE 1   A sorting problem

Consider the problem of sorting a fixed data set of N integers A. If the array a[1..N] is used to store the sorted result a possible postcondition specification is:

R : perm(a,A)

This specification tells us is that the sorted result is a permutation of the original data set A of N integers. The predicate perm(a,A) can be expressed as

$$perm(a,A) \equiv (\forall k : 1 \leqslant k \leqslant N : \#(j : 1 \leqslant j \leqslant N : a_k = a_j) = \#(j : 1 \leqslant j \leqslant N : a_k = A_j))$$

This specification is *too weak* for the sorting problem. It admits numerous other permutations of A in addition to the sorted result. To exclude unwanted permutations it is necessary to include a relation which specifies that the array elements must be ordered. We then get

$$R_1 : (\forall k : 1 \leqslant k < N : a_k \leqslant a_{k+1}) \wedge perm(a,A)$$

This specification tells us that the elements in the sorted array a[1..N] must be ordered and a permutation of the original data set A. Many people, when asked to provide a specification for the sorting problem, are quick to give the response:

$$R_2 : (\forall k : 1 \leqslant k < N : a_k \leqslant a_{k+1})$$

Unfortunately, as a specification for sorting, R_2 is again too weak. It admits unacceptable solutions. A program which established the configuration:

$$a_1 = 0, a_2 = 0, ..., a_N = 0$$

would establish the postcondition R_2. This discussion suggests that *both* the ordering component and the permutation component are needed to correctly describe the sorting postcondition. As it happens, there are other more useful specifications for sorting. They will be considered later in Chapter 9.

This example has shown us the importance of making specifications strong enough to exclude erroneous final states. In general, additional conjuncts make a specification stronger.

EXAMPLE 2   A search specification_____

A well-known problem in computing involves searching an unordered fixed data sequence $(A_1, A_2, ..., A_N)$ for the first occurrence of an element equal to the fixed element X. A postcondition that might be proposed for this problem is

$$R : X = A_{i+1}$$

It tells us that X is equal to the $(i+1)$th element. There are several things about this postcondition that do not conform to the guidelines given in the previous section. The most obvious deficiency is that it does not tell us anything about the index variable i. There are clearly some values that i cannot assume (e.g. $i = -327$), yet the postcondition gives no hint of any such restriction. This problem can be overcome by constraining i to a range of N values, that is

$$R_1 : 0 \leqslant i < N \wedge X = A_{i+1}$$

This is a stronger specification than R because of the restrictions that it places on the final values of i. The condition R_1 is acceptable provided the precondition that X is definitely a member of the sequence holds. A more general, and presumably more useful postcondition, is one that can also accommodate X being absent. To do this we weaken R_1 to obtain

$$R_2 : 0 \leqslant i \leqslant N \wedge (i = N \vee X = A_{i+1})$$

This postcondition allows X to be in any of the positions in the sequence, that is 1,2,...,N. For example, when the first element in A is equal to X we will have $i = 0$, and when X is equal to the last element A_N, we will have $i = N - 1$. When X is not present, after the search, i will be equal to N, and there will be no ambiguity.

Another way to account for X not being present is not to break the direct correspondence between the value of the index and the position of the element equal to X. To make this possible it is necessary to *displace* the elements in the sequence so that they are stored in the segment $A[0..N - 1]$†. This scheme does not allow an element at the index position N. The corresponding specification is

$$R_3 : 0 \leqslant i \leqslant N \wedge (i = N \vee X = A_i)$$

† A $[0..N - 1]$ defines the sequence $A_0, A_1, A_2, ..., A_{N-1}$.

With R_3, when there is no element equal to X present, i will assume the value N after the search. This method of index shifting has been employed by Dijkstra and Gries in their writing of specifications. Both of these approaches are acceptable. We prefer to use A[1..N] for storage, for, among other things, reasons of symmetry. (Then the result of the 'shift' does not appear unnatural when a search is conducted from the index N downwards.)

Both R_2 and R_3 to be useful as postconditions must be made stronger. In their present form both can be established by the program i := N which is clearly not a search. If X is not present, or at position i + 1, then all the elements A[1..i] must not be equal to X. Adding this constraint to R_2, we get

$$R_4 : 0 \leq i \leq N \wedge (\forall j : 0 < j \leq i : X \neq A_j) \wedge (i = N \vee X = A_{i+1})$$

This form of specification is usually given for the linear search problem. It presumes that the data sequence will be searched from left to right, and, that i + 1 will be used to identify the first position of an element equal to X, if one exists.

There still is a problem with R_4. The expression $X = A_{i+1}$ admits an out-of-range subscript when i = N. The way this sort of defect is usually overcome is by the introduction of conditional connectives.

To correct the defect in R_4 the $\vee$ needs to be replaced by a **cor**, the conditional **or**. This yields

$$R_5 : 0 \leq i \leq N \wedge (\forall j : 0 < j \leq i : X \neq A_j) \wedge (i = N \textbf{ cor } X = A_{i+1})$$

Notice in this specification, and some of the earlier ones, it is possible for i to assume the value 0. This results in universal quantification over an *empty* range which, by definition, is always true.

EXAMPLE 3   The greatest common divisor problem_____

It is apparent from the discussion thus far that there may be a number of different ways of describing and representing the postcondition for a particular problem. That such a possibility exists does not make the task of providing guidelines for constructing postconditions any easier.

In our next example three different specifications for the greatest common divisor problem will be considered and compared. Earlier, in our discussion of preconditions, the following postcondition was proposed for the greatest common divisor problem. The free variable x is the greatest common divisor.

$$R : x = \textbf{MAX}(d : 1 \leq d \leq \textbf{min}(X, Y) : X \textbf{ mod } d = 0 \wedge Y \textbf{ mod } d = 0)$$

This postcondition suggests a systematic search with a set of trial divisors to find the one that satisfies the constraints.

Another approach is to use an axiomatic specification. The following relations hold for $x \neq 0$ and $y \neq 0$.

$$gcd(x, y) = gcd(x, y - x)$$
$$gcd(x, y) = gcd(x - y, y)$$
$$gcd(x, y) = gcd(y, x)$$
$$gcd(x, x) = x$$

The accompanying postcondition that must be satisfied to establish the greatest common divisor of two fixed positive integers X and Y is

$$R_1 : x = gcd(X, Y) \wedge 1 \leqslant x \leqslant \textbf{min}(X, Y)$$

Even though the conjunct $1 \leqslant x \leqslant \textbf{min}(X,Y)$ is implied by the definition of the gcd it is still useful to include it to guide the initialization of x.

This sort of specification is appropriate where axioms are available or can be discovered. It is usually only applied to problems supported by a strong theoretical background (for example problems from number theory). The postcondition R_1, in its present form, gives little or no support for the development of a program. As we shall see later in the next chapter there are several manipulations that can be made on R_1 that lead to a postcondition that is well suited to deriving a program. The specification resulting from these manipulations on R_1 is

$$R_1' : x = y \wedge y = gcd(x,y) \wedge gcd(x,y) = gcd(X,Y) \wedge 1 \leqslant x, y \leqslant \textbf{min}(X,Y)$$

This specification R_1' implies R_1. So if a program can be derived that establishes R_1', it will also establish R_1. In this example, because we have not been content with the usefulness of a given specification, we have sought to transform it. This option should always be considered as a possible source of more useful specifications. Furthermore, as there are usually various transformations possible, *different* algorithms may be possible. This prospect should not be overlooked.

Attention will now be given to the development of a third possible specification of the gcd problem. In some ways, constructing the postcondition for a problem is like developing a program. Just as a program can have meaningful structure, so too can a postcondition. Furthermore, just as complex programs need to be built by stepwise refinement, so also do complex specifications. The choices for doing this are either a top-down or bottom-up stepwise refinement. While not attempting the construction of a complex specification, the method of top-down specification refinement will be illustrated for the gcd problem. From the requirement that the *greatest* common divisor is sought it is apparent that a maximizing qualification on the common divisors of X and Y is needed, that is

$$R : \gcd(X,Y) = \textbf{MAX}(d : 1 \leqslant d \leqslant \textbf{min}(X,Y) : \text{common\_divisor}\,(X,Y,d))$$

In this specification, a function common_divisor(X,Y,d) occurs which has yet to be defined. The range of this function is {true, false}. This means it is just a predicate. Our next concern is to make a refinement to the postcondition that defines a common divisor. For positive integers m and n to share a common divisor d the following definition will need to be satisfied:

$$\text{common\_divisor}(m,n,d) \equiv \text{divisor}(m,d) \wedge \text{divisor}(n,d)$$

All that remains to complete the gcd definition in a top-down fashion is to define the predicate divisor. This can be done using the **mod** operator, whose definition we will assume:

$$\text{divisor}(a,b) \equiv (a \textbf{ mod } b = 0)$$

The original specification of R is now fully supported by the definitions of common_divisor and divisor.

If the specifier **MAX** had not been used in the specification it would have assumed the more involved form

$$R : \text{common\_divisor}(X,Y,\gcd) \wedge \neg(\exists d : \gcd < d \leqslant \textbf{min}(X,Y) :$$
$$\text{common\_divisor}(X,Y,d))$$

Obviously for a problem as simple as the greatest common divisor it is sufficient to define the postcondition in the more direct manner:

$$R : \gcd = \textbf{MAX}(\,d : 1 \leqslant d \leqslant \textbf{min}(X,Y) : X \textbf{ mod } d = 0 \wedge Y \textbf{ mod } d = 0)$$

The approach we have used in this example, and in its bottom-up counterpart, is not too different from the axiomatic approach to constructing specifications. For more complex problems, introducing abstracted components into the specification of a postcondition by the definition of structurally significant predicates can prove a valuable tool. Such an approach adds clarity to a specification.

4.3.3   Commonly encountered postcondition types

Although there is great diversity among computing problems, many fit loosely into two broadly recognizable categories, in which

- some systematic search or examination is made of a problem space until a recognizable state or condition or set of conditions is established at which termination of the mechanism takes place;
- a systematic mechanism is applied repeatedly until some defined configuration or result is established either for data initially associated with the problem or for data that may have been generated during the course of the computation.

These two categories are obviously not mutually exclusive. More complex problems may consist of a mix of these problem categories associated with identifiable sub-problems within the main problem. It is, nevertheless, often useful when trying to formulate a postcondition to ask the question whether it fits into one of these categories. The advantage of trying to make such a loose classification is that it may provide insights not only into how postconditions may be expressed formally but also, by analogy, how the problem might subsequently be solved. In what follows we will refer to problems in the first category as inherently **search problems** while problems in the second category may be considered as **constructive problems.** Some simple problems that fit into these two broad categories will now be considered.

Search problems

Problems that fall into this category can usually be divided further into two sub-categories. In the first of these categories the *whole* of some predefined search space must be searched to establish a single solution or a set of solutions that satisfy some desired precondition/postcondition pair. A simple example of a search problem with a single solution is that of finding the maximum m in a fixed array A[1..N] of distinct integers. A postcondition for this problem is

$$R : 1 \leqslant i \leqslant N \wedge m = A_i \wedge (\forall j : 1 \leqslant j \leqslant N : m \geqslant A_j)$$

A search problem in this category with potentially more than one solution is one that involves finding the set of all pairs (x,y) of natural numbers which satisfy the relation

$$x^2 + y^2 = N \wedge x \geqslant y \geqslant 0$$

To characterize *all* pairs the postcondition may be expressed using standard set notation, that is

$$R : s = \{ (x,y) \mid 0 \leqslant y \leqslant x \wedge N = x^2 + y^2 \}$$

The structure of these last two postconditions is fairly typical of problems where the whole of a defined search space needs to be searched. Either a set must be defined or quantification is used to identify a single solution.

The other common type of search problem is that where only part of a predefined search space may need to be searched to satisfy some desired relation. The integer square root problem is a very simple example of this type. One possible postcondition for this problem is

$$R : 0 \leq a \leq N \wedge a^2 \leq N < (a + 1)^2$$

where a is the integer square root of the fixed natural number N. Another way of expressing the postcondition for this problem is

$$R : a = \textbf{MAX}(b : 0 \leq b \leq N : b^2 \leq N)$$

Another search problem where only part of the search space may need to be examined is that of deciding whether a fixed array A[1..N] of integers is in non descending order. A specification for this problem is

$$R : (\forall j : 1 < j \leq i : A_{j-1} \leq A_j) \wedge (i = N \textbf{ cor } A_i > A_{i+1})$$

If i is equal to N the array is in nondescending order, otherwise the (i + 1)th element is out of order.

Notice the similar structure of this postcondition to that for the linear search discussed earlier and shown below:

$$R : (\forall j : 0 < j \leq i : A_j \neq X) \wedge (i = N \textbf{ cor } X = A_{i+1})$$

Such search specifications consist of two components, one describing that part of the space where the relation sought does not apply, and the other component describing the conditions for terminating the search. These two problems exhibit something of the flavour of examples that require algorithms that may terminate before examining all of a predefined search space. A number of factoring problems also belong to this category (for example determining whether or not a number is prime). We will now turn our attention to problems that belong to the constructive category.

Constructive problems

There are several varieties of constructive problem. Two common types are those involving organization of data according to some predefined rule, and those involving computation upon or transformation of data according to some predefined rule. Typical examples of problems in the first constructive category are building a heap (see Chapter 9), sorting an array of data, partitioning an array of data, and constructing a minimum spanning tree. The form of the postconditions for these problems, and others like them, usually requires that some relationship which defines the data arrangement at an element level is universally quantified over an appropriate range. Sometimes it is necessary to add the qualification that the final data configuration is a permutation of the original one. As we saw earlier a sorting specification is

$$R : (\forall j : 1 \leqslant j < N : a_j \leqslant a_{j+1}) \wedge \text{perm}(a,A)$$

For building a heap the defining rule is

$$a_j \leqslant a_{2j}, a_{2j+1} \qquad \text{for subscripts within range.}$$

The corresponding postcondition for building a heap therefore takes the form

$$R : (\forall j : 1 < j \leqslant N : a_{\lfloor j/2 \rfloor} \leqslant a_j) \wedge \text{perm}(a,A)$$

where $\lfloor j/2 \rfloor$ refers to the integer formed by discarding the fractional part when j is divided by 2.

Examples of problems belonging to the second constructive category are matrix multiplication, discrete convolution, and summing an array of elements. For matrix multiplication the entity relations is

$$c_{i,j} = \Sigma \, (a_{i,k} \times b_{k,j} : 0 < k \leqslant p)$$

and the corresponding postcondition may take the form

$$R : (\forall i : 0 < i \leqslant M : (\forall j : 0 < j \leqslant N : c_{i,j} = \Sigma(a_{i,k} \times b_{k,j} : 0 < k \leqslant p \,))$$

This concludes the present discussion of postconditions.

4.3.4   Writing formal specifications

One of the most difficult steps in the process of deriving programs is often the task of writing an accurate formal specification. The process is difficult because there is no well-defined set of steps that can be applied to arrive at a formal specification. There is no doubt that with lots of practice the process becomes somewhat easier. In what follows we will consider a case study involving a class of simple related specifications in an effort to shed some light on the process.

The starting point for a specification is often

- an idea, or collection of ideas that can be expressed in a natural language;
- or a schematic diagram or sketch which captures the intent of a specification;

- or a specific collection of data or a schematic representation of a collection of data and operations on that data.

The first consideration is how to proceed from one of these or some other starting point. There are two underlying strategies that we can employ in developing a specification: either a top-down approach or a bottom-up approach, or some mixture of both. In the top-down approach we operate on the basis that we will subsequently be able to define relations employed at the current level of description. In the bottom-up approach we start by defining the basic vocabulary that will subsequently be used to create the specification. In both cases, the precision of the high and low-level vocabulary is crucial. Most people, while in the process of learning how to write specifications, usually find the bottom-up process easier to manage, although, as their skills improve, they become more confident about switching to the top-down approach.

In what follows, we will illustrate some of the things that can be tried in making progress with the writing of specifications, using the predicate calculus.

Consider the following list of related problems which we want to formally specify.

(1)   None of the elements in an array A[1..N] is multiply-occurring.

(2)   One of the elements in an array A[1..N] is multiply-occurring.

(3)   Some of the elements in the array A[1..N] are multiply-occurring.

(4)   c of the elements in the array A[1..N] are multiply-occurring.

(5)   All of the elements in the array A[1..N] are multiply-occurring.

In all of these descriptions, the definition of *multiply-occurring* is of central importance, as are the qualifications *none, one, some,* c, and *all*.

Problem 1

Starting with the first problem, it is essential to define precisely what we mean by *none*, and *multiply-occurring*.

No elements, or *none*, possessing some property can be expressed using the complementary terminology by

all do not have some property P

Whenever *all* is referred to in relation to properties, it is suggestive of a need to employ universal quantification in the formal specification. In this case we may require:

$(\forall j : \text{in the range} : \neg P_j)$

Having got this far we need to tackle the notion of multiply-occurring or in this case 'not multiply-occurring'. Our final objective is to express formally the sentence

> All elements in the array A[1..N] are *not multiply-occurring*

Rather than focus directly on *all* of the elements being not multiply-occurring, let us first try to describe formally that a single element is not multiply-occurring. To try to come to terms with this a diagram may be of some use.

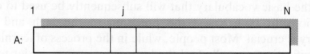

What we are interested in describing is that the jth element, A_j is not multiply-occurring. This suggests we require a relation that describes the situation where:

> the jth element is not equal to *all* the other elements in the array A[1..N]

In other words

$$A_1 \neq A_j \wedge A_2 \neq A_j \wedge \dots A_N \neq A_j$$

Using a universal quantifier we might try to express this as

$$1 \leq j \leq N \wedge (\forall k : 1 \leq k \leq N : A_j \neq A_k)$$

A careful examination of this relation reveals that it is not quite what we want because it permits the situation where $A_j \neq A_k \wedge j = k$ which is clearly false. A way around this difficulty is to introduce an implication, that is

$$1 \leq j \leq N \wedge (\forall k : 1 \leq k \leq N : j \neq k \Rightarrow A_j \neq A_k)$$

In this case when the condition $j = k$ arises because the antecedent (i.e. $j \neq k$) is false, the implication holds, and therefore the relation holds for all k in the specified range.

This most recent quantified expression corresponds to $\neg P_j$. All that remains is to ensure that the relation holds for *all* elements in the array and so we arrive at the formal specification:

$$(\forall j : 1 \leq j \leq N : (\forall k : 1 \leq k \leq N : j \neq k \Rightarrow A_j \neq A_k))$$

for the requirement that none of the elements in the array A[1..N] are multiply-occurring.

Problem 2

The next case we have to deal with is where exactly one of the elements in the array A[1..N] is multiply-occurring. Our initial response to this problem might be to provide the following formula, which indicates that an element occurs at position j and some later position.

$$1 \leqslant j \leqslant N \wedge (\exists k : j < k \leqslant N : A_j = A_k)$$

Unfortunately this specification is not strong enough to guarantee that there is only one multiply-occurring element in an array. To understand the problem let us again introduce a diagram where we have marked a group

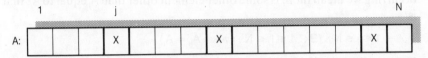

of multiply-occurring elements with an 'x'. Any such configuration should register a count of one for the element x. A way to achieve such a count is to focus on the *first* (leftmost positioned) member of the multiply-occurring group. If the first member of the group is at position j, the first j − 1 elements must not be equal to A_j, that is, the relation

$$(\forall k : 0 < k < j : A_j \neq A_k) \wedge 1 \leqslant j \leqslant N$$

must hold and there must be one or more elements equal to A_j in the range j + 1 to N. That is, the relation:

$$(\exists k : j < k \leqslant N : A_k = A_j)$$

must also hold.

These last two relations can be used with the counting specifier to obtain the required specification

$$\#(j : 0 < j \leqslant N : (\forall k : 0 < k < j : A_k \neq A_j) \wedge (\exists k : j < k \leqslant N : A_k = A_j)) = 1$$

Problem 3

Handling the case where *some* of the elements in the array A[1..N] are multiply-occurring is relatively straightforward. Our initial response to Problem 2 is sufficient for this specification, that is:

$$1 \leqslant j \leqslant N \wedge (\exists k : j < k \leqslant N : A_j = A_k)$$

Problem 4

The case where there are c multiply-occurring elements in the array is also easily handled, given the groundwork done in Problem 2. We simply replace one by c to obtain

$$c = \#(j : 0 < j \leqslant N : (\forall k : 0 < k < j : A_k \neq A_j) \wedge (\exists k : j < k \leqslant N : A_k = A_j))$$

Problem 5

Where all the elements in the array are multiply-occurring we simply have to universally quantify the multiply-occurring definition. By multiply-occurring we mean there is some other element other than A_j equal to A_j, that is:

$$1 \leqslant j \leqslant N \wedge (\exists k : 1 \leqslant k \leqslant N : j \neq k \wedge A_k = A_j)$$

Universally quantifying this expression we obtain the desired relation

$$(\forall j : 1 \leqslant j \leqslant N : (\exists k : 1 \leqslant k \leqslant N : j \neq k \wedge A_k = A_j))$$

At this point it is useful to try to summarize steps that can be taken when attempting to write a specification.

- When starting with a natural language description for which a formal specification is required, the first step is to re-phrase the description using the English equivalents of the various quantifiers and specifiers. (We used this strategy in Problem 1 when we replaced 'None have some property' by 'All do not have some property'.)

- The next step is to try to identify the various properties or predicates associated with the problem. A property or predicate normally corresponds to a statement or relation that can be either true or false (in Problem 1, 'multiply-occurring' is a property that requires formal definition).

- To formally define identified properties and predicates we try to use the various quantifiers and specifiers. These tools have been used to define multiply-occurring.

- Whenever problems arise in trying to create a complex formal specification, it is advisable to construct a diagram that captures the essence of the problem. It is then often a lot easier to use the diagram to build up the corresponding formal specification. Diagrams have been used in our examples to aid understanding of the concept of multiply-occurring.

4.4   Loop Invariants[†]

A **loop invariant,** or **invariant** as it is sometimes called, is a **secondary specification** used to model or characterize the dynamic behaviour of loops.

[†]We will use the terms 'loop invariant' and 'invariant' interchangeably throughout the text.

Important roles that a loop invariant can play in program derivation are as follows

- It should provide a concise and preferably formal description of the properties of a loop (expressed in terms of the variables associated with the loop) that are established on initialization of the loop variables, maintained with each iteration of the loop, and held to be true upon termination of the loop. *A loop invariant is therefore both a precondition and a postcondition of a loop.*
- It can be used to reason about the correctness of a loop.
- It can provide a basis for the constructive derivation of the loop body when used in conjunction with weakest precondition calculations (see Chapter 5).

Before discussing the role of the loop invariant as a specification let us try to refine our understanding of what is meant by a loop invariant. An invariant is a relationship between (or among) variables that is *not changed* even when the values of those variables are changed. It models the relationships between the variables of a loop during the lifetime of the loop. This does not imply that the values of variables can be arbitrarily changed with the expectation of still maintaining the invariant. Our original statement should be qualified by saying that an invariant is a relation between variables that is not changed when the values of those variables are changed in a constrained way. This, as a definition, although useful, is still not precise enough. Consideration of loop invariants as specifications can help to clarify the situation.

4.4.1   Loop invariants and specification

A loop invariant characterizes the initial state, the final state, and the intermediate states of a sequential iterative process. It describes properties that remain true in all these states. These characteristics give the loop invariant a role very much like the inductive hypothesis employed in mathematical induction. As with preconditions and postconditions the detailed nature of a loop invariant is dependent on the particular problem being specified. The loop invariants of most interest to us in program design are those derivable from postcondition specifications. Any detailed study of postconditions reveals that only some of them are able to yield useful loop invariants. When a postcondition does not, by transformation, yield a suitable loop invariant, we should either look for a more appropriate (usually stronger) postconditon or try to make transformations on that postcondition. Transformed postconditions are more likely to yield a suitable invariant. This discussion suggests that the relationship between the postconditon and the loop invariant is of central importance. To gain a deeper understanding of just what a loop invariant is, it is appropriate to study the loop invariants and postconditions for a sample of small problems. At this stage we will not concern ourselves in detail with how these loop invariants have been derived from the corresponding postconditions.

EXAMPLE 1

For the problem of finding the maximum m, and its position p, in a fixed array A[1...N] of integers the following precondition Q, postcondition R, loop invariant P_D, and loop may be used:

$$Q : N \geq 1$$
$$R : 1 \leq p \leq N \wedge m = A_p \wedge (\forall j : 1 \leq j \leq N : m \geq A_j)$$

The postcondition R is not directly useful for obtaining a suitable loop invariant. We therefore choose to transform it by introducing a new free variable i in place of N. We also record the identity i = N. When R is transformed in this way we get

$$R_D : 1 \leq p \leq i \wedge m = A_p \wedge (\forall j : 1 \leq j \leq i : m \geq A_j) \wedge i = N$$

The loop invariant P_D is obtained from R_D by identifying those components of R_D made true by the initialization of p, i, and m and then including the range for i, that is:

$$P_D : 1 \leq p \leq i \wedge m = A_p \wedge (\forall j : 1 \leq j \leq i : m \geq A_j) \wedge 1 \leq i \leq N$$

The basic setup is

```
'Initialize variables to establish P_D'
do i ≠ N →
    'Try to increase i to N while maintaining P_D'
od
'Terminate loop with i = N and P_D still true'
```

What the invariant P_D is able to maintain with each iteration of the loop is that

'm is the maximum of the i elements examined so far and p is the position among the first i positions where the maximum m occurs'

In other words these two properties are kept *invariant* by the loop. The initialization of the loop is

p := 1; m := A_p; i := 1

Substituting the values for p, m, and i in P_D we get

$1 \leqslant 1 \leqslant 1 \wedge A_1 = A_1 \wedge (\forall j : 1 \leqslant j \leqslant 1 : A_1 \geqslant A_j) \wedge 1 \leqslant 1 \leqslant N$

which simplifies to

TRUE $\wedge$ TRUE $\wedge A_1 \geqslant A_1$

which is true. It follows that this initialization will always establish the loop invariant. The task then is to construct a loop that makes progress towards establishing the goal R_D while maintaining P_D. The way this is done will be discussed in detail in the next two chapters. For the present we are interested in what makes P_D an invariant. The program derived using P_D is :

```
p := 1; m := A_p ; i := 1;
do i ≠ N → {P_D}
    if m ≥ A_{i+1} → i := i + 1
    [] m < A_{i+1} → p, i, m := i + 1, i + 1, A_{i+1}†
    fi
od
{P_D ∧ i = N }
```

Here, the development of the program (assumed as given) has been made based on the derived postcondition R_D which implies the original postcondition R. Therefore if the program is able to establish R_D, it will also have established R.

Spelling things out we have

After initialization (i =1)   m is equal to the first element A_1 and p is equal to 1

After one iteration (i = 2)   m is equal to the larger of A_1 and A_2 and p is the position (1, 2) of the larger of A_1 and A_2

After two iterations (i = 3)   m is equal to the largest of A_1, A_2 and A_3 and p is the position (1, 2, or 3) of the largest of A_1, A_2 and A_3

.

.

.

---

† In this example we have used guarded commands (see Chapters 3 and 5) which incorporates the idea of a multiple or concurrent assignment.

After iteration until termination (i = N)   m is equal to the largest of A_1, A_2, ..., A_N, and p is the position (1, 2,.., or N) of the largest of A_1, A_2, ..., A_N

This example shows how, by maintaining invariant properties (that is by making appropriate updates of variables in step with the iterations) from initialization through to termination, it is possible for an iterative process to establish a desired postcondition. It also makes it clear that the invariant is weaker than the postcondition. The postcondition describes just *one* of the allowable states that the invariant describes.

EXAMPLE 2

As a second example consider the problem of summing the elements in a fixed array A[1....N] of integers. We may use:

R : $s = \Sigma(A_j : 0 < j \leq N)$ (original postcondition)
R_D : $s = \Sigma(A_j : 0 < j \leq i) \wedge i = N$ (by transformation from R)
P_D : $s = \Sigma(A_j : 0 < j \leq i) \wedge 0 \leq i \leq N$ (loop invariant derived from R_D)

The program that can be derived using P_D is

```
i := 0 ; s := 0 ;
do i ≠ N → {P_D}
    i, s := i + 1, s + A_{i+1}
od
{P_D ∧ i = N }
```

Spelling things out more specifically we have:

After initialization (i = 0)   s is equal to the sum of zero array elements
        (i.e. s = 0)
After one iteration (i = 1)   s is equal to the sum of one array element
        (i.e. s = A_1)
After two iterations (i = 2)   s is equal to the sum of two array elements
        (s = $A_1 + A_2$)
.
.
.
After iteration until termination (i = N)   s is equal to the sum of N array
        elements (s = $A_1 + A_2 + ... + A_N$)

This example again shows how by maintaining invariant properties from initialization, through to termination, it is possible for an iterative process to establish a desired postcondition.

In this case, the invariant tells us that after i iterations s is the sum of the first i array elements A[1..i]. After N iterations s represents the sum of the N array elements and so the postcondition is satisfied.

Principle
The invariant should characterize the role of all variables in a loop.

4.4.2   The strength of loop invariants

Loop invariants are predicates. This means each loop invariant has a certain strength associated with it. What this strength does is provide a measure of the number of states that the loop invariant characterizes. This section investigates the properties of strength that a loop invariant must exhibit in order to accurately characterize the behaviour of a loop.

To proceed let us consider the following problem which is defined by the specification

$$Q : N \geqslant 0$$
$$R_1 : x = y + 2 \wedge y = N$$

The postcondition R_1 can be trivially established by the assignments:

$$y := N;$$
$$x := y + 2$$

Here, for the purpose of illustration, we will assume that the variables x and y can only be changed by *one* by an assignment†. With these restrictions a loop is needed to establish the postcondition. The loop invariant P_1 that can be derived from R_1 is

$$P_1: x = y + 2 \wedge 0 \leqslant y \leqslant N$$

This loop invariant contains two variables x and y which may be changed and a constant N which is fixed. The program that can be derived that will maintain P_1 and establish R_1 is:

```
x := 2; y := 0;
do y ≠ N → {P₁}
   x := x + 1;
   y := y + 1
od
{R₁}
```

† We will however let x be initialized to 2.

If we examine this loop carefully we discover that the following relation holds initially, after each iteration, and upon termination:

$$y < x$$

If this relation is combined with a restriction on the range of y we come up with another possible invariant for our loop:

$$P_2: y < x \land 0 \leqslant y \leqslant N$$

This specification P_2 indeed identifies invariant properties of our loop. There is, however, an important way in which it is lacking. To understand this it is necessary to consider a second related problem which has the specification.

$$Q : N \geqslant 0$$
$$R_3: x = 2y + 2 \land y = N$$

An invariant that can be derived from R_3 in this case is

$$P_3 : x = 2y + 2 \land 0 \leqslant y \leqslant N$$

and the loop that will maintain P_3 and establish R_3 is

```
x := 2; y := 0;
do y ≠ N → {P₃}
   x := x + 2;
   y := y + 1
od
{R₃}
```

This second loop, like the first loop, also maintains the *same* invariant P_2:

$$P_2: y < x \land 0 \leqslant y \leqslant N$$

Clearly it would be possible to write numerous other loops that could maintain the loop invariant P_2. The problem with P_2 as a loop invariant for the two problems we have just considered is that it is not strong enough to accurately characterize the relationships among the variables associated with the two loops. In contrast P_1 and P_3 both characterize stronger relationships between x and y, that is

$$P_1 \Rightarrow P_2$$

and

$$P_3 \Rightarrow P_2$$

In program design the most useful loop invariants are those that define the strongest relationships among all the variables that are changed by a loop. Loop invariants like P_1 and P_3 that retain the form of their respective postconditions preserve the strongest relationships among their variables.

In Section 4.4.5 we will take a closer look at the most desirable relationship between a loop invariant and a postcondition.

4.4.3   Loop invariants and loop structure

At this point we want to continue our efforts to characterize loop invariants by considering examples that show characteristics that a loop invariant *should not* possess, and the relationship of these to loop structure.

Loop progress

To demonstrate these characteristics we will consider the following problem defined by the specification:

$$Q : N \geqslant 0$$
$$R : a = N! \times N^N$$

Four different attempts at solving this problem will be given. The first two of these implementations have serious design flaws. The third design is satisfactory but lacks the quality of the fourth design where the postcondition and invariant have been employed to arrive at the final implementation.

For a loop to be properly formed at least one variable must change with each iteration of the loop. The example below illustrates that this condition alone is not strong enough to define a properly formed loop.

The following represents an *unsuccessful* attempt to establish R. Its development has clearly not been based on a loop invariant.

Implementation 1 (flawed design – nonterminating program)

```
i := 0; a := 1; N2 := 2 * N;
do i ≠ N2→
   if i < N → i := i + 1; a := a * i
   [] i ≥ N → a := a * i
   fi
od
{ R : a = N ! × N^N }† where N! = N × (N−1) × (N−2) × ... × 1 and 0! = 1
```

---

† In this section we have taken the licence of using the complex terms, factorial, and exponentiation, in our specification language. In general, careful consideration must be given to such practices.

This loop will not terminate because it reaches a state where i is no longer changed. At least one variable that ensures progress towards termination must be changed with each iteration of a loop. More will be said later about this issue when variant functions are discussed.

Loop inhomogeneity

In implementation 1, the variable i would need to be changed with each iteration to guarantee termination. The loop could be 'corrected' so that it terminated and established the postcondition by introducing a variable c, and adding the statement i := i + 1 to the command guarded by i ≥ N. Once again, no attempt has been made to use a loop invariant to guide the development.

Implementation 2

```
i := 0; a := 1; c := 0; N2 := 2 * N;
do i ≠ N2 →
   if i < N → i := i +1; a := a * i; c := i
   [] i ≥ N → a := a * c; i := i +1
   fi
od
{ R : a = N! × N^N }
```

The invariant for this rather 'simple' loop is surprisingly complicated. To formulate it, it is necessary to account for the roles of the variables a, c, and i, that is:

$$P : 0 \leqslant i \leqslant N2 \wedge ((0 \leqslant i \leqslant N \wedge (a = i! \wedge c = i))$$
$$\vee (N < i \leqslant N2 \wedge (a = N! \times N^{i-N} \wedge c = N))$$

Examining the specification P carefully reveals that the variables a and c are characterized in *two* ways. In other words, a *single property* or relation has not been used to characterize these variables initially and after each iteration of the loop. Loop invariants that admit property changes for any of their variables are said to be *inhomogeneous*. Inhomogeneity in a loop invariant is symptomatic of a poorly formulated loop structure. It is usually caused by trying to do more than one well-defined task requiring iteration in a single loop.

Unnecessary decomposition

The following implementation overcomes the problem of inhomogeneity by using two loops. The two loop invariants for the loops are

$$P_1 : 0 \leqslant i \leqslant N \wedge a = i!$$
$$P_2 : 0 \leqslant j \leqslant N \wedge a = N! \times N^j$$

Implementation 3 (unnecessary decomposition)

```
i := 0; a := 1;
do i ≠ N → {P₁}
    i := i + 1; a := a * i
od;
{ R₁ : a = N! }
j := 0;
do j ≠ N → {P₂}
    a := a * N; j := j + 1
od
{ R₂ : a = N! × Nᴺ}
```

Comparing implementations 2 and 3 it is apparent that 3 has two much simpler loop invariants. Also implementation 3 is more efficient and logically cleaner. It avoids the need for the variable c and the need to keep resetting it on each of the first N iterations without using it. The latter is a logically spurious step which makes implementation 2 harder to understand. Implementation 3 also avoids the need for the alternative command below in both of its loops.

```
if i < N ...
[] i ≥ N ...
```

What can be learned from this example? It shows us how the loop invariant can and should be used for designing the structure of loops. Any hint of inhomogeneity indicates a problem has not been structurally decomposed properly. In general, we should strive to work with *homogeneous* loop invariants. All variables in a homogeneous loop invariant have a single property associated with them. This property is established on initialization, and maintained throughout the lifetime of the loop.

Postcondition – invariant loop design

The structure of the loop invariant in implementation 2 is probably symptomatic of the fact that it was constructed *after* the loop had been implemented. The appropriate way to proceed is to start with the postcondition

$$R : a = N! \times N^N$$

transform this to a new postcondition R_D (where $R_D \Rightarrow R$)

$$R_D : a = i! \times N^i \wedge i = N$$

This postcondition may be used to derive the loop invariant. Finally the loop is derived from the resulting invariant and we end up with an even cleaner implementation for this problem. The loop invariant P_D that follows directly from R_D is

$P : a = i! \times N^i \wedge 0 \leqslant i \leqslant N$

An implementation that follows from this latest invariant is

Implementation 4 (derived from specification)
```
i := 0; a := 1;
do i ≠ N → {P_D}
   i := i + 1 ; a : = a * N * i
od
{ R : a = N! x N^N }
```

What this and the previous implementation suggest is that there are two ways of trying to avoid inhomogeneity in loop invariants. Either we look for a structural change or better still we always try to conform to the rule of attempting to derive loop invariants directly from postconditions.

4.4.4   Invariant ranges

To complete the present discussion of loop invariants a series of invariants and their accompanying implementations is provided for the simple array summation problem. The examples illustrate how subtle variations in postconditions and loop invariants can influence the structure of loops. We will list the variations on this problem and then compare them

Case 1
$R : s = \Sigma(A_j : 0 < j \leqslant N)$
$R_D : s = \Sigma(A_j : 0 < j \leqslant i) \wedge i = N$ (derived from R)
$P_D : s = \Sigma(A_j : 0 < j \leqslant i) \wedge 0 \leqslant i \leqslant N$ (derived from R_D)

```
i, s := 0, 0;
do i ≠ N → {P_D}
   i, s := i + 1, s + A_{i+1}
od
```

Case 2
$R : s = \Sigma(A_j : 0 < j \leqslant N)$
$R_D : s = \Sigma(A_j : i < j \leqslant N) \wedge i = 0$ (derived from R)
$P_D : s = \Sigma(A_j : i < j \leqslant N) \wedge 0 \leqslant i \leqslant N$ (derived from R_D)

```
i, s := N, 0;
do i ≠ 0 → {P_D}
   i, s := i − 1, s + A_i
od
```

Case 3

R : $s = \Sigma(A_j : 1 \leqslant j < N + 1)$
R_D : $s = \Sigma(A_j : 1 \leqslant j < i) \wedge i = N + 1$
P_D : $s = \Sigma(A_j : 1 \leqslant j < i) \wedge 1 \leqslant i \leqslant N + 1$

```
i, s := 1, 0;
do i ≠ N + 1 → {P_D}
    i, s := i + 1, s + A_i
od
```

Case 4

R : $s = \Sigma(A_j : 1 \leqslant j < N + 1)$
R_D : $s = \Sigma(A_j : i \leqslant j < N + 1) \wedge i = 1$
P_D : $s = \Sigma(A_j : i \leqslant j < N + 1) \wedge 1 \leqslant i \leqslant N + 1$

```
i, s := N + 1, 0;
do i ≠ 1 → {P_D}
    i, s := i - 1, s + A_{i-1}
od
```

Case 5 (cf. Case 1)

R : $s = \Sigma(A_j : 0 < j \leqslant N)$
R_D : $s = \Sigma(A_j : 0 < j \leqslant i) \wedge i = N$
P_D : $s = \Sigma(A_j : 0 < j \leqslant i) \wedge 0 \leqslant i \leqslant N$

```
i, s := 0, 0;
do i ≠ N → {P_D}
    i := i + 1;
    s := s + A_i
od
```

Case 6 (using an array index shift, that is A[0..N−1])

R : $s = \Sigma(A_j : 0 \leqslant j < N)$
R_D : $s = \Sigma(A_j : 0 \leqslant j < i) \wedge i = N$
P_D : $s = \Sigma(A_j : 0 \leqslant j < i) \wedge 0 \leqslant i \leqslant N$

```
i, s := 0, 0;
do i ≠ N →
    i, s := i + 1, s + A_i
od
```

Case 7 (array A[0..N−1])

$$R: \quad s = \Sigma(A_j : 0 \leqslant j < N)$$
$$R_D : s = \Sigma(A_j : i \leqslant j < N) \wedge i = 0$$
$$P_D : s = \Sigma(A_j : i \leqslant j < N) \wedge 0 \leqslant i \leqslant N$$
$$i, s := N, 0;$$
do $i \neq 0 \rightarrow i, s := i - 1, s + A_{i-1}$ **od**

Our preferred way of specifying and solving the problem of summing an array of N elements is to use the specification and implementation described in Case 1. We reject Case 3 on the grounds that the variable i in the invariant does not directly reflect the number of elements that have been summed. For example, when $i = 7$ only six of the elements have been summed. This 'lagging' in an invariant can be confusing. The specifications for Case 5 are the same as for Case 1 but the two implementations differ. The multiple assignment in Case 1 preserves the invariant whereas after the assignment $i := i + 1$ in Case 5 the invariant is destroyed then subsequently restored by the second assignment $s := s + A_i$. In Case 6, the array elements are displaced from the counting sequence 1, 2, 3, ... N. This convention of giving arrays an origin of zero is advocated by some authors, but once again it can lead to confusion. The only thing in its favour compared with Case 1 is that it avoids the need to refer to subscripts like $i + 1$. This yields a slight efficiency gain but little else. Cases 2, 4 and 7 tackle the summation from the other end. With the exception of Case 4, they introduce factors of confusion.

4.4.5   The relationship between loop invariants and postconditions

The relationship between loop invariants and postconditions is of fundamental importance in program derivation. In Chapters 5 and 6 we will discuss how invariants are derived from postconditions. To illustrate the relationship here we will use a postcondition for the exponentiation problem. To solve this problem a fixed X must be raised to a fixed power Y and the result stored in z. The specification for the problem is

$$Q: \quad X \geqslant 0 \wedge Y \geqslant 0$$
$$R: \quad z = X^Y$$
$$R_D: z = X^y \wedge y = Y \qquad \text{(obtained from R by transformation)}†$$

X and Y are fixed natural numbers. Important considerations are as follows:

- The postcondition R_D is only true when the loop terminates and $y = Y$.
- The loop invariant P_D must be true

---

† Note R_D implies R and so if we can establish it R will also be established.

- *before* the first iteration of the loop
- *after* every iteration of the loop
- and upon *termination* of the loop.

- The loop invariant P_D must be weaker than the postcondition. It should include R_D.

The loop invariant P_D derived from R_D has the form

$$P_D : z = X^y \wedge 0 \leqslant y \leqslant Y$$

It can be seen that P_D includes R_D by rewriting it in the equivalent form:

$$P_D : z = X^y \wedge (y = 0 \vee y = 1 \vee \ldots \vee y = Y)$$

This can be expanded to

$$P_D : (z = X^y \wedge y = 0) \vee (z = X^y \wedge y = 1) \vee \ldots \vee \underbrace{(z = X^y \wedge y = Y)}_{\leftarrow \quad R_D \quad \rightarrow}$$

The postcondition R_D (underlined) is just one of the disjuncts of P_D. The invariant P_D will always be true as long as one of its disjuncts is true. The stronger predicate R_D is true only when $y = Y$.

An implementation that maintains P_D and establishes R_D is

```
y := 0; z := 1;
do y ≠ Y → {P_D}
   y, z := y + 1, z * X
od
{R_D}
```

The invariant P_D is true upon initialization because the assignments $y := 0$; $z := 1$ make the first disjunct (that is, $z = X^y \wedge y = 0$) true. After the first iteration P_D is still true because the second disjunct is true. Upon termination when $y = Y$ the last disjunct of P_D (that is, $z = X^y \wedge y = Y$) is true and hence R_D is established as required.

Postcondition-Invariant Relation
The situation where the postcondition is a disjunct of the invariant provides the most desirable relationship between these two specifications.

4.5 Variant Functions

A **variant function**, or **bound function** as it is sometimes called, is a function of the natural numbers used to characterize the termination properties of a loop. Variant functions play the following important roles in program development:

- They can be used to assess the suitability of a given command or commands for making progress towards termination.
- They can be used in the construction of a formal proof to show that a given loop terminates.
- They can sometimes provide an upper bound on the number of iterations that a given loop will make before it terminates.

4.5.1   Nature of variant functions

Prior to the work of Dijkstra (1976) on constructive program development a variant function was usually assigned to a loop mechanism only *after* the development of the loop had been completed. Its main role then was in an *a posteriori* proof that the loop terminated in a finite number of iterations. A definition used in this context is as follows.

Variant function (first definition)
A variant function is an integer function t of the program variables that is monotonically decreased (by at least one) with each iteration of the loop. It is bounded below by 0.

If a function possessing these properties can be found for a loop, that loop must terminate. While this view of the variant function is useful it is not necessarily adequate to be of assistance in program development. What we require is a definition that is more directly related to specifications if it is to play a constructive role in the development of a program from those specifications. The following definition tries to make this more direct link.

Variant function (second definition)
The variant function is an integer function t of a subset of the free variables used to describe the precondition, invariant, and postcondition. It must admit at least one command (which is also a function of the same free variables) which, if executed repeatedly, would guarantee to monotonically decrease t by integer amounts while maintaining it bounded below by 0 so long as the invariant is maintained and the loop guard is true.

Every loop that always terminates possesses a variant function. Working from this latest definition construction of a variant function is one of the first steps taken in program derivation. It should be identified directly after an invariant has been derived from the postcondition. It will involve variables from the invariant. The properties that the variant function needs to possess have been identified but this does not help us much in constructing such functions. While the form of the variant function is usually heavily problem-dependent there are several basic forms that recur frequently. These will be examined.

Subtractive variants

There are three basic forms for subtractive variants. Given two expressions e1 and e2, and the following conventions:

e ↑	denotes an expression whose value is repeatedly increased by a loop
e ↓	denotes an expression whose value is repeatedly decreased by a loop
e	denotes a fixed expression whose value is not changed by execution of a loop

The three basic forms are:

$$e1 - e2 \uparrow \dots (S1) \quad \text{where e1 is fixed}$$
$$e1 \downarrow - e2 \dots (S2) \quad \text{where e2 is fixed}$$
$$e1 \downarrow - e2 \uparrow \dots (S3)$$

In each case the invariant relation $e2 \leq e1$ is maintained throughout the execution of the loop. Some examples that exhibit these basic forms of variant are as follows:

EXAMPLE 1 (S1) ────────────────────────────────

Consider the problem of summing an array A[1..N] of N integers. We have as a variant function

$$t : N - i$$

The accompanying, postcondition, invariant, and implementation are

$$R_D : s = \Sigma(A_j : 0 < j \leq i) \wedge i = N$$

$$P_D : s = \Sigma(A_j : 0 < j \leq i) \wedge 0 \leq i \leq N$$

```
i := 0; s := 0;
do i ≠ N →
    s := s + A_{i+1};
    i := i + 1
od
```

In this example the variant function follows directly from the condition $i = N$ in R_D. In general this condition can be established only by increasing i to N while maintaining P_D. When the loop terminates i is equal to N and $N - i$ is zero.

EXAMPLE 2 (S2)

Another way of summing an array of $A[1..N]$ integers is to start summing from the end of the array. In this case we have

$$R_D : s = \Sigma(A_j : i \le j < N + 1) \wedge i = 1$$

$$P_D : s = \Sigma(A_j : i \le j < N + 1) \wedge 1 \le i \le N + 1$$

An appropriate variant function in this case is:

$$t : i - 1$$

and the accompanying implementation is

```
i := N + 1; s := 0;
do i ≠ 1 → { P_D }
  s := s + A_{i-1};
  i := i - 1
od
{ R_D }
```

Again, in this example, the variant function follows directly from the condition $i = 1$ in R_D. In this case $i = 1$ can only be established by decreasing i to one while maintaining P_D.

EXAMPLE 3 (S3)

It is possible to construct an S3-variant for the array-sum problem by splitting the range over which the sum is taken.

$$R_D : s = \Sigma(A_k : 0 < k \le i) + \Sigma(A_k : j \le k < N + 1) \wedge i = j - 1$$
$$P_D : s = \Sigma(A_k : 0 < k \le i) + \Sigma(A_k : j \le k < N + 1) \wedge 0 \le i < j \le N + 1$$

The S3-variant in this case is

$$t : j - i - 1$$

and the corresponding implementation is

```
if even(N) → s := 0; i := 0; j := N + 1
[] ¬even(N) → s := A_1; i := 1; j := N + 1
fi;
do i ≠ j - 1 →
  s := s + A_{i+1} + A_{j-1};
  i := i + 1; j := j - 1
od
```

The condition $i = j - 1$ is again used directly to obtain the variant function. We could have used just $j - 1$ as a variant function. However we prefer, where possible, for such functions to have a value of zero when the loop terminates.

EXAMPLE 4 (S3)

The well-known binary search problem also has an S3-variant. The relevant specifications are as follows. Given an ordered array $A[1..N]$, and a fixed search value X, we have

$$Q : (\forall k : 1 \leqslant k < N : A_k \leqslant A_{k+1})$$

$$R_D : A[1..i] < X \wedge A[j..N] \geqslant X \wedge i = j - 1\dagger$$

$$P_D : A[1..i] < X \wedge A[j..N] \geqslant X \wedge 0 \leqslant i < j \leqslant N + 1$$

$$t : j - i - 1$$

```
i := 0; j := N + 1;
do i ≠ j − 1 → {P_D}
  m := (i + j) div 2 ;
  if A_m < X → i := m
  [] A_m ≥ X → j := m
  fi
od
{R_D}
```

EXAMPLE 5 (S3)

Another problem with an S3–variant is the partitioning problem. Detailed specifications are

$$R_D : a[1..i] \leqslant X \wedge a[j..N] \geqslant X \wedge i = j - 1 \wedge \text{perm}(a, A)$$

$$P_D : a[1..i] \leqslant X \wedge a[j..N] \geqslant X \wedge 0 \leqslant i < j \leqslant N + 1 \wedge \text{perm}(a, A)$$

$$t : j - i - 1;$$

```
i := 0; j := N + 1;
do i ≠ j − 1 → {P_D}
  if a_{i+1} ≤ X → i := i + 1
  [] a_{j−1} ≥ X → j := j − 1
  [] a_{i+1} > X ∧ a_{j-1} < X → swap(a_{i+1}, a_{j-1}); i := i + 1; j := j − 1
  fi
od
{R_D}
```

---

†In this section we have used a shorthand notation for specifying array relations. A detailed discussion of such conventions is given by Reynolds (1981). Here we have
$$A[1..i] < X \equiv (\forall j : 0 < j \leqslant i : A_j < X)$$
From time to time we will use these shorthand conventions for array specifications.

Notice in Examples 4 and 5 that it is sufficient with each iteration for either i to increase or j to decrease or for both to change.

Additive variants

Additive variants are less common. There are two basic forms for the additive variants. Adopting the same conventions as previously they are

$$e1 \downarrow + e2 \ldots (A1) \quad \text{(where e2 is fixed)}$$

$$e1 \downarrow + e2 \downarrow + \ldots \ldots (A2)$$

In the case of A1, the invariant relation $e1 + e2 \geq 0$ is maintained throughout the lifetime of execution of the loop. A similar relation holds for the more general variant A2. Some examples that exhibit these basic forms of variant are as follows.

EXAMPLE 6 (A1)

The quotient–remainder problem provides a very simple example of an A1-variant. The detailed specifications are

$$Q \; : X \geq 0 \land D > 0$$

$$R_D : X = q \times D + r \land 0 \leq r \land r < D \land 0 \leq q \leq X$$

$$P_D : X = q \times D + r \land 0 \leq r \land 0 \leq q \leq X$$

The associated A1-variant is

$$t : r$$

and the accompanying implementation is

```
r := X ; q := 0 ;
do r ≥ D → {P_D}
  r := r − D ;
  q := q + 1
od
{R_D}
```

With each iteration of the loop r is decreased. However, the loop keeps the relation $r \geq 0$ invariant.

EXAMPLE 7 (A2)_____

The greatest common divisor solution below exhibits an A2-invariant. The specifications are

$$R_D : x = y \wedge y = gcd\ (x,y) \wedge gcd(x,y) = gcd\ (X,Y)$$

$$P_D : gcd(x,y) = gcd(X,Y) \wedge 1 \leqslant x \leqslant \textbf{min}(X,Y) \wedge 1 \leqslant y \leqslant \textbf{min}(X,Y)$$

and the A2-variant is

$$t : x + y$$

The accompanying implementation has the form

```
do x > y → x := x − y
[] y > x → y := y − x
od
```

4.5.2   Deriving variant functions

There is no universal procedure for deriving a variant function from a specification. Fortunately, there is a relatively straightforward method that will in many cases yield appropriate variant functions from specifications. The process used to derive a variant function is not unlike that employed to derive a loop invariant from a postcondition. To obtain a loop invariant from a postcondition we take a specification that is true upon termination of a loop and weaken it to obtain a specification that is true upon initialization, after each iteration, and upon termination of the loop (see Section 4.4.5). Similarly to derive a variant function we start with the **termination condition**. The termination condition is that part of the postcondition not guaranteed to be made true by an initialization of free variables that will establish the postcondition. In other words it corresponds to the negation of the guard for a loop. For example in the specification

$$(\forall j : 1 < j \leqslant i : a_{j-1} \leqslant a_j) \wedge perm(a,A) \wedge i = N$$

the condition i=N is the termination (or equivalence) condition (see Chapter 5).

The first step in deriving a variant function is to rewrite the termination condition so that it forms a relation that is equal to (or greater than) zero. For the termination condition i=N we have:

Termination Condition:	i=N
Grounded Termination Condition:	N−i = 0

The next step is to weaken the grounded termination condition which is true upon termination to form a new relation that is greater than or equal to zero upon initialization, after each iteration, and upon termination, that is

Variant Condition: $N - i \geqslant 0$

The variant function may be obtained directly from the variant condition. In this case we have

Variant Function: $t : N - i$

As a second example given the postcondition

$R : a[1 .. i] \leqslant x \wedge a[j .. N] \geqslant x \wedge perm(a,A) \wedge i = j - 1$

we have

Termination Condition: $i = j - 1$
Grounded Termination Condition: $j - 1 - i = 0$
Variant Condition: $j - 1 - i \geqslant 0$
Variant Function t: $j - 1 - i$

SUMMARY

- Specifications serve a number of important functions in program design. They are used to define a problem precisely, and to identify the limitations of a program. However, probably the most important role that specifications play is that of providing a constructive framework for the development of programs and their proofs of correctness.

- Specifications also serve a documenting role by identifying certain critical states or sub-goals of a program.

- The primary program specifications are the precondition, and the postcondition. The other important program specifications are invariants, and variant functions.

- A precondition identifies and makes explicit constraints that must be satisfied by the input data if it is to be used correctly by the program. Put another way, the precondition is a predicate which characterizes the set of initial states for which a problem must be solved.

- Preconditions characterize such things as problem size, bounds for variables and properties and assumptions about input data.

- A postcondition provides a formal statement of what a program is required to accomplish. It also provides the primary basis for the constructive development of a program and its proof of correctness.

- In formulating postconditions it is desirable to construct specifications for a problem that are as general as possible. At the same time programs should always be developed for the strongest specification of a problem. In other words a postcondition should be as tightly constrained as possible.

- Important postcondition forms are those that characterize either systematic searches or systematic organization of data.

- A loop invariant is a secondary specification that is used to model the dynamic behaviour of loops.

- With reference to variables, an invariant is a relationship among variables that is not changed even when the values of those variables are changed in a constrained way. A loop invariant should characterize the role of all variables in a loop.

- A loop invariant is a precondition, incondition and postcondition of a loop. In other words a loop invariant should be true upon initialization of the loop variables, and true after each iteration of the loop, and also true upon termination of the loop.

- A loop invariant can be used to reason about the correctness of a loop and whether the loop terminates.

- A loop invariant can also provide the basis for the constructive derivation of the associated loop body when weakest precondition calculations are employed.

- The most useful loop invariants are those derived directly from postconditions.

- Variant functions are used to characterize the termination properties of loops.

- A variant function is an integer function of the program variables that is monotonically decreased by at least one with each iteration of a loop.

- All loops that terminate have an associated variant function.

■ *EXERCISE 4.1 Interpretation of specifications*

It is at least as important to be able to read and interpret specifications as it is to be able to write them. Before attempting to write specifications of any complexity it is necessary to gain considerable experience in reading such specifications. The following problems are designed to give experience in reading and understanding specifications.

All the problems refer to the following array data set A[1..N], where N = 9:

6	1	2	3	−1	9	5	−7	−2

1. For the given data set, what value of p satisfies

    $p = \text{MAX} \, (i : 1 \leqslant i \leqslant N : A_i > 0)$

2. For the given data set, what value of p satisfies

    $p = \text{MIN} \, (i : 1 \leqslant i \leqslant N : A_i < 0)$

3. For the given data set, what value of p satisfies

    $p = \text{MIN} \, (i : 1 \leqslant i \leqslant N : A_i > 0)$

4. For the given data set, what value of p satisfies

    $p = \text{MAX} \, (i : 1 \leqslant i \leqslant N : A_i < 0)$

5. For the given data set, what value of p satisfies

    $p = \text{MAX} \, (i : 1 \leqslant i \leqslant N : (\forall j : 0 < j \leqslant i : A_j > 0))$

6. For the given data set, what value of p satisfies

    $1 \leqslant p \leqslant N \wedge (\forall j : 0 < j \leqslant N : A_j \geqslant A_p)$

7. For the given data set, what value of p satisfies

    $1 \leqslant p \leqslant N \wedge (\forall j : 1 \leqslant j \leqslant N : A_p \geqslant A_j)$

8. For the given data set, what is the largest value of m which satisfies

    $(\forall j : 1 \leqslant j \leqslant N : m \leqslant A_j)$

9. For the given data set provide a second array a which satisfies

    $(\forall j : 1 \leqslant j \leqslant N : a_j = A_{N-j+1})$

10. For the given data set provide a value p and array values b[1..p] which satisfy the relation

    $0 \leqslant p \leqslant N \wedge (\forall j \in [1..N]) \, (A_j > 0 \Rightarrow (\exists k : 0 < k \leqslant p : b_k = A_j))$

11. For the given data set supply values of c which satisfy

    (a) $c = \#(j : 1 \leqslant j \leqslant N : A_j \leqslant 0)$
    (b) $c = \#(j : 1 \leqslant j \leqslant N : A_j < 0)$
    (c) $c = \#(j : 1 \leqslant j \leqslant N : A_j > 0)$
    (d) $c = \#(j : 1 \leqslant j \leqslant N : A_j \geqslant 0)$
    (e) $c = \#(j : 1 \leqslant j < N : A_j \leqslant A_{j+1})$

12. What is wrong with the relation

    $1 \leqslant p \leqslant N \wedge (\forall j : 1 \leqslant j \leqslant N : A_p \neq A_j)$

13. For the given data set provide values for the array b[1..N] whose elements satisfy the relation

    $(\forall j : 1 \leqslant j \leqslant N : b_j = \Sigma(A_k : 1 \leqslant k \leqslant j))$

14. Provide a sample data set that satisfies the relation†

    $(\forall j : 1 \leqslant j < N : A_j = A_{j+1})$

    for a chosen value of N.

† Problems 14, 15 and 16 do not refer to the original data set.

15. · Provide a sample data set that satisfies the relation

$$(\forall j : 1 \leq j \leq N : (\forall k : j < k \leq N : A_j \neq A_k))$$

16. Provide a sample array data set and values for A and N which satisfy the relation

$$(\forall j : 1 \leq j < N : A_j \geq A_{j+1})$$

■ **EXERCISE 4.2   Positional specifications**

It is often necessary to identify the position in a sequence where some condition holds. This position may be the first such position, the last such position, or a position that satisfies some other condition. In describing such specifications it is often convenient to use the **MIN** and **MAX** specifiers, although in some instances other means are the most practical. The following problems are typical of those involving position specifiers.

1. Write a specification that identifies the position of the *first* occurrence of an element equal to X in an array A[1..N], using

   (a) the **MIN** specifier
   (b) the **MAX** specifier
   (c) only the universal quantifier.

2. Write a specification that identifies the first occurrence of an element equal to X in an array A[1..N] if such an element is present (an implication may be used).

3. Write a specification that identifies the position of the *last* occurrence of an element equal to X in an array A[1..N] using

   (a) the **MIN** specifier
   (b) the **MAX** specifier
   (c) only the universal quantifier.

4. Given that an array A[1..N] is in nondescending order, and that some of its elements may be multiply-occurring write a specification that:

   (a) identifies the position of the first element equal to X
   (b) identifies the position of the last element equal to X.

5. Given an array A[1..N] write a specification that identifies the position of

   (a) the first element that is greater than zero
   (b) the last element that is greater than zero
   (c) an arbitrary element that is greater than zero.

6. Given an array A[1..N] write a specification that identifies the position of

   (a) the first occurrence of the minimum element in the array
   (b) the last occurrence of the minimum element in the array
   (c) an arbitrary occurrence of the minimum element in the array.

■ **EXERCISE 4.3   Search specifications**

In formulating appropriate specifications for search problems it is usually necessary to consider whether the search may be successful or unsuccessful. Furthermore, to provide specifications suitable for program derivation it is necessary to characterize where the search condition *does not* apply as well as where it *does* apply when the search terminates. This corresponds to providing a stronger specification. In general we should strive to write the strongest specification for a problem. This should be the most precise specification. The following problems are typical search problems.

Examples

(a) The following specification indicates that all the elements in the array A[1..N] are not equal to X

$$(\forall j : 0 < j \leqslant N : X \neq A_j)$$

It may be read as 'For all j in the range one to N, X is not equal to the jth array element A_j'.

(b) The following specification indicates that all elements in the array A[1..N] are sorted in nondescending order

$$(\forall j : 1 \leqslant j < N : A_j \leqslant A_{j+1})$$

It may be read as 'For all j in the range 1 to N−1, the element A_j is less than or equal to the element A_{j+1}.

Problems

1. (a) Write a predicate that describes the situation where the first i elements in the array A[1..N] are not equal to X and the (i+1)th element is equal to X.

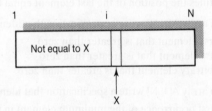

(b) Modify the answer to 1(a) so that it allows for the *possibility* (but not certainty) that none of the elements in the array may be equal to X.

2. (a) Write a predicate that describes the situation where the first i elements in the array A[1..N] are in nondescending (⩽) order and the (i + 1)th element is out of order (this problem represents a search for the first element that is 'out-of-order').

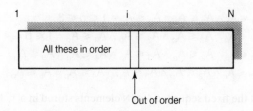

Out of order

(b) Modify the answer in 2(a) so that it allows for the possibility (but not certainty) that all the elements in the array A[1..N] are in nondescending (≤) order.

3. Write a specification for a program that must determine whether or not X is the maximum value in the array A[1..N].

4. (a) Write a predicate that describes the situation where the first i elements in the array A[1..N] are equal to X and the (i + 1)th element is not equal to X.

(b) Modify the answer in 4(a) so that it allows for the possibility (but not certainty) that all the elements in the array A[1..N] are equal (this corresponds to a search for an element that is not equal to its predecessor).

5. (a) Write a specification that describes the situation where the first i elements in the array A[1..N] match the first i elements in the array B[1..N], i.e. A[1] = B[1], A[2] = B[2], ... Note that A[i+1] is not equal to B[i+1].

(b) Modify the specification in 5(a) so that it allows for the possibility that all the elements in the two arrays match.

(c) Modify the specification in 5(b) to account for the fact that the array A is of length M and the array B is of length N.

6. (a) Write a specification that indicates that X does not occur in the first i rows of a two-dimensional array A[1..M, 1..N].

(b) Modify the specification in 6(a) so that it will allow for the possibility that X occurs in the (i + 1)th row of the array.

■ *EXERCISE 4.4   Interpreting loop invariants*

The following problems give experience in initializing and interpreting loop invariants.

1. Given the array A[1..N]

10	4	11	8	14	6

What value would p need to assume to maintain each of the following relations?

(a) $A_1 \leq A_p \wedge 1 \leq p \leq 1$

(b) $A_1 \leq A_p \wedge A_2 \leq A_p \wedge 1 \leq p \leq 2$

(c) $A_1 \leqslant A_p \wedge A_2 \leqslant A_p \wedge A_3 \leqslant A_p \wedge 1 \leqslant p \leqslant 3$

(d) $A_1 \leqslant A_p \wedge A_2 \leqslant A_p \wedge A_3 \leqslant A_p \wedge A_4 \leqslant A_p \wedge 1 \leqslant p \leqslant 4$

(e) $A_1 \leqslant A_p \wedge A_2 \leqslant A_p \wedge A_3 \leqslant A_p \wedge A_4 \leqslant A_p \wedge A_5 \leqslant A_p \wedge 1 \leqslant p \leqslant 5$

(f) $A_1 \leqslant A_p \wedge A_2 \leqslant A_p \wedge A_3 \leqslant A_p \wedge A_4 \leqslant A_p \wedge A_5 \leqslant A_p \wedge A_6 \leqslant A_p \wedge 1 \leqslant p \leqslant 6$

2.   Given the fixed sequence A of N elements stored in a[1..N] and the invariant P

a:	10	5	6	12	16	14	23	15

P: $(\forall p : 0 < p \leqslant i : a_p \leqslant x) \wedge (\forall q : j \leqslant q < N+1 : a_q \geqslant x) \wedge \text{perm}(a,A)$

(a) If x is equal to 11 what is the smallest value i could be given and the largest value j could be given that would establish P?

(b) If x is equal to 11 what is the maximum value that i could be given that would maintain P?

(c) If x is equal to 11 what is the minimum value j could be given that would maintain P?

(d) If x is equal to 15 what is the smallest value given to i and the largest value given to j that would establish P?

(e) If x is equal to 15 what is the minimum value that could be given to j that would maintain P?

(f) If x is equal to 15 what is the maximum value that could be given to i that would maintain P?

(g) For x = 9, given i was initially zero, what is the maximum value i could be increased to while maintaining P without changing a[1..N]?

(h) For x = 9, given j was initially N + 1, what is the minimum value j could be decreased to while maintaining P without changing a[1..N]?

3.   Given the array a[1..N] and the invariant P

a:	10	14	27	31	29	33	36	40

P: $(\forall j : 1 \leqslant j < i : a_j \leqslant a_{j+1}) \wedge 1 \leqslant i \leqslant N$

(a) What is the smallest value that could be given to i that would establish P?

(b) Given the initialization in (a), what is the maximum value i can be increased to while maintaining P?

4.   Given the array A[1..N] and the invariant P

A:	10	5	6	12	16	14	23	15

P: $1 \leqslant p \leqslant i \wedge (\forall j : 1 \leqslant j \leqslant i : A_j \geqslant A_p) \wedge 1 \leqslant i \leqslant N$

what value would p need to assume in order to maintain P for

(a)	$i = 1$	(e)	$i = 5$
(b)	$i = 2$	(f)	$i = 6$
(c)	$i = 3$	(g)	$i = 7$
(d)	$i = 4$	(h)	$i = 8$

5. Given the invariant P and that $N = 23$

$$P: a^2 \leqslant N < b^2 \wedge 0 \leqslant a \leqslant N \wedge a+1 \leqslant b \leqslant N+1$$

(a) What is the smallest value of a that will help establish the invariant P?

(b) What is the largest value of b that will help establish P?

(c) Given the initial value of a in (a), what is the maximum value that a can be increased to while still maintaining P?

(d) What is the minimum value b can be decreased to that will maintain P?

6. Given the invariant P

$$P: a^2 < N \leqslant b^2 \wedge 0 \leqslant a < N$$

(a) What is the smallest value N could have if a is always initialized within its range?

(b) If N is 25 what is the largest value of a that will satisfy the invariant P?

(c) Suggest an appropriate initialization for b that will establish P.

7. Given the invariant

$$P: (\forall j : 0 < j \leqslant i : A_j \neq X) \wedge (n=N \textbf{ cor } X=A_{i+1}) \wedge 0 \leqslant i \leqslant n \leqslant N$$

and the array $A[1..N]$ and $X = 16$

A:	10	15	7	42	16	53	18

(a) What is the smallest value that i can be given and the largest value n can be given that will establish the invariant P?

(b) What is the maximum value i can be increased to while maintaining P?

8. Given the invariant P below and the array given in Problem 7

$$P: (\forall j : 1 \leqslant j < i : A_j \neq X) \wedge (n=N \textbf{ cor } X=A_i) \wedge 1 \leqslant i \leqslant n \leqslant N$$

(a) What is the smallest value that i can be given and the largest value n can be given that will establish P?

(b) What is the maximum value i can be increased to while maintaining P given $X=42$?

9. It is claimed that the following loop maintains the invariant P_D

```
r, q := X, 0;
do r ⩾ D → {P_D}
    r, q := r - D, q + 1
od
P_D : X = q × D + r ∧ 0 ⩽ r
```

Establish whether or not this is true by completing the following execution table which records values of variables initially and after each iteration of the loop together with the loop invariant. Assume X is 28 and D is 5.

D	X	r	q	$X = q \times D + r$
5	28	28	0	$28 = 0 \times 5 + 28$

10.   It is claimed that the following loop maintains the invariant P_D

$$f, i := 1, N;$$
$$\textbf{do } i \neq 0 \rightarrow \{P_D\}$$
$$f, i := f * i, i - 1$$
$$\textbf{od}$$
$$P_D : f \times i! = N! \wedge 0 \leqslant i \leqslant N$$

Establish whether or not this is true by completing the following execution table. Assume N = 5.

N	i	f	$f \times i! \wedge 0 \leqslant i \leqslant N$
5	5	1	$1 \times 5! = 5! \wedge 0 \leqslant 5 \leqslant 5$

■ *EXERCISE 4.5   Interpreting loop invariants*

1.   Given the following loop invariant P_D, the implementation below

$$P_D : s = \Sigma(A_j : 0 < j \leqslant i) \wedge 0 \leqslant i \leqslant N$$
$$i, s := 0, 0;$$
$$\textbf{do } i \neq N \rightarrow \{P_D\}$$
$$i, s := i + 1, s + A_{i+1}$$
$$\textbf{od}$$

and the array A[1..N]

10	5	12	9	2	14	8	6

write down the values of s and i that maintain P_D after

(a) initialization of the loop
(b) one iteration of the loop
(c) two iterations of the loop
(d) three iterations of the loop
(e) N iterations of the loop.

What is a suitable postcondition of this loop?

2.   Given the following loop invariant P_D, the same array A[1..N] as in Problem 1 and the implementation

$P_D : s = \Sigma(A_j : 1 \leqslant j \leqslant i) \wedge 1 \leqslant i \leqslant N$

$i, s := 1, A_1;$

do $i \neq N \rightarrow \{P_D\}$

$\quad i, s := i + 1, s + A_{i+1}$

od

write down the values of s and i that maintain P_D after

(a) initialization of the loop

(b) one iteration of the loop

(c) two iterations of the loop

(d) three iterations of the loop

(e) N − 1 iterations of the loop.

What is a suitable postcondition of this loop?

3.   Given the following loop invariant P_D, the implementation

$P_D : s = \Sigma(A_j : i < j \leqslant N) \wedge 0 \leqslant i \leqslant N$

$i, s := N, 0;$

do $i \neq 0 \rightarrow \{P_D\}$

$\quad i, s := i - 1, s + A_i$

od

and the same data set as in Problem 1, write down values of s and i that maintain P_D after

(a) initialization of the loop

(b) one iteration of the loop

(c) two iterations of the loop

(d) three iterations of the loop

(e) N iterations of the loop.

What is a suitable postcondition of this loop?

4.   Given the following loop invariant P_D, the array A[1 ..N] in Problem 1, and the implementation below:

$P_D : 1 \leqslant p \leqslant i \wedge m = A_p \wedge (\forall j : 1 \leqslant j \leqslant i : m \geqslant A_j) \wedge 1 \leqslant i \leqslant N$

$i, p, m := 1, 1, A_1;$

do $i \neq N \rightarrow \{P_D\}$

$\quad$ **if** $A_{i+1} > m \rightarrow i, p, m := i + 1, i + 1, A_{i+1}$

$\quad [] \ A_{i+1} \leqslant m \rightarrow i := i + 1$

$\quad$ **fi**

od

write down the values of i, p and m that maintain P_D after

(a) initialization of the loop

(b) one iteration of the loop

(c) two iterations of the loop

(d) three iterations of the loop

(e) N − 1 iterations of the loop.

What is a suitable postcondition of this loop?

5.   Given the array A[1..N] in Problem 1, the following loop invariant P_D,

$$P_D : c = \#(j : 0 < j \leqslant i : A_j > X) \wedge 0 \leqslant i \leqslant N$$

and that $X = 9$, write down values of c, and i that maintain P_D as i is initialized then increased. Consider the cases where

(a) i = 0   (d) i = 3   (g) i = 6
(b) i = 1   (e) i = 4   (h) i = 7
(c) i = 2   (f) i = 5   (i) i = 8

6.   Given the array A[1..N] in Problem 1 and the following loop invariant P_D,

$$P_D : c = \#(j : 1 \leqslant j < i : A_j \leqslant A_{j+1}) \wedge 1 \leqslant i \leqslant N$$

write down values of c and i that maintain P_D as i is initialized then increased. Consider the cases where

(a) i = 1   (e) i = 5
(b) i = 2   (f) i = 6
(c) i = 3   (g) i = 7
(d) i = 4   (h) i = 8

■ **EXERCISE 4.6   *Interpretation of array properties***

1.   Given the two arrays A[1..M] and B[1..N]

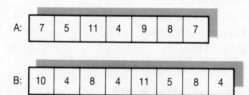

and that k = 2, which element in A ensures that the following relation holds?

$$(\exists j : 1 \leqslant j \leqslant M : k = \#(i : 1 \leqslant i \leqslant N : A_j = B_i))$$

2.   Given the two arrays

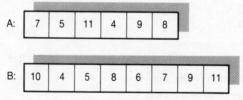

which values of the array B ensure that the following relation holds?

$$(\forall j : 1 \leqslant j \leqslant M : (\exists k : 1 \leqslant k \leqslant N : A_j = B_k))$$

3.   Given the two arrays A[1..M] and B[1..N]

A:	7	5	11	4	9	8

B:	10	6	3	22	13	5	12

which of the values in the array A ensure that the following relation holds?

$(\exists j : 1 \leqslant j \leqslant M : (\exists k : 1 \leqslant k \leqslant N : A_j = B_k))$

4.   Given the arrays A[1..M] and B[1..N]

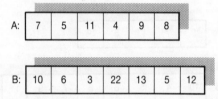

(a) does the relation below hold?
(b) indicate which value or values in the array ensure the result in (a);
(c) what value could A[2] be changed to that would make the relation hold?
(d) what value could A[2] be changed to so that the relation would not hold?

$(\forall j : 1 \leqslant j \leqslant M : (\forall k : 1 \leqslant k \leqslant N : A_j \neq B_k))$

5.   Given the two arrays A[1..M] and B[1..N]

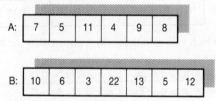

(a) which of the following relations hold?

$(\exists j : 1 \leqslant j \leqslant M : (\forall k : 1 \leqslant k \leqslant N : A_j < B_k))$
$(\exists j : 1 \leqslant j \leqslant N : (\forall k : 1 \leqslant k \leqslant M : B_j < A_k))$

(b) for the relation identified as true in (a) which corresponding array element ensures the truth of the relation?

6.   Given the array A[1..M]

A:	10	4	8	4	11	5	8	4

(a) which values in the array ensure that the following relation holds?

(b) Suggest a change or changes to the array A which would make the following relation false

$$(\exists j : 1 \leqslant j \leqslant M : (\forall k : 1 \leqslant k \leqslant M : j \neq k \Rightarrow A_j \neq A_k))$$

7.   Given the array A[1..M]

A:

7	5	11	4	9	8

(a) which values in the array ensure that the following relation holds?

(b) suggest a change to A[4] that would make the following relation false:

$$(\forall j : 1 \leqslant j \leqslant M : (\forall k : 1 \leqslant k \leqslant M : j \neq k \Rightarrow A_j \neq A_k))$$

8.   Given the two arrays A[1..M] and B[1..N]

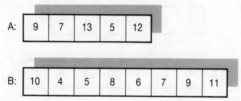

A:

9	7	13	5	12

B:

10	4	5	8	6	7	9	11

which values in the array B ensure that p = 3 for the following relation?

$$p = \#(j : 1 \leqslant j \leqslant M : (\exists k : 1 \leqslant k \leqslant N : A_j = B_k))$$

9.   Given the two arrays A[1..M] and B[1..N]

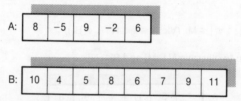

A:

8	−5	9	−2	6

B:

10	4	5	8	6	7	9	11

in each case which values in the array A ensure that the following relations hold?

(a) $(\forall j : 1 \leqslant j \leqslant M : A_j > 0 \Rightarrow (\exists k : 1 \leqslant k \leqslant N : A_j = B_k))$

(b) $(\exists j : 1 \leqslant j \leqslant M : A_j > 0 \wedge (\exists k : 1 \leqslant k \leqslant N : A_j = B_k))$

10.   Given the array A[1..N]

A:

1	7	4	3	8	2	5	6

give a value of i that satisfies the following relation:

$$0 \leqslant i \leqslant N \wedge \#(j : 0 < j \leqslant i : A_j > i) = \#(j : i < j \leqslant N : A_j < i)$$

Give an explanation for your answer.

■ EXERCISE 4.7   Completing formal specifications

For each of the following problems fill in the missing parts of the formal specifications provided.

1.   X occurs p times in the array A[1..N].

   $p = \#(j : \underline{\quad} : X = \underline{\quad})$

2.   X occurs p times in the first k positions in the array A[1..N].

   $1 \leqslant k \leqslant N \wedge p = \#(j : 0 < \underline{\quad} : X = \underline{\quad})$

3.   The array A[1..N] contains at least p zeros.

   $\#(j : \underline{\quad} : \underline{\quad} = 0) \geqslant p$

4.   The first k elements in the array A[1..N] are all less than X.

   $0 \leqslant k \leqslant N \wedge (\forall j : 0 < j \leqslant k : \underline{\quad} > \underline{\quad})$

5.   The element in position k is less than or equal to all elements located at positions greater than k in the array A[1..N].

   $1 \leqslant k \leqslant N \wedge (\forall j : k \underline{\quad} : \underline{\quad} \leqslant \underline{\quad})$

6.   All the elements in the array A[1..N] occur at least h times.

   $(\forall j : \underline{\quad} : \#(k : \underline{\quad} : \underline{\quad} = A_k) \geqslant \underline{\quad})$

7.   All the elements in the array B[1..M] are greater than z.

   $(\forall j : \underline{\quad} M : \underline{\quad} < \underline{\quad})$

8.   The last k elements in the array A[1..N] are in nondescending order.

   $(\forall j : \underline{\quad} < j < N : \underline{\quad} \leqslant A_{j+1})$

9.   The first c elements in the array A[1..N] are positive and c is the maximum value for which this condition holds.

   $c = \textbf{MAX}(j : \underline{\quad} : (\forall k : \underline{\quad} : \underline{\quad} \geqslant 0))$

10.   The minimum in the array B[1..N] which occurs at position p is unique.

   $1 \leqslant p \leqslant N \wedge (\forall k : 1 \leqslant k \leqslant N : p \neq \underline{\quad} \Rightarrow \underline{\quad} < B_k)$

11.   c is a count of the number of elements in the array A[1..N] that occur more than once.

   $c = \#(j : \underline{\quad} : (\exists k : 1 \leqslant k \leqslant N : j \neq k \wedge \underline{\quad} = A_k))$

12.   p is the position of the last occurrence of the minimum in the array A[1..N].

   $p = \textbf{MAX}(k : \underline{\quad} : (\forall j : \underline{\quad} : A_k \leqslant \underline{\quad}))$

13.   The minimum in the array A[1..N] occurs c times.

   $c = \#(k : \underline{\quad} : (\forall j : \underline{\quad} < \underline{\quad} \leqslant N : \underline{\quad} \leqslant A_j))$

14.   Each of the elements in the array B[1..N] is present in the array A[1..M].

   $(\forall j : \underline{\quad} : (\exists k : \underline{\quad} : A_k = \underline{\quad})$

15.   One or more of the elements in the array A[1..M] is not present in the array B[1..N].

   $(\exists j : \underline{\quad} : (\forall k : \underline{\quad} N : \underline{\quad} \neq B_k))$

16.   One or more elements in the array B[1..N] is greater than or equal to the rest.

$$(\exists k : \underline{\quad} : (\forall j : 1 \leqslant j \leqslant N : \underline{\quad} \geqslant B_j))$$

■ **EXERCISE 4.8   Specification using quantifiers I**

Write formal specifications for the following problems.

1.   X occurs the same number of times in an array A[1..N] as in another array C[1..M].

2.   The largest element in the array A[1..N] occurs somewhere in the first k positions.

3.   The array A[1..N] contains at least two zeros.

4.   Every element in a[1..j] is less than X and every element in a[j+1..N] exceeds X.

5.   The first k elements in the array a[1..N] are negative.

6.   At least one of the elements in the array A[1..N] is equal to X.

7.   Every element in the array A[1..N] occurs twice.

8.   y is the smallest element in an array A[1..N] that is greater than X.

9.   The first p elements in an array a[1..N] are in nondescending order and p is the maximum value for which this condition is true.

10.   c is a count of the number of times the maximum element occurs in an array a[1..N].

11.   The maximum value in the array a[1..N] only occurs once.

12.   p is a count of the number of unique elements in the array A[1..N].

13.   The array a[1 .. N] is a permutation of the array A[1..N].

■ **EXERCISE 4.9   Specification using quantifiers II**

Write formal specifications for the following problems.

1.   c represents the number of distinct elements in the array A[1..N].

2.   m represents the number of distinct elements in the array A[1..N] that are multiply-occurring.

3.   p is the position of the *first* occurrence of the maximum m in an array A[1..N].

4.   f is the position of the *third* occurrence of the maximum m in an array A[1..N] if the maximum occurs at least three times.

5.   p is the position of the *last* occurrence of an element equal to X in an array A[1..N].

6.   v is the average of the elements in the array A[1..N].

7.   k is the length of longest sequence of elements in the array A[1..N] starting at position one that are in nondescending order.

8.   c is a count of the number of times the maximum occurs in the array A[1..N].

9.   i is the position where an element equal to X *first* occurs in the array A[1..N] which is arranged in nondescending order.

10.   j is the position where an element equal to X *last* occurs in an array A[1..N] which is in nondescending order.

11.   All the positive elements in an array A[1..N] are identified and stored in another array b.

12.   The array b contains a copy of the sequence of characters in the array A[1..N] but with *all* the trailing spaces at the end of the array removed.

■ *EXERCISE 4.10   Array properties specifications*

Write formal specifications for the following problems using specifiers and quantifiers where necessary.

1.   At least one of the members of the array A[1..M] is a member of the array B[1..N].

2.   All of the members of the array A[1..M] are members of the array B[1..N].

3.   None of the elements in the array A[1..M] are present in the array B[1..N].

4.   At least one of the members of the array A[1..M] occurs k times in the array B[1..N].

5.   At least one of the elements in the array A[1..M] is less than all the elements in the array B[1..N].

6.   p of the elements in the array A[1..M] occur in the array B[1..N].

7.   Elements in the array A[1..M] that are greater than zero also occur in the array B[1..N].

8.   Elements in the array A[1..M] that are positive in value are all greater than 100.

9.   All the elements in the array A[1..M] are unique.

10.   None of the elements in the array A[1..M] are unique.

11.   At least one of the elements in the array A[1..M] is unique.

■ *EXERCISE 4.11   Strength of predicates*

In each of the following examples indicate which of the pairs of predicates is weaker, or indicate they are the same strength.

1.   (a) $N > 0$ (b) $N \geq 0$

2.   (a) $1 \leq i \leq N$ (b) $0 < i \leq N$

3.   (a) $i = N$ (b) $1 \leq i \leq N$

4.   (a) $x < 0 \vee x > 10$ (b) $x < 0$

5.   (a) $x < 0 \wedge x > 10$ (b) $x < 0$

6.   (a) $x > 0 \wedge x < 10$ (b) $x > 0$

7.   (a) $x > 0 \wedge x < 10$ (b) $x > 0 \vee x < 10$

8.   (a) $(\forall j : 1 \leq j \leq i : x \neq A_j) \wedge i = N$ (b) $(\forall j : 1 \leq j \leq i : x \neq A_j) \wedge 1 \leq i \leq N$

9.   (a) $x \geq y$ (b) $x > y$

10.   (a) $(\forall j : 1 \leq j \leq i : x \neq A_j)$ (b) $(\forall j : 1 \leq j \leq i+1 : x \neq A_j)$

11.   (a) $(\forall j : 1 \leq j < N : A_j \leq A_{j+1})$ (b) $(\forall j : 1 < j \leq N : A_{j-1} \leq A_j)$

Bibliography

Alagic, S. and M. A. Arbib, (1978), *The Design of Well-structured and Correct Programs*, Springer-Verlag, New York.

Dijkstra, E.W. (1976), *A Discipline of Programming*, Prentice-Hall, Englewood Cliffs, N.J.

Gehani, N. and A.D. McGetterick, (eds) (1986), *Software Specification Techniques*, Addison-Wesley.

Hehner, E.C.R. (1984), *The Logic of Programming*, Prentice-Hall, London.

Reynolds, J.C. (1981), *The Craft of Programming*, Prentice-Hall, London.

Turski, W.M. and T.S.E. Maibaum, *The Specification of Computer Programs*, Addison-Wesley.

Part 2
MODEL FOR PROGRAM DERIVATION

The model that we will consider for program derivation is a relatively simple one. It is best understood in terms of the state model for computation. For each refinement or derivation step that we make there is an expansion of the set of initial states for which the postcondition is established. The propelling force behind the derivation process is the weakest precondition calculation. These calculations identify conditions under which progress towards predefined goals is made. To support the program derivation process a number of rules and conventions are needed – these are identified and demonstrated in Chapter 5.

To give the model for program derivation some constructive power it is appropriate to identify constructive transformations that can be applied to specifications. In Chapter 6 we confront this issue by examining the links between specification transformations and traditional problem-solving strategies. Having explored these connections we then go on to consider a number of derivations for problems requiring single and nested loop solutions.

Chapter 5
Program Derivation

Methodological abstraction is a wise long term investment

R.W.Floyd

5.1 Introduction
5.2 State Model
5.3 The Weakest Precondition
5.4 Guarded Comments
5.5 Program Derivation – An Example
5.6 Model for Program Derivation
5.7 Systematic Decomposition
Summary
Exercises
Bibliography

5.1 Introduction

For program derivation to become more effective it needs to be specification driven. This means a precondition and a postcondition should be supplied or constructed *before* program derivation is started. Such specifications support the state model for computation. The precondition Q formally characterizes the set of initial states associated with a problem while the postcondition R characterizes the final states.

The precondition and postcondition, as well as defining problems, may also be used to guide the derivation of programs. As we have seen in the previous chapter, before a postcondition can be used constructively in aiding program derivation it often needs to undergo a number of transformations to an equivalent or stronger form on an extended state space. Such transformations guarantee that the original problem is solved. It must

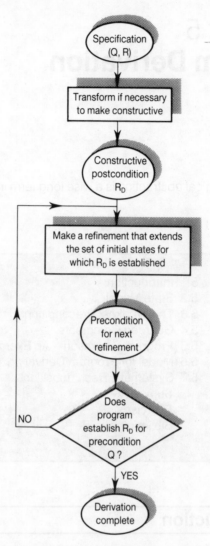

Figure 5.1 Program derivation strategy.

always be remembered that we cannot go ahead and simply adjust the specification to suit the program we want to derive.

The state model for computation allows the semantics of a program to be conveniently interpreted in terms of a mapping between the set of initial states and the set of final states. Once a suitable specification has been established the task is then to make a sequence of refinements until an implementation is obtained which solves the problem given. If, in carrying out these refinements, the conventional strategy of top-down design is employed, no correspondence with the sets of initial and final states is achieved by the decomposition process. This is unfortunate because the state concept is the basic structural currency we have for understanding programs. In what follows we will describe a method of program derivation that is strongly dependent on the state model.

When the state model is used to provide a supporting framework, one systematic way to compose a program in a stepwise manner is by a sequence of refinements, each of which enlarges the set of initial states for which the postcondition is established until finally a mechanism has been composed that will establish the postcondition for the given precondition. This refinement strategy, when combined with a means for identifying an appropriate starting point, a set of rules for manipulating specifications, a means for partitioning the set of initial states, and a set of composition rules for incorporating new refinements, provides a constructive method for program derivation from specifications. A sketch of this derivation strategy is given in Figure 5.1.

Before considering program derivation in detail it is necessary to have an understanding of the state concept and the state model for computation.

5.2   State Model

The free variables or identifiers associated with a computation can be used to characterize completely the state of a computation. A **state** may be defined as a function from a set of identifiers (all the named variables in a computation) to a set of values. Put another way, a state is made up of a set of ordered pairs of the form (identifier, value) with the requirement that all the identifiers be distinct.

When defining specifications it is important to distinguish between two types of identifiers, the **input** or **data variables**, and the **output** or **program variables**.

The input or data variables have two important properties. They may assume different values from one computation (or application) of the program to the next. However, with respect to a given computation, their values are completely frozen. In other words *the input variables of a particular computation act as unspecified constants of that computation.* We apply this restriction to input variables in order to reason constructively about programs. The most important reason for adopting this convention is to provide a suitable reference point so that relations between the input and the output can be adequately expressed. For deterministic computations there is only one output state associated with a given input state.

To distinguish between input variables and output variables in a specification it is useful to adopt the convention that capital letters (for example N, A[1..N] etc.) are used for input data and small letters (for example n, a[1..n] etc.) are used for output or program variables. In practice, in the implementation of programs, we do not always maintain the distinction that is needed in the specification. For example, to sort a fixed array of integers A[1..N] we may only mention the output array a[1..N] in the implementation of the program. In the specification however, it is essential to refer to the two sets of data. As another example, to indicate that a program accepts as input two fixed integers X and Y, and stores them in the program variables x and y, and then is required to swap the values of the variables, the following relationship between the input and output is used:

$$Q : x = X \wedge y = Y$$
$$R : x = Y \wedge y = X$$

Again in the implementation there is no need to mention the input variables X and Y, for example

```
procedure swap (var x , y ; integer);
var t: integer;
{It is assumed that the parameter passing establishes Q}
    t := x ;
    x := y ;
    y := t
    {R}
end
```

Each of the variables associated with a particular computation may in general assume a number of different values. In combination, a set of variables and their ranges of values defines a **state space.** For example, suppose we have two input variables A and B with allowable sets of values {1,2,3} and {10, 11} respectively. The possible input states or initial state space is formed from the Cartesian product of the sets of values associated with each input variable. In this particular case the input state space is defined by the following set of states:

A	B	
1	10	
1	11	
2	10	Initial
2	11	states
3	10	
3	11	

Now suppose the computation being modelled consisted only of the following step which assigns a value to the program variable s:

$$s := A + B$$

then the allowable set of final states would be:

A	B	s	
1	10	11	
1	11	12	
2	10	12	Final
2	11	13	states
3	10	13	
3	11	14	

The individual states are represented by sets of ordered pairs; for example $\{(A, 1), (B, 10), (s, 11)\}$ is a possible final state of the program. For other than trivial computations we do not explicitly seek to enumerate all possible states. Instead, we settle for precondition and postcondition predicates which define the allowable initial and final state spaces. A particular set of allowable values of the program variables corresponds to a **point** in the state space. For each allowable point in a state space the corresponding predicate must be *true*. States where the defining precondition and postcondition predicates are *false* are ignored as they are not part of the goal of the computation.

As an example, the precondition $N \geq 1$ defines an initial state space:

State	Defining predicate ($N \geq 1$)
(N, 1)	TRUE
(N, 2)	TRUE
(N, 3)	TRUE
.	
.	
.	

The following states:

State	Defining predicate ($N \geq 1$)
(N, 0)	FALSE
(N, −1)	FALSE
(N, −2)	FALSE
.	
.	
.	

are disqualified as members of the state space because the defining predicate is *false* for these states.

For our example described previously by enumeration, the defining predicate Q for the initial state space is:

Q : 1 ⩽ A ⩽ 3 ∧ 10 ⩽ B ⩽ 11

and the final states R are described by the predicate:

R : s = A + B

5.3   The Weakest Precondition

We now need to introduce a new concept called the **weakest precondition.** This concept has at least three important roles in programming.

- It can be used to characterize the semantics of, and hence verify, simple programs.
- It can provide a means for defining the semantics of a programming language.
- It can be used in a constructive role to help build program statements that satisfy certain constraints.

All of these roles will be explored but as a lead up to this an intuitive introduction to the concept will be given. The idea derives from the state model of a program described earlier, where we saw that a program functions by accepting data from a set of allowable initial states and transforms the data in some way to produce a resultant configuration that belongs to a set of allowable final states.

5.3.1   Weakest preconditions and the state model

One way of viewing the state model is to ask the question: *what, for a given initial state, will be the corresponding final state produced by the program?* This relation between input and output is an obvious one to consider as it captures the semantics of a program. Unfortunately it is usually not easy to manipulate. In fact it is usually difficult and tedious to predict a program's final state given just the program and an initial state. Anyone who has tried to hand-execute other than a very simple program for some given input data quickly comes to this realization.

A far more fruitful way to use the state model is to ask what is essentially the opposite question: *given some set of final states what corresponding set of initial states would produce those final states when transformed by a given program?* It is this question that embodies the

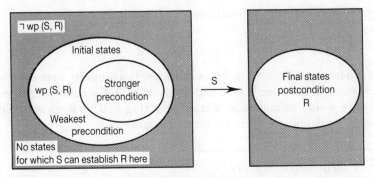

Figure 5.2   State space representation involving the precondition and postcondition.

essence of the weakest precondition. A more precise working definition of the weakest precondition is the following.

Weakest Precondition
For a terminating program statement S, and a required postcondition R, wp(S,R) symbolizes the weakest precondition such that execution of S is certain to establish the postcondition R.

In this context a precondition is a condition that applies *before* S is executed. The *weakest* precondition is the precondition which characterizes *all* the admissible initial states from which execution of S will be able to establish R. A *stronger* precondition with respect to wp(S,R) will characterize only a *subset* of the initial states for which the mechanism S can establish R. These relationships are shown schematically in Figure 5.2.

5.3.2   Properties of weakest preconditions

In order to use the weakest preconditon concept as the basis for defining programming language constructs the following two fundamental axioms are required:

Law of the excluded miracle (1)
There are no states in which the execution of a mechanism S can begin and guarantee to terminate in a state satisfying FALSE.

Symbolically this property may be expressed as

wp(S, F) ≡ F

This can be proved by contradiction. Suppose this property were not true. It would mean at least one state could satisfy wp(S,F). Execution of S begun in this state would terminate in a state satisfying F. This is a contradiction because, by definition, there are no states satisfying F.

Law of conjunction (2)
For a mechanism S and postconditions R1 and R2 the following equivalence holds:
  wp(S, R1) ∧ wp(S, R2) ≡ wp(S, R1 ∧ R2)

This law tells us that the weakest precondition distributes through conjunction. It may be proved using the equivalence rule and the definition of wp.

wp(S, R1 ∧ R2) describes the set of all initial states that guarantee termination of S in a state satisfying R1 ∧ R2. Any such initial state must guarantee both

wp(S, R1 ∧ R2) ⇒ wp(S, R1)

and

wp(S, R1 ∧ R2) ⇒ wp(S, R2)

It follows that

wp(S, R1 ∧ R2) ⇒ wp(S, R1) ∧ wp(S, R2)   (Tautology – Rule 14, Chapter 2)

Conversely an initial state satisfying wp(S,R1) ∧ wp(S, R2) will guarantee termination of S in a state satisfying R1 ∧ R2 and therefore

wp(S, R1) ∧ wp(S, R2) ⇒ wp(S, R1 ∧ R2)

It follows by the distributivity rule that the law of conjunction is proved.

As an example suppose we have

R1 : c = X
R2 : c = Y
S : c := a

then

$$wp(S, R1) \equiv wp(\text{"c := a"}, c = X)$$
$$\equiv a = X$$
$$wp(S, R2) \equiv wp(\text{"c := a"}, c = Y)$$
$$\equiv a = Y$$

and

$$wp(S, R1 \wedge R2) \equiv wp(\text{"c := a"}, c = X \wedge c = Y)$$
$$\equiv a = X \wedge a = Y$$

and so the equivalence with respect to conjunction is seen to follow.

The above two laws can be used to prove two other useful properties of weakest preconditions given below.

Law of disjunction (3)
For a mechanism S and postconditions R1 and R2

$$wp(S, R1) \vee wp(S, R2) \Rightarrow wp(S, R1 \vee R2)$$

This law holds for commands that are *nondeterministic* (that is, the execution of a command begun in the same initial state may not always be the same). For deterministic commands the law can be strengthened to

$$wp(S, R1) \vee wp(S, R2) \equiv wp(S, R1 \vee R2)$$

The proof of this law is left as an exercise.

Law of monotonicity (4)
For a mechanism S and postconditions R1 and R2 the following relation applies:

$$(R1 \Rightarrow R2) \Rightarrow (wp(S, R1) \Rightarrow wp(S, R2))$$

Activation of a mechanism S in a state satisfying wp(S, R1) guarantees to establish R1 and if R1 $\Rightarrow$ R2 it will also establish R2. Such behaviour is an indication of monotonicity. This law tells us that wp preserves implication. This law is a consequence of the law of conjunction.

As an illustration of this law suppose we have

$$R1 : x > 0$$
$$R2 : x \geqslant 0$$
$$S \; : x := x + 1$$

it follows that R1 $\Rightarrow$ R2 holds and we have

$$wp(S, R1) \equiv wp("x := x + 1", x > 0)$$
$$\equiv x > -1$$

and

$$wp(S, R2) \equiv wp("x := x + 1", x \geq 0)$$
$$\equiv x \geq -1$$

where

$$x > -1 \Rightarrow x \geq -1$$

and so if R1 $\Rightarrow$ R2 we have that

$$wp(S, R1) \Rightarrow wp(S, R2)$$

What this law is saying is that if postcondition R1 is stronger than another postcondition R2 and there is a mechanism S capable of establishing both R1 and R2, then the corresponding weakest precondition for S establishing R1 will be stronger than the weakest precondition for S establishing R2.

5.3.3   Computation of weakest preconditions

Formal computation of weakest preconditions can be used for two purposes;

- assisting with the verification of programs;
- assisting with the construction of program statements that satisfy particular desired specifications.

Before weakest preconditions can be used for these tasks it is necessary to define the required programming language constructs in terms of weakest preconditions.

The central construct that we need to define is the assignment statement

$$x := e \tag{1}$$

where x is a variable and e is an expression of the same type. When this assignment statement is executed the expression e is evaluated and the result is assigned to x. Now suppose that execution of the assignment statement (1) guarantees to establish the postcondition R.

For this to be true the predicate R, with all free occurrences of x *simultaneously* replaced by e (symbolized by R_e^x) must have held *directly before*

$$x := e$$

was executed. Otherwise, this assignment could not guarantee to establish R. Computing R_e^x allows us to characterize completely the semantics of the assignment statement $x := e$ because R_e^x is the precondition that holds directly before the assignment executes and establishes the postcondition R, that is

$$\{R_e^x\} \qquad \qquad \text{precondition}$$
$$x := e \qquad \qquad \text{assignment}$$
$$\{R\} \qquad \qquad \text{postcondition}$$

The condition R_e^x is in fact the *weakest precondition* for which execution of the assignment $x := e$ will guarantee to establish the postcondition R. This is written as

$$wp("x := e", R) \equiv R_e^x$$

To be strictly formal in defining the weakest precondition for assignment a predicate should be included which characterizes the set of all initial states in which e may be evaluated (that is dom(e)). The more formal definition could then be written following Dijkstra:

$$wp("x := e", R) \equiv dom(e) \ \textbf{cand} \ R_e^x$$

The mechanism for computing R_e^x is usually referred to as **textual substitution.** As an example suppose we have

$$R : x + x \times y = c + y$$
$$S : x := y + c$$

then when the textual substitution rule is applied, the result is

$$wp("x := y + c", R) \equiv (y + c) + (y + c) \times y = c + y$$
$$\equiv y \times (y + c) = 0$$

An approximate geometric interpretation of weakest preconditions and their computation can help improve our understanding of the concept. Suppose our goal R is to construct a circular disc. Also let us assume that we have in hand a mechanism S that is capable of constructing a *sector* of the disk R. We therefore have the requirement R for a disk, and the component S as shown

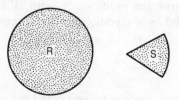

'Computing' the weakest precondition for S being able to *establish* (or complete the construction of) R corresponds to *removing* S from R.
R with S removed has the form shown below:

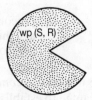

It follows that if wp(S, R) applies and S is 'executed' a complete disk R will result, that is†

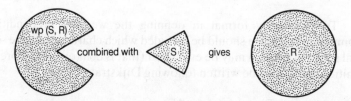

wp(S, R) is the necessary and sufficient condition that must apply if execution of S is to guarantee to establish R. Once we have determined wp(S, R) we have completely captured the semantics of S in predicate form. In other words, the weakest precondition for S establishing R, that is wp(S, R), is just R with the contribution of S removed from it.

In an effort to make things still clearer it is useful to examine several other examples.

EXAMPLE 1   The unconstrained weakest precondition

Suppose

$$R : x = 3 \qquad \text{postcondition}$$
$$S : x := 3 \qquad \text{assignment}$$

† That the geometric interpretation is only approximate is seen from the fact the wp(S,R) is a condition while S is a mechanism.

Then applying the first definition for wp(S, R) gives

wp("x := 3", x = 3) ≡ 3 = 3 ≡ TRUE

The corresponding program is

{ wp(S, R) : TRUE }	precondition
x := 3	assignment
{ R : x = 3 }	postcondition

What this example shows is that no matter what initial state this computation is begun in, it will always terminate with the postcondition x = 3 established. The set of *all possible initial states* is characterized by the weakest precondition TRUE.

EXAMPLE 2   The empty weakest precondition_____

This example illustrates the completely complementary situation to that shown by the first example. Suppose

R : x = 3	postcondition
S : x := 4	assignment

then applying the definition for wp(S, R) gives

wp("x := 4", x = 3) ≡ 4 = 3 ≡ FALSE

The *incorrect* program is

{wp(S,R) : FALSE }	
x := 4	
{R : x = 3 }	

This example shows that there is *no initial state* in which the computation x := 4 can be executed and establish the postconditon x = 3. The set of *no* initial states is characterized by the weakest preconditon FALSE.

EXAMPLE 3   The independent weakest precondition_____

When weakest preconditions are computed for other than limiting cases new subtleties enter into consideration. Suppose:

R : x > 0	postcondition
S : x := y + z	assignment

then:

$$wp("x := y + z", x > 0) \equiv y + z > 0$$

and the program is:

{ wp(S, R) : y + z > 0 }	precondition
x := y + z	assignment
{ R : x > 0 }	postcondition

This example shows that when the final state involves a new variable (i.e. x) not set in the initial state, the weakest precondition tells us essentially the *same thing* as the postcondition, but it is expressed in terms of the variables of the precondition state space (i.e. y, z).

EXAMPLE 4   The dependent weakest precondition_____

Yet another subtlety is exhibited by the weakest precondition when characterizing an assignment that *changes* the value of a variable defined in the initial state in order to arrive at the prescribed postcondition. As an example of this situation suppose

R : x > 0	postcondition
S : x := x + 2	assignment

then

$$wp("x := x + 2", x > 0) \equiv x + 2 > 0 \equiv x > - 2$$

Here, in order to best understand what is happening, it is useful to distinguish between initial and final values of x. To make this distinction we will use x' to refer to the initial state and x" to refer to the final state.

{ wp(S, R) : x' + 2 > 0 }	precondition
x" := x' + 2	assignment
{ R : x" > 0 }	postcondition

and when no distinction is made between initial and final values of x

{ wp(S, R) : x > −2 }	precondition
x := x + 2	assignment
{ R : x > 0 }	postcondition

To re-emphasize, suppose the condition x > −2 applies, and then the statement "x := x + 2" is executed. It will guarantee to establish the condition $x > 0$. This example follows the form of the earlier geometric interpretation of the weakest precondition where wp(S, R) *is just the postcondition with the effects of the statement* S *removed.*

5.3.4   Constructive weakest precondition calculations

In using weakest precondition calculations for program derivation there are three principal types of construction:

- identification of a guard for a command;
- identification of a command that will ensure that an invariant is maintained;
- identification of a sub-goal that needs to be established before a command can be executed.

Guard identification

To illustrate how a weakest precondition calculation can be used to identify a suitable guard for a command, suppose we have the following invariant P, loop guard B, command S, and variant function t:

$P : (\forall j : 0 < j \le i : A_j \ne X) \wedge 0 \le i \le N$
$B : i \ne N$
$t : N - i$
$S : i := i + 1$

Our objective is to find a guard B_s that will allow S to be executed while maintaining P and decreasing t, that is

$$i := 0;$$
$$\textbf{do } i \ne N \rightarrow \{P\}$$
$$\textbf{if } B_s \rightarrow S \textbf{ fi}$$
$$\textbf{od}$$

The first step in our search for a guard is to do a weakest precondition calculation using S and P, that is

$$wp(\text{"}i := i + 1\text{"}, (\forall j : 0 < j \le i : A_j \ne X) \wedge 0 \le i \le N) \equiv (\forall j : 0 < j \le i + 1 : A_j \ne X) \wedge 0 \le i + 1 \le N$$

The second step in our search for a guard for S is to rewrite wp(S,P) in the form

$$P \wedge \text{'some other term(s)'}$$

The reason for doing this is to *identify that component of* wp(S,P) *that is not implied by the invariant* P (remember in weakest precondition calculations P is assumed to be true before S is executed). Any part of wp(S,P) other than P itself will need to be taken care of with a guard (or guards) if S is to safely execute and maintain P. In this case we have

$$wp(S,P) \equiv (\forall j : 0 < j \leq i + 1 : A_j \neq X) \wedge 0 \leq i + 1 \leq N$$

$$\equiv (\forall j : 0 < j \leq i : A_j \neq X) \wedge A_{i+1} \neq X \wedge 0 \leq i + 1 \leq N$$
$$\leftarrow \text{ belongs to P } \rightarrow$$

Examination of this latest form for wp(S,P) reveals that the term

$$A_{i+1} \neq X$$

is not implied by P and the loop guard $i \neq N$. The term $A_{i+1} \neq X$ is the condition B_S we are seeking. For those uncertain how $A_{i+1} \neq X$ was obtained from wp(S, P), consider rewriting both P and wp(S,P) in the expanded form:

$$P : A_1 \neq X \wedge A_2 \neq X \wedge ... \wedge A_i \neq X \wedge 0 \leq i \leq N$$

$$wp(S, P) : A_1 \neq X \wedge A_2 \neq X \wedge ... \wedge A_i \neq X \wedge A_{i+1} \neq X \wedge 0 \leq i + 1 \leq N$$

A comparison of P and wp(S,P) reveals that wp(S,P) has the additional conjunct $A_{i+1} \neq X$. Furthermore, if P is true and the loop guard is $i \neq N$, then

$$0 \leq i \leq N \wedge i \neq N \Rightarrow 0 \leq i + 1 \leq N$$

The technique of expanding P and wp(S,P) and comparing them can always be used if there is any doubt about the identity of B_S.

An invariant is applied in the context of a loop. The loop guard B which controls termination of the loop, conjoined with the invariant, represents the necessary and sufficient precondition for executing the loop body. Therefore S will need to be guarded by $A_{i+1} \neq X$ if it is to preserve P when it is executed.

This leads to the construction of a guarded command which preserves P:

$$\{P\} \textbf{ if } A_{i+1} \neq X \rightarrow i := i + 1 \textbf{ fi } \{P\}$$

To complete the development of this command the case where $A_{i+1} = x$ must be dealt with.

Command identification

To illustrate how a weakest precondition calculation can be used for command identification, suppose we have the following invariant P, command S, and variant function t.

$$P : f = i! \wedge 0 \le i \le N\dagger$$
$$t : N-i$$
$$S : i := i + 1$$

We also have

do $i \ne N \rightarrow \{P\}$
  S1   {S1 includes S together with some other unknown command}
od

Our objective in this case is to find a command (or commands) that will allow t to be decreased while maintaining P. Obviously S will decrease t, but it may not necessarily ensure P is preserved. Therefore wp(S,P) must be investigated. In this case

$$wp(S,P) \equiv wp(\text{"}i := i + 1\text{"}, f = i! \wedge 0 \le i \le N)$$
$$\equiv f = (i + 1)! \wedge 0 \le i + 1 \le N$$

Rewriting wp(S,P) to identify components of P we get

$$wp(S,P) \equiv f = i! \times (i + 1) \wedge 0 \le i + 1 \le N$$

Comparing the term $f = i!$ from P with the term

$$f = i! \times (i + 1)$$

from wp(S,P) reveals that the RHS of the equality has been multiplied by (i+1). Therefore if the equality relation is to be maintained, and thence P preserved, the LHS (i.e. f) will need to be multiplied by (i + 1), that is

$$f \times (i + 1) = i! \times (i + 1)$$

The 'other' command that makes up S1 is therefore $f := f \times (i + 1)$.

This suggests that a suitable multiple assignment command S1 that will change both f and i in a way that preserves P is

$$S1: i, f := i + 1, f \times (i + 1)$$

† Here i! symbolizes i factorial where i! = i × (i−1)× ... × 1.

A check can be made to confirm that this new command S1 will preserve P by computing

$$wp(S1,P) \equiv wp("i, f := i + 1, f \times (i + 1)", f = i! \wedge 0 \le i \le N)$$
$$\equiv f \times (i + 1) = (i + 1)! \wedge 0 \le i+1 \le N$$
$$\equiv f = i! \wedge 0 \le i + 1 \le N$$

From this verification we find that $P \wedge i \ne N$ implies $wp(S1,P)$.

An alternative way of reasoning to identify the additional command that will preserve the invariant P is as follows.

We have the partial command:

$$S : i := i + 1$$

and

(1) $P: f = i! \wedge 0 \le i \le N$ {invariant true **before** commands executed}
'Execution of command(s) that preserve P'

(2) $P : f' = i'! \wedge 0 \le i - \le N$ {invariant true **after** commands executed}

where f' and i' represent the values of the variables f and i *after* execution of commands that preserve P. We already know:

$$i' = i + 1$$

substituting for i' in (2) we get:

$$f' = (i + 1)! \wedge 0 \le i + 1 \le N$$
$$f' = (i + 1) \times i! \wedge 0 \le i + 1 \le N$$

and from (1) assuming P is initially true we know that i! can be replaced by f so we get:

$$f' = (i + 1) \times f$$

The complete command that preserves P is therefore:

$$i, f := i + 1, (i + 1) \times f$$

In this command f' and f are not distinguished.

Sub-goal identification

A particularly important application of weakest precondition calculations is to assist with the systematic decomposition of complex problems. To illustrate how a weakest precondition calculation can be used to identify a sub-goal, suppose we have the following invariant P, command S, and variant function t:

$P : (\forall k : 1 \leqslant k < i : a[1..k] \leqslant a[k + 1..N]) \wedge 1 \leqslant i \leqslant N$†
$t : N - i$
$S : i := i + 1$

As with guard identification, our objective here is to find a sub-goal (complex guard) that will need to be satisfied before S can be executed to maintain P.

We have:

```
i := 1;
do i ≠ N → {P}
   {P} S₁ {R₁}                        {R₁ established}
   i := i + 1                         {P re-established}
od
```

The notation $\{P\} S_1 \{R_1\}$ indicates that we wish to find a sequence of statements S_1, which when executed in a state satisfying P will terminate with R_1 established. To identify the sub-goal R_1 we will use a weakest precondition calculation.

Our first step is to compute wp(S,P) where S is $i := i + 1$, i.e.,

$$wp(S,P) : (\forall k : 1 \leqslant k < i + 1 : a[1..k] \leqslant a[k + 1..N]) \wedge 1 \leqslant i + 1 \leqslant N$$

The second step in our search for a sub-goal R_1, is to rewrite wp(S,P) in the form:

$P \wedge$ 'some other term'

This will allow us to identify the component of wp(S,P) that is not implied by P. This component will correspond to the sub-goal R_1, that will need to be established first if S is to safely execute and maintain P. In this case we have:

$$wp(S,P) \equiv (\forall k : 1 \leqslant k < i + 1 : a[1..k] \leqslant a[k + 1..N]) \wedge 1 \leqslant i + 1 \leqslant N$$

$$\equiv (\forall k : 1 \leqslant k < i : a[1..k] \leqslant a[k + 1..N]) \wedge a[i] \leqslant a[i + 1..N] \wedge 1 \leqslant i + 1 \leqslant N$$

It follows that the sub-goal:

$$R_1 : a[i] \leqslant a[i + 1..N]$$

†Here again we have used a shorthand array notation where
$(\forall k : 1 \leqslant k < i : (\forall p : 1 \leqslant p \leqslant k : (\forall q : k + 1 \leqslant q \leqslant N : a_p \leqslant a_q))) \equiv (\forall k : 1 \leqslant k < i : a[i..k] \leqslant a[k + 1..N])$.

is not implied by P. Therefore R_1 will need to be established before i := i + 1 can be executed.

A diagram can in this case help us identify those parts of wp(S,P) not implied by P.

P tells us that the following relations hold:

a[1] ≤ a[2..N]
∧ a[1..2] ≤ a[3..N]
.
.
∧ a[1..i−1] ≤ a[i..N]

When i := i + 1 is taken into account in the wp calculation it adds the term:

a[1..i] ≤ a[i + 1..N]

that is:

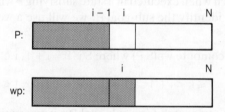

where all the shaded elements are less than or equal to all the elements in the un-shaded area. P and wp(S, P) differ only in that:

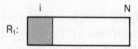

and

R_1 : a[i] ≤ a[i + 1..N]

is not implied by P. The job of establishing R_1 is a separate task that will need to be treated on its own merits (see Chapter 9 where this process is carried out). Basically what R_1 requires is that the smallest element in a[i ..N] be found and placed in a[i], with the value originally in a[i] being moved elsewhere in a[i ..N]. Before taking the computation of weakest preconditions any further it is necessary to define some other programming language constructs in terms of weakest preconditions.

5.4   Guarded Commands

The programming notation developed by Dijkstra and referred to as 'guarded commands' is a primitive language defined in terms of weakest preconditions. It accommodates three means for composition of program statements; **sequence, selection,** and **iteration.** The fundamental building block in this notation is the *guarded command.* A guarded command may take the form:

$$<\text{guard}> \rightarrow <\text{statement}> \tag{1}$$

where the *guard* is simply a Boolean expression. With this form, the *statement* is executed only when the guard evaluates to true. We will now examine the various means for composition of program statements.

5.4.1   Sequential composition

Sequential composition provides a primary mechanism for program construction. Given two commands S1 and S2 it is possible to compose these commands to construct a new command S1; S2 which has the same effect as executing S1 followed by S2. The semicolon serves as the operator for sequential composition. Given that the execution of S1 followed by S2 establishes the postcondition R, the formal definition of sequential composition in terms of weakest preconditions is

$$wp(\text{"S1; S2"}, R) \equiv wp(S1, wp(S2, R)) \tag{2}$$

What this definition captures is the fact that the postcondition of S1 must exactly match the weakest precondition for S2 establishing R. Imagine that we have two pipes, A and B, through which fluid is to be conducted. A and B can only be successfully composed without loss if the diameter of the pipe at A's output matches B's input diameter. Figure 5.3 crudely defines the requirements for sequential composition.

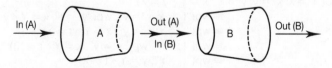

Figure 5.3   Schematic representation of sequential composition.

As an example, suppose S1 is a := b and S2 is c := a and R is c = X, then

```
{wp(S1 ; S2 , R) ≡ ?}
 a := b;
 c := a
{R : c = X}
```

Applying our definition for sequential composition (2) we get

$$wp("a := b; c := a", c = X) \equiv wp("a := b", wp("c := a", c = X))$$
$$\equiv wp("a := b", a = X)$$
$$\equiv b = X$$

The resulting weakest precondition b = X would need to have applied initially in order for the combined mechanism to establish the postcondition. These tools have allowed us to capture the essence of sequential composition. That is, the statement a := b (i.e. S1) must establish the condition a = X in order for the second statement c := a (i.e. S2) to establish the postcondition c = X. The complete semantics of the sequentially composed statements a := b; c := a is

```
{wp : b = X}
 a := b;                (S1)
{a = X}                 postcondition S1 ≡ precondition S2
 c := a                 (S2)
{R : c = X}             postcondition S2
```

As another example, let us reconsider the swap mechanism. We may take as the postcondition in this case

R : x = Y ∧ y = X

and the mechanism S is

```
 t := x;
 x := y;
 y := t
{R}
```

To characterize the semantics of S we will compute wp(S, R) by repeatedly applying the sequential composition rule:

$$wp("t := x; x := y; y := t", x = Y \wedge y = X)$$
$$\equiv wp("t := x; x := y", wp("y := t", x = Y \wedge y = X))$$
$$\equiv wp("t := x; x := y", x = Y \wedge t = X)$$
$$\equiv wp("t := x", wp("x := y", x = Y \wedge t = X))$$
$$\equiv wp("t := x", y = Y \wedge t = X)$$
$$\equiv y = Y \wedge x = X$$

Therefore, in order for the swap mechanism S to establish the postcondition $x = Y \wedge y = X$, the precondition

$$x = X \wedge y = Y$$

would need to have held directly before S was executed.

5.4.2 Multiple assignment

In our earlier discussion of assignment in terms of weakest preconditions we neglected to define the weakest precondition for what is called the **multiple assignment** command. Such a command may be used to describe a state change that involves more than one variable.

Given a set $X = \{x_1, x_2, ..., x_N\}$ of N distinct variables and a corresponding set of expressions $E = \{e_1, e_2, ..., e_N\}$ (the e's need not be distinct) then the notation:

$$x_1, x_2, ..., x_N := e_1, e_2, ..., e_N \qquad \text{(or } X := E) \tag{3}$$

represents simultaneous execution of the assignments

$$x_1 := e_1$$
$$x_2 := e_2$$
$$.$$
$$.$$
$$.$$
$$x_N := e_N$$

The multiple assignment (3) is considered to execute as follows. All of the expressions $e_1, e_2, ..., e_N$ are first evaluated and then the resulting values are assigned to the variables $x_1, x_2, ..., x_N$. The semantics for a multiple assignment (3) which establishes a postcondition R may be described in a similar way to a single assignment. We have:

$$wp(\text{``}x_1, x_2, ..., x_N := e_1, e_2, ..., e_N\text{''}, R) \equiv R\begin{matrix}x_1, ..., x_N \\ e_1, ..., e_N\end{matrix} \tag{4\dagger}$$

provided all the e's are well-defined.

An often-quoted example of multiple assignment involves the swap of the values of two variables. Using multiple assignment we have:

$$x, y := y, x$$

which, from the user's viewpoint, eliminates the usual need for an extra temporary variable to complete the swap.

† This is an extension of the notation introduced in Section 5.3.3

When variables are *shared* among a number of assignments, such statements may have a different semantics depending on whether they are executed by multiple assignment or sequentially. As an example suppose we have the postcondition

$R : x > y$

and the two assignments

$x := x + y$ and $y := x + c$

If these statements are executed by multiple assignment we have

$$wp("x, y := x + y, x + c", x > y)$$
$$\equiv x + y > x + c$$
$$\equiv y > c$$

Whereas if these statements are executed sequentially we get

$$wp("x := x + y; y := x + c", x > y)$$
$$\equiv wp("x := x + y", x > x + c)$$
$$\equiv wp("x := x + y", c < 0)$$
$$\equiv c < 0$$

5.4.3   Selective composition

There are many instances in deriving programs where we want to select and execute just one of a number of possible commands $S_1, S_2, \ldots, S_N$. This method of composition may be implemented using an **alternative command**.

The alternative command is composed of a set of guarded commands $\{(B_i \rightarrow S_i) \mid 1 \leq i \leq N\}$. The general form for the alternative command, designated by **IF** is:

$$
\begin{aligned}
&\textbf{if } B_1 \rightarrow S_1 \\
&[] \ B_2 \rightarrow S_2 \\
&\cdot \\
&\cdot \\
&[] \ B_N \rightarrow S_N \\
&\textbf{fi}
\end{aligned}
\tag{5}
$$

The command S_i is guarded by the Boolean expression B_i, and S_i may be executed only if B_i is true.

A *nondeterministic* model is usually assumed for the execution of the alternative command. What this means in practical terms is that the guards

B_i are selected *in arbitrary order* and evaluated. The first guard B_i selected according to this rule which evaluates to true results in the execution of the corresponding command S_i. If a precondition exists where more than one of the guards is true, then there is no *a priori* way of telling which of the commands with true guards will be selected for execution. If all the guards are false the command is designed to abort as it implies that the composition has not been properly formulated. A program with an alternative command that aborts is incorrect. Furthermore if any guard is undefined the command may also abort.

The most primitive way in which we use an alternative command is to handle the situation where, if some condition B applies, the command S is executed, otherwise no action is taken.

In this case we may use the following version of the alternative command:

$$\begin{aligned}
&\{Q\}\\
&\textbf{if } B \rightarrow S\\
&[] \neg B \rightarrow \text{skip}\\
&\textbf{fi}\\
&\{R\}
\end{aligned} \tag{6}$$

What this command tells us is that S will establish the postcondition R if the condition B holds before **IF** is executed, whereas if $\neg B$ holds before **IF** is executed, then no change of state is needed to establish R. The command skip does not alter the state of a computation – in other words it 'does nothing'. The command skip may be formally defined in terms of weakest preconditions as follows:

$$\text{wp("skip", R)} \equiv R \tag{7}$$

That is, for skip to guarantee that R is established, R will need to have been established *before* skip is executed. In our case R would have had to be part of the precondition Q for **IF**. The following shorthand for (6) will be used when appropriate:

$$\textbf{if } B \textbf{ then } S \textbf{ fi} \tag{8}$$

This command *does not* abort when the guard B is FALSE.

Another very common use of the alternative command is where a choice is made between two alternatives. In this case we have:

$$\begin{aligned}
&\textbf{if } B \rightarrow S_1\\
&[] \neg B \rightarrow S_2\\
&\textbf{fi}
\end{aligned} \tag{9}$$

For example to choose the larger of two fixed integers X and Y we could write

```
if X ≥ → m := X
[] X < → m := Y
fi
```

where m is given the value of the larger of the two integers. It is interesting to see that in this case we could also have used the command

```
if X ≥ Y → m := X
[] X ≤ Y → m := Y
fi
```
(10)

For this command, if X = Y, because of the nondeterministic execution we cannot predict in advance whether m:= X or m := Y will be executed. Either way, the same value is assigned to m.

If instead of (10) we had used the command

```
if X > Y → m := X
[] X < Y → m := Y
fi
{R}
```
(11)

then there would be the risk of abortion if a situation could arise where the condition X = Y applied before (11) was executed. The definition of the **abort** command in terms of the weakest precondition for establishing R is

$$\text{wp(``abort''}, R) \equiv \text{FALSE} \tag{12}$$

What this tells us is that there is *no* set of initial states from which execution of abort can guarantee to execute and establish any postcondition R. The only precondition under which (11) could guarantee to execute safely and establish R would be if

$$X \neq Y$$

held *before* (11) was executed.

As for assignment, it is possible to treat the alternative command **IF** formally in terms of weakest preconditions. If we assume that all the guards B_i are well-defined in all states, then the weakest precondition for **IF** establishing R may be defined as

$$\text{wp(\textbf{IF}}, R) \equiv (\exists i : 1 \leq i \leq N : B_i) \wedge (\forall i : 1 \leq i \leq N : B_i \Rightarrow \text{wp}(S_i, R)) \tag{13}$$

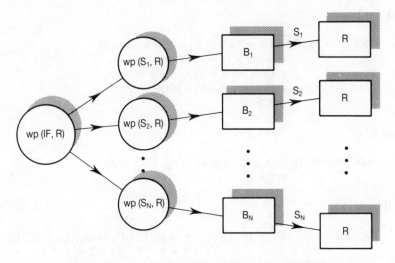

Figure 5.4   Schematic representation of wp(**IF**,R).

In this definition the existentially quantified conjunct tells us that at least one of the guards must be true. The universally quantified expression tells us that for each guarded command $B_i \rightarrow S_i$ the guard B_i must imply the weakest precondition for the command S_i establishing the postcondition R. A schematic representation for wp(**IF**, R) is shown in Figure 5.4.

As an example, suppose we have the required postcondition

$$R : (m = X \wedge X \geqslant Y) \vee (m = Y \wedge Y \geqslant X)$$

where for fixed X and Y the task is to assign m the value of the larger of X and Y. A possible alternative command for establishing R is

if $X \geqslant Y \rightarrow m := X$
[] $X \leqslant Y \rightarrow m := Y$
fi
{R}

Now we may proceed to calculate wp(**IF**, R) according to the definition given in (13).

We have

$B_1 : X \geqslant Y$
$B_2 : X \leqslant Y$

and

$$wp(\text{"m} := X\text{"}, R) \equiv (X = X \wedge X \geqslant Y) \vee (X = Y \wedge Y \geqslant X)$$
$$\equiv X \geqslant Y \vee (X = Y \wedge Y \geqslant X)$$
$$\equiv (X \geqslant Y \vee X = Y) \wedge (X \geqslant Y \vee Y \geqslant X)$$
$$\equiv (X \geqslant Y \vee X = Y) \wedge \text{TRUE}$$
$$\equiv X \geqslant Y$$

Similarly

$$wp(\text{"m} := Y\text{"}, R) \equiv (X \geqslant Y \wedge Y = X) \vee (Y = Y \wedge Y \geqslant X)$$
$$\equiv Y \geqslant X$$

And so we get

$$wp(\textbf{IF}, R) \equiv (B_1 \vee B_2) \wedge ((B_1 \Rightarrow wp(\text{"m} := X\text{"}, R) \wedge B_2 \Rightarrow wp(\text{"m} := Y\text{"}, R))$$
$$\equiv (X \geqslant Y \vee X \leqslant Y) \wedge ((X \geqslant Y \Rightarrow X \geqslant Y) \wedge (Y \geqslant X \Rightarrow Y \geqslant X))$$
$$\equiv \text{TRUE}$$

Since $wp(\textbf{IF}, R) \equiv \text{TRUE}$ it follows that **IF** will establish R for *all* initial states.

In many instances when applying the alternative command the postcondition of the previous command is known. This postcondition becomes the precondition Q for applying the **IF** command. It is then not necessary to calculate $wp(\textbf{IF}, R)$ but instead we must show that:

$$Q \Rightarrow wp(\textbf{IF}, R) \tag{14}$$

This can be done in two stages by first showing

$$Q \Rightarrow B_1 \vee B_2 \vee ... \vee B_N \tag{15}$$

and then showing

$$Q \wedge B_i \Rightarrow wp(S_i, R) \qquad \text{holds for all } i \in 1 .. N \tag{16}$$

An example of using (15) and (16) to show that

$$Q \Rightarrow wp(\textbf{IF}, R)$$

is as follows. Suppose we are given the postcondition

$$R : (m = X \wedge m \geqslant Y) \vee (m = Y \wedge m \geqslant X)$$

and we know that the command m := X has been previously executed to establish the condition

$$Q : m = X$$

Then, in order to establish R, we propose to add an alternative construct, that is

        m := X; {Q}
        if m ≥ Y → skip
        [] m ≤ Y → m := Y
        fi
        {R}

where

        Q : m = X
        B_1: m ≥ Y
        B_2: m ≤ Y

Now we need to show

        Q ⇒ wp(**IF**, R)

To do this, first we must show

        Q ⇒ B_1∨ B_2

that is

        m = X ⇒ m ≥ Y ∨ m ≤ Y ≡ m = X ⇒ TRUE
                                ≡ ¬(m = X) ∨ TRUE
                                ≡ TRUE

and so (15) is established.

The second step in the proof requires that

        Q ∧ B_i ⇒ wp(S_i, R)   holds for all i ∈ 1..N

In showing this we need to use the fact that

        wp(skip, R) ≡ R

We have

(1)   m = X ∧ m ≥ Y ⇒ wp(skip, R)
                        ⇒ (m = X ∧ m ≥ Y) ∨ (m = Y ∧ m ≥ X)

The latter implication is of the form A ⇒ A ∨ B, which is a tautology.

(2)   m = X ∧ m ≤ Y ⇒ wp("m := Y", R)
                        ⇒ Y ≥ X

which is also true by the principle of extensionality and so we can conclude

$Q \Rightarrow$ wp($\mathbf{IF}$, R)

as required to complete the proof.

5.4.4   Iterative command

Frequently in deriving programs we want to repetitively select and execute one of a number of possible commands S_1, S_2, ..., S_N. This method of composition may be implemented using an **iterative command** .

The iterative command is composed of a set of guarded commands $\{(B_i \rightarrow S_i)| 1 \leqslant i \leqslant N\}$. The general form for the iterative command, designated by **DO** is

$$
\begin{array}{ll}
\mathbf{do}\ B_1 \rightarrow S_1 \\
[]\ B_2 \rightarrow S_2 & \quad (17) \\
. \\
. \\
. \\
[]\ B_N \rightarrow S_N \\
\mathbf{od}
\end{array}
$$

where each $B_i \rightarrow S_i$ is a guarded command. A single iteration of **DO** is executed in the following way. Guards from the set B_1, B_2, ..., B_N are selected until one is found that is true then the command that is guarded is executed (that is if B_i is true then S_i is executed). Execution proceeds until an iteration is attempted where *all* guards are false. The loop then terminates.

If we define BB as

$BB \equiv B_1 \lor B_2 \lor ... \lor B_N$

then (17) is equivalent to

$$
\begin{array}{ll}
\mathbf{do}\ BB \rightarrow \\
\quad \mathbf{if}\ B_1 \rightarrow S_1 \\
\quad []\ B_2 \rightarrow S_2 & \quad (18) \\
\quad . \\
\quad . \\
\quad . \\
\quad []\ B_N \rightarrow S_N \\
\quad \mathbf{fi} \\
\mathbf{od}
\end{array}
$$

As with the alternative command, the guards in (17) are considered to be selected nondeterministically.

A very simple and often-used form of iterative composition involves just one guarded command, that is

do B →
    S   (19)
od

This is the fundamental **guarded loop** mechanism common to many programming languages. Iteration of the loop (19) continues while the guard B is true. As soon as the mechanism finds B false, when the guard is tested, the loop terminates.

In its more general form, the iterative command allows composition with more than one guarded command. For example, the following loop with two guarded commands can be used to compute the greatest common divisor (gcd) of two fixed natural numbers X and Y.

x, y := X, Y;
do x > y → x := x − y   (20)
[] x < y → y := y − x
od

This loop terminates when *both* guards are false, that is, when the condition x = y holds. This loop structure, which supports more than one guarded command, often leads to considerable economy in the expression of algorithms. Using Pascal to express this gcd algorithm we would require the description

x := X; y := Y;
while x <> y **do begin**   (21)
    if x > y **then** x := x − y **else** y := y − x
end

which is a somewhat more clumsy representation of the algorithm.

As another example, to order four elements a_1, a_2, a_3 and a_4 we could use

do a_1 > a_2 → swap (a_1, a_2)
[] a_2 > a_3 → swap (a_2, a_3)   (22)
[] a_3 > a_4 → swap (a_3, a_4)
od

This mechanism (22) can only terminate when all the guards are false, that is when

$$a_1 \leqslant a_2 \wedge a_2 \leqslant a_3 \wedge a_3 \leqslant a_4$$

which is the required ordering condition.

As with the alternative command it is possible to define the iterative command **DO** using the weakest precondition for establishing some goal R in at most k iterations. Following Dijkstra and Gries, if we let $H_k(R)$ represent the set of all states in which **DO** will establish R in at most k iterations we can formally define **DO** using

$$wp(\textbf{DO}, R) \equiv (\exists k : 0 \leqslant k \wedge H_k(R)) \tag{23}$$

Our only problem now is to find a way to define $H_k(R)$. This can be accomplished by making use of our definition for **IF.**

If we limit **DO** to at most k iterations it can be thought of as k *sequentially composed* alternative commands. That is,

> **IF;**   {1 iteration}
> **IF;**   {2 iterations}
>
> .
>
> .
>
> .
>
> **IF**   {k iterations}
> {R}

Also, to make the definition complete, it will be necessary to define the predicate $H_0(R)$ which represents the set of initial states in which **DO** will terminate in zero iterations with R true. This can only be possible if we have the precondition that R is already true and all the guards for **DO** (i.e. BB) are false.

Symbolically this is represented by

$$H_0(R) = \neg BB \wedge R \tag{24}$$

Interpreting **DO** as k sequentially composed **IF** commands $H_k(R)$ may be given the recursive definition

$$H_k(R) = H_0(R) \vee wp(\textbf{IF}, H_{k-1}(R)) \qquad \text{for } k > 0 \tag{25}$$

In deriving programs it is not practical to solve a set of recursive equations every time we want to use the **DO** command. Given this situation, we will still be able to achieve our objective if we can work in terms of some other stronger predicate that implies $wp(\textbf{DO}, R)$. The loop invariant P, introduced in the previous chapter, can fulfil this role. Let us now try to understand the role of the invariant P.

Consider the iterative command

> { P – true upon initialization }
> **do** $B_1 \rightarrow S_1$
> [] $B_2 \rightarrow S_2$
>
> .
>
> .   where $BB = B_1 \vee B_2 \vee ... \vee B_N$
>
> .
>
> [] $B_N \rightarrow S_N$
> **od**
> { $P \wedge \neg BB$ – true upon termination}

In our previous discussion in Chapter 4 we saw that a predicate P was an invariant of an iterative command provided that it was true before execution of the loop, after each iteration of the loop, and upon termination of the loop. In other words provided it was a *precondition*, *incondition*, and *postcondition* of the loop. Since P is always true when the loop terminates, a postcondition of the loop must be

$$P \wedge \neg BB \quad \text{where it is hoped to show } P \wedge \neg BB \Rightarrow R$$

It is also possible to establish the following important result:

$$P \Rightarrow \text{wp}(\textbf{DO}, P \wedge \neg BB) \tag{26}$$

The detailed proof of (26) is beyond the scope of the present discussion.

Requirements for loop correctness

To establish that (26) does indeed hold and that the loop is correct the following will be needed.

(1)   Show that P is true after execution of the command S_{INIT} which initializes the free variables in P before execution of the loop is commenced. This can be done by computing

$$\text{wp}(S_{INIT}, P) \tag{27}$$

(2)   Show that execution of each guarded command $B_i \rightarrow S_i$ terminates leaving P true, and therefore an invariant of the loop. To do this formally we must establish that

$$P \wedge B_i \Rightarrow \text{wp}(S_i, P) \tag{28}$$

holds for *all* the guarded commands in the **DO** construct.

(3)   Show that the truth of P, and the condition for termination of the loop, $(\neg BB)$ implies the postcondition R. That is, we need to establish that

$$P \wedge \neg BB \Rightarrow R \tag{29}$$

Our discussion has ignored whether the loop with invariant P terminates. To prove it does we must show there is a positive integer function t of the variables in the loop which is decreased by at least one with each iteration of the loop. This function must be bounded below by zero. If such a function t can be found then the loop must terminate.

These requirements translate formally as follows.

(4)   Show that the truth of P and at least one of the guards implies that the integer function t is strictly greater than zero, that is

$$P \wedge BB \Rightarrow t > 0 \qquad\qquad (30)$$

The condition $P \wedge BB$ is a precondition for there being at least one more iteration of the loop (which will decrease t by at least one). If an iteration of the loop can decrease t by δ then it is necessary to show

$$P \wedge BB \Rightarrow t - \delta \geqslant 0 \qquad\qquad (31)$$

(5)   Show that each iteration of the loop decreases the variant function t. Formally for this to be true we must show

$$P \wedge B_i \Rightarrow wp(\text{"t1} := t\,;\,S_i\text{"}, t < t1) \qquad\qquad (32)$$

holds for all guarded commands in the **DO** construct. Here the device t1 := t has been used to establish the condition t1 = t prior to execution of the command S_i. Note that S_i has the responsibility for decreasing the variant function t.

These five requirements complete our obligations for establishing that a loop is correct. We will now apply these requirements to a simple example.

Proving a loop correct – an example

The problem that we wish to consider is that of summing a fixed array of elements A[1..N]. The specification for the problem is

$$Q : N \geqslant 0$$
$$R : s = \Sigma(A_j : 0 < j \leqslant N)$$

In discussing this example, attention will be focused on just trying to prove that the following implementation is correct rather than attempting a constructive proof. The latter approach is the far better practice. The additional specifications and implementation to be considered are as follows:

$$R_D : s = \Sigma(A_j : 0 < j \leqslant i) \wedge i = N$$
$$P_D : s = \Sigma(A_j : 0 < j \leqslant i) \wedge 0 \leqslant i \leqslant N$$
$$t : N - i$$

```
{Q}
i , s := 0 , 0;
do i ≠ N → {P_D}
    i , s := i + 1 , s + A_{i+1}
od
{P_D ∧ i = N}
```

The following five steps are needed to establish the correctness of this loop.

(1)   First we must compute

$$\text{wp}(S_{\text{INIT}}, P_D) \equiv \text{wp}(\text{"i, s := 0, 0"}, s = \Sigma(A_j : 0 < j \leqslant i) \wedge 0 \leqslant i \leqslant N)$$
$$\equiv 0 = \Sigma(A_j : 0 < j \leqslant 0) \wedge 0 \leqslant 0 \leqslant N$$
$$\equiv 0 = 0 \wedge 0 \leqslant N$$
$$\equiv 0 \leqslant N$$

This tells us that S_{INIT} will establish P_D *provided* Q holds before S_{INIT} is executed. Since Q is assumed in our original specification it follows that the initialization establishes P_D.

(2)   Next we must show that the loop body maintains P_D. That is, we must show

$$P_D \wedge B_i \Rightarrow \text{wp}(S_i, P_D)$$

We have

$$\text{wp}(S_i, P_D) \equiv \text{wp}(\text{"i, s := i + 1, s + A}_{i+1}\text{"}, s = \Sigma(A_j : 0 < j \leqslant i) \wedge 0 \leqslant i \leqslant N))$$
$$\equiv s + A_{i+1} = \Sigma(A_j : 0 < j \leqslant i + 1) \wedge 0 \leqslant i + 1 \leqslant N$$
$$\equiv s + A_{i+1} = \Sigma(A_j : 0 < j \leqslant i) + A_{i+1} \wedge 0 \leqslant i + 1 \leqslant N$$
$$\equiv s = \Sigma(A_j : 0 < j \leqslant i) \wedge 0 \leqslant i + 1 \leqslant N$$

Now we must show

$$P_D \wedge i \neq N \Rightarrow s = \Sigma(A_j : 0 < j \leqslant i) \wedge 0 \leqslant i + 1 \leqslant N$$

This is of the form $p \wedge q \Rightarrow p \wedge r$ which can be simplified to $\neg p \vee \neg q \vee r$. Thus we get

$$\neg(0 \leqslant i \leqslant N) \vee \neg(i \neq N) \vee 0 \leqslant i + 1 \leqslant N \equiv i > N \vee i < N \vee 0 \leqslant i \leqslant N - 1$$
$$\equiv 0 \leqslant i \leqslant N \vee i > N$$
$$\text{(tautology)}$$
$$\equiv \text{TRUE}$$

and so it is established that the loop body maintains the invariant P_D.

(3)   Our third obligation is to show

$$P \wedge \neg BB \Rightarrow R$$

In this case we have

$$s = \Sigma(A_j : 0 < j \leqslant i) \wedge 0 \leqslant i \leqslant N \wedge i = N \Rightarrow s = \Sigma(A_j : 0 < j \leqslant N) \quad \textbf{(33)}$$

To establish that this implication holds we will assume the truth of its LHS. It follows that

$$s = \Sigma(A_j : 0 < j \leqslant i) \wedge i = N$$

holds. Using the identity rule which allows us to replace i by N this simplifies to

$$s = \Sigma(A_j: 0 < j \leqslant N)$$

Since we have been able to reduce the LHS to the same form as the RHS by assuming the truth of its conjuncts, it follows that the original implication (33) is established.

(4)   Our next obligation is to show that the variant function t is bounded below by zero. In other words we must show that:

$$P \wedge BB \Rightarrow t > 0$$

For our example we must establish:

$$s = \Sigma(A_j: 0 < j \leqslant i) \wedge 0 \leqslant i \leqslant N \wedge i \neq N \Rightarrow t > 0$$
$$\Rightarrow N - i > 0$$

Assuming the LHS of the implication the validity of this implication follows directly since

$$0 \leqslant i \leqslant N \wedge i \neq N \Rightarrow N - i > 0$$

This latter result can be confirmed by assuming a maximum value for i (that is $i = N - 1$) that will hold the LHS true.

(5)   The remaining task to complete the proof is to show that each iteration of the loop decreases the variant function t. We must show

$$P \wedge B_i \Rightarrow wp(\text{"t1} := t; S_i\text{"}, t < t1)$$

In our case we have

$$\Sigma(A_j: 0 < j \leqslant i) \wedge 0 \leqslant i \leqslant N \wedge i \neq N \Rightarrow wp(\text{"t1} := N - i; i, s := i + 1, s +$$
$$A_{i+1}\text{"}, N - i < t1)$$
$$\Rightarrow wp(\text{"t1} := N - i\text{"}, N - (i + 1) < t$$
$$\Rightarrow N - (i + 1) < N - i$$
$$\Rightarrow N - i - 1 < N - i$$
$$\Rightarrow \text{TRUE}$$

It follows that the implication holds, and so the proof of correctness for the loop is complete. We will now examine another method of composition that allows repetition of certain actions.

5.4.5   Recursive composition

A powerful alternative to iterative composition is to apply recursion. Here we are only interested in a very simple form of recursive composition called **tail recursion**. This form of recursion involves labelling or naming a sequence of statements and subsequently, *within* the sequence, using the label instead of the sequence to force execution of the sequence again. This allows a change in the flow of control in the execution of the mechanism.

As a simple example of tail recursion consider the following implementation which searches an array A[1..N] for an element equal to X. The label introduced is search

```
i := 0;
search: if i ≠ N then
            if A_{i+1} ≠ X then i := i + 1; search fi
        fi
```

This mechanism executes by first evaluating the guard $i \neq N$. If this guard is true the guard $A_{i+1} \neq X$ is evaluated. If the latter guard is true i is increased by one and control switches to evaluating the first guard for the new value of i. The inclusion of the label search after the command $i := i + 1$ signals the requirement for control to be switched to the labelled statement.

Usually wp(S, R) exhibits just one solution. However, using the mode of composition exhibited by tail recursion means in formal terms that the equations requiring solution become recursive. This also means there is the possibility that there may be more than one solution. In such circumstances wp(S, R) needs to be defined as the strongest predicate that satisfies the equations. If we can work with a stronger predicate than wp we can circumvent the difficult task of having to solve a set of recursive equations. The formal treatment of tail recursion may be dealt with using the *least fixed-point method* of Scott and Strachey. This formal treatment will not be pursued here. Our interest in tail recursion arises from the fact that it is often the most natural and most practical way to compose a solution to a problem. Even for our recursive search implementation the termination problems of an iterative solution (see Section 7.2) are avoided. Tail recursion sometimes provides a cleaner and more powerful control mechanism.

5.4.6   Procedure command

We saw in Chapter 3 that a procedure was a device for describing a sequence of statements that perform some well-defined task. It is possible to use weakest preconditions to formally characterize the semantics of a procedure command.

Suppose we have

{Q}	precondition
procedurename (actual parameters)	procedure command
{R}	postcondition

and suppose the sequence of statements in the body of the procedure is S.

The set of *actual parameters* is made up from the union of two possibly overlapping sets i, and o:

$$i_1, i_2, ..., i_M \qquad \text{input parameters}$$
$$o_1, o_2, ..., o_N \qquad \text{output parameters}$$

To simplify the reasoning we will assume that all the variables in a procedure are local variables (that is, their use is confined to the procedure body) which belong to the set

$$l_1, l_2, ..., l_p$$

We will also define subsets of the local variables l', and l''. Using sequence representations of these subsets we give the following description of the procedure command:

$$\text{wp("procedurename(actualparameters)",R)} \equiv \text{wp(" l' := i ; S ; o := l''', R)}$$

where the assignments in the definition may be multiple assignments if more than one parameter is involved. The procedure executes by first copying all the input parameters i to the local variable subset l', then the sequence of statements S is executed, then finally the results of the computation (that is l'')are copied to the output parameters o.

Having previously defined multiple assignment and sequential composition in terms of weakest preconditions the right-hand side of the equivalence relation can be easily evaluated.

5.5   Program Derivation – An Example

The necessary foundations have now been laid to enable us to consider the formidable task of program derivation. Before describing the method in detail, a simple example will be used to convey some of the notions upon which it is based. The problem is that of developing a program which will order a fixed sequence A of one or more integers using an array a[1..N]. An informal treatment of this problem was given earlier in Chapter 1. The specification is

$$Q : N \geqslant 1$$
$$R : (\forall j : 1 < j \leqslant N : a_{j-1} \leqslant a_j) \wedge \text{perm(a,A)}$$

where perm(a,A) indicates that the final result stored in the array a must be a permutation of the original data A.

Notation associated with the program derivation is given in the following table and in Figure 5.5

Q	precondition for the original problem
R	postcondition for the original problem
R_D	derived constructive postcondition
X	set of non-fixed free variables in R
D	equivalence condition
P	invariant
a	array with elements $a_1, a_2, ..., a_N$
A	fixed array of integers $A_1, A_2, ..., A_N$
A_i	precondition associated with program $S_i(X_i)$
a_i	precondition for the ith refinement $s_i(x_i)$
x_i	smallest finite subset of non-fixed free variables in X_i which when changed is sufficient to establish the postcondition R_D at least in some limiting circumstance
t	variant function
$s_i(x_i)$	the ith refinement acting on variable subset x_i
$S_i(X_i)$	program after i refinements. Acts on variable subset X_i
R_i	a sub-goal for establishing R_D
P_0	base invariant
$P_1, P_2,...$	derivative invariants constructed from P_0

Given a specification (Q , R) before development can proceed, it is necessary for the postcondition R to be in a form where

(1)   it is easy to make an initialization of some non-fixed free variables in R that is sufficient to establish R, at least in some limiting circumstance, and

(2)   having made such an initialization, for some given data configuration, it is easy to check whether or not the initialization has established R.

By 'easy' in (1) we mean by a simple assignment or assignments and by 'easy' in (2) we mean by a simple conditional test involving free variables. If the given postcondition is not of this form it should be transformed preferably to a form on an extended state space where (1) and (2) are satisfied. When a postcondition satisfies the requirements (1) and (2) it is said to be **constructive**. A constructive postcondition is needed to start the derivation of a program.

     In our example, the set of *non-fixed* free variables is X = {a}. The variables N and A are also free but they are *fixed* (i.e. not to be changed by the program). *Fixed free variables will be identified throughout the text by capital letters*. When an attempt is made to initialize the smallest subset of free variables in X that would be sufficient to establish R (in this case there is only one such free variable in the set, a), we find that although the array

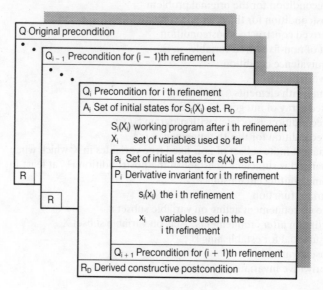

Figure 5.5 Stages of refinement.

assignment a := A is sufficient to establish R, the latter is not in a constructive form. This can be seen by computing

$$wp(\text{``a := A''}, R) \equiv (\forall j : 1 < j \leqslant N : A_{j-1} \leqslant A_j)$$

To confirm this condition a check must be made to see if the array is sorted. This requires more than a simple conditional test. Hence R needs to be transformed. The principle of extensionality (see Chapter 2) can provide the basis for a simple state space extension where a new free variable i is introduced in place of N and the conjunct i = N is included to record the identity for the replacement. This leads to the constructive postcondition R_D given below:

$$R_D : i = N \wedge (\forall j : 1 < j \leqslant i : a_{j-1} \leqslant a_j) \wedge perm(a,A)$$

Because R_D is stronger than R, that is

$$R_D \Rightarrow R$$

we are free to base our derivation of the program on R_D. The condition i = N in R_D is referred to as the **equivalence condition**.

For the example, when all the occurrences of i in R_D are replaced by N and the result is simplified, R is retrieved. This is expressed as

$$R_D(i,a)_N^i \equiv R(a)$$

where the variable list in parentheses identifies only the non-fixed free variables in the predicates. The conventions used here are similar to those employed by Gries for textual substitution except that assignment has been replaced by identity.

The set of non-fixed free variables in R_D is $X_0 = \{i, a\}$. An initialization can now be made for the smallest finite subset of non-fixed free variables x_0 in X_0 that is sufficient to establish R_D, at least in some limiting circumstance. In this instance the assignment $i := 1; a := A$ is sufficient to establish R_D, and the equivalence condition $i = N$ is sufficient to determine whether the initialization has established R_D, and hence R.

A program $S_0(X_0)$, which includes the initialization refinement $s_0(x_0)$ and accommodates the fact that the initialization chosen may not always be sufficient to establish R_D given the precondition Q, can be written

$S_0(X_0)$ Initialization $x_0 = \{i, a\}$

$i := 1; a := A; \{P_0\}$
if $i = N \rightarrow$ skip $\{R_D \text{ established}\}$
[] $i \neq N \rightarrow \{Q_1\}\ s_1(x_1)\ \{R_D\}$
fi

The condition P_0 that the initialization guarantees to establish is R_D apart from the equivalence condition D_0 (where $D_0 : i = N$) together with the equalities corresponding to the assignments. So

$$P_0 : i = 1 \wedge a = A \wedge (\forall j : 1 < j \leqslant i : a_{j-1} \leqslant a_j) \wedge \text{perm}(a, A)$$

Also

$$P_0 \wedge i = N \Rightarrow R_D$$

and Q_1 is identified as

$$Q_1 : P_0 \wedge i \neq N$$

Evaluating $P_0(i, a)$ at $i = N$, $a = A$ and simplifying the result gives the set of initial states A_0 for which the initialization will be sufficient to imply R_D. It follows that R is also established.

The **base invariant** P_0, is defined as the relation established by the initialization of the smallest finite subset of free variables x_0 from X_0 that is sufficient to imply that R_D is established, at least in some limiting circumstance. The base invariant, like conventional loop invariants, is at once a precondition and a postcondition.

The strategy for development, once a base invariant has been constructed, is as follows:

> **Refinement strategy**
> A sequence of further refinements $s_1(x_1), \ldots, s_i(x_i)$ is made until
> we have a mechanism that is general enough to establish the
> postcondition at least for the given precondition Q. Each of
> these successive refinements should be made for specifica-
> tions that correspond to either progressively weakening the
> base invariant or to making state-space extensions by
> introducing additional free variables. Both of these manip-
> ulations lead to refinements that can extend the number of
> initial states for which the mechanism will establish the
> postcondition.

The base invariant P_0, and the **derivative invariants** constructed from it, P_1, P_2, ..., P_i, characterize the set of initial states for which the mechanisms constructed from the refinements $s_0(x_0), s_1(x_1), \ldots, s_i(x_i)$ will establish R_D. With this form for the P_i the goal of the progressive refinement process is to expand monotonically the set of initial states until a mechanism has been constructed that will establish the postcondition R_D for a set of initial states that at least includes the set of initial states characterized by the precondition Q.

Returning to our example we have

$$A_0 : N = 1$$

and

$$A_0 \Rightarrow Q$$

As A_0 does not characterize anywhere near as many initial states as Q further refinements are needed. The next refinement must be made for the instance where Q_1 applies, that is

$$Q_1 : P_0 \wedge i \neq N$$

To establish R_D when Q_1 applies i will need to be increased to establish i = N. A suitable variant function that follows from the equivalence condition is

$$t : N - i$$

To guide the next refinement $s_1(x_1)$ for establishing R_D the base invariant P_0 needs to be weakened. This can be done by allowing a subset of its non-fixed free variables to be changed. To keep refinements as simple as possible we choose to adopt a form of the *principle of least action*. That is, we make a refinement that changes only the *smallest* finite subset of non-fixed free variables sufficient to establish R_D given Q_1 (note that the smallest finite subset of non-fixed free variables x_1 may not always be unique – Section 5.6.3 describes how such cases are handled).

For our example, given Q_1, we have a choice of changing i, or a, or both. Increasing just i while holding a constant will decrease the variant function. This will establish R_D provided i can be increased to N (that is to satisfy the equivalence condition). Altering P_0 accordingly gives

$$P_1: a = A \land (\forall j : 1 < j \leq i : a_{j-1} \leq a_j) \land perm(a,A) \land 1 \leq i \leq N$$

The relation P_1 is an invariant for next refinement $s_1(x_1)$ which has the responsibility of changing i (i.e. $x_1 = \{i\}$). At this point we need to investigate how i can be increased while maintaining P_1. The simplest way to increase i is to use $i := i + 1$. We may therefore investigate

$$\begin{aligned} wp \, ("i := i + 1", P_1) &\equiv a = A \land (\forall j : 1 < j \leq i + 1 : a_{j-1} \leq a_j) \land perm(a,A) \\ &\quad \land 1 \leq i + 1 \leq N \\ &\equiv a = A \land (\forall j : 1 < j \leq i : a_{j-1} \leq a_j) \land a_i \leq a_{i+1} \land \\ &\quad perm(a,A) \land 1 \leq i + 1 \leq N \end{aligned}$$

Clearly $a_i \leq a_{i+1}$ is not implied by P_1. This condition must prevail if $i := i + 1$ is to execute and still maintain P_1. We therefore obtain:

if $a_i \leq a_{i+1} \rightarrow i := i + 1$ **fi**

There is no guarantee that $a_i \leq a_{i+1}$ will hold and so this construct may abort. The requirement of making a refinement that guarantees to establish $P_1 \land i = N$ (and hence R_D) simply by increasing i is too ambitious. A way out of this situation is to settle for guaranteeing to establish something less ambitious. To proceed on this less demanding course we can first introduce a new free variable n in place of i in $i = N$ and add the equivalence condition $i = n$. This yields the constructive relation:

$$P_1 \land n = N \land i = n$$

The relation $P_1 \land n = N$ is easily established. We may then seek to establish the more easily realizable sub-goal:

$$R_1: P_1 \land i = n$$

This implies $P_1 \land i = N$ provided $n = N$ holds. There is however no obligation to preserve $n = N$ so long as the refinement preserves P_1 and decreases the variant function. We adjust the variant function associated with increasing i:

$$t : n - i$$

to accommodate a change in the new variable n. When $a_i \leq a_{i+1}$ does not hold

$a_i > a_{i+1}$ must hold. Our less ambitious sub-goal opens up the possibility of an alternative way of decreasing the variant function by executing $n := i$. It can be confirmed that this command preserves P_1 by computing $wp("n := i", P_1)$. Initializing n to N we get a command that will preserve P_1, decrease the variant function, and not abort, that is

```
n := N;
if a_i ≤ a_{i+1} → i := i + 1 {P_1}
[] a_i > a_{i+1} → n := i
fi
```

In making the refinement $s_1(x_1)$ our immediate concern is to test whether the sub-goal R_1 has been established. This is checked by testing if $i = n$ holds. Given that this refinement may not establish $i = n$ we write the new program $S_1(X_1)$ (where $S_1(X_1) = s_0(x_0) \circ s_1 x_1$)) which incorporates $s_1(x_1)$ as follows:

$S_1(X_1)$ First refinement $x_1 = \{i, n\}$

```
i := 1; a := A;
if i = N → skip
[] i ≠ N →
    n := N; {P_1}
    if a_i ≤ a_{i+1} → i := i + 1
    [] a_i > a_{i+1} → n := i
    fi; {P_1}
    if i = n → skip {R_1 established}
    [] i ≠ n → {Q_2} s_2(x_2) {R_1}
    fi
fi
```

From P_1 we find that the refinement $s_1(x_1)$ will be sufficient to establish the postcondition R_D for the precondition

$$a_1: N = 2 \land A_1 \leq A_2$$

The overall program at this stage, $S_1(X_1)$, will be sufficient to establish the postcondition R_D for the precondition

$$A_1: (N = 1) \lor (N = 2 \land A_1 \leq A_2)$$

The precondition A_1 is weaker than A_0 but still much stronger than Q so further refinements are needed.

To establish the sub-goal R_1, when Q_2 applies, we may increase i further, under the invariance of P_1. For this purpose a loop or recursive call to the alternative command in $s_1(x_1)$ may be used. Using a loop, we end up with a mechanism that guarantees to establish R_1. We may then test $i = N$ to see if R_D has been established. Implementing the refinement $s_2(x)_2$ using a loop we get the new program $S_2(X_2)$.

$S_2(X_2)$ Second refinement

```
i := 1; a := A;
if i = N → skip
[] i ≠ N →
    n := N;
    repeat {P₁}
        if aᵢ ≤ aᵢ₊₁ → i := i + 1
        [] aᵢ > aᵢ₊₁ → n := i
        fi
    until i = n; {R₁}
    if i = N → skip {R_D established}
    [] i ≠ N → {Q₃} s₃(x₃) {R_D}
    fi
fi
```

In this refinement we have deliberately used a **repeat ...until** loop instead of a loop of the form

```
do i ≠ n →
    if aᵢ ≤ aᵢ₊₁ → i := i + 1
    [] aᵢ > aᵢ₊₁ → n := i
    fi
od
```

because this latter implementation involves an initial unnecessary test of the guard $i \neq n$ directly after $i \neq n$ has been established to be true. Throughout the text when this form of redundancy occurs we use repeat-loops.

From P_1 we discover that the refinement $s_2(x_2)$ will be sufficient to establish the postcondition R_D for the precondition

$$a_2 : N \geqslant 2 \wedge (\forall j : 1 < j \leqslant N : A_{j-1} \leqslant A_j)$$

The overall program, at this stage $S_2(X_2)$, will therefore establish the postcondition R_D for the precondition

$$A_2 : N \geqslant 1 \wedge (\forall j : 1 < j \leqslant N : A_{j-1} \leqslant A_j)$$

This tells us is that if the original data set A was initially ordered then the mechanism $S_2(X_2)$ would be sufficient to establish R_D and hence R.

The precondition A_2 is weaker than A_1 but still stronger than Q, and so it is necessary to seek a further refinement.

We have

$$R_1 : P_1 \wedge (i = N \textbf{ cor } i < N \wedge a_i > a_{i+1})$$

and

$$P_1 \wedge i = N \Rightarrow R_D$$
$$P_1 \wedge i \neq N \Rightarrow P_1$$

and we identify Q_3 as

$$Q_3 : P_1 \wedge (i < N \wedge a_i > a_{i+1} \wedge N > 1)$$

Q_3 is the precondition for which the next refinement $s_3(x_3)$ must be made. However, allowing just i to increase when Q_3 applies violates P_1, since $s_2(x_2)$ has established $a_i > a_{i+1}$. Therefore to guide the next refinement, P_1 must be weakened to admit more initial states for which R_D can be established. The condition $a_i > a_{i+1}$ suggests a must be changed. Weakening P_1 by dropping the restriction a = A gives

$$P_2 : (\forall j : 1 < j \leq i : a_{j-1} \leq a_j) \wedge 1 \leq i \leq N \wedge \text{perm}(a, A)$$

Given Q_3, to change a will involve inserting a_{i+1} into the ordered sequence a[1..i] under the invariance of P_2. We therefore need to establish the sub-goal R_2

$$R_2 : (\forall j : 1 < j \leq i + 1 : a_{j-1} \leq a_j) \wedge 1 \leq i + 1 \leq N \wedge \text{perm}(a, A)$$

in order to be able to execute $i := i + 1$ under the invariance of P_2.

The derivation of the program component for the specification (Q_3, R_2) may be treated as an entirely separate problem. It involves several more sophisticated transformations to incorporate the influence of Q_3 into the invariant for the problem. Consideration of this sub-problem has therefore been deferred until later (see Section 6.4.3) when the reader has a better understanding of specification transformations. For the present purposes it will be assumed that insert is available which will establish R_2 and therefore allow us to execute $i := i + 1$ under the invariance of P_2. The refinement that incorporates insert may be sufficient to establish R_D and so we get

$S_3(X_3)$ Third refinement $x_3 = \{a, i\}$

```
i := 1; a := A;
if i = N → skip
[] i ≠ N →
  n := N;
  repeat {P₁}
    if a_i ≤ a_{i+1} → i := i + 1
    [] a_i > a_{i+1} → n := i
    fi
  until i = n; {R₁}
  if i = N → skip
  [] i ≠ N →
    insert( a, i + 1); i := i + 1; {P₂}
    if i = N → skip {R_D established}
    [] i ≠ N → {Q₄} s₄(x₄) {R_D}
    fi
  fi
fi
fi
```

The refinement $s_3(x_3)$ will be sufficient to establish the postcondition for the precondition

$$a_3 : N \geqslant 2 \wedge (\forall j : 1 < j < N : A_{j-1} \leqslant A_j) \wedge A_{N-1} > A_N$$

The current program, $S_3(X_3)$, will establish the postcondition R_D for the precondition

$$A_3 : (N \geqslant 1 \wedge (\forall j : 1 < j \leqslant N : A_{j-1} \leqslant A_j) \vee (N \geqslant 2 \wedge (\forall j : 1 < j < N: A_{j-1} \leqslant A_j)$$
$$\wedge (A_{N-1} > A_N))$$

The latest refinement will establish the postcondition if only the *last* element A_N is out of order. The precondition A_3, although weaker than A_2, is still stronger than Q and so a further refinement is needed.

We have

$$P_2 \wedge i = N \Rightarrow R_D$$

and we identify Q_4 as

$$Q_4 : P_2 \wedge i \neq N$$

Increasing just i will be sufficient to establish R_D when Q_4 applies provided i can be increased to N. The refinement $s_1(x_1)$ would be sufficient to use as the next refinement $s_4(x_4)$. This suggests that the development process has uncovered *a cycle* in the structure of the program.

Further investigation tells us that a loop or recursive call which includes the mechanism $s_1(x_1) \circ s_2(x_2) \circ s_3(x_3)$ can be used to make the next refinement under the invariance of P_2. We get

$S_4(X_4)$ Fourth refinement $x_4 = \{a, i\}$

```
i := 1; a := A;
do i ≠ N → {P₂}
    n := N ;
    repeat
        if aᵢ ≤ aᵢ₊₁ → i := i + 1
        [] aᵢ > aᵢ₊₁ → n := i
        fi
        until i = n; {R₁}
        if i = N → skip
        [] i ≠ N → insert(a, i + 1); i := i + 1
        fi
od
{R_D}
```

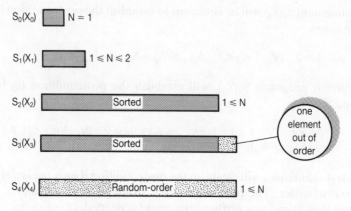

Figure 5.6   Preconditions for which postcondition is established

The refinement $s_4(x_4)$ yields a program $S_4(X_4)$ which has the properties

$$P_2 \wedge i = N \Rightarrow R_D$$
$$P_2 \wedge i \neq N \Rightarrow P_2$$

This program is sufficient to establish the postcondition R_D for the precondition

$$N \geq 1$$

No restriction at all is placed on the configuration of the original data set. The derivation of the program is therefore complete.

The staged derivation of this algorithm shows very clearly how a mechanism may be built from components that establish the postcondition for a sequence of stronger preconditions

a_0: $N = 1$	for a single element
a_1: $N = 2 \wedge A_1 \leq A_2$	for two elements sorted
a_2: $N \geq 2 \wedge (\forall j: 1 < j \leq N: A_{j-1} \leq A_j)$	for the whole array sorted
a_3: $N \geq 2 \wedge (\forall j: 1 < j < N: A_{j-1} \leq A_j)$	for only the last element out
$\wedge A_{N-1} > A_N$	of place

than the given weaker precondition

$$Q : N \geq 1 \qquad\qquad \text{for an arbitrary array of elements}$$

Figure 5.6 gives a pictorial representation of these preconditions.

In the derivation of the insertionsort we have seen how the solution to a problem can be built up in a stepwise fashion by a sequence of refinements, each of which extends the set of initial states for which the postcondition is established. We will now examine in some detail a model for program derivation based on the use of specifications.

5.6 Model for Program Derivation

The solution of a complex problem is not something that can be understood 'all-at-once'. *Elements of it must be grasped over a period of time and fitted into an overall framework.* Our objective here is to provide a concrete realization of this underlying problem-solving strategy built upon extensive use of primary specifications (preconditions and postconditions) and secondary specifications (invariants and sub-goals).

Progress relative to the nature of problem

To understand this method for program derivation we may start by considering how progress is made towards the final solution of a problem. In simplest terms progress is made

- by moving in steps from the most restricted solution to a problem to the most general solution, or
- by moving stepwise from the simplest or easiest version of a solution to a problem to the most complex or most comprehensive solution, or
- by proceeding from a solution to the smallest version of the problem to a solution of a much larger version of the problem.

This interpretation of the method does not tell us all that much. What we need is an interpretation of progress that relates directly to the use of specifications.

Progress as measured by specifications

There are four elements to this second interpretation.

- Firstly, successive refinements result in the postcondition being established for progressively weaker preconditions. In other words *there is a progression from the strongest precondition to the weakest precondition.* For each refinement there is a corresponding weakening transformation applied to a specification. Quite often the strongest useful precondition is the postcondition itself. The task then is to try to decide whether R applies for the given data set.

- A related interpretation is that *successive refinements expand the set of initial states for which the mechanism will establish the postcondition.* Again expanding the set of initial states corresponds directly to transformations on a specification.

- There is another link between specifications and progress with a solution. What we find very often is that there is a progression from a solution for a precondition that *looks most like* the postcondition to other solutions for increasingly more general preconditions. An example of this would be a refinement where the postcondition was established in the first instance by *confirming* it rather than by having to construct it, e.g. 'sorting' a set of data by simply checking to see if it was *already* sorted.

- There is one other important way in which progress is made towards a final solution. This relates to the structure of the data. For problems involving structured data each refinement *extends* the match between the program control structure and the data structure it processes. It is interesting to note that we get the same sort of match with the structure of the data as is achieved by another of the constructive program development methods – Michael Jackson's top-down data-driven method (see the Bibliography at the end of the chapter) development. In fact the present method of refinement captures not only *explicit data structure* but also *implicit structure* in data. More will be said about this later.

The refinement process

Two other important operational elements of the method which relate to specifications are:

- how the refinement process is initiated
- how successive refinements are made.

A practical way to begin the refinement process is to look for an initialization of free variables that will establish the truth of the postcondition at least in some limiting circumstance. An initialization refinement of this form serves two purposes. If it is successful it provides a starting point for the derivation of a program from a specification. If, on the other hand, it is not possible to make such an initialization, either there is an error in the specification (it is not *satisfiable*) or the specification needs to be transformed to some equivalent or related form.

Our concern with initialization is always to make a refinement capable of establishing the postcondition. Subsequent refinements should also establish the postcondition at least in some limiting circumstance (see Figures 5.7 and 5.8).

This will be called the **refinement invariant.** Figures 5.7 and 5.8 illustrate the strategy. This refinement strategy has several advantages:

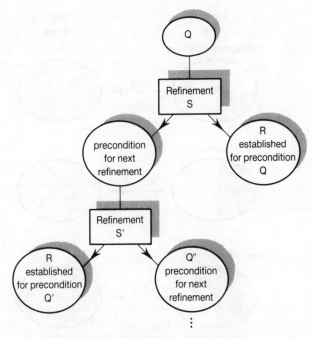

Figure 5.7   Limited top-down design

- After each refinement there is a working but limited program.
- Each refinement either establishes the postcondition for the given precondition or establishes the precondition for making the next refinement.
- The need to make refinements that require either recursive or iterative composition is discovered naturally when the precondition for the next refinement matches the precondition for an earlier refinement (i.e. the refinement has preserved an invariant).

To achieve a match between program control structure and the structure of data being processed further restrictions on how refinements are made are needed. Each refinement changes a subset of the free variables associated with the problem.

To keep these refinements as simple as possible and ensure a match between program control structure and data structure, always make refinements that change or set the smallest finite subset of free variables that will be sufficient to establish the postcondition for the given precondition. This strategy is a realization of a principle loosely analogous to the *principle of least action* known in physics. Our principle will be given the same name.

This refinement strategy depends on a method for finding the base invariant, a set of postcondition transformations, a method for partitioning the initial and final states, and another set of rules for incorporating new

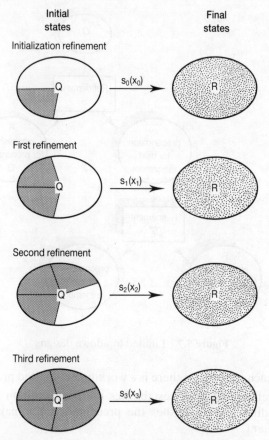

Figure 5.8 Successive refinements expand the set of initial states for which the postcondition is established.

refinements into an existing program structure. These issues will now be considered.

5.6.1 State-space extension

A specification given for a problem, although accurate, is often not in a form that is directly useful for developing a program which satisfies that specification. For example, consider the postcondition R in the following specification:

$$Q : X > 0 \wedge Y > 0$$
$$R : x = \gcd(X,Y)$$

It specifies that an x be found which is the greatest common divisor of two fixed positive integers X and Y but does not give much insight into how the program could be developed. Faced with this sort of situation a good program designer should always be prepared to meet the need to transform a specification into a form that can aid the program's derivation.

The first problem is recognizing when a postcondition is not in a form that easily aids development of the program. Frequently the criteria suggested in the previous section can signal this situation. That is, if

- it is not easy to initialize a subset of free variables that will establish R,

or

- it is not easy to check that the initialization has established R,

then the postcondition needs to be transformed. In making transformations on a postcondition the objective is to introduce more accessible freedom into the specification which may subsequently be exploited in the development of the program.

A simple way to do this is by making a state-space extension to give an *equivalent* or *related stronger form*. One way of interpreting how such a state-space extension is achieved in general is as follows. A higher-dimensional state space is first constructed for which the current state space is a projection. The equivalence condition is then the equation in the larger state space whose solution is the current state space. A state space extension transformation involves two steps. Firstly, one or more fixed free variables (i.e. constants) or other variables, or expressions, in the original postcondition is replaced by new free variables. Then a conjunction of this new form is made with an equivalence condition which establishes the equivalence under variable substitution. The principle of extensionality also permits us to make such transformations. This principle, which was mentioned earlier (see Section 2.4.8) may be stated as follows:

$$(\forall x)(\forall y)\,(x = y \Rightarrow (P(x) \equiv P(y)))$$

Using the definition of equivalence this formula implies

$$(\forall x)(\forall y)\,(x = y \Rightarrow (P(x) \Rightarrow P(y)))$$

The latter expression is equivalent in the predicate calculus to

$$(\forall x)(\forall y)\,((x = y \wedge P(x)) \Rightarrow P(y))$$

The several different types of state-space extension based on these ideas will now be illustrated.

Constant replacement

In this extension a constant is replaced directly by a variable and the equivalence condition specifies the equality between the constant and the variable. Given a formula P(F) containing a constant or fixed free variable F, one or more occurrences of the F can be replaced by a new free variable f to yield a new formula P(f) provided the equality f = F is preserved. We have

$$P(f) \wedge f = F \tag{1}$$

where

$$P(f) \wedge f = F \Rightarrow P(F) \tag{2}$$

Because the new formula (1) implies the original formula P(F) it can be used as a basis for program derivation.

EXAMPLE 1

The postcondition

$$R : s = \Sigma(A_j : 0 < j \le N)$$

can be transformed to a constructive form by replacing the constant N by the variable i to give

$$R_D : s = \Sigma(A_j : 0 < j \le i) \wedge i = N$$

where i = N is the equivalence condition.

EXAMPLE 2

The postcondition for raising a fixed integer X to a fixed natural number Y is

$$R : z = X^Y$$

Replacing the constant Y by the free variable y yields

$$R_D : z = X^y \wedge y = Y$$

where y = Y is the equivalence condition.

Expression replacement

In this extension an expression e in a formula P(e) is replaced by a new variable f. We have

$$P(f) \wedge f = e \tag{3}$$

where

$$P(f) \wedge f = e \Rightarrow P(e) \tag{4}$$

Again because of the implication (4) the formula (3) can be used as a basis for program derivation.

EXAMPLE 3

The postcondition for finding the integer square root a of a fixed natural number N may be given as

$$R : a^2 \leqslant N < (a + 1)^2$$

Replacing the expression $(a + 1)$ by b gives

$$R_D : a^2 \leqslant N < b^2 \wedge (b = a + 1)$$

where $b = a + 1$ is the equivalence condition.

EXAMPLE 4

The postcondition for finding the quotient q and remainder r for a fixed integer X and a fixed divisor D may be given as

$$R : X = q \times D + r \wedge 0 \leqslant r < D$$

The expression $q \times D$ may be replaced by a new free variable d to yield

$$R_D : X = d + r \wedge 0 \leqslant r < D \wedge d = q \times D$$

Splitting a variable

In this extension an occurrence of a variable is replaced by another variable. Given a formula $P(f)$ containing a free variable f, one or more occurrences of f can be replaced by a new free variable g to yield a new fomula $P(g)$ provided the equality $g = f$ is preserved. We have

$$P(g) \wedge g = f \tag{5}$$

where

$$P(g) \wedge g = f \Rightarrow P(f) \tag{6}$$

Because the new formula (5) implies the original formula $P(f)$ it can be used as a basis for program derivation.

EXAMPLE 5

The postcondition for searching a fixed integer array A[1..N] to see if X is present may be given as

$$R : (\forall j : 0 < j \leq i : X \neq A_j) \wedge (i = N \textbf{ cor } X = A_{i+1})$$

Replacing the variable i by a new variable n in i = N gives a form that can be easily initialized with equivalence condition i = n, that is

$$R_D : (\forall j : 0 < j \leq i : X \neq A_j) \wedge (n = N \textbf{ cor } X = A_{i+1}) \wedge i = n$$

This form provides the basis for forced termination of loops which is discussed in Chapter 12.

Image extension

A more interesting form of state-space extension involves incorporating a free variable 'image' of an existing sub-expression within the postcondition. Image extension is a generalization of the idea of replacing a constant by a variable. The following examples illustrate the technique.

EXAMPLE 6

For the greatest common divisor problem discussed earlier the following specification is often given:

$$R : x = gcd(X,Y)$$

This postcondition has the underlying structure

$$x = CONSTANT$$

where the CONSTANT is gcd(X,Y) and the free variable is x.

To transform this postcondition to a more useful form we first introduce a variable y and split the '=' relation to obtain

$$x = y \wedge y = gcd(X,Y)$$

We then replace the second y by the variable image of gcd(X,Y), and include the equivalence condition y = gcd(x,y) to obtain

$$R_D : x = y \wedge gcd(x,y) = gcd(X,Y) \wedge y = gcd(x,y)$$

The equivalence under variable replacement of R_D with R can easily be checked by replacing the new free variable y in R_D by x which gives

$$x = x \wedge gcd(x,x) = gcd(X,Y) \wedge x = gcd(x,x)$$

which simplifies to

$$x = gcd(X,Y) \qquad \text{since } gcd(x,x) = x$$

It is very easy to obtain an invariant from R_D that includes $gcd(x,y) = gcd(X,Y)$. In most treatments of this problem the origin of the invariant is usually a mystery.

EXAMPLE 7

There is often another motivation for doing a state-space expansion. We introduce more freedom into a postcondition in an effort to discover a more efficient algorithm. In the quest for greater efficiency for the exponentiation problem (i.e. $R : z = X^Y$) we can apply an image transformation by introducing x^y as the image of the constant X^Y. The first step is to do an *identity transformation* to obtain

$$z \times 1 = X^Y$$

We then replace the constant 1 by the variable image of X^Y and include the necessary equivalence condition to obtain

$$R_D : z \times x^y = X^Y \wedge y = 0 \wedge x = X$$

with $y = 0 \wedge x = X$ acting as the equivalence condition. The equivalence with R under variable substitution is easily confirmed. This new specification admits the possibility of changing X indirectly via x. A doubling strategy can be used for this purpose.

EXAMPLE 8

The following postcondition is often given for the problem of multiplying two fixed natural numbers X and Y without using multiplication:

$$R : z = X \times Y$$

To make this more useful we first do an identity transformation to obtain

$$z + 0 = X \times Y$$

We may then replace the constant 0 by the *complete* variable image of
$X \times Y$ and include the equivalence condition to obtain

$$R_D : z + x \times y = X \times Y \wedge y = 0 \wedge x = X$$

This formula can be used to construct an efficient multiplication-by-
addition algorithm that applies a doubling strategy. If instead of using
a complete image of $X \times Y$ we use only a *partial* variable image $X \times y$
where X is fixed, and y is a free variable, we get

$$R : z + X \times y = X \times Y \wedge y = 0$$

This partial image transformation leads to a simpler but less efficient
algorithm. For this problem we can also use the constant replacement
rule to give

$$R_D : z = X \times y \wedge y = Y.$$

but the loop invariant which follows from this (that is, $z = X \times y$) is
perhaps not quite as pleasing. As a final comment about the use of
state-space extensions it should be noted that they may be applied not
only to the postcondition but also to the base invariant and derivative
invariants encountered in the course of the refinement process.

Complement extension

State-space extensions involving the introduction of new free variables are
not alone sufficient to cover all the transformations needed to put
postconditions into a constructive form. There is another important type of
transformation on the existing state space that is sometimes needed when a
problem requires a search to establish some relation (for example, even the
greatest common divisor problem may be re-phrased as a search problem).
The form of the postcondition that is often given for such problems is a
description of just the final state relation (e.g. $R : x = \gcd(X,Y)$). This relation
characterizes a set of states in a given universe of discourse. It also splits the
universe of discourse into two parts, namely the states that belong to the set,
and the states that do not belong to the set. The latter part forms another set
of states C correlative to the one given, called its **complement**. A
specification that characterizes all or part of the complement set as well as
the original specification is often a more useful stronger form that will assist
program derivation.

Establishing the truth of

$$R \wedge C$$

is a sufficient condition for establishing the truth of R. We may base our derivation on R ∧ C rather than simply on R. Adding the conjunct C strengthens the specification. We should always try to base program derivation on the strongest possible specification for a problem.

EXAMPLE 9

Consider the problem of searching a fixed integer array A[1..N] to find where a fixed integer X occurs (it is known to be present). The specification often given is

$$R : X = A_i$$

The complement C may assume the form

$$C : (\forall j : 1 \leqslant j < i : X \neq A_j)$$

A complement extension of R is then

$$R_D: X = A_i \wedge (\forall j : 1 \leqslant j < i : X \neq A_j)$$

This specification R_D may be used in place of R to develop the program. The conjunct C may be easily established by the assignment $i := 1$. It is then only a matter of maintaining C in the search to establish $X = A_i$.

EXAMPLE 10

A similar situation applies with the gcd problem if we choose to do a complement extension of $x = \gcd(X,Y)$. After identifying C we end up with

$$R_D : (\forall z : x < z \leqslant \min(X,Y) : z \neq \gcd(X,Y)) \wedge x = \gcd(X,Y)$$

This specification may be used to conduct a descending linear search to find $\gcd(X,Y)$. An appropriate initialization is $x = \min(X,Y)$.

Range and bound extensions

Appropriate initializations of free variables that can establish a postcondition frequently correspond to bounds associated with those free variables. We should therefore try to include at least a bound or preferably a range for free variables in a postcondition. This suggestion reinforces the advice that the strongest appropriate specification should always be used for program development

Applying this advice to several of our earlier specifications we get

$$R_D : 1 \leqslant x \leqslant min(X,Y) \wedge x = y \wedge gcd(x,y) = gcd(X,Y) \wedge y = gcd(x,y)$$

where $1 \leqslant x \leqslant min(X,Y)$ has been added. This upper limit for the greatest common divisor follows directly from the definition of the gcd.

For the quotient–remainder problem we have:

$$R_D : X = q \times D + r \wedge 0 \leqslant r < D \wedge 0 \leqslant q \leqslant eX$$

where $0 \leqslant q \leqslant X$ has been appended. Note that q can reach a maximum value of X when $D = 1$ and $X < D$.

Deeper insights into a problem are often gained by attempting to attach either bounds or ranges to free variables in specifications.

5.6.2   Base invariant construction

The simplest way to identify a suitable base invariant P_0 is by a weakest precondition calculation. This requires first finding an initialization of free variables that can establish R and then computing the weakest precondition for which that initialization will establish the postcondition. In making this calculation the objective is quite different from that usually sought from such calculations. We are interested in identifying those components of R that are guaranteed to be made TRUE by the chosen initialization of free variables. Those components of R constitute one of two major parts of the base invariant. The other part comes directly from any equalities that the initialization establishes (for example, the initialization $i := 0$ establishes the condition $i = 0$). The conjunction of the components identified as TRUE in the weakest precondition calculation for the initialization, with the condition established directly by the initialization, form the **base invariant**. Figure 5.9 provides a sketch of the steps in the process.

To illustrate the process consider the sorting example given earlier:

$$Q : N \geqslant 1$$
$$R : (\forall j : 1 \leqslant j < N : a_j \leqslant a_{j+1}) \wedge perm(a,A)$$

It is required to sort a fixed array of integers A. To proceed with our search for a suitable base invariant we need to find an initialization of free variables that can establish the postcondition. The only free variable in R is the array variable a. We might therefore propose the initialization

$$a := A$$

Computing the weakest precondition for this initialization establishing R we get

$$wp("a := A", R) \equiv (\forall j : 1 \leqslant j < N : A_j \leqslant A_{j+1}) \wedge perm(A,A)$$

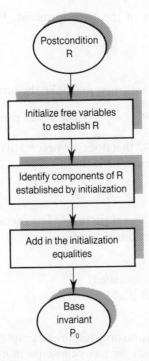

Figure 5.9 Base invariant identification.

This tells us that if the original data A is already sorted our initialization will be sufficient to establish the postcondition. However, the test to confirm that this initialization has established R is complicated – it involves a test to see if the array is sorted. In these circumstances it is appropriate to see if the postcondition can be transformed to a form that is easier to work with. Doing a state-space extension in which N is replaced by i yields the constructive postcondition

$$R_D : (\forall j : 1 \leq j < i : a_j \leq a_{j+1}) \land perm(a,A) \land i = N$$

A possible initialization that can establish R_D under certain circumstances is:

$$i, a := 1, A$$

Computing the weakest precondition for which this initialization will establish R_D we get

$$wp(\text{"i, a := 1, A"}, R) \equiv (\forall j : 1 \leq j < 1 : A_j \leq A_{j+1}) \land perm(A,A) \land 1 = N$$
$$\equiv TRUE \land TRUE \land 1 = N$$

which indicates that the weakest precondition is N = 1. This tells us that the first two conjuncts evaluate to TRUE. Therefore

$$(\forall j : 1 \leq j < i : a_j \leq a_{j+1}) \land perm(a,A)$$

may be used as one part of the base invariant. For the other part, the initialization establishes

$$i = 1 \land a = A$$

and so the complete base invariant may take the form

$$P_0 : i = 1 \land a = A \land (\forall j : 1 \leqslant j < i : a_j \leqslant a_{j+1}) \land \mathrm{perm}(a, A)$$

The component in R_D that does not necessarily evaluate to TRUE in the weakest precondition calculation is the condition

$$i = N$$

This latter condition may therefore be used to check whether the initialization establishes the postcondition, that is

```
i, a := 1, A;
if i = N → skip {R_D established}
[] i ≠ N → {Q_1} s_1(x_1) {R_D}
fi
```

The fact that this initialization only requires a simple test (i.e. $i = N$) to check if R_D is established suggests we have chosen a more suitable form for the postcondition. Appropriate initialization values for use in constructing the base invariant are often bounds on the ranges of free variables.

5.6.3   Decomposition rules

The partitioning strategy suggested consists of three hierarchical decomposition rules. For a program $S(X)$, described by a free variable set X, and composed by a sequence of refinements $s_0(x_0), s_1(x_1), \dots, s_N(x_N)$, where $x_i \subseteq X_i$, and X_i is the set of free variables available at the ith refinement, the following rules apply:

Primary decomposition rule (sufficiency rule)
Each member of the sequence of refinements $s_0(x_0), \dots,$ $s_N(x_N)$ needed to compose the program $S_N(X_N)$ should extend the set of initial states for which the postcondition is established beyond that established by all previous refinements.

Expressed more pragmatically, what the primary decomposition rule suggests is that we should always try to make refinements that will establish the postcondition at least in some limiting circumstance.

The primary decomposition rule provides a basic framework for making refinements. Two other rules are provided. Their intent is to make the partitioning and refinement processes more explicit. The first of these additional rules is a minimum progress rule, based on the principle of least action. It is stated as follows:

Secondary decomposition rule (correspondence rule)
Given a precondition Q_i that has previously been established, the next refinement in the sequence $s_i(x_i)$ should be made by assigning values to or changing the smallest subset x_i (where $x_i \subseteq X_i$) of free variables which is sufficient to extend the set of initial states for which the postcondition is established.

This rule serves two important functions:

- It provides an explicit rule for refinement in terms of free variables used to define the postcondition, the base invariant, and derivative invariants.
- It allows a match to be made between program control structure and data structure in the sense advocated by Jackson.

The principle that this rule embodies represents a generalization and abstraction of Jackson's correspondence principle. It suggests that the limiting conditions under which particular subsets of variables may be changed frequently identifies and characterizes important structure that may be realized in the stepwise implementation of a program. It also provides a departure from trying to base program development on a loose or incomplete set of semantic tags. As there is no appeal to known semantic structure tags it is possible to identify and exploit structure which has no semantic label. When a refinement is made which changes other than a minimum subset of free variables that is sufficient to establish R it is likely that the match between the program control structure and the data structure will be destroyed. *Subsets of free variables, and the relations which they describe, provide an abstract description of structure.* This way of characterizing structure is more powerful than rules based only on semantics as it allows structures for which there is no semantic equivalent to be captured and exploited.

Although explicit, the secondary decomposition rule is not always strong enough to uniquely define the minimum subset x_i of free variables which are candidates for change in a particular refinement. At this point we can either make an arbitrary choice among the candidate minimum subsets of the same cardinality or introduce a third finer decomposition rule. One such rule, which is again an extension of the principle of least action, takes the following form:

> **Tertiary decomposititition rule (simplification rule)**
> The refinement $s_i(x_i)$ (which changes the variable subset x_i) chosen when variable subsets of equal size are selected by the secondary rule is that refinement which needs to reference but not necessarily change the least number of free variables from X_i.

Of course this rule, like the secondary decomposition rule, cannot always guarantee to yield a unique subset x_i. In such instances an arbitrary choice can be made as to which subset is used for the refinement. More elaborate refinement rules could be included but this would be an unnecessary complication of the method. There are instances where symmetries exist in a problem that can only be dealt with by arbitrary choice.

The main function of this tertiary rule is to try to ensure that the simplest refinements are always made first, the tacit assumption being, if more variables are involved, a refinement is more complex. Other criteria may be preferred for simplification. A schematic representation of the complete refinement context is given in Figure 5.10.

What has emerged from this discussion is that useful structure in a problem can be characterized by relations defined in terms of variables and

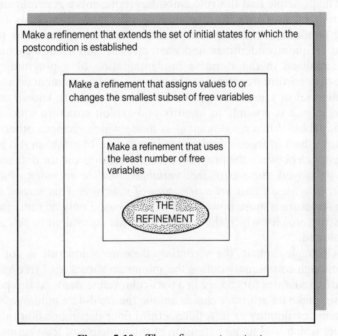

Figure 5.10   The refinement context.

conditions applied to particular domains. Furthermore, the structure in programs is built from just these materials and so it is reasonable to view decomposition of a problem in terms of changing certain subsets of variables.

5.6.4   Refinement composition rules

We can characterize how goal-establishing refinements may be composed by relating each such refinement to the alternative construct which guards the next refinement. The rules are very simple; the current refinement $s_i(x_i)$ is either *prefix*, *infix*, or *postfix* with respect to the alternative construct which guards the next refinement. It is important with the infix refinement that $s_i(x_i)$ does not destroy the equivalence condition, D_i. With P_i defined as the condition that the refinement $s_i(x_i)$ guarantees to establish or maintain, and D_i defined such that $P_i \wedge D_i \Rightarrow R$ the composition rules assume the form given below.

(1) Prefix refinement (Q)

$s_i(x_i)$;
if $D_i \rightarrow$ skip
[] $\neg D_i \rightarrow$ "make next refinement capable of establishing R"
fi

(2) Infix refinement (I)

if $D_i \rightarrow s_i(x_i)$
[]$\neg D_i \rightarrow$ "make next refinement capable of establishing R"
fi

(3) Postfix refinement (R)

if $\neg D_i \rightarrow$ "make next refinement capable of establishing R"
[] $D_i \rightarrow$ skip
fi; $\{D_i\}$
$s_i(x_i)$

(4) Recursive or iterative refinement (P)

$s_j(x_j), \ldots , s_{i-1}(x_{i-1})$ where $0 \leqslant j \leqslant i-1$

Here the refinement $s_i(x_i)$ is made by either putting the program text consisting of the last $i-j$ refinements $s_j(x_j), \ldots s_{i-1}(x_{i-1})$ in a loop or by achieving the same effect using tail recursion.

For the most part, prefix refinements are used to add another component to an existing program structure. Any refinement that involves initialization of free variables almost invariably requires a prefix refinement. The other type of refinement frequently used is the recursive or iterative refinement. Infix and postfix refinements are less commonly used. A postfix refinement is used when some subsequent refinement will guarantee to establish a condition D_i that is needed for $s_i(x_i)$ to establish R at least in some limiting circumstance. An example of a postfix refinement is given later which, it is hoped, clarifies how this rule is applied. An infix refinement, like the postfix refinement, requires that a condition D_i be established before it can be used to establish R. It should be used in preference to a postfix refinement when subsequent refinements cannot guarantee to establish the condition D_i.

The need for recursive or iterative refinement is discovered during the development process only after the compound loop-body or recursive-body has been developed in earlier refinements. It is signalled by the need to make a refinement that changes a subset of variables equivalent to a subset that had been changed or assigned previously. This is an important attribute of the method. Implementation of this refinement may be made using either a loop or tail recursion.

A generalization of the composition rules allows $s_i(x_i)$ to be replaced by $S_i(X_i)$ in each of the rules. For example, this results in another prefix rule:

$S_i(X_i)$;
if $D_i \rightarrow$ skip
[] $\neg D_i \rightarrow$ "make next refinement capable of establishing R"
fi

This rule is applied quite frequently. It indicates that a composite set of refinements may serve as a prefix, infix, or postfix refinement with respect to a new refinement.

EXAMPLE 1   Refinements for a simple loop

The following example illustrates the three composition steps to construct a simple loop.

$$S_0(X_0) = Q(s_0(x_0))$$ Initialization of loop
$$S_1(X_1) = S_0(X_0) \circ Q(s_1(x_1))$$ Development of the loop body
$$S_2(X_2) = S_1(X_1) \circ P(s_1(x_1))$$ Iterative or recursive call to loop body

EXAMPLE 2   Refinements for insertion sort

This second example shows the composition steps needed to construct the insertion sort implementation derived in Section 5.5.

$$S_0(X_0) = Q (s_0(x_0))$$

Initialization of outermost loop

$$S_1(X_1) = S_0(X_0) \circ Q(s_1(x_1))$$

Development of the loop body for sort check

$$S_2(X_2) = S_1(X_1) \circ P (s_1(x_1))$$

Iterative call to sort check loop body

$$S_3(X_3) = S_2(X_2) \circ Q(s_3(x_3))$$

Development of insertion mechanism

$$S_4(X_4) = S_3(X_3) \circ P$$
$$(s_{1..3}(x_{1..3}))$$

Iterative call to sort check/ insertion loop body

5.6.5   Comparison with top-down design

The refinement model that has been described provides the basis for a limiting form of top-down design in that the remaining problem is always split into two. This can simplify both the development process and the construction of the accompanying proof. As a method for program derivation, the present method of stepwise refinement lies at the boundary between top-down and bottom-up design although, as the composition rules show, it is strictly a top-down refinement method.

Individual goal-establishing refinements may identify sub-problems that require further decomposition. In this situation, the original decomposition/refinement strategy can be applied to the sub-problem. A solution to the sub-problem is constructed by a sequence of refinements, each of which enlarges the set of initial states for which the sub-goal is established – *the method is recursive* in its application.

It is useful to make a superficial comparison of this method with conventional top-down design. In the conventional method progress from an abstract specification to a concrete realization is made by replacing a defined, but as yet unwritten, component of a program by one or more sub-components which are again well defined but not necessarily at the implementation level. This process is repeated until the entire program is expressed at the implementation level in a programming language. With the proposed method of derivation, each refinement yields a realization or implementation that is capable of establishing the postcondition for an expanded set of initial states. Final states are usually not accessible until most, if not all, refinements are made in conventional top-down design. In contrast to this, with the proposed method, right from the first refinement, final states are accessed. More graphically, conventional refinement is like trying to reach the heart (centre) of an onion by starting at the outside and peeling off the body layer by layer whereas with the present method a part of all of the heart is reached with each refinement by slicing out a wedge of the onion. It should be stressed that *with the present method there is always a working program* $S_i(X_i)$ *after each refinement* $s_i(x_i)$. Figure 5.14 highlights the difference.

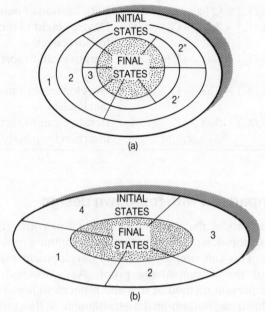

Figure 5.14   Comparison of top-down design with limited top-down design.

In the top part of the figure the numbers 1, 2, refer to the levels of refinement in the hierarchical decomposition of the problem, whereas in the lower part of the figure the numbers simply indicate successive refinements and their impact on the set of initial states for which the postcondition is established.

5.7   Systematic Decomposition

The decomposition of a large problem into manageable sub-problems is not something that can be done 'all at once'. Such a decomposition must be accomplished in a stepwise manner. In this section we will show how a problem requiring a nested loop structure solution is systematically decomposed. The strategy that we will employ for decomposition relies on the use of:

- state-space extensions, and
- weakest precondition calculations

The problem chosen, although somewhat artificial, illustrates in the simplest way a strategy that can be employed to solve more complex problems. The problem requires the row sums for a fixed integer array A[1..M,1..N] to be computed and the results stored in a one–dimensional array s[1..M]. The specification can be written as follows:

$$Q : M \geqslant 0 \wedge N \geqslant 0$$
$$R : (\forall p : 0 < p \leqslant M : s_p = \Sigma(A_{p,q} : 0 < q \leqslant N))$$

It is not easy to make an initialization of free variables that can establish R. This suggests that R needs to be transformed. Using the constant replacement rule we can do a state-space extension where we introduce a new free variable i to replace M. This yields R_D, which implies R:

$$R_D : (\forall p : 0 < p \leqslant i : s_p = \Sigma(A_{p,q} : 0 < q \leqslant N)) \wedge i = M$$

An initialization can now be made that may establish R_D and which can be easily checked by the equivalence condition i = M. We get

$S_0(X_0)$ Initialization $x_0 = \{i\}$

```
i := 0 ; {P0}
if i = M → skip {RD established}
[] i ≠ M → {Q1} s1(x1) {R}
fi
```

The initialization guarantees to establish the base invariant P_0 :

$$P_0 : i = 0 \wedge (\forall p : 0 < p \leqslant i : s_p = \Sigma(A_{p,q} : 0 < q \leqslant N))$$

and we have

$$P_0 \wedge i = M \Rightarrow R_D$$

and we identify Q_1 as

$$Q_1 : P_0 \wedge i \neq M$$

To establish R_D when Q_1 applies i will need to be increased in order to establish i = M. A suitable variant function that follows from the equivalence condition is

$$t : M - i$$

A simple way to decrease the variant function is to use the command i := i + 1. Weakening P_0 to allow i to increase we get

$$P_1 : 0 \leqslant i \leqslant M \wedge (\forall p : 0 < p \leqslant i : s_p = \Sigma (A_{p,q} : 0 < q \leqslant N))$$

To investigate how progress may be made we compute

$$wp("i := i + 1", P_1)$$

When we do this we find that the sub-goal R_1

$$R_1 : s_{i+1} = \Sigma(A_{i+1,q} : 0 < q \leqslant N)$$

is not implied by P_1. The weakest precondition calculation has assisted us with the decomposition by identifying the sub-goal R_1. It will be necessary to develop a mechanism to establish the sub-goal R_1 before $i := i + 1$ can be executed under the invariance of P_1. We will now attend to this task.

It is easy to initialize the free variable s_{i+1}, but to check if the initialization we have made has established R_1 it is necessary to compute the sum

$$\Sigma(A_{i+1,q} : 0 < q \leqslant N)$$

and then test if the value of s_{i+1} is equal to this sum. This begs the question as it requires the original problem to be solved before making the test. To make progress we need to look for a transformation on R_1. We want a simple initialization of free variables that can establish the sub-goal, at least in some limiting circumstance, which requires a *simple* rather than a difficult test to see if the sub-goal has been established.

A state-space extension that replaces the N by a new free variable j will do the job. We get

$$R_1' : s_{i+1} = \Sigma(A_{i+1,q} : 0 < q \leqslant j) \wedge j = N$$

where

$$R_1' \Rightarrow R_1$$

In this case, noting that the sum over an empty range is zero, the initialization

$$j := 0; \, s_{i+1} := 0$$

will be sufficient to establish R_1' and the test $j = N$ will be sufficient to confirm whether or not the initialization has established R_1'. We may now make the second initialization refinement.

$S_1(X_1)$ Second initialization $x_1 = \{j,s\}$

```
i := 0;
if i = M → skip
[] i ≠ M →
    j := 0; s_{i+1} := 0;
    if j = N → skip {R'_1 established}
    [] j ≠ N → {Q_2} s_2(x_2) {R'_1}
    fi
fi
```

This second initialization guarantees to establish the sub-goal invariant P'_1:

$$P'_1 : j = 0 \wedge s_{i+1} = 0 \wedge s_{i+1} = \Sigma(A_{i+1,q} : 0 < q \leq j)$$

where

$$P'_1 \wedge j = N \Rightarrow R'_1$$

and

$$P'_1 \wedge j \neq N \Rightarrow P'_1$$

Before i can be increased j = N will need to be established. The simplest way to do this is use $j := j + 1$. This condition P'_1 needs to be weakened to accommodate the change in j and a possible change in s_{i+1}. This yields

$$P''_1 : 0 \leq j \leq N \wedge s_{i+1} = \Sigma (A_{i+1,q} : 0 < q \leq j)$$

Investigating $wp("j := j + 1", P''_1)$ we find that $A_{i+1, j+1}$ needs to be added to s_{i+1} in order to maintain the relation

$$s_{i+1} = \Sigma(A_{i+1,q} : 0 < q \leq j)$$

in P''_1 when j is increased by one. Our command then becomes

$$j, s_{i+1} := j + 1, s_{i+1} + A_{i+1, j+1}$$

We can now make another refinement that can establish the sub-goal R'_1.

$S_2(X_2)$ First refinement $x_2 = \{j,s\}$

```
i := 0;
if i = M → skip
[] i ≠ M →
    j := 0; s_{i+1} := 0;
    if j = N → skip
    [] j ≠ N →
        j, s_{i+1} := j + 1 , s_{i+1} + A_{i+1,j+1};
        if j = N → skip {R'_1 established}
        [] j ≠ N → {Q_3} s_3(x_3) {R'_1}
        fi
    fi
fi
```

To establish R'_1 when Q_3 applies, a loop or recursive call to $s_2(x_2)$ can be used. Such a loop will guarantee to establish R'_1. This will also mean that the sub-goal has been established which permits i to be increased and hence there is the chance to switch again to making a refinement that can establish R_D.

Making this refinement and including the increase in i we get

$S_3(X_3)$ Second refinement $x_3 = \{i, j, s\}$

```
i := 0;
if i = M → skip
[] i ≠ M →
    j := 0; s_{i+1} := 0;
    do j ≠ N → {P''_1}
        j, s_{i+1} := j+1 , s_{i+1} + A_{i+1, j+1}
    od; {R'_1}
    i := i + 1; {P_1}
    if i = M → skip {R_D established}
    [] i ≠ M → {Q_4} s_4(x_4) {R_D}
    fi
fi
```

where

$$P_1 \wedge i = M \Rightarrow R_D \quad \text{and} \quad P''_1 \wedge j = N \Rightarrow R'_1$$
$$P_1 \wedge i \neq M \Rightarrow P_1 \quad \text{and} \quad P''_1 \wedge j \neq N \Rightarrow P''_1$$

To establish R_D when Q_4 applies, a loop or recursive call to $s_1(x_1) \circ s_2(x_2) \circ s_3(x_3)$ can be applied as it embodies a mechanism that allows us to safely increase i while maintaining P_1.

Incorporating this refinement as a loop we get the following.

$S_4(X_4)$ Third refinement

```
i := 0;
do i ≠ M → {P_1}
    j := 0; s_{i+1} := 0;
    do j ≠ N → {P''_1}
        j, s_{i+1} := j + 1 , s_{i+1} + A_{i+1, j+1}
    od; {R'_1}
    i := i + 1
od
{R_D}
```

where

$$P_1 \wedge i = M \Rightarrow R_D$$
$$P_1 \wedge i \neq M \Rightarrow P_1$$

and

$$P_1 \Rightarrow wp(S_4(X_4), R_D)$$

A summary of the composition refinement steps for the derivation of this program is as follows:

$S_0(X_0) = Q(\ s_0(x_0)\ )$	Initialization of row-sum loop
$S_1(X_1) = S_0(X_0) \circ Q(\ s_1(x_1)\ )$	Initialization for column-sum
$S_2(X_2) = S_1(X_1) \circ Q(\ s_2(x_2)\ )$	Development of column-sum loop body
$S_3(X_3) = S_2(X_2) \circ P(\ s_2(x_2)\ )$	Iterative call to column-sum loop body
$S_4(X_4) = S_3(X_3) \circ P\ (\ s_{1..3}(x_{1..3})\ )$	Iterative call to row-sum loop body

The interesting thing about this example and other problems like it is that a situation was encountered where it was not possible directly to make a refinement that established the postcondition. The command $i := i + 1$ could not be executed directly – another relation, which required the changing of a second variable j, had to be dealt with first. The weakest precondition computation with $i := i + 1$ was able to identify the required decomposition for the problem and the sub-goal that needed to be established before i could be safely increased. The strategy employed for development with this problem has provided a more formal approach to problem decomposition for problems that require nested loops than the Wirth–Dijkstra strategy for stepwise refinement.

In deriving a solution to the matrix row-sum problem we have chosen to go through three detailed stages in developing a loop:

- an initialization refinement
- a single-step refinement
- an iterative refinement.

Often, although not always, after making an initialization, it is apparent that a loop is required. In such cases it is appropriate to combine the second and third refinements into a single refinement. The task then becomes one of using a weakest precondition calculation on an invariant to derive a loop body that will maintain the invariant and at the same time make progress towards termination by decreasing the associated variant function. Where appropriate we will adopt this more streamlined approach to program derivation. However, when in doubt it is safer to fall back on the more detailed approach.

SUMMARY

- Precondition and postcondition specifications can be used to guide the development of programs.

- The precondition characterizes the set of initial states associated with a problem and the postcondition characterizes the final states associated with a problem.

- The state model for computation allows the semantics of a program to be interpreted in terms of a mapping between the set of initial states and the set of final states.

- A systematic way to compose a program in a stepwise manner is to make a sequence of refinements each of which expands the set of initial states for which the postcondition is established.

- A state may be defined as a function from a set of identifiers to a set of values.

- Weakest preconditions play an important role in program derivation. They may be used to characterize and hence verify simple programs, to define the semantics of a programming language and to play a constructive role in building program statements that satisfy certain constraints. Weakest preconditions can also be used to help decompose complex problems.

- The weakest precondition is a precondition which characterizes all the admissible initial states from which execution of a statement (or statements) S will be able to establish a postcondition R.

- Guarded commands is a primitive program design language which has been defined in terms of weakest preconditions.

- Guarded commands supports three possible means for the composition of program statements: sequence, selection, and iteration.

- To derive programs using formal specifications it is necessary for the postcondition to be in a form where it is possible to make an initialization of free variables that will establish the postcondition, and it is easy to check whether the initialization has established the postcondition.

- To manipulate specifications in the process of deriving programs it is often necessary to perform equivalence transformations on a specification and to inject new variables into a specification by doing a state-space extension.

- Each refinement carried out in deriving a program should be made by assigning values to, or changing, the smallest subset of free variables which is sufficient to extend the set of initial states for which the postcondition is established. This refinement strategy allows a match to be made between program control structure and data structure in the sense advocated by Jackson.

- Refinements made may be characterized as prefix, infix or postfix with respect to the alternative construct which guards the next refinement.

- Making goal-establishing refinements that can establish the post-condition ensures that each refinement either establishes the postcondition or sets up the precondition for making the next refinement.

■ **EXERCISE 5.1   *The weakest precondition concept***

1.   Given the operation

'Add 4 marbles to the existing number of marbles'

and that after execution of the operation there are *exactly* 6 marbles, how many marbles must there have been *before* execution of the operation?

2.   Given the operation

'Add 4 marbles to the existing number of marbles'

and that after execution of the operation there are at least 6 marbles, what condition must have applied before execution of the operation?

3.   Given the operation

'Paint the garage green'

what condition would have to have applied *before* this operation was executed, if after executing it the car was painted red?

4.   Complete the following weakest precondition calculations.

(a) wp ("i := 3", i = 3)   (f) wp ("i := i − 2", i = 3)
(b) wp ("i := i + 1", i = 3)   (g) wp ("j := j + 1", i = 3)
(c) wp ("i := i + 2", i = 3)   (h) wp ("j := i + 1", i = 3)
(d) wp ("i := i + 3", i = 3)   (i)   wp ("i := j+1", i = 3)
(e) wp ("i := i − 1 ", i = 3)

5.   Determine the weakest precondition wp(S,R) for the following commands S and postconditions R.

	S	R
(a)	$i := i + 2$	$i > 1$
(b)	$i := i + 2; j := j - 2$	$i + j = 0$
(c)	$z := z * j; i := i - 1$	$z * j^i = c$
(d)	$i := i + 1; j := j - 1$	$i * j = 0$
(e)	$a[i] := 1$	$a[i] = a[j]$

6.   Determine and simplify wp(S,R) for the following (S,R) pairs.

S	R
(a) z, x, y := 1, c, d	$z * x^y = c^d$
(b) i, s := 1, a[1]	$1 \leq i < N \wedge s = \Sigma(a_j : 0 < j \leq i)$
(c) a, n := 0, 1	$a^2 < n \wedge (a + 1)^2 \geq n$
(d) i, s := i + 1, s + a[i]	$1 \leq i \leq N \wedge s = \Sigma(a_j : 0 < j < i)$
(e) i := i + 2; j := j + 1	$i = j$
(f) i, j := i + 2, j + 1	$i = j$

■ *EXERCISE 5.2   Weakest precondition calculations*

1.   Use weakest precondition calculations to identify suitable guards that will
ensure that the invariant P is maintained when S is executed for the
following (P,S) pairs.

(a) $P : (\forall j : 1 \leq j \leq i : m \geq A_j) \wedge 1 \leq i \leq N$
    $S : i := i + 1$

(b) $P : (\forall j : 0 \leq j < i : m \geq A_j) \wedge 0 \leq i \leq N$
    $S : i := i + 1$

(c) $P : (\forall j : 1 \leq j \leq i : A_p \geq A_j) \wedge 1 \leq p \leq i \wedge 1 \leq i \leq N$
    $S : i := i + 1$

(d) $P : (\forall j : 0 \leq j < i : A_p \geq A_j) \wedge 0 \leq p \leq i \wedge 0 \leq i \leq N$
    $S : i := i + 1$

(e) $P : (\forall j : i \leq j \leq N : m \geq A_j) \wedge 1 \leq i \leq N$
    $S : i := i - 1$

(f) $P : (\forall j : i < j \leq N : m \geq A_j) \wedge 0 \leq i \leq N$
    $S : i := i - 1$

(g) $P : (\forall j : 0 < j \leq i : A_j \neq X) \wedge 0 \leq i \leq N$
    $S : i := i + 1$

(h) $P : (\forall j : 0 \leq j < i : A_j \neq X) \wedge 0 \leq i \leq N$
    $S : i := i + 1$

(i) $P : a^2 \leq N \wedge 0 \leq a \leq N$
    $S : a := a + 1$

(j) $P : (\forall j : 1 \leq j < i : a_j \leq a_{j+1}) \wedge 1 \leq i \leq N$
    $S : i := i + 1$

(k) $P : (\forall j : 1 < j \leq i : a_{j-1} \leq a_j) \wedge 1 \leq i \leq N$
    $S : i := i + 1$

2.   Use weakest precondition calculations to identify suitable *additional
commands* needed to maintain P when S is executed for the following (P,S)
pairs.

(a) $P : f = i! \wedge 0 \leq i \leq N$
    $S : i := i + 1$

(b) $P : f \times i! = N! \wedge 0 \leq i \leq N$
    $S : i := i - 1$

    (c) $P : p = X \times y \wedge 0 \leqslant y \leqslant Y$
         $S : y := y + 1$

    (d) $P : p + X \times y = X \times Y$
         $S : y := y - 1$

    (e) $P : f = (i-1)! \wedge 1 \leqslant i \leqslant N+1$
         $S : i := i + 1$

    (f) $P : e = X^y \wedge 0 \leqslant y \leqslant Y$
         $S : y := y + 1$

    (g) $P : e \times X^y = X^Y \wedge 0 \leqslant y \leqslant Y$
         $S : y := y - 1$

    (h) $P : s = i^2 \wedge 0 \leqslant i \leqslant N$
         $S : i := i+1$

    (i) $P : s = i(i+1)/2 \wedge 0 \leqslant i \leqslant N$
         $S : i := i + 1$

    (j) $P : s = \Sigma(A_j \times j : 0 < j \leqslant i) \wedge 0 \leqslant i \leqslant N$
         $S : i := i + 1$

    (k) $P : s = \Sigma(A_j \times j : i \leqslant j \leqslant N) \wedge 1 \leqslant i \leqslant N$
         $S : i := i - 1$

3.   Use weakest precondition calculations to identify *sub-goals* that need to be established before S can be executed and still maintain P.

    (a) $P : (\forall p : 0 < p \leqslant i : (\forall q : 0 < q \leqslant N : X \neq A_{p,q})) \wedge 0 \leqslant i \leqslant M$
         $S : i := i + 1$

    (b) $P : (\forall p : 0 \leqslant p < i : (\forall q : 0 < q \leqslant N : X \neq A_{p,q})) \wedge 0 \leqslant i \leqslant M$
         $S : i := i + 1$

    (c) $P : (\forall p : 0 < p \leqslant i : s_p = \Sigma(A_{p,q} : 0 < q \leqslant N)) \wedge 0 \leqslant i \leqslant M$
         $S : i := i + 1$

    (d) $P : (\forall p : i < p \leqslant M : s_p = \Sigma(A_{p,q} : 0 < q \leqslant N)) \wedge 0 \leqslant i \leqslant M$
         $S : i := i - 1$

    (e) $P : (\forall k : 1 \leqslant k < i : a[1..k] \leqslant a[k+1..i])$
         $S : i := i + 1$

    (f) $P : (\forall k : 1 \leqslant k < i : (\forall q : i \leqslant q < N+1 : a_k \leqslant a_q))$
         $S : i := i + 1$

4.   Given

$$P : 0 \leqslant r \leqslant X \wedge X = q \times D + r \wedge 0 \leqslant q \leqslant X$$

compute

$$wp(\text{“ } r := r - D \text{ ”}, P)$$

and thereby determine a suitable additional command involving q that will maintain P when r is changed. Verify that the resulting command maintains P.

5.   Given
$$P : z \geqslant 1 \wedge z = X^y \wedge 0 \leqslant y \leqslant Y$$
compute

wp(" y := y+1 ", P)

and thereby determine a suitable additional command involving z that will maintain P when y is changed. Verify that the resulting command maintains P.

6.   Given
$$P : 0 \leqslant r \leqslant X \wedge X = q \times D + r \wedge 0 \leqslant q \leqslant X$$
compute

wp(" q := q+1 ", P)

and thereby determine a suitable additional command that will maintain P when q is changed.

7.   Given
$$R : X = q \times D + r \wedge 0 \leqslant r < D$$
compute the weakest precondition that the initialization

r, q := X, 0

will establish R.

■ *EXERCISE 5.3   Postcondition initialization*

Write down an initialization of free variables that could be used to establish each of the following postconditions. Also write down a simple test that could be used to check whether or not the initialization has established the postcondition. Fixed free variables (data supplied to program) are in upper case and non-fixed free variables (to be assigned by program) are in lower case.

1. $R_D : z = X \times y \wedge y = Y$

2. $R_D : z + X \times y = X \times Y \wedge y = 0$

3. $R_D : z = X^y \wedge y = Y$

4. $R_D : z \times X^y = X^Y \wedge y = 0$

5. $R_D : z \geqslant X \wedge z \geqslant Y \wedge (z = X \vee z = Y)$

6. $R_D : z \leqslant X \wedge z \leqslant Y \wedge (z = X \vee z = Y)$

7. $R_D : c^2 \leqslant N < d^2 \wedge d = c+1 \wedge N \geqslant 0$

8. $R_D : c^2 < N \leqslant d^2 \wedge d = c+1 \wedge N \geqslant 1$

9. $R_D : s = i \times (i+1) / 2 \wedge i = N \wedge N \geqslant 0$

10. $R_D : A = b \times C + d \wedge d \geqslant 0 \wedge d < C$

11. $R_D : 1 \leqslant p \leqslant i \wedge (\forall j : 1 \leqslant j \leqslant i : A_j \leqslant A_p) \wedge i = N$

12. $R_D : 1 \leqslant p \leqslant i \wedge m = A_p \wedge (\forall j : 1 \leqslant j \leqslant i : m \geqslant A_j) \wedge i = N$

13. $R_D : (\forall j : 1 \leqslant j \leqslant i : m < A_j) \wedge i = N$

14. $R_D : i \leqslant p \leqslant N \wedge m = A_p \wedge (\forall j : i \leqslant j \leqslant N : m \geqslant A_j) \wedge i = 1$

15. $R_D : (\forall j : 1 \leqslant j < i : A_j \leqslant A_{j+1}) \wedge i = N$

16. $R_D : (\forall j : i < j \leq N : A_{j-1} \geq A_j) \wedge i = 1$
17. $R_D : (\forall p : 0 < p \leq i : A_p \neq X) \wedge (i = N \textbf{ cor } X = A_{i+1})$
18. $R_D : (\forall q : j \leq q < N+1 : A_q \neq X) \wedge (j = 1 \textbf{ cor } X = A_{j-1})$
19. $R_D : (\forall p : 0 < p \leq i : a_p \leq X) \wedge (\forall q : j \leq q < N+1 : a_q \geq X) \wedge i = j-1$

Bibliography

Alagic, S. and M.A. Arbib (1978), *The Design of Well-structured and Correct Programs*, Springer-Verlag, N.Y.

Berglund, G.D. (1981), A Guided Tour of Program Design Methodologies, *Computer*, **14**, 13-37, (Oct.)

Dijkstra, E.W. (1971), A Short Introduction to the Art of Programming, Report EWD316, Technological University of Eindhoven, (Aug.)

Dijkstra, E.W.(1972), Notes on Structured Programming, In: O.J. Dahl, E.W. Dijkstra and C.A.R. Hoare, *Structured Programming*, Academic Press, London.

Dijkstra, E.W. (1975), The Development of Programming Methodology, in *Programming Language Systems*, Eds., M.C. Newey, R.B. Stanton, G.L. Wolfendale, ANU Press, Canberra.

Dijkstra, E.W. (1976), *A Discipline of Programming*, Prentice-Hall, Englewood Cliffs, N.J.

Dromey, R.G. (1985a), Forced Termination of Loops, *Software Practice and Experience,* **15**, 29-40.

Dromey, R.G. (1985b), Program Development by Inductive Stepwise Refinement, *Software Practice and Experience*, **15**, 1-28.

Dromey, R.G. (1988), Systematic Program Development, *IEEE Trans. on Soft. Eng.,* **24**(1), 12-29.

Floyd, R.W. (1967), Assigning Meanings to Programs, In: *Proc. Sym. in App. Math.,* **19**, *Mathematical Aspects of Computer Science* (J.T. Schwartz, ec.) Am. Math. Soc. 19-32.

Gries, D.(1981), *The Science of Programming*, Springer-Verlag, N.Y.

Hehner, E. (1979), do considered od, *Acta Informatica*, **11**, 287-304.

Hoare, C.A.R. (1971), Proof of a Program: Find, *Comm. ACM*, **14**, 39-45.

Jackson, M.A. (1975), *Principles of Program Design*, Academic Press, London.

Jackson, M.A. (1976), Constructive Methods of Program Design, *Lecture Notes in Computer Science*, **44**, 236-62, Springer-Verlag, Berlin.

Jackson, M.A. (1983), *Systems Development*, Prentice-Hall, London.

Mayer, A. (1877), *Geschichte des Prinzips der kleinston Action*, Leipzig.

Polya, G. (1973), *Induction and Analogy in Mathematics*, Princeton University Press, N.J.

Turski, W.M. (1978), *Computer Programming Methodology*, Heyden, London.

Turski, W.M. (1984), On Programming by Iterations, *IEEE Trans. Software Eng.*, **SE-10**, 175-8, (Mar.)

Warnier, J.D. (1974), *Logical Construction of Programs*, van Nostrand, Reinhold, N.Y.

Wirth, N. (1971), Program Development by Stepwise Refinement, *CACM*, **14**, 221-7.

Chapter 6
From Specifications to Programs

Programming is a mathematical activity ... [whose] successful
practice requires the determined and meticulous application
of traditional methods of mathematical understanding,
calculation, and proof.

C.A.R. Hoare

6.1 Introduction
6.2 Specification Transformations
6.3 Generating Sub-problems
6.4 Generating Auxiliary Problems
6.5 Basic Examples
6.6 Simple Loops
6.7 Nested Loops
     Summary
     Exercises
     Bibliography

6.1 Introduction

A clear understanding of the relationship between problem-solving
strategies and specification transformations is essential if we are to maximize
the benefits of applying formal techniques to program derivation. The
fundamental question that needs to be addressed is: *do formal methods of
program derivation have correspondences with intuitive problem-solving
strategies and top-down design?* In the discussion which follows we will
attempt to address this issue.

Top-down design suggests that a complex problem may be solved by
breaking it down into simpler sub-problems. Each of the sub-problems may

325

then in turn be solved by employing essentially the same approach. In other words, the decomposition strategy is recursive.

The usefulness of top-down design as a guiding principle for program development rests with the support it gives for dividing a problem into sub-problems. Unfortunately the traditional formulation of top-down design gives us precious little advice beyond the need to divide a problem up into sub-problems. In fact top-down design provides essentially no advice on:

- how the decomposition should be carried out;
- how many sub-problems a problem should be decomposed into;
- what criteria should be used to identify suitable sub-problems of a problem.

Our objective here is not to debunk top-down design as a method which is of little constructive value. What we are interested in doing is preserving the strategy of solving complex problems using simpler problems and sub-problems – this has to be sound advice for handling complexity. However, we want to go further than this by giving the top-down strategy some teeth and constructive power.

One way of achieving our objective requires top-down design to be integrated with formal manipulations that can be applied to specifications. This synthesis can lead to a constructive form of top-down design which accommodates both formality and traditional problem-solving strategies. To try to establish the connections between problem-solving and formal program derivation it is necessary to examine the nature of the transformations that can be applied to specifications. The most useful currency for conducting such a discussion is in terms of the notion of **specification strength**.

The strength of a specification may be measured in terms of the number of states that the specification describes. A state in this context is just a set of ordered pairs of the form (identifier, value). The stronger a specification, the fewer states it will describe. In our discussion we will focus on specifications that have been written in the predicate calculus.

In terms of strength, the specifications of interest to us when we are attempting to derive a program are

- *weaker* specifications than our original specification;
- *stronger* specifications than our original specification;
- *equivalent* specifications.

Figure 6.1 provides a schematic representation of the specification dimension.

When talking about equivalent specifications it is useful to introduce another property of a specification – its **explicitivity**, ϵ. Equivalent specifica-

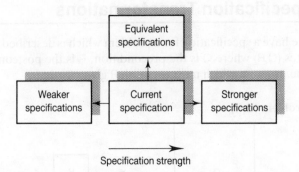

Figure 6.1 The relative strength of specifications compared with the current specifications.

tions very often have different explicitivities. The explicitivity of a specification is just a measure of the number of atomic formulae (see Chapter 2) in the specification. Conjuncts and disjuncts that involve TRUE or FALSE or that simplify to TRUE or FALSE do not contribute to a specification's explicitivity.

As an example, consider the two incomplete sorting specifications:

(1) $(\forall j : 1 < j \leqslant N : a_{j-1} \leqslant a_j)$ $\epsilon = N - 1$

(2) $(\forall p : 1 \leqslant p < N : (\forall q : p < q \leqslant N : a_p \leqslant a_q))$ $\epsilon = N(N - 1)/2$

These specifications are equivalent and therefore of the same strength (note that (1) relies on the fact that the relation '$\leqslant$' is transitive). However, using the notion of explicitivity we get quite a different picture, that is

(1) $a_1 \leqslant a_2, a_2 \leqslant a_3, \dots\dots\dots\dots\dots\dots\dots\dots\dots\dots\dots\dots\dots\dots\dots\dots, a_{N-1} \leqslant a_N$

(2) $a_1 \leqslant a_2, a_1 \leqslant a_3, \dots\dots\dots\dots\dots\dots\dots\dots\dots\dots\dots\dots\dots\dots\dots, a_1 \leqslant a_N$
        $a_2 \leqslant a_3, a_2 \leqslant a_4, \dots\dots\dots\dots\dots\dots\dots\dots\dots\dots\dots\dots\dots\dots, a_2 \leqslant a_N$
            •
                •
                    •
        $a_{N-2} \leqslant a_{N-1}, a_{N-2} \leqslant a_N$
            $a_{N-1} \leqslant a_N$

Clearly (2) makes explicit a lot of extra terms that are only implicit in (1). As will be shown in Chapter 9 specifications with a greater explicitivity often allow the derivation of a richer set of algorithms that can satisfy their specification.

Our next task is to show how weaker, stronger, and equivalent specifications may be exploited in program derivation. We will also show how such transformations relate to traditional ideas on top-down design and problem-solving.

6.2 Specification Transformations

Suppose we have a specification for a problem which is described by the pair of predicates (Q,R) where Q is the precondition, R is the postcondition and S(Q,R) is the program which must establish R given Q, that is

Original problem (Q,R)

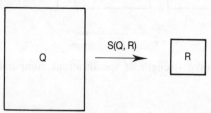

In general, the postcondition for a problem is more restrictive and hence stronger than the corresponding precondition (i.e. $R \Rightarrow Q$). If this were not the case Q could possibly imply R and there would be no need to derive a program. This suggests that we may view a program as a device for imposing additional restrictions on a set of data.

To derive a program S(Q,R) there are several alternative classes of sub-problems and auxiliary problems that we may consider. These follow directly from transformations that can be applied to the original specification (Q,R).

6.2.1 Sub-problem: stronger precondition Q_s

A powerful strategy for decomposing a problem into two sub-problems is to split the original precondition for the problem. The idea is to derive a mechanism $S(Q_s,R)$ that will establish the postcondition R, for a precondition Q_s which is stronger and hence more restrictive that Q (i.e. $Q_s \Rightarrow Q$)

Sub-problem (Q_s,R)

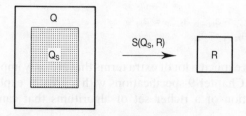

Solving a problem with a more restrictive precondition usually involves the derivation of a simpler and less challenging mechanism.

The consequences that result from establishing the postcondition R for a precondition Q_s that is stronger than Q are as follows.

- A decomposition of the original problem is achieved by dividing the original precondition into two components Q_s, and Q_t (where $Q_t \equiv \neg Q_s \wedge Q$ and $Q_s \Rightarrow Q$).

- A new sub-problem with specification (Q_t, R) is identified. Because Q_t is also stronger than Q it should again involve the solution of a simpler and easier problem than the original problem with precondition Q.

Schematically the problem decomposition achieved by precondition splitting has the form

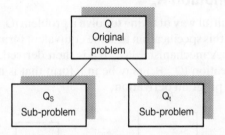

6.2.2   Auxiliary problem: weaker postcondition R_w

Decomposition is not the only way of identifying a simpler problem. What we can do instead is solve an **auxiliary** or **intermediate problem**. The strategy in this case is to derive a mechanism $S(Q, R_w)$ that will establish a weaker sub-goal R_w (where $R \Rightarrow R_w$) for the original precondition Q. Schematically we have as our overall strategy

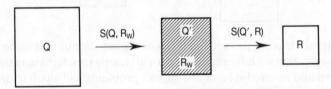

In deriving $S(Q, R_w)$ progress towards establishing R is made because R_w will be stronger than Q but not as strong as R. Having solved the intermediate problem and thereby established R_w, the next objective is to exploit this solution in solving the original problem. Adopting this strategy the postcondition R_w that defines the solution to the intermediate problem becomes the precondition Q' for the next refinement $S(Q', R)$ directed at establishing R.

6.2.3   Auxiliary problem: stronger postcondition R_s

Rather than directly trying to solve a problem (Q, R) it is sometimes useful to try to establish R_s as a stronger postcondition than R. The reason for adopting this strategy is often to create a solution that is more efficient. In our subsequent discussion we will give an example illustrating this strategy.

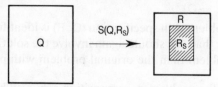

6.2.4   Auxiliary problem: equivalent precondition Q_e and postcondition R_e

Often the most fruitful way of trying to solve a problem (Q, R) is to look for a transformation of this specification to some equivalent form (Q_e, R_e) where $Q \equiv Q_e$ and $R \equiv R_e$. A mechanism $S(Q_e, R_e)$ is then derived. In this case the equivalent specification (Q_e, R_e) may be in a form that is more suitable for manipulation and program derivation.

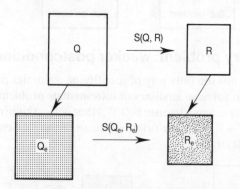

Before leaving this section it is worth pointing out that some or all of the strategies that we have mentioned for attacking problems may need to be employed and re-employed in solving sub-problems and auxiliary problems identified in the course of solving a problem.

6.3   Generating Sub-problems

Having outlined the principal strategies for generating sub-problems and auxiliary problems for a given problem our next task is to focus on various constructive tools and techniques that can be used to implement these strategies.

There are four fairly straightforward ways of identifying sub-problems that possess stronger preconditions. Each involves the direct use of formal specifications. We will now discuss and illustrate each of the techniques.

6.3.1   Confirming a postcondition

An obvious stronger precondition to consider as a candidate sub-problem is the postcondition itself, that is

$$Q_s \equiv R†$$

Assuming the given data for a problem already satisfies the postcondition identifies a sub-problem where it is simply necessary to try to *confirm* the postcondition. The simplest way of establishing a postcondition is often by confirmation.

EXAMPLE 1

In Section 5.5 we have already seen how a confirmation strategy can be employed in the design of a mechanism to sort a set of data. In that case the sub-problem to be solved involved checking whether or not a set of data was already sorted (i.e. $Q_s \equiv R$).

EXAMPLE 2

The idea of trying to confirm a postcondition may also be used in the construction of an algorithm for partitioning a set of data about some pivot element. Here the sub-problem would involve checking whether the data was already partitioned with respect to the pivot element. Many implementations of the Quicksort algorithm use this strategy (see Section 9.3).

6.3.2   Identifying the initialization sub-problem

The simplest sub-problem associated with a problem is usually identified by finding an initialization of free variables that can establish the postcondition for at least one initial state. Such a refinement often establishes the postcondition for the strongest useful precondition. A consequence of identifying the **initialization sub-problem** is that it splits the original precondition into two. It also identifies another sub-problem that will need to be established in order to satisfy the postcondition.

EXAMPLE

Suppose we have the following specification for the quotient/remainder problem:

$$Q : X \geq 0 \land D > 0$$
$$R : X = q \times D + r \land 0 \leq r < D$$

---

† Here 'equivalence' is used loosely because Q_s and R will have a different state space.

This specification requires that a quotient q and remainder r be found that satisfy R. An initialization of free variables q and r which can establish R is

$$r := X \quad \text{and} \quad q := 0$$

A weakest precondition calculation

$$wp("r, q := X, 0", R)$$

indicates that the initialization establishes the postcondition for the strong precondition

$$Q_s : X < D$$

Identification of the initialization sub-problem also tells us that the remaining precondition for which it will be necessary to establish R is

$$Q_t : X \geq D$$

6.3.3   Decomposition by calculation

Constructive weakest precondition calculations have been widely used to identify components of simple loops. A less well-known but equally important use of weakest precondition calculations is for problem decomposition. The outcome of such calculations is quite often a sub-goal that needs to be established before some other variable is changed.

EXAMPLE_____

As an example suppose we have the invariant specification

$$P : (\forall k : 1 \leq k < i : (\forall p : 1 \leq p \leq k : (\forall q : k + 1 \leq q \leq N : a_p \leq a_q)))$$
$$\wedge \, 1 \leq i \leq N$$

and suppose we investigate

$$wp("i := i + 1", P)$$

When we do this we discover that the sub-goal

$$R_w : (\forall q : i + 1 \leq q \leq N : a_i \leq a_q)$$

is not implied by P. It will therefore be necessary to derive a mechanism to establish the sub-goal R_w before proceeding to increase the variable i by one. To establish R_w in this case will require the implementation of a separate loop.

6.3.4   Strengthening a Precondition

In our search for simpler sub-problems there is always the option of applying direct transformations to a precondition. To obtain a simpler sub-problem using this approach it is necessary to directly strengthen the precondition. There are two ways of doing this. We can

- delete disjuncts from the precondition Q;
- add conjuncts to Q.

The latter transformation corresponds to adding constraints or restrictions to the precondition while the former transformation corresponds to removing alternatives.

As an example, suppose Q was of the form

$Q : p \vee q$

then it could be strengthened either by deleting q to obtain the stronger precondition

$Q' : p$ where $Q' \Rightarrow Q$

or by adding the conjunct r to obtain the stronger conjunct

$Q'' : (p \vee q) \wedge r$ where $Q'' \Rightarrow Q$

Both of these transformations split the original precondition into two (i e. Q' and $\neg Q' \wedge Q$ or Q'' and $\neg Q'' \wedge Q$) where (Q',R) and (Q'',R) are respectively the intermediate sub-problems that need to be solved.

6.4   Generating Auxiliary Problems

The strategy of generating auxiliary problems as a way of solving a problem is undervalued as a problem-solving strategy for use in program derivation. Auxiliary problems provide a way of 'staging' the solution to a problem.

6.4.1   Weakening a postcondition

The most fruitful way of finding a useful auxiliary problem is to directly weaken the postcondition. There are three ways of doing this. We can

- delete conjuncts from the postcondition R;
- remove a universal quantifier from the postcondition R;
- add disjuncts to the postcondition R.

EXAMPLE 1

Suppose we have a postcondition of the form

$$R : p \wedge q$$

then it could be weakened by simply deleting the conjunct q to obtain the new postcondition

$$R' : p$$

which is the postcondition of the auxiliary problem. The approach that can be used to start the derivation of a mergesort illustrates the strategy of deleting conjuncts to obtain a weaker postcondition.

Suppose we have the sorting postcondition

$$R : (\forall j : 1 \leqslant j < N : a_j \leqslant a_{j+1}) \wedge \text{perm}(a,A)$$

It can be written in longhand form as

$$R : a_1 \leqslant a_2 \wedge a_2 \leqslant a_3 \leqslant a_3 \leqslant a_4 \wedge ... \wedge a_{N-1} \leqslant a_N \wedge \text{perm}(a,A)$$

If we now delete every second conjunct from R we get a new weaker specification

$$R' : a_1 \leqslant a_2 \wedge a_3 \leqslant a_4 \wedge a_5 \leqslant a_6 \wedge ... \wedge a_{N-1} \leqslant a_N \wedge \text{perm}(a,A)$$

Solving the auxiliary problem (Q,R') corresponds to doing a 'two-sort' on the data. The next refinement will involve a 'four-sort' and so on. If we continue with this development it is possible to derive a merge sort.

EXAMPLE 2

To illustrate the technique of deleting a quantifier to obtain a weaker postcondition, suppose we have the sorting specification

$$R : (\forall k : 1 \leqslant k < N : (\forall p : 1 \leqslant p \leqslant k : (\forall q : k + 1 \leqslant q \leqslant N : a_p \leqslant a_q))) \\ \wedge \text{perm}(a,A)$$

If we delete the quantifier involving k we obtain the weaker postcondition

$$R' : 1 \leqslant k < N \Rightarrow (\forall p : 1 \leqslant p \leqslant k : (\forall q : k + 1 \leqslant q \leqslant N : a_p \leqslant a_q)) \\ \wedge \text{perm}(a,A)$$

It is shown in Section 9.5 that R′ can be used as the basis for making a partitioning refinement. If this derivation is pursued we can end up with an implementation of the well-known sorting algorithm, Quicksort.

EXAMPLE 3_____

To illustrate the technique of adding a disjunct to obtain an auxiliary problem with a weaker postcondition we will again focus on a sorting specification. Suppose we have the sorting specification

$$R : (\forall j : 1 < j \leq i : a_{j-1} \leq a_j) \wedge i = N \wedge \text{perm}(a,A)$$

We can add a disjunct to this specification to obtain

$$R'' : (\forall j : 1 < j \leq i : a_{j-1} \leq a_j) \wedge (i = N \; \textbf{cor} \; a_i > a_{i+1}) \wedge \text{perm}(a,A)$$

This new weaker postcondition can be used to guide a search to see if there are any of the elements out of order. Pursuing this line of development from this auxilary problem can lead to the derivation of an insertion sort (see Section 5.5).

6.4.2 Strengthening a postcondition

Provided a problem has been properly specified it is unusual to contemplate trying to establish a stronger postcondition. As a general rule establishing a stronger postcondition will require a greater computational effort and a more extensive derivation. However, this is not always the case. Occasionally greater efficiency can be achieved by establishing a stronger postcondition.

EXAMPLE 1_____

To illustrate the strategy of solving a problem by establishing a stronger postcondition suppose it is necessary to identify one of the duplicates known to be present in a sequence A[1...N] of integers. A possible specification for this problem is

$$Q : 1 \leq j \leq N \wedge (\exists k : 1 \leq k \leq N : j \neq k \wedge A_j = A_k)$$
$$R : 1 \leq j \leq N \wedge 1 \leq i \leq N \wedge j \neq i \wedge A_j = A_i$$

Rather than attempt to establish this postcondition directly we can instead derive a mechanism to establish the stronger postcondition

$$R_s : 1 \leqslant j < N \wedge i = j + 1 \wedge a_j = a_i \wedge (\forall k : 1 \leqslant k < N : a_k \leqslant a_{k+1})$$
$$\wedge \, perm(a,A)$$

In R_s the relation between i and j is much stronger than the corresponding relation in R. The first step towards establishing R_s will involve ordering the original sequence. Once the sequence has been ordered a simple linear search may be used to find a duplicate pair that will satisfy R_s. The gain in average case efficiency will be achieved because the sort has an $O\,(N \log N)$ cost, whereas to find a duplicate pair without sorting is most likely to have an $O(N^2)$ cost.

EXAMPLE 2

Another interesting case where establishing a stronger postcondition pays off handsomely is with the Kth largest element problem (an important special case of this problem is finding the median). A possible specification for the problem is

$$Q : (\forall p : 0 < p \leqslant N : (\forall q : p < q \leqslant N : p \neq q \Rightarrow A_p \neq A_q))$$
$$R : K - 1 = \# \, (j : 0 < j \leqslant N : A_j < A_s) \wedge 1 \leqslant s \leqslant N \wedge 1 \leqslant K \leqslant N$$

In this specification A_s is the Kth largest element. Rather than attempt to establish this postcondition directly we can instead derive a mechanism to establish the stronger postcondition R_s, that is

$$Q : 1 \leqslant K \leqslant N$$
$$R_s : (\forall p : 0 < p \leqslant K : a_p \leqslant a_K) \wedge (\forall q : K + 1 \leqslant q < N + 1 : a_K \geqslant a_q)$$
$$\wedge \, perm\,(a,A)$$

In this specification a_K is the Kth largest element. As is shown in Section 8.5, this specification leads to the derivation of partitioning algorithms with an average case complexity of $O(N)$. Once again, the use of a stronger postcondition has led to the derivation of a more efficient algorithm.

In conclusion, while it is unusual that it is more effective to establish a stronger postcondition there are enough instances where the strategy works for us not to discount the idea.

6.4.3   Precondition–postcondition conjunction

A very useful transformation for generating a stronger postcondition and hence stronger invariant is to begin by forming the conjunction of the precondition with the postcondition. There are two important reasons for wanting to create such a specification.

- Firstly we may need to make direct use of the postcondition established in the most recent refinement – it becomes the precondition for the next refinement. This can be particularly important when a situation arises where Q *does not* imply R.

- Secondly we may want to take advantage of structure in data to guide the derivation of a program whose control structure matches that data structure.

Given the specification (Q,R) our stronger *combined* postcondition R_c is

$$R_c : Q \wedge R$$

The specification R_c needs to be transformed in order to incorporate the influence of Q. The reason for this simple. The variables in Q are all *fixed* and therefore cannot be changed directly to establish R. To make progress new free variables that can be changed need to be introduced into the 'Q-component' of R_c. This will allow the influence of Q to take effect in the next refinement. Using these transformations the strategy for derivation is

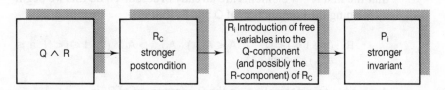

This compares with the more usual strategy for derivation

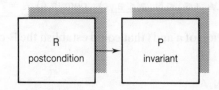

where

$$P_i \Rightarrow P$$

The stronger invariant P_i will retain the influence of Q in the program component that is derived from it. To illustrate these ideas we will consider a problem identified in Section 5.5 in the course of deriving an insertion sort.

EXAMPLE 1

Here we will treat the sub-problem identified in Section 5.5 as a problem in its own right. The problem is defined by the specification

$$Q : (\forall j : 1 \leqslant j < N - 1 : A_j \leqslant A_{j+1}) \wedge A_{N-1} > A_N$$
$$R : (\forall j : 1 \leqslant j < N : a_j \leqslant a_{j+1}) \wedge perm(a,A)$$

Schematically we have

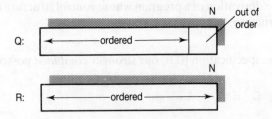

The task requires that the Nth element (which is out of order) be inserted in the ordered sequence

$$(A_1, A_2, ..., A_{N-1}).$$

In solving this problem we want to take advantage of the fact that the first $N - 1$ elements are already ordered. To do this we begin by forming the conjunction of Q and R, that is

$$R_c : (\forall j : 1 \leqslant j < N - 1 : A_j \leqslant A_{j+1}) \wedge A_{N-1} > A_N \wedge (\forall j : 1 \leqslant j < N : a_j \leqslant a_{j+1}) \wedge perm(a,A)$$

A possible transformation on the R-component of R_c is

$$R_1 : (\forall j : 1 \leqslant j < N - 1 : A_j \leqslant A_{j+1}) \wedge A_{N-1} > A_N$$
$$\wedge (\forall j : i \leqslant j < N : a_j \leqslant a_{j+1}) \wedge perm(a,A) \wedge i = 1$$

An initialization of a and i that could establish the R-component of R_1 (and hence R_c) is

$$i, a := N, A$$

Our next task is to make a transformation that incorporates the influence of the Q-component of R_1 (and hence R_c). We do this by introducing the variable substitutions that correspond to the initializations of the R-component (i.e. a = A and i = N). This yields

$$R_2 : (\forall j : 1 \leqslant j < i - 1 : a_j \leqslant a_{j+1}) \wedge a_{i-1} > a_i$$
$$\wedge (\forall j : i \leqslant j < N : a_j \leqslant a_{j+1}) \wedge perm(a,A) \wedge a = A \wedge i = 1$$

The specification R_2 does not imply R because $a_{i-1} > a_i$. However, if the two universally quantified components are maintained while i and a are changed until either i = 1 or $\neg a_{i-1} > a_i$ is established, then R will be established. The postcondition, invariant, and guard that follow from R_2 are

$$R_D : (\forall j : 1 \leqslant j < i - 1 : a_j \leqslant a_{j+1}) \wedge (\forall j : i \leqslant j < N : a_j \leqslant a_{j+1})$$
$$\wedge \text{ perm } (a,A) \wedge (i = 1 \textbf{ cor } a_{i-1} \leqslant a_i)$$
$$P_D : (\forall j : 1 \leqslant j < i - 1 : a_j \leqslant a_{j+1}) \wedge (\forall j : i \leqslant j < N : a_j \leqslant a_{j+1})$$
$$\wedge \text{ perm } (a,A) \wedge 1 \leqslant i \leqslant N$$
$$B : a_{i-1} > a_i \wedge i \neq 1$$

where $R_D \Rightarrow R$. The condition a = A has been dropped from R_D because we may need to alter the order of the elements in a. Provided this is done using swaps of pairs of elements perm(a, A) will be preserved. The implementation that can be derived for the insertion using P_D and investigating wp("i := i − 1", P_D) is

```
i, a := N, A;
do i ≠ 1 cand a_{i-1} > a_i →
    swap (a_{i-1}, a_i);
    i := i − 1
od
```

For this problem if development had to depend on R alone, we would not have been able to exploit the order in the sequence $(a_1, a_2, ..., a_{i-1})$ that can allow termination as soon as insertion is completed (this is signalled by $a_{i-1} \leqslant a_i$ or i = 1). It is important with this example to note the initialization/substitution strategy that has been employed to factor the influence of the precondition Q into the postcondition and the invariant. Without the influence of Q the invariant would have been simply

$$P : (\forall j : i \leqslant j < N : a_j \leqslant a_{j+1}) \wedge \text{ perm } (a,A) \wedge 1 \leqslant i \leqslant N$$

which is considerably weaker than the P_D we have used.

EXAMPLE 2

In Section 11.3 another example of precondition–postcondition conjunction is used to factor the influence of the structure of the input data into the postcondition and the invariant. In that case it leads to the derivation of a program whose control structure matches the structure of the input data.

6.4.4 Solving an equivalent problem

The idea of solving an equivalent but different formulation of a problem is a time-honoured problem-solving strategy employed by mathematicians and others (Polya, 1945). There are basically two ways of trying to generate equivalent problems. We can:

- try to apply equivalence transformations to an existing specification (often this involves increasing the explicitivity of a specification);
- attempt to create an entirely different formulation of a problem.

EXAMPLE 1

Different formulations of a problem usually lead to the derivation of quite different solutions to a problem. A very simple example illustrating this is the greatest common divisor problem. Suppose it is necessary to find the greatest common divisor x of two fixed positive integers X and Y. One possible specification of the problem is

$$R : x = max(d : 1 \leqslant d \leqslant min(X,Y) : X \textbf{ mod } d = 0 \wedge Y \textbf{ mod } d = 0)$$

If a derivation is pursued using this specification we end up with an algorithm based on a linear search. In contrast to this if we start out with the specification

$$R' : x = gcd(X,Y) \wedge 1 \leqslant x \leqslant min(X,Y)$$

and make transformations on this specification we end up with a more efficient algorithm that performs division by subtraction (see algorithm [17], Section 6.7.7).

The thrust of our discussion has been to show that formal methods of program derivation do have correspondences with top-down design and well-known problem-solving strategies. It is quite surprising that the links between specification transformations and different problem-solving strategies are as simple as we have shown them to be. Our objective in demonstrating these relationships has been to encourage program designers to take a more systematic approach to problem decomposition, and to the generation of auxiliary problems. Using specifications and specification transformations to do this can give us a richer and more powerful set of tools to assist with the derivation of programs.

6.5 Basic Examples

In this chapter we will derive a number of simple programs using the techniques and the tools developed in the last two chapters. The first two examples we will consider have been discussed elsewhere by Gries. We will present a different approach to them which demonstrates the value of always attempting to make refinements that can establish the postcondition. Gries' solutions to these problems may be consulted to give a different perspective.

6.5.1 Pair – maximum [1]

For this problem, given two fixed integers X and Y, it is required to assign to the variable z the maximum of these two integers. The specification which follows from defining the maximum is

> Q : TRUE
> R : $z \geqslant X \wedge z \geqslant Y \wedge (z = X \vee z = Y)$

The precondition TRUE indicates that the program should establish R for all initial states, that is, for all fixed integer pairs X and Y. Our first step in the development is to look for a simple initialization of z that can establish R and be easily checked to see if R is established. From R we see that one possible initialization is $z := X$. This initialization will be sufficient to establish R provided $z \geqslant Y$ is true. Our initialization refinement is therefore

$S_0(X_0)$ Initialization

> $z := X$; $\{R_0\}$
> **if** $z \geqslant Y \rightarrow$ skip $\{R$ established$\}$
> [] $z < Y \rightarrow \{Q_1\}$ $s_1(x_1)$ $\{R\}$
> **fi**

The components of R established are

> $R_0 : z = X \wedge z \geqslant X$

and

> $R_0 \wedge z \geqslant Y \Rightarrow R$
> $R_0 \wedge z < Y = Q_1$

The predicate characterizing the set of initial states for which $z := X$ will establish R can be computed using wp("$z := X$", R):

> wp ("$z := X$" , R) $\equiv X \geqslant X \wedge X \geqslant Y \wedge (x = X \vee X = Y)$
> $\equiv T \wedge X \geqslant Y \wedge (T \vee X = Y)$
> $\equiv X \geqslant Y$

The set of initial states for which the initialization will establish R is therefore

$A_0 : X \geqslant Y$

For the refinement $s_1(x_1)$ when $z < Y$, to ensure z is assigned to the maximum it needs to be reassigned, that is we end up with

$S_1(X_1)$ First refinement

$z := X; \{R_0\}$
if $z \geqslant Y \rightarrow$ skip
$[] z < Y \rightarrow z := Y \{R_1\}$
fi

This most recent refinement, i.e. $z := Y$, will be sufficient to establish R when $X \leqslant Y$. This can be shown using similar steps to those above, therefore

$A_1 : X \geqslant Y \vee X \leqslant Y \equiv \text{TRUE}$

Hence, the mechanism will establish R for all initial states, which is just the given precondition Q.

6.5.2   Pair – relation [2]

This problem requires a program which, given a pair of fixed integers X and Y, assigns the smaller of the pair to x and the larger of the pair to y. The program should work for all fixed pairs X and Y. The formal specification is therefore

$Q : \text{TRUE}$
$R : x \leqslant y \wedge ((x = X \wedge y = Y) \vee (x = Y \wedge y = X))$

R needs to be examined to establish whether a simple initialization of the free variables x and y can be made which is sufficient to establish it. One possible initialization is $x,y := X,Y$ The condition $x \leqslant y$ may serve as a test to determine whether the initialization establishes R.

Computing the weakest precondition that this initialization will establish R we get

$$\text{wp}(\text{``} x,y := X,Y\text{''} ; R) \equiv X \leqslant Y \wedge ((X = X \wedge Y = Y) \vee (X = Y \wedge Y = X))$$
$$\equiv X \leqslant Y$$

Making the initialization refinement we get

$S_0(X_0)$ Initialization

$x , y := X , Y ; \{R_0\}$
if $x \leq y \rightarrow$ skip {R established}
[] $x > y \rightarrow \{Q_1\}\ s_1(x_1)\ \{R\}$
fi

where

$R_s : x = X \wedge y = Y$

and

$R_0 \wedge x \leq y \Rightarrow R$
$R_0 \wedge x > y \Rightarrow Q_1$

The set of initial states for which this initialization will establish R is therefore $X \leq Y$. Given Q_1 and R, it is necessary to swap x and y for the $s_1(x_1)$ refinement, that is

$S_1(X_1)$ First refinement

$x , y := X , Y ; \{R_0\}$
if $x \leq y \rightarrow$ skip
[] $x > y \rightarrow x , y := y , x\ \{R_1\}$
fi

where

$R_1 : x < y \wedge x = Y \wedge y = X$

and

$A_1 : X \leq Y \vee Y \leq X \equiv$ TRUE

6.5.3 Exchange [3]

An elementary operation that is frequently used in programming involves the exchange of the values of two variables. Given fixed X and Y the specification is

$Q : x = X \wedge y = Y$
$R : x = Y \wedge y = X$

For this specification, since Q is not initially established, we are obliged first to establish it. An appropriate initialization is

$x , y := X , Y\ \{Q\}$

With Q established our task is to change x and y so that R is established. This can be handled directly by the following concurrent assignment:

$$x, y := y, x$$

The complete implementation is therefore

```
x , y := X , Y;   {Q established}
x , y := y , x    {R established}
```

We now need to compute the weakest precondition for these assignments establishing R. We find

$$\text{wp}("x, y := y, x", R) \equiv x = X \wedge y = Y$$

Happily the weakest precondition that $x, y := y, x$ will establish R is just Q, the condition established by the initialization of x and y. Our refinement will therefore establish R for all initial states defined by Q. It is interesting to note that the initialization that established Q would be sufficient to establish R for the precondition that $X = Y$. In our implementation we have refrained from checking whether the initialization did indeed establish R on the grounds that it is very unlikely that X and Y would be equal in general.

A common implementation of the exchange operation involves the use of a temporary variable t. For this implementation we have:

```
x , y := X , Y;   {Q established}
t := x;
x := y;
y := t           {R established}
```

It is interesting to check that this mechanism also establishes R by computing the weakest precondition for it establishing R. We can do this using the sequential composition rule:

$$
\begin{aligned}
\text{wp}("t := x ; x := y ; y := t", R) &\equiv \text{wp}("t := x ; x := y ; y := t", x = Y \wedge y = X) \\
&\equiv \text{wp}("t := x ; x := y", \text{wp}("y := t", x = Y \wedge y = X)) \\
&\equiv \text{wp}("t := x ; x := y", x = Y \wedge t = X) \\
&\equiv \text{wp}("t := x"; \text{wp}("x := y", x = Y \wedge t = X)) \\
&\equiv \text{wp}("t := x", y = Y \wedge t = X) \\
&\equiv y = Y \wedge x = X
\end{aligned}
$$

Therefore

$$\text{wp}("t := x ; x := y ; y := t", R) \equiv y = Y \wedge x = X$$

But $y = Y \wedge x = X$ is just Q, the condition established by the initialization of x and y. The second exchange mechanism will therefore also establish R for all initial states as defined by Q. Weakest precondition calculations for sequential composition have been able to completely capture the meaning of the exchange mechanism.

6.6   Simple Loops

The development strategy for programs requiring simple loops is usually clear-cut. However, since more complicated structures are built largely from simple loops it is important to gain fluency in applying elementary loop-

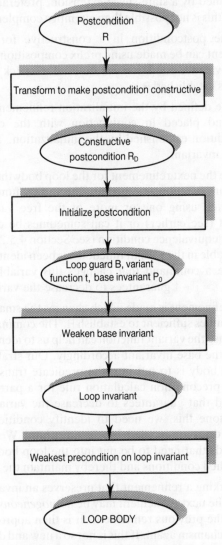

Figure 6.2   Steps in designing a loop.

design principles first. The steps shown in Figure 6.2 represent a set of useful guidelines for deriving mechanisms that employ iteration.

In more detail the steps in designing a loop are as follows.

(1)   First obtain or construct a precondition/postcondition pair (Q,R).

(2)   Try to make a simple initialization of the smallest number of free variables in R that is sufficient to establish R at least in some circumstances. If it is not easy to make such an initialization, or it is not easy to check that it has established R then R needs to be transformed by a state-space extension, preferably to an equivalent form. If this is not possible then attempt a complement extension of R.

(3)   With the postcondition in a constructive form an initialization refinement can be made using prefix composition, and at least part of the equivalence condition can be used to check whether the refinement has established R.

(4)   The state defined by the initialization refinement should be written down and placed in conjunction with the components of the postcondition established by the initialization. This combination is the base invariant.

(5)   To make the next refinement for the loop body the base invariant and the variant function are needed. The variant function can usually be constructed using one or more of the free variables in the base invariant (see earlier) or it can sometimes be constructed directly from the equivalence condition (see Section 4.5.2). Once at least one free variable in the variant function has been identified the next step is to create a command that changes this variable or variables (for example $i := i + 1$ guarantees to decrease the variant function $N - i$).

(6)   Next a refinement is made which changes the smallest finite subset of free variables sufficient to establish R. The command that guarantees to decrease the variant function can help us to identify this subset, and weaken the base invariant accordingly. Our strategy for developing the loop body is to put into the predicate transformer (that is the weakest precondition calculation rule for a particular command) a command that guarantees to decrease the variant function. Then, having done this, we need to identify conditions in the weakest precondition not implied by the invariant. We must then invent commands that need to be put into the loop body to guarantee the non-implied conditions and thereby maintain the loop invariant.

(7)   After making a refinement that preserves an invariant the precondition for the next refinement may be *homogeneous* with the precondition for the previous refinement. It is then appropriate to apply the same mechanism again. If this is not so a new and different refinement must be made.

(8)   To resolve the situation in (7) the refinement process needs to be repeated until a mechanism is obtained that will establish the postcondition for all the initial states defined by the precondition.

We can now consider the derivation of a number of simple loop programs. The first six problems that we will consider all involve an accumulative computational strategy in which the value of a variable (or variables) v is modified with each iteration of a loop. In each case the basic form for the computation is

"Initialize";
do B $\rightarrow$

.
.
.
    v := v $[\frac{+}{\times}]$ term;

.
.
.

od

The examples chosen illustrate a variety of simple transformations that can be applied to specifications.

6.6.1   Array summation [4]

One of the simplest repetitive strategies involves applying some computation to a sequence of data. Finding the sum of an array of fixed integers A[1..N] where N is also fixed is an elementary problem in this category. It is instructive to see how a solution to this problem is developed as a similar framework can be used for many other simple problems. The specification is

$Q : N \geqslant 0$
$R : s = \Sigma(A_j : 0 < j \leqslant N)$

R is not in a form which admits a simple initialization of s that can be easily checked to see if R is established. It would be very easy to initialize s to some value but it would be necessary to sum all the array elements to determine whether the initialization of s had indeed established the equality in R. This begs the original question. A transformation of R is therefore needed.

The fixed variable N can be replaced by i and the equivalence i = N can be added to give a constructive postcondition that implies R, that is

$R_D : s = \Sigma(A_j : 0 < j \leqslant i) \wedge i = N$

Using the fact that the sum of an empty array is 0 an appropriate initialization that can establish R_D is as follows:

$S_0 (X_0)$ Initialization

> $i, s := 0, 0; \{P_0\}$
> **if** $i = N \rightarrow$ skip $\{R_D$ established$\}$
> $[\!] \; i \neq N \rightarrow \{Q_1\} \; s_1(x_1) \; \{R_D\}$
> **fi**

The initialization will establish the postcondition R_D for $N = 0$. It also guarantees to establish the first conjunct in R_D. Coupling this with the condition established by the initialization assignments the base invariant becomes

$$P_0 : i = 0 \wedge s = 0 \wedge s = \Sigma(A_j : 0 < j \leq i)$$

and we have

$$P_0 \wedge i = N \Rightarrow R_D$$
$$P_0 \wedge i \neq N \equiv Q_1$$

To establish R_D when Q_1 applies we know at least that i will need to be increased in order to satisfy the equivalence condition $i = N$. This also raises the possibility that the condition $s = 0$ cannot be maintained.

Weakening P_0 accordingly we get P_1 which we hope may serve as the basis for the next refinement, that is

$$P_1 : s = \Sigma(A_j : 0 < j \leq i) \wedge 0 \leq i \leq N$$

Our next concern is to consider how i should be incremented. A simple way to do this is to use the assignment $i := i + 1$. Our objective in increasing i is to do so while maintaining P_1. To check the conditions under which increasing i in this way will maintain P_1 the corresponding weakest precondition needs to be computed, that is

$$wp(i := i + 1, P_1) \equiv s = \Sigma(A_j : 0 < j \leq i + 1) \wedge 0 \leq i + 1 \leq N$$

When i is replaced by $i + 1$ the RHS of the equality is increased by A_{i+1} while s on the LHS remains unchanged. This destroys the equality in the expression for s. To remedy this situation and preserve the equality, and P_1 too, it is necessary to add A_{i+1} to s. The following steps are therefore needed when i is increased:

$$i, s := i + 1, s + A_{i+1}$$

Making this refinement and checking if R_D is established we get

$S_1(X_1)$ First refinement

  i , s := 0 , 0 ; {R_D}
  if i = N → skip
  [] i ≠ N →
   i , s := i + 1 , s + A_{i+1};
   if i = N → {R_D established}
   [] i ≠ N → {Q_1} $s_1(x_1)$ { R_D }
   fi
  fi

This latest refinement cannot guarantee to establish R_D. It does however establish a precondition for the next refinement that is homogeneous with the precondition for the last refinement.

  In other words, the latest refinement preserves P_1 and we have

$$P_1 \wedge i = N \Rightarrow R_D$$

and we identify Q_1 as

$$P_1 \wedge i \neq N \equiv Q_1$$

To establish R_D when Q_1 applies i will need to be increased in order to establish i = N. A suitable variant function that follows from the equivalence condition is

$$t : N - i$$

A suitable way to proceed is to make a loop or recursive call on the command

$$i , s := i + 1 , s + A_{i+1}$$

This will be sufficient to preserve P_1 and, at the same time, decrease the variant function. Making this refinement gives

$S_2(X_2)$ Second refinement

  i , s := 0 , 0 ; {R_D}
  if i = N → skip
  [] i ≠ N →
   repeat {P_1}
    i , s := i + 1 , s + A_{i+1}
   until i = N {$P_1 \wedge i = N$}
  fi

where

$$P_1 \Rightarrow wp(S_2(X_2), R_D)$$

and

$$P_1 \wedge i = N \Rightarrow R_D$$
$$P_1 \wedge i \neq N \Rightarrow P_1$$

Each iteration increases i, and hence decreases the variant function. Termination is therefore assured. The implementation can be made simpler by replacing the **if** ... **repeat** structure by the equivalent **do** ... **od** representation, that is

```
i , s := 0 , 0;
do i ≠ N → {P₁}
    i , s := i + 1, s + A_{i+1}
od
{R_D}
```

In this example, and others that we will consider in this chapter, we have chosen to give very detailed refinements. We could have taken the shortcut of going directly to a **do** ... **od** loop after the initialization.

6.6.2   Factorial computation [5]

With this next example we again want to illustrate the value of making simple manipulations of a specification to assist the development of the program. The constructive value of starting the development by making an initialization that can establish R is also shown. The problem is, given a fixed natural number N, compute N! (that is, N factorial). The following axioms are given:

(1) $0! = 1$

(2) $N! = N \times (N - 1)!$ for $N > 0$

The accompanying specification is

```
Q : N ⩾ 0
R : f = N !
```

The postcondition in its present form is of no help in guiding the development because it is not possible to make an initialization of f that can be easily checked to see if R is established. In fact such an initialization would beg the question as it would require N! to be computed in order to check whether the value given f did establish R. A transformation of R to a constructive form is therefore needed. One possibility is to replace the fixed natural number N by a free variable i and record the equivalence condition. This yields

$$R_D : f = i! \wedge i = N$$

which implies R and can therefore be used to develop the program. Using the given axioms an appropriate initialization that can establish R_D and which can be easily checked by the equivalence condition $i = N$ is

$S_0(X_0)$ Initialization $\{f,i\}$

$\quad$ i, f := 0, 1 ; $\{P_0\}$
$\quad$ **if** i = N → skip $\{R_D$ established$\}$
$\quad$ **[]** i ≠ N → $\{Q_1\}$ $s_1(x_1)$ $\{R_D\}$
$\quad$ **fi**

The condition that the initialization guarantees to establish is the base invariant:

$$P_0 : i = 0 \wedge f = 1 \wedge f = i!$$

and we have

$$Q_1 : P_0 \wedge i \neq N$$

To make the next refinement, that is to establish R_D when Q_1 applies, will at least require that i be increased, if it is to satisfy the equivalence condition. If i is increased then the condition $f = 1$ will not be able to prevail. Weakening P_0 accordingly gives

$$P_1 : f = i! \wedge 0 \leq i \leq N$$

P_1 may serve as the basis for the next refinement since it permits both i and f to be changed. We want to make changes to i and f that maintain P_1. For this purpose we compute

$$wp(\text{"i} := i + 1\text{"}, P_1) \equiv f = (i + 1)! \wedge 0 \leq i + 1 \leq N$$

as we may be unsure at this stage how to change f. When i is replaced by $i + 1$ the RHS of the equality is increased by the factor $(i + 1)$ while f on the LHS remains unchanged. This *destroys* the equality in the expression for f. To remedy this situation and preserve the equality, and P_1 too, it is necessary to multiply f by the factor $(i + 1)$. The following steps are therefore needed when i is increased:

$$i, f := i + 1, f * (i + 1)$$

This new command can be checked using

$$\text{wp}(\text{"}i\,,f:=i+1\,,f*(i+1)\text{"}\,,P_1) \equiv f*(i+1) = (i+1)\,!\,\wedge\,0 \leqslant i+1 \leqslant N$$

which is implied by $P_1 \wedge i \neq N$ since the $(i+1)$ factors on both sides of the equality cancel to leave $f = i\,!$. As in our last example, simply increasing i by one cannot guarantee to establish the equivalence condition $i = N$ and hence R_D. A loop or recursive call on the command

$$i\,,f:=i+1\,,f*(i+1)$$

is needed with P_1 serving as the loop invariant and

$$t:N-i$$

as the variant function. Again the equivalence conditon may be used to guard the refinement. We get

$S_1(X_1)$ First refinement

```
    i , f := 0 , 1;
    if i ≠ N → skip
    [] i ≠ N →
        repeat {P₁}
            i , f := i + 1 , f * (i + 1)
        until i = N
    fi
```

No further refinements are needed as the loop guarantees to increase i to N, whereupon it terminates. For this refinement the following relations apply:

$$P_1 \Rightarrow \text{wp}\,(S_1(X_1),\,R_D)$$

and

$$P_1 \wedge i = N \Rightarrow R_D$$
$$P_1 \wedge i \neq N \Rightarrow P_1$$

Each iteration increases i, decreasing the variant function and so termination is assured.

Rewriting the implementation in **do** ... **od** form we get

```
    i , f := 0 , 1;
    do i ≠ N → {P₁}
        i , f := i + 1 , f * (i + 1)
    od
    {R_D}
```

6.6.3   Quotient and remainder problem [6]

The quotient–remainder problem is similar to the previous problems but its specification does not require any manipulation because it is already in a constructive form. It is included because we want to contrast its development with a more efficient algorithm to be given later. Given a fixed natural number X and a fixed divisor D (a positive integer) and compute the quotient q and remainder r that results from dividing X by D. Direct division should be avoided in the implementation. The specification is

$$Q : X \geqslant 0 \wedge D > 0$$
$$R : X = q \times D + r \wedge 0 \leqslant r < D$$

It is possible to add a range for the free variable q to give

$$R_D : X = q \times D + r \wedge 0 \leqslant r < D \wedge 0 \leqslant q \leqslant X$$

An initialization of r and q that can establish R_D is

$$r, q := X, 0$$

As no equivalence condition was previously identified we can compute the weakest precondition for this initialization to be able to establish R_D.

This will identify a suitable test to check if the initialization has established R_D. We get

$$\text{wp}(\text{``} r, q := X, 0\text{''}, R_D) \equiv X = 0 \times D + X \wedge 0 \leqslant X < D \wedge 0 \leqslant 0 \leqslant X$$
$$\equiv X < D \wedge 0 \leqslant X$$

This tells us that provided that X is less than D the initialization will be sufficient to establish R_D. The condition $X < D$ on the program variable state space $\{X, D, q, r\}$ has the form $r < D$. This form can be used to check whether the initialization refinement has established R_D and so we get

$S_0(X_0)$ Initialization

```
r, q := X, 0;
if r < D → skip {R_D established}
[] r ≥ D → {Q_1} s_1(x_1) {R_D}
fi
```

The initialization guarantees to establish the base invariant P_0 :
$$P_0 : r = X \wedge q = 0 \wedge X = q \times D + r \wedge 0 \leqslant r \wedge 0 \leqslant q \leqslant X$$

and we have

$$P_0 \wedge r < D \Rightarrow R_D$$
$$P_0 \wedge r \geqslant D \equiv Q_1$$

To establish R_D when Q_1 applies we know that at least r will need to be decreased and possibly q will also need to be changed. Weakening the base invariant P_0 accordingly we get

$$P_1 : 0 \leqslant r \leqslant X \wedge X = q \times D + r \wedge 0 \leqslant q \leqslant X$$

A possible variant function is

$$t : r$$

In order to maintain $X = q \times D + r$ the variable r will need to be decreased by multiples of D. To do this we may propose the command

$$r := r - D$$

We can now investigate the effect of this command on P_1 by computing $wp("r := r - D", P_1)$.

$$wp("r := r - D", P_1) : 0 \leqslant r - D \leqslant X \wedge X = q \times D + (r - D) \wedge 0 \leqslant q \leqslant X$$

This change in r breaks the equality in the expression for X since the RHS is decreased by D. One way to restore the equality would be to change q. Simply increasing q by 1 would have the effect of adding D to the RHS of the expression and restoring the equality. We may therefore propose the command

$$r, q := r - D, q + 1$$

to decrease the variant function while maintaining P_1. We see that in order to maintain the equality $X = q \times D + r$, a corresponding increase in q by one is needed. It is important to note in this case that we do not try to restore the equality by subtracting D from the LHS of the equality, that is

$$X - D = q \times D + (r - D)$$

because the LHS contains no variable (it contains only X which is fixed). Reducing r just by D cannot guarantee to establish $r < D$ and hence R_D. A loop or recursive call is therefore needed with P_1 as the invariant. We can show

$$P_1 \Rightarrow wp("r, q := r - D, q + 1", P_1)$$

and

$$P_1 \wedge r < D \Rightarrow R_D$$
$$P_1 \wedge r \geqslant D \Rightarrow P_1$$

The accompanying refinement we propose is therefore:

$S_1(X_1)$ First refinement

```
r, q := X, 0 ;
if r < D → skip
[] r ≥ D →
    repeat {P₁}
        r, q := r - D, q + 1
    until r < D
fi
```

It extends the set of initial states for which the mechanism will establish R_D to include those where $X \geqslant D$ and so we have a mechanism that will establish R_D for $X < D \wedge X \geqslant D \wedge X \geqslant 0$. This reduces to simply $X \geqslant 0$ as required by the original precondition.

If we wish this can be transformed to the equivalent form

```
r, q := X, 0 ;
do r ≥ D → {P₁}
    r, q := r - D, q + 1
od
{R_D}
```

This loop guarantees to decrease the variant function r with each iteration and so it will eventually terminate. The development is therefore complete.

6.6.4 Exponentiation [7a]

The exponentiation problem is interesting because it can be tackled in several different ways depending on the type of transformation we make on the given postcondition. We will consider two possible transformations. The problem requires that X^Y be computed for fixed natural numbers X and Y. The given specification is

$$Q : X \geqslant 0 \wedge Y \geqslant 0$$
$$R : z = X^Y$$

A simple constant replacement state-space extension yields the constructive postcondition R_D which implies R:

$$R_D : z = X^y \wedge y = Y$$

An initialization of the free variables z and y that can establish R_D and can be easily checked by the equivalence condition is as follows:

$S_0(X_0)$ Initialization

```
z , y := 1 , 0 ;
if y = Y → skip {R_D established}
[] y ≠ Y →{Q_1} s_1(x_1) {R_D}
fi
```

The initialization guarantees to establish the base invariant

$$P_0 : z = 1 \wedge y = 0 \wedge z = X^y \wedge 0 \leq y \leq Y \quad \text{(note } 0^0 = 1 \text{ by definition)}$$

where

$$P_0 \wedge y = Y \Rightarrow R_D$$
$$P_0 \wedge y \neq Y \equiv Q_1$$

To establish R_D when Q_1 applies y will need to be increased to establish the equivalence condition. A suitable variant function that can be constructed from the equivalence condition is

$$t : Y - y$$

The change in y will need to be accompanied by an increase in z. Weakening P_0 to accommodate these changes we get a new derivative invariant:

$$P_1 : z \geq 1 \wedge z = X^y \wedge 0 \leq y \leq Y$$

A simple command that will increase y is $y := y + 1$. The weakest precondition for this command maintaining P_1 is

$$\text{wp (“}y := y + 1\text{ ”}, P_1) \equiv z \geq 1 \wedge 0 \leq y + 1 \leq Y \wedge z = X^{y+1}$$

The replacement of y by $y + 1$ means that $z = X^{y+1}$ is no longer an equality. The right hand side expression is

$$X^y * X$$

which is just the old value (X^y) of the RHS multiplied by X. To restore the equality the LHS will also need to be multiplied by X and so we get

$$\text{wp}(\text{``}y,z:=y+1,z*X\text{''},P_1) \equiv z*X \geqslant 1 \wedge 0 \leqslant y+1 \leqslant Y \wedge z*X = X^{y+1}$$

which is implied by P_1 and $y \neq Y$. A refinement that can establish R_D which follows using this command is

$S_1(X_1)$ First refinement

```
z , y := 1 , 0
if y = Y → skip
[] y ≠ Y → {P₁}
   y , z := y + 1 , z * X;
   if y = Y → skip {R_D established}
   [] y ≠ Y → {Q₂} s₂(x₂) {R_D}
   fi
fi
```

where

$$P_1 \wedge y = Y \Rightarrow R_D$$
$$P_1 \wedge y \neq Y \Rightarrow P_1$$

The invariant P_1 will still hold after changing y and z and so for the next refinement $s_2(x_2)$ either a loop or recursive call may be made on the $s_1(x_1)$ mechanism. This will further decrease the variant function and may eventually satisfy the equivalence condition. Using a loop to make this refinement gives

$S_2(X_2)$ Second refinement

```
z , y := 1 , 0 ;
do y ≠ Y → {P₁}
   y , z := y + 1 , z * X
od
{R_D}
```

where

$$P_1 \Rightarrow \text{wp}(S_2(X_2), R_D)$$
$$P_1 \wedge y = Y \Rightarrow R_D$$
$$P_1 \wedge y \neq Y \Rightarrow P_1$$

6.6.5   Exponentiation [7b]

Given once again the same specifications as in our last example:

$$Q : X \geqslant 0 \wedge Y \geqslant 0$$
$$R : z = X^Y$$

another way to proceed with the development of an exponentiation algorithm is to employ a partial image extension by taking the partial image X^y of X^Y to yield a constructive form of the postcondition R_D which implies R :

$$R_D : z \times X^y = X^Y \wedge y = 0$$

where $y = 0$ is the equivalence condition.

An initialization of the free variables y and z which can establish R_D and which can be easily checked by the equivalence condition is

$S_0(X_0)$ Initialization

```
z , y := 1 , Y ;
if y = 0 → skip {R_D established}
[] y ≠ 0 → {Q_1} s_1(x_1) {R_D}
fi
```

The base invariant established is

$$P_0 : z = 1 \wedge y = Y \wedge z \times X^y = X^Y$$

and

$$P_0 \wedge y = 0 \Rightarrow R_D$$
$$P_0 \wedge y \neq 0 \equiv Q_1$$

If we follow the refinements through for this development we end up with the implementation

```
z , y := 1 , Y ;
do y ≠ 0 → {P_1}
   y , z := y − 1 , z * X
od
{R_D}
```

What the two exponentiation algorithms demonstrate is the value of state-space extensions as a source for exploring different solutions to a problem. Later a full image state-space extension will be used to construct a more efficient exponentiation algorithm. As an exercise try to develop such an algorithm.

6.6.6   Multiplication by addition [8a]

The multiplication-by-addition problem, like the exponentiation problem, can be approached in several different ways depending on the type of transformation we make on the given postcondition. We will consider two transformations in this section. The problem requires that $X \times Y$ be computed for fixed natural numbers X and Y without resorting to multiplication. The given specification is

$$Q : X \geqslant 0 \wedge Y \geqslant 0$$
$$R : z = X \times Y$$

A constant replacement state-space extension yields a constructive postcondition

$$R_D : z = X \times y \wedge y = Y$$

An initialization of the free variables z and y that can establish R_D and which can be checked by the equivalence condition is

$S_0(X_0)$ Initialization

$$z , y := 0 , 0 \, ;$$
if $y = Y \rightarrow$ skip {R_D established}
[] $y \neq Y \rightarrow$ {Q_1} $s_1(x_1)$ {R_D}
fi

The initialization guarantees to establish the base invariant

$$P_0 : z = 0 \wedge y = 0 \wedge z = X \times y \wedge 0 \leqslant y \leqslant Y$$

where

$$P_0 \wedge y = Y \Rightarrow R_D$$
$$P_0 \wedge y \neq Y \equiv Q_1$$

To establish R_D when Q_1 applies y will need to be increased to establish the equivalence condition. A variant function that can be constructed from the equivalence condition is

$$t : Y - y$$

Weakening P_0 to accommodate the change in y and the accompanying change in z we get

$$P_1 : z \geqslant 0 \wedge 0 \leqslant y \leqslant Y \wedge z = X \times y$$

Choosing $y := y + 1$ as our command to increase y and computing the weakest precondition for this command to change y, we get

$$wp("y := y + 1", P_1) \equiv z \geqslant 0 \wedge 0 \leqslant y + 1 \leqslant Y \wedge z = X \times (y + 1)$$

The replacement of y by $y + 1$ means that $z = X \times (y + 1)$ destroys the original equality in P_1. The RHS of the expression is

$$X \times y + X$$

which is just the old value $(X \times y)$ of the RHS with X added. To restore the original equality the LHS will need to have X added, so we get

$$wp("y, z := y + 1, z + X", P_1) \equiv z + X \geqslant 0 \wedge 0 \leqslant y + 1 \leqslant Y$$
$$\wedge z + X = X \times (y + 1)$$

which is implied by P_1 and $y \neq Y$. A refinement that can establish R_D which follows from using this command is

$S_1(X_1)$ First refinement

```
y := 0 ; z := 0 ;
if y = Y → skip
[] y ≠ Y → {P₁}
   y , z := y + 1, z + X;
   if y = Y → skip {R_D established}
   [] y ≠ Y → {Q₂} s₂(x₂) {R_D}
   fi
fi
```

where

$$P_1 \wedge y = Y \Rightarrow R_D$$
$$P_1 \wedge y \neq Y \Rightarrow P_1$$

After changing y and z, P_1 still holds and so for the refinement $s_2(x_2)$ a loop over $s_1(x_1)$ is in order, as it can eventually establish the equivalence condition. We get

$S_2(X_2)$ Second refinement

```
y , z := 0 , 0 ;
do y ≠ Y → {P₁}
   y , z := y + 1, z + X
od
{R_D}
```

where

$$P_1 \Rightarrow wp(S_2(X_2), R_D)$$

and

$$P_1 \wedge y = Y \Rightarrow R_D$$
$$P_1 \wedge y \neq Y \Rightarrow P_1$$

The development for this algorithm has closely paralleled that for the exponentiation algorithm.

6.6.7 Multiplication by addition [8b]

Another way to proceed from the specification

$$Q : X \geqslant 0 \wedge Y \geqslant 0$$
$$R : z = X \times Y$$

is to take a partial image of $X \times Y$ to give a constructive form for the postcondition:

$$R_D : z + X \times y = X \times Y \wedge y = 0$$

with $y = 0$ acting as the equivalence condition.

If the complete development is followed through for this specification we get the implementation

```
z , y := 0 , Y ;
do y ≠ 0 →
    y , z := y − 1, z + X
od
{R_D}
```

6.6.8 Generating squares and cubes [9]

The problems of generating successive squares and cubes provide an interesting illustration of the value of making transformations on specifications. Consider first the problem of generating and storing all the squares of the first N positive integers. We have

$$R : (\forall j : 0 < j \leqslant N : a_j = j^2)$$

An obvious solution to this problem via the constructive postcondition R_D is as follows:

$$R_D : (\forall j : 0 < j \leq i : a_j = j^2) \wedge i = N$$
$$P_D : (\forall j : 0 < j \leq i : a_j = j^2) \wedge 0 \leq i \leq N$$

```
i := 0;
do i ≠ N → {P_D}
   i, a_{i+1} := i + 1, (i + 1)²
od
{R_D}
```

The question arises can we derive an alternative implementation for this problem that tries to build on previous computations as we have tried to do in most of our previous examples?

Suppose we know i^2 and we want to generate $(i + 1)^2$. We have

$$a_{i+1} = i^2 + 2i + 1$$

The next term clearly includes the current term, i^2.

The aim is to relate the next term to the current term. To do this new free variables x and y (and their successors x′ and y′ respectively) are introduced.

This yields the relations

$$a_{i+1} = i^2 + 2i + 1$$

or

$$x' = x + y' \wedge x = i^2 \wedge y' = 2i + 1$$

We can then write a loop to generate the successive squares in the form below, provided we can work out how to generate y′ from its predecessor y, i.e.

```
x := 1; i := 1; y := ?;
do i ≠ N →
   y := ?;
   x := x + y;
   i, a_{i+1} := i + 1, x
od
```

Now consider how we can generate the term

$$2i + 1$$

from its predecessor.

The predecessor term, as a function of i, is

$$y = 2(i - 1) + 1$$

and we have

$$y' = y + 2$$

Incorporating these results, together with the fact that y will need to be initially 1, we get:

```
i := 1; x := 1; y := 1;
do i ≠ N →
   y := y + 2;
   x := x + y;
   i, a_{i+1} := i + 1, x
od
```

This latest implementation has the virtue that it avoids the need for multiplication. The algorithm captures the fact that the sum of the odd sequence generates successive squares. Let us now extend these ideas to the problem of generating successive cubes to see if a similar sort of algorithm can be achieved by again building on previous computations.

Suppose we know i^3 and we want to generate $(i + 1)^3$. We have

$$a_{i+1} = i^3 + 3i^2 + 3i + 1$$

We can again try to relate the next term to the current term. For this purpose we will introduce new free variables x and y and their successors.

This yields the relations

$$a_{i+1} = i^3 + 3i^2 + 3i + 1$$
$$x' = x + y' \land x = i^3 \land y' = 3i^2 + 3i + 1$$

Our next concern is to find a way of generating the term

$$3i^2 + 3i + 1$$

from its predecessor.

The predecessor term as a function of i is:

$$y = 3(i - 1)^2 + 3(i - 1) + 1$$

and we have

$$y' = y + 6i$$

Introducing a new free variable z and its successor z' we can write the last equality as

$$y' = y + z' \wedge z' = 6i$$

Our task now reduces to generating z' from its predecessor which, as a function of i, is

$$z = 6(i - 1)$$

and so we can write

$$z' = z + 6 \wedge z = 6(i - 1)$$

So from z, we can compute y, and from y we can compute x and thereby generate the next cube from the current cube. Collecting these results into an implementation and including appropriate initializations we get an algorithm for generating successive cubes without multiplications:

```
i := 1; x := 1; y := 1; z := 0;
do i ≠ N →
    z := z + 6;
    y := y + z;
    x := x + y;
    i, a_{i+1} := i + 1, x
od
```

This basic idea can obviously be extended to generating successive integral terms for any polynomial without the need to resort to multiplication. This corresponds to the familiar differencing technique employed frequently by numerical analysts. We have however arrived at the result differently by our now familiar technique of determining how the next term (or state) in the computation relates to the current term.

6.6.9   Integer square root (linear) [10a]

The integer square root problem gives a clear demonstration of the influence of transformations on the efficiency of the algorithms that may be derived from a specification. The problem may be stated as follows. For a fixed natural number N it is required to find an integer square root a that satisfies the specification:

$$Q : N \geqslant 0$$
$$R : a^2 \leqslant N < (a + 1)^2$$

This problem is a search problem. There are two possible ways of transforming the postcondition to a constructive form:

(1) $R_D : a^2 \leq n < (a + 1)^2 \wedge n = N \wedge 0 \leq a \leq N$ (by constant replacement and range inclusion)

(2) $R_D : a^2 \leq N < b^2 \wedge b = a + 1 \wedge 0 \leq a \leq N$ (by replacement of a variable expression by a variable and range inclusion)

For development using (1), if n assumes only a sequence of values that are perfect squares, then there is no guarantee that n = N will ever be satisfied. Care must therefore be taken with such an implementation. The method of termination we will use is at best unusual. Carrying out the development based on (1) we end up with

```
a := 0 ; n := 0 ;
do n ≠ N → {P₁}
    if (a + 1)² ≤ N → a , n := a + 1, (a + 1)²
    [] (a + 1)² > N → n := N
    fi
od
```

where

$$P_1 : a^2 \leq n < (a + 1)^2 \wedge 0 \leq a \leq N$$

and

$$P_1 \wedge n = N \Rightarrow R_D$$
$$P_1 \wedge n \neq N \Rightarrow P_1$$

Dijkstra, using his technique of weakening a postcondition by deleting a conjunct to get an invariant rather than trying to find an equivalent or stronger postcondition, derives the following invariant P from R:

$$P : a^2 \leq N$$

This invariant is easily initialized by the assignment $a := 0$.

Computing wp("a := a + 1", P) he is led to the implementation below that is based on P as the loop invariant.

```
a := 0 ;
do (a + 1)² ≤ N → a := a + 1 od
```

This implementation is more efficient than our implementation based on (1). Usually there is no advantage to be gained by basing the development on a weakened form that results from deleting a conjunct from a postcondition. Methodologically it is far better to weaken a postcondition by retaining its original form. The following example reiterates the recommended strategy of weakening the postcondition

$$R_D : z = X^y \wedge y = Y$$

to obtain an invariant P_D, not by deleting the conjunct $y = Y$, but by expanding the range of y, that is

$$P_D : z = X^y \wedge 0 \leqslant y \leqslant Y$$

This form for P_D *includes* R_D. A more detailed discussion of this point has been given in Section 4.4.5.

6.6.10   Integer square root (binary) [10b]

A much more efficient integer square root algorithm can be derived from the constructive postcondition (2)

(2) $R_D : a^2 \leqslant N < b^2 \wedge b = a + 1 \wedge 0 \leqslant a \leqslant N$

An initialization of the free variables a and b that can establish R_D and which can be easily checked by the equivalence condition $b = a + 1$ is

$S_0(X_0)$ Initialization

$$a := 0 \; ; b := N + 1 \; ; \{P_0\}$$
$$\textbf{if } b = a + 1 \rightarrow \text{skip } \{R_D \text{ established}\}$$
$$[\!]\; b \neq a + 1 \rightarrow \{Q_1\} \; s_1(x_1) \; \{R_D\}$$
$$\textbf{fi}$$

The initialization guarantees to establish the base invariant

$$P_0 : a = 0 \wedge b = N + 1 \wedge a^2 \leqslant N < b^2 \wedge 0 \leqslant a \leqslant N$$

where

$$P_0 \wedge b \neq a + 1 \equiv Q_1$$

To make the next refinement that can establish R_D when Q_1 applies either a will need to be increased, or b decreased, or both changed, in order to establish the equivalence condition. An appropriate variant function constructed from the equivalence condition is therefore

$$t : b - a - 1$$

To eliminate on average the largest part of the region between a and b, in our search for the integer square root, we can choose the mid-range m where

$$m = (a + b) \, \textbf{div} \, 2$$

Consider first a change in a. The condition P_0 must be weakened to

$$P_1' : a \geqslant 0 \wedge b = N + 1 \wedge a^2 \leqslant N < b^2 \wedge 0 \leqslant a \leqslant N$$

We can compute the weakest precondition that assigning a to m will maintain P_1':

$$wp(\text{``}a := m\text{''}, P_1') \equiv m \geqslant 0 \wedge b = N + 1 \wedge m^2 \leqslant N < b^2 \wedge 0 \leqslant m \leqslant N$$

Now the condition $m^2 \leqslant N$ is not implied by P_1' and so a refinement that sets $a := m$ will need to ensure first that $m^2 \leqslant N$ holds. We therefore get

$$m := (a + b) \, \textbf{div} \, 2;$$
$$\textbf{if} \, m^2 \leqslant N \rightarrow a := m$$

Since there is nothing about the problem that suggests changing a should have any preference over changing b, we can weaken P_1' accordingly:

$$P_1 : a \geqslant 0 \wedge b \leqslant N + 1 \wedge a^2 \leqslant N < b^2 \wedge 0 \leqslant a \leqslant N$$

Computing $wp(\text{``}b := m\text{''}, P_1)$ shows that $N < m^2$ is not implied by P_1 and so it will need to be included in the refinement, that is

$$m := (a + b) \, \textbf{div} \, 2;$$
$$\textbf{if} \, N < m^2 \rightarrow b := m$$

There is nothing to guarantee that either $m^2 \leqslant N$ or $m^2 > N$ will hold and so it is appropriate to combine the steps that change a and b into a single construct. The equivalence condition is sufficient to check whether the assignment either to a or to b will establish R_D.

$S_1(X_1)$ First refinement

```
a := 0 ; b := N + 1;
if b = a + 1 → skip
[] b ≠ a + 1 → {P₁}
   m := (a + b) div 2;
   if m² ≤ N → a := m
   [] m² > N → b := m
   fi;
   if b = a + 1 → skip {R_D established}
   [] b ≠ a + 1 → {Q₂} s₂(x₂) { R_D }
   fi
fi
```

The invariant still holds after changing a or b and so either a loop or recursive call may be employed when Q_2 applies. Using a loop to make the refinement we get

$S_2(X_2)$ Second refinement

$$a := 0; b := N + 1$$
$$\textbf{do } b \neq a + 1 \rightarrow \{P_1\}$$
$$m := (a + b) \textbf{ div } 2;$$
$$\textbf{if } m^2 \leqslant N \rightarrow a := m$$
$$[] \ m^2 > N \rightarrow b := m$$
$$\textbf{fi}$$
$$\textbf{od}$$
$$\{R_D\}$$

where

$$P_1 \Rightarrow wp(S_2(X_2), R_D)$$

and

$$P_1 \wedge b = a + 1 \Rightarrow R_D$$
$$P_1 \wedge b \neq a + 1 \Rightarrow P_1$$

The structure of this algorithm is similar to the binary search which is discussed in Chapter 7. Both implementations have $O(\log_2 N)$ complexity.

6.7   Nested Loops

In this section we will examine a number of examples that involve the derivation of programs that contain nested loops. In deriving these programs inner loops are usually associated with the identification of a sub-goal that must be established before progress can be made with an outer loop. Weakest precondition calculations with an invariant can be used to identify more complex sub-goals that require a loop for their resolution. Figure 6.3 sketches the strategy for deriving programs that require nested loops.

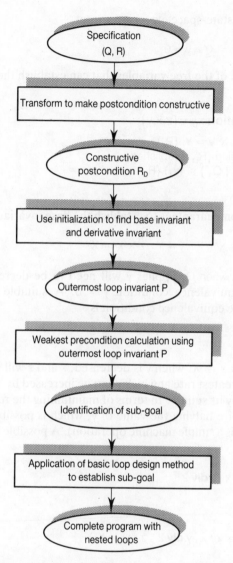

Figure 6.3   Program derivation for nested loops

6.7.1   Fast exponentiation [11]

The exponentiation problem discussed earlier can be solved using a different state-space extension which leads directly to a more efficient algorithm because there is more accessible freedom in the postcondition. The given specification was

$Q : X \geqslant 0 \wedge Y \geqslant 0$
$R : z = X^Y$

Using an image state-space extension we get

$$R_D : z \times x^y = X^Y \wedge y = 0$$

An initialization of the free variables that can establish the postcondition is

$S_0(X_0)$ Initialization $x_0 = \{z,x,y\}$

> $z := 1; x := X; y := Y; \{P_0\}$
> **if** $y=0 \rightarrow$ skip $\{R_D$ established$\}$
> $[] \ y \neq 0 \rightarrow \{ Q_1 \} \ s_1 (x_1) \{R_D\}$
> **fi**

This initialization guarantees to establish the base invariant:

$$P_0 : z = 1 \wedge x = X \wedge y = Y \wedge z \times x^y = X^Y$$

To establish R_D when Q_1 applies y will need to be decreased in order to establish the equivalence condition $y = 0$. A suitable variant function derived from the equivalence condition is

$$t : y$$

To maintain $z \times x^y = X^Y$ when y is decreased, x and z will be candidates for increase. The greatest rate at which x can be increased by a single operation is to replace it by its square. In terms of maintaining the relation $z \times x^y = X^Y$ this would require halving the value of y, which is possible only when y is even (the latter is a simple machine operation). A possible command for this is

$$x , y := x * x , y \ \textbf{div} \ 2$$

Computing

$$wp(\text{"}x , y := x * x , y \ \textbf{div} \ 2\text{"}, z * x^y = X^Y)$$

confirms that y must be *even*. In fact while y is even it is possible to repeatedly execute this command. Weakening P_0 to accommodate these changes we get

$$P_1 : z = 1 \wedge x \geq X \wedge y \leq Y \wedge z \times x^y = X^Y$$

A refinement based on changing just x and y cannot be one that will establish R_D. It can however hopefully be exploited in a subsequent refinement to establish R_D. The most recent refinement establishes the condition

$$R_1 : P_1 \wedge \neg even (y)$$

It is now possible to incorporate the results of the last refinement into another refinement which changes z and therefore has a chance of establishing R_D provided y is also decreased. Allowing for z to change we get

$$P_2 : z \geqslant 1 \wedge x \geqslant X \wedge y \leqslant Y \wedge z \times x^y = X^Y$$

z can be changed by incorporating the current value of x (which is x raised to a binary power).

Computing

$$wp(\text{"}z := z * x\text{"}, P_2)$$

we find that y will need to be reduced by 1 in order to maintain the condition

$$z \times x^y = X^Y$$

and hence P_2. Incorporating this step into our command we can make a refinement that will establish R_D provided the equivalence condition $y = 0$ is also satisfied:

$S_2(X_2)$ Second refinement $x_2 = \{ z, y \}$

```
z := 1; x := X; y := Y;
if y = 0 → skip
[] y ≠ 0 →
    do even(y) →
        x , y := x * x , y div 2
    od;
    z , y := z * x , y − 1;
    if y = 0 → skip {R_D established}
    [] y ≠ 0 → {Q_3} s_3(x_3) {R_D}
    fi
fi
```

When Q_3 applies a loop or recursive call to the mechanism $s_1(x_1) \circ s_2(x_2)$ can be used to decrease y and hence establish the equivalence condition while maintaining P_2.

Making this refinement yields

$S_3 (X_3)$ Third refinement

```
z := 1 ; x := X ; y := Y;
do y ≠ 0 → {P_2}
    do even (y) →
        x , y := x * x , y div 2
    od;
    z , y := z * x , y − 1
od
{R_D}
```

where

$$P_2 \Rightarrow wp(S_3(X_3), R_D)$$

and

$$P_2 \wedge y = 0 \Rightarrow R_D$$
$$P_2 \wedge y \neq 0 \Rightarrow P_2$$

In this development a more efficient algorithm than our original solution has resulted because we have introduced into the specification the possibility of changing X (via x) as well as Y (via y) and z. We have ended up with an $O(\log Y)$ algorithm compared with our original $O(Y)$ algorithm. As this example demonstrates certain state-space extensions can introduce more freedom into a specification, thereby allowing efficiency gains. State-space extension should therefore be seen as a tool for helping us discover more efficient algorithms as well as simply a tool that allows us to make initializations of free variables.

6.7.2.   Fast multiplication by addition [12]

Like the exponentiation problem, multiplication by addition can be solved more efficiently by making a different transformation on the original postcondition. The original specification was

$$Q : X \geqslant 0 \wedge Y \geqslant 0$$
$$R : z = X \times Y$$

Making an image state-space extension we get the following constructive postcondition with an equivalence condition $y = 0$:

$$R_D : z + x \times y = X \times Y \wedge y = 0$$

An initialization of free variables that can establish the postcondition and which can be confirmed by the equivalence condition is

$S_0(X_0)$ Initialization

```
z := 0; x := X; y := Y; {P_0}
if y = 0 → skip {R_D established}
[] y ≠ 0 → {Q_1} s_1(x_1) {R_D}
fi
```

This initialization guarantees to establish the base invariant:

$$P_0 : z = 0 \wedge x = X \wedge y = Y \wedge z + x \times y = X \times Y$$

To establish R_D when Q_1 applies y needs to be decreased to establish the equivalence condition $y = 0$. A suitable variant function derived from the equivalence condition is

$$t : y$$

To maintain $z + x \times y = X \times Y$ when y is decreased x and z are candidates for being increased. The greatest useful rate at which x can be increased by a single operation is to replace it by its sum with itself (i.e. $x + x$). To maintain the relation $z + x \times y = X \times Y$ this requires halving y. A possible command is

$$x, y := x + x, y \textbf{ div } 2$$

Computing wp("$x, y := x + x, y$ **div** 2", $z + x * y = X * Y$) indicates that y must be even. Under these circumstances the command can be repeatedly executed. Weakening P_0 to accommodate these changes yields the invariant

$$P_1 : z = 0 \wedge x \geqslant X \wedge y \leqslant Y \wedge z + x \times y = X \times Y$$

The refinement based on the above command cannot establish R_D but it suitably decreases the variant function:

$S_1(X_1)$ First refinement $x_1 = \{x, y\}$

```
z := 0; x := X; y := Y;
if y = 0 → skip
[] y ≠ 0 →
    do even (y) →
        x , y := x + x , y div 2
    od ;
    {Q₂} s₂(x₂) {R_D}
fi
```

The most recent refinement establishes the condition

$$R_1 : P_1 \wedge \neg even(y)$$

The gains of the last refinement can now be incorporated into a new refinement which changes z and thereby has a chance of establishing R_D, provided y is also changed to maintain the relation $z + x \times y = X \times Y$. Weakening P_1 to allow for z to change gives

$$P_2 : z \geqslant 0 \wedge x \geqslant X \wedge y \leqslant Y \wedge z + x \times y = X \times Y$$

Computing wp("z := z + x", P_2) reveals that y will need to be decreased by one to maintain P_2. Incorporating this step into our command we can make a refinement that will establish R_D provided the equivalence condition y = 0 is also satisfied:

$S_2(X_2)$ Second refinement $x_2 = \{z, y\}$

```
z := 0; x := X; y := Y;
if y = 0 → skip
[] y ≠ 0 →
    do even(y)→
        x , y := x + x , y div 2
    od;
    z , y := z + x , y − 1;
    if y = 0 → skip {R_D established}
    [] y ≠ 0 → {Q_3} s_3(x_3) {R_D}
    fi
fi
```

where

$$P_2 \wedge y = 0 \Rightarrow R_D$$
$$P_2 \wedge y \neq 0 \Rightarrow P_2$$

When Q_3 applies a loop or recursive call to the mechanism $s_1(x_1) \circ s_2(x_2)$ can be used to decrease y under the invariance of P_2 and hence establish the equivalence condition, and R_D. Making this refinement we get

$S_3(X_3)$ Third refinement

```
z := 0; x := X; y := Y;
do y≠0 → {P_2}
    do even(y) →
        x , y := x + x , y div 2
    od;
    z , y := z + x , y − 1
od
{R_D}
```

where

$$P_2 \Rightarrow wp(S_3(X_3), R_D)$$

and

$$P_2 \wedge y = 0 \Rightarrow R_D$$
$$P_2 \wedge y \neq 0 \Rightarrow P_2$$

Our new implementation is $O(\log Y)$ compared with our original algorithm which was $O(Y)$. It is interesting to compare the parallels in the development of this algorithm with the previous algorithm for fast exponentiation.

6.7.3 Matrix multiplication [13]

The problem of multiplying two two-dimensional matrices typifies a simple problem well suited to solution by top-down stepwise refinement. We will now examine this problem. The accompanying specifications are

$$Q : M \geqslant 0 \wedge N \geqslant 0 \wedge R \geqslant 0$$
$$R : (\forall p : 0 < p \leqslant M : (\forall q : 0 < q \leqslant N : c_{p,q} = \Sigma(A_{p,r} \times B_{r,q} : 0 < r \leqslant R)))$$

It is not easy to make an initialization of free variables that will establish this postcondition. Applying the constant replacement rule yields the following constructive postcondition, with equivalence condition $i = M$.

$$R_D : (\forall p : 0 < p \leqslant i : (\forall q : 0 < q \leqslant N : c_{p,q} = \Sigma(A_{p,r} \times B_{r,q} : 0 < r \leqslant R))) \wedge i = M$$

An initialization refinement that can establish R_D is:

$S_o(X_0)$ Initialization $x_0 = \{i\}$

    i := 0;
    if i = M → skip {R_D established}
    [] i ≠ M → {Q_1} $s_1(x_1)$ {R_D}
    fi

The initialization establishes the following base invariant :

$$P_0 : i = 0 \wedge (\forall p : 0 < p \leqslant i : (\forall q : 0 < q \leqslant N : c_{p,q} = \Sigma(A_{p,r} \times B_{r,q} : 0 < r \leqslant R)))$$

where

$$P_0 \wedge i = M \Rightarrow R_D$$
$$P_0 \wedge i \neq M \equiv Q_1$$

Given P_0 and Q_1 in order to make progress towards establishing $i = M$ and hence R_D, i will need to be increased. The simplest way to do this is with the command $i := i + 1$.

P_0 can be weakened to allow for this change, i.e.

$$P_1 : 0 \leqslant i \leqslant M \wedge (\forall p : 0 < p \leqslant i : (\forall q : 0 < q \leqslant N : c_{p,q} = \Sigma(A_{p,r} \times B_{r,q} : 0 < r \leqslant R)))$$

To investigate how progress can be made we examine:

$$wp(\text{"}i := i + 1\text{"}, P_1)$$

When we do this we find that the term:

$$R_1 : (\forall q : 0 < q \leqslant N : c_{i+1,q} = \Sigma(A_{i+1,r} \times B_{r,q} : 0 < r \leqslant R))$$

is not implied by P_1. A mechanism that guarantees to establish this sub-goal will be needed before we can safely execute $i := i + 1$ under the invariance of P_1. There is a difficulty with making this refinement with R_1 in its present form. We must therefore look to a state-space extension on R_1. Replacing the fixed N by a new free variable j and including the equivalence condition $j = N$ yields:

$$R_1' : (\forall q : 0 < q \leqslant j : c_{i+1,q} = \Sigma(A_{i+1,r} \times B_{r,q} : 0 < r \leqslant R)) \wedge j = N$$

From this condition we obtain the invariant:

$$P_1' : (\forall q : 0 < q \leqslant j : c_{i+1,q} = \Sigma(A_{i+1,r} \times B_{r,q} : 0 < r \leqslant R)) \wedge 0 \leqslant j \leqslant N$$

R_1' can be trivially established by the assignment $j := 0$ provided the equivalence condition $j = N$ is true.

Making this initialization yields the structure

$S_1(X_1)$ Second initialization

```
i := 0; {P₀}
if i = M → skip
[] i ≠ M →
    j := 0; {P₁'}
    if j = N → skip {R₁' established}
    [] j ≠ N → {Q₂} s₂(x₂) {R₁'}
    fi
fi
```

With this refinement we cannot execute $i := i + 1$ yet as we do not have a mechanism that guarantees $j = N$.

To make progress when Q_2 applies and $j \neq N$ we therefore need to investigate the conditions under which $j := j + 1$ can be executed. We find that the following component is not implied by P_1'

$$R_2 : c_{i+1,j+1} = \Sigma(A_{i+1,r} \times B_{r,j+1} : 0 < r \leqslant R))$$

To deal with this sub-goal R_2 another state-space extension is needed. Replacing the fixed R by the new free variable k yields

$$R_2' : c_{i+1,j+1} = \Sigma(A_{i+1,r} \times B_{r,j+1} : 0 < r \le k)) \wedge k = R$$

An initialization that establishes this sub-goal is

$$k := 0 \; ; \; c_{i+1,j+1} := 0$$

since summation over an empty range is zero. It follows that the invariant is

$$P_2' : c_{i+1,j+1} = \Sigma(A_{i+1,r} \times B_{r,j+1} : 0 < r \le k)) \wedge 0 \le k \le R$$

$S_2(X_2)$ Third initialization $x_2 = \{k,c\}$

```
i := 0;
if i = M → skip
[] i ≠ M →
    j := 0;
    if j = N → skip
    [] j ≠ N →
        k := 0; c_{i+1,j+1} := 0;
        if k = R → skip
        [] k ≠ R → {Q_3} s_3(x_3) {R_2'}
        fi
    fi
fi
```

Having made this most recent refinement we are still not in a position where we can safely execute either $j := j + 1$ as $k = R$ is not guaranteed or $i := i + 1$ as $j = N$ and hence R_2' is not guaranteed. Our most immediate concern is to increase k in order to establish $k = R$. To do this we must examine

$$wp(\text{``}k := k + 1\text{''}, P_2')$$

where we find that $A_{i+1,k+1} * B_{k+1,j+1}$ will need to be added to $c_{i+1,j+1}$ in order to preserve the equality with the Σ term. The resulting command which may possibly establish $k = R$ is

$$k , c_{i+1,j+1} := k + 1 , c_{i+1,j+1} + A_{i+1,k+1} * B_{k+1,j+1}$$

Making this refinement and including the check whether $k = R$ we get

$S_3(X_3)$ First refinement $x_3 = \{k,c\}$

```
i := 0;
if i = M → skip
[] i ≠ M →
    j := 0;
    if j = N → skip
    [] j ≠ N →
        k := 0; c_{i+1,j+1} := 0;
        if k = R → skip
        [] k ≠ R →
            k , c_{i+1,j+1} := k + 1 , c_{i+1,j+1} + A_{i+1,k+1} * B_{k+1,j+1};
            if k = R → skip {R'_2 established}
            [] k ≠ R → {Q_4} s_4(x_4) {R'_2}
            fi
        fi
    fi
fi
```

As this most recent refinement does not guarantee R'_2 a further refinement is needed when Q_4 applies. A loop or recursive call to $s_3(x_3)$ can be used for this purpose. The loop will guarantee to establish $k = R$ and hence R'_2. We are therefore at liberty to include "$j := j + 1$" subsequently and test whether $j = N$ and hence R'_1 has been established.

Making this refinement we get

$S_4(X_4)$ Second refinement $x_4 = \{k, c\}$

```
i := 0;
if i = M → skip
[] i ≠ M →
    j := 0;
    if j = N → skip
    [] j ≠ N →
        k := 0; c_{i+1,j+1} := 0;
        do k ≠ R →
            k , c_{i+1,j+1} := k + 1, c_{i+1,j+1} + A_{i+1,k+1} * B_{k+1,j+1}
        od; {R'_2}
        j := j + 1;
        if j = N → skip {R'_1 established}
        [] j ≠ N → {Q_5} s_5(x_5) {R'_1}
        fi
    fi
fi
```

The most recent refinement does not yet guarantee R'_1 and so a further refinement is needed when $\{Q_5\}$ applies. A loop or recursive call over $s_2(x_2) \circ s_3(x_3) \circ s_4(x_4)$ is needed to guarantee $j = N$ and hence R'_1. We will then be at liberty to include $i := i + 1$ subsequently and test whether $i = M$ and hence R_D has been established.

Making this refinement we get

$S_5(X_5)$ Third refinement $x_5 = \{k,c,j\}$

```
i := 0;
if i = M → skip
[] i ≠ M →
     j := 0;
     do j ≠ N →
        k := 0; c_{i+1,j+1} := 0;
        do k ≠ R →
           k , c_{i+1,j+1} := k+1 , c_{i+1,j+1} + A_{i+1,k+1} * B_{k+1,j+1}
        od; {R'_2}
        j := j + 1
     od; {R'_1}
     i := i + 1;
     if i = M → skip {R established}
     [] i ≠ M → {Q_6} s_6(x_6) {RD}
     fi
fi
```

To complete the development a further refinement is needed when Q_6 applies. A loop over $s_1(x_1) \circ ... \circ s_5(x_5)$ can guarantee to establish R_D. Making this refinement gives the final implementation.

$S_6(X_6)$ Fourth refinement

```
     i := 0;
     do i ≠ M →
        j := 0;
        do j ≠ N →
           k := 0; c_{i+1,j+1} := 0;
           do k ≠ R →
              k , c_{i+1,j+1} := k + 1, c_{i+1,j+1} + A_{i+1,k+1} * B_{k+1,j+1}
           od; {R'_2}
           j := j + 1
        od; {R'_1}
        i := i + 1
     od
     {R_D}
```

6.7.4   Fast quotient–remainder computation [14]

It is possible to obtain a more efficient solution to the quotient–remainder problem discussed earlier by using a more elaborate state-space extension that introduces more accessible freedom into the specification. The original specification was

$$Q : X \geqslant 0 \wedge D > 0$$
$$R : X = q \times D + r \wedge 0 \leqslant r < D$$

Dijkstra, in his discussion of the problem, suggests that an efficient solution can be achieved by reducing r by larger multiples of D. The aim here is to show how suitable state-space extensions lead us to this idea. An initialization of free variables that can establish R is

$$r := X; \ q := 0$$

This initialization will establish R provided the condition $r < D$ holds. We get

$S_0(X_0)$ Initialization

```
r := X; q := 0;
if r < D → skip {R established}
[] r ⩾ D → {Q₁} s₁(x₁) {R}
fi
```

This initialization guarantees to establish the base invariant:

$$P_0 : r = X \wedge q = 0 \wedge X = q \times D + r \wedge 0 \leqslant r$$

A suitable variant function is

$$t : r$$

In making the next refinement we want to try to reduce r by multiples of D. Furthermore the most we can reduce r by in a single operation (that does not use multiplication) is by its sum with itself (i.e $D + D$). With each doubling we can expect to subtract the following multiples of D:

$$1D, 2D, 4D, 8D, \ldots \tag{1}$$

Subtracting these multiples of D will have the cumulative effect of removing the following multiples of D from r:

$$1D, 3D, 7D, 15D, \ldots \tag{2}$$

This cumulative effect corresponds to an *exponential* growth in the rate of subtraction of multiples of D from r. To try to accommodate this exponential growth rate we will introduce a new free variable q1 by way of a partial-image state-space extension on P_0. Allowing also for q and r to change we get

$$P_1 : X = q \times D + r + q1 \times D \wedge 0 \leqslant r$$

where q1 is intended to specify the cumulative multiples of D, that is 1, 3, 7, 15, ... in (2). To make this specification stronger we need to include the doubling values indicated in sequence (1). For this purpose we will use the variable d. Investigating the relationship between the sequences (1) and (2) we find

$$d = ((q1 + 1) / 2) \times D$$

Adding this relationship to P_1 we get

$$P_1' : X = q \times D + r + q1 \times D \wedge d = ((q1 + 1) / 2) \times D \wedge 0 \leqslant r$$

The aim now is to make a refinement when Q_1 applies. To do this the first step is to attempt to establish P_1' so as to base our doubling strategy on this specification. In making this refinement, as part of our initialization of q1 and d, advantage can be taken of the fact that $r \geqslant D$. This means r can be decreased as part of the initialization.

Allowing for this a refinement can be made that establishes P_1' and decreases r and which could ultimately establish R. We get

$S_1(X_1)$ First refinement $x_1 = \{r, d, q1\}$

```
r := X; q := 0;
if r < D → skip
[] r ≥ D→
    r, d, q1 := r − D, D, 1; {P₁'}
    if r < d + d → skip
    [] r ≥ d + d → {Q₂} s₂(x₂) {R}
    fi
fi
```

If $r \geqslant d + d$ and Q_2 applies (i.e where $Q_2 : P_1' \wedge r \geqslant d + d$) r can be reduced further by at least d + d, and d can be doubled. We can then build the complete command for doing this by calculating the weakest precondition that captures these changes (that is q1 must also be changed to maintain P_1' and decrease the variant function).

In order to determine the changes for q1 we will compute

$$wp(\text{"}d := d + d\text{"}, P_1')$$

When we do this we find that in order to maintain the equality

$$d = ((q1 + 1) / 2) \times D$$

the variable q1 needs to be increased by (q1 +1), and so the command for q1 that will maintain P'_1 becomes

$$q1 := q1 + (q1 + 1)$$

Including these steps we can make the next refinement. In fact while $r \geqslant d+d$ we can continue to subtract exponentially growing multiples of D.

For this purpose we may use a loop. This refinement can establish the postcondition R provided the loop terminates with the condition $r < D$ true. We get:

$S_2(X_2)$ Second refinement $x_2 = \{r, d, q1\}$

```
r := X; q := 0;
if r < D → skip
[] r ⩾ D →
   r, d, q1 := r − D, D, 1;
   do r ⩾ d + d → {P₁}
      r, d, q1 := r − (d + d), d + d, q1 + q1 + 1
   od;
   q := q + q1;
   if r < D → skip {R established}
   [] r ⩾ D → {Q₃} s₃(x₃) {R}
   fi
fi
```

This mechanism establishes $P'_1 \wedge r < d + d$. After the doubling loop has terminated the number of cumulated multiples of D held by q1 can be added to q. Incorporating this step we can restore a situation where P_1 applies again. In this situation, when Q_3 also applies, a loop over the mechanism $s_1(x_1) \circ s_2(x_2)$, can be used to decrease r while maintaining P_1 and hence ultimately establish $r < D$. Making this refinement we get

$S_3(X_3)$ Third refinement $x_3 = \{r, d, q, q1\}$

```
r := X; q := 0;
do r ⩾ D →
   r, d, q1 := r − D, D, 1;
   do r ⩾ d + d →
      r, d, q1 := r − (d + d), d + d, q1 + q1 + 1
   od;
   q := q + q1;
od
{R}
```

At first glance it would seem we have perhaps introduced more free variables than may be needed. Originally when the problem was considered an integrating state-space extension was attempted directly on R. This yields the simpler constructive postcondition

$$R_D : X = d + r \wedge d = q \times D \wedge 0 \leqslant r < D$$

Unfortunately this postcondition does not lead to an invariant where it is easy to maintain both $X = d \times D + r$ and $d = q \times D$ and at the same time re-apply the loop that affects the doubling strategy on d. When d gets reset to D the above two equalities both get destroyed. The only way to overcome this problem is to use the two state-space extensions that we have employed in the development. Dijkstra in his discussion of the problem avoids the issue by not bothering to determine q in his speeded-up algorithm. The d + d in the guard could be replaced but we have left it to emphasize what is happening.

6.7.5   Fermat's algorithm [15]

The present problem and the next problem illustrate ways of changing variables in order to maintain somewhat more complex relationships. In each case the idea of changing a variable to its fullest extent is exploited in the design of loops. Fermat discovered a set of relations that can be used to find the largest factor u of an odd natural number N that is less than or equal to the square root of N. The basic specification may be written as:

$$Q : N \geqslant 0$$
$$R : N = u \times v \qquad \text{where } u \leqslant v$$

Following the suggestion made by Fermat we can do a state-space extension on R replacing u by $x - y$ and v by $x + y$ to yield the following form:

$$R' : N = x^2 - y^2 \wedge u = x - y \wedge v = x + y$$

Since it is difficult to make an initialization of free variables that will establish R' we can make a further state-space extension to obtain

$$R_D : r = x^2 - y^2 \wedge u = x - y \wedge v = x + y \wedge r = N$$

A suitable initialization of free variables that can establish R_D is then

```
x := 0; y := 0; r := 0;
if r = N → skip {R_D established if u and v assigned}
[] r ≠ N → {Q_1} s_1(x_1) {R_D}
fi
```

In making this initialization it has been decided not to set u and v as they can be conveniently set after $N = x^2 - y^2$ has been established. The initialization guarantees to establish the following base invariant:

$$P_0 : x = 0 \wedge y = 0 \wedge r = 0 \wedge x^2 - y^2 = r$$

To make the next refinement which may possibly establish R_D when Q_1 applies we need to consider what subset of the free variables $\{r, x, y\}$ may be changed. At least r must be changed if we are to establish $r = N$. Furthermore r cannot be increased without increasing x. The derivative invariant that follows from modifying P_0 to allow x and r to change is

$$P_1 : x \geq 0 \wedge y = 0 \wedge r \geq 0 \wedge x^2 - y^2 = r$$

When x is increased the relation $r = x^2 - y^2$ in P_1 will not be preserved unless r is re-computed for the new value of x. This can be seen from computing $wp("x := x + 1", P_1)$. Just increasing x by one may not be sufficient to establish R_D. We will therefore combine two refinements into one and use a loop to increase x. Making this refinement we get

$S_1(X_1)$ First refinement $x_1 = \{r, x\}$

```
x := 0; y := 0; r := 0;
if r = N → skip
[] r ≠ N →
    repeat {P₁}
        x := x + 1;
        r := x² - y²
    until r ≥ N;
    if r = N → skip {R_D established if u and v assigned}
    [] r > N → {Q₂} s₂(x₂) {R}
    fi
fi
```

The refinement $s_1(x_1)$ maintains P_1. To establish R_D when Q_2 applies there is no point in increasing x further if $r = N$ is to be established. The only other alternative is to increase y so that r may in turn be decreased. Weakening P_1 to permit y to increase

$$P_2 : x \geq 0 \wedge y \geq 0 \wedge r \geq 0 \wedge x^2 - y^2 = r$$

Again when we increase y the relation $x^2 - y^2 = r$ will not be maintained and hence P_2 will not be maintained unless a new value of r is computed for the new value of y. A loop may also be used to increase y. Making this refinement and changing the **if** $r > N$ ... **repeat** ... into a **do** ... **od** loop gives

S$_2$(X$_2$) Second refinement $x_2 = \{r, y\}$

```
x := 0; y := 0; r := 0;
if r = N → skip
[] r ≠ N →
    repeat
        x := x + 1; r := x² − y²
    until r ⩾ N;
    do r > N →
        y := y + 1; r := x² − y²
    od;
    if r = N → skip {R_D established if u and v assigned}
    [] r ≠ N → {Q₃} s₃(x₃) {R_D}
    fi
fi
```

The refinement $s_2(x_2)$ results in a mechanism that terminates with P_2 preserved but $r = N$ not guaranteed. To establish R_D when Q_3 applies x will need to be increased again. For the next refinement we may use a loop or recursive call to $s_1(x_1) \circ s_2(x_2)$.

Making this refinement and including the assignments to u and v that are necessary to establish R_D gives

S$_3$(X$_3$) Third refinement $x_3 = \{r, x, y\}$

```
x := 0; y := 0; r := 0;
do r ≠ N → {P₂}
    repeat
        x := x + 1; r := x² − y²
    until r ⩾ N;
    do r > N →
        y := y + 1; r := x²−y²
    od
od;
u := x − y; v := x + y
{R_D}
```

where

$$P_2 \Rightarrow wp(S_3(X_3), R_D)$$

and

$$P_2 \wedge r = N \Rightarrow R_D$$
$$P_2 \wedge r \neq N \Rightarrow P_2$$

This algorithm can be improved if the repeated recomputation of $r = x^2 - y^2$

can be avoided. To do this requires the insight that successive squares can be generated using the sum of the odd natural number sequence. Simple additions and subtractions can then be used to maintain the relation $r = x^2 - y^2$.

An implementation that follows from making these improvements is

Fermat's algorithm (Version 2)
```
xx := 1; yy := 1; r := 0;
do r ≠ N →
  repeat
    r := r + xx; xx := xx + 2
  until r ≥ N;
  do r > N →
    r := r − yy; yy := yy + 2
  od
od;
u := (xx − yy) div 2; v := (xx + yy) div 2
```

This implementation does less guard-testing than the other implementations. If textual simplicity were our prime objective then the following implementation could have been used. It is obtained by derivation when we discard the strategy of always trying to change variables in a single refinement to the maximum extent that will preserve the invariant. Details of this derivation are left as an exercise.

Fermat's algorithm (Version 3)
```
xx := 1; yy := 1; r := 0;
do r < N → r := r + xx; xx := xx + 2
[] r > N → r := r − yy; yy := yy + 2
od
```

What a comparison between the solutions for this problem reveals is the influence of program control structure on efficiency. The second version recognizes that x must be initially increased until it reaches a value equal to the integer square root of N. Only then is it necessary to give consideration to the introduction of y into the computation. This second solution also recognizes that after the square root of x has been computed subsequent unit increases in x are sufficient. They can be accompanied by multiple increases in y because x is greater than y. The other solutions do not recognize these considerations. Another thing that this example serves to underline is that textual simplicity and mechanistic simplicity do not always go hand in hand.

6.7.6   Two-squares sum [16]

The problem of finding *all* the ways in which a natural number N can be written as the sum of two squares has a lot of similarities with the last problem discussed. In the present problem we are concerned with the relation $x^2 + y^2 = N$ whereas in Fermat's problem we were concerned with $x^2 - y^2 = N$. A suitable specification is

$Q : N \geq 1$
$R : s = \{x, y \mid x^2 + y^2 = N y x \geq \vee \geq 0\}$

We may direct our attention to the following relation as it determines the set membership for a pair (x, y):

$R' : x^2 + y^2 = N \wedge x \geq \wedge \geq 0$

It is not easy to find an initialization of free variables that may establish R'. Doing a state-space extension in which we replace N by a new free variable r we get

$R_D : x^2 + y^2 = r \wedge x \geq y \geq 0 \wedge r = N$

A suitable initialization of free variables which can establish R_D and which can be checked by the equivalence condition is as given below. Technically we need a way of building the set s, but in this case we will simply write out the (x, y) pairs.

$S_0(X_0)$ Initialization $x_0 = \{x, y, r\}$

$x := 1; y := 0; r := 1;$
if $r = N \rightarrow$ writeln(x, y) $\{R_D$ established$\}$
$[] r \neq N \rightarrow \{Q_1\}$ $s_1(x_1)$ $\{R_D\}$
fi

This initialization guarantees to establish

$P_0 : x = 1 \wedge y = 0 \wedge x^2 + y^2 = r$

To establish R_D when Q_1 applies we may seek to increase x while holding y constant. A suitable command is:

$x := x + 1; r := x^2$ $\{ x^2 + y^2 = r\}$

As a single increase in x may not be sufficient to establish $r = N$ we may use a loop for this refinement where the following derivative invariant holds:

$P_1 : x \geq 1 \wedge y = 0 \wedge x^2 + y^2 = r \wedge x \geq y \geq 0$

$S_1(X_1)$ First refinement

```
x := 1; y := 0; r := 1;
if r = N → writeln(x,y)
[] r < N →
    repeat
        x := x + 1; r := x²
    until r ≥ N;
    if r = N then writeln(x, y) fi
fi;
if x ≤ y + 1 → skip {R_D established}
[] x > y + 1 → {Q_2} s_2(x_2) {R_D}
fi
```

When Q_2 applies the following relation holds:

$$Q_2 : P_1 \wedge r \geq N \wedge x > y + 1$$

Our task is then to systematically search for all (x, y) that satisfy $x^2 + y^2 = N \wedge x > y$. What is required is to decrease x and increase y in such a way that no pairs which satisfy $x^2 + y^2 = N$ are missed until $x \leq y + 1$ at which point *all* (x, y) will have been found. Anticipating that y will need to be changed we can weaken P_2 to

$$P_2 : x \geq 1 \wedge y \geq 0 \wedge x^2 + y^2 = r \wedge x \geq y \geq 0$$

A suitable variant function for the overall development of generating all pairs is

$$t : x - y$$

In making our next refinement since the current pair has been dealt with we can safely decrease x by one and recompute r so that P_2 is preserved. A check can then be made to see if R_D has been established. After rearrangement of $S_1(X_1)$ and inclusion of this new refinement we get

$S_2(X_2)$ Second refinement

```
x := 1; y := 0; r := 1;
do r < N → x := x + 1; r := x² od;
if r = N then writeln(x, y) fi;
if x ≤ y + 1 → skip
[] x > y + 1 →
    x := x − 1; r := x² + y²;
    do r < N → y := y + 1; r := x² + y² od;
    if r = N then writeln(x,y) fi;
    if x ≤ y + 1 → skip {R_D established}
    [] x > y + 1 → {Q_4} s_4(x_4) {R_D}
    fi
fi
```

We now have completed a mechanism that both decreases x and increases y. To establish R_D when Q_4 applies a loop or recursive call to $s_2(x_2)$ may be made. Making this refinement yields

$S_3(X_3)$ Third refinement

```
x := 1; y := 0; r := 1;
do r < N → x := x + 1; r := x² od;
if r = N then writeln(x, y) fi;
do x > y + 1 → {P₂}
   x := x − 1; r := x² + y²;
   do r < N → y := y + 1; r := x² + y² od;
   if r = N then writeln(x, y) fi
od
```

where

$$P_2 \wedge x \leqslant y + 1 \Rightarrow R$$

There are a number of ways of comparing solutions to this problem. The present solution could be improved in the same way as Fermat's algorithm by using the odd sequence sum to generate squares. Dijkstra uses a somewhat different way of ensuring that all pairs that satisfy $x^2 + y^2 = r$ are found. The structure of the present algorithm makes it abundantly clear that no pairs will be missed. It is claimed that the structure of the algorithm matches the structure of the problem, that is, with each decrease in x by 1 there is the potential for an increase in y of more than one.

6.7.7   Greatest common divisor [17]

The greatest common divisor (gcd) problem is one of the classic problems in computing science. Our interest in presenting it here is to illustrate how it can be solved by making a sequence of refinements each of which expands the set of initial states for which the postcondition is established. Given fixed finite positive integers X and Y, it is required to develop a program to compute their greatest common divisor x without using division. The specification is

```
Q : X > 0 ∧ Y > 0
R : x = gcd(X,Y)
```

As was suggested in Section 4.3 the postcondition is not in a constructive form and so a transformation to a constructive form is needed. Using the results directly from Section 5.6 we get:

$$R_D : 1 \leq x \leq \min(X,Y) \wedge x = y \wedge \gcd(x,y) = \gcd(X,Y) \wedge y = \gcd(x,y)$$

An initialization that can establish R_D and which, at the same time, is easily checked is

$S_0(X_0)$ Initialization $x_0 = \{x, y\}$

> $x := \min(X,Y); y := \max(X,Y); \{P_0\}$
> **if** $x = y \rightarrow$ skip $\{R_D$ established$\}$
> $[\!]\ x < y \rightarrow \{Q_1\}\ s_1(x_1)\ \{R_D\}$ $\{$note $\neg(x = y) \wedge x \leq y \Rightarrow x < y\}$
> **fi**

The base invariant that this mechanism guarantees to establish is:

$$P_0 : x = \min(X,Y) \wedge y = \max(X,Y) \wedge 1 \leq x \leq \min(X,Y) \wedge \gcd(x,y) = \gcd(X,Y)$$

and

$$P_0 \wedge x = y \Rightarrow R_D$$

and we identify Q_1 as:

$$Q_1 : P_0 \wedge x \neq y$$

The set of initial states for which $s_0(x_0)$ will establish R_D can be obtained by first evaluating

$$P_0(x,y)_x^y : x = \min(X,Y) \wedge x = \max(X,Y) \wedge 1 \leq x \leq \min(X,Y) \wedge x = \gcd(X,Y)$$

which yields $P_0(x)$. Now since

$$x = \min(X,Y) \wedge x = \max(X,Y) \Rightarrow X = Y$$

we find after evaluating $P_0(x)$ at $x = X$ that the set of initial states for which R_D is established by the initialization is

$$A_0 : X = Y \wedge 1 \leq \min(X,Y) \wedge X = \gcd(X,Y)$$

Given P_0 and Q_1 the next refinement may be made by changing a subset of $\{x, y\}$. The condition Q_1 and the principle of least action suggest making a refinement to establish R_D by decreasing just y. Weakening P_0 to reflect this gives P_1:

$$P_1 : x = \min(X,Y) \wedge 1 \leq y \leq \max(X,Y) \wedge 1 \leq x \leq \min(X,Y) \wedge \gcd(x,y)$$
$$= \gcd(X,Y)$$

P_1 should act as an invariant in developing a refinement that changes y. Simply decreasing y in steps of 1 cannot guarantee to maintain P_1. Other properties of the gcd are needed to make the refinement. It is obvious that the sum of X + Y and Y will have the same gcd as X and Y, that is

$$gcd(X + Y,Y) = gcd(X + Y,X) = gcd(X,Y)$$

and it also follows that

$$gcd(Y - X,X) = gcd(X,Y) \text{ for } Y > X$$
$$gcd(X - Y,Y) = gcd(X,Y) \text{ for } X > Y$$

These properties suggest that decreasing y in multiples of x will maintain P_1 and establish R_D provided y can be decreased to x. Again the equivalence condition x = y can be used to test whether R_D has been established. It is necessary to take into account that decrementing y by x may take y below x. Adding the new refinement $s_1(x_1)$ yields:

$S_1(X_1)$ First refinement $x_1 = \{y\}$

```
x := min(X,Y); y := max(X,Y);
if x = y → skip
[] x < y →
    repeat {P₁}
        y := y − x
    until y ≤ x;
    if x = y → skip {R_D established}
    [] x > y → {Q₂} s₂(x₂) {R_D}
    fi
fi
```

The condition established by this most recent refinement is just $P_1 \wedge y \leqslant x$.

$$P_1 \wedge x = y \Rightarrow R_D$$

and we identify Q_2 as

$$Q_2 : P_1 \wedge y < x$$

Evaluating $P_1(x,y)$ at y = x gives

$$P_1(x,y)_x^y : x = min(X,Y) \wedge 1 \leqslant x \leqslant max(X,Y) \wedge 1 \leqslant x \leqslant min(X,Y) \wedge x = gcd(X,Y)$$

Then, evaluating the resultant $P_1(x)$ at x = min(X,Y) gives the set of initial states for which it will establish R_D:

$$P_1(X)_{min(X,Y)}^x : 1 \leqslant min(X,Y) \wedge min(X,Y) = gcd(X,Y)$$

and so the set of initial states for which R_D can be established has expanded to

$$A_1 : 1 \leqslant \min(X,Y) \wedge ((X = Y \wedge X = \gcd(X,Y)) \vee (\min(X,Y) = \gcd(X,Y)))$$

Therefore if the fixed integers X and Y are equal, or one is a multiple of the other, the mechanism $S_1(X_1)$ will be sufficient to establish R_D.

To guide the next refinement $s_2(x_2)$, where Q_2 applies, P_1 needs to be weakened to accommodate the possibility that the gcd may be less than $\min(X,Y)$. We therefore get for P_2:

$$P_2 : 1 \leqslant x \leqslant \min(X,Y) \wedge 1 \leqslant y \leqslant \max(X,Y) \wedge \gcd(x,y) = \gcd(X,Y)$$

P_2 may act as an invariant for the next refinement which has the job of changing x by multiples of y. For this next refinement again we can apply the standard loop construction technique to get:

$S_2(X_2)$ Second refinement $x_2 = \{x\}$

```
x := min(X,Y); y := max(X,Y);
if x = y → skip
[] x < y →
  repeat {P₁}
    y := y − x
  until y ≤ x;
  if x = y → skip
  [] x > y →
    repeat {P₂}
      x := x − y
    until x ≤ y;
    if x = y → skip {R_D established}
    [] x < y → {Q₃} s₃(x₃) {R_D}
    fi
  fi
fi
```

The condition established by this most recent refinement is just

$$P_2 \wedge x \leqslant y$$

and

$$P_2 \wedge x = y \Rightarrow R_D$$

with Q_3 identified as

$$Q_3 : P_2 \wedge x < y$$

After evaluating $P_2(x,y)$ first at $y = x$ and then $P_2(x)$ at $x = \max(X,Y)$ **mod** $\min(X,Y)$ we find that the set of initial states for which R_D is established has expanded to

$$A_2 : 1 \leq \min(X,Y) \wedge ((X = Y \wedge X = \gcd(X,Y)) \vee (\min(X,Y) = \gcd(X,Y))$$
$$\vee (\max(X,Y) \textbf{ mod } \min(X,Y) = \gcd(X,Y)))$$

What has been added to the set of initial states, is the set corresponding to the gcd being a multiple of $\max(X,Y)$ **mod** $\min(X,Y)$. To make the next refinement $s_3(x_3)$, we find that y again needs to be changed. Examining our mechanism carefully we find that a *cycle* in the program structure has been detected and $s_1(x_1) \circ s_2(x_2)$ can be used to make the next refinement. This can be implemented by a loop or recursive call, for which P_2 may serve as the loop invariant. Using a loop and replacing the **if**...**repeat**...**until** by the equivalent **do** ... **od** construct we get

$S_3(X_3)$ Third refinement $x_3 = \{x, y\}$

```
x := min(X,Y); y := max(X,Y);
do x < y → {P₂}
  repeat
    y := y − x
  until y ≤ x;
  do x > y →
    x := x − y
  od
od
{R_D}
```

where we end up with

$$P_2 \wedge x = y \Rightarrow R_D$$
$$P_2 \wedge x < y \Rightarrow P_2$$

and

$$P_2 \Rightarrow wp(S_3(X_3), R_D)$$

The development is now complete. It is interesting to note that the strategy for development that we have used has led to an implementation that is more efficient than the other alternatives that are generally quoted for this problem, i.e.

```
(1)   x := Y; y := Y;
      do x ≠ y →
        do x > y → x := x − y od;
        do y > x → y := y − x od;
      od
```

(2)   x := X; y := Y;
    do x ≠ y →
      if x > y → x := x−y
      [] y > x → y := y−x
      fi
    od

    With (1), after the first iteration of the outer loop, applying the guard x > y directly after x ≠ y is unnecessary. This problem is avoided in our implementation which takes advantage of a repeat loop. With (2) x ≠ y can be applied more times than needed. The important thing that this example shows is how the need for a compound loop structure was arrived at by refinement, rather than by proposing the need for it in advance. The burden of having to propose a loop invariant for a compound loop structure prior to its development has therefore been removed.

    On the question of efficiency here it is worthwhile trying to put things a little better into perspective. In general gcd algorithms are a linear function of the magnitude of the numbers whose gcd is being sought. When dealing with very large numbers the sort of gains we have been speaking of do not help much. An open question is: could a large number of processors, operating in parallel, be used to speed up gcd computations to, say, a logarithmic dependency on the size of the numbers? Given the importance of the gcd algorithm in factoring this would be a significant breakthrough if it were possible.

SUMMARY

- In deriving programs it is important to exploit the relationship between problem-solving strategies and specification transformations.
- For any given specification for a problem there are three other types of specifications that are important: weaker, stronger and equivalent specifications for the problem.
- For a given problem weaker and stronger problems may be of interest.
- Simple loops may be designed by first making an initialization refinement that can establish the postcondition.
- The initialization refinement can be used to identify a suitable loop invariant from a postcondition.
- A weakest precondition calculation involving a loop invariant can be used to help construct the bodies of simple loops.
- To derive programs that involve nested loop structures weakest precondition calculations can be used to identify complex sub-goals that need to be established. The sub-goals in turn can be

treated as separate problems that can be solved using the same techniques at a different level.

■ **EXERCISE 6.1   Program derivation I**

1. Provide an implementation using guarded commands that establishes the postcondition R while maintaining the invariant P for the following problems:

   (a) $R \; : s = \Sigma(A_j : 1 \leq j < N + 1)$
   $P_D : s = \Sigma(A_j : i \leq j < N + 1) \land 1 \leq i \leq N + 1$

   (b) $R \; : c = \#(j : 1 \leq j < N + 1 : A_j > x)$
   $P_D : c = \#(j : i \leq j < N + 1 : A_j > x) \land 1 \leq i \leq N + 1$

2. Write down a loop invariant, variant function, and postcondition for the following problems:

   (a) i := 1;
   do i ≠ N→
     if a[i] ≤ a[i + 1] → i := i + 1
     [] a[i] > a[i + 1] → i, a[i], a[i + 1] := i + 1, a[i + 1], a[i]
     fi
   od

   (b) i := N; l := 1; x := a[N]
   do l ≠ i →
     if a[i − 1] > x → i, a[i] := i − 1, a[i − 1]
     [] a[i − 1] ≤ x → l := i
     fi
   od;
   a[i] := x

   (c) i := N + 1; l := 1
   do l ≠ i →
     if a[i − 1] ≠ X → i := i − 1
     [] a[i − 1] = X → l := i
     fi
   od

3. Derive a program that will satisfy the following specification:

   $Q \; : \;\; (\exists j : 0 < j \leq N : A_j > X)$
   $R_D : \;\; y > X \land (\forall j : 0 < j \leq i : A_j > X \Rightarrow y \leq A_j) \land y \in A[1..i] \land i = N$

■ **EXERCISE 6.2   Program derivation II**

Specify, design, and implement solutions to the following problems. Include preconditions, postconditions, invariants, variants, and implementations using guarded commands.

1. Find the minimum in an array A[1..N].

2. Find the minimum and the maximum in an array A[1..N].

3. Find the minimum and how many times it occurs in the array A[1..N].

4. Find the longest consecutive sequence containing a single element in the array A[1..N].

5. Find the longest consecutive sequence consisting of only two values in an array A[1..N].

6. Delete adjacent duplicates from an ordered array A[1..N].

7. Delete all occurrences of X from an array A[1..N] and contract the array accordingly.

8. Check whether the elements in two arrays A[1..N] and B[1..N] are pairwise equal (that is, A[1] = B[1], A[2] = B[2] etc.).

9. Given a fixed integer array A[1..N] whose elements satisfy the condition

    $$(\forall j : 1 \leqslant j < N : A_j \leqslant A_{j+1})$$

    specify, derive and implement using guarded commands

    (a) an $O(\log_2 N)$ mechanism that locates the *position* of the *first* element in this array that is equal to X. Indicate specifically which variable identifies the required position.

    (b) an $O(\log_2 N)$ mechanism that locates the *position* of the *last* element in this array that is equal to X. Indicate specifically which variable identifies the required position.

Bibliography

Alagic, S. and M.A. Arbib (1978), *The Design of Well-structured and Correct Programs*, Springer-Verlag, N.Y.

Dijkstra, E.W. (1976), *A Discipline of Programming*, Prentice-Hall, Englewood Cliffs, N.J.

Dromey, R.G. (1988), *Systematic program development, IEEE Trans. Software Eng.*, **14**(1), 12–29.

Gries, D. (1981), *The Science of Programming*, Springer-Verlag, N.Y.

Polya, G. (1945), *How to Solve It*, Princeton University Press, N.J.

Wirth, N. (1971), *Program development by stepwise refinement, Comm. ACM*, **14**, 221–7.

Part 3
THE DERIVATION OF PROGRAMS

To demonstrate the application of formal methods for program specification and program derivation a series of case studies has been made in what are often regarded as foundational areas in the study of programming. These studies cover a variety of issues that relate to searching, partitioning, sorting, and sequential processing.

In the consideration of the sorting problem we have demonstrated how different transformations on a sorting specification lead to the derivation of different sorting algorithms. Most of the well-known sorting algorithms have been derived.

A recurring theme in these case studies is the idea of matching program control structure with the structure of the data that must be processed. This is particularly relevant for text processing and sequential problems. From a development perspective some of the structurally more complex problems considered show up clearly the advantage of the strategy of always trying to make refinements which expand the set of initial states for which the postcondition is established. A number of the more complex problems also require some of the more interesting specification transformations outlined in Chapter 6 which identify auxiliary problems and sub-goals.

Chapter 7
Searching

Programmers must stop regarding errors in programs as an
inevitable feature of their daily lives.

C.A.R. Hoare

7.1 Introduction
7.2 Linear Search
7.3 Binary Search
7.4 Two-dimensional Search
7.5 Common Element Search
7.6 Rubin's Problem
7.7 Saddleback Search
   Summary
   Exercise
   Bibliography

7.1 Introduction

The searching of data is probably the most frequently used computational
strategy. How searches are conducted depends very much on

- how the data is organized, and
- how much data must be searched.

Both of these factors can significantly influence search strategies. When the
data has been ordered in some way, it is very often possible to take
advantage of that order and thereby significantly improve the efficiency of
the search. This is usually done by identifying large segments of the data that
will not need to be searched. On the other hand, when there is little or no

399

organization in the data, the only option is to make a tedious element-by-element search. For large amounts of data such searches can be very costly. In this chapter we will examine a variety of ordered and unordered searches. We will show how the specification of search problems can play an important role in their derivation.

7.2   Linear Search

The linear search problem is one of the fundamental problems in computing science. It recurs time and time again in program design in a variety of guises. It is therefore desirable that we fully understand how best to solve the linear search problem. One way of viewing it is as an array searching problem, where it is required that a fixed integer array $A[1..N]$ be searched for a fixed element X which may or may not be present. A program is required to satisfy the following specification:

$$Q : N \geq 0$$
$$R : (\forall j : 0 < j \leq i : X \neq A_j) \wedge (i = N \text{ cor } X = A_{i+1})$$

An obvious initialization that could establish the postcondition would be to set i to zero. This suggests the invariant

$$P : (\forall j : 0 < j \leq i : X \neq A_j)$$

In making this choice we have had to discard all of the second conjunct because it is difficult to establish it in concert with the first conjunct. This is a pity because as a general design rule it is best to try to retain as much as possible of the form of the postcondition in the invariant that is derived from it. One way to make progress in this regard is to use the variable replacement rule to replace the variable i in $i = N$ by n and add the equivalence condition $i = n$. We then get the following constructive form

$$R_D : (\forall j : 0 < j \leq i : X \neq A_j) \wedge (n = N \text{ cor } X = A_{i+1}) \wedge i = n$$

An initialization that can establish R_D which can also be easily checked by the equivalence condition is

$S_0(X_0)$ Initialization

```
i := 0; n := N; {P_0}
if i = n → skip {R_D established}
[] i ≠ n → {Q_1} s_1(x_1) { R_D }
fi
```

The initialization guarantees to establish the base invariant

$$P_0 : i = 0 \land n = N \land (\forall j : 0 < j \leqslant i : X \neq A_j) \land (n = N \textbf{ cor } X = A_{i+1})$$

and

$$P_0 \land i = n \Rightarrow R_D$$

$$P_0 \land i \neq n \equiv Q_1$$

The strategy of introducing n to obtain R_D allows us to extract the strongest possible invariant from the postcondition.

To make the next refinement $s_1(x_1)$ that can establish R_D when Q_1 applies either i will need to be increased or n decreased or both changed in order to establish the equivalence condition i = n. An appropriate variant function that follows from the equivalence condition is

$$t : n - i$$

Weakening P_0 to accommodate these possible changes we get

$$P_1 : 0 \leqslant i \leqslant n \leqslant N \land (\forall j : 0 < j \leqslant i : X \neq A_j) \land (n = N \textbf{ cor } X = A_{i+1})$$

The simplest way to increase i is with the command i := i + 1. Computing wp("i := i + 1", P_1) we find that it is implied by P_1 and i ≠ n, provided $X \neq A_{i+1}$. We can therefore write

$$\textbf{if } X \neq A_{i+1} \rightarrow i := i + 1$$

Unfortunately we cannot guarantee that the condition $X \neq A_{i+1}$ will always hold and so there is a risk of this command aborting. To avoid this we need to add the guard $X = A_{i+1}$ and investigate how the variant function can be decreased under these conditions while still maintaining the invariant P_1. There is obviously no prospect of increasing i as this would violate P_1. Our only alternative is therefore to investigate changing n. To decrease the variant function n will need to be decreased. The assignment n := i can be used to decrease n and establish i = n. This assignment makes the guard false and thereby forces the loop to terminate. Computing wp("n := i", P_1) we find that it will maintain P_1 provided $X = A_{i+1}$ holds and so we can write

$$\textbf{if } X = A_{i+1} \rightarrow n := i$$

Since neither $X \neq A_{i+1}$ nor $X = A_{i+1}$ can be guaranteed but the condition $X \neq A_{i+1} \lor X = A_{i+1}$ will always hold, the assignments to n and i can be combined into a single refinement. The equivalence condition is sufficient to confirm whether either command will establish R_D. We therefore get

$S_1(X_1)$ First refinement

```
i := 0; n := N;
if i = n → skip
[] i ≠ n → {P₁}
   if X ≠ A_{i+1} → i := i + 1
   [] X = A_{i+1} → n := i
   fi;
   if i = n → skip {R_D established}
   [] i ≠ n → {Q₂} s₂(x₂) {R_D}
   fi
fi
```

The invariant P_1 alone holds after changing either i or n so for the next refinement $s_2(x_2)$ either a loop or recursive call may be made when Q_2 applies. Using a loop to make this refinement we get:

$S_2(X_2)$ Second refinement

```
i := 0 ; n := N;
do i ≠ n → {P₁}
   if X ≠ A_{i+1} → i := i + 1
   [] X = A_{i+1} → n := i
   fi
od
```

where

$$P_1 \Rightarrow wp(S_2(X_2), R_D)$$

and

$$P_1 \wedge i = n \Rightarrow R_D$$
$$P_1 \wedge i \neq q\, n \Rightarrow P_1$$

A simple additional test whether i = N can be added to this implementation to decide if X is present. What is interesting about this solution to the linear search problem is the way termination is forced when an array element equal to X is encountered. More will be said about **forced termination** in Chapter 12.

7.3   Binary Search

The binary search problem will now be considered because it illustrates several interesting aspects of loop development including the handling of alternative cases. For ordered data it is a lot more efficient than a linear search. We will first consider a simplified version of the problem and subsequently a more general version. Given a fixed integer array in non-descending order $A[1..N]$ and a fixed integer X it is required to find where X belongs in the array assuming its magnitude is within the range of the elements in the array. The specification is

$$Q : N > 1 \wedge A_1 \leqslant X < A_N$$

$$R : 1 \leqslant i < N \wedge A_i \leqslant X < A_{i+1}$$

It is not easy to make an initialization of i that can establish R. We may therefore make a state-space extension on R by replacing $i + 1$ by j to yield a constructive form

$$R_D : 1 \leqslant i < N \wedge A_i \leqslant X < A_j \wedge j = i + 1$$

where $j = i + 1$ is the equivalence condition that links the two state spaces. Given Q an initialization that can establish R_D which can be easily checked by the equivalence condition is

$S_0(X_0)$ Initialization

```
i := 1; j := N;
if j = i + 1 → skip {R_D established}
[] j ≠ i + 1 → {Q_1} s_1(x_1) { R_D }
fi
```

This initialization guarantees to establish the base invariant

$$P_0 : i = 1 \wedge j = N \wedge 1 \leqslant i < N \wedge A_i \leqslant X < A_j$$

and

$$P_0 \wedge j = i + 1 \Rightarrow R_D$$
$$P_0 \wedge j \neq i + 1 \equiv Q_1$$

To make the next refinement that can establish R_D when Q_1 applies, either i will need to be increased, or j decreased, or both changed, in order to establish the equivalence condition. An appropriate variant function constructed from the equivalence condition is

$$t : j - i - 1$$

On average, we can guarantee to eliminate the most elements in our search by considering the middle element m in the range defined by i and j, that is

$$m := (i + j) \textbf{ div } 2$$

Committing ourselves to changing i we must weaken P_0 to give

$$P_1 : i \geqslant 1 \wedge j = N \wedge 1 \leqslant i < N \wedge A_i \leqslant X < A_i\dagger$$

We can then compute the weakest precondition for assigning i to m to maintain P_1:

$$wp("i := m", P_1) = 1 \leqslant m < N \wedge A_m \leqslant X \wedge X < A_i$$

Now the condition $A_m \leqslant X$ is not implied by P_1 and so a refinement that sets i := m will need to first ensure that $A_m \leqslant X$ holds. We therefore get

$$m := (i + j) \textbf{ div } 2;$$
$$\textbf{if } A_m \leqslant X \rightarrow i := m$$

As there is nothing about the problem that suggests changing i should have any preference over changing j we can weaken P_1 accordingly

$$P_1' : i \geqslant 1 \wedge j \leqslant N \wedge 1 \leqslant i < N \wedge A_i \leqslant X < A_i$$

We are also free to compute

$$wp("j := m", P_1') = 1 \leqslant i < N \wedge A_i \leqslant X \wedge X < A_m$$

In this case the condition $X < A_m$ is not implied by P_1 and so it will need to be included in the refinement, i.e.

$$m := (i + j) \textbf{ div } 2;$$
$$\textbf{if } X < A_m \rightarrow j := m$$

There is nothing to guarantee that either $A_m \leqslant X$ alone or $A_m > X$ alone will hold but $A_m \leqslant X \vee A_m > X$ will hold and so it is appropriate to combine the two steps that change i and j into a single construct. The equivalence condition is again sufficient to check whether an assignment to either i or j will establish R_D.

$S_1(X_1)$ First refinement

```
i := 1 ; j := N;
if j = i + 1 → skip
[] j ≠ i + 1 → {P₁'}
    m := (i + j) div 2;
    if Aₘ ≤ x → i := m
    [] Aₘ > x → j := m
    fi;
    if j = i + 1 → skip {R_D established}
    [] j ≠ i + 1 → {Q₂} s₂(x₂) { R_D }
    fi
fi
```

---

† The first conjunct $i \geqslant 1$ is now redundant but we have left it in to emphasize the strategy.

The invariant P'_1 will still hold after changing i or j and so for the next refinement $s_2(x_2)$ either a loop or recursive call may be employed when Q_2 applies.

Using a loop to make this refinement we get

$S_2(X_2)$ Second refinement

```
i := 1; j := N;
do j ≠ i + 1 → {P'₁}
    m := (i + j) div 2;
    if Aₘ ≤ X → i := m
    [] Aₘ > X → j := m
    fi
od
{ R_D }
```

where

$$P'_1 \Rightarrow wp(S_2(X_2), R_D)$$

and

$$P'_1 \wedge j = i + 1 \Rightarrow R_D$$
$$P'_1 \wedge j \neq i + 1 \Rightarrow P_1$$

$S_2(X_2)$ will establish R_D for all cases where Q applies and $N \geq 2$. A simple check whether $A_i = X$ can be used to decide whether X is present.

The solution to the binary search problem that we have presented is not a general solution in that it requires the precondition:

$$A_1 \leq X < A_N$$

It is desirable to have a solution that can handle arbitrary X values – that is, where X may be outside the bounds of the array.

Returning to our original postcondition we see that it has the form

$$R : 1 \leq i < N \wedge A_i \leq X < A_{i+1}$$

A suggestion made earlier was that for searching problems a complement extension to R is usually appropriate.

Including the complement over the closed range yields

$$R' : 1 \leq i < N \wedge A_i \leq X < A_{i+1} \wedge (\forall k : 1 \leq k < i : A_k \leq X)$$
$$\wedge (\forall k : i + 1 < k \leq N : X < A_k)$$

This can be simplified further by including $A_i \leqslant X$ and $X < A_{i+1}$ in the quantified expressions. This yields

$$R'' : 1 \leqslant i < N \wedge (\forall k : 1 \leqslant k \leqslant i : A_k \leqslant X) \wedge (\forall k : i + 1 \leqslant k \leqslant N : X < A_k)$$

The expression can now be generalized to account for the possibility that all the array values may be either less than X or greater than X. This corresponds to extending the range of i by one in both directions

$$R''' : 0 \leqslant i \leqslant N \wedge (\forall k : 0 < k \leqslant i : A_k \leqslant X) \wedge (\forall k : i + 1 \leqslant k < N + 1 : X < A_k)$$

From this specification we are led to the constructive postcondition

$$R_D : (\forall k : 0 < k \leqslant i : A_k \leqslant X) \wedge (\forall k : j \leqslant k < N + 1 : X < A_k) \wedge j = i + 1$$

The derivation of an implementation to satisfy this postcondition follows along the lines of the derivation of the simple binary search. From this postcondition we end up with the invariant P_1:

$$P_1 : (\forall k : 0 < k \leqslant i : A_k \leqslant X) \wedge (\forall k : j \leqslant k < N + 1 : X < A_k) \wedge 0 \leqslant i < j \leqslant N + 1$$

The implementation that follows from this invariant is:

```
i := 0; j := N + 1;
do j ≠ i + 1 → {P₁}
    m := (i + j) div 2;
    if Aₘ ≤ X → i := m
    ▯ Aₘ > X → j := m
    fi
od
```

This solution neatly handles the situation where X is outside the bounds of the array. In these cases one of the conjuncts involves universal quantification over an empty range which is always true.

Both implementations of the binary search algorithm considered do not attempt to stop as soon as the value sought is found. Instead they continue until the two integers defining the current relevant search range assume adjacent positions. As half the elements essentially are in the 'leaf-nodes' of the imaginary search tree that we may superimpose on the array this is an appropriate strategy on the grounds of efficiency.

If we start out with the specifications

$$R_D : (\forall k : 0 < k \leqslant i : A_k \leqslant X) \wedge (\forall k : j \leqslant k < N + 1 : X \leqslant A_k) \wedge (i = j \vee i = j - 1)$$
$$P_D : (\forall k : 0 < k \leqslant i : A_k \leqslant X) \wedge (\forall k : j \leqslant k < N + 1 : X \leqslant A_k) \wedge i \leqslant j$$

and we choose to use guards that distinguish elements less than X, equal to X, and greater than X, then a derivation along similar lines to the one above leads to the implementation:

```
i := 0; j := N + 1;
do i < j − 1 →
   m := (i + j) div 2;
   if Aₘ < X → i := m
   [] Aₘ = X → i := m, j := m
   [] Aₘ > X → j := m
   fi
od;
found := (i = j)
```

The interesting thing about this binary search is that it terminates as soon as an element equal to X is encountered. The cost of early termination is the need for a third guard in the body of the loop. The usual way of achieving early termination of a binary search is to use a Boolean flag. This is clumsier and less efficient than the present proposal.

7.4 Two-dimensional Search

The linear search problem considered earlier can be extended to two-dimensions. To solve this problem it is required to search a fixed two-dimensional integer array A[1..M, 1..N] for a fixed value X. The accompanying specification is

$$Q : M \geqslant 0 \wedge N \geqslant 0$$
$$R : (\forall p : 0 < p \leqslant i : (\forall q : 0 < q \leqslant N : X \neq A_{p,q})) \wedge (i = M \text{ cor } (0 \leqslant j < N \wedge X = A_{i+1,j+1})) \wedge i = m$$

The variable replacement rule permits us to replace i in "i = M" by m to yield the following constructive postcondition with equivalence condition "i = m":

$$R_D : (\forall p : 0 < p \leqslant i : (\forall q : 0 < q \leqslant N : X \neq A_{p,q})) \wedge (m = M \text{ cor } (0 \leqslant j < N \wedge X = A_{i+1, j+1})) \wedge i = m$$

This postcondition is very similar to that for the R_D used in the linear search except that $X \neq A_k$ has been replaced by a more complex two-dimensional term. An initialization that can establish the postcondition which is also easy to check by the equivalence condition is

$S_0(X_0)$ Initialization $x_0 = \{i,m\}$

> $i := 0; m := M;$
> **if** $i = m \rightarrow$ skip $\{ R_D$ established$\}$
> **[]** $i \neq m \rightarrow \{Q_1\}$ s_1 (x_1) $\{ R_D \}$
> **fi**

In making this refinement we have applied the principle of least action. We have tried to establish the postcondition by initializing the smallest number of free variables. At the first stage of development there has been no need to consider the other free variable j.

The initialization guarantees to establish the following base invariant:

$$P_0 : i = 0 \wedge m = M \wedge (\forall p : 0 < p \leqslant i : (\forall q : 0 < q \leqslant N : X \neq A_{p,q}))$$
$$\wedge\, (m = M\ \textbf{cor}\ (0 \leqslant j < N \wedge X = A_{i+1,\ j+1}))$$

and

$$P_0 \wedge i = m \Rightarrow R_D$$
$$P_0 \wedge i \neq m \equiv Q_1$$

To establish R_D when Q_1 applies i will need to be increased in order to establish $i = m$. A suitable variant function that follows from the equivalence condition is

$$t : m - i$$

A simple way to decrease the variant function is to use the command $i := i + 1$. Weakening P_0 to allow i to increase we get

$$P_1 : 0 \leqslant i \leqslant m \wedge m = M \wedge (\forall p : 0 < p \leqslant i : (\forall q : 0 < q \leqslant N : X \neq A_{p,q}))$$
$$\wedge\, (m = M\ \textbf{cor}\ (0 \leqslant j < N \wedge X = A_{i+1,\ j+1}))$$

To investigate how progress may be made we compute

$$\text{wp}(\ "i := i + 1"\ , P_1)$$

When we do this we find that the sub-goal

$$R_1 : (\forall q : 0 < q \leqslant N : X \neq A_{i+1,q})$$

is not implied by P_1. It will be necessary to develop a mechanism to establish the sub-goal R_1 before $i := i + 1$ can be executed under the invariance of P_1.

Because X may be present there is no guarantee that it will always be possible to establish R_1. The weaker sub-goal R_2 (see below) more accurately characterizes the situation:

$$R_2 : (\forall q : 0 < q \leq j : X \neq A_{i+1,q}) \wedge (j = N \textbf{ cor } X = A_{i+1,j+1})$$

We may introduce a new free variable n to obtain

$$R_2' : (\forall q: 0 < q \leq j : X \neq A_{i+1,q}) \wedge (n = N \textbf{ (cor } X = A_{i+1,j+1}) \wedge j = n$$

From this sub-goal postcondition we obtain the invariant

$$P_2' : (\forall q : 0 < q \leq j : X \neq A_{i+1,q}) \wedge (n = N \textbf{ cor } X = A_{i+1,j+1}) \wedge 0 \leq j \leq n \leq N$$

A suitable initialization of free variables that can establish R_2' and which can be checked by the guard $j = n$ is

$S_1(X_1)$ First refinement $x_1 = \{j,n\}$

```
i := 0; m := M;
if i = m → skip
[] i ≠ m →
    j := 0; n := N;
    if j = n → skip
    [] j ≠ n → {Q₂} s₂(x₂) {R₂'}
    fi
fi
```

where

$$P_2' \wedge j = n \Rightarrow R_2'$$
$$P_2' \wedge j \neq n \equiv Q_2$$

An appropriate variant function for the mechanism constructed from the equivalence condition is

$$t : n - j$$

To make the next refinement $s_2(x_2)$ that can establish R_D when Q_2 applies, either j will need to increase, or n decrease, or both be changed in order to establish the equivalence condition $j = n$. Computing $wp(\text{"}j := j + 1\text{"}, P_2')$ we find $X \neq A_{i+1,j+1}$ is not implied by P_2' and we are led to a similar refinement to that for the linear search:

$S_2(X_2)$ Second refinement

```
i := 0; m := M;
if i = m → skip
[] i ≠ m →
    j := 0; n := N;
    if j = n → skip
    [] j ≠ n → {P'_2}
        if X ≠ A_{i+1,j+1} → j := j + 1
        [] X = A_{i+1,j+1} → n := j
        fi; {P'_2 maintained, variant decreased}
        if j = n → skip
        [] j ≠ n → {Q_3} s_3(x_3) {R'_2}
        fi
    fi
fi
```

Changing j by one under the invariance of P_2 cannot guarantee to establish $j = n$ and so for our next refinement when Q_3 applies we can choose to use either a loop or a recursive call.

$S_3(X_3)$ Third refinement

```
i := 0; m := M;
if i = m → skip
[] i ≠ m →
    j := 0; n := N;
    do j ≠ n → {P'_2}
        if X ≠ A_{i+1,j+1} → j := j + 1
        [] X = A_{i+1,j+1} → n := j
        fi
    od; {R'_2}
    {check if R_D established and make next refinement}
fi
```

The condition established by $s_3(x_3)$ is R'_2. Examining this condition if $j = N$ it signifies a row has been processed without finding X and therefore i needs to be increased by one. Whereas if $j \neq N$ it signifies that X has been found, in which case all that remains to do is to establish the equivalence condition $i = m$ by the assignment $m := i$. Accounting for the two possible states in which $S_3(X_3)$ can terminate and checking whether or not the equivalence condition (i.e. $i = m$) has been established we end up with

$S_4(X_4)$ Fourth refinement

```
i := 0; m := M;
if i = m → skip
[] i ≠ m → {P₁}
    j := 0; n := N;
    do j ≠ n → {P₂'}
        if X ≠ A_{i+1,j+1} → j := j + 1
        [] X = A_{i+1,j+1} → n := j
        fi
    od; {R₂'}
    if j = N → i := i + 1
    [] j ≠ N → m := i
    fi;
    if i = m → skip { R_D established}
    [] i ≠ m → {Q₅} s₅(x₅) { R_D }
    fi
fi
```

where

$$P_1 \wedge i = m \Rightarrow R_D$$
$$P_1 \wedge i \neq m \Rightarrow P_1$$

For the next refinement when Q_5 applies a loop or recursive call to $s_1(x_1) \circ \ldots \circ s_4(x_4)$ with P_1 as the invariant is needed either to increase i or decrease m to establish R_D. Making this latest refinement with a loop we end up with

$S_5(X_5)$ Fifth refinement

```
i := 0; m := M;
do i ≠ m → {P₁}
    j := 0; n := N;
    do j ≠ n → {P₂'}
        if X ≠ A_{i+1,j+1} → j := j + 1
        [] X = A_{i+1,j+1} → n := j
        fi
    od; {R₂'}
    if j = N → i := i + 1
    [] j ≠ N → m := i
    fi
od;
{R_D}
found := ( i ≠ M)
```

7.5 Common Element Search

The search for a common element in two ordered arrays involves a linear search that exploits order. It demonstrates the importance of using the strongest possible specification for a problem to guide the development. Like other search problems this involves precisely stating where something 'is not' as well as well as where it 'is'. The detailed requirements of the problem are as follows. We are given two arrays A[1..M] and B[1..N] both in non-descending order and we are required to find the first occurrence of an element that is known to be present in both.

A formal specification for the problem is

$$Q : (\exists \, p \, , q : 0 < p \leqslant M, 0 < q \leqslant N : A_p = B_q) \wedge \text{ordered}(A) \wedge \text{ordered}(B)$$
$$R : 0 < p \leqslant M \wedge 0 < q \leqslant N \wedge A_p = B_q$$

Examining the postcondition carefully we see that it can be strengthened by including two other implicit relations, that is

$$R' : 0 < p \leqslant M \wedge 0 < q \leqslant N \wedge A_p = B_q \wedge A[1..p-1] < B_q \wedge B[1..q-1] < A_p$$

where

$$R' \Rightarrow R$$

These additional relations are not easily established directly so we introduce new free variables i and j to obtain:

$$R_D : 0 < p \leqslant M \wedge 0 < q \leqslant N \wedge A_i = B_j \wedge A[1..i-1] < B_j \wedge B[1..j-1] < A_i \wedge i = p \wedge j = q$$

An initialization of i to 1 and j to 1 will guarantee to establish all of the conjuncts except

$$A_i = B_j \wedge i = p \wedge j = q$$

It follows that a suitable invariant is

$$P_D : A[1..i-1] < B_j \wedge B[1..j-1] < A_i \wedge 1 \leqslant i \leqslant p \wedge 1 \leqslant j \leqslant q$$

Given the conditions for termination a suitable variant function that follows from R_D is:

$$t : p - i + q - j$$

and we need to establish:

$$A_i = B_j \wedge i = p \wedge j = q$$

in order to establish R_D and hence R.

To make progress with the development we need to look at ways of increasing i, and j while maintaining P_D. Investigating:

$$wp("i := i + 1", P_D) \equiv A[1..(i + 1) - 1] < B_j \wedge B[1..j - 1] < A_{i+1} \wedge 1 \le i + 1 \le p$$
$$\wedge 1 \le j \le q$$
$$\equiv A[1..i] < B_j \wedge B[1..j - 1] < A_{i+1} \wedge 1 \le i + 1 \le p \wedge 1 \le j \le q$$
$$\equiv A[1..i - 1] < B_j \wedge A_i < B_j \wedge B[1..j - 1] < A_{i+1} \wedge 1 \le i + 1 \le p \wedge 1 \le j \le q$$

This calculation tells us that

$$A_i < B_j$$

is not implied by P_D. Therefore, in order to safely increase i while maintaining P_D we need the guarded command

if $A_i < B_j \to i := i + 1$

We may also investigate

$$wp("j := j + 1", P_D)$$

from which we quickly discover that

$$B_j < A_i$$

is not implied by P_D. Therefore in order to safely increase j while maintaining P_D we need the guarded command:

if $B_j < A_i \to j := j + 1$

The conjunction of the guards

$$A_i < B_j \wedge B_j < A_i$$

leaves us only with the condition

$$A_i = B_j$$

unaccounted for. This latter condition is the termination condition.

The two guarded commands may therefore be combined to obtain the implementation:

```
i := 1; j := 1; {P_D}
do A_i < B_j → i := i + 1
[] B_j < A_i → j := j + 1
od
{A_i = B_j}
```

This implementation is linear with respect to M and N.

7.6 Rubin's Problem

The problem of determining whether or not all the elements in one row of an $M \times N$ matrix are all zero is another example of a search in two dimensions. This problem provoked a lot of debate among computing scientists in the letters section of the leading journal *Communications of the Association for Computing Machinery* during 1987. The problem was cited by Frank Rubin as an example of a problem that was most easily solved using 'goto' statements. Perhaps somewhat surprisingly many people responded to Rubin's original article, some supporting his position, and others criticizing his stand. The perceived difficulty with the problem is centred around the issue of how to bring about termination of a nested loop structure. Our intention here is to show that the problem causes no trouble when tackled formally.

To solve the problem it is required to search a fixed two-dimensional integer array $A[1..M, 1..N]$. The accompanying specification is

$Q : M > 0 \wedge N > 0 \wedge (\forall p : 0 < p \leq M : (\forall q : 0 < q \leq N : A[p,q] \in \mathbb{Z}))$
$R : (\forall k : 0 < k \leq i : \text{Nonzero}(A,N,k)) \wedge (i = M \textbf{ cor } \text{Allzero}(A,N,i+1))$

where the relations $\text{Nonzero}(A,N,p)$ and $\text{Allzero}(A,N,q)$ are defined as:

$\text{Nonzero}(A,N,p) : (\forall l : 0 < l \leq j : A[p,l] = 0) \wedge (j = N \textbf{ cor } A[p,j+1] \neq 0)$
$\text{Allzero}(A,N,q) : (\forall r : 0 < r \leq N : A[q,r] = 0)$

The variable replacement rule permits us to replace i in $i = M$ by m to yield the following constructive postcondition with equivalence condition $i = m$

$R_D : (\forall k : 0 < k \leq i : \text{Nonzero}(A,N,k)) \wedge (m = M \textbf{ cor } \text{Allzero}(A,N,i+1)) \wedge i = m$

An initialization that can establish the postcondition R_D, which is also easy to check using the equivalence condition is:

$S_0(X_0)$ Initialization $x_0 = \{i,m\}$

```
i := 0; m := M;
if i = m → skip {R_D established}
[] i ≠ m → {Q_1} s_1(x_1) {R_D}
fi
```

The initialization guarantees to establish the following base invariant:

$P_0 : i = 0 \wedge m = M \wedge (\forall k : 0 < k \leq i : \text{Nonzero}(A,N,k))$
$\wedge (m = M \textbf{ cor } \text{Allzero}(A,N,i+1))$

where

$$P_0 \wedge i = m \Rightarrow R_D$$
$$P_0 \wedge i \neq m \equiv Q_1$$

To establish R_D when Q_1 applies, i will need to be increased in order to establish $i = m$. A suitable variant function that follows from the equivalence condition is

$$t : m - i$$

A simple way to decrease the variant function is to use the command $i := i + 1$. Weakening P_0 to allow i to increase we get

$$P_1 : 0 \leqslant i \leqslant m \wedge m = M \wedge (\forall k : 0 < k \leqslant i : \text{Nonzero}(A,N,k))$$
$$\wedge (m = M \text{ cor Allzero}(A,N,i + 1))$$

To investigate how progress is made we may compute

$$\text{wp}(\text{"}i := i + 1\text{"}, P_1)$$

When we do this we find that the sub-goal R_1

$$R_1 : \text{Nonzero}(A,N,i + 1)$$

is not implied by P_1. It will therefore be necessary to develop a mechanism to establish the sub-goal R_1 before $i := i + 1$ can be executed under the invariance of P_1. Describing R_1 in detail we get:

$$R_1 : (\forall l : 0 < l \leqslant j : A[i + 1,l] = 0) \wedge (j = N \text{ cor } A[i + 1, j + 1] \neq 0)$$

Because of the difficulty of establishing R_1 by an initialization we may introduce a new free variable n to obtain

$$R_2 : (\forall l : 0 < l \leqslant j : A[i + 1,l] = 0) \wedge (n = N \text{ cor } A[i + 1, j + 1] \neq 0) \wedge j = n$$

From this sub-goal we obtain a new invariant:

$$P_2 : 0 \leqslant j \leqslant n \wedge (\forall l : 0 < l \leqslant j : A[i + 1,l] = 0) \wedge (n = N \text{ cor } A[i + 1, j + 1] \neq 0)$$

A suitable initialization of free variables that can establish R_2 and which can be checked by the guard $j = n$ is

$S_1(X_1)$ First refinement $x_1 = \{j,n\}$

```
    i := 0; m := M;
    if i = m → skip
    [] i ≠ m →
        j := 0; n := N;
        if j = n → skip
        [] j ≠ n → {Q₂} s₂(x₂) {R₂}
        fi
fi
```

where

$$P_2 \wedge j = n \Rightarrow R_2$$
$$P_2 \wedge j \neq n \equiv Q_2$$

An appropriate variant function for the mechanism constructed from the equivalence condition is

$$t : n - j$$

To make the next refinement $s_2(x_2)$ that can establish R_D when Q_2 applies, either j will need to increase, or n decrease, or both be changed in order to establish the equivalence condition $j = n$. Computing wp("j := j + 1", P_2) we find $A[i + 1, j +1] = 0$ is not implied by P_2 and so we get the following refinement:

$S_2(X_2)$ Second refinement

```
i := 0; m := M;
if i = m → skip
[] i ≠ m →
    j := 0; n := N;
    if j = n → skip
    [] j ≠ n → {P₂}
        if A_{i+1,j+1} = 0 → j := j + 1
        [] A_{i+1,j+1} ≠ 0 → n := j
        fi; {P₂ maintained, variant decreased}
        if j = n → skip
        [] j ≠ n → {Q₃} s₃(x₃) {R₂}
        fi
    fi
fi
```

Changing j by one under the invariance of P_2 cannot guarantee to establish $j = n$ and so for our next refinement when Q_3 applies we can choose to use either a loop or a recursive call.

$S_3(X_3)$ Third refinement

```
i := 0; m := M;
if i = m → skip
[] i ≠ m →
    j := 0; n := N;
    do j ≠ n → {P₂}
        if A_{i+1,j+1} = 0 → j := j + 1
        [] A_{i+1,j+1} ≠ 0 → n := j
        fi
    od; {R₂}
    {check if R_D established and make next refinement}
fi
```

The condition established by $s_3(x_3)$ is R_2. Examining this condition, if $j = N$ it signifies a zero row has been found and therefore all that remains is to establish $i = m$, whereas if $j \neq N$ it signifies that a non-zero has been found, in which case all that remains to do is to increase i by one. Accounting for the two possible states in which $s_3(x_3)$ can terminate and checking whether or not the equivalence condition (i.e. $i = m$) has been established we end up with

$S_4(X_4)$ Fourth refinement

```
i := 0; m := M;
if i = m → skip
[] i ≠ m → {P₁}
    j := 0; n := N;
    do j ≠ n → {P₂}
        if A_{i+1,j+1} = 0 → j := j + 1
        [] A_{i+1,j+1} ≠ 0 → n := j
        fi
    od; {R₂}
    if j = N → m := i
    [] j ≠ N → i := i + 1
    fi;
    if i = m → {R_D established}
    [] i ≠ m → {Q₅} s₅(x₅) { R_D }
    fi
fi
```

where

$$P_1 \wedge i = m \Rightarrow R_D$$
$$P_1 \wedge i \neq m \Rightarrow P_1$$

For the next refinement when Q_5 applies a loop or recursive call to $s_1(x_1) \circ \ldots \circ s_4(x_4)$ with P_1 as the invariant is needed to either increase i or decrease m in order to establish R_D.

Making this latest refinement with a loop we end up with

$S_5(X_5)$ Fifth refinement

```
i := 0; m := M;
do i ≠ m → {P₁}
    j := 0; n := N;
    do j ≠ n → {P₂}
        if A_{i+1,j+1} = 0 → j := j + 1
        [] A_{i+1,j+1} ≠ 0 → n := j
        fi
    od; {R₂}
    if j = N → m := i
    [] j ≠ N → i := i + 1
    fi;
od;
{R_D}
found := ( i ≠ M )
```

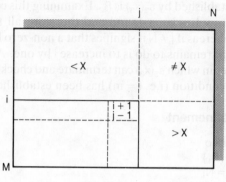

Figure 7.1

7.7 Saddleback Search

In multiplying sparse polynomials it is sometimes necessary to search a two-dimensional array that is ordered both by its row elements and its column elements. This problem, which has been discussed elsewhere by Gries, provides an interesting contrast to the problem of searching a two-dimensional array. Stated more specifically it is required to search a two-dimensional array $A[1..M, 1..N]$ for an element X that is known to be present. The rows and columns of the array are ordered by $\leq$. A possible formal specification for the problem is

$Q : X \in A[1..M, 1..N]$
$R : X = A[i + 1, j - 1] \wedge 0 \leq i < M \wedge 1 < j \leq N + 1$

The problem with this postcondition is that it is not strong enough. It can be strengthened by accurately describing where X is not to be found. A diagram can help us in formulating a stronger specification. Figure 7.1 suggests that X is not contained in the first i rows and the columns from j to N of the array.

Incorporating these conditions we get

$R' : X = A[i + 1, j - 1] \wedge X \notin A[1..i, 1..N] \wedge X \notin A[1..M, j..N] \wedge 0 \leq i < M$
$\wedge 1 \leq j \leq N + 1$

It is possible to strengthen our postcondition specification even further by identifying the regions of the array where values are *less* than X and *greater* than X.

When we do this we get the following specification:

$R_D : X = A[i + 1, j - 1] \wedge X \notin A[1..i, 1..N] \wedge X \notin A[1..M, j..N] \wedge A[1..i, 1..j - 1] < X$
$\wedge A[i + 1..M, j..N] > X \wedge 0 \leq i < M \wedge 1 \leq j \leq N + 1$

An appropriate initialization of the free variables i and j which guarantees to establish all of R_D except the first conjunct is

   $i, j := 0, N + 1$

This initialization suggests that an appropriate invariant would be

   $P_D : X \notin A[1..i, 1..N] \wedge X \notin A[1..M, j..N] \wedge A[1..i, 1..j-1] < X$
   $\wedge A[i+1..M, j..N] > X \wedge 0 \leqslant i < M \wedge 1 \leqslant j \leqslant N + 1$

An appropriate variant function is

   $t : M - i + j$

The variant function can be decreased either by increasing i or decreasing j. We are therefore interested in investigating conditions under which $i := i + 1$ can be executed while maintaining P_D. We are also interested in investigating conditions under which $j := j - 1$ can be executed while maintaining P_D.

   To do this we may compute

   $wp("i := i + 1", P_D)$

from which we discover that

   $A_{i+1, j-1} < X$

is not implied by P_D. This condition will need to be used as a guard when i is increased, that is

   if $A_{i+1,j-1} < X \rightarrow i := i + 1$

Similarly when we investigate:

   $wp("j := j - 1", P_D)$

we find that

   $A_{i+1,j-1} > X$

is not implied by P_D. Therefore to decrease j we require:

   if $A_{i+1,j-1} > X \rightarrow j := j - 1$

Combining the guards

   $A_{i+1,j-1} < X \wedge A_{i+1,j-1} > X$

we see that only the condition

$$A_{i+1, j-1} = X$$

is not accounted for. Combining the two guarded commands for changing i and j we may propose the following implementation for a saddleback search:

```
i := 0 ; j := N + 1 ; {P_D}
do A_{i+1,j-1} < X → i := i + 1 {P_D}
[] A_{i+1,j-1} > X → j := j - 1 {P_D}
od
{R_D}
```

The interesting thing about this algorithm, compared with the search of an unordered two-dimensional array, is that it is possible to take advantage of the order to achieve a linear $O(M + N)$ implementation.

SUMMARY

- Searching of data is probably the most frequently used computational strategy.

- The strategy for conducting searches depends on how the data is organized and how much data needs to be searched.

- The linear search strategy is one of the fundamental computational strategies in computing science. It requires that elements be examined sequentially and exhaustively until an element is found that satisfies some condition that allows a termination mechanism to be invoked. Forced termination may be used for this purpose.

- The binary search strategy, which can be applied to ordered data, involves the classic divide-and-conquer strategy.

- Most search problems including those that involve more than one dimension are usually variants of either a linear search or a divide-and-conquer search.

■ EXERCISE 7   Searching Derivations

Provide specifications, derivations, and implementations for each of the following problems

1.   Check if a fixed array A[1..N] is in non-ascending order.

2.   Check whether all the elements in the array A[1..N] are equal.

3.   Check whether m is greater than or equal to all the elements in the array A[1..N].

4.   For an array A[1..N] find the largest index k such that all the first k elements are zero.

5.   For an array A[1..N] find the smallest index k such that all the elements in the segment A[k + 1..N] are zero.

6.   Check whether X occurs exactly k times in the array A[1..N].

7.   Check whether there are no duplicates in an ordered array A[1..N].

8.   Find the maximum index i such that the first i elements of A[1..N] are sorted in non-descending order.

9.   Check whether all the elements in the array A[1..N] are greater than or equal to X and less than or equal to Y.

10.   Sum the first k elements in an array A[1..N]. Terminate the summation process if the addition of the (k + 1)th would cause the sum s to exceed the value M.

11.   Design and implement a version of the common element search that handles the situation where there may or may not be a common element in the two arrays.

12.   Design and implement a version of the common element search that finds all common elements in two ordered arrays.

13.   Design and implement a version of the common element search where it is known that there is a common element present in *three* ordered arrays.

Bibliography

Dijkstra, E.W. (1975), The development of programming a methodology, in *Programming Language Systems*, (Eds., M.C. Newey, R.B. Stanton, and G.L. Wolfendale), ANU Press, Canberra.

Dromey, R.G. (1985), Forced termination of loops, *Software: Practice and Experience*, **15**(1), 30–40.

Gries, D. (1981), *The Science of Programming*, Springer-Verlag, N.Y.

Rubin, F. (1987), 'GOTO consider harmful' considered harmful, *ACM*, **30**(3), 195–6.

Chapter 8
Partitioning

Adjusting to the requirement for perfection is the most difficult part of learning to program.

F.P. Brooks

8.1 Introduction
8.2 Simple Pivot Partitioning
8.3 Straight Pivot Partitioning
8.4 Pivot Partitioning
8.5 Interval Partitioning
8.6 Finding the Kth Largest Element
8.7 Dutch National Flag
      Summary
      Exercise
      Bibliography

8.1 Introduction

Partitioning is used in a number of important applications including sorting. It is a strategy for imposing a weak ordering on data. To satisfy a partitioning postcondition the constraints on the data are less stringent than the requirements for sorting a set of data. Most often it involves separating components of an array according to whether they satisfy some predetermined constraint (for example the first i elements in the array a[1..n] are all less than or equal to X). There are several well-known variations on the basic problem. Here we will examine several of these problems and algorithms to illustrate different strategies. Later in Chapter 9 we will consider the application of partitioning to sorting.

8.2   Simple Pivot Partitioning

In one form of the problem a pivot value X is given and it is required to find an i to partition the fixed array of elements A[1 . . N] using an array a[1 . . N], that is

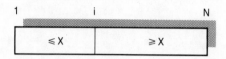

The specifications for the problem can be expressed as

$Q : N \geqslant 0$
$R : 0 \leqslant i \leqslant N \wedge (\forall p : 0 < p \leqslant i : a_p \leqslant X) \wedge (\forall q : i + 1 \leqslant q < N + 1 : a_q \geqslant X)$
$\quad \wedge \text{perm}(a, A)$

This postcondition is not easy to establish directly but if we make a state-space extension where i + 1 is replaced by a new free variable j we get the following constructive postcondition:

$R_D : 0 \leqslant i \leqslant N \wedge (\forall p : 0 < p \leqslant i : a_p \leqslant X) \wedge (\forall q : j \leqslant q < N + 1 : a_q \geqslant X)$
$\quad \wedge \text{perm}(a, A) \wedge j = i + 1$

An appropriate initialization that can establish the postcondition R_D is:

$S_0(X_0)$ Initialization

```
{Q}
i := 0; j := N + 1; a := A;
if j = i + 1 → skip {R_D established}
[] j ≠ i + 1 → {Q_1} s_1(x_1) {R_D}
fi
```

The initialization guarantees to establish the base invariant

$P_0 : i = 0 \wedge j = N + 1 \wedge a = A \wedge (\forall p : 0 < p \leqslant i : a_p \leqslant X)$
$\quad \wedge (\forall q : j \leqslant q < N + 1 : a_q \geqslant X)$

To establish R_D when Q_1 applies we need to consider what subset of the free variables {i, j, a} need to be changed in order to establish j = i + 1.

The associated variant function derived from the equivalence condition is

$t : j - i - 1$

To decrease the variant function either j can be decreased or i increased or both changed. Weakening P_0 to permit i to be increased we get

$$P_1' : 0 \leq i \leq N \wedge j = N + 1 \wedge a = A \wedge (\forall p : 0 < p \leq i : a_p \leq X)$$
$$\wedge (\forall q : j \leq q < N + 1 : a_q \geq X)$$

To guide our next refinement we may investigate wp("i := i + 1", P_1'). This tells us that $a_{i+1} \leq X$ is not implied by P_1'. One possible command for decreasing the variant function is therefore

if $a_{i+1} \leq X \rightarrow i := i + 1$

There is no guarantee that $a_{i+1} \leq X$ will hold so we must accommodate the situation where $a_{i+1} > X$ applies. Under these conditions i cannot be increased directly without violating P_1'. However, the condition $a_{i+1} > X$ tells us that a_{i+1} belongs with the right partition a[j .. N]. A swap can be used to achieve this transfer, extend the j-partition, and decrease the variant function. Combining these two steps, and adjusting P_1' to allow j to decrease we get

$$P_1'' : 0 \leq i < j \leq N + 1 \wedge (\forall p : 0 < p \leq i : a_p \leq X) \wedge (\forall q : j \leq q < N + 1 : a_q \geq X)$$

and the corresponding refinement is:

$S_1(X_1)$ First refinement $x_1 = \{i, j, A\}$

```
i := 0; j := N + 1; a := A;
if j = i + 1 → skip
[] j ≠ i + 1 →
    if a_{i+1} ≤ X → i := i + 1
    [] a_{i+1} > X → swap(a_{i+1}, a_{j-1}); j := j - 1
    fi; {P_1''}
    if j = i + 1 → skip {R_D established}
    [] j ≠ i + 1 → {Q_2} s_2(x_2) {R_D}
    fi
fi
```

where

$$P_1'' \wedge j = i + 1 \Rightarrow R_D$$
$$P_1'' \wedge j \neq i + 1 \equiv Q_2$$

To establish R_D when Q_2 applies a loop or recursive call to $s_1(x_1)$ will be sufficient for the next refinement as it will decrease the variant function and maintain P_1''.

Making this refinement with a loop we get

S₂(X₂) Second refinement $x_2 = \{i, j, A\}$

Pivot partitioning (Version 1)

```
i := 0; j := N + 1; a := A;
do j ≠ i + 1 → {P″₁}
   if a_{i+1} ≤ X → i := i + 1
   [] a_{i+1} > X → swap(a_{i+1}, a_{j−1}); j := j − 1
   fi
od
{R_D}
```

where

$$P_1'' \Rightarrow wp(S_2(X_2), R_D)$$

and

$$P_1'' \wedge j = i + 1 \Rightarrow R_D$$
$$P_1'' \wedge j \neq i + 1 \Rightarrow P_1''$$

This implementation has several weaknesses, including the fact that it may move elements at $a_{j−1}$ that belong in the j-partition. In the derivation below we will see how this problem is overcome.

8.3 Straight Pivot Partitioning

In considering an alternative to our last derivation we may pick up the discussion where, having investigated wp("i := i + 1", P_1'') we found that it was not possible to guarantee the condition $a_{i+1} \leq X$. Our original choice of changing i instead of j was an arbitrary one. We may therefore weaken P_1' to give

$$P_1'' : 0 \leq i < j \leq N + 1 \wedge a = A \wedge (\forall p : 0 < p \leq i : a_p \leq X)$$
$$\wedge (\forall q : j \leq q < N + 1 : a_q \geq X)$$

and then investigate wp("j := j − 1", P_1''). This tells us that $a_{j−1} \geq X$ is not implied by P_1''. Both of these refinements can establish the postcondition under certain circumstances; however, they alone are not sufficient to guarantee that the variant function is decreased, and so a further construct at least is needed.

What we have so far for this refinement is:

```
if a_{i+1} ≤ X → i := i + 1
[] a_{j−1} ≥ X → j := j − 1
```

In the situation where both guards are false the condition

$$a_{i+1} > X \wedge a_{j-1} < X$$

applies and neither i can be increased, nor j decreased, without violating P''_1. Our only option then is to drop the constraint $a = A$ from P''_1 to yield

$$P'''_1 : 0 \leq i < j \leq N + 1 \wedge (\forall p : 0 < p \leq i : a_p \leq X) \wedge (\forall q : j \leq q < N + 1 : a_q \geq X)$$

A swap of a_{i+1} and a_{j-1} can then be performed which will establish $a_{i+1} < X$, and $a_{j-1} > X$, which allows both i to be increased and j decreased. Including this construct in our refinement we end up with

$S_1(X_1)$ First refinement $x_1 = \{i, j, A\}$

```
i := 0; j := N + 1; a := A;
if j = i + 1 → skip
[] j ≠ i + 1 →
    if a_{i+1} ≤ X → i := i + 1
    [] a_{j-1} ≥ X → j := j - 1
    [] (a_{i+1} > X ∧ a_{j-1} < X) → swap(a_{i+1}, a_{j-1}); i := i + 1; j := j - 1
    fi; {P'''_1}
    if j = i + 1 → skip {R_D established}
    [] j ≠ i + 1 → {Q_2} s_2(x_2) {R_D}
    fi
fi
```

where

$$P'''_1 \wedge j = i + 1 \Rightarrow R_D$$
$$P'''_1 \wedge j \neq i + 1 \equiv Q_2$$

To establish R_D when Q_2 applies we find that a loop or recursive call to $s_1(x_1)$ will be sufficient for the next refinement as it will decrease the variant function and maintain P'''_1.

Making this refinement with a loop we get

$S_2(X_2)$ Second refinement $x_2 = \{i, j, A\}$

Pivot partitioning (Version 2)

```
i := 0; j := N + 1; a := A;
do j ≠ i + 1 → {P'''_1}
    if a_{i+1} ≤ X → i := i + 1
    [] a_{j-1} ≥ X → j := j - 1
    [] a_{i+1} > X ∧ a_{j-1} < X → swap(a_{i+1}, a_{j-1}); i := i + 1; j := j - 1
    fi
od
{R_D}
```

where

$$P_1''' \Rightarrow wp(S_2(X_2), R_D)$$

and

$$P_1'' \wedge j = i + 1 \Rightarrow R_D$$
$$P_1''' \wedge j \neq i + 1 \Rightarrow P_1$$

The implementation of the partitioning algorithm that we have ended up with, although clean and concise, is usually not favoured when efficiency is a concern. It uses a complex alternative construct and, on average, it is possible to achieve essentially the same postcondition with executions of the guard $j \neq i + 1$.

8.4   Pivot Partitioning

The central importance of partitioning in fast sorting algorithms (see Quicksort, Section 9.5) has led to the discovery of more efficient methods of partitioning than those proposed in the last section. In this section we will derive a more efficient and more often-quoted partitioning algorithm. We will start the development of this alternative implementation from the point where P_1' had been established, that is

$$P_1' : i \geq 0 \wedge j = N + 1 \wedge a = A \wedge (\forall p : 0 < p \leq i : a_p \leq X)$$
$$\wedge (\forall q : j \leq q < N + 1 : a_q \geq X)$$

As we are interested in establishing the postcondition for an arbitrary positioning of the partitioning index i we can choose to make a refinement that changes both i and j to the maximum degree. Loops can be used for this purpose. A possible refinement that can establish the postcondition is

S$_1$(X$_1$) First refinement $x_1 = \{i, j\}$

```
{ Q : X ∈ A[1..N] }
i := 0; j := N + 1; a := A;
if j = i + 1 → skip
[] j ≠ i + 1 →
   do a_{i+1} < X → i := i + 1 od;
   do a_{j−1} > X → j := j − 1 od;
   if j ≤ i + 1 → skip {R_D established}
   [] j > i + 1 → {Q_2} s_2(x_2) {R_D}
   fi
fi
```

The refinement $s_1(x_1)$ guarantees to establish the condition

$$R_1 : P'_1 \wedge a_{i+1} \geqslant X \wedge a_{j-1} \leqslant X$$

Clearly if the data is already partitioned in advance, then $s_1(x_1)$ will guarantee to establish the postcondition. In making the refinement $s_1(x_1)$, in our quest for efficiency, we have taken several liberties. We have neglected to use guards that will guarantee that the i and j array subscripts remain within range. The assumption that X is present in the array and the use of the stronger loop guards $a_{i+1} < X$ and $a_{j-1} > X$ instead of $a_{i+1} \leqslant X$ and $a_{j-1} \geqslant X$ ensure a sentinel effect that will always terminate both loops. To make the next refinement when Q_2 applies, we find that neither i nor j can be changed directly without violating P'_1. The only option is therefore to weaken P'_1 to permit a to change (i.e. we drop a = A). A swap of a_{i+1} and a_{j-1} is needed. This will allow i to be increased and j to be decreased. Making this refinement we get

$S_2(X_2)$ Second refinement $x_2 = \{i, j, a\}$

```
i := 0; j := N + 1; a := A;
if j = i + 1 → skip
[] j ≠ i + 1 →
   do a_{i+1} < X → i := i + 1 od;
   do a_{j-1} > X → j := j - 1 od;
   if j ≤ i + 1 → skip
   [] j > i + 1 →
      swap(a_{i+1}, a_{j-1}); i := i + 1; j := j - 1;
      if j ≤ i + 1 → skip {R established}
      [] j > i + 1 → {Q_3} s_3(x_3) {R}
      fi
   fi
fi
```

This refinement can lead to a situation where either i = j or i + 1 = j in certain circumstances. It is therefore necessary to replace the equivalence condition by i ⩾ j + 1 where we have upon termination j ≤ i ≤ j + 1. This situation arises because of the way in which we have used stronger loop guards compared with our original implementation (which guaranteed to terminate with i + 1 = j).

For the next refinement, when Q_3 applies, a loop or recursive call to $s_1(x_1) \circ s_2(x_2)$ can be applied.

If, in our quest for efficiency, we ignore that the swap can establish the postcondition, then we can arrive at the following more efficient recursive implementation which does less guard testing.

S₃(X₃) Third refinement

```
{ Q: N ≥ 1 ∧ X ∈ A[1..N] }
i := 0; j := N + 1; a := A;
partition:
    do a_{i+1} < X → i := i + 1 od;
    do a_{j−1} > X → j := j − 1 od;
    if j ≤ i + 1 → skip
    [] j > i + 1 →
        swap (a_{i+1}, a_{j−1}); i := i + 1; j := j − 1;
        partition
    fi
```

This implementation of pivot partition is equivalent to the implementation of a loop with an exit in the middle. A loop implementation (which can be obtained by refinement) that achieves the same level of efficiency is given below.

Pivot partitioning (Version 4)

```
i := 0; j := N + 1; a := A;
do a_{i+1} < X → i := i + 1 od;
do a_{j−1} > X → j := j − 1 od;
do j > i + 1 →
    swap(a_{i+1}, a_{j−1}); i := i + 1; j := j − 1;
    do a_{i+1} < X → i := i + 1 od;
    do a_{j−1} > X → j := j − 1 od
od
```

A more often-quoted but less efficient implementation of pivot partitioning is given below. It follows from the second refinement for Version 2. Version 5 is less efficient than Version 4 because it uses an extra guard for the swap.

Pivot partitioning (Version 5)

```
i := 0; j := N + 1; a := A;
do j > i + 1 →
    do a_{i+1} < X → i := i + 1 od;
    do a_{j−1} > X → j := j − 1 od;
    if j ≤ i + 1 → skip
    [] j > i + 1 → swap (a_{i+1}, a_{j−1}); i := i + 1; j := j − 1
    fi
od
```

The last three implementations for partitioning all establish the postcondition

$$R : 0 \leqslant i \leqslant N \wedge (\forall p : 0 < p \leqslant i : a_p \leqslant X) \wedge (\forall q : j \leqslant q < N + 1 : a_q \geqslant X)$$
$$\wedge \, perm\,(a, A) \wedge j - 1 \leqslant i \leqslant j$$

where there are two possibilities for the relation between i and j (i.e. $i = j$ or $i + 1 = j$) which are data dependent. The quest for efficiency has led to an implementation that establishes a weaker postcondition. For practical reasons we are sometimes willing to pay this price.

To summarize: the version 2 implementation is useful when it is essential to establish a stronger postcondition or when it cannot be guaranteed that X is either present or within the range of the array values. In other applications, such as partitioning in Quicksort (see Section 9.5), where efficiency is important, the version 4 implementation is to be preferred.

8.5   Interval Partitioning

In sorting applications performance is optimal when the partitioning algorithm divides the segment being partitioned into two smaller segments of equal size (that is, where half the elements are less than the partitioning element x and the other half are greater than x). With the algorithms discussed in the previous sections, because the partitioning element x is usually chosen in some arbitrary way we can end up with badly uneven partitioned segments. When this happens it reduces the optimality of the sort. A way to minimize this problem is to use a partitioning strategy that is able to update partitioning elements dynamically during the course of the partitioning process. We will begin our derivation of such an algorithm with the R_D established earlier:

$$R_D : 0 \leqslant i \leqslant N \wedge (\forall p : 0 < p \leqslant i : a_p \leqslant x) \wedge (\forall q : j \leqslant q < N + 1 : a_q \geqslant x)$$
$$\wedge \, j = i + 1 \dagger$$

An initialization that can establish R_D is

$S_0(X_0)$ Initialization
```
i := 0; j := N + 1; a := A;
if i = j − 1 → skip {R_D established}
[] i ≠ j − 1 → {Q_1} s_1(x_1) {R_D}
fi
```

† In this case we will assume x is no longer fixed.

The initialization guarantees to establish the base invariant

$$P_0 : i = 0 \land j = N + 1 \land a = A \land (\forall p : 0 < p \leq i : a_p \leq x)$$
$$\land (\forall q : j \leq q < N + 1 : a_q \geq x)$$

We can introduce more accessible freedom into our original R_D by replacing the rightmost x by a new free variable y which satisfies the relation $x \leq y$. This yields R_D' which implies R_D.

$$R_D' : 0 \leq i \leq N \land (\forall p : 0 < p \leq i : a_p \leq x)\,(\forall q : j \leq q < N + 1 : a_q \geq y)$$
$$\land x \leq y \land j = i + 1$$

If we can establish the truth of R_D' then R_D and hence R will be guaranteed. As the free variables x and y have yet to be initialized they can be considered for the next refinement. The variant function for the problem follows from the equivalence condition. It has the form

$$t : j - i - 1$$

In the initialization of x and y we are also interested in trying to make a refinement that decreases the variant function and thus has a chance of establishing R_D'. This will mean that P_0 will need to be weakened.

A possible initialization that follows is

$$i, j, x, y := i + 1, j - 1, a_{i+1}, a_{j-1}$$

However, this initialization does not guarantee $x \leq y$. If a_{i+1} were greater than a_{j-1} the two elements would need to be swapped to guarantee $x \leq y$, hence a must also be allowed to change. We therefore require

$$P_1 : 0 \leq i < j \leq N + 1 \land (\forall p : 0 < p \leq i : a_p \leq x) \land (\forall q : j \leq q < N + 1 : a_q \geq y)$$
$$\land x \leq y$$

An initialization of x, and y that can establish R_D' and make progress towards termination is then

$S_1(X_1)$ Initialization $x_1 = \{x, y, i, j, a\}$

```
    i := 0; j := N + 1; a := A;
    if i = j − 1 → skip
    [] i ≠ j − 1 →
        if a_{i+1} ≤ a_{j−1} → i, j, x, y := i + 1, j − 1, a_{i+1}, a_{j−1}
        [] a_{i+1} > a_{j−1} → swap(a_{i+1}, a_{j−1}); i, j, x, y := i + 1, j − 1, a_{i+1}, a_{j−1}
        fi;
        if i = j − 1 → skip {R_D' established}
        [] i ≠ j − 1 → {Q_2} s_2(x_2) {R_D'}
        fi
    fi
```

where

$$P_1 \wedge i = j - 1 \Rightarrow R'_D$$
$$P_1 \wedge i \neq j - 1 \equiv Q_2$$

For the next refinement, as we are still interested in establishing $i = j - 1$, we can investigate wp("i := i + 1", P_1) and wp("j := j − 1", P_1). We find that $a_{i+1} \leq x$ not implied by P_1 for the increase in i and $a_{j-1} \geq y$ is not implied by P_1 for the decrease in j. Both these refinements could establish R'_D under certain circumstances, but they are not sufficient to guarantee that the variant function is always decreased. Paralleling our development of the first pivot-partitioning algorithm, what we have so far for this refinement is:

    if $a_{i+1} \leq x \rightarrow i := i + 1$
    [] $a_{j-1} \geq y \rightarrow j := j - 1$
    ⋮

However, in the situation where both the guards are false, that is the condition

$$a_{i+1} > x \wedge a_{j-1} < y$$

applies, neither i can be increased nor j decreased without violating P_1. To overcome the problem a_{i+1} and a_{j-1} will need to be swapped. Consequently x and y may also need to be updated to preserve P_1.

Incorporating these steps the next refinement can be made:

$S_2(X_2)$ First refinement

    i := 0; j := N + 1; a := A;
    if i = j − 1 → skip
    [] i ≠ j−1
        if $a_{i+1} \leq a_{j-1} \rightarrow$ i, j, x, y := i + 1, j − 1, a_{i+1}, a_{j-1}
        [] $a_{i+1} > a_{j-1} \rightarrow$ swap (a_{i+1}, a_{j-1}); i, j, x, y := i + 1, j − 1, a_{i+1}, a_{j-1}
        fi;
        if i = j − 1 → skip
        [] i ≠ j − 1 →
            if $a_{i+1} \leq x \rightarrow$ i := i + 1
            [] $a_{j-1} \geq y \rightarrow$ j := j − 1
            [] $a_{i+1} > x \wedge a_{j-1} < y \rightarrow$ swap (a_{i+1}, a_{j-1});
                                i, j, x, y := i + 1, j − 1, max (x, a_{i+1}), min (y, a_{j-1})
            fi;
            if i = j − 1 → skip {R'_D established}
            [] i ≠ j − 1 → {Q_3} $s_3(x_3)$ {R'_D}
            fi
        fi
    fi

To establish R'_D when Q_3 applies a loop or recursive call to $s_2(x_2)$ can be applied. This will maintain P_1 and decrease the variant function. Making this next refinement with a loop gives the following implementation.

$S_3(X_3)$ Second refinement

```
i := 0; j := N + 1; a := A;
if a_{i+1} ≤ a_{j-1} → i, j, x, y := i + 1, j - 1, a_{i+1}, a_{j-1}
[] a_{i+1} > a_{j-1} → swap( a_{i+1}, a_{j-1}); i, j, x, y := i + 1, j - 1, a_{i+1}, a_{j-1}
fi;
do i ≠ j - 1 → {P_1}
    if a_{i+1} ≤ x → i := i + 1
    [] a_{j-1} ≥ y → j := j - 1
    [] a_{i+1} > x ∧ a_{j-1} < y → swap( a_{i+1}, a_{j-1});
                            i, j, x, y := i + 1, j - 1, max(x, a_{i+1}), min(y, a_{j-1})
    fi
od
{R'_D}
```

where

$$P_1 \Rightarrow wp(S_3(X_3), R'_D)$$

and

$$P_1 \wedge i = j - 1 \Rightarrow R'_D \quad \text{(and } R'_D \Rightarrow R)$$
$$P_1 \wedge i \neq j - 1 \Rightarrow P_1$$

The close parallel between this implementation and the original pivot partitioning algorithm (version 2) should be noted. This implementation will on average partition the data such that the two partitions are more even in size than partitioning with an arbitrary element x from the array. There is a price for this better partitioning performance – additional testing when the partitioning elements x and y are updated. As with pivot partitioning it is possible to obtain a more efficient implementation. This development follows closely the path taken in finding a more efficient pivot-partitioning algorithm (version 4).

The final implementation obtained when this latter derivation is pursued is given below:

```
{N ⩾ 2}
i := 0; j := N + 1; a := A;
if a_{i+1} ⩽ a_{j-1} → i, j, x, y := i + 1, j − 1, a_{i+1}, a_{j-1}
[] a_{i+1} > a_{j-1} → swap( a_{i+1}, a_{j-1}); i, j, x, y := i + 1, j − 1, a_{i+1}, a_{j-1}
fi;
  do a_{i+1} < x → i := i + 1 od;
  do a_{j-1} > y → j := j − 1 od;
  do i < j − 1 →
    swap( a_{i+1}, a_{j-1}); i, j, x, y := i + 1, j − 1, max(x, a_{i+1}), min(y, a_{j-1});
    do a_{i+1} < x → i := i + 1 od;
    do a_{j-1} > y → j := j − 1 od
od
```

This implementation does less guard testing than the previous implementation. It also establishes a weaker postcondition than R'_D (i.e., $i = j$ or $i = j − 1$ rather than just $i = j − 1$).

8.6   Finding the Kth Largest Element

It is often necessary to find the Kth largest element in a fixed array $A[1..N]$. An important special case of this problem is that of finding the median (that is when $K = N/2$) in a given data set. A possible specification for this problem is

$$Q : (\forall p : 0 < p ⩽ N : (\forall q : p < q ⩽ N : p \neq q \Rightarrow A_p \neq A_q))$$
$$R : K − 1 = \#(j : 0 < j ⩽ N : A_j < A_s) \wedge 1 ⩽ s ⩽ N \wedge 1 ⩽ K ⩽ N$$

where A_s is the Kth largest element assuming all the elements in $A[1..N]$ are unique.

Rather than attempting to solve this problem directly a more fruitful approach in this case is to solve an auxiliary problem with a stronger postcondition. Finding the Kth largest element then becomes a variation on the idea of partitioning.

A new, stronger specification for the problem is

$$Q : 1 ⩽ K ⩽ N$$
$$R_A : (\forall p : 0 < p ⩽ K : a_p ⩽ a_K) \wedge (\forall q : K + 1 ⩽ q < N + 1 : a_K ⩾ a_q)$$
$$\wedge \; perm(a, A)$$

This postcondition is a partitioning specification a_K being the Kth largest element. What differentiates this problem from a straight partitioning problem is that here the partitioning position K is *fixed* and the partitioning element x is *unknown*, whereas with straight partitioning, the partitioning element is *known* and the partitioning position is *unknown*. This postcondition cannot be easily initialized and confirmed. We will therefore introduce new free variables I and u which replace the K and the K + 1 respectively.

The following constructive postcondition can then be written. We have dropped perm(a, A) because the operation swap, the mechanism which changes the array, does not alter its truth value.

$$R_D : (\forall p : 0 < p \leq l : a_p \leq a_K) \wedge (\forall q : u \leq q < N + 1 : a_K \leq a_q)$$
$$\wedge ((l = K \wedge u = K + 1) \vee (l = K - 1 \wedge u = K))$$

An initialization of free variables that can establish the postcondition and which also can be easily confirmed is

$S_0(X_0)$ Initialization $x_0 = \{l, u, a\}$

```
l := 0; u := N + 1; a := A;
if (l = K ∨ u = K) → skip {R_D established}
[]¬(l = K ∨ u = K) → {Q_1} s_1(x_1) {R_D}
fi
```

The initialization guarantees to establish the base invariant

$$P_0 : l = 0 \wedge u = N + 1 \wedge a = A \wedge (\forall p : 0 < p \leq l : a_p \leq a_K)$$
$$\wedge (\forall q : u \leq q < N + 1 : a_K \leq a_q)$$

In proceeding we will try to exploit some sort of partitioning strategy. To this end, we can make the specification R_D look even more like the one that is used for partitioning by replacing a_K by x to obtain the following specification which implies R_D:

$$R'_D : (\forall p : 0 < p \leq l : a_p \leq x) \wedge (\forall q : u \leq q < N + 1 : x \leq a_q)$$
$$\wedge ((l = K \wedge u = K + 1) \vee (l = K - 1 \wedge u = K)) \wedge x = a_K$$

To establish R'_D when Q_1 applies we need to consider what subset of free variables need to be changed in order to establish $l = K \vee u = K$. The associated variant function derived from the equivalence condition is

$$t : u - l$$

To decrease the variant function either u must be decreased or l increased or both may need to be changed. Given the form of P_0 one strategy that is possible is to partition the data set. To do this an x must be chosen. If we are very lucky, the x chosen will partition the data such that $(l = K \vee u = K) \wedge x = a_K$. If the x chosen is not the one we want it must be either too small or too large. In either case we will be able to discard one of the segments produced by the partitioning mechanism. This will correspond to increasing l or decreasing u. For the purposes of partitioning we can introduce new free variables i and j to replace l and u as the latter cannot be used directly for partitioning. We will also replace a_K by x.

$$P_1 : I \geqslant 0 \wedge u \leqslant N + 1 \wedge (\forall p : 0 < p \leqslant I : a_p \leqslant a_K)$$
$$\wedge (\forall q : u \leqslant q < N + 1 : a_K \leqslant a_q)$$
$$\wedge (\forall p : I < p \leqslant i : a_p \leqslant x)$$
$$\wedge (\forall q : j \leqslant q < u : x \leqslant a_q) \wedge x = a_K$$

We can now make a refinement $s_1(x_1)$ that partitions the data and hence establishes $P_1 \wedge i \geqslant j - 1$. Then, if $j < K$, the x used was too small and so I can be increased to i. Otherwise if $i > K$ the x is too large and so u can be decreased to j. And if $I = K \vee u = K$ is true the postcondition is established.

Making this partitioning refinement using a partitioning algorithm very like the one described earlier we get

$S_1(X_1)$ First refinement

```
I := 0; u := N + 1; a := A;
if (I = K ∨ u = K) → skip {R_D established}
[] ¬(I = K ∨ u = K) → {P_1}
  i := I; j := u; x := a_K;
  do i < j − 1 →
    if a_{i+1} < x → i := i + 1
    [] a_{j−1} > x → j := j − 1
    [] a_{i+1} ⩾ x ∧ a_{j−1} ⩽ x → swap(a_{i+1}, a_{j−1}); i := i + 1, j := j − 1
    fi
  od;
  if (i = K ∨ j = K) → skip {R_D established}
  [] ¬(i = K ∨ j = K) → {Q_2} s_2(x_2) {R_D}
  fi
fi
```

This mechanism will establish R_D if the x chosen is the Kth largest element. To establish R_D when Q_2 applies either a loop or recursive call to $s_1(x_1)$ can be applied. This yields, after some rearrangement, the following algorithm:

$S_2(X_2)$ Second refinement

```
I := 0; u := N + 1; a := A;
Kselect:
  i := I; j := u; x := a_K;
  do i < j−1 →
    if a_{i+1} < x → i := i + 1
    [] a_{j−1} > x → j := j − 1
    [] a_{i+1} ⩾ x ∧ a_{j−1} ⩽ x → swap(a_{i+1}, a_{j−1}); i := i + 1, j := j − 1
    if
  od;
  if (i = K ∨ j = K) → skip {R_D established}
  [] i > K → u := j; Kselect
  [] j < K → I := i; Kselect
  fi
```

There are considerable similarities between the algorithm we have just developed and the strategy employed in the binary search algorithm (see Section 7.3). In the binary search the next element for consideration is found by averaging the range that currently defines the limits which contain the value sought. With the present problem the next value for consideration is instead selected by partitioning, rather than m := (i + j) **div** 2. Subtle differences follow from the guarantee that the Kth largest element will always be present.

8.7   Dutch National Flag

The extension of partitioning from the more usual two partitions to three partitions provides an interesting variation on the basic problem. This problem has been presented by Dijkstra and others in a form that has come to be known as the Dutch national flag problem. In this form a fixed bag A[1..N] is given which contains elements that are designated RED, WHITE or BLUE. It is required to partition the elements using a swap mechanism and an array a[1..N] so that all the red elements appear before all the white elements, which in turn appear before all the blue elements. Schematically we require

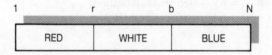

A suitable specification using an abbreviated notation for quantification over the three ranges is

Q : N ⩾ 1
R : a[1 . . r] = RED ∧ a[r + 1 . . b − 1] = WHITE ∧ a[b . . N] = BLUE
    ∧ perm(a, A)

where r denotes the upper limit for the RED partition and b denotes the lower limit for the BLUE partition. The WHITE partition is consequently defined by default. However, if we make a state-space extension in which b − 1 is replaced by w the following constructive postcondition with equivalence condition w = b − 1 is obtained:

R_D : a[1 . . r] = RED ∧ a[r + 1 . . w] = WHITE ∧ a[b . . N] = BLUE ∧ perm(a , A)
    ∧ w = b − 1

A suitable initialization that can establish R_D and which can be easily confirmed by the equivalence condition is

$S_0(X_0)$ Initialization

r := 0; w := 0; b := N + 1; a := A;
if w = b − 1 → skip {R_D established}
[] w ≠ b − 1 → {Q_1} $s_1(x_1)$ {R_D}
fi

The initialization guarantees to establish the base invariant below as we have universal quantification over three empty ranges:

P_0 : r = 0 ∧ w = 0 ∧ b = N + 1 ∧ a = A ∧ a[1 . . r] = RED ∧ a[r + 1 . . w]
    = WHITE ∧ a[b . . N] = BLUE

A suitable variant function that follows from the equivalence condition is

t : b − w − 1

To establish R_D when Q_1 applies either w must be increased or b decreased in order to arrive at w = b − 1. At this point we will weaken P_0 to allow w and b to change. We will also anticipate changes in r and a.

We then get

P_1 : 0 ≤ r ≤ w < b ≤ N+1 ∧ a[1 . . r] = RED ∧ a[r + 1 . . w] = WHITE
    ∧ a[b..N] = BLUE

To guide our next refinement we may investigate wp("w := w + 1", P_1). When we do this we find that a_{w+1} = WHITE is not implied by P_1. What we have so far is then

if a_{w+1} = WHITE → w := w + 1

.

.

Now it is only possible for a_{w+1} to be RED, WHITE or BLUE. What is of concern to us is how the variant function can be decreased when a_{w+1} is either RED or BLUE. Consider first the situation where a_{w+1} is BLUE. Clearly w cannot be advanced so we are left with the question, can b be decreased to reduce the variant function? The answer is yes, because the BLUE element at a_{w+1} can be swapped with a_{b-1}, thereby allowing b to be decreased.

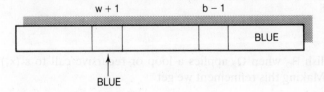

Our mechanism for the $s_1(x_1)$ refinement can be extended to

```
if a_{w+1} = WHITE → w := w + 1
[] a_{w+1} = BLUE → swap(a_{w+1}, a_{b-1}); b := b - 1
    .
    .
    .
```

These two steps alone are not sufficient to guarantee that the variant function will always be reduced. We must consider the situation where a_{w+1} = RED, and try to discover how the variant function might be decreased in these circumstances. We have

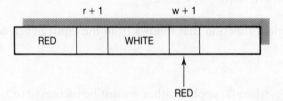

The RED at a_{w+1} can be swapped to the position a_{r+1}, thereby extending the RED region by one. To complete this swap the WHITE element at a_{r+1} (if there is one) can be moved to a_{w+1}. This has the effect of extending the rightmost position of the WHITE region by one. The index w can therefore be increased by one and so we have a refinement that once again can decrease the variant function. Now that all possibilities are accounted for we can complete this refinement.

It has a chance of establishing R_D and so we get:

$S_1(X_1)$ First refinement $x_1 = \{r, w, b, a\}$

```
r := 0; w := 0; b := N + 1; a := A;
if w = b - 1 → skip
[] w ≠ b - 1 →
    if a_{w+1} = WHITE → w := w + 1
    [] a_{w+1} = BLUE → swap(a_{w+1}, a_{b-1}); b := b - 1
    [] a_{w+1} = RED → swap(a_{w+1}, a_{r+1}); w := w + 1; r := r + 1
    fi;
    if w = b - 1 → skip {R_D established}
    [] w ≠ b - 1 → {Q_2} s_2(x_2) {R_D}
    fi
fi
```

To establish R_D when Q_2 applies a loop or recursive call to $s_1(x_1)$ can be applied. Making this refinement we get

$S_2(X_2)$ Second refinement

```
r := 0; w := 0; b := N + 1; a := A;
do w ≠ b − 1 → {P₁}
    if a_{w+1} = WHITE → w := w + 1
    [] a_{w+1} = BLUE → swap(a_{w + 1}, a_{b−1}); b := b − 1
    [] a_{w+1} = RED → swap(a_{w+1}, a_{r+1}); w := w + 1; r := r + 1
    fi
od
{R_D}
```

where

$$P_1 \wedge w \neq b - 1 \Rightarrow P_1$$
$$P_1 \wedge w = b - 1 \Rightarrow R_D$$

This algorithm has an interesting analogue for pivot partitioning which we saw earlier, i.e.

```
i := 0; j := N + 1;
do i ≠ j − 1 → {P₁}
    if a_{i+1} ≤ x → i := i + 1
    [] a_{i+1} ≥ x → swap(a_{i+1}, a_{j−1}); j := j − 1
    fi
od
```

This implementation of partitioning, like the implementation of the Dutch national flag, is simpler than other implementations for the same problem. Unfortunately it can engage in unnecessary swapping of data, because the value $a_{j−1}$ may be swapped when it is greater than or equal to x. More efficient implementations of the Dutch national flag may be pursued by using loops to change the individual colour boundaries.

SUMMARY

- Partitioning involves a weak ordering strategy that is significantly less costly than sorting – it has linear complexity.

- Partitioning forms the basis of the divide-and-conquer Quicksort algorithm, and of a well-known algorithm for finding the median.

- Partitioning is important in sorting because it allows data to be moved over large distances in the early stages of a sort.

- There are several different partitioning algorithms that follow from making different transformations on the basic postcondition specification.

- Interval partitioning is particularly interesting in that it partitions data without employing a fixed partitioning element.

- To find the Kth largest element in a data set an extension of the partitioning idea is employed.
- The Dutch national flag problem represents a more difficult partitioning problem in that it involves the maintenance of a floating partition segment.

■ *EXERCISE 8   Partitioning Problems*

Provide specifications, derivations, and implementations for each of the following problems.

1.   Given an array consisting only of 0's and 1's partition the array so that all the 0's come before all the 1's.

2.   Given a fixed sequence A of N elements, partition the elements using an array a[1..N] such that all the negative elements are in the range a[1..i] and all the positive elements are in the range a[i +1..N].

3.   Given a fixed sequence A of N elements, partition the sequence with respect to X using an array a[1..N] such that the following arrangement is achieved

4.   For an array A[1..N] find the largest index k such that the sum of the first k elements is less than or equal to the sum of the remaining elements in the array.

5.   For an array A[1..N] find the largest index k such that the number of positive elements in the first k positions is less than or equal to the number of positive elements in the remainder of the array. The array may contain positive and negative elements.

6.   Check whether the array A[1..N] has been partitioned about X such that

$$A[1..i] \leqslant X \wedge A[j..N] \geqslant X \wedge j = i + 1$$

7.   The implementation of the Dutch national flag algorithm in Section 8.7 does a number of unnecessary swaps. Try to provide an implementation of this algorithm that avoids these.

8.   Implement a version of Kselect (Section 8.6) which employs a partitioning mechanism that terminates as soon as either i reaches K first or j reaches K first. As soon as either of these situations is detected it is known that the current partitioning value is not the correct one.

Bibliography

Dijkstra, E.W. (1976), *A Discipline of Programming,* Prentice-Hall, N.J.

Dromey, R.G. (1986), An algorithm for the selection problem, *Software: Practice and Experience,* **16**(11), 981–6.

Hoare, C.A.R. (1962), Quicksort, *Computer Journal* **5,** 10–15.

Hoare, C.A.R. (1971), Proof of a program : FIND, *Comm. ACM,* **14,** 39–45.

Van Emden, M.(1970), Increasing the efficiency of Quicksort, *Comm ACM,* **13,** 563–7.

Wirth, N. (1976), *Algorithms + Data Structures = Programs*, Prentice-Hall, N.J.

Chapter 9
Sorting

> The intelligent use of equivalent forms is the touchstone of
> logical insight.
>
> *S.K. Langer*

9.1 Introduction
9.2 Transformations of a Sorting Specification
9.3 The Selection Algorithms
9.4 The Insertion Algorithms
9.5 The Partitioning Algorithms
Summary
Exercise
Bibliography

9.1 Introduction

We must learn to use specifications more effectively in program development. The usual scenario is to define a specification and then manipulate it to aid in the development of a program. Our objective in this chapter is to go beyond this scenario and explore the use of a specification as a vehicle for developing a number of alternative solutions to a problem. There are several things that can stand in the way of such an endeavour. Firstly, specifications are often not in a form that will directly permit the development of even a single solution, let alone a number of alternatives. It is therefore necessary to be able to recognize this situation when it occurs and do something about it.

This recognition problem has been discussed in detail in Chapter 5. To recapitulate, a specification is considered suitable for program derivation if

- it is easy to make an initialization of free variables that will establish the postcondition, and

- it is easy to check if the initialization has established the postcondition.

Our primary concern here is to develop a number of different solutions to a problem from a single base specification. There are two ways in which manipulations of a specification can influence the development of different algorithmic solutions to a problem. The differentiation is provided by the *transformations* that are made on a specification, and the *order* in which those transformations are made in the course of development of a program. An attempt will be made to show that variability with respect to these two factors can, in some instances at least, lead to a rich variety of strategies for satisfying a given base specification. This variability is possible because a transformation on a specification translates in the program domain into a set of constraints under which a particular subset of a program's variables may be changed. It is the changing of particular subsets of variables, under a set of constraints, which ultimately defines the corresponding structure in a program and the strategy or algorithm that will satisfy the specification.

If what is suggested is to have any credence different manipulations of a single sorting specification should lead to the derivation of a number of sorting algorithms. In the sections which follow we will show how this is indeed the case.

9.2 Transformations of a Sorting Specification

A simple formulation of the sorting problem involves the requirement of ordering a fixed bag A of integers using an array a[1..N]. The corresponding specification for this problem, phrased in terms of a precondition Q, and a postcondition R, may take the form

$$Q : N \geq 1$$
$$R : (\forall k)\,(1 \leq k < N \Rightarrow a_k \leq a_{k+1}) \wedge perm(a,A)$$

where perm(a,A) is a predicate indicating that the sorted result must be a permutation of the original fixed bag of integers A.

The postcondition R is not in a form where it is possible to make an initialization of free variables which can establish R and be shown to have done so. However, making a state-space extension on R, by introducing a new free variable i , we get

$$R_D : (\forall k)\,(1 \leq k < i \Rightarrow a_k \leq a_{k+1}) \wedge perm(a,A) \wedge i = N\dagger$$

†We will drop perm(a,A) to keep the specification simpler. It will be assumed in each case.

where

$$R_D \Rightarrow R$$

Because R_D implies R, R_D may be used as a basis for program development. The invariant that follows from R_D is

$$P_D : (\forall k)\,(1 \leqslant k < i \Rightarrow a_k \leqslant a_{k+1}) \wedge 1 \leqslant i \leqslant N$$

Computing

$$wp(\text{"i} := i + 1\text{"}, P_D)$$

we are quickly led to the derivation of an insertion sort algorithm. This derivation has been shown in detail in Chapter 5.

The question that this raises is how can we make any useful transformations on R or R_D that would lead to the derivation of a selectionsort, a bubblesort, a quicksort or any other kind of sort. To make progress we will re-examine the original specification R more carefully. We have

$$R : (\forall k)\,(1 \leqslant k < N \Rightarrow a_k \leqslant a_{k+1})$$

The following sequence of manipulations can be made on R and its descendants. Each transformation leads to a new specification which is at least as strong as its predecessor.

Transformation (I)   Introduction of a new free variable.

$$R^I : (\forall k)\,(1 \leqslant k < N \Rightarrow (q = k + 1 \Rightarrow a_k \leqslant a_q))$$

where

$$R^I \Rightarrow R$$

Transformation (II)   Introduction of a quantifier over q

$$R^{II} : (\forall k)\,(1 \leqslant k < N \Rightarrow (\forall q)\,(k + 1 \leqslant q \leqslant N \Rightarrow a_k \leqslant a_q))$$

where

$$R^{II} \Rightarrow R^I$$

Transformation (III)   State-space extension, introduction of a new free variable p

$$R^{III} : (\forall k)(1 \leqslant k < N \Rightarrow (p = k \Rightarrow (\forall q)(k + 1 \leqslant q \leqslant N \Rightarrow a_p \leqslant a_q)))$$

where

$$R^{III} \Rightarrow R^{II}$$

Transformation (IV)   Introduction of a quantifier over p

$$R^{IV}: (\forall k)(1 \leqslant k < N \Rightarrow (\forall p)(1 \leqslant p \leqslant k \Rightarrow (\forall q)(k + 1 \leqslant q \leqslant N \Rightarrow a_p \leqslant a_q)))$$

where

$$R^{IV} \Rightarrow R^{III}$$

It is also relatively easy to show that

$$R^{IV} \Rightarrow R$$

and therefore any sorting algorithms that we develop which satisfy R^{IV} will also satisfy R.

There are several ways of expressing the relation R^{IV} with varying degrees of formality, that is

$$(\forall k : 1 \leqslant k < N : (\forall p,q : 1 \leqslant p \leqslant k < k + 1 \leqslant q \leqslant N : a_p \leqslant a_q))$$

and

$$(\forall k : 1 \leqslant k < N : a[1..k] \leqslant a[k + 1..N])$$

These specifications state that for each partition defined by k, the elements in the left partition, (i.e. a[1..k]) are less than or equal to the elements in the right partition (i.e. a[k + 1..N]). Quantification over k ensures that the 'sorted condition' expressed in R is still implied by the various versions of R^{IV}.

The postcondition R^{IV} is sufficiently rich in its degrees of freedom to allow manipulations that lead to the development of a variety of different sorting algorithms. We will focus on the last version of R^{IV}, that is

$$R^{IV}: (\forall k : 1 \leqslant k < N : a[1..k] \leqslant a[k + 1..N])$$

as the base specification from which to develop different sorting algorithms. It should be noted that R^{II} is also a perfectly reasonable specification from which to develop a number of different sorting algorithms.

Before considering the constructive development of any particular sorting algorithm a brief summary will be provided of the main lines of manipulation of R^{IV} that we will use.

Three primary transformations on R^{IV} will be considered. Each leads to a family of sorting algorithms that share an underlying strategy. The strategies are sorting by selection, sorting by insertion, and sorting by partitioning.

9.2.1   The transformation for selection

An obvious manipulation on R^{IV} we can make is a simple state-space extension in which the leftmost N is replaced by a new free variable i and the accompanying equivalence condition i = N is appended to give

$$R_D : (\forall k : 1 \leqslant k < i : a[1..k] \leqslant a[k + 1..N]) \wedge i = N$$

where

$$R_D \Rightarrow R^{IV}$$

The first conjunct in R_D is easily established by the assignments i := 1; a := A but it is much more difficult to establish the second conjunct i = N in concert with the first.

The condition established by the initialization is therefore

$$P_1 : (\forall k : 1 \leqslant k < i : a[1..k] \leqslant a[k + 1..N]) \wedge 1 \leqslant i \leqslant N$$

To make progress towards establishing the remaining conjunct i = N and hence R_D, i will need to be increased. One possibility is to investigate the effect of executing the command i := i +1 under the invariance of P_1. We compute

$$wp ("i := i + 1", P_1)$$

which immediately tells us that the following component is *not* implied by P_1, that is

$$R_1 : a[i] \leqslant a[i + 1..N]   \text{is not implied by } P_1$$

Therefore in order to safely execute the command i := i + 1 under the invariance of P_1 the sub-goal R_1 will need to be established first. Pursuit of this goal leads to the derivation of mechanisms that apply a strategy of locating and putting in place first the smallest element in the array, then the second smallest element in the array, and so on. The particular transformations made on R_1 to derive a refinement that will establish it determine whether we end up with a **direct selectionsort**, an **indirect selectionsort**, a **bubblesort**, or a **heapsort**. We will pursue these derivations in Section 9.3.

9.2.2 The transformation for insertion

Returning to our original postcondition R^{IV}, a second possible state-space extension is to replace not just one but *both* occurrences of N by i, and include the equivalence condition i = N. This yields

$$R_D : (\forall k : 1 \leqslant k < i : a[1..k] \leqslant a[k + 1.. i]) \wedge i = N$$

where again

$$R_D \Rightarrow R^{IV}$$

The first conjunct in R_D is easily established by the assignments i := 1; a := A but it is much more difficult to establish the second conjunct i = N in concert with the first. The condition established by the initialization is therefore

$$P_1 : (\forall k : 1 \leqslant k < i : a[1..k] \leqslant a[k + 1..i]) \wedge 1 \leqslant i \leqslant N$$

With this specification it is also possible to investigate conditions under which the command i := i + 1 can be executed. When we compute

$$wp (\text{``i} := i + 1\text{''}, P_1)$$

we find that the sub-goal

$$R_1 : (\forall k : 1 \leqslant k < i + 1 : a[1..k] \leqslant a[k + 1..i + 1] \wedge 1 \leqslant i + 1 \leqslant N$$

will need to be established before we can safely execute the command i := i + 1 under the invariance of P_1. In contrast to the previous development, the focus here is not on finding the minimum, and then the second smallest, and so on. Rather it is on keeping the segment a[1..i] in non-descending order. The particular transformations that are made on R_1 in order to derive a refinement that will establish it determine whether we end up with a **direct insertionsort**, or an **indirect insertionsort**. These derivations will also be pursued in Section 9.4.

9.2.3 The transformation for partitioning

Both of the previous primary manipulations of the postcondition have focused on building up the sorted or ordered array one element at a time, from the left. Another approach is to be more arbitrary about the order in which the partitioning is done by allowing it to be data driven.

The focus then is upon some *arbitrary* k value in the range $1 \leqslant k < N$ such that the array is partitioned into two segments a[1..k] and a[k + 1..N]. In other words, the 'for all k' is replaced by 'for one k' and so we have

$$R_1 : 1 \leqslant k < N \wedge a[1..k] \leqslant a[k + 1..N]$$

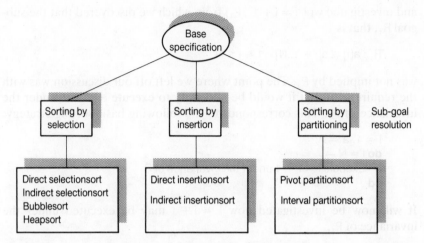

Figure 9.1. The diagram shows how, at the sub-goal level, specification transformations, separate the various sorting algorithms into classes.

The task is then, in the first instance, to construct a mechanism which achieves the split into two partitions (that is, the array a must be transformed, and a k found for which relation R_1 is satisfied). This leaves two sub-problems to which the same partitioning strategy can be applied. Depending on how the specifications are manipulated we end up with the derivation of a quicksort algorithm based either on **pivot partitioning** or **interval partitioning** (see also Sections 8.3 and 8.4). The partitioning algorithm needs to be applied in such a way that it achieves partitioning for all k in the range $1 \leq k < N$ in order to guarantee the relation R_D with its quantification over k.

Now some of the sorting algorithms mentioned in the previous section will be derived. What will be shown is the underlying principles which relate the various algorithms and also the influence of specification manipulations in deriving these algorithms. Figure 9.1 shows the basic topology for the various sorting algorithms resulting from resolution of sub-goals in the way we have outlined.

9.3 The Selection Algorithms

The first family of sorting algorithms whose derivation we will consider comprises selectionsort, bubblesort, and heapsort. The postcondition that we will use for these derivations is

$$R_D : (\forall k : 1 \leq k < i : a[1..k] \leq a[k + 1..N]) \wedge i = N$$

Earlier we derived the invariant

$$P_1 : (\forall k : 1 \leq k < i : a[1..k] \leq a[k + 1..N]) \wedge 1 \leq i \leq N$$

and investigated wp("i := i + 1", P_1) from which we discovered that the sub-goal R_1, that is

$$R_1 : a[i] \leqslant a[i + 1..N] \wedge 1 \leqslant i \leqslant N$$

was not implied by P_1. The point where we left off our discussion was with the requirement that it would be necessary to execute i := i + 1 under the invariance of P_1. This corresponds to the following basic sorting strategy:

```
i := 1; a := A;
do i ≠ N →
   "Execute i := i + 1 under the invariance of P₁"
od
```

It will now be investigated how i := i + 1 may be executed under the invariance of P_1.

9.3.1   Direct selectionsort derivation

It is not easy to establish the sub-goal R_1 by an initialization of free variables. In response to this situation, one way to proceed is to introduce a new free variable j into R_1 along with the equivalence condition j = N.

This transformation yields

$$R_1^1 : a[i] \leqslant a[i + 1..j] \wedge j = N$$

where $R_1^1 \Rightarrow R_1$

The first conjunct of R_1^1 is easily established by the initialization j := i. It is however much more difficult to establish this conjunct in concert with the second conjunct j = N. We will therefore work with the first conjunct of R_1^1 as an invariant P_1^1

$$P_1^1 : a[i] \leqslant a[i + 1..j] \wedge i \leqslant j \leqslant N$$

and attempt to establish the second conjunct. Our basic sorting loop is therefore decomposed to

```
i := 1; a := A;
do i ≠ N → {P₁}
   j := i;
   do j ≠ N → { P₁¹ }
      "Execute j := j + 1 under the invariance of P₁¹"
   od; {R₁¹}
   i := i + 1 {P₁}
od
```

Investigating wp("j := j + 1", P_1^1) we find that $a[i] \leqslant a[j + 1]$ is not necessarily implied by P_1^1. When $a[i] \leqslant a[j + 1]$ prevails we can simply execute j := j + 1, but when a[i] > a[j + 1] occurs we will need to execute swap(a_i, a_{j+1}) † together with a j-increment in order to preserve P_1^1. Incorporating these refinements we arrive at a description of the main elements of a version of direct selectionsort.

Direct selectionsort
```
i := 1; a := A;
do i ≠ N → {P₁}
    j := i;
    do j ≠ N → { P₁¹ }
        if aᵢ ≤ aⱼ₊₁ → j := j + 1
        [] aᵢ > aⱼ₊₁ → swap(aᵢ, aⱼ₊₁); j := j+1 †
        fi
    od; {R₁¹}
    i := i + 1
od
```

9.3.2   Indirect selectionsort derivation

To obtain the more familiar and efficient version of selectionsort two further manipulations of R_1^1 are needed. First we introduce a new free variable x, in place of a_i, and we record the identity $x = a_i$ as a conjunct:

R_1^{11} $x = a_i \land x \leq a[i + 1..j] \land j = N$ ‡

We then introduce a new free variable m in place of i in $x = a_i$ and add the conjunct m = i. This yields

R_1^{111} $x = a_m \land x \leq a[i + 1..j] \land m = i \land j = N$

This relation can be weakened by dropping the conjuncts $m = i \land j = N$ which leaves the invariant

P_1^{111}: $x = a_m \land x \leq a[i + 1..j] \land i \leq j \leq N$

The selection sort derived using this new loop invariant P_1^{111} is as follows:

Indirect selectionsort
```
i := 1; a := A;
do i ≠ N → {P₁}
    x, m, j := aᵢ, i, i;
    do j ≠ N → { P₁¹¹¹ }
        if x ≤ aⱼ₊₁ → j := j + 1
        [] x > aⱼ₊₁ → x, m, j := aⱼ₊₁, j + 1, j + 1
        fi
    od; {x = aₘ ∧ x ≤ a[i + 1..j] ∧ j = N}
    aₘ := aᵢ;
    aᵢ = x; {R₁¹¹}
    i := i + 1
od
```

† swap is a procedure which swaps its arguments.
‡ Strictly a conjunct indicating that x is a member of a[i..j], that is x ∈ a[i..j] is also needed.

9.3.3   Bubblesort derivation

For the derivation of a bubblesort we will again work with the same P_1 and R_1 derived earlier, that is

$$P_1 : (\forall k : 1 \leqslant k < i : a[1..k] \leqslant a[k + 1..N]) \wedge 1 \leqslant i \leqslant N$$
$$R_1 : a[i] \leqslant a[i + 1..N]$$

Only after first establishing R_1 is it possible to execute $i := i + 1$ under the invariance of P_1. Because we cannot guarantee to establish the sub-goal R_1 directly by an initialization of free variables, or simply by increasing i, a state-space extension is needed. We replace *both* i's by j's and include the equivalence condition $j = i$.
This yields

$$R_1^1 : a[j] \leqslant a[j + 1..N] \wedge j = i$$

where

$$R_1^1 \Rightarrow R$$

The first conjunct is easily established by the initialization $j := N$. It may be used as an invariant P_1^1

$$P_1^1 : a[j] \leqslant a[j + 1..N] \wedge i \leqslant j \leqslant N$$

which will allow j to be decreased in order to establish $j = i$. The basic structure of the algorithm that follows from this is

```
i := 1; a := A;
do i ≠ N →
  j := N;
  do j ≠ i →
    "Execute j := j − 1 under the invariance of P₁¹"
  od;
  i := i + 1
od
```

Investigating $wp(\text{"}j := j - 1\text{"}, P_1^1)$ we find $a_{j-1} \leqslant a_j$ is not necessarily implied by P_1^1. When $a_{j-1} \leqslant a_j$ prevails we can safely execute $j := j - 1$ but when $a_{j-1} > a_j$ occurs we will need to execute $swap(a_{j-1}, a_j)$ together with the j-decrement to decrease the variant function $j - i$ while preserving P_1^1. Incorporating these refinements we arrive at a description of the main elements of a version of bubblesort.

Bubblesort

```
i := 1; a := A;
do i ≠ N → {P₁}
  j := N;
  do j ≠ i → { P¹₁ }
    if aⱼ₋₁ ≤ aⱼ → j := j − 1
    [] aⱼ₋₁ > aⱼ → swap (aⱼ₋₁,aⱼ); j := j − 1
    fi
  od; {R¹₁}
  i := i + 1
od
```

Bubblesort is one of the least efficient sorting algorithms. Only when data is nearly sorted is bubblesort an effective algorithm to use.

9.3.4   Heapsort derivation

The same underlying selection strategy for sorting is employed in heapsort as in the selectionsorts and bubblesort. All three algorithms repeatedly find the minimum in the unsorted part of the array a[i..N]. The difference with heapsort is that it uses a more sophisticated and more efficient method for establishing

$$R_1 : a[i] \leq a[i + 1..N]$$

To begin its derivation we will adopt the problem-solving strategy of directly weakening the postcondition to create a weaker sub-goal.

Starting out with the postcondition

$$R : (\forall k : 1 \leq k < N : a[1..k] \leq a[k + 1..N]) \wedge perm(a,A)$$

and replacing the range 1..k by k we obtain another sorting specification

$$R_1 : (\forall k : 1 \leq k < N : a[k] \leq a[k + 1..N]) \wedge perm(a,A)$$

For *each* value of k in R_1 we have

$$a_k \leq a_{k+1} \wedge a_k \leq a_{k+2} \wedge ... \wedge a_k \leq a_N.$$

In Chapter 6 it was suggested that it is sometimes useful to explore weaker relations (i.e. those with less conjuncts) as a means of identifying suitable sub-goals that can contribute to solving the original problem. One such weaker relation for each k is

$$a_k \leq a_{2k} \wedge a_k \leq a_{2k+1} \quad \text{for } k < 2k, 2k + 1 \leq N$$

It introduces a tree-like dependency for the elements.

The R_1 order dependency is

whereas the R_2 order dependency is

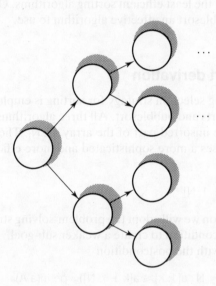

This weaker relation R_2 could be written as

$$R_2 : (\forall k : 1 \leq k < N : (2k \leq N \Rightarrow a_k \leq a_{2k}) \wedge (2k + 1 \leq N \Rightarrow a_k \leq a_{2k+1}))$$
$$\wedge \; perm(a,A) \; \dagger$$

It is difficult to make an initialization of free variables in R_2 that will establish it directly. We will therefore introduce a new free variable j in place of 1 to obtain:

$$R_3 : (\forall k : j \leq k < N : (2k \leq N \Rightarrow a_k \leq a_{2k}) \wedge (2k + 1 \leq N \Rightarrow a_k \leq a_{2k+1}))$$
$$\wedge \; perm(a,A) \wedge j = 1$$

† Note $R_1 \Rightarrow R_2$

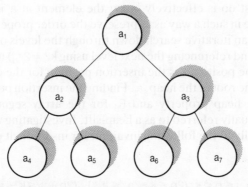

The relation R_3 describes the heap data structure (an example for $N = 7$ is shown above) where $a_k \leq a_{2k}$ and $a_k \leq a_{2k+1}$. Notice that the elements beyond $N/2$ (here 3) satisfy the heap property because $2k$ and $2k + 1$ are out of range.

An initialization of free variables that can establish R_3 is

$$j, a := N/2 + 1, A$$

Setting j to $N/2 + 1$ makes both $2k \leq N$ and $2k + 1 \leq N$ false and hence the corresponding implications are true. In other words the *leaves* of the heap $a_{N/2+1},\ldots,a_N$ already form a heap. The corresponding invariant identified by this initialization is

$$P_3 : 1 \leq j \leq N/2 + 1 \wedge (\forall k : j \leq k < N/2 + 1 : (2k \leq N \Rightarrow a_k \leq a_{2k})$$
$$\wedge (2k + 1 \leq N \Rightarrow a_k \leq a_{2k+1})) \wedge \mathrm{perm}\,(a,A)\dagger$$

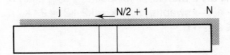

To make progress in establishing R_3 we need to decrease j while maintaining P_3, that is

```
j, a := N/2 + 1, A;
do j ≠ 1 →
    "decrease j while maintaining P₃"
od
```

Maintaining P_3 for a given j value involves more than ensuring that

$$a_j \leq a_{2j} \quad \text{and} \quad a_j \leq a_{2j+1}$$

---

† It is unnecessary to consider k values beyond $N/2$ as they will always provide true conjuncts because of the implications.

What we must do is effectively insert the element at a_j into the tree-like heap structure in such a way as to preserve the order properties of the heap. This involves an iterative search down through the levels of the heap (using initially $k = j$ and referencing the next level using $k2 = 2 * j$) until $a_k \leq a_{k2}$, and $a_k \leq a_{k2+1}$. The position k is the insertion position for the element that was originally at the root of the heap, a_j. Finding the insertion position in this way preserves the heap property and P_3 for the array segment $a[j..N]$. This insertion is usually referred to as a heap-sift. Investigating $wp("j := j - 1", P_3)$ leads eventually to the following invariant for insertion at position j

$$P_4 : (\forall p : j \leq p < k : (2p \leq k \Rightarrow a_p \leq a_{2p}) \wedge (2p + 1 \leq k \Rightarrow a_p \leq a_{2p+1})) \wedge j \leq k$$
$$\wedge (n = N \textbf{ div } 2 \textbf{ cor } (a_k \leq a_{2k} \wedge a_k \leq a_{2k+1})) \wedge perm(a, A)$$

Investigating $wp("k := 2 * k", P_4)$ leads to the following heap-insertion implementation. The loop can make at most $\log_2 N$ steps to perform the insertion

```
Sift(a, j, N):
    .
    .  declarations
    .
    k := j; k2 := 2 * j; n := N div 2;
    do k < n → { P₄ }
        if k < N div 2 then k2 := Minpos(a_k2, a_k2+1, k2) fi;
        if a_k > a_k2 → swap(a_k, a_k2); k := k2; k2 := 2 * k
        [] a_k ≤ a_k2 → n := k
        fi
    od
end
```

where the function Minpos(x, y, p) has the form

```
Minpos(x, y, p):
    .
    .  declarations
    .
    if x > y then p := p + 1 fi;
    return p
end
```

Our mechanism for building a heap and thereby establishing R_3 then takes the form:

```
Buildheap(a, N):
    .
    .   declarations
    .
    j, a := N/2 + 1, A;
    do j ≠ 1 → {P₃}
        j := j − 1;
        Sift(a, j, N)
    od
    {R₃}
end
```

The process of establishing R_3 produces a weak-ordering of the array in which the minimum value in the array is located at the root of the heap in position one, that is

$$a[1] \le a[2..N]$$

The process of building the heap has 'selected' the minimum element in the array. The question that must be asked is, having established a weaker sub-goal, how can it be exploited to establish the original goal R_1? The simplest strategy for achieving a sort from a heap involves 'selecting' the elements from the heap one by one in increasing order of magnitude. The Sift procedure can be used for this purpose i.e.

```
Heapsort(a, N):
    .
    .   declarations
    .
    Buildheap(a, N);
    do N ≠ 1 →
        swap(a[1], a[N]);
        N := N − 1;
        Sift(a, 1, N)
    od
end
```

This heapsort selects the elements in non-descending order as our original postcondition required. If we choose to store the sorted data in the same array (as we have done here) then we end up establishing the following postcondition:

$$R_4 : (\forall k : 1 \le k < N : a[k] \ge a[k + 1..N])$$

The establishment of the sub-goal R_3 has not enabled us to establish our original goal R_1 but instead it has led us to a goal R_4 from which the goal R_1 can be easily achieved by a further refinement that reverses the order of the elements in the array. A different definition of the heap property, in which the root of the heap was at a[N], would have allowed the direct accomplishment of the sort without the need for the order reversal at the end. This alternative is left as an exercise.

While it is unlikely that other than an experienced designer would be able to see all the steps used here, the derivation of an algorithm of this sophistication is still within the reach of the formal methods we have been using.

9.4   The Insertion Algorithms

The two insertionsort algorithms that we will derive here result from using two different methods for inserting an element into an ordered sequence so as to preserve the order of the extended sequence. The methods for insertion arise directly from making different transformations on the subgoal that must be established in order to extend the ordered sequence by one element.

9.4.1   Direct insertionsort derivation

Earlier we saw that a second basic form of postcondition to work with was

$$R_D : (\forall k : 1 \leqslant k < i : a[1..k] \leqslant a[k + 1..i]) \wedge i = N$$

From this we were led to the invariant

$$P_1 : (\forall k : 1 \leqslant k < i : a[1..k] \leqslant a[k + 1..i]) \wedge 1 \leqslant i \leqslant N$$

Our investigation of increasing i under the invariance of P_1 led to the discovery that R_1, that is

$$R_1 : (\forall k : 1 \leqslant k < i + 1 : a[1..k] \leqslant a[k + 1..i + 1]) \wedge 1 \leqslant i + 1 \leqslant N$$

will need to be established before we can safely execute the command $i := i + 1$ under the invariance of P_1. Our basic loop structure at this stage is therefore

```
i := 1; a := A;
do i ≠ N →
    "Execute i := i + 1 under the invariance of P₁"
od
```

As there is no guarantee of being able to establish R_1 directly we may seek transformations to other more useful specifications. This specification can be rewritten in the form

R_1^1: ordered(a[1..i]) $\wedge$ a[1..i] $\leq a_{i+1}$†

To proceed with the development we may introduce a new free variable j to obtain

R_1^{11}: ordered(a[1..j]) $\wedge$ a[1..j] $\leq a_{i+1} \wedge j = i$

where

$R_1^{11} \Rightarrow R_1$

Weakening R_1^{11} we obtain the invariant

P_1^{11}. ordered(a[1..j]) $\wedge$ a[1..j] $\leq a_{i+1} \wedge 0 \leq j \leq i$

Carrying out the necessary loop development using a weakest precondition computation with P_1^{11} we obtain an implementation of *direct insertionsort*.

Direct insertionsort

```
i := 1;
do i ≠ N → {P₁}
    j := 0;
    do j ≠ i → { P₁¹¹ }
        if a_{j+1} ≤ a_{i+1} → j := j + 1
        [] a_{j+1} > a_{i+1} → swap(a_{j+1}, a_{i+1}); j := j + 1
        fi
    od; { R₁¹¹ }
    i := i + 1
od
{ R_D }
```

9.4.2   Indirect insertionsort derivation

The more familiar implementation of an insertion sort can be derived by starting out with a different transformation on R_1. Writing R_1^1 in the shorthand form we have

R_1^1: ordered(a[1..i +1])

† ordered(a[1..i]) is shorthand for $(\forall k : 1 \leq k < i : a[1 .. k] \leq a [k + 1 .. i])$.

Introducing a new free variable j we get

R_1^{11}: ordered(a[j..i + 1]) $\wedge$ j = 1

where

$R_1^{11} \Rightarrow R_1$

An initialization that can establish R_1^{11} is "j := i+1". It is also possible to take advantage of the fact that a[1..i] is already ordered. Strengthening R_1^{11} accordingly and incorporating j we get

R_1^{111}: ordered(a[1..j − 1]) $\wedge$ ordered(a[j..i + 1]) $\wedge$ j = 1

This will imply R_1 even if j = 1 does not apply *provided* $a_{j-1} \leq a_j$. Strengthening R_1^{111} with this condition we get

R_1^{IV} : ordered(a[1..j − 1]) $\wedge$ ordered(a[j..i + 1]) $\wedge$ (j = 1 **cor** $a_{j-1} \leq a_j$)

Introducing a new free variable I we get

R_1^V: ordered(a[1..I −1]) $\wedge$ ordered(a[j..i + 1]) $\wedge$ (I = 1 **cor** $a_{j-1} \leq a_j$) $\wedge$ j = I

Weakening R_1^V: we get

P_1^V : ordered(a[1..I − 1]) $\wedge$ ordered(a[j..i + 1]) $\wedge$ (I = 1 **cor** a_{j-1}) $\leq a_j$
    $\wedge$ 1 $\leq$ I $\leq$ j $\leq$ i + 1

Carrying out the necessary loop development using weakest precondition calculations with P_1^V we obtain the following implementation of an insertion sort:

Indirect insertionsort

```
i := 1; a := A;
do i ≠ N → {P₁}
  I := 1; j := i + 1;
  do I ≠ j → { P₁ᵛ }
    if a_{j−1} > a_j → swap (a_{j−1}, a_j); j := j − 1
    [] a_{j−1} ≤ a_j → I := j
    fi
  od; {R₁ᵛ}
  i := i + 1
od
```

9.5 The Partitioning Algorithms

The two versions of quicksort that we will derive here result from using two different methods for partitioning a sequence. The different methods for partitioning arise directly from making different transformations on the sub-goal that must be established in order to extend the number of partitions established by one.

9.5.1 Quicksort derivation (using pivot partitioning)

In our earlier discussion of quicksort we found that the first step was to establish the sub-goal

$$R_0 : 1 \leqslant k < N \wedge a[1..k] \leqslant a[k + 1..N]$$

for some arbitrary k value.

As it is difficult to make an initialization of free variables that will establish R_0 directly we will choose to split the variable k by introducing two new free variables i and j to obtain

$$R_0^1: 1 \leqslant i < N \wedge a[1..i] \leqslant a[j..N] \wedge i = k \wedge j = k + 1$$

where

$$R_0^1 \Rightarrow R_0$$

From R_0^1 we can obtain

$$R_0^{11} : 1 \leqslant i < N \wedge a[1..i] \leqslant a[j..N] \wedge i = j - 1$$

The last conjunct of R_0^{11} is difficult to establish in concert with the first two conjuncts by initialization of free variables. We therefore have the choice of trying to work with this specification or of seeking other transformations. Here we will choose the latter course.

Before proceeding further we will illustrate a new transformation which we refer to as **splitting a relation.** Suppose, for example we have the relation

$$a_i \leqslant a_j$$

The a_j in this relation can be replaced by x to yield $a_i \leqslant x$ provided $x \leqslant a_j$ also holds. We can then write

$$a_i \leqslant x \wedge x \leqslant a_j \Rightarrow a_i \leqslant a_j$$

Applying a similar transformation to R_0^{11} we obtain

$$R_0^{111}: 1 \leqslant i < N \wedge a[1..i] \leqslant x \wedge x \leqslant a[j..N] \wedge i = j - 1$$

where

$$R_0^{111} \Rightarrow R_0$$

We are free to base our derivation upon R_0^{111}. All but the last conjunct is easily established by the initialization

$$i := 0; x := a[1]; j := N + 1$$

This leads to the invariant

$$P : 0 \leq i < N \wedge a[1..i] \leq x \wedge x \leq a[j..N] \wedge 0 \leq i < j \leq N + 1$$

and variant function

$$t : j - i - 1$$

This invariant is very close to the familiar invariant employed to develop a partitioning algorithm which serves as the central computational element of quicksort. Below we provide an implementation of quicksort that employs both binary recursion and tail recursion that is based on the specifications given and the associated weakest precondition calculations for $i := i + 1$ and $j := j - 1$.

Quicksort

```
quicksort (var a: nelements; l,u: integer);
var i, j, x: integer;
    i := l−1; j := u + 1; x := a[l]; †
    if i < j − 1 then {P}
    partition:
        do a_{i+1} < x → i := i + 1 od;
        do a_{j−1} > x → j := j − 1 od;
        if i < j − 1 then swap(a_{i+1},a_{j−1}); i :=i + 1; j :=j − 1; partition fi;
        quicksort (a, l ,i);
        quicksort (a, j, u)
    fi
end
```

In carrying out this derivation we chose to introduce two new free variables i and j. We could have arrived at essentially the same implementation by the introduction of just one variable j to replace $k + 1$ in R_0. The invariant requires $a[1..i] \leq x$ should be maintained; however, the stronger loop guard $a_{i+1} < x$ is used to avoid the termination problems that the weaker guard $a_{i+1} \leq x$ would introduce. The stronger guard is also commonly used in most published implementations of quicksort. The same reasoning applies to the guard involving j.

† Our relations should indicate x is a member of the array.

9.5.2   Quicksort derivation (using interval partitioning)

There is an interesting alternative to the pivot partitioning method that we
have just derived. To see how it may be obtained we will also start out with

$$R_0^{11}: 1 \leq i < N \wedge a[1..i] \leq a[j..N] \wedge i = j - 1$$

Again it is necessary to use a relation-splitting technique. To understand
how the technique is applied consider again the relation

$$a_i \leq a_j$$

From this relation we can move to

$$a_i \leq x \wedge x \leq a_j$$

We can then make a further state-space extension by replacing the x in $x \leq a_j$
by a new free variable y which must satisfy $x \leq y$. We can then write

$$a_i \leq x \wedge y \leq a_j \wedge x \leq y \Rightarrow a_i \leq a_j$$

Applying essentially the same manipulations to R_0^{11} yields

$$R_0^{111}: 1 \leq i < N \wedge a[1..i] \leq x \wedge y \leq a[j..N] \wedge x \leq y \wedge i = j - 1$$

Weakening the 'hard-to-establish' conjunct we arrive at the invariant

$$P_0^{111}: 0 \leq i < N \wedge a[1..i] \leq x \wedge y \leq a[j..N] \wedge x \leq y \wedge 0 \leq i < j \leq N + 1$$

This invariant, when used to make weakest precondition computations for
increasing i and decreasing j, leads to an **interval partitioning** algorithm. An
implementation of quicksort that employs interval partitioning is

```
quicksort2 (var a : nelements; l, u : integer);
var i, j, x, y : integer;
    i := l; j := u + 1;
    if i < j − 1 then
        if a_i ⩾ a_{j−1} then swap(a_i, a_{j−1}) fi;
        x := a_i ; y := a_{j−1}; j := j − 1;
        intpartition : { P_0^{111} }
            do a_{i+1} < x → i := i + 1 od;
            do a_{j−1} > y → j := j − 1 od;
            if i < j − 1 then
                if a_{i+1} ⩾ a_{j−1} then swap(a_{i+1}, a_{j−1}) fi;
                i, j, x, y := i + 1, j − 1, max(x, a_{i+1}), min(y, a_{j−1});
                intpartition
            fi;
        quicksort2 (a,l,i);
        quicksort2 (a, j, u)
    fi
end
```

SUMMARY

- We have used manipulations of a specification to derive implementations for a variety of well-known sorting algorithms. The investigation has identified specific transformations that separate the well-known sorting algorithms. A number of these transformations should be applicable to other problems.

- The primary objective of this exercise has been to show the potential that specification manipulations have for guiding and exploring different possible solutions to problems. If the techniques that we have used here are more widely applicable, then they raise the prospects of a reasonably systematic strategy for exploring different solutions to well-specified problems.

- We need to go beyond the strategy of simply taking a postcondition and weakening it directly in some simple way. What the present discussion shows is that it is sometimes necessary to go through a considerable manipulation of a specification by introducing new free variables and accompanying conditions before arriving at a form suitable to obtain an invariant form. The process of transforming specifications allows more alternatives to be explored when applying weakest precondition techniques.

- The derivations indicate that weakest precondition calculations may serve as a tool for guiding and ordering the decomposition of a problem. They can do this by identifying parts of a specification that may not be satisfied under the influence of a change in certain variables. What the present examples show is that weakest precondition investigations can identify larger and more complex components of a program as well as the simple components of a loop body that they are usually used to identify.

- The refinement process that the weakest precondition investigations propagate is accompanied by the stepwise introduction of new free variables which in turn need to be changed under some invariant condition. Different choices made in taking these steps lead naturally to the derivation of different algorithms. There is some pedagogical merit in explaining the differences between sorting algorithms in these terms even though the algorithms were obviously not originally derived in this way. Discovering new and different solutions to problems remains a central and difficult concern for computing science.

■   **EXERCISE 9**   *Sorting derivations*

1.   Design and implement a sorting algorithm that establishes the postcondition

$$R : (\forall p : 1 \leqslant p \leqslant N : (\forall q : 1 \leqslant q \leqslant N : p < q \Rightarrow a_p \leqslant a_q)) \wedge \text{perm}(a, A)$$

2.   Design and implement a sorting algorithm that establishes the postcondition

$$R : (\forall k : 1 \leqslant k < N : (\forall q : k + 1 \leqslant q \leqslant N : a_k \leqslant a_q)) \wedge \text{perm}(a, A)$$

3.   Design and implement a sorting algorithm that establishes the postcondition

$$R : (\forall k : i \leqslant k < N : a[i..k] \leqslant a[k + 1..N]) \wedge i = 1 \wedge \text{perm}(a, A)$$

Bibliography

Darlington, J. (1978), A synthesis of several sorting algorithms, *Acta Informatica*, 11, 1–30

Dijkstra, E.W. (1976), *A Discipline of Programming*, Prentice-Hall, N.J.

Dijkstra, E.W. and van Gasteren, A.J. (1982), An introduction to three algorithms for sorting in situ, *Inf. Proc. Letts.*, **15**(3), 129–34.

Dromey, R.G. (1988), Systematic program development, *IEEE Trans. Software Eng.*, **14**(1), 12–29.

Dromey, R.G. (1987), Derivation of sorting algorithms from a specification, *Computer Journal* **30**(6), 512–18.

Hoare, C.A.R. (1962), Quicksort, *Computer Journal* **5**, 10–15.

van Emden, M. (1970), Increasing the efficiency of quicksort, *Comm. ACM,* **13,** 563-7.

Williams, J. (1964), *Heapsort* (Algorithm 232), *Comm. ACM* **7**(6), 347-8.

Wirth, N. (1976), *Algorithms + Data Structures = Programs,* Prentice-Hall, N.J.

Chapter 10
Text Processing

The price of complexity cannot be overestimated.

E.W. Dijkstra

10.1 Introduction
10.2 Simple Pattern Match
10.3 Simple Pattern Search
10.4 Boyer and Moore Algorithm
10.5 Text Editing
10.6 Text Formatting
10.7 Comment Skipping
     Summary
     Exercise
     Bibliography

10.1   Introduction

Processing textual information is a major computational activity. There are three principal operations that we want to perform on text.

- We want to search texts of varying structures and look for patterns or words.
- We want to modify, manipulate, and format text in a variety of ways.
- We want to analyse certain characteristics of text.

In this chapter we will focus primarily on the specification and derivation of searching and formatting algorithms. In Chapters 11 and 12 some other text-processing algorithms are discussed.

The specification of text problems is often most easily handled using EBNF. For editing and searching operations on text the predicate calculus is

469

still a viable option. In constructing specifications it is important that we end up with a description that captures the structure of the text. Only if specifications capture structure is it possible subsequently to derive programs that match that structure.

The options for searching text are fairly limited. The obvious approach is to use a linear character-by-character strategy similar to that used to search arrays. To identify more sophisticated and more efficient text-searching algorithms it is necessary to look for ways to move through the text without examining all the characters. To pursue this line we make use of weakest precondition calculations which can identify conditions that must be satisfied in order to achieve greater efficiency. The interesting thing about such investigations is that they do not lead directly to the derivation of a more efficient algorithm. Instead they point to the condition that must be satisfied in order to achieve the greater efficiency. This is the next best thing to direct derivation. Provided we have the insight to create a mechanism that will satisfy the condition identified we will achieve the outcome we are seeking.

10.2   Simple Pattern Match

Testing whether one pattern matches another pattern is fundamental to many text-processing problems. The simplest of the matching problems involves deciding whether or not two strings of characters, equal in length, match. The most primitive form of postcondition specification for this problem is:

R : match $\lor$ mismatch

A solution to this problem will now be developed in a fairly formal style.

Assuming we are dealing with two strings A[1..N] and B[1..N], we can refine this specification to the familiar search specification form used in Section 7.2.

$Q : N \geqslant 0$
$R_1 : (\forall j : 0 < j \leqslant i : A_j = B_j) \land (i = N \textbf{ cor } A_{i+1} \neq B_{i+1})$

Here if $i = N$ we have a match, otherwise there is a mismatch.

Transforming this specification R_1 by introducing a new free variable n we get the following constructive postcondition R_D from which we can extract the strongest useful invariant

$R_D : (\forall j : 0 < j \leqslant i : A_j = B_j) \land (n = N \textbf{ cor } A_{i+1} \neq B_{i+1}) \land i = n$

An initialization that can establish R_D which can also be easily checked by the equivalence condition $i = n$ is:

$S_0(X_0)$ Initialization

> i, n := 0, N; {P_0}
> **if** i = n → skip {R_D established}
> [] i ≠ n → {Q_1} $s_1(x_1)$ {R_D}
> **fi**

The initialization guarantees to establish the base invariant

$$P_0 : i = 0 \wedge n = N \wedge (\forall j : 0 < j \leq i : A_j = B_j) \wedge (n = N \textbf{ cor } A_{i+1} \neq B_{i+1})$$

and

$$P_0 \wedge i = n \Rightarrow R_D$$
$$P_0 \wedge i \neq n \equiv Q_1$$

To make the next refinement when Q_1 applies either i will need to be increased, or n decreased, or both changed, in order to establish the equivalence condition i = n. An appropriate variant function that follows from the equivalence condition is

$$t : n - i$$

Weakening P_0 to accommodate these possible changes we get

$$P_1 : 0 \leq i \leq n \leq N \wedge (\forall j : 0 < j \leq i : A_j = B_j) \wedge (n = N \textbf{ cor } A_{i+1} \neq B_{i+1})$$

Our basic loop structure becomes

> i, n := 0, N;
> **do** i ≠ n →
>   "Increase i under the invariance of P_1"
> **od**

The simplest way to increase i is with the command i := i + 1. Computing wp("i := i + 1", P_1) we find that it is implied by P_1 and i ≠ n provided $A_{i+1} = B_{i+1}$. We can therefore write

> **if** $A_{i+1} = B_{i+1}$ → i := i + 1

Unfortunately we cannot guarantee that the condition $A_{i+1} = B_{i+1}$ will always hold and so there is a risk of the command aborting. To avoid this we need to add the guard $A_{i+1} \neq B_{i+1}$ and investigate how the variant function can be decreased under this condition while still maintaining P_1. It is not possible to increase i under these circumstances without violating P_1, and so we are left with decreasing n.

A possibility is

if $A_{i+1} \neq B_{i+1} \rightarrow n := i$

Since neither $A_{i+1} = B_{i+1}$ nor $A_{i+1} \neq B_{i+1}$ can be guaranteed, but the condition $A_{i+1} = B_{i+1} \lor A_{i+1} \neq B_{i+1}$ will always hold, the assignments to n and i can be combined into a single refinement. And so we then get:

$S_1(X_1)$ First refinement

```
i, n := 0, N;
do i ≠ n → {P₁}
   if A_{i+1} = B_{i+1} → i := i + 1
   ] A_{i+1} ≠ B_{i+1} → n := i
   fi
od;
{R_D}
match := (i = N)
```

This basic pattern-matching strategy can be adapted to other situations for example where the two patterns differ in length, or where it is necessary to search for the presence of one pattern in another longer pattern. The latter problem we will consider next because it is also a fundamental problem in text processing.

10.3 Simple Pattern Search

Searching for a fixed pattern in a line of text is a simple extension of the problem of searching a sequence for a particular element (see Section 7.2). The underlying similarity between the two problems can be seen in the form of their specification and in the strategy used to bring about a solution. The difference lies in the complexity of the test for a match that is made at each position in the sequence being searched.

What we try to do in the simple pattern search is effectively to 'position' the pattern at each location in the text and then test if there is a

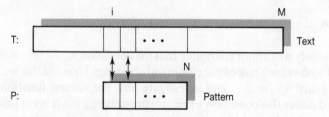

Figure 10.1   Positioning of pattern in text.

match. Figure 10.1 shows this schematically. Our style of treatment for this problem will be more abbreviated than for the previous example.

The basic postcondition specification is

$$R : (\forall q : 0 < q \leqslant i : Trymatch(q))$$
$$\wedge (i = M - N + 1 \textbf{ cor } (\forall l : 0 < l \leqslant N : T[i + l - 1] = P[l]))$$

where Trymatch(i) is defined as follows

$$Trymatch(i) : (\forall l : 0 < l \leqslant j : P[l] = T[i + l - 1]) \wedge (j = N \textbf{ cor } P[j + 1] \neq T[i + j])$$

This specification indicates that the search should continue until a match is found or the text is exhausted.

Introducing a new free variable m into R we get the constructive specification

$$R_D : (\forall q : 0 < q \leqslant i : Trymatch(q))$$
$$\wedge (m = M - N + 1 \textbf{ cor } (\forall l : 0 < l \leqslant N : T[i + l - 1] = P[l])) \wedge i = m$$

A suitable variant function that follows from R_D is

$$t : m - i$$

and an initialization of free variables that can establish R_D is

$$i, m := 0, M - N + 1$$

The initialization leads to the identification of the invariant

$$P_D : (\forall q : 0 < q \leqslant i : Trymatch(q))$$
$$\wedge (m = M - N + 1 \textbf{ cor } (\forall l : 0 < l \leqslant N : T[i + l - 1] = P[l]))$$
$$\wedge 0 \leqslant i \leqslant m \leqslant M - N + 1$$

The basic loop structure may therefore take the form

```
i, m := 0, M − N + 1;
do i ≠ m →
    "Increase i while maintaining P_D"
od
```

Computing

$$wp("i := i + 1", P_D)$$

we find that the sub-goal Trymatch(i + 1) is not implied by P_D. It will therefore be necessary to establish this subgoal R_1 *before* i can safely be increased by one. We have:

$$R_1 : (\forall l : 0 < l \leqslant j : P[l] = T[i + l]) \wedge (j = N \textbf{ cor } P[j + 1] \neq T[i + j + 1])$$

To make this sub-goal specification constructive we introduce a new free variable n to obtain

$$R_2 : (\forall l : 0 < l \leqslant j : P[l] = T[i + l]) \wedge (n = N \textbf{ cor } P[j + 1] \neq T[i + j + 1]) \wedge j = n$$

A suitable variant function that follows from R_2 is

$$t_2 : n - j$$

and an initialization of free variables that can establish R_2 is:

$$j, n := 0, N$$

The initialization leads to the identification of the invariant:

$$P_2 : (\forall l : 0 < l \leqslant j : P[l] = T[i + l])$$
$$\wedge (n = N \textbf{ cor } P[j + 1] \neq T[i + j + 1]) \wedge 0 \leqslant j \leqslant n \leqslant N$$

Our loop structure therefore refines to

```
i, m := 0, M - N + 1;
do i ≠ m → {P_D}
  j, n := 0, N;
  do j ≠ n → {P_2}
    "Increase j while maintaining P_2"
  od
  "Test if complete match"
od
```

Computing

$$wp("j := j + 1", P_2)$$

we find that

$$P[j + 1] = T[i + j + 1]$$

is not implied by P_2. It follows that the command for increasing j will need to be

if $P[j + 1] = T[i + j + 1] \rightarrow j := j + 1$

Since the condition $P[j + 1] = T[i + j + 1]$ cannot be guaranteed we end up with the following implementation:

```
i, m := 0, M − N + 1;
do i ≠ m → {P_D}
    j, n := 0, N;
    do j ≠ n → {P_2}
        if P[j + 1] = T[i + j + 1] → j := j + 1
        [] P[j + 1] ≠ T[i + j + 1] → n := j
        fi
    od; {R_2}
    if j ≠ N → i := i + 1
    [] j = N → m := i {complete match}
    fi
od
{R_D}
match := (i < M − N + 1)
```

This completes the derivation of our simple $O(M \times N)$ pattern-searching algorithm. There are various other pattern-searching algorithms with significantly better efficiency than our present algorithm.

10.4 Boyer and Moore Algorithm

In the simple pattern search we saw how the pattern $P[1..N]$ being searched for was effectively placed at each consecutive position in the text $T[1..M]$ and a test for a match was applied. An obvious strategy for trying to improve on the efficiency of this basic algorithm is to try to move the pattern greater distances after each test for a match. The question that needs to be asked is what are the implications of this in terms of specifications?

The specification that we will start out with for this problem is one that captures the fact that there is no match at any of the first i positions in the text being searched.

$Q : 0 < N \leqslant M$
$R : (\forall q : 0 < q \leqslant i : \text{Nomatch}(q)) \land (i = M − N + 1 \text{ cor } \neg \text{Nomatch}(i + 1))$

where

$\text{Nomatch}(i) : (\exists r : 0 < r \leqslant N : P[r] \neq T[i + r − 1])$

Here we have chosen initially to use a slightly different specification to the one employed in the previous pattern-search problem.

Introducing a new free variable m into R we get the constructive specification

$$R_D : (\forall q : 0 < q \leqslant i : \text{Nomatch}(q)) \wedge (m = M - N + 1 \text{ cor } \neg\text{Nomatch}(i + 1))$$
$$\wedge\, i = m$$

A suitable variant function that follows from R_D is

$$t : m - i$$

and an initialization of free variables that can establish R_D is

$$i, m := 0, M - N + 1$$

The initialization leads to the identification of the invariant

$$P_D : (\forall q : 0 < q \leqslant i : \text{Nomatch}(q)) \wedge (m = M - N + 1 \text{ cor } \neg\text{Nomatch}(i + 1))$$
$$\wedge\, 0 \leqslant i \leqslant m \leqslant M - N + 1$$

Our basic loop structure may therefore take the form

```
i, m := 0, M − N + 1
do i ≠ m →
    "Increase i while maintaining P_D"
od
```

In our previous discussion of the search problem we made progress with deriving a solution by computing wp("$i := i + 1$", P_D). If we are to achieve greater efficiency we will need to look for a way of increasing i by larger amounts than one while still maintaining P_D.

Candidate values for increasing i by are 2, 3, ... N. An increase of i by more than N, the pattern length, is clearly out of the question because it will allow possible matches to be missed. To proceed, as a first step, let us investigate the consequences of increasing i by N, the search-pattern length. To do this we perform the calculation

$$wp("i := i + N", P_D)$$

This investigation tells us that the condition

$$R_1 : (\forall q : i < q \leqslant i + N : \text{Nomatch}(q))$$

is not implied by P_D. In other words the condition

$$\text{Nomatch}(i + 1) \wedge \text{Nomatch}(i + 2) \wedge ... \wedge \text{Nomatch}(i + N)$$

will need to be established before i can be increased by N if we are to guarantee that P_D is maintained. The most obvious way to establish this rather formidable condition would be to establish $\text{Nomatch}(i + 1)$ then

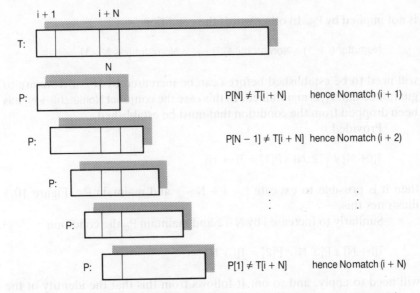

Figure 10.2   This figure shows that if $P[N] \neq T[i + N]$ and the character $T[i + N]$ is not the pattern $P[1..N]$ then there can be no possible matches for the pattern at the positions shown.

Nomatch($i + 2$) and so on, but this will leave us with our simple pattern-search algorithm. We can however take advantage of the fact that establishing a mismatch involves a weaker condition. If it happens that $T[i + N]$ is not equal to $P[N]$ and furthermore the stronger condition

$$T[i + N] \in P[1..N] \dagger$$

holds, then it is possible to execute "$i := i + N$" and maintain P_D. Figure 10.2 illustrates the situation.

Clearly it will not always be possible to execute the command $i := i + N$. To proceed further let us examine next the conditions under which it is possible to execute the command

$$i := i + N - 1$$

which will permit the second greatest rate of progress. To investigate the consequences of increasing i by $N - 1$ we perform the calculation

$$wp(\text{``}i := i + N - 1\text{''}, P_D)$$

This investigation tells us that the condition

$$R_2 : (\forall q : i < q \leqslant i + N - 1 : \text{Nomatch}(q))$$

† This notation indicates that the $T[i+N]$ character is not in the pattern $P[1..N]$.

is not implied by P_D. In other words the condition

$$\text{Nomatch}(i + 1) \wedge \text{Nomatch}(i + 2) \wedge ... \wedge \text{Nomatch}(i + N - 1)$$

will need to be established before i can be increased by $N - 1$ if we are to guarantee that P_D is maintained. In this case the conjunct $\text{Nomatch}(i + N)$ has been dropped from the condition that must be established.

Provided

$$T[i + N] \notin P[2..N] \wedge P[1] = T[i + N]$$

then it is possible to execute $i := i + N - 1$ and maintain P_D. Figure 10.3 illustrates this.

Similarly to increase i by $N - 2$ and maintain P_D the condition

$$T[i + N] \notin P[3..N] \wedge P[2] = T[i + N]$$

will need to apply, and so on. It follows from this that the identity of the character at $T[i + N]$ in relation to the pattern $P[1..N]$ will determine how far the pattern can be 'shifted' through the text after a test for a match.

Our next concern is to work out how tests of the form

$$T[i] \notin P[k..N] \text{ for } 1 \leq k \leq N \text{ and arbitrary i}$$

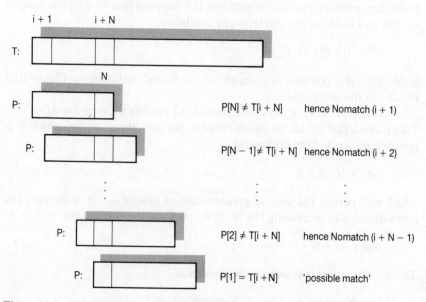

Figure 10.3   This figure shows that if $P[N] \neq T[i + N]$ and the character $T[i + N]$ is not in the pattern $P[2..N]$ and $P[1] = T[i + N]$ then there can be no possible matches at the positions shown.

can be easily and efficiently performed, for this represents the key to the gain in efficiency of the Boyer and Moore algorithm over the simple pattern-search algorithm. Because, in general, we are dealing with only relatively small character sets (for example the ASCII† character set has only 128 characters), the 'code value' of the text character being matched (e.g. $T[i]$) can be used to directly index into a skip-table $S[0..L]$ which tells us how far the pattern can be shifted for each character in the alphabet, including those characters in the search pattern. This skip-table is shown schematically in Figure 10.4.‡

It follows from our analysis that the shift values in the table $S[0..L]$ will need to satisfy the specification below for a search pattern $P[1..N]$.

$$Q : (\forall l : 0 \leqslant l < L : S[l] = N)$$
$$R_s : (\forall k : 1 \leqslant k < N : P[k] \notin P[k+1..N] \Rightarrow S[ORD(P[k])] = N - k)$$

This specification ensures that when a character occurs more than once in the search pattern it will have associated with it the smallest of its possible skip values. With this precaution it is not possible to 'miss' any potential matches.

This set-up for the skip-table allows us to 'shift' the pattern *forward* in all instances except when the current text character matches the character $P[N]$. In this instance it will not be possible to skip forward without first matching *backwards* to see if there is a complete match. To distinguish the $P[N]$ character in the table $S[0..L]$ it is convenient to make its skip value negative. As we will see later this simplifies the testing involved in the

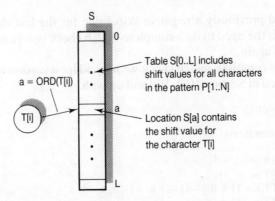

Figure 10.4   Shift table for complete character set. The ordinal value of a character determines its position in the table.

† ASCII is short for 'American Standard Code for Information Interchange'. This character code is extensively used by computer systems.
‡ The function ORD returns the ASCII value of its argument.

search. An implementation that can be used to build the skip-table and therefore establish R_s is

```
l := 0;
do l ≠ L → S[l] = N; l := l + 1 od;
{Q}
j := 1;
do j ≠ N →
    ascii := ORD(P[j]);
    S[ascii] := N − j;
    j := j + 1
od
{R_s}
ascii := ORD(P[j]);
S[ascii] := − S[ascii]
```

Examples of skip values for patterns are

Pattern (1)

P:	F	e	b	r	u	a	r	y
S:	7	6	5	1	3	2	1	−8

Pattern (2)

P:	c	h	a	r	a	c	t	e	r
S:	3	7	4	−5	4	3	2	1	−5

As mentioned previously a negative skip value for the last character in a pattern signals the need to do a complete-match check before attempting to skip forwards again.

For this complete-match check we may adapt a version of the simple match provided in Section 10.2. We end up with

```
Backmatch(i);
.
.   declarations
.
j := N; k := i; l := 1;
do l ≠ j →
    if T[k − 1] = P[j − 1] → j, k := j − 1, k − 1
    [] T[k − 1] ≠ P[j − 1] → l := j
    fi
od;
return(j = 1)    {if j = 1 then is a match}
end
```

Our next task is to examine how the skip-table may be used to conduct the Boyer and Moore pattern search.

To proceed with our derivation of the Boyer and Moore search that uses the skip-table S[0..L] it is convenient to redefine our postcondition slightly to take into account that the complete-match check is a 'backward' match rather than a forward match as used in Section 10.2. Incorporating this modification our search specification becomes

$$R : (\forall q : 1 \leqslant q < i : \text{Nomatch}(q)) \land (i > M \textbf{ cor } \neg\text{Nomatch}(i))$$

where

$$\text{Nomatch}(i) : 0 \leqslant i < N \textbf{ cor } (\exists r : 0 < r \leqslant N : T[i - N + r] \neq P[r])$$

Introducing a new free variable m into R we get the constructive specification

$$R_D : (\forall q : 1 \leqslant q < i : \text{Nomatch}(q)) \land (m > M \textbf{ cor } \neg\text{Nomatch}(i)) \land i = m$$

A suitable variant function that follows from R_D is

$$t : m - i$$

and an initialization of free variables that can establish R_D is

$$i, m := N, M + 1$$

The initialization i to N is appropriate because there cannot be a complete-match *terminating* at a value of q that is less than N, and so Nomatch(q) will be true for all q values less than N.

The initialization leads to the identification of the invariant:

$$P_D : (\forall q : 1 \leqslant q < i : \text{Nomatch}(q)) \land (m > M \textbf{ cor } \neg\text{Nomatch}(i))$$
$$\land N \leqslant i \leqslant m \leqslant M + N$$

Our basic loop structure may therefore take the form

```
i, m := N, M + 1;
do i < m →
    "Increase i while maintaining P_D"
od
```

We have previously determined that i can be increased by:

$$S[\text{ORD}(T[i])]$$

whenever the skip-table value is positive. Our implementation of the Boyer and Moore pattern searching algorithm may therefore take the form

```
Quicksearch(P, T, M, N);
    declarations
    i, m := N, M + 1;
    do i < m → {P_D}
      a := ORD(T[i]);
      if S[a] > 0 → i := i + S[a]
      [] S[a] < 0 → present := Backmatch(i);
        if present → m := i
        [] ¬present → i := i − S[a]
        fi
      fi
    od
    {R_D}
```

Several comments about this implementation are in order. The simple guard S[a] > 0 effectively establishes that there can be no possible matches of the text with P[1..N] terminating at positions

$$T[i], T[i + 1], ..., T[i + S[a] - 1]$$

which means that

$$Nomatch(i), Nomatch(i + 1), ..., Nomatch(i + S[a] - 1)$$

will all be true when S[a] > 0. It follows that i can safely be increased by S[a] and still maintain P_D. When, after an unsuccessful Backmatch it is necessary to shift forward again, it is necessary to take into account that the prevailing S[a] is negative and so i := i − S[a] must be executed to advance forward.

The order complexity for the average case approximates to $O(M/N)$. Typically when this algorithm is applied to English text it will need to examine only 10–20% of characters in the text. This is a significant improvement over the simple pattern search described in Section 10.3. Note that it is necessary to use a much more sophisticated back-matching algorithm to guarantee optimum performance from this algorithm in the general case. In this example we have seen how a weakest precondition calculation can sometimes be used as a vehicle for exploring a more efficient solution to a problem. What the weakest precondition calculation can do is identify the condition that must be satisfied; the challenge is then to discover an efficient way of satisfying the condition, as is done with the Boyer and Moore algorithm.

10.5   Text Editing

Inserting, deleting, and changing one component for another are frequently used text-processing operations. Here we are interested in providing specifications for each of these operations. In each case we will assume the edit operation has been preceded by a search of the text T[1..M] and that a match has been established at position i. The match at position i in the text is defined by

$$\text{Match}(i, P) : 1 \leqslant i \leqslant M - N + 1 \wedge (\forall j : 0 < j \leqslant N : P[j] = T[i + j - 1])$$

Single delete

Suppose we wish to delete P[1..N] from the original text T[1..M] to obtain the final text t[1..M − N](see Figure 10.5).

The required specification is

$$Q : \text{Match}(i, P) \wedge (\forall k : 0 < k \leqslant M : t[k] = T[k])$$
$$R : (\forall k : 0 < k < i : t[k] = T[k]) \wedge (\forall k : i + N \leqslant k \leqslant M : t[k - N] = T[k])$$

Details of the corresponding implementation to establish R are straightforward, and are therefore left as an exercise for the reader.

Single insert

Suppose we wish to insert the pattern P[1..N] into the text T[1..M] at position i. See Figure 10.6.

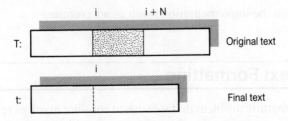

Figure 10.5   Deletion of a pattern from a text array.

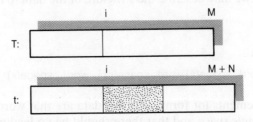

Figure 10.6   Insertion of a pattern into a text array.

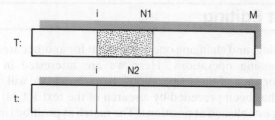

Figure 10.7 Replacement of one pattern by another in a text array.

The appropriate specification is

Q : (∀k : 0 < k ≤ M : t[k] = T[k]) ∧ 1 ≤ i ≤ M + 1
R : (∀k : 0 < k < i : t[k] = T[k]) ∧ (∀j : 0 < j ≤ N : t[i + j − 1] = P[j])
    ∧ (∀k : i + N ≤ k ≤ M + N : t[k] = T[k − N])

This implementation is also straightforward and therefore left as an exercise.

Single change

Here we are concerned with replacing one pattern P1[1..N1] at position i in text T[1..M] by a new pattern P2[1..N2]. Figure 10.7 illustrates this.

The corresponding specification is

Q : (∀k : 0 < k ≤ M : t[k] = T[k]) ∧ Match(i, P1)
R : (∀k : 0 < k < i : t[k] = T[k]) ∧ (∀j : 0 < j ≤ N2 : t[i + j − 1] = P2[j])
    ∧ (∀j : 1 ≤ j ≤ M − N1 : t[i + N2 + j − 1] = T[i + N1 + j − 1])

Once again the implementation is left as an exercise.

10.6 Text Formatting

The text formatting problem that we wish to consider involves re-formatting a line of text consisting of words each separated by one or more spaces. There may also be spaces preceding the first word and spaces trailing the last word. Informally we may describe the structure of the data to be processed as:

Unformatted line:

space(s) word$_1$ space(s) word$_2$ space(s) ... word$_M$ space(s)

The requirements for formatting this data are that words should be separated by a *single* space and that there should be no leading or trailing spaces.

Formatted line:

$$\text{word}_1 \text{ space word}_2 \text{ space ... space word}_M$$

Essentially the same problem has been discussed in detail by Dijkstra. It has been generalized here so that the data does not contain a sentinel. The other issues raised by Dijkstra's informal specification of the problem are peripheral and have therefore been ignored.

To proceed we will first try to specify the problem a little more formally. Unfortunately it is not straightforward to use the standard universal and existential quantifiers to specify problems of this type. We shall instead use EBNF. The following basic definitions are needed:

    <space> ::= ' '
    <char> ::= "a" | "b" | "c" ... | "z"
    <word> ::= <char> | <char> <word>

They can be used to build descriptions for unformatted and formatted lines of text:

$$\text{Q} : \text{U} = \{<\text{spaces}>\}[<\text{word}>\{[<\text{space}>]^+<\text{word}>\}^{M-1}] \{<\text{spaces}>\}$$
$$\text{R} : \text{f} = [<\text{word}>\{<\text{space}><\text{word}>\}^{M-1}]\wedge \text{form(f, U)}$$

where form(f, U) indicates that the word sequences for f and U are the same.

We could pursue sequence definitions for the problem based on sets and ordered pairs, but the present descriptions are sufficient. For the purpose of development we will assume the formatted output is simply written out. It is possible, with the specification given, for either or both of the text-lines to be empty. Using the array u[1..N] to store the unformatted line, an index j to reference the array, and a standard output for f, an appropriate initialization that can establish R is:

$S_0(X_0)$ Initialization $x_0 = \{u, j, f\}$† { Empty line }

    j := 0; u := U;
    if j = N → skip {R established}
    [] j ≠ N → {Q₁} s₁(x₁) {R}
    fi

The initialization guarantees to establish the base invariant:

$$P_0 : \text{u}[1..j] = \{<\text{spaces}>\}^0[<\text{word}>...]^0\{<\text{spaces}>\}^0 \wedge \text{f} = [<\text{word}>...]^0$$
$$\wedge \text{form(f,u)}$$

---

† f can be thought of as having been assigned to the empty output.

To make progress we are interested in making a new refinement that will establish R by changing the smallest subset of free variables. Just changing j while holding f constant will be sufficient to establish R provided the input consists *only* of one or more spaces. A loop can be used to change j under these conditions. In making this next refinement we will need to accommodate the possibility that simply consuming spaces may not always be sufficient to establish R. The base invariant needs to be weakened to:

$$P\,1: u[1..j] = \{<\text{space}>\}\ [<\text{word}>...]^o\{<\text{space}>\}^o \wedge \text{form}(f,U)$$

The precondition Q_1 for which R will be established is:

$$Q_1 : u[1..j] = \{<\text{space}>\}$$

Employing forced termination to handle the encounter with a non-space we get

$S_1(X_1)$ First refinement $x_1 = \{j, n\}$ { Zero words }

```
j := 0; u := U;
if j = N → skip
[] j ≠ N →
  n := N;
  repeat {P₁}
    if u_{j+1} = space → j := j + 1
    [] u_{j+1} ≠ space → n := j
    fi
  until j = n;
  if j = N → skip {R established}
  [] j ≠ N → {Q₂} s₂(x₂) {R}
  fi
fi
```

For convenience we will replace the implementation for this most recent refinement by a procedure getspaces. In our implementation of getspaces we will replace the **if...repeat...** by a **do...od** loop. We can then write what is essentially $S_1(X_1)$ as:

```
j := 0; u := U;
getspaces(u, j, N);
if j = N → skip {R established}
[] j ≠ N → {Q₂} s₂(x₂) {R}
fi
```

and

$$P_1 \wedge j = N \wedge j = n \Rightarrow R$$
$$P_1 \wedge j \neq N \wedge j = n \equiv Q_2$$

Interestingly, this most recent refinement has enlarged the set of initial states for which R is established, *without* enlarging the set of final states.

To establish R when Q_2 applies it will be necessary to deal with at least one word. In making this refinement we propose the use of a procedure that consumes characters of a word from u and writes them out until either a space is encountered or the end of the unformatted line is reached. An implementation for this procedure called getword is

```
getword(u[1..N]:char; var k:int; N:int);
var n : int;
  n := N;
  do k ≠ n →
    if u_{k+1} ≠ space → write(u_{k+1}); k := k + 1
    [] u_{k+1} = space → n := k
    fi
  od
end
```

In making this refinement the variable f must effectively be allowed to change as output is produced. Weakening P_1 accordingly we get

$$P_2 : u = U \wedge u[1..j] = \{<\text{space}>\} \, [\, <\text{word}> \,] \wedge f = [<\text{word}>]$$
$$\wedge \, f = \text{form}(f,U)$$

Making the refinement that uses getword we get:

$S_2(X_2)$ Second refinement $x_2 = \{j, f\}$ { One word }

```
j := 0; u := U; space := ' ';
getspaces(u, j, N);
if j = N → skip
[] j ≠ N →
  getword(u, j, N);
  if j = N → skip {R established}
  [] j ≠ N → {Q_3} s_3(x_3) {R}
  fi
fi
```

The most recent refinement will establish R provided there is at most one word present. To establish R when Q_3 applies we again seek to change the smallest subset of variables. Simply changing j while spaces are encountered will be sufficient to establish R provided j can be increased to N. As with $s_1(x_1)$ this will correspond to enlarging the set of initial states for which R is established without enlarging the set of final states (that is f will be kept constant). Making this new refinement using getspaces we get:

$S_3(X_3)$ Third refinement $x_3 = \{j\}$† { One word at most }

```
j := 0; u := U; space := ' ';
getspaces(u, j, N);
if j = N → skip
[] j ≠ N →
    getword(u, j, N);
    getspaces(u, j, N);
    if j = N → skip {R established}
    [] j ≠ N → {Q_4} s_4(x_4) {R}
    fi
fi
```

$$P_3 : u = U \wedge u[1..j] = \{<space>\} [<word>] \{<space>\} \wedge f = [<word>]$$
$$\wedge f = form(f,U)$$

The mechanism $S_3(X_3)$ will establish R for all unformatted data sets consisting of at most one word, where there is the possibility of either or both leading and trailing spaces.

To establish R when Q_4 applies we need to generalize our mechanism to handle one or more words. Q_4 indicates that the start of another word has been encountered. Recalling the form for R, this new word cannot be written until after a space is written out. Writing a space must therefore be the first part of our next refinement.

With the space written out we process the next (second) word. The procedure getword may be used for this purpose. The strongest precondition corresponding to an expansion of the set of initial states for which R is established involves processing at most *two* input words.

$$P_4 : \quad u = U \wedge u[1..j] = \{<spaces>\} [<word> \{ [<space>] \,^+ <word>\} \,^i]$$
$$\{<spaces>\} \wedge f = [<word> \{ <space> <word> \} \,^i]$$
$$\wedge form (f, U) \wedge 0 \leq i \leq 1$$

The accompanying implementation is:

$S_4 (X_4)$ Fourth refinement $x_4 = \{j, f\}$ { Zero, one, or two words }

```
j := 0; u := U;
getspaces(u, j, N);
if j ≠ N then
    getword(u, j, N);
    getspaces(u, j, N);
    if j ≠ N →
        write(space);
        getword(u, j, N);
        getspaces(u, j, N);
        if j = N → skip {R established}
        [] j ≠ N → {Q_5} S_5(x_5){R}
        fi
    [] j = N → skip
    fi
fi
```

† In making this refinement we have put getspaces directly after getword at the expense of making an extra guard test in some cases.

To handle more than two words P_4 will need to be weakened by dropping the upper limit of 1 on i. We get

$$P_5 : u = U \wedge u[1..j] = \{<spaces>\} [<word> \{ [<space>] + <word>\} ^i]$$
$$\{<spaces>\} \wedge f = [<word> \{ <space> <word> \}^i]$$
$$\wedge \text{ form } (f, U) \wedge 0 \leqslant i$$

For this next refinement a loop or recursive call on the refinement $s_4(x_4)$ can be made. The loop implementation is

$S_5(X_5)$ Fifth refinement $x_5 = \{j, f\}$ {Zero, one, two, or more words}

```
j := 0; u := U;
getspaces(u, j, N);
if j ≠ N then
    getword(u, j, N);
    getspaces(u, j, N);
    do j ≠ N → {P₄}
        write(space);
        getword(u, j, N);
        getspaces(u, j, N)
    od
fi
```

Two things complicate the structure of this problem, the need to avoid writing a space after the last word and the possibility that there can be trailing spaces in the unformatted line after the last word.

A textually simpler although more inefficient solution to this problem would follow from making a different composition after $S_3(X_3)$ was constructed. We would then get

```
j := 0; u := U;
getspaces(u, j, N);
do j ≠ N →
    getword(u, j, N);
    getspaces(u, j, N);
    if j ≠ N then write(space) fi
od
```

This seemingly more attractive solution has the defect of having to include an extra guard to protect against writing the space after the last word. The guard in **if** j − N **then** ... is always false except on the *last* iteration of the loop. The preceding solution represents a way of avoiding the extra guard testing. Essentially the same problem arises with pivot partitioning. The structure of the solution can remain the same if the unformatted line is being read from a text file if the techniques used in Section 12.4 on forced termination are employed.

It is interesting to recap the stages in the development for this problem. They were as follows:

(1)   Empty unformatted line and empty formatted line.

(2)   One or more input spaces and empty formatted line.

(3)   Leading input spaces, one input word and one output word.

(4)   The configuration in (3) plus trailing input spaces after first word.

(5)   The configuration in (4) plus next input word and trailing spaces consumed and single space followed by next word output.

(6)   Repeated application of the invariant extension made in step (5).

The underlying principle that has guided the derivation of this program has been the idea of making successive refinements that establish the postcondition for progressively weaker preconditions. In going from one refinement to the next we have chosen to weaken the precondition for which R is established by the minimum amount that will allow progress. This keeps refinements as simple as possible, while achieving the best match between the program control structure and the data structure. In our implementation the control structure matches both the structure of the input data and the structure of the output data.

For the output the first word is treated specially while for all other words there is repetition over the structure:

{<space>}<word>

This provides the control structure/data structure match for the output.

For the processing of the input, after treating the leading spaces specially, along with the first word, there is then repetition over the structure:

<word>{<space>}

This provides the control structure/data structure match for the input.

We will finish off this section by providing the implementation that is obtained by making a recursive refinement for the fourth refinement.

S$_4$(X$_4$) Fourth refinement $x_4 = \{j, f\}$ { Zero or more words }

```
j := 0; u := U;
getspaces(u, j, N);
if j ≠ N then
   nextword:
      getword(u, j, N);
      getspaces(u, j, N); {P₄}
      if j ≠ N then write(space); nextword fi
fi
```

10.7 Comment Skipping

In some implementations of the programming language Pascal comments are parenthesized using left and right parentheses in combination with an asterisk, that is

(* a Pascal comment *)

where '(*' signals the start of the comment and '*)' signals the end of the comment. In processing Pascal programs it is frequently necessary simply to ignore any comments in the program text. In developing a general mechanism to skip comments it is very easy to get into trouble if considerable care is not taken. The difficulty arises because it is possible for asterisks and right parentheses to appear in the body of the comment.

A specification for the problem is

Q : IN = <'(*'> { {<NONAST>} [< AST>]}^{M} [<')'>] <EOF> ∧ M ⩾ 0
R : EOF ∧ out = <"BAD COMMENT" > | out = <"GOOD COMMENT">

where <NONAST> refers to any character other than an asterisk and
< AST> ::= '*'. EOF refers to the end-of-file.

This specification takes into account that there may not be a properly formed comment that begins with '(*'. Since the task of recognizing '(*', the start of a comment, is purely clerical we will begin our development for this problem assuming this character pair has been recognized. For this problem, the precondition (or data) has considerable structure whereas there is little associated with the postcondition that can help us. In making refinements to solve the problem we will therefore try to take advantage of the precondition's structure in making our refinements by forming the conjunction of the precondition with the postcondition to construct a stronger postcondition. We will start by making refinements that establish the postcondition for stronger preconditions than the one given precondition.

A state-space extension on the Q-component of $Q \wedge R$ is needed to make an initialization that can establish both the precondition and the postcondition. Including this transformation we get

$$R_c : IN = <'('*'> \{ \{<NONAST>\} [< AST>] \}^i [<')'>] [<EOF>]$$
$$\wedge M \geq 0 \wedge i = M \wedge R$$

The initialization of i must be indirect because what we are really testing for is whether we are at the end of the file IN. To do this we introduce another free variable j.

$S_0(X_0)$ Initialization

```
{i := 0}; j := eof(IN); N := TRUE †
if j = N → skip {R can be established}
[] j ≠ N → {Q₁} s₁(x₁) {R}
fi
```

The initialization of this new postcondition guarantees to establish the base invariant

$$P_0 : i = 0 \wedge j = eof(IN) \wedge IN = <'('*'> \{ \{<NONAST>\} [< AST>] \}^i \wedge M \geq 0$$

To make progress when Q_1 applies we need to effectively increase i until it reaches M. In the first instance we want to increase i just by 1 (i.e. $i := i + 1$). Weakening P_0 to allow i to increase we get

$$P_1 : i \geq 0 \wedge j = eof(IN) \wedge IN = <'('*'> \{ \{<NONAST>\} [< AST>] \}^i \wedge M \geq 0$$

Now we can compute wp("$i := i + 1$", P_1). When we do this we get

$$wp("i := i + 1", P_1) \equiv i + 1 \geq 0 \wedge j = eof(IN) \wedge$$
$$IN = <'('*'>\{ \{<NONAST>\}[<AST>]\}^{i+1} \wedge M \geq 0$$

Examining this carefully we find that

$$\{ \{<NONAST>^P [< AST>] \}^1$$

is not implied by P_1. It will need to be consumed before we can execute $i := i + 1$. Once again it is not easy to make a suitable initialization. We can overcome the problem by introducing a new free variable k. We then get

$$P_2 : i \geq 0 \wedge k \geq 0 \wedge j = eof(IN) \wedge IN = <'('*'>\{\{<NONAST>\}^k[< AST>] \}^i$$
$$\wedge M \geq 0$$

---

† The variable i is not needed in the implementation but is needed to characterize the base invariant and its derivatives.

For our next refinement (assuming the initialization of k has been done) we can seek to execute effectively $k := k + 1$. The precondition for doing this is that the next input character, if there is one, is not an asterisk. Again the variable k is needed only for development and not in the actual implementation. A loop can be used to read the non-asterisk characters. Termination of this loop should be forced if an asterisk is encountered. Writing this mechanism as a procedure we get

```
getnonast(in: TEXT; var j: boolean; N: boolean);
var n: boolean;
  n := N;
  do j ≠ n →
    if in↑ ≠ AST → get(in); j := eof(in)
    [] in↑ = AST → n := j
    fi
  od
```

We can now write our first refinement. In making this refinement, since it has the guard $j = n$, we will drop the guard used in the initialization.

$S_1(X_1)$ First refinement

```
{Q: IN = <(*>}
j := eof(IN); N := true;
getnonast(IN, j, N);
if j = N → skip {R can be established}
[] j ≠ N → {Q₂} s₂(x₂) {R}
fi
```

This refinement guarantees to establish

$$R_2 : i \geqslant 0 \wedge k \geqslant 0 \wedge j = eof(IN) \wedge IN = <'(*'>\{ \{<NONAST>\}^k\}^1 \wedge M \geqslant 0$$

If $j - N$ applies then the next character to be consumed in the input will be an asterisk. To establish R when Q_2 applies a first step will therefore be to consume the asterisk (i.e. with get(IN); j := eof(IN)). This can be followed directly by a check for a ')' to complete the comment if $j \neq N$. If however the next character after the asterisk is not a ')' we can clearly make a recursive call to the mechanism for processing non-asterisks as our next refinement. Combining these two refinements into one yields

S₃(X₃) Second and third refinements

```
j := eof(IN); N := TRUE;
NEXT:
    getnonast(IN, j, N);
    if j ≠ N then
        get(IN); j := eof(IN);
        if j ≠ N then if IN↑ ≠ ')' then NEXT fi fi
    fi;
    if j = N → writeln(' BAD COMMENT')
    [] j ≠ N → writeln(' GOOD COMMENT')
    fi
```

The most recent refinements extend the range of i . The ')' on the end of a valid comment is not consumed by the mechanism.

To solve this problem it has been necessary to exploit the structure in the input data. We have done this by taking the conjunction of the precondition with the postcondition to obtain a new postcondition that is useful to assist with the derivation. Many data-processing problems and recognition problems that involve the processing of structured data can be fruitfully handled by starting out with a $Q \land R$ transformation.

SUMMARY

- Principal text-processing operations are matching one pattern against another, searching for some pattern, and changing or editing text in some way.

- Searching of text is a sequential process involving the examination of a stream of characters.

- The simplest form of text searching requires the examination of each character in the text until a match is made.

- A weakest precondition calculation can be used to help derive an efficient text searching algorithm – the Boyer and Moore algorithm. The Boyer and Moore text-searching algorithm will, on average, need to examine only a small percentage of the characters in the text.

- Reformatting of text shows the value of developing programs with control structures which match the structure of the data.

- The development of a program for skipping comments in Pascal programs is an interesting problem in that refinements are guided by making transformations on the precondition rather than the postcondition. A number of recognition problems share this characteristic.

■ **EXERCISE 10   Text-processing derivations**

1. Specify and derive an implementation that deletes leading blanks from a line of text.

2. Given a person's name which consists of a sequence of initials followed by a surname, for example

     J. S. Bach

   process the line so as to write out only the surname. Specify and derive an implementation that matches the structure of the data. Note the name may have one or more initials.

3. A common problem that occurs when entering text is that words are mistakenly repeated, for example

     "This text text contains a repeating word"

   Design a program that detects such repetitions.

4. Design a program that deletes all words of less than four characters from a line of text A[1 .. N].

5. Devise a mechanism that reads a line of text of unknown length and prints out only the last n characters.

Bibliography

Boyer R.S., and J.S. Moore (1977), A fast string searching algorithm, *Comm. ACM,* **20,** 762-72.

Dijkstra E.W. (1972), *Structured Programming,* Academic Press, London.

Dromey R.G., (1982), *How To Solve It By Computer,* Prentice-Hall, London.

Floyd R.W., (1979), The paradigms of programming, *Comm. ACM,* **22**(8), 455–60.

Knuth D.E., J.H. Morris, and V.R. Pratt (1977), Fast pattern matching in strings, *SIAM J. Comp,* **6,** 322–50.

Chapter 11
Sequential Problems

The essence of programming lies in finding the right structure.

N. Wirth

11.1 Introduction
11.2 The Majority-element Problem
11.3 The Maximum Sum-section Problem
11.4 The Stores-movement Problem
11.5 Two-way Merge
11.6 Sequential File Update
11.7 The Telegrams Analysis Problem
Summary
Exercise
Bibliography

11.1   Introduction

The most common way of storing and processing data is sequentially. To process data sequentially we must move from one data element to the next carrying out any necessary computations in the process. Sequential data very often has conditions and structure associated with it. In deriving programs to process such data it is important to be able to exploit such information.

Our plan in this chapter is to consider several problems where structure and specifications are important in guiding the derivation of programs. With the first two problems we will show how the strategy of solving a problem with a weaker postcondition is employed initially to get a foothold on the problem. The solutions that evolve using this strategy are superior to others that are usually proposed when these problems are tackled head-on.

497

The third problem considered, the stores-movement problem, provides a very clear illustration of the technique of combining the precondition with the postcondition in order to create a stronger invariant that allows us to exploit the structure in the input data in deriving the program. The fourth and fifth problems illustrate the importance of taking advantage of order in processing sequential data. They also pose some interesting questions about specification and decomposition. The last problem, the telegrams analysis problem, has been included because it represents a more challenging problem that can be tackled systematically by making a sequence of refinements each of which expands the set of initial states for which the postcondition can be established.

11.2   The Majority-element Problem

The majority-element problem is an interesting and challenging problem that underlines the importance of

- providing a detailed formal specification;
- establishing a weaker sub-goal before solving the original problem.

To solve the problem we must determine *whether* there is an element in a fixed array A[1..N] that is in the majority. For an element to be in the majority it must occur *more than* 50% of the time. The obvious way to solve this problem is to sort the array and then look for the longest plateau.

Fortunately there is a much more elegant way to solve the problem, which we will show can be discovered by formal derivation. An obvious specification for the majority property is

$$R_1 : c \geq N \textbf{ div } 2 + 1$$

where c is the number of times the majority element occurs. This is a weak formal specification, as it does not define what c represents. Strengthening the specification R_1 by including a definition for c we get

$$R_2 : 1 \leq p \leq N \wedge x = A_p \wedge c = \#(j : 0 < j \leq N : x = A_j) \wedge c \geq N \textbf{ div } 2 + 1$$

This specification can be strengthened further by identifying c as the count of the element that occurs most in the array. Including this additional qualification we get

$$R_3 : 1 \leq p \leq N \wedge x = A_p \wedge c = \#(j : 0 < j \leq N : x = A_j) \wedge c \geq N \textbf{ div } 2 + 1$$
$$\wedge (\forall k : 0 < k \leq N : c \geq \#(j : 0 < j \leq N : A_j = A_k))$$

Unfortunately the specification R_3 is too strong because there is no guarantee that there is a majority element in the array. To overcome this problem we could delete the conjunct

$$c \geqslant N \text{ div } 2 + 1$$

There is, however, a more attractive way to weaken R_3 that retains its original form (as a general rule, transformations that conserve the form of a specification appear to be more useful). We do this by introducing a new free variable e that satisfies the relation

$$e \geqslant c$$

Making this weakening transformation we get

$$R_w : 1 \leqslant p \leqslant N \wedge x = A_p \wedge e \geqslant \#(j : 0 < j \leqslant N : x = A_j) \wedge e \geqslant N \text{ div } 2 + 1$$
$$\wedge (\forall k : 0 < k \leqslant N : e \geqslant \#(j : 0 < j \leqslant N : A_j = A_k)) \wedge e \geqslant c$$

where

$$R_3 \Rightarrow R_w$$

The specification R_w no longer demands that there is a majority element present. The obvious question to ask next is what role does the variable e have? If e is to satisfy the relation $e \geqslant N \text{ div } 2 + 1$ it can only serve as an *upper limit* on the number of occurrences of the element x that occurs most in the array. Assuming this role for e we will attempt to solve the problem by first establishing a weaker sub-goal than R_w. Having established R_w the task remaining is to check whether the x identified is the majority element.

An initialization of p, x, and e that can establish R_w directly which is also easy to check is hard to find. We therefore introduce a new free variable i in place of N to obtain

$$R_D : 1 \leqslant p \leqslant i \wedge x = A_p \wedge e \geqslant \#(j : 0 < j \leqslant i : x = A_j) \wedge e \geqslant i \text{ div } 2 + 1$$
$$\wedge (\forall k : 0 < k \leqslant i : e \geqslant \#(j : 0 < j \leqslant i : A_j = A_k)) \wedge e \geqslant c \wedge i = N$$

An initialization of free variables that can establish R_D is

$$i, e, x := 1, 1, A_1 \qquad \text{(p is not needed in the implementation)}$$

The initialization identifies the invariant as

$$P_D : 1 \leqslant p \leqslant i \wedge x = A_p \wedge e \geqslant \#(j : 0 < j \leqslant i : x = A_j) \wedge e \geqslant i \text{ div } 2 + 1$$
$$\wedge (\forall k : 0 < k \leqslant i : e \geqslant \#(j : 0 < j \leqslant i : A_j = A_k)) \wedge e \geqslant c \wedge 1 \leqslant i \leqslant N$$

Our basic strategy for establishing R_D will therefore be to increase i under the invariance of P_D. The variant function that follows from R_D is

$$t : N - i$$

and we have

$$i, e, x := 1, 1, A_1;$$
$$\textbf{do } i \neq N \rightarrow \{P_D\}$$
"Increase i under the invariance of P_D"
$$\textbf{od}$$
$$\{R_D\}$$

To proceed we may investigate

$$wp("i := i + 1", P_D)$$

This investigation reveals that the following conditions (in addition to $1 \leq i + 1 \leq N$) are not implied by the weakest precondition:

$$e \geq \#(j : 0 < j \leq i : x = A_j) \wedge e \geq \#(j : 0 < j \leq i + 1 : A_{i+1} = A_j)$$
$$\wedge e \geq (i + 1) \textbf{ div } 2 + 1$$

Now assuming P_D, and then executing "$i := i + 1$", there is no guarantee that these conjuncts will hold, but somehow P_D must be maintained when i is increased.

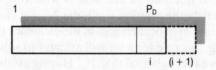

Two situations are possible:

(1) $A_{i+1} = x$
(2) $A_{i+1} \neq x$

In case (1) we can safely execute

$$i, e := i + 1, e + 1$$

and guarantee to maintain P_D. In the second case things are more complicated. If e, the upper bound on the number of occurrences of x, satisfies

$$e \geq (i + 1) \textbf{ div } 2 + 1$$

then the command

$$i := i + 1$$

alone can be executed and P_D will still be preserved. The difficult situation to handle is where increasing i forces the condition

$$e < (i + 1) \textbf{ div } 2 + 1$$

The only inference we can draw from this situation is that the x that satisfied P_D at position i is no longer a possible majority element at the present stage of the computation. This situation leaves two questions open

(1)   how do we decide on a new possible majority element?

(2)   what estimate do we place on its number of occurrences?

The only choice for x has to be A_{i+1} and if it satisfies P_D it will need to have occurred (i + 1) **div** 2 + 1 times in the first (i + 1) positions in the array. Incorporating these refinements we get the implementation

```
i, e, x := 1, 1, A₁;
do i ≠ N → {P_D}
   if A_{i+1} = x → i, e := i + 1, e + 1
   [] A_{i+1} ≠ x →
      if e ≥ (i + 1)div 2 + 1 → i := i + 1
      [] e < (i + 1) div 2 + 1 → i, e, x := i + 1, (i + 1) div 2 + 1, A_{i+1}
      fi
   fi
od
{R_D}
```

Once R_D is established, x will hold the value of the *only possible* majority element. It is then only a matter of counting how many times x occurs in the array to decide whether or not x is really a majority element, and thereby establish R_3. This detail of the implementation is left as an exercise for the reader. The overall algorithm is linear in its behaviour and therefore much more efficient than the sorting strategy for solving the problem. What has been important about this example is that it has shown the value of first establishing a weaker sub-goal. It has also shown the value of focusing on maintaining an invariant as a means for uncovering the solution to an otherwise difficult problem.

11.3   The Maximum Sum-section Problem

The maximum sum-section problem lends itself to solution via a number of computational strategies that are widely different in their relative efficiencies. Here we are interested in showing how formal specifications can guide us to a simple and efficient solution. To solve this problem the data must be viewed and processed as a sequence.

Informally the problem may be stated as follows. Given a fixed array of numbers (they may be positive or negative) it is required to find the contiguous subsection A[l + 1..u] of the array A[1..N] which has the maximum sum m for its elements. More formally we have

$$R : 0 \leqslant l \leqslant u \leqslant N \wedge m = \Sigma(A_j : l < j \leqslant u)$$
$$\wedge (\forall p : 0 \leqslant p \leqslant N : (\forall q : p < q \leqslant N : m \geqslant \Sigma(A_k : p < k \leqslant q)))$$

An example is

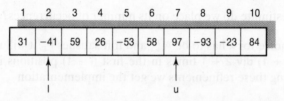

The variable l identifies the array position *immediately before* the start of the maximum sum-section. This specification device has been used to allow us to characterize sum-sections with an empty range (i.e. when l = u).

The difficulty when considering this problem is seeimg how to manage systematically the changes in the l and u variables while trying to identify the maximum sum-section. One approach in a situation like this is to *fix* one of the variables and investigate changing the other. In this case we could fix l, the lower limit on the sum-section, and at the same time try to increase u, the upper limit for the sum-section.

The impact of *fixing* l corresponds to dropping the quantifier over all p. The resulting weaker specification for one p value, that is, l, then becomes

$$R_1 : 0 \leqslant l \leqslant u \leqslant N \wedge m = \Sigma(A_j : l < j \leqslant u)$$
$$\wedge (\forall q : l < q \leqslant N : m \geqslant \Sigma(A_k : l < k \leqslant q))$$

Our strategy will be to try to establish this sub-goal R_1 before establishing the stronger postcondition R. This specification suggests that if all the elements were negative the maximum section would be the empty sum-section (i.e. we would have l = u).

A further consideration is the question what would happen should the sum for a contiguous subsection ever become negative? If this situation does arise the summing process will be terminated because the elements that force the sum-section to become negative will never be included in the maximum sum-section. Making this refinement to the specification we get

$$R_2 : 0 \leqslant l \leqslant u \leqslant N \wedge m = \Sigma(A_j : l < j \leqslant u)$$
$$\wedge (\forall q : l < q \leqslant i : m \geqslant \Sigma(A_k : l < k \leqslant q))$$
$$\wedge \Sigma(A_k : l < k \leqslant i) \geqslant 0 \wedge (i = N \text{ cor } \Sigma(A_k : l < k \leqslant i + 1) < 0)$$

It is convenient to rewrite this specification using a shorthand informal notation where

$$\Sigma A[1..p] \equiv \Sigma(A_j : 0 < j \leqslant p)$$

Making these substitutions we get

$$R_3 : 0 \leqslant l \leqslant u \leqslant N \wedge m = \Sigma A[l + 1..u] \wedge (\forall q : l < q \leqslant i : m \geqslant \Sigma A[l + 1..q])$$
$$\wedge \Sigma A[l + 1..i] \geqslant 0 \wedge (i = N \text{ cor } \Sigma A[l + 1..i + 1] < 0)$$

In order to extract the strongest invariant we can from R_3 we will introduce a new free variable n into the last conjunct to obtain

$$R_D : 0 \leqslant l \leqslant u \leqslant N \wedge m = \Sigma A[l + 1..u] \wedge (\forall q : l < q \leqslant i : m \geqslant \Sigma A[l + 1..q])$$
$$\wedge \Sigma A[l + 1..i] \geqslant 0 \wedge (n = N \text{ cor } \Sigma A[l + 1..i + 1] < 0) \wedge i = n$$

A suitable initialization of free variables that can establish R_D is

$$l, u, m, i, n := 0, 0, 0, 0, N;$$

This initialization will be sufficient to establish R_D provided the condition $i = n$ holds. If this condition does not hold a further refinement is needed. The initialization identifies the following invariant:

$$P_D : 0 \leqslant l \leqslant u \leqslant N \wedge m = \Sigma A[l + 1..u] \wedge (\forall q : l < q \leqslant i : m \geqslant \Sigma A[l + 1..q])$$
$$\wedge \Sigma A[l + 1..i] \geqslant 0 \wedge (n = N \text{ cor } \Sigma A[l + 1..i + 1] < 0) \wedge 0 \leqslant i \leqslant n \leqslant N$$

and the variant function that follows from R_D is

$$t : n - i$$

Our basic strategy for establishing R_D will involve increasing i under the invariance of P_D, that is

```
l, u, m, i, n := 0, 0, 0, 0, N;
do i ≠ n → { P_D }
    "Increase i under the invariance of P_D"
od
{ R_D }
```

To proceed we may investigate

$$wp("i := i + 1", P_D)$$

This investigation reveals that the two conditions

$$m \geqslant \Sigma A[l + 1..i + 1]$$

and

$$\Sigma A[l + 1..i + 1] \geq 0$$

are both not implied by P_D. They will both need to be guaranteed before it would be possible to execute $i := i + 1$ and maintain P_D.

To assist with the sequential processing of the array it is useful to introduce a new free variable s in place of $\Sigma A[l + 1..i]$. (The variable s will need to be given the initial value of 0.)

Making this replacement the invariant becomes

$$P'_D : 0 \leq l \leq u \leq N \wedge m = \Sigma A[l + 1..u] \wedge (\forall q : l < q \leq i : m \geq \Sigma A[l + 1..q])$$
$$\wedge s \geq 0 \wedge (n = N \textbf{ cor } s + A_{i+1} < 0) \wedge s = \Sigma A[l + 1..i] \wedge 0 \leq i \leq n \leq N$$

The condition involving m then becomes

$$m \geq s + A_{i+1} \tag{1}$$

and the condition involving s becomes

$$s + A_{i+1} \geq 0 \tag{2}$$

To make the refinement for increasing i or decreasing n we need to take into account four possible situations because both (1) and (2) can be either true or false.

In the situation where the condition $s + A_{i+1} < 0$ applies the loop must be forced to terminate. This can be achieved by executing the command

$$n := i$$

There is no need to consider updating m or u in this case because A_{i+1} cannot contribute to the maximum sum-section.

The situation is different when $s + A_{i+1} \geq 0$ applies. Then both possibilities for (1) must be taken into account. To maintain the invariant P_D for $m < s + A_{i+1}$ the necessary command is

$$u, m, s, i := i + 1, s + A_{i+1}, s + A_{i+1}, i + 1$$

When $m \geq s + A_{i+1}$ applies to maintain P_D, only s and i will need to be updated, that is

$$i, s := i + 1, s + A_{i+1}$$

Putting these components together we get

```
Sum-Section (A, i, s, m, u, N);
.
.   declarations
.
    u, m, s, n := i, 0, 0, 0, N;
    do i ≠ n → { P_D }
       if s + A_{i+1} < 0 → n := i
       [] s + A_{i+1} ≥ 0 →
          if m ≥ s + A_{i+1} → i, s := i + 1, s + A_{i+1}
          [] m < s + A_{i+1} → u, m, s, i := i + 1, s + A_{i+1}, s + A_{i+1}, i + 1
          fi
       fi
    od
    { R_D }
end
```

The question that now arises is, having developed a mechanism to establish the weaker sub-goal R_D, how can this be used to help solve the original problem when termination occurs with i = n but i ≠ N? Recapping the situation, we have derived a mechanism for establishing the postcondition R for the case where l is fixed (i.e. l = 0).

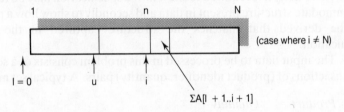

$$i ≠ N ∧ ΣA[l + 1..i+1] < 0$$

When this mechanism terminates with

$$i ≠ N ∧ ΣA[l + 1..i+1] < 0$$

it suggests three things:

- A new contiguous sum-section defined by the tuple (m1, l1, u1, s) will need to be started and extended until s again goes negative.

- The current maximum sum-section defined by the tuple (m, l, u) will need to be compared with subsequent contiguous sum-sections (m1, l1, u1) and updated if the latter are greater.

- The mechanism derived for a sum-section with a fixed lower limit l, can be used to identify subsequent contiguous sum-sections. The new invariant P_D'' for this mechanism will have the same form as P_D' except that l1 replaces l, u1 replaces u, and m1 replaces m.

Making these refinements the implementation to establish R may take the form:

```
i, m, l, u := 0, 0, 0, 0;
do i ≠ N →
    m1, l1, u1, s := 0, i, i, 0;
    Sum-section (A, i, s, m1, u1, N);
    if i ≠ N ∧ m1 > m → m, l, u, i := m1, l1, u1, i + 1
    [] i = N ∧ m1 > m → m, l, u := m1, l1, u1
    [] i ≠ N ∧ m1 ≤ m → i := i + 1
    fi
od
```

Here solving a weaker auxiliary problem has led us via a straightforward path to the solution of the original problem. Attempting to solve this problem without fixing the lower limit is very difficult.

11.4   The Stores-movement Problem

The stores-movement problem is well known in data-processing circles. It has been used by several authors to discuss the issue of matching program control structure and data structure. This problem is discussed with two intentions. Firstly it is required to show how a specification may be refined to accommodate structure present in data and secondly to show how a program can be derived that matches the structure captured in the refined specification.

The input data to be processed in this problem consists of a sequence of transactions of (product identifier, quantity) pairs. A typical set might be:

Product	Quantity		
product1	23	↑	
product1	29	.	
product1	48		all transactions for product1
product1	10	.	
product1	4	↓	
product2	33	↑	
product2	17		all transactions for product 2

To process this data a second sequence of (product identifier, sum) pairs needs to be produced. The first pair in this output sequence for the above data is

(product1, 114)

where 114 is the sum of all the quantities for product1.

If there are M transactions t in the input sequence T a TDSD description (see Section 3.6.3) of the input data is

$$Q : T = Seq^M(t)$$

where the ith transaction t_i is of the form

(p, q)

where

p is the product identifier
q is the associated quantity for the transaction

We will use the notation

$t_i(p)$ to refer to the product identifier of the ith transaction

$t_i(q)$ to refer to the quantity associated with the ith transaction

For the output sequence b if there are N different products, there will be N transactions u in that sequence, that is

$$R : b = Seq^N(u)$$

where the jth output transaction u_j is of the form

(prod,s)

where

prod is the product identifier
s is the sum of all quantities for the product

The specification (Q,R) is deficient in several ways. Most importantly it does not capture the structured view of the data. It will therefore need to be strengthened in this regard. A definition of s in terms of its relation to the input transactions is also needed.

Strengthening our description of the input sequence to reflect the top-down structured view of the data, we get

$$Q_c : T = Seq^M(t) \wedge T = Seq^N(g)$$

This description represents T as both a sequence of transactions, and as a sequence of product groups (g). Each product group represents all the transactions for a single product, that is

$$g = Seq^n(t(P,q))$$

Here the conventions of TDSD (that is the uppercase P) are used to indicate that the product identifier is *fixed* for the n members of the particular product group.

In strengthening the postcondition we need to define s and add a new sequence a to capture that T has been processed in producing the output sequence b. This corresponds to making a $Q \wedge R$ transformation to obtain R_c. In the process the variable a has been introduced. Making these refinements we get

$$R_c : b = Seq^N (u(p,s)) \wedge a = Seq^M(t) \wedge a = Seq^N(g) \wedge a = T$$

where

$$s = \Sigma t(q) : Seq^n (t(P,q))\dagger$$

It is not easy to initialize the free variables a and b to establish R_c. New free variables i, and j are therefore introduced to obtain a constructive postcondition R_D.

$$R_D : b = Seq^j (u(p,s)) \wedge a = Seq^i(t) \wedge a = Seq^i(g) \wedge i = M \wedge j = N \wedge a = T$$

We will now sketch the major steps in the derivation.

An initialization that will establish R_D will involve setting i, and j to zero and a, and b to the empty sequence.

$S_0(X_0)$ Initialization

```
i := 0; j := 0; b := ();‡
if i = M → skip {R_D established}
[] i ≠ M → {Q_1} s_1(x_1){R_D}
fi
```

This mechanism will only be sufficient to establish R_D if the input sequence is empty.

A suitable invariant that can be derived from R_D by initialization is:

$$P_D : b = Seq^i(u(p,s)) \wedge a = Seq^i(t) \wedge a = Seq^i(g) \wedge 0 \leqslant i \leqslant M \wedge 0 \leqslant j \leqslant N$$

To make progress towards establishing R_D we can first look at increasing i by one, that is, we compute wp ("i := i + 1", P_D). This investigation tells us that such a refinement may be used as part of a mechanism to establish R_D provided there is only a single transaction for a single product. This will involve another initialization, in this case of s and prod.

---

† This notation is used to indicate that the Q-components for the product P are extraced and summed.
‡ In our implementation it is not necessary to explicity include the sequence a. Also () refers to the empty sequence.

$S_1(X_1)$ One product, one transaction at most

```
i := 0; j := 0; b := ();
if i = M → skip
[] i ≠ M →
    i, prod, s := i + 1, t_{i+1}(P), t_{i+1}(q);
    if i = M → skip
    [] i ≠ M → {Q_2} s_2(x_2) {R_D}
    fi;
    j, b_{j+1}(prod), b_{j+1}(s) := j + 1, prod, s
fi
```

For the next refinement, we will try to establish R_D by changing the transactions variable i while holding the product variable (and hence j) constant. This leads to a mechanism that will establish R_D for one product, involving one or more transactions. A loop can be used for this purpose. Full details of this loop derivation have not been provided as they follow an already familiar pattern. The accompanying sub-goal R_2 and loop invariant P_2 are

$$R_2 : s = \Sigma t(q) : Seq^n (t(P,q)) \wedge a = Seq^{i+1}(g) \wedge a = Seq^i(t)$$
$$P_2 : s = \Sigma t(q) : Seq^k (t(P,q)) \wedge 1 \leq k \leq n$$

After updating the output sequence we have P_D restored. The implementation that follows is given below.

$S_2(X_2)$ One product, one or more transactions

```
i := 0; j := 0; b := (); {P_D}
if i = M → skip
[] i ≠ M →
    i, prod, s := i + 1, t_{i+1}(P), t_{i+1}(q);
    m := M;
    do i ≠ m → {P_2}
        if prod = t_{i+1}(P) → i, s := i + 1, s + t_{i+1}(q);
        [] prod ≠ t_{i+1}(P) → m := i
        fi
    od; {R_2}
    j, b_{j+1}(prod), b_{j+1}(s) := j + 1, prod, s; {P_D}
    if i = M → skip {R_D established}
    [] i ≠ M → {Q_3} s_3(x_3) {R_D}
    fi
fi
```

Our next refinement needs to look at changing the product variable (and hence j). A loop over the mechanism derived in the last two refinements will achieve the desired effect. It will lead to a mechanism that will establish R_D for one or more products each containing one or more transactions. The details of the implementation are as follows.

$S_3(X_3)$ One or more products

```
i := 0; j := 0; b := ();
do i ≠ M → {P_D}
   i, prod, s := i + 1, t_{i+1}(P), t_{i+1}(q);
   m := M;
   do i ≠ m → {P_2}
      if prod = t_{i+1}(P) → i, s := i + 1, s + t_{i+1}(q)
      [] prod ≠ t_{i+1}(P) → m := i
      fi
   od; (R_2}
   j, b_{j+1} (prod), b_{j+1}(s) := j + 1, prod, s
od
{R_D}
```

The stores-movement problem has been discussed in detail by Berglund (he calls it the McDonald's problem), who illustrates how it is solved by a number of different program development methods. The program structure of the present solution conforms to the data structure; there is one loop over transactions for a given product and another loop over products. What makes the solution interesting is that the correspondence between program control structure and data structure has been achieved by a goal-directed, limited top-down refinement method. This contrasts with Jackson's method, which achieves essentially the same program structure by matching the control structure with the data structure.

The strategy we have used here for refining a specification to incorporate structure in data is important. Many data-processing problems in particular need a similar treatment. In such cases deriving a stronger invariant from $Q \wedge R$ rather than directly from R provides a much more satisfactory treatment. A solution to this problem where there has been no attempt to match the data structure is as follows:

```
i := 0; j := 0; b := ();
if i ≠ M →
   i, prod, s := i + 1, t_{i+1}(P), t_{i+1}(q);
   do i ≠ M →
      if prod = t_{i+1}(P) → s := s + t_{i+1}(q);
      [] prod ≠ t_{i+1}(P) → j, b_{j+1}(prod), b_{j+1}(s) := j + 1, prod, s;
                              prod := t_{i+1}(P); s := t_{i+1}(q)
      fi;
      i := i + 1
   od;
   j, b_{j+1}(prod), b_{j+1}(s) := j + 1, prod, s
[] i = M → skip
fi
```

The match between program control structure and data is destroyed because the loop changes more than the smallest subset of variables that is sufficient to establish the postcondition (that is the product variable as well as the transaction variable is changed in the loop). Superficially this implementation with its single loop may appear simpler than our original solution. It does however have a more complex loop invariant and considerable duplication of program statements. With structurally more complex problems, the symptoms shown by this example can be greatly magnified if attention is not paid to structural integrity. Further discussion of this problem is given in Section 12.5.1.

11.5 Two-way Merge

The merging of ordered data is one of the classic sequential data-processing problems. It provides the framework for solving many other data-processing problems including the sequential file update. Our interest in the problem here is related to the difficulties in specifying the postcondition for a merge. Given two ordered arrays A[1..M] and B[1.. N], it is required to produce a third ordered array c[1..M + N] whose elements are a permutation of the elements in the two original arrays. There may be repeating elements in the two original arrays and other elements that are common to the two arrays. It is this multiplicity of elements that causes some problems in writing a specification for the merged array.

We will begin this specification by defining a predicate labelled ordered:

$$\text{ordered}(a,h) = (\forall i : 1 \leqslant i < h : a_i \leqslant a_{i+1})$$

The precondition for the merge can now be defined as

$$Q : M \geqslant 0 \wedge N \geqslant 0 \wedge \text{ordered}(A,M) \wedge \text{ordered}(B,N)$$

The description of the postcondition is more difficult. We will start it by defining another array S[1..M + N] equal in length to the merged array c but satisfying the following predicate:

$$(\forall p : 1 \leqslant p \leqslant M : S_p = A_p) \wedge (\forall q : 1 \leqslant q \leqslant N : S_{M+q} = B_q)$$

We can now define the merged array c as a permutation of the array S with the additional requirement that it is ordered. Our postcondition then takes the form

$$R : \text{ordered}(c,M + N) \wedge \text{perm}(c,S)$$

To be strictly formal in defining this postcondition the predicate defining S should be conjoined to the other relations in the postcondition. This postcondition provides the basis for constructing a postcondition R_D that can be used for program development. The latter has the form

$$R_D : \text{ordered}(c,k) \wedge \text{merged}(A[1..i]) \wedge \text{merged}(B[1..j]) \wedge \text{pperm}(c,S,k)$$
$$\wedge k = i + j \wedge i = M \wedge j = N$$

where merged(A[1..i]) is a predicate indicating that the first i elements of the array A have been used in producing the first k elements in the merged array c. The predicate pperm(c,S,k) indicates that the first k elements of c match the first k elements of the ordered permutation of S. The array $S[1..M + N]$ plays no role in the implementation of the program.

The derivation of the program for the two-way merge is relatively straightforward. A suitable invariant that follows from the postcondition is

$$P_D : \text{ordered}(c,k) \wedge \text{merged}(A[1..i]) \wedge \text{merged}(B[1..j]) \wedge \text{pperm}(c,S,k)$$
$$\wedge\, k = i + j$$

To establish the postcondition four variables must be changed. The variable i must be increased to M, the variable j increased to N, and the variable k increased to $M + N$ as the merged array c is created.

In making a sequence of refinements to establish the postcondition we want each refinement to change the least number of variables. This means that if either $i = M$ or $j = N$ the merge degenerates to a simpler copy operation. Because there is nothing to guarantee $i = M$ over $j = N$ a refinement consisting of two copies is needed.

Making this refinement using postfix composition we get

```
i := 0; j := 0; k := 0;
if i ≠ M ∧ j ≠ N → {Q₁} s₁(x₁) {R_D}
[] i = M ∨ j = N → skip {R_D established by copy below}
fi;
do i ≠ M → k, i, c_{k+1} := k + 1, i + 1, A_{i+1} od;
do j ≠ N → k, j, c_{k+1} := k + 1, j + 1, B_{j+1} od
{R_D}
```

For the next refinement we want to establish R_D when the condition $i \neq M \wedge j \neq N$ applies. We have the choice of changing i or j or both in an attempt to make a refinement that will establish the postcondition at least in some limiting circumstances. We will choose to make several steps at once and do an iterative refinement that changes both i and j. Thus we get the following implementation:

Two-way merge (Version 1)
```
i := 0; j := 0; k := 0;
do i ≠ M ∧ j ≠ N →
    if A_{i+1} ≤ B_{j+1} → k, i, c_{k+1} := k + 1, i + 1, A_{i+1}
    [] A_{i+1} ≥ B_{j+1} → k, j, c_{k+1} := k + 1, j + 1, B_{j+1}
    fi
od;
do i ≠ M → k, i, c_{k+1} := k + 1, i + 1, A_{i+1} od;
do j ≠ N → k, j, c_{k+1} := k + 1, j + 1, B_{j+1} od
{R_D}
```

Here we have ignored our own advice of trying to change only the smallest number of variables in an effort to obtain the more often quoted version of the two-way merge. Our implementation therefore ends up doing more guard testing on average than is necessary. The implementation below, which includes refinements that always change the smallest number of variables does less guard testing.

Two-way merge (Version 2)

```
i := 0; j := 0; k := 0 ; m := i; n := j;
if j ≠ N then m := M fi;
do i ≠ m →
   repeat
      if A_{i+1} ≤ B_{j+1}→ k, i, c_{k+1} := k + 1, i + 1, A_{i+1}
      [] A_{i+1} > B_{j+1}→ m := i; n := N
      fi
   until i = m;
   do j ≠ n →
      if B_{j+1} ≤ A_{i+1} → k, j, c_{k+1} := k + 1, j + 1, B_{j+1}
      [] B_{j+1} > A_{i+1} → n := j; m := M
      fi
   od
od;
do i ≠ M → k, i, c_{k+1} := k + 1, i + 1, A_{i+1} od;
do j ≠ N → k, j, c_{k+1} := k + 1, j + 1, B_{j+1} od
{R_D}
```

Unlike the previous implementation, this algorithm, when it changes i, does not need to test the guard $j \neq n$, and when it changes j, the guard $i \neq m$ is not tested. This factoring can on average reduce guard testing in version 2 relative to that in version 1. Another interesting aspect of this mechanism is the way each loop controls whether or not the next loop to be executed will be entered again.

11.6   Sequential File Update

Sequential file updating is one of the most widely used data-processing techniques. Most forms of transaction processing involve a sequential file update. The variation of the problem which allows the possibility of more than one transaction on a single key is often regarded as non-trivial. It involves a specialized file merge. Three files are used, a file of transactions records trans which specifies amendments to be made to an old master file old to produce a new master file new. Successive records in the old and new files have monotonically increasing values of their keys. Each transaction record includes a sub-field which identifies whether the transaction for that particular key is to be an insert, update or delete. Records in the old master file not involved in transactions should be copied to the new master file in a way that maintains the order of the new file. Keys in the new master file should be unique.

The postcondition for this problem can be stated informally as follows:

> *All transactions and all records in the old master file have been read and processed to produce a new ordered master file.*

The record structures of the three files are

```
oldⱼ ::= <key> <data>
newᵢ ::= <key> <data>
transᵢ ::= <action> <key> <data>
```

The formal specifications for this problem are similar to the specifications for the the last problem, but somewhat more complicated. The intention here is to illustrate the stages in the development of the solution. The starting point will be a refinement that establishes the postcondition for a very strong precondition and this leads to a sequence of refinements that establish the postcondition for progressively weaker preconditions until we eventually have a solution that will establish the postcondition for the more general given precondition.

The first development step involves the identification and implementation of the most elementary mechanism that can establish the postcondition. The precondition suggests that either of the files might be empty. To decide upon the initial refinement a choice must be made between a mechanism that establishes the postcondition for zero transactions and one that establishes the postcondition for zero old master records. Analysis of the data indicates that the very strong precondition corresponding to zero transactions is simpler as it requires no identification of the type of the transaction.

A_0 Zero transactions – initial refinement†

To establish the postcondition for zero transactions in general we will go straight to an iterative mechanism to copy records from the old master file to the new master file. For this the procedure copyold may be used:

```
procedure copyold(var old, new: master; j, N: boolean);
    do j ≠ N →
        new↑ := old↑ ; put(new);
        get(old); j := eof(old)
    od
end;
```

---

† To emphasize the precondition for which refinements are made the A-notation is used from Chapter 5.

The initial refinement using postfix composition then becomes:

Zero transactions

```
const EOF = true;
var i, j, M, N : boolean;
M := EOF; N := EOF; i := eof(trans); j := eof(old);
if i ≠ M → {Q₁} s₁(x₁) {R}
[] i = M → skip {R established by copy below}
fi;
copyold(old,new,j,N)
{R}
```

A₁ One transaction at most – first generalization†

In general we must handle preconditions where the transaction file is not empty (i.e. $i \neq M$). This implies one or more transactions must be processed. We will consider first a *single transaction* as this represents the minimum weakening of the precondition with respect to the initial refinement.

To establish R for a single transaction an additional iterative mechanism is required. It must search the old master file to locate the 'transaction position'. In the process, records in the old file need to be copied to the new master file. Once the transaction position has been located the transaction may be performed. Treating these two components separately we get:

Search and copy

```
procedure searchcopy(old, new : master; trans: transaction; var j, N :
boolean);
    var n : boolean;
    n := N;
    do j ≠ n →
        if old↑.key < trans↑.key → new↑ := old↑ ; put(new); get(old);
                                    j := eof(old)
        [] old↑.key ≥ trans↑.key n := j
        fi
    od
end
```

Transaction

The transaction mechanism can be appended to the search mechanism as a finalization mechanism. Three possible actions firstinsert(ins), firstdelete(del) and firstupdate(upd) must be accommodated depending on whether the transaction involves an insert (ins), a delete (del) or an update (upd). The transaction mechanism has the form

```
if trans↑.action = ins → firstinsert(....,valid)
[] trans↑.action = upd → firstupdate(....,valid)
[] trans↑.action = del → firstdelete(....,valid)
fi;
get(trans); i := eof(trans);
if valid → put(new)
[] ¬valid → skip
fi
```

Details are needed for each of the three possible transactions, and are given for **firstinsert**.

The sequential search terminates in one of two states:

(1)   With eof(old) true (i.e. j = N).

(2)   With eof(old) false (i.e. j ≠ N).

If the old master file is not exhausted, then the condition trans↑.key < old↑.key must also hold for it to be possible to make a valid insertion. With both these conditions true the following actions are appropriate:

```
new↑.key := trans↑.key; new↑.data := trans↑.data; valid := true
```

The same steps are appropriate if the old master file is exhausted. However, if the condition trans↑.key ≥ old↑.key applies, an invalid transaction is being attempted. To ensure the corresponding old master record is not lost due to an invalid transaction the following steps are needed:

```
new↑ := old↑; get(old); j := eof(old); valid := true;
writeln('Insertion error', trans↑.key)
```

Details of firstinsert are therefore:

```
procedure firstinsert(old, new: master; trans: transaction; var j, N, valid :
boolean);
    if j ≠ N →
    if trans↑.key<old↑.key → new↑.key:= trans↑.key;
                                new↑.data : = trans↑.data
    [] trans↑.key → ≥old↑.key → new↑ := old↑; get(old); j:= eof(old);
                                writeln ('Insertion error', trans↑.key)
    fi
    [] j = N → new↑.key := trans↑.key; new↑.data := trans↑.data
    fi;
    valid := true
end
```

The structure of firstupdate and firstdelete follow a similar pattern, except that valid will be false after a deletion. A mechanism that will establish the postcondition R in the general case for a single transaction may therefore take the form

One transaction

```
var i, j, M, N:boolean;
  M := true; N := true; i := eof(trans); j := eof(old);
  if i ≠ M →
    searchcopy(old, new, trans, j, N);
    if trans↑.action = ins → firstinsert(old, new, trans, j, N, valid)
    [] trans↑.action = upd → firstupdate(old, new, trans, j, N, valid)
    [] trans↑.action = del → firstdelete(old, new, trans, j, N, valid)
    fi;
    get(trans); i := eof(trans);
    if i ≠ M → "further processing – same key"
    [] i = M → skip {R established by put, and copy below}
    fi;
    if valid → put(new)
    [] ¬valid → skip
    fi
  [] i = M → skip
  fi;
  copyold(old,new,j,N)
  {R}
```

A₂ More than one transaction for single key – second generalization

To accommodate more than one transaction there are two possible generalizations to consider:

(1)   a number of transactions for a single key;

(2)   transactions for more than one key.

The first of these cases is more elementary because it does not involve a change in the key variable. It is therefore used to make the next refinement.

In the first generalization a mechanism was developed to handle the first transaction for a given key. We must next decide whether this mechanism:

(a)   can be applied iteratively to handle many transactions for a single key, or

(b)   it may serve as the initializing step for handling many transactions for a single key.

Investigation reveals that situation (b) applies because it requires no sequential search of the old master file. The validity of the next transaction for the same key will depend only on the most recent valid transaction and not on whether the old master file is exhausted.

	Transaction currently in buffer	*Possible transaction*		
		Insert	*Delete*	*Update*
valid		×	✔	✔
not valid		✔	×	×

The rules above summarize valid (✔) and invalid (×) transactions. Subsequent insertions for a particular key after the first transaction for that key may be handled by the following procedure:

```
procedure insert(new : master; trans : transaction; var valid : boolean);
    if valid → writeln ('Insertion error', trans↑.key)
    [] ¬valid → new↑.key := trans↑.key; new↑.data := trans↑.data; valid :=
    true
    fi
end
```

The delete and update procedures are similar. They can be derived from the table of rules. The complete mechanism to establish R for a single key in the general case may therefore take the form:

More than one transaction for a single key

```
    var i, j, M, N : boolean; ckey : name;
    M := true; N := true; i := eof(trans); j := eof(old);
    if i ≠ M →
        searchcopy(old, new, trans, j, N);
        if trans↑.action = ins → firstinsert(old, new, trans, j, N, valid)
        [] trans↑.action = upd → firstupdate(old, new, trans, j, N, valid)
        [] trans↑.action = del → firstdelete(old, new, trans, j, N, valid)
        fi;
        get(trans); i := eof(true);
        m := M; ckey := new↑.key;
        do i ≠ m →
            if trans↑.key = ckey →
                if trans↑.action = ins → insert(new, trans, valid)
                [] trans↑.action = upd → update(new, trans, valid)
                [] trans↑.action = del → delete(new, trans, valid)
                fi;
                get(trans); i := eof(trans)
            [] trans↑.key ≠ ckey → m := i
            fi
        od;
        if valid → put(new)
        [] ¬valid → skip
        fi;
        if i ≠ M → "further processing – other keys"
        [] i = M → skip {R established by copyold}
        fi
    [] i = M → skip
    fi;
    copyold(old, new, j, N)
    {R}
```

A₃ Many transactions for one or more keys – third generalization

The mechanism for more than one transaction for a single key can terminate in a state where R has not been established (i.e. i ≠ M). This implies that more than one key must be accommodated in the general case. We have already developed a mechanism which will handle a single key in the general case. Examination of this mechanism reveals that it can be applied iteratively to handle more than one key. Making this refinement gives

Many transactions for one or more keys

```
var i, j, M, N; boolean; ckey : name;
M := true; N := true; i := eof(trans); j := eof(old);
do i ≠ M →
    searchcopy(old, new, trans, j, N);
    if trans↑.action = ins → firstinsert(old, new, trans, j, N, valid)
    [] trans↑.action = upd → firstupdate(old, new, trans, j, N, valid)
    [] trans↑.action = del → firstdelete(old, new, trans, j, N, valid)
    fi;
    get(trans); i := eof(trans);
    m := M; ckey := new↑.key;
    do i ≠ m →
        if trans↑.key = ckey →
            if trans↑.action = ins → insert(new, trans, valid)
            [] trans↑.action = upd → update(new, trans, valid)
            [] trans↑.action = del → delete(new, trans, valid)
            fi;
            get(trans); i := eof(trans)
        [] trans↑.key ≠ ckey → m := i
        fi
    od;
    if valid → put(new)
    [] ¬valid → skip
    fi
od;
copyold(old, new, j, N)
{R}
```

Several comments about this implementation are in order. We could have broken up the refinement for a single transaction into a sequence of simpler steps. The logical structure reflected in the development of this algorithm is clearly visible in the final implementation. With successive generalizations the guards for a previous development step do not change. What may change is whether the guard protects a mechanism that is applied iteratively or a mechanism that is part of an alternative construct. This is important for constructive proof development.

The choice of the initial refinement for this problem may have seemed unusual. If instead, a single transaction for a single key had been chosen as the focus the same algorithm structure would have resulted. Then the original development step would have been a compound and more complex step. Therefore, although the initial refinement is important, other choices may be acceptable provided they establish the postcondition at least for a very strong precondition.

The complexity for this non-trivial problem has been controlled by first making a refinement that establishes the postcondition for a very strong precondition and then making a sequence of refinements that establish the postcondition for progressively weaker preconditions.

Although we have not relied on formal specifications to guide the refinement process we have still achieved a result that is easy to prove correct. The implementation also matches the structure of the data. The formal specifications for this problem are fairly detailed because of the difficulty in describing multiple transactions on a single key.

11.7   The Telegrams Analysis Problem

The telegrams analysis problem has been used by several authors to discuss program development methods. It requires a program to process a stream of telegrams each terminated by the string 'ZZZZ'. The data are stored in blocks of size M. Words are separated by one or more spaces, and they *do not* extend across block boundaries. The words in each telegram (excluding 'ZZZZ') must be counted. Each telegram must also be printed with a single space between words and no leading or trailing blanks.† As with the last problem, our interest is in showing how a viable solution can be developed by making a sequence of refinements each of which expands the set of initial states for which the postcondition is developed. Very informally we have

Q : At least the NULL TELEGRAM is present in the INPUT FILE.

R : The INPUT FILE has been read including the terminating NULL TELEGRAM and a corresponding OUTPUT TELEGRAM FILE has been produced.

The format of the telegrams closely follows that for the text-formatting problem discussed earlier (see Chapter 10). The null telegram consists of zero or more spaces followed by 'ZZZZ'.

A_0 Initial refinement – null telegram
The simplest way to establish the postcondition would be to encounter and

---

† In Henderson's original specification there were also STOP words which were not to be counted and over-size words which were to be specially noted. These considerations do not influence the structure of the problem and so they have been omitted.

process the NULL TELEGRAM. No output is required to establish the postcondition R in these circumstances. A procedure fillbuffer, which reads data from a file and fills a buffer buff with M characters, and a second procedure getspaces, which consumes the leading spaces in the buffer, are assumed. The consecutive application of fillbuffer and getspaces cannot guarantee to consume all leading spaces preceding the first word because there could be multiple lines consisting only of spaces. The provision for repeated application of fillbuffer and getspaces is therefore needed to deal with all leading white space. The procedure preword embodies this refinement:

```
procedure preword(var data : textfile; var buff : array[1..M] of char; var j,
M : int);
    getspaces(buff, j, M);
    do j = M →
        fillbuffer(data, buff, M); j := 0;
        getspaces(buff, j, M)
    od
end
```

The procedure preword terminates with $j \neq M$ implying that a word in buff is available for access.

Assuming a procedure getword that moves the next available word of length w from buff to the array word, a mechanism that can establish R for the NULL TELEGRAM may be defined as follows:

A_0 Initial refinement – null telegram †

```
const M = buffsize;
var data : textfile; buff, word : array[1..M] of char; j, w : integer;
    fillbuffer(data,buff,M); j := 0;
    preword(data, buff, j, M);
    getword(buff, word, w, j, M);
    if word = 'ZZZZ' → skip {R established}
    [] word ≠ 'ZZZZ' → "further processing"
    fi
    {R}
```

It is assumed that the language can match the word array with 'ZZZZ'. This mechanism will establish R for all configurations of the NULL TELEGRAM. In the more general case it terminates with only the first word in the first telegram read and stored in word.

† The variable "j" is passed to getword as a value parameter and therefore is not changed by getword.

A₁ One telegram with one word – first generalization

There are two possible states of termination for the NULL TELEGRAM mechanism. Termination with word ≠ 'ZZZZ' implies that there is at least one telegram with at least one countable word that needs to be processed. The word that has just been consumed can be written out by the following mechanism:

```
writeheader; writeword(word, w); wc := 1; j := j + w;
if j ≠ M → "further processing – current buffer"
[] j = M → "further processing – next buffer"
fi
```

Development can continue by adding an iterative mechanism to find the next word (if any) in the current buffer or beyond. The stages in this phase of the development follow closely those employed in dealing with the NULL TELEGRAM. The mechanism for one telegram with one countable word can then be defined.

A₁ One telegram with one word

```
const M = buffsize; SPACE = ' ';
var data: textifle; buff, word : array[1..M] of char; j, w,wc : integer;
fillbuffer(data, buff, j, M); j := 0;
preword(data, buff, j, M);
getword(buff, word, w, j, M);
if word ≠ 'ZZZZ' then
  writeheader; writeword(word, w); wc := 1; j := j + w;
  if j ≠ M →
    preword(data, buff, j, M);
    getword(buff, word, w, j, M);
    if word ≠ 'ZZZZ'→"further processing – current telegram"
    [] word = 'ZZZZ' → skip {"finished – current telegram"}
    fi;
  [] j = M → "further processing – next buffer"
  fi;
  write(wc); writetail
fi
```

A₂ One telegram with one or more words – second generalization

The most elementary generalization (or expansion of initial states for which R can be established) is one that allows the handling of a single telegram with one or more words. For this purpose the mechanism in the segment guarded by if j ≠ M → ... can be iteratively applied until either the current buffer is exhausted (that is j = M) or an end-of-telegram word 'ZZZZ' is encountered. Incorporating these steps we get

One telegram

```
const M = buffsize; SPACE = ' ';
var data : textfile; buff, word : array[1..M] of char; j, w, wc, m, M : integer;
    fillbuffer(data, buff, j, M); j := 0;
    preword(data, buff, j, M);
    getword(buff, word, w, j, M);
    if word ≠ 'ZZZZ' then
        writeheader; writeword(word, w); wc := 1, j := j + w;
        m := M;
        do j ≠ m →
            preword(data, buff, j, M);
            getword(buff, word, w, j, M);
            if word ≠ 'ZZZZ' → write(SPACE); writeword(word,w);
                                wc := wc + 1, j := j + w
            [] word = 'ZZZZ' → m := j
            fi
        od;
        if = M → "further processing – current telegram"
        [] j ≠ M → skip {end-of-telegram established}
        fi;
        write(wc); writetail;
        "further processing – to handle more than one telegram"
    fi
```

At this point we could add a mechanism to detect the null telegram
that would follow if we only had to deal with a single telegram. It is however
appropriate at this point to consider a further refinement to handle the
current telegram. Termination of the most recently added loop with the
condition "j = M" implies that the single telegram terminating with a word at
the end of the buffer extends across another buffer. To handle this situation
a new procedure will first be defined processrest that incorporates the steps
in the last refinement:

```
processrest(var data : textfile; var buff : array[1..M] of char; var j, w, wc, M :
int);
var m : int;
    m := M;
    do j ≠ m →
        preword(data, buff, j, M);
        getword(buff, word, w, j, M);
        if word ≠ 'ZZZZ' → write (SPACE); writeword(word, w);
                            wc := wc + 1, j := j + w
        [] word = 'ZZZZ' → m := j
        fi
    od
end
```

The procedure processrest will handle the processing of other than the
first word in any telegram in a single buffer. As soon as the end of a telegram

is encountered the loop is forced to terminate. When processrest terminates with j = M another buffer must be filled and processed. The steps to do this are

```
if j = M →
    fillbuffer(data, buff, j, M); j := 0;
    processrest(data, buff, j, w, wc, M);
    .
    .
    .
```

Potentially processrest could, after this second call, terminate again with j = M. A refinement that involves a loop over these last two steps is therefore in order. The underlying form of the loop structure required is

```
A;
do j = M →
    B;
    A
od
```

These loop structures are discussed in Chapter 12. Making this most recent refinement we end up with a mechanism that will process all the data in a single telegram.

One complete telegram in general

```
const M = buffsize; SPACE = ' ';
var data : textfile; buff, word : array[1..M] of char; j, w, wc, m, M : integer;
    fillbuffer(data, buff, j, M); j := 0;
    preword(data, buff, j, M);
    getword(buff, word, w, j, M);
    if word ≠ 'ZZZZ' then
        writeheader; writeword(word, w); wc := 1; j := j + w;
        processrest(data, buff, j, w, wc, M);
        do j = M →
            fillbuffer(data, buff, j, M); j := 0;
            processrest(data, buff, j, w, wc, M)
        od;
        write(wc); writetail;
        "further processing – to handle more than one telegram"
    fi
```

This mechanism will read, reformat and write out a single telegram in the general case. However, to establish the postcondition for a single real telegram it is necessary to subsequently detect a NULL TELEGRAM (see specification for INPUT FILE). As for the first refinement, the steps to detect a null telegram are:

```
preword(data,buff,j,M);
getword(buff,word,w,j,M);
if word = 'ZZZZ' → " Null telegram detected – R established "
[] word → 'ZZZZ' → "Start of another telegram detected"
fi
```

These steps match the steps at the start of our program. Rather than repeat the code we can make an iterative refinement which takes in these steps. Such a refinement will allow us to handle more than one real telegram as well as detect the null telegram that terminates the file. Forced termination is needed when the null telegram is detected. Making these refinements we get:

One real telegram at most in general

```
const M = buffsize; SPACE = ' ';
var data : textfile; buff, word : array[1..M] of char; j, w, wc, m, M : integer;
    fillbuffer(data, buff, j, M); j:= 0;
    preword(data, buff, j, M);
    getword(buff, word, w, j, M);
    if word ≠ 'ZZZZ' then
       writeheader; writeword(word, w); wc := 1; j := j + w;
       processrest(data, buff, j, w, wc, M);
       do j = M →
          fillbuffer(data, buff, j, M); j:= 0;
          processrest(data, buff, j, w, wc, M)
       od;
       write(wc); writetail; j := j + w;
       preword(data, buff, j, M);
       getword(buff, word, w, M);
       if word ≠ 'ZZZZ' → "further processing – next telegram"
       [] word = 'ZZZZ' → skip {R established}
       fi
    fi
```

The most recent generalization leads to a mechanism that will establish the postcondition in the general case for at most a single real telegram.

A₃ One or more telegrams – third generalization

If the mechanism developed for a single real telegram terminates with word ≠ 'ZZZZ' it implies that there is at least one more telegram to be processed. A mechanism has already been developed for a single telegram. It is therefore appropriate to consider whether a segment of this mechanism can be iteratively applied to handle more than one telegram. In pursuing this next generalization it should be noted that the steps

```
    .
    .
    preword(data,buff,j,M);
    getword(buff,word,w,M);
    if word ≠ 'ZZZZ' → "further processing – next telegram"
    [] word = 'ZZZZ' → skip
    fi
```

at the end of the mechanism duplicate the same structure at the beginning of the program text. Taking this into account the mechanism to handle more than one telegram may take the form:

More than one telegram

```
    const M = buffsize; SPACE = ' ';
    var data: textfile; buff, word: array[1..M] of char; j, w, wc, m, M : integer;
    fillbuffer(data, buff, j, M); j := 0;
    repeat
        preword(data, buff, j, M);
        getword(buff, word, w, j, M);
        if word ≠ 'ZZZZ' →
            writeheader; writeword(word,w); wc := 1; j = j + w;
            processrest(data, buff, j, w, wc, M);
            do j = M →
                fillbuffer(data, buff, j, M); j := 0;
                processrest(data, buff, j, w, wc, M)
            od;
            write(wc); writetail; j := j + w;
        [] word = 'ZZZZ' → m = j
        fi
    until j = m
    {R}
```

This mechanism will establish the postcondition R in the general case for a file of one or more telegrams and so the development is complete. The control structure needed to solve this problem has been nontrivial. However, as we have demonstrated, the problem is still amenable to solution by a sequence of refinements each of which expands the set of initial states for which the postcondition is established.

SUMMARY

- Formal methods of specification and derivation can sometimes lead to the discovery of sophisticated algorithms. The majority-element problem is in this category.

- The majority-element problem also illustrates the value of solving a problem by first solving an auxiliary problem with a weaker postcondition.

- As with the majority-element problem, the maximum sum-section problem demonstrates how formal specifications can guide us to a simple and efficient solution.

- The maximum sum-section problem illustrates the value of always trying to fix as many variables as possible while changing other variables that allow a computation to progress.

- Sequential data often has considerable structure associated with it. The cleanest solutions to such problems are obtained when an attempt is made to derive solutions in which the program control structure matches the data structure.

- Some sequential data-processing problems involve merging strategies in various guises. In specifying merge problems it is necessary to accommodate a degree of indeterminancy.

- Two somewhat more complex problems, the sequential file update and the telegrams analysis problem, illustrate the value of making a sequence of goal-directed refinements, each of which expands the set of initial states for which the postcondition is established.

■ EXERCISE 11   Sequential problems

1. Given an ordered array of integers specify, derive, and implement a mechanism that deletes all duplicates.

2. Given an array of numbers (they may be positive or negative) find the sum of the contiguous subsection of the array that has the maximum sum.

3. Given two arrays A[1..N] and B[1..N] of alphabetic characters check whether one array is a cyclic permutation of the other array, that is the character sequence in B may be displaced relative to that in A.

4. Given a sequence of arbitrary positive integers which have been stored in an array A[1..N] specify, design and implement a program that detects the smallest absent positive integer. Assume there are no duplicates in the sequence. Note the sequence is *not* ordered.

5. Write an EBNF specification for the telegrams analysis problem.

Bibliography

Backhouse, R.C. (1986), *Program Construction and Verification,* Prentice-Hall, London.

Berglund, G. (1981), A guided tour of programming methodologies, *Computer,* **14,** (October.)

Dijkstra, E.W. (1976), *A Discipline of Programming,* Prentice-Hall, Englewood Cliffs, N.J.

Henderson, P. and R.A. Snowden (1972), "An experiment in structured programming, *BIT* **12,** 38–53.

Jackson, M. (1976), *Principles of Program Design,* Academic Press.

Part 4
PROGRAM IMPLEMENTATION

The final part of this book is devoted to a range of issues, techniques, and advice that can have a significant influence on the quality of derived programs. Issues of form, structure and appearance are all considered.

For a loop we study initialization problems, its body, and techniques for termination. We also look at matching explicit and implicit structure in data, and the problem of looping over data structures that are not synchronized. In the course of this wide-ranging discussion we end up considering a diverse selection of algorithms.

Chapter 12
Program Implementation

> Style, in its finest sense is the last acquirement of the
> educated mind; it is also the most useful.
>
> *A. N. Whitehead*

12.1 Introduction
12.2 Programming Style
12.3 Initialization of Loops
12.4 Termination of Loops
12.5 Loop Structuring
12.6 Lookahead Implementation
12.7 Forced Synchronization of Loops
Summary
Exercise
Bibliography

12.1 Introduction

In the preceding chapters we have provided an array of tools that can assist us with the derivation of programs. There are still other disciplines needed for effective program design. Much of what we will be concerned with in this chapter could be described as cosmetic. The cosmetic element is of vital importance in program design for the following reasons.

- Programs must be designed to be read and understood by people.
- The intricate logic of programs means they cannot be 'read' like a book. Structure, and organization, are of central importance in making programs understandable.

531

- Certain classes of problems are best treated by known systematic methods. We will examine some of the important classes of problems that submit to systematic treatment.

Conventions, programming style, consistency, and systematic methods add an important and useful dimension to programs derived from formal specifications. They give the final product of a derivation its seal of quality. Some of what we will be discussing comes down to a sense of taste and a quest for elegance in design. The suggestions made are not to be taken as rules and conventions that should not be broken. Instead, they have been put forward in the hope that they may provoke readers to raise their level of consciousness about matters which some dismiss as merely cosmetic.

The first issue we will turn to in the present discussion is probably the most controversial – programming style. Everyone has an opinion about this but often these opinions lack any real depth. The only way to proceed is to confront the tiger head on.

12.2 Programming Style

An obvious place to start a discussion on programming style is with the question 'what is programming style?' Before addressing the issue properly it is pertinent to raise the matter of why style in programming, or style in anything else for that matter, is important. One of the best responses to this has been succinctly put by A.N. Whitehead in his classic essay 'The Aims of Education'. He makes the following observations.

- (Style) is an aesthetic sense, based on admiration for the direct statement of a foreseen end, simply and without waste.
- Style in art, literature, science, logic, and practical execution have fundamentally the same aesthetic qualities, attainment and restraint.
- 'Style, in its finest sense is the last acquirement of the educated mind; it is also the most useful ... style is the ultimate morality of mind."
- Style enables an end to be attained without side issues, without raising undesirable inflammations. With style you attain your end and nothing but your end.
- With style your power is increased, for your mind is not distracted with irrelevancies, and you are more likely to attain your object.
- Style is always the product of specialist study, the peculiar contribution of specialism to culture.

These comments give some insight into the relevance of asking 'What is programming style?' However, they also imply that a deep insight into programming style is not attainable without considerable specialist study.

Returning now to our original question, rather than attempt to answer it directly, it is more productive to address the issue *'what determines or contributes to the style of a program?'*

Much of what we want to say about programming style is covered in the rest of this chapter and for that matter in Chapters 4–12. Here we will concentrate on some of the more general aspects of programming style. The first that we will consider has no influence at all on the behaviour of the program. Instead it relates only to the documentation and textual layout of the program.

12.2.1   Documentation conventions

It is very easy to fall into the trap of thinking that the object of program design is just to construct programs that will run correctly when executed on a computer. While this objective is central it is far from the whole story. It has been claimed by many authors that in practice, somewhere between 50% and 70% of all programming effort goes into program maintenance. This means that programs have to be changed a lot, and, before a program can be successfully changed, it must be thoroughly understood. Therefore, if maintenance of a program is to be efficient, that program must be easy to unravel and understand.

Layout Conventions

In this section we will focus on documenting conventions for

- the textual layout of programs;
- incorporating comments;
- naming variables, constants and procedures, etc.

Making a program understandable is not something that can be achieved without very considerable effort, attention to detail, consistency, and form. In this regard, the actual textual layout and appropriate indenting of the significant structural elements of a program plays an important role. There are two dimensions, the **horizontal** and the **vertical**, to be catered for in defining the layout of a program.

The objective of the horizontal layout is to align vertically all statements that are on the same semantic and structural level. It is convenient to think of the screen or paper on which the program appears as being divided up into a number of adjacent columns. *A level change and a shift to the right should be applied when a set of statements is prefixed or postfixed by a guard.* This means loops and alternative constructs always force another level of indentation (a tab perhaps) with respect to other statements that are on the same level. For example, consider the statements $S_1, S_2, \ldots, S_5$ and their use with **IF** and **DO** statements.

IF – statement indenting	**DO** – statement indenting
S_1;	S_1;
S_2;	S_2;
if B **then**	**do** B $\rightarrow$
$\quad S_3$;	$\quad S_3$;
$\quad S_4$	$\quad S_4$
fi;	**od**;
S_5	S_5

Because statements S_3 and S_4 are guarded they are considered not to be on the same level as the statements S_1, S_2 or S_5. In the examples if S_3 were an **IF** or **DO** statement, it would invoke a third level of indentation, and so on. Keywords signalling the start and end of a statement should line up at the *same* level of indentation. In cases where we are dealing with very simple constructs (e.g. a simple loop, **IF** statement, or sequence of assignments), it is sometimes convenient to ignore the suggested conventions for indenting and write the statement or statements on a single line, e.g.

```
i := 0; f := 1;
do i ≠ N → i := i + 1; f := f * i od
```

This convention is *not* used when we have statements of different form (e.g. assignments and a loop) on the same level. The above implementation follows this convention by putting the initializations on a separate line to the loop. Some programmers use a tab (8 spaces) to differentiate the different levels of a program. This is rather generous – three or four spaces per level is adequate to identify the different levels.

The vertical layout conventions for programs relate mostly to the modularity of the program. Each procedure in a program can be likened to a paragraph in a text. At least one blank line should be left between procedures to allow them to stand out and be easily recognized.

Commenting conventions

The second central documentation issue that we need to consider relates to the use of **comments** in the program text. The primary uses of comments in a program text are

- to explain the nature of the computational strategy employed by some mechanism, for example 'This procedure uses a binary search to locate NAME in the array';
- to identify the purpose or role of some mechanism or procedure, for example 'This procedure sorts a file of names into non-descending order';

- to identify certain conditions or requirements that apply or need to apply at a specified point in a program, for example 'p defines the position of the maximum in the array A[1..N]";
- to describe specifications (for example preconditions, postconditions and invariants) associated with the design of a program. These should be either formal or semi-formal:

> PRECONDITION : N ⩾ 1
> POSTCONDITION : m ⩾ A[1..N] ∧ m ∈ A[1..N]

When working with large systems it is necessary to include other status information to support the management, testing, and maintenance of the software. In this context, it is necessary to include such things as:

- the author of the program or procedure;
- when the code was completed;
- when it was last altered;
- whether it was tested;
- what other procedure(s) uses the procedure;
- details of the interface with other modules or procedures.

In the present discussion we will focus on the primary uses of comments. What usually is of most concern in relation to comments is just how much commenting is needed in a program. The two obvious problems programmers have with commenting practice are

- comments are over-used;
- comments are under-used.

Typical examples of the over-use of comments are

```
i := i + 1;                                    { Add one to i }
s := s div 2                                   {Divide s by 2}
if maximum < a[i] then maximum := a[i] fi      {Update the maximum}
```

These sort of comments are stating the obvious and therefore unnecessary. Where a complex or unusual expression is being evaluated, like computing compound interest, then a comment may be in order, for example

```
interest := . . . ;      {compute the compound interest}
```

One rule of thumb that some programmers advocate is that half of the text of a program should be devoted to comments. As a general rule this suggestion seems to be too generous, although for large complex systems such a high level of commenting may be needed. What is important in constructing comments is that they be precise, succinct, and yet complete.

In practice programmers are much more likely to under-use than over-use comments. In fact some programmers go to the extreme of not bothering to comment their programs at all. This practice is always much worse than over-commenting.

Some practical suggestions for commenting are as follows.

- Always provide a comment defining each important variable. Such comments should be located where the variable is first declared, for example

```
procedure compare (w1, w2: word, ...)
var p : integer;     {p is the length of the prefix match for words w1
                     and w2}
  .
  .
```

- Sometimes good choices for identifiers can reduce the need for comments.
- Almost every loop in a program deserves a comment which defines its role and characterizes its behaviour.
- Where possible keep comments to one line in length although sometimes it is preferable to use longer comments to explain a complex component of a program.
- Every procedure or function or module deserves a comment describing its functional role.

Functional comments are located either just *before* the procedure text, for example

```
* ----------------------------------------------------------------------- *
*                                                                          *
* This procedure sorts an array of integers into non-descending
  order                                                                    *
*                                                                          *
* ----------------------------------------------------------------------- *
procedure sort (var a : nelements; ...)
```

or just *inside* the procedure

```
procedure sort (var a : nelements; ...)
* ----------------------------------------------------------------------- *
*                                                                          *
* This procedure sorts an array of integers into non-descending
  order                                                                    *
*                                                                          *
* ----------------------------------------------------------------------- *
```

Variable declarations ...

- Include preconditions, postconditions, and loop invariant comments for important loops and composite mechanisms. Use of formal specifications can reduce the need for other forms of commenting, although where an informal comment is more concise it may be justified as an alternative. In some cases a combination of formal and informal comments is appropriate. Throughout this text we have focused mostly on the use of formal comments.

Naming conventions

The choice of names for the variables and procedures etc. in a program can provide a simple yet powerful means for making a program easier to comprehend. As with commenting there are two extreme positions that are taken which can cause problems:

- under-use of naming conventions;
- over-use of naming conventions.

Some programmers make no conscious effort to select variable names that can improve the documentation of a program. For example, they might supply the following implementation for finding the maximum in an array:

Version 1

```
g := 1; w := d[1];
do g ≠ T →
  if d[g + 1] > w → g, w := g + 1, d[g + 1]
  [] d[g + 1] ≤ w → g := g + 1
  fi
od
```

The variable name w in no way indicates that it is used for the maximum, nor is the variable T suggestive of the array size. As a contrast, consider the following implementation:

Version 2

```
arrayindex := 1; maximumvalue := dataset[1];
do arrayindex ≠ arraysize →
  if dataset[arrayindex + 1] > maximumvalue →
    arrayindex, maximumvalue :=
      arrayindex + 1, dataset[arrayindex + 1]
  [] dataset[arrayindex + 1] ≤ maximumvalue →
    arrayindex := arrayindex + 1
  fi
od
```

In this second version the choice of variable names, by trying to be over-explicit actually makes the program harder to read.

A more balanced approach to naming probably gives the best results. To illustrate this consider the following implementation for the maximum finding problem.

Version 3

```
i := 1; max := a[1];
do i ≠ N →
    if a[i] > max → i, max := i + 1, a[i + 1]
    [] a[i] ≤ max → i := i + 1
    fi
od
```

Here max is sufficient to convey the notion of maximum, i is suggestive of an index, and N is frequently used to indicate the size of an array. In contrast with version 2, the mechanism is not buried in a sea of characters.

In this book we have tended to err on the crisp and concise side in presenting algorithms, on the grounds that less detail can often make things easier to understand. Other programmers have a tendency towards the version 2 style in choosing variable names.

One of the greatest dangers in choosing variable names is that the choice is inaccurate. As an example, consider the following implementation:

```
max := 1; i := 1;
do i ≠ N →
    if a[i + 1] > a[max] → i, max := i + 1, i + 1
    [] a[i + 1] ≤ a[max] → i := i + 1
    fi
od
```

Unlike the last three examples this implementation finds the *position of the maximum* rather than the maximum itself. However, the choice of the variable name max would appear to suggest that the implementation finds the maximum itself. Loose naming like this can cause serious problems when making changes to programs because our natural tendency is to jump to conclusions about what things mean and what they are needed for. A few people use this argument to condemn the practice of trying to choose meaningful names for variables and procedures etc.

There are several simple conventions for naming in *specifications* and *program implementations* that are used in this book.

- Constants and variables that are *not changed* in a program are represented either by single capital letters or upper-case words. Examples are

N	for the size of an array
PI	the value of π
STACKSIZE	limiting value for size of stack
$(\forall j : 1 \leq j < N...$	where N is the array upper limit

- All variables whose values are changed by a program are given lower-case representations, for example

sum	variable used to sum the elements in an array
pos	position of maximum in an array
ch	an ASCII character

- For array subscripts and loop indices the following variables are often used:

  i, j, k, p, q

This is a convention left over from the days of FORTRAN. For the most part it seems to be a simple and practical convention that has some merit.

- For array sizes the variables M and N are frequently used while for array names we often use A, a, B, b, C, c for arrays of numbers, depending on whether they are fixed or changed by the program. For example, when an array is being searched but not changed, we refer to it in the specification and implementation as A[1..N]. On the other hand, when an array is used for sorting, a[1..N] is used.

- Procedures and functions start with a capital letter but subsequent letters (apart from the start of other words) are in lowercase, for example

ReadWord(word, N)	reads a word of text
WriteWord(word, N)	writes out a word
CompareWords(w1, w2, N)	compares two words of length N

These simple naming conventions if rigorously followed can make programs and specifications a lot easier to read.

The actual naming conventions that one settles upon when writing programs are not all that important. What is important though, is that a *consistent style* is used throughout. For example it would be poor style to *sometimes* use all upper-case characters to represent constants and other times use all lower-case. The best advice is to adopt a convention and stick to it.

12.2.2   Input/output conventions

Above all else programs are written to be used by people. The acceptance of a program by users rests very heavily on how much care has been put into the design of the user interface. A program with the most elegant algorithms in the world is likely to be rejected or regarded as a 'lousy program' if it interacts poorly with its users. Many good programs requiring years of toil have met this fate simply because their designers tacked on a poor user interface at the end when they realized their program might be useful to others.

The role of the user-interface component of a program is

- to signal users whenever data is required and to indicate clearly what parameters, in which particular format, must be supplied;
- to protect users from entering data that will cause the program to fail or produce erroneous results;
- to provide informative feedback whenever a user enters inappropriate data;
- to ensure any output produced by a program is properly labelled and formatted;
- to provide a meaningful and informative context for user interactions with the program;
- to provide a novice user of the program with access to detailed documentation which describes clearly what the program is used for, and the results that can be expected from it. This requirement is most relevant for large programs that are likely to have many users. Back-up systems of this order are often referred to as 'Help' systems.

A very simple example will now be used to discuss and illustrate the design of a user interface. Suppose for example we want to design one for a program that computes the greatest common divisor of two positive integers. Given that a function gcd is available that performs the computation the following program steps (borrowing Pascal's I/O) would be sufficient to do the job.

Version 1

```
read(X, Y);
d := gcd(X, Y);
writeln(d)
```

The 'Screen interaction' that takes place when this program is executed is shown below.

Screen interaction
```
36 54
18
```

It consists of two numbers on one line (36 and 54) and a third number 18 on a second line. To an observer examining the screen after the execution of the program there is little to suggest what might have taken place. This program is very likely to trouble not only its observers but also its users. It provides no help to a would-be user about what the program will do, what input the user must provide or what output the program provides. In short, its user interface is virtually non-existent.

To overcome these criticisms the following implementation may be proposed:

Version 2

```
writeln("Function: Computes Greatest Common Divisor of Two Positive
Integers");
writeln;
write("Enter first positive integer X : "); readln(X);
write("Enter second positive integer Y : "); readln(Y);
d := gcd (X, Y);
writeln;
writeln("Greatest Common Divisor of X and Y = ", d);
```

The screen interaction for this second implementation is as follows.

Screen interaction

Function: Computes Greatest Common Divisor of Two Positive Integers

Enter first positive integer X : 36
Enter second positive integer Y : 54

Greatest Common Divisor of X and Y = 18

This second implementation provides a much better user interface than our original implementation. It informs the user what the program does, what inputs are required, and what format should be used to enter the inputs (in the original version there was no indication that the two integers should be entered on a single line or on separate lines). The output is also clearly labelled.

We might be encouraged to think that a good job has been done and that the design of this user interface could be put to rest. Unfortunately, this interface, although informative, makes no allowance for the user making an error when entering data into the program. For example, if the user responded with either a zero or negative integer to either of the requests for input the program would fail badly.

This latest problem can be overcome by including tests to see whether the data entered is positive. Recovery from a negative or zero input can be achieved by combining the test with a repeat loop. Making these modifications we get

Version 3

```
      .
      .
      .
    writeln("Function: Computes Greatest Common Divisor of Two Positive
    Integers");
    writeln;
    repeat
        write("Enter first positive integer X :"); readln(X);
    until X > 0;
    repeat
        write("Enter second positive integer Y : "); readln(Y);
    until Y > 0;
    d := gcd (X, Y);
    writeln;
    writeln("Greatest Common Divisor of X and ∧ = ", d);
```

This latest implementation will not allow the gcd computation to proceed until two positive integers X and Y have been entered by the user. Cycling on the input as we have done here is a commonly used technique for improving the robustness of a program. In most cases, it is desirable for a program to attempt to recover when it detects bad input data.

This last implementation is still vulnerable to bad input from the user. It will recover from the input of negative or zero integers but it will fail when a user accidently or otherwise types a non-digit (e.g., a user may accidently type the digit one, followed by the alphabetic character o, thinking that the number 10 has been typed).

The only way to protect against this sort of bad input is for the program to treat the expected numbers as strings of characters and then construct the corresponding integers. This will allow checking of each character to ensure that it is a digit and responding accordingly when a non-digit (and hence bad input) is encountered. To handle the character input and integer construction in Pascal a mechanism getinteger that includes the following steps could be used:

```
    i := eoln(input); N := true; n := N;
    int := 0; base := ord('0');
    while i <> n do begin
       ch := input↑ ;
       d := ord(ch) – base;
       if (d >= 0) and (d <= 9) then begin
          int := int * 10 + d;
          get(input); i := eoln(input)
          end
       else
          n := i
    end;
    writeln;
    if i = N then getinteger := int else begin
       getinteger := –1
       writeln;
       writeln ("Input Error non-digit or negative number entered")
    end
```

Our final implementation, incorporating the function getinteger may take the following form.

Version 4

```
    .
    .
    .
    writeln("FUNCTION: Computes the Greatest Common Divisor of
    two positive integers")
    writeln;
    repeat
        write ("Enter first positive integer X : "); X := getinteger();
    until X > 0;
    repeat
        write ("Enter second positive integer Y : "); Y := getinteger();
    until Y > 0;
    d := gcd (X,Y);
    writeln("Greatest Common Divisor of X and Y = ",d);
    .
    .
    .
```

This final implementation is more robust. It has most of the attributes of a sound and effective user interface. Believe it or not there are still chinks in this program's armour. It offers no protection against the user entering a number that is larger than the maximum integer the particular hardware can store. Incorporating this addition check on the input is left as an exercise for the reader.

This very simple example has illustrated a number of the common problems with user interfaces along with various ways of overcoming them.

12.2.3 Modularization

The modularity of a program makes a significant contribution

- to the understandability of the program, and
- to the ease with which it can be modified.

The amount of code that can be comprehended as a whole at any one time is small. Modularization can be used to break programs down into relatively small easily understood units. Modern programming languages like Modula-2 and Ada provide a number of syntax conventions for assisting with the modularization of a program. They provide a means for the controlled sharing of information and functions as well as preserving the hierarchical structure of a program.

In program design there are two kinds of modularity that we must be concerned with:

- hierarchical modularity;
- functional modularity.

Hierarchical modularity

Breaking a large program into modules which in turn may be further broken down into even smaller modules, and so on is the technique used to model the hierarchical organization of a program. A broader view of some large programs is to regard them as directed acyclic graphs rather than as trees. In both kinds of organization the issues are the same. A typical hierarchical organization is illustrated in Figure 12.1

In creating a hierarchical organization for a program it is necessary to be able to model two levels of interaction and modularity, **strong localized interaction** with the sharing of information between small modules, and much **weaker global interactions** between large functionally independent modules. These two kinds of interaction are modelled and distinguished nicely in Modula-2 using procedure/function constructs and the MODULE construct. Procedures, with their parameter passing and scope rules are well suited for the efficient high-volume localized sharing of information. Modules, on the other hand, are well suited for encapsulating or providing an umbrella around well-defined functional entities built from procedures/

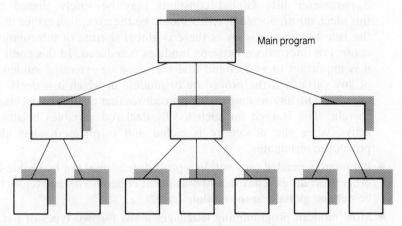

Main program

Figure 12.1   Hierarchical program organization.

functions and shared data structures. IMPORT and EXPORT mechanisms associated with modules provide an effective way of sharing procedures and data structures on a more global scale. Modules, being largely self-contained, should define intellectually manageable functional components of a program.

There are several useful guidelines for achieving modularity at the procedure/function level.

- The primary criterion for identifying a procedure/function is singularity of function. In other words, at the base level a procedure is a mechanism that carries out a *single* well-defined task. (This does not preclude the use of higher-level procedures that model more complex functions built from simple functions.)

- Even at the level of localized modularization, interaction between procedures should be kept to a minimum. Parameter passing within an encapsulating module framework should provide the primary vehicle for defining and controlling interactions between procedures.

- Information required by a procedure should be passed to it via a parameter list. A mechanism that yields a single result parameter should be implemented using a function. Whenever a mechanism yields more than one result, procedure parameter passing should be used to model the information flow. Greater simplicity and modularity can be achieved by striving to use functions in preference to procedures whenever possible.

- Within a localized module or procedure there are sometimes critical parameters that are used by most of the procedures. Such parameters may be given global status within the local module. This allows procedures to use such parameters without including them within a parameter list. Global constants may be safely shared by this mechanism. Such a practice should be the exception rather than the rule because as soon as there is global sharing of information control of interactions between modules is reduced. In this context it is important to understand that the *scope* or extent of influence of any variable is the procedure or module in which it is declared together with any accompanying procedures that have been declared therein. The storage for such locally declared variables becomes active when the procedure is called and is released when the procedure terminates

- Parameters needed only within a procedure should not be visible to other procedures. They should not appear either in a parameter list or be defined globally at the module level.

- Most modern programming languages allow for two types of parameters to be passed to procedures and functions; those whose values are *changed* by the procedure/function, and those whose values are *not changed* by the procedure/function. In Pascal and Modula-2 for example, the VAR declaration within the procedure parameter list declaration is used to identify variables that are changed by the procedure. We need to qualify what we mean by 'changed' because any parameter passed to a procedure can be changed *within* that procedure. What distinguishes VAR parameters is that the changes to the values of such parameters within the procedure are propagated back to the module that called the procedure:

EXAMPLE 1 (Parameter passing)_____

Consider the following Modula-2 procedure declaration

```
PROCEDURE Sumdiff (VAR s, d : INTEGER; A, B: INTEGER);
BEGIN
    s := A + B;
    d := ABS(A − B)
END
```

The variables s and d serve as place holders for values that are passed back to the calling procedure. The variables A and B are value parameters which are not changed.

_____

A good convention is to make value parameters capitalized in the declaration of the procedure.

If the procedure Sumdiff was called using

```
Sumdiff(sum, diff, X, Y)
```

Only the values of sum and diff would be changed in the calling module.

EXAMPLE 2_____

Suppose the following function was used to compute N factorial:

```
PROCEDURE Factorial (N : CARDINAL) : CARDINAL;
VAR f : CARDINAL;
BEGIN
  f := 1;
  WHILE N > 0 DO
    f := f * N;
    N := N – 1
  END;
  RETURN f
END
```

In this implementation, although the value of N is changed within Factorial, the corresponding parameter is *not* changed in the module that calls Factorial. For example, if the call is

```
fact := Factorial(n)
```

then n will not be changed in the module that calls factorial even though a copy of it is changed *locally* within Factorial.

EXAMPLE 3 (Singularity of function)_____

To illustrate these ideas consider how we might solve the problem of reading a line of text consisting of words separated by one or more spaces with possibly leading and trailing spaces in the line. The task is to read this text and write out the words one per line.

One way to solve the problem would be to implement a single loop mechanism that was able to detect the end of words, for example

Version 1

```
w := 0; i := eoln(input); N := true;
do i ≠ N →
   if input↑ = SPACE → get(input); if w > 0 then writeln; w := 0 fi
   [] input↑ ≠ SPACE → w := w + 1; ch := input↑ ; write(ch);
                       get(input); i := eoln(input)
   fi
od;
if w > 0 then writeln fi
```

The second way to solve this problem is to use procedures that deal respectively with the *word* and *spaces* structures in the text. We then get the implementation

Version 2

```
i := getspaces(i);
do i ≠ N →
  i := getword(i);
  writeln;
  i := getspaces(i)
od
```

The function getspaces will consume a sequence of adjacent spaces from the input, and the function getword will consume a sequence of adjacent alphabetic characters. Both getspaces and getword contain loops which means that there are three loops used in the second implementation compared with only one loop in the first implementation. However, because the purpose of the mechanism is to process words and spaces, the use of functions to highlight the two forms of processing required is justified. It can be seen at a glance what the second implementation is doing whereas the detail of the first implementation is more subtle.

If the problem had been one of simply reading a line of text and writing it out again, with no distinction accorded to words, then a single loop implementation would have been appropriate. More is said about this sort of issue in the section on loop structuring.

EXAMPLE 4

Consider the problem of summing an array of N elements. One way we could do this would be to use the procedure sum

Version 1

```
procedure sum (A : nelements; N : integer; var s: integer);
var i : integer;
begin
  i := 0; s := 0;
  do i ≠ N →
    i, s := i + 1, s + A[i + 1]
  od
end
```

An alternative implementation for this problem would involve using a function:

Version 2

```
function sum(a : nelements; N : integer): integer;
var i,s : integer;
begin
  i := 0; s := 0;
  do i ≠ N →
    i, s := i + 1, s + a[i + 1]
  od;
  sum := s
end
```

The call to this function would be of the form

```
s1 := sum(a, N)
```

Because only a *single* parameter is returned, the function implementation with the assignment is to be preferred, as it provides a more explicit description of the role of the mechanism.

EXAMPLE 5 (Using procedures, local variables)

For some problems using a function is just not appropriate. Consider the problem of swapping the values of two variables. To implement this mechanism two parameters must be passed to the procedure, both of which have their values changed. The most appropriate way to handle this problem is to use a **var** declaration for the two parameters.

```
procedure swap (var a, b : integer);
var t : integer;
begin
  t := a;
  a := b;
  b := t
end
```

EXAMPLE 6 (Local procedures)

The textual organization of procedures/functions within a program should model the hierarchical organization of the program. This suggests that when a procedure is used only within the confines of another procedure then it should be *declared* within that procedure.

For example, consider the use of the procedure swap in a selection sort – it should be declared within the sort.

```
procedure selectsort (var a : nelements; N : integer);
var i, j : integer;
    procedure swap (var x, y : integer);
    var t : integer;
    begin
      t := x;
      x := y;
      y := t
    end; {swap}
begin {selectsort}
    i := 1;
    do i ≠ N →
      j := i;
      do j ≠ N →
        if aᵢ ≤ aⱼ₊₁ → j := j + 1
        [] aᵢ > aⱼ₊₁ → swap (aᵢ, aⱼ₊₁) ; j := j + 1
        fi
      od;
      i := i + 1
    od
end {selectsort}
```

Local procedures should be declared and used much in the same way as local variables are employed.

Functional modularity

Functional modularity is most often associated with the implementation of abstract data types. In such implementations the objective is to gather together the declarations for a data structure along with *all* the operations that are performed on that data structure. For example, when a stack is declared, the accompanying operations to *push* another element onto the stack, *pop* an element off the top of the stack, test whether the stack is empty, and so on are all defined at the same time. The definition and use of abstract data types are simply and practically supported by the language Modula-2; the data structure, its operations, and initializations are all *encapsulated* in a module. An EXPORT and IMPORT syntax allows the data structure and its operations to be used by other modules without regard for the details associated with the implementation. In other words functional modularity allows us to reduce complexity by decoupling implementation from application. Details irrelevant to an application are *hidden* from the user.

A very simple example of this programming technique is illustrated by the application of a random-number generator. Random numbers are usually implemented by providing an initial *seed* value. The most desirable situation for a user of a random-number generator is not to have to bother about the details of providing an initial seed, etc. All the user wants to be able to do is simply call the generator and have it supply new random numbers. Modula-2 allows the seed initialization to be hidden from the user inside an implementation module. Where possible we should strive for this sort of decoupling. A sketch of this implementation is as follows:

```
MODULE UseRandom;
FROM DefRandom IMPORT Random;
.
.

BEGIN

.
  x := Random( );      (* no need to initialize seed *)

.
END UseRandom.
IMPLEMENTATION MODULE DefRandom;
VAR seed : INTEGER;

.
PROCEDURE Random( ) : INTEGER;
BEGIN

.    (*body of random number generator*)

END;
.
.

BEGIN
  seed := 457     (*seed initialized*)
END DefRandom.
```

12.2.4 Use of variables and constants

In general programs are required to be used many times on many different sets of data often on many different computer systems. To allow maximum flexibility, durability, and portability of programs it is essential to adopt sound and consistent practices for employing constants and variables.

Most of the practices and suggestions that we wish to make about program parameterization can be best illustrated by examples illustrating good and bad practices.

Use of constants

We often see arrays in a program declared in the following way:

Bad practice

> **VAR** a : ARRAY [1 . . 100] OF INTEGER

The problem with this is that subsequently we may wish to expand the array. If our program is large this is likely to involve more than a simple replacement of 100 by, say, 200. It is far better practice to localize changes by employing constants to parameterize array sizes and so on.

Good practice

> **CONST** NA = 100;
>   NB = 200;
>
> **VAR** a : ARRAY [1 . . NA] OF INTEGER;
>   b : ARRAY [1 . . NB] OF CHAR;
>   c : ARRAY [1 . . NA] OF CARDINAL

With constant parameterization, when a change is required it is localized to a single place (e.g. to change the lengths of arrays a and c we simply change the constant declaration).

Another bad practice along similar lines is illustrated by the following example:

Bad practice

> **FOR** i := 1 **TO** 20 **DO** ...

To obtain maximum flexibility the 20 should be replaced either by a constant or variable parameter as illustrated below.

Good practice

> CONST N = 20;
> .
> .
> .
> **FOR** i := 1 **TO** N **DO** ...

As a general rule *numerical constants should appear only in constant declarations*. Rigorous application of this rule can markedly improve the flexibility of programs. Furthermore, carefully chosen names for constants and parameters can make a useful contribution to the self-documentation of programs.

There is one practice in the use of variables that takes precedence over everything else. A variable in a program should be used for *one purpose*, and one purpose only, in a given program context. Neglect of this practice results in a confusing style of programming. The following example illustrates the problem.

Bad practice

Consider the problem of computing the average of an array of N integers. A possible implementation is

```
i := 0; sum := 0;
do i ≠ N →
    i, sum := i + 1, sum + a[i + 1]
od;
sum := sum / N;       (*compute average*)
WriteString("Average ="); Write(sum); WriteLn
```

What is confusing about this implementation is that the variable sum is used for the sum of the array elements and subsequently also to hold the average of the array elements. This doubling up of usage can in more complicated cases lead to considerable confusion. In this case, a second variable for the average is justified as illustrated by the following implementation.

Good practice

```
i := 0; sum := 0;
do i ≠ N →
    i, sum := i + 1, sum + a[i + 1]
od;
average := sum / N;
WriteString("Average ="); Write(average); WriteLn
```

The opposite problem of using two or more identifiers to play the role of a single variable should also be avoided as it too can lead to confusion.

A useful set of documenting conventions for variables, constants, and procedures is as follows.

- Variables in a program are represented by *lower-case* names or abbreviations, for example, max, ch, top
- Constants in a program and data that is processed but not changed by a program are represented by upper-case names or abbreviations, for example, N, SIZE
- Procedures and functions start with a capital letter but the rest of the letters in each word are lower-case, for example, PROCEDURE Fibonacci, PROCEDURE GetWord

We will now turn to a discussion of the initialization problem in some detail.

12.3   Initialization of Loops

> The initialization of the environment for iterations is one of the most important aspects of robust programming ... it is difficult, perhaps impossible, to formulate universal rules on this aspect and the guidelines seem to be somewhat contradictory
>
> *W. Turski*

The appropriate initialization for loops is of central importance in the implementation of programs. There are four main functions that the initialization of a loop serves.

- It must provide appropriate initial values for all variables that are to be used in the loop (*except* those that may only be used in an internal loop).
- It must establish the loop invariant.
- It should be sufficient to establish the postcondition of the loop in the instance where a state of the computation can force the guard of the loop to be false prior to entry into the loop. That is, in some sense, initialization must solve the smallest, or simplest class of problems that the mechanism may encounter for data that satisfies the precondition.

Initialization can also play an important constructive role in the development and implementation of algorithms for defined postconditions. In particular, an initialization can be used to derive an invariant from a postcondition. Rather than simply attempting to provide a list of rules for making 'good' initializations of loops we will discuss a number of mistakes that are commonly made. Usually it is only the initialization of compound loops that causes problems.

12.3.1   Under-initialization

In making an initialization of the free variables associated with a loop a common mistake is not to provide appropriate initial values for variables. **Under-initialization** of a loop occurs when the free variables associated with the loop are not given values that will enable the postcondition to be established in the instance where the body of the loop is not executed.

EXAMPLE 1_____

As an example consider the problem of finding the maximum in an array of N integers. An initialization and loop implementation for this problem might be

```
{ N ⩾ 1 }
i := 0; max:= − 9999;      { Initialization }
do i ≠ N →
  i := i + 1;
  if aᵢ > max → max := aᵢ
  [] aᵢ ⩽ max → skip
  fi
od
```

This is an example of under-initialization. Although this program will, in many cases, correctly find the maximum, it carries the risk of failure should all the numbers be less than −9999. The postcondition for finding the maximum is

$$R : 1 \leqslant i \leqslant N \wedge max = a_i \wedge (\forall j : 1 \leqslant j \leqslant N : max \geqslant a_j)$$

The smallest problem is therefore the instance where N = 1. An appropriate initialization and implementation is

```
i := 1; max := aᵢ;
do i ≠ N →
  if aᵢ₊₁ > max → i, max := i + 1, aᵢ₊₁
  [] aᵢ₊₁ ⩽ max → i := i + 1
  fi
od
```

This implementation is not vulnerable to the situation where all the integers are less than some fixed constant that has been used for initialization.

EXAMPLE 2_____

Implementations given for generating the Fibonacci sequence frequently exhibit under-initialization. Successive members of this sequence are generated by adding together their two predecessors.
    The Fibonacci sequence is

$$1, 1, 2, 3, 5, 8, 13, \ldots$$

To generate the Nth Fibonacci number the following under-initialized loop structure is often given:

```
if N ≤ 2 → c := 1
[] N > 2 →
   i := 1; a := 1; b := 1;
   do i < N →
      c := a + b;
      a := b;
      b := c;
      i := i + 1
   od
fi
```

This implementation functions correctly for all cases where $N \geq 1$. However, the implementation involves some redundant computations and some clumsy guard testing. On the last iteration of the loop the variable c holds the value of the Nth Fibonacci number. However, *after* c is computed redundant assignments to a and b are made on the last iteration. Notice also that c is not initialized prior to entry into the loop. If these defects are corrected we get a much cleaner implementation that does not suffer from under-initialization.

```
b := 0; c := 1; i := 1;
do i ≠ N →
   a := b;
   b := c;
   c := a + b;
   i := i + 1
od
```

Notice that this second implementation works correctly for all values of $N \geq 1$. It avoids the redundant computations and does not treat $N = 2$ as a special case that must be guarded. The initialization assigns a value to c and thereby solves the smallest problem where $N = 1$.

EXAMPLE 3

Another interesting example of under-initialization of loops is illustrated by the following implementation of the *stores movement* problem (see also Section 11.4). Stated in its simplest form, we are given two arrays of length N. The first array is a product-identifier array p[1 . . N], which contains a set of incoming and outgoing transactions for various products that are ordered by their identifier. The elements in a second array trans[1 . . N] form a one-to-one correspondence with the elements in the first array. They are positive or negative quantities each representing a particular transaction for the associated product in the first array. A mechanism is needed to process this data and produce a report indicating the net quantity of each product currently held in stock.

The following solution to this problem exhibits under-initialization.

```
j := 0;
do j ≠ N →
    net := 0; prod := p[j + 1]; n := N;    { initialization for inner loop }
    do j ≠ n →
        if prod = p[j + 1] → j, net := j + 1, net + trans[j + 1]
        [] prod ≠ p[j + 1] → n := j
        fi
    od;
    writeln(prod, net)
od
```

The defect in this case is not that the mechanism does not function correctly in all cases but rather that it involves redundant computations, and involves some confusing logic. It is the under-initialization of the inner loop that causes the problems. The role of the inner loop is to process all the transactions of a product. The initialization of the inner loop here does not solve the smallest problem – that of processing a *single* transaction for a product. A consequence of the lack of progress made by the initialization is that the assignment

```
prod := p[j + 1]
```

is made and then, immediately upon entering the inner loop, the test

```
if prod = p[j + 1] → ...
```

is made. This test must *always* be true for the first iteration of each invocation of the inner loop. Furthermore, the guard test on the inner loop

```
do j ≠ n → ...
```

is redundant on first entering the inner loop since j is not increased on passing through the guard of the outer loop to the guard of the inner loop.

These defects are overcome in the following implementation

```
j := 0;
do j ≠ N →
   net, prod, j := trans[j + 1], p[j + 1], j + 1; n := N;
   do j ≠ n →
      if prod = p[j + 1] → j, net := j + 1, net + trans [j + 1]
      [] prod ≠ p[j + 1] → n := j
      fi
   od;
   writeln(prod, net)
od
```

In this case the initialization of the inner loop solves the smallest problem – that of processing a *single* transaction. Also, the initialization increases j and thereby makes progress towards termination. Consequently the test

```
if prod = p[j + 1] →...
```

no longer involves the initialized value of the product identifier but instead its successor. The test is no longer redundant. It will not necessarily be true for the first iteration of each invocation of the inner loop. Furthermore, the guard test on first entering the inner loop is no longer redundant but a necessity since j has been increased in the initialization. Redundancy aside, a further problem with under-initialized loops is that they are often harder to maintain when a program has to be altered.

EXAMPLE 4

Another example of an under-initialized loop is given by the following implementation of a divide-and-conquer strategy for computing the remainder of X divided by D without using multiplication (see also the quotient–remainder problem, algorithm [14], Section 6.7.4).

Version 1   Under-initialized inner loop

```
{X ≥ 0 ∧ D > 0}
r := X;
do r ≥ D →
   d := D;      {initialization of inner loop}
   do r ≥ d →
      r, d := r − d, d + d
   od
od
```

In Version(1) the initialization of the inner loop again makes no progress towards termination. As a consequence, the guard test

$$\textbf{do } r \geqslant d \rightarrow$$

immediately after the assignment d := D is redundant, as the test on the outer loop

$$\textbf{do } r \geqslant D \rightarrow$$

already accounts for the status of the variable r.

The second implementation, with an initialization that can solve the smallest problem when $r \geqslant D$ applies, is as follows:

Version 2
```
r := X;
do r ≥ D →
   r, d := r – D, D + D;
   do r ≥ d →
      r, d := r – d, d + d
   od
od
```

In this second implementation, the inner loop guard test $r \geqslant d$ is no longer redundant as r has been reduced on passing from the outer to the inner loop. In other words this initialization for the inner loop makes measurable progress towards termination.

When the Version (2) implementation is examined carefully we see that the steps in the inner loop and in the initialization for the inner loop are essentially the same. In such cases it is possible to collapse the loop body and the initialization into one by using a repeat loop as is done below in Version (3).

Version 3
```
r := X;
do r ≥ D →
   d := D;
   repeat
      r, d := r – d, d + d
   until r < d
od
```

This implementation retains the efficiency of Version (2).

EXAMPLE 5_____

Another form of under-initialization is illustrated by the following implementation (the procedure swap simply exchanges the elements at the specified indices) of the well-known partitioning algorithm (see also Section 8.1). This basic implementation strategy for partitioning has been advocated elsewhere. This implementation will not work for all equal keys. Accompanying specifications are as follows:

$$R : a[1 .. i - 1] < x \wedge a[j + 1 .. N] \geqslant x \wedge i > j$$
$$P : a[1 .. i - 1] < x \wedge a[j + 1 .. N] \geqslant x$$
$$t : j - i + 1$$

The implementation is

```
k := Xfind (a,N);
{k is the index of the larger of the first two different keys in a[1 .. N] }
{ Q : a[1 .. l−1] < x ∧ a[r + 1 .. N] ⩾ x }
i := l; j := r; x := a[k]; {P}
repeat
   swap(a[i], a[j]);
   do a[i] < x → i := i + 1 od;
   do a[j] ⩾ x → j := j − 1 od
until i > j
```

At first sight this looks like a clever, elegant and textually simple implementation of a partitioning algorithm. Unfortunately because the outermost loop is under-initialized, the implementation is inefficient and logically loose. To convince yourself, hand execute this algorithm for N = 2, x = 20, and a[1] = 10, a[2] = 20.

The problem with this implementation is that the initialization does not establish a strong enough precondition for the loop body to function effectively. We see that upon *first* entering the main loop the procedure

```
swap(a[i], a[j])
```

is executed. This *unconditionally* swaps the ith and jth elements irrespective of whether or not they need swapping to achieve the final partitioning. A consequence of this under-initialization defect is that the variant function t cannot be decreased directly (e.g. by i := i + 1 and j := j − 1) after the swap. Subsequent to the first iteration of the outer loop a stronger precondition exists that would permit the variant function to be decreased after the swap. However, because of the under initialization we *cannot* modify Version (1) to

```
repeat
   swap(a[i], a[j]); i := i + 1; j := j − 1;
   do a[i] < x → i := i + 1 od;
   do a[j] ⩾ x → j := j − 1 od
until i > j
```

because there are initial data configurations for which the implementation will fail. The fact that i does not increase and j does not decrease after the swap introduces a significant inefficiency into the algorithm. The reason for this is as follows. After the swap (on all iterations other than the first) the conditions

$$a[i] < x \quad \text{and} \quad a[j] \geq x$$

are both guaranteed to be true. However, the inner loop guard tests applied directly after the swap are

do a[i] < x → ...
do a[j] ≥ x → ...

These inner-loop guard tests are therefore redundant on the first iteration of both of the inner loops each time they are invoked.

The only way to remove this inefficiency and still retain essentially the same loop body for the inner loop is to employ an initialization mechanism that establishes a stronger precondition for the main loop. It is required to establish an initialization precondition consistent with the precondition maintained on subsequent iterations of the main loop.

There are two ways to accomplish this stronger precondition. The first and simplest way to proceed is to conditionally 'undo' what the swap does. This idea, although solving the problem introduces another defective initialization technique called *backstep initialization*. We will have more to say about this in the next section. The other way around the problem is to invoke for the initialization that part of the loop body which establishes the desired stronger precondition. When this is done i and j can be changed directly after the swap and the inefficiency is removed. This corresponds to matching the data structure and the program control structure (see also Section 12.6).

The resulting implementation is

```
.
.
.
do a[i + 1] < x → i := i + 1 od;        { iterative initialization}
do a[j − 1] > x → j := j − 1 od;
do i < j − 1 → {P}
   swap (a[i + 1], a[j − 1]); i := i + 1; j := j − 1;
   do a[i + 1] < x → i := i + 1 od;
   do a[j − 1] > x → j := j − 1 od
od
```

This implementation operates with the invariant

$$P : a[1 \ldots i] \leq x \land a[j \ldots N] \geq x \land 0 \leq i \leq j \leq N + 1$$

In this case we have cured an under-initialization problem by using an *iterative initialization* mechanism, that is

do a[i + 1] < x → i := i + 1 **od**;   { iterative initialization }
do a[j − 1] > x → j := j − 1 **od**

12.3.2   Backstep initialization

The discussion of the partitioning implementation in the last section identified what was called backstep initialization. **Backstep initialization** is really a form of under-initialization where it is necessary to invoke an action which is the *inverse* of an action that will be carried out as soon as the loop is entered. There are two primary defects with backstep initialization. The most significant defect is the confusion that can be introduced by a seemingly 'contrary' set of steps prior to entry into the loop body. Such steps can be very misleading to anyone who wishes to understand or modify a back-stepped implementation. The other defect of backstep initialization is that it involves some unnecessary computations.

To illustrate backstep initialization we will use a slightly different variation on the partitioning problem to that discussed in the previous section. When partitioning is used in sorting (i.e. with Quicksort) it is often advocated that the partitioning elements should be chosen to be the median of the first, middle, and last elements in the section to be partitioned.

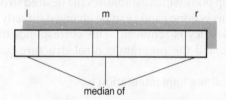

median of

In this case the backstepped **median-of-three** initialization mechanism establishes the data configuration below.

Backstep initialization

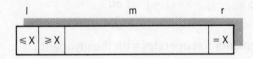

After the swap upon entering the loop we end up with the configuration

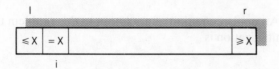

In the case where there were only three elements the swap would establish the postcondition.

The actual partitioning implementation that employs the backstep median-of-three initialization is as follows:

```
{r ≥ 3}
i := l − 1; j := r + 1; m := (i + j) div 2;
median of three(a, x, i, m, j); i := l;
{Q : N ≥ 3 ∧ a[i] ≤ x ∧ a[l + 1] ≥ x ∧ a[r] = x}
do i < j − 1 →
    swap (a[i + 1], a[j − 1]); i := i + 1; j := j − 1;
    do a[i + 1] < x → i := i + 1 od;
    do a[j − 1] > x → i := j − 1 od
od;
```

With care it is possible to combine a median-of-three mechanism with partitioning that avoids backstep initialization.

The backstep initialization needed for the partitioning algorithm in the last section is as follows:

```
if a[i] < a[j] then swap(a[i], a[j]) fi;
do i < j →
    swap (a[j], a[j]); i := i + 1; j := j − 1;
    do a[i] < x → i := i + 1 od;
    do a[j] > x → j := j − 1 od
od
```

12.3.3 Over-initialization of loops

Over-initialization of loops occurs when *more* is done in the initialization step than is required to solve the smallest or simplest problem that the mechanism is designed to handle. What usually happens with over-initialization is that all or part of the action for the next step (in the loop) is completed in the initialization. Once a loop has been over-initialized, it is then necessary to provide a step for the next iteration at the end of the loop. The following example illustrates this initialization defect.

EXAMPLE 1

Consider the task of evaluating a polynomial that satisfies the specification

```
Q : N ≥ 0
R : y = X⁰ + X¹ + X² + ... + Xᴺ
```

for some arbitrary N and an arbitrary X.

An implementation of a solution to this problem that exhibits over-initialization is

Version 1

```
i := 0; p := X; y := 1;
do i ≠ N → {P}
   y := y + p;
   p := p * X;
   i := i + 1
od
{R_D}
```

where

$$R_D : y = X^0 + X^1 + ... + X^i \wedge p = X^{i+1} \wedge i = N$$

The smallest problem for this example corresponds to the case where $N = 0$. It is true that the initialization

$$y := 1$$

will establish R_D. However the assignment $p := X$ over-initializes the variable p. A consequence of this is that at the end of the loop we have the statement

$$p := p * X$$

When the loop terminates *one more* p value is generated than is needed to compute y and thereby establish R. The invariant P for the loop makes this quite clear. It has the form

$$P : y = X^0 + X^1 + ... + X^i \wedge p = X^{i+1} \wedge 0 \leq i \leq N$$

when $i = N$ and termination occurs p has the value

$$p = X^{N+1}$$

It might be argued that the sort of defects exhibited by this implementation are very minor. However, when we are dealing with much more complex problems that have this defect, it may contribute adversely to the efficiency and complexity of an implementation. In addition, over-initialization contributes badly to the logic of the solution to a problem. In this case a reader of this program would be left wondering what the significance of the extra computation of p was after the last y value had been computed. Programs with these sort of defects are harder to maintain and understand because of the lingering doubts they often leave in the programmer's mind.

A solution to the polynomial evaluation problem that avoids over-initialization is

Version 2

```
i := 0; p := 1; y := 1;
do i ≠ N → {P}
  p := p * X;
  y := y + p;
  i := i + 1
od
{R_D}
```

where

$$R_D : y = X^0 + X^1 + ... + X^i \wedge p = X^i \wedge i = N$$

and

$$P : y = X^0 + X^1 + ... + X^i \wedge 0 \leq i \leq N$$

When $i = N$ and termination occurs p has the value

$$p = X^N$$

In this case there is no overshoot in the p computation.

EXAMPLE 2

Another slightly more complex example of over-initialization occurs with the implementation below of Hamming's problem (Dijkstra, 1976). To solve this problem it is necessary to generate the first N members of the following sequence:

$$S = \{1, 2, 3, 4, 5, 6, 8, 9, 10, 12, ... \}$$

Members of the sequence S consist only of natural numbers that are divisible by no other primes than 2, 3 and 5. Using an inductive definition members of the sequence satisfy the relations

$$1 \in S$$
$$x \in S \Rightarrow 2x \in S \wedge 3x \in S \wedge 5x \in S$$

Clever solutions to this problem are presented elsewhere by Dijkstra and Gries. To solve this problem they introduce the invariant

$$P : 0 \leq i < N \wedge S[0 .. i] \text{ contains the first } i \text{ values of } S$$

New free variables x2, x3 and x5 satisfy the relations

$$P2 : x2 = y * 2 \land y = MIN (x : x \in S[0 .. i] : 2 * x > S[i])$$
$$P3 : x3 = y * 3 \land y = MIN (x : x \in S[0 .. i] : 3 * x > S[i])$$
$$P5 : x5 = y * 5 \land y = MIN (x : x \in S[0 .. i] : 5 * x > S[i])$$

and

$$P' : P2 \land P3 \land P5$$

An implementation of the sequence generator that exhibits over-initialization is given below. Variables j2, j3 and j5 are introduced to locate the y values.

Version 1
```
i := 0; S[0] := 1;
j2 := 0, j3 := 0; j5 := 0;
x2 := 2; x3 := 3; x5 := 5;
do i ≠ N →
    i , S[i + 1] := i + 1 , min(x2, x3, x5);
    do x2 ≤ S[i] → j2, x2 := j2 + 1, 2 * S[j2 + 1] od;
    do x3 ≤ S[i] → j3, x3 := j3 + 1, 3 * S[j3 + 1] od;
    do x5 ≤ S[i] → j5, x5 := j5 + 1, 5 * S[j5 + 1] od
od
```

This implementation, on its last iteration, calculates new values of x2, x3 and x5 that are never used. The implementation below avoids over-initialization.

Version 2

Choosing an initialization that solves the smallest problem (N=1) and maintains the invariant

P : S[1 .. i] contains the first i values in S

We propose the following underlying computational strategy

```
i, S[1] := 1 , 1;
do i ≠ N
    "Calculate next-value-in-sequence"
    i, S[i+1] := i + 1, next-value-in-sequence
od
```

Our implementation then becomes

```
j2, j3, j5 := 0, 0, 0;
i, S[1] := 1, 1;
do i ≠ N → {P'}
    do 2 * S[j2 + 1] ≤ S[i] → j2 := j2 + 1 od;
    do 3 * S[j3 + 1] ≤ S[i] → j3 := j3 + 1 od;
    do 5 * S[j5 + 1] ≤ S[i] → j5 := j5 + 1 od;
    i, S[i+1] := i + 1, min(2 * S[j2 + 1], 3 * S[j3 + 1],5 * S[j5 + 1])
od
```

For this implementation the component invariants are quite different, i.e.

$$P2 : j2 = MAX (j : 0 < j \leq i : 2 * S_j \leq S_i)$$
$$P3 : j3 = MAX (j : 0 < j \leq i : 3 * S_j \leq S_i)$$
$$P5 : j5 = MAX (j : 0 < j \leq i : 5 * S_j \leq S_i)$$

and

$$P' = P \wedge P2 \wedge P3 \wedge P5$$

With these conditions the next member of the sequence must be one of

$$2 * S[j2 + 1], 3 * S[j3 + 1] \text{ and } 5 * S[j5 + 1].$$

In this implementation we have neglected to introduce new free variables x2, x3 and x5. Their use is an unnecessary complication of the algorithm.

EXAMPLE 3

Not all over-initialization problems are programmer generated. For example, the syntax usually used for reading from input in Modula-2 forces programmers to construct reading loops that are over-initialized. In Modula-2 a Read must be invoked before a test can be made for the end-of-file via the Done variable. The usual structure for repetitive input until end-of-file is as follows:

Version 1   Modula-2 implementation

```
Read(x);
WHILE Done DO
    .
    .
    .
    Read(x)
END
```

Because of the over-initialization that requires the Read outside the loop, it is then necessary for a second Read at the end of the loop. The Done variable is set to FALSE by the system when a Read is invoked that fails because the end-of-file is reached. When an invocation of Read is successful the system sets Done to TRUE.

With Pascal, over-initialization is avoided because the available systems function eof allows a test for end-of-file to be made without first invoking a read.

For repetitive input with Pascal, we may use the following implementation

Version 2   Pascal implementation

```
while not eof(input) do
  begin
    read (x)
    .
    .
    .
  end
```

In the second version the read is required only once in the program text, as opposed to twice in the over-initialized Modula-2 version.

The method for handling repetitive input in Pascal can be simulated in Modula-2 by defining a function EOF and a procedure Pread, that is

```
PROCEDURE EOF(): BOOLEAN;
BEGIN
  Read(x); (* the variables x and Done are global *)
  RETURN (NOT Done)
END;

PROCEDURE Pread (VAR x : INTEGER);
BEGIN
END
```

Using these tools repetitive input in Modula-2 may take the following form:

Version 3   Modula-2

```
VAR x : INTEGER;
  .
  .
  .
  WHILE NOT EOF() DO
    Pread(x);
    .
    .
    .
  END
```

With this simulated Pascal input there is only one read, but it is hidden inside the function EOF. The dummy procedure Pread serves merely as a vehicle for making the variable x read in EOF *visible* at the time when it would be assigned by a Pascal read. Using this arrangement, the problem of over-initialization is no longer apparent.

12.3.4   Premature initialization

Premature initialization is a common defect in programming style. It is a form of over-initialization that can occur where there are nested loops. The following example of a two-dimensional search taken from Gries and written in a Pascal dialect illustrates the form that premature initialization usually takes.

Version 1
```
    i := 0; j := 0;
    while i < m do
      begin
        while j < n do
          if x = b[i, j] then
            goto loopexit
          else
            j := j + 1;         {end of inner loop}
          i := i + 1; j := 0
      end;
loopexit:
```

Premature initialization occurs when a variable (or variables) that is used only in an inner loop is initialized *outside* an outer loop. It clearly violates generally accepted program structuring and decomposition practices. In our example, the variable j suffers from premature initialization. It has been initialized *outside* the outer loop rather than *just before* the inner loop.

The conventional schematic structure for initialization of nested loops is as follows:

Conventional nested loop initialization
> **Initialization for outer loop**;
> Outer loop guard
>   **Initialization for inner loop**;
>   Inner loop guard
>
>   .
>   .
>
>   Inner loop body
>
>   .
>   .
>
>   End of inner loop
> End of outer loop

In contrast to this structure, when there is premature initialization of an inner loop we end up with the following schematic arrangement:

Nested loops with premature initialization

    Initialization for outer loop;
    Initialization for inner Loop;
    Outer loop guard
      Inner loop guard

      Inner loop body
.

     End of inner loop;
     Initialization for inner loop

    End of outer loop

When there is premature initialization of an inner loop, it is necessary to duplicate the initialization *after* the inner loop. In our two-dimensional search example, the initialization $j := 0$ for the inner loop must be duplicated after the inner loop. The need for this duplication is avoided when the inner loop is initialized just prior to its guard test. The following example shows an implementation that avoids premature initialization.

Version 2   Appropriate initialization

```
    i := 0;
    while i < m do
      begin
      j := 0;      {initialization for inner loop}
      while j < n do
        if x = b[i, j] then
          goto loopexit
        else
          j := j + 1;
      { end of inner loop }
      i := i + 1
      end
loopexit:
```

The problems that premature initialization in particular, and over-initialization in general, raise may be summarized as follows.

- It results in unnecessary duplication of code.
- It complicates the formal reasoning about loops particularly with respect to representing appropriate loop invariants.

- It separates actions that belong together.
- It complicates the structure of a program unnecessarily.
- The *first* execution of the inner loop initialization may need to be protected by additional guards because of the environment in which it is located.

It is apparent from the preceding discussion on loop initialization that considerable care is needed if the sort of defects that we have highlighted here are to be avoided. More than anything else this comes back to the strict application of the guidelines suggested in the introduction to this section.

12.4   Termination of loops

The termination of loops is one of the most vulnerable aspects of program implementation. When loops are designed and implemented from post-conditions and invariants etc., problems with termination should be minimized. However, there are some ground rules and implementation techniques that are worth noting in the interests of good programming. We will now explore some of these issues.

12.4.1   Choosing loop guards

Of central importance in designing a loop is the choice of the loop guard. If the guard is not chosen with absolute precision several things can happen.

(1)   The loop can do *more* iterations than it should and thereby risk side-effects. We call this **over-iteration.**

For example, the following implementation, which is intended to check whether or not a given data set is sorted, exhibits over-iteration.

```
i := 1; n := N;
do i ≤ n →
    if a_i ≤ a_{i+1} → i := i + 1
    [] a_i > a_{i+1} → n := i
    fi
od;
sorted := i > N
```

What happens with this implementation is that when the data is sorted the guard allows one more iteration than it should. As a consequence, on the last iteration, in the test

$$\textbf{if } a_i \leq a_{i+1} \cdots$$

with $i = N$, an attempt is made to reference a_{N+1} which will cause a subscript error. With this loop body an appropriate guard is

do $i < n \rightarrow$

Proper design from a specification would avoid this problem. The sort-check problem will be discussed in detail in Section 12.4.2 on forced termination.

The greatest risks of over-iteration occur when an implementation involves nested loops. This usually happens because the guards of the loops are not precisely synchronized.

(2)   A second problem that can arise from poor choice of a loop guard is that it can end up doing *fewer* iterations than it should and thereby risk not completing the task it was designed to do. We call this **under-iteration.**

(3)   A third problem that can happen with the choice of loop guards is that the guard may be unsatisfiable. What then happens is that a loop will not terminate at all. It gets into a state where no variables can change with further iterations. Implementations that exhibit this behaviour are said to possess an **infinite loop**. Infinite loops are usually data dependent. For some data configurations they function correctly while in other cases they become infinite. An example that exhibits this problem is the following attempt at implementing a binary search (see also Section 7.3).

```
i := 0; j := N + 1;
do i < j →
    m := (i + j) div 2;
    if a[m] < X → i := m
    [] a[m] ⩾ X → j := m
    fi
od
```

In this case the required guard is

do $i \neq j - 1 \rightarrow$

because it is impossible for i and j to ever get closer than one apart due to the way m is calculated.

(4)   Another problem with choice of loop guards relates to the practice of using Boolean variables as guards. For example we frequently see in Pascal and Modula-2 programs statements like

while not found **do** ...
WHILE Done **DO** ...

The use of Boolean variables as guards is often used to exit from an iterative process. To handle such problems a common approach employed in most programming languages has been to use a goto statement or a break or exit command which transfers control *out* of the loop. These solutions have caused many problems and heated debates about when to, and when not to, use goto statements. In this discussion we are not interested in extending the debate but rather we will try to suggest a simple viable, language-independent solution to the problem. Much of the problem has arisen because of the semantics used to discuss the problem. The discussion has always focused on the need to 'jump out of' loops when certain conditions apply. If instead we look at the problem as one of *needing to terminate a loop when certain conditions apply* the whole attack on the problem becomes much simpler. This problem will now be examined as a termination problem.

12.4.2   Forced termination of loops

It is frequently desirable to force termination of an iterative process if certain conditions are encountered. For example, in searching an unordered array for an element X it is usually desirable to terminate the loop as soon as an element equal to X is found. Problems like this raise some interesting practical and philosophical questions about loop invariants, proof of correctness, representation-independent control structures, and programming style. These issues will be explored.

The starting point will be a program transformation that originally led to the idea of forced termination of loops. The binary search implementation given below together with its conversion to a linear search suggests the method:

```
{N > 0}
i := 0, j := N + 1;
do i < j − 1
    m := (i + j) div 2;
    if a[m] < X → i := m
    [] a[m] ⩾ X → j := m
    fi
od;
found := (a[m] = X)
```

A postcondition R, and loop invariant P for this mechanism are

$$R : a[1 .. i] < X \wedge a[j .. N] \geq X \wedge i = j - 1$$
$$P : a[1 .. i] < X \wedge a[j .. N] \geq X \wedge 0 \leq i < j \leq N + 1$$

The search element is X and the array is stored in a[1..N]. This binary search can be converted into a linear search for an ascending-order array by replacing the assignment $m := (i + j)$ **div** 2 by

$$m := i + 1$$

The resulting linear search algorithm is

```
{N > 0}
i := 0, j := N + 1;
do i < j − 1 →
    m := i + 1;
    if a[m] < X → i := m
    [] a[m] ⩾ X → j := m
    fi
od;
found := (a[m] = X)
```

Operationally the variable i is increased in single steps while the guard $i < j − 1$ is true and $a[m] < X$. If an element $a[m]$ greater than or equal to X is encountered the variable j is immediately reduced to $i + 1$ by the assignment $j := m$. This assignment makes the guard $i < j − 1$ false, forcing termination of the loop.

Interpretation of this mechanism using the loop invariant (which is the same as that for the binary search) suggests that the least upper bound j for the segment of array elements greater than or equal to X is reduced to preserve the invariant when a value greater than or equal to X is encountered. This technique of decreasing the upper bound (or increasing a lower bound) in a guard to force termination of a loop can be widely applied.

The unordered array-search problem can be considered in the light of the preceding discussion. Modelling the solution to this problem on the solution to the linear ordered-array search yields

```
(1)    i := 0, n := N;
       do i ≠ n →
           if a[i + 1] ≠ X → i := i + 1
           [] a[i + 1] = X → n := i
           fi
       od;
       found := i ≠ N
```

In this implementation it has been possible to exclude the extra variable m and replace it directly by $i + 1$. A postcondition and invariant for this implementation are

$$R : (\forall p: 0 < p \leqslant i : a[p] \neq X) \wedge (n = N \textbf{ cor } X = a[i + 1]) \wedge i = n$$
$$P : 0 \leqslant i \leqslant n \leqslant N \wedge (\forall p: 0 < p \leqslant i : a[p] \neq X) \wedge (n = N \textbf{ cor } X = a[i + 1])$$

The variable n assumes the role of the least known upper bound on the array segment not containing X; potentially it has a maximum value of N. It is initialized to this maximum value.

There are two ways the loop in (1) can terminate. The first, when X is absent, involves i increasing stepwise to N. We refer to this as **natural termination**. The second, when X is present, involves reducing n, the upper bound on the array segment not containing X. This is referred to as **forced termination**. Use of the assignment i := n (rather than n := i) to force termination is rejected because it would destroy the loop invariant.

The role of the finalization mechanism

A loop that admits both forced termination and natural termination is said to terminate in an **unresolved** state. Resolution of such states is usually necessary (for example, in our linear search above it is necessary to decide whether X is present). It is suggested that this resolution should be made by a *finalization mechanism* located *outside* the loop body. An associated loop design principle follows:

Principle
Any condition or mechanism that can obtain in only a single iteration of a loop should be separated from the loop body.

Another way of interpreting this principle is to say that the loop invariant defines the set of variables that may be used in the loop body. Justification for this rule comes from the examination of an alternative implementation to (1) given below. Here resolution of the termination state is carried out *within* the loop body.

```
i := 0; n := N; found := FALSE;
do i ≠ n →
   if a[i + 1] ≠ X → i := i + 1
   [] a[i + 1] = X → n := i; found := TRUE
   fi
od
```

The loop invariant for this implementation is the same as for (1). Notice that found (or not found) is not and cannot be part of the loop invariant. This suggests that the assignment to found should be made outside the loop. In fact the absence of a variable from a meaningful loop invariant for a loop is probably the best criterion for indicating that the step involving the omitted variable belongs in a finalization mechanism. Another argument against this second implementation is that it may make two assignments to found when one is sufficent. The first assignment to found in the initialization is premature because only after either forced or natural termination is it meaningful to make a decision on the presence of X – hence the assignment to found in the finalization mechanism of (1). This loop design principle conforms to the more general **law of separation of concerns**. Consistent application of this principle often cleans up and simplifies loop bodies and loop invariants. This is a desirable design goal because loops are conceptually more difficult to characterize and understand than non-iterative mechanisms. This principle also helps to define when the use of a finalization mechanism is appropriate and what steps are required for finalization. It can raise the status of the finalization mechanism to a level comparable to that currently enjoyed by initialization in the construction of loops.

In passing it may be noted that there is an important class of problems where the complementary situation applies; that is, a component of the loop body apparently needs to be executed in all but the last iteration of a loop. A methodology for handling such problems is discussed in the section on loop structuring.

Forced termination and programming style

It is instructive to compare the implementation (1) given above with two traditional solutions to the problem presented by Feuer and Gehani. Their solutions are presented below. Their first solution is implemented in Pascal and the second using Dijkstra's guarded commands (Feuer and Gehani used C for their second implementation (3)).

```
(2)    found := false; i := 1;
       while (i ≤ N) and (not found) do
          begin
             found := (a[i] = x);
             i := i + 1
          end;
       if found then i := i − 1
```

```
(3)    i := 1;
       do i ≤ N cand a[i] ≠ x → i := i + 1 od;
       found := (i ≤ N)
```

A meaningful loop invariant for solution (2) is elusive. We might expect that part of the loop invariant will indicate that the array segment a[1 . . i − 1] does not contain x. Unfortunately this breaks down if x is present. The repeated assignment to found and the repeated testing of not found in (2) are avoided in (1). The clumsiness of this solution is attributed to Pascal's lack of conditional logical operators (in this case **cand**).

The solution (3) which employs a **cand** is considered a 'better' program by Feuer and Gehani. The question then arises which of (1) and (3) is to be preferred? If the decision is made simply on the grounds of textual simplicity then (3) would be the choice. Textual simplicity has however only been gained at a price – the introduction of an asymmetric logical operator or partial function. The latter complicates the formal reasoning about programs. A more practical reason favouring (1) is the language independence of its control structure. At a time when not all languages admit conditional logical operators it is prudent to use language-independent solutions to problems of this type for no other reason than preservation of generality. The approach adopted in (1) is offered as a solution to the forced-termination problem consistent with the minimum set of language constructs needed for structured programming.

Other deeper but debatable philosophical reasons for favouring (1) over (3) may be suggested. The spirit of structured programming is upheld by loops with single points of entry and exit. A guard with a single condition conforms more closely to this ideal than one made up of the conjunction or disjunction of conditions. These ideas are reinforced by the observation that the proof of termination is simplified if there is a direct relationship between the variant function (e.g. for the linear search case $(t: n - i)$ and the guard for the loop. Components of guards such as a[i] $\neq$ x and not found bear no direct relationship to the variant function and therefore belong elsewhere. Expressed another way *the preferred guard is the condition defined for natural termination of a loop*.

The technique we have used for forced termination can be generalized to handle nested loops. Consider the problem of searching a two-dimensional array A[1...M, 1...N] for some value X. If X is present in the array the mechanism should return indices that can be used to identify the row and column where X is located. A Boolean variable found should be set to TRUE if X is present and set to FALSE otherwise. Termination should be forced as soon as X is found if it is present.

In the implementation below m is the least known upper bound on the number of complete leading rows not containing X, and n is the least known upper bound on the number of leading columns not containing X for a given row specification. A detailed implementation for this problem is

```
i := 0, m := M;
do i ≠ m →
  j := 0, n := N;
  do j ≠ n →
    if a[i + 1, j + 1] ≠ X → j := j + 1
    [] a[i + 1, j + 1] = X → n := j
    fi
  od;
  if j ≠ N → m := i
  [] j = N → i := i + 1
  fi
od;
found := (i ≠ M)
```

This problem is in essence relatively simple but it can cause adherents of structured programming difficulty if they are unwilling to resort to **cand**s, **goto**s or **break**s. The solution offered here, which is language independent, overcomes the difficulty and still conforms to structured programming principles. A detailed derivation for this problem has been given in Section 7.4.

It is interesting to compare the present implementation with Gries' solution, which employs a single loop and a **cand** to solve the problem. It could be argued that on the one hand the single-loop implementation represents a superior simplification of the problem, or on the other hand, that because the data structure is two-dimensional a nested loop solution is more appropriate. The single-loop solution has to simulate a second loop. The choice is therefore between two explicit loops and a single loop with a 'hidden' loop. These issues are discussed further in Section 12.5, which is on loop structuring.

Another problem that illustrates these principles is a procedure that checks whether an array A[1...N] is sorted. Using the suggested technique of forced termination we get

```
{N > 0}
i := 1; n := N;
do i < n →
    if A[i] ≤ A[i + 1] → i := i + 1
    [] A[i] > A[i + 1] → n := i
    fi
od;
sorted := (i = N)
```

In contrast a Pascal solution that neglects forced termination in the way we have suggested will take the form

```
{N > 1}
i := 1;
while (i < N − 1) and (A[i] ≤ A[i + 1]) do i := i + 1;
if i = N − 1 then
    sorted := A[i] ≤ A[i + 1]
else
    sorted := false
```

The latter solution is clumsy. Furthermore it cannot handle the case where N = 1 without an extra guard.

Another Pascal implementation that uses a Boolean flag rather than forced termination is

```
i := 1; sorted := true;
while sorted and (i < N) do
    if A[i] ≤ A[i + 1] then
        i := i + 1
    else
        sorted := false
```

This still involves more testing than the forced-termination example. With each iteration sorted is tested as well as i < N. In contrast, using forced termination only i < n is tested.

A final example is included in this section to illustrate the use of increasing a lower bound to force termination. The example considered is the conventional insertion sort. The central part of its implementation is

```
{N ⩾ 1}
i := 1;
do i < N →
    x := a[i + 1];
    l := 1; j := i + 1;
    do l < j →
        if a[j − 1] > x → j, a[j] := j − 1, a[j − 1]
        [] a[j − 1] ⩽ x → l := j
        fi
    od;
    a[l] := x; i := i + 1
od
```

This implementation needs no further discussion other than to note the role of the variable l (see also Chapter 9).

Data structures and forced termination

The principles for forced termination described can be generalized to handle other data structures. For example, consider the three search implementations for an element X in an array, text-line and linked list, respectively (note that language constructs for text and linked lists have been borrowed from Pascal).

(1) **Array**
```
i := 0, n := N;
do i ≠ n →
    if A[i + 1] ≠ X → i := i + 1
    [] A[i + 1] = X → n := i
    fi
od;
found := (i ≠ N)
```

(2) **Text-line**
```
N := TRUE;
i := eoln(input), n := N;
do i ≠ n →
    if input↑ ≠ X → get(input); i := eoln(input)
    [] input↑ = X → n := i
    fi
od;
found := (i ≠ N)
```

(3)   **Linked List**
```
N := nil;
i := listhead; n := N;
do i ≠ n →
    if i↑.info ≠ X → i := i↑.link
    [] i↑.info = X → n := i
    fi
od;
found := (i ≠ N)
```

All three implementations use the *same* control structure.

A solution to the problem of searching an ordered binary tree for a key value equal to X also has a surprisingly similar implementation which is cleaner than other alternatives.

(4)   **Binary tree**
```
N := nil;
i := root; n := N
do i ≠ n →
    if i↑.info < X → i := i↑.left
    [] i↑.info = X → n := i
    [] i↑ .info > i := i↑ .right
    fi
od;
found := (i ≠ N)
```

An alternative control structure could be proposed to that used in implementations (2) and (3). For (2) this alternative implementation would take the form

(5)   **Text-line**
```
done := eoln(input);
do ¬done →
    if input↑ ≠ X → get(input); done := eoln(input)
    [] input↑ = X → done := true
    fi
od;
found := ¬eoln(input)
```

This implementation is rejected in favour of (2) for two reasons. First done may assume two different roles in the course of execution of the loop (i.e. the status of eoln and a forced value of true). In comparison with this i in (2) invariantly assumes the status of eoln. Implementation (5) always terminates with done true, and so done cannot be used directly to decide whether the termination was natural or forced. A separate check of the eoln status outside the loop is needed to resolve this issue. The variable done also bears no relationship to the variant function for the array solution.

The use of representation-independent control structures has a number of advantages. In many applications the array can provide the prototype solution to a class of problems defined for different data structures. Modification of the prototype solution to accommodate other data structures (e.g. files, lists, textlines, etc.) is then essentially a mechanical process that does not require a change in the control structure of the loop. Correspondences among such constructs as a[i + 1], input↑, i↑.info, etc. can be easily made. In each case we 'look ahead' at the next value in the sequence.

12.5   Loop Structuring

The structure of a program determines its quality. There are, however, few guidelines for structuring programs. Many program designers ignore, or are ignorant of, program structuring principles. They take the view that each problem should be dealt with on its merits. While this is in part true, the discussion which follows will illustrate several useful and fairly widely applicable program structuring principles that can be used when designing loop structures.

Probably the best known and most widely used program structuring principle is Jackson's **correspondence principle.** In essence, what Jackson suggests is as follows

---

Correspondence principle

The control structure (loop structure) of a program should be designed to match the structure of the data that the program has to process.

This principle is a very powerful one that works exceptionally well for certain classes of problems (notably transaction-based data-processing problems). There are, however, many problems for which it is not obvious how Jackson's structuring principle could be applied. The present discussion will attempt to go further than matching program control structure with data structure.

To understand what it would be most desirable to achieve by program structuring, it is useful to make an analogy with Codd's theory of relational database organization. What Codd was able to achieve by applying a set of normalization rules was a means for factoring data into a set of relations (structured components) that minimized redundancy and maximized the independence of the relations. When this factoring is applied to data, it keeps update operations simple and it minimizes the risk of updates introducing inconsistencies into the database. From a structural perspective, it leads to the construction of relations with strongly localized intra-relational bonds and weak inter-relational bonds.

What is sought in program structuring is something very similar to Codd's ideal. It is required to factor programs into components that are computationally highly localized, and independent, with only weak interactions with other program components. Programs that exhibit such characteristics are usually easier to understand and modify, because it is hoped that the effects of a local change are kept local due to the high independence of the components in the program structure.

The redundancy that we are seeking to remove by appropriate program structuring is

- the unnecessary assignment to, or change in, values of variables;
- the unnecessary testing of conditions.

Removal of these forms of computational redundancy is usually achieved when there is a match between the structure of the data or the problem and the structure of the program.

Much of the localization and redundancy removal we require can be achieved by applying the program decomposition principles advocated in Chapter 5. To proceed we start by taking the fundamental position that *structure in a program is realized by changing or setting particular subsets of a program's variables under certain prescribed conditions.*

Once this definition of structure is adopted, the process of choosing the program structure for a particular problem can be viewed as one of

- deciding which variables to change or set, and
- deciding under what conditions these variables should be changed or set.

This view of the program structuring process needs further qualification to make it useful. In the last chapter, the qualifications chosen for structuring were

- that any refinement made should extend the set of initial states for which the postcondition is established;
- refinements should also satisfy the principle of least action.

The interpretation of the principle of least action adopted for program design is that progress towards a solution should be made at all times by the simplest and least costly means possible. This interpretation translates further. It requires that individual structural components in a program should be constructed by changing or setting the least number of variables under the simplest possible conditions consistent with making a refinement that can establish the postcondition at least in some limiting circumstance.

Enough background has now been covered to make it possible to look at some of the various facets of loop and program structuring. To do this two types of data structure will be distinguished:

- *explicit* data structure
- *implicit* data structure

It is suggested that Jackson's correspondence principle tries to take advantage of explicit data structure in determining how the control structure to process such data should be arranged. The correspondence principle does not, however, allow us to achieve a match of program control structure with implicit data structure. To achieve a control structure that matches implicit data structure, we must focus on designing program components that change minimum subsets of variables. The application of this structuring principle represents a generalization and abstraction of Jackson's correspondence principle. It also allows us to design control structures that match both implicit and explicit data structure. Before coming to terms with matching implicit structure in data, we need to examine examples of explicit data-structure matching.

12.5.1   Matching explicit data structure

Consider the data for the stores-movement problem (see Section 11.4):

Product	Quantity	
product1	23	
product1	29	
product1	48	
product1	−10	
product1	4	all transactions for product1
product2	33	
product2	17	
product2	−8	
product2	19	all transactions for product2
product3	6	
product3	41	all transactions for product3

which represents a list of stores movement transactions for a set of products

product1, product2, ...

There are two ways to view this data:

- as simply a sequence of transactions of the form (product, amount);

- as a sequence of transactions for product1, followed by a sequence of transactions for product2, and so on.

The second interpretation imposes a higher order on the structure of the data. To illustrate the difference consider Figures 12.2a and 12.2b.

In the flat or unstructured view of the data there is potential multiplicity only of the transactions. In contrast, in the structured view of the data there is

- multiplicity over the products (i.e. one or more products);
- multiplicity over the transactions for each product (i.e. one or more transactions for each product).

Now suppose, to process this data set of product/amount transactions, it was necessary to add up and print out the amounts for *each* product. In constructing an iterative mechanism to perform this processing, we have potentially two possible control structures that we can use:

(a)

(b)

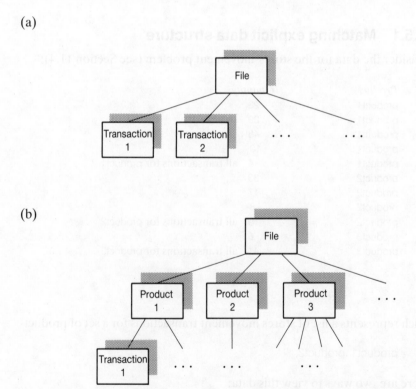

Figure 12.2   (a) Unstructured view of data; (b) structured view of data.

(1)   *A single loop control structure*

WHILE still more transactions **DO**
"Process the next transaction and do any necessary printing"
END

(2)   *A nested loop structure that matches the structure of the data*

WHILE still more products **DO**
  WHILE still more transactions for current product **DO**
    "Process next transaction"
  END
  Write out result for current product
END

Detailed implementations of the two different solutions to the problem are given below. In the implementations we have used Pascal's record and I/O facilities. A full specification and derivation of the solution for this problem is provided in Section 11.4.

Implementation 1   (No match between control structure and data structure)

```
M := true; i := eof(T);
if i ≠ M then
    prod := T↑.p; s := T↑.q;
    get(T); i := eof(T);
    do i ≠ M →
        if prod = T↑.p → s := s + T↑.q
        [] prod ≠ T↑.p → writeln(prod, s); prod := T ↑ .p; s := T ↑ .q
        fi;
        get(T); i := eof(T)
    od;
    writeln(prod, s)
fi
```

Implementation 2   (Match between program control structure and data structure)

```
M := true; i := eof(T);
do i ≠ M →
    prod := T↑.p; s := T↑.q;
    get(T); i := eof(T); m := M;
    do i ≠ m →
        if prod = T↑.p → s := s + T↑.q; get(T); i := eof(T)
        [] prod ≠ T↑.p → m := i
        fi
    od;
    writeln (prod, s)
od
```

It is interesting to make a comparison of these two implementations and assess their relative strengths and weaknesses. Superficially at least, the single-loop solution may appear to be simpler.

It does, however, have a much more complex loop invariant and there is some duplication of code, that is

- the output appears in two places (i.e. writeln(prod, s));
- the initialization appears in two places (i.e. prod := T↑.p; s := T↑.q).

Duplication of code has a consequence for maintaining a program. For example if we have to alter the output, changes must be made in *two* places rather than one. This arises purely because the control structure is not matched with the structure of the data.

The loop invariant for the single loop is complicated by the fact that it can change two variables, the *product* variable and the *quantity* variable. The difficulty arises because the product variable is not changed with every iteration – it only changes when a transaction for a new product is encountered.

Things are quite different with the second implementation. Its inner loop only changes the *quantity* variable while holding the *product* variable constant. The role of the outer loop is also very simple. With each new iteration a new product is processed. This structure makes the second implementation much easier to understand and change. The use of lookahead (T↑.p) here has contributed to the simplification of the loop structure.

Although this example is relatively simple it illustrates quite clearly most of the consequences of matching program control structure with the structure of the data to be processed.

Another observation is that the control structure we employ is dependent on the type of processing we wish to do on the data. If we had only wanted to add up all the quantities irrespective of their product, then a single-loop implementation would have been entirely appropriate. This sort of consideration should always be borne in mind.

Single verses multiple loop implementations

Programs that contain more than one loop can always be reduced to a version that contains only a *single* loop. Our stores-movement example has identified only some of the consequences of not resolving control structures.

This exploration needs to be taken further. The best way to do this is to try to understand the mechanisms of single-loop solutions to problems and relate them to multiple-loop solutions.

When matching the data structure in a single-loop implementation suggests a nested loop, then the implementation must somehow simulate what is otherwise achieved by an extra loop.

To illustrate these ideas let us again consider the row-sums problem discussed in Section 5.7. To solve this problem, it is required to compute the row-sums for a fixed integer, two-dimensional array A[1..M, 1..N] and store the results in a one-dimensional array s[1..M].

The specification is

$$Q : M \geqslant 0 \wedge N \geqslant 0$$
$$R : (\forall p : 0 < p \leqslant M : s_p = \Sigma \, (A_{p,q} : 0 < q \leqslant N))$$

The multiplicity in the data structure is matched by the following nested loop implementation:

Structured solution

```
i := 0;
do i ≠ M →
   j := 0; s_{i+1} := 0;
   do j ≠ N →
      j, s_{i+1} := j + 1, s_{i+1} + A_{i+1, j+1}
   od;
   i := i + 1
od
```

In this implementation there is an inner loop over the columns and an outer loop over the rows. A single-loop implementation is given below:

Flat solution

```
i := 0; j := 0; if i ≠ M then s_{i+1} := 0 fi;
do i ≠ M →
   if j ≠ N → j, s_{i+1} := j + 1, s_{i+1} + A_{i+1, j+1}
   [] j = N → i, j := i + 1, 0; if i ≠ M then s_{i+1} := 0 fi
   fi
od
```

In the flat solution it has been necessary to simulate a j-loop by setting j to zero whenever it reaches N. A complication is also introduced in initializing the array element s_{i+1} that stores the sum. These complications often make a flat solution harder to understand than a structured solution.

There are also significant efficiency differences between the two implementations. With the structured solution the guard i ≠ M is tested only when a whole row has been summed, whereas with the flat solution the guard i ≠ M is tested with *each* iteration. There are also additional guard tests introduced when s_{i+1} is set to zero at the end of each row. These inefficiencies are avoided in the structured solution because it matches the structure of the data and thereby separates the concerns of summing the elements in a row from moving to a new row. Put another way the main processing is done in a loop that changes s and j while holding i constant. The flat solution must look after changing i, j and s in a single loop and therefore pay the price of increased complexity and inefficiency. Our argument here is that, in general, a loop that changes fewer variables is easier to understand and characterize, and more efficient than one that changes more variables.

A guarded commands dilettante may have offered the following more elegant flat solution:

```
i := 0; j := 0; if i ≠ M then s_{i+1} := 0 fi;
do i ≠ M ∧ j ≠ N → j, s_{i+1} := j + 1, s_{i+1} + A_{i+1, j+1}
[] i ≠ M ∧ j = N → i, j := i + 1, 0; if i ≠ M then s_{i+1} := 0 fi
od
```

However, this solution has the same drawbacks as the original flat solution.

12.5.2   Matching implicit data structure

Dealing with implicit structure in data is not as clear cut as trying to match explicit structure. In such cases we have to rely upon:

- the minimum variable change rule, and
- an intimate knowledge of the data

for guidance in designing suitable matching control structures. To illustrate implicit data structure matching we will consider several examples.

EXAMPLE 1   Prime factorization_____

The problem of finding the prime factors of a natural number is well known. Alagic and Arbib give an implementation for this problem with the following structure:

Flat solution

```
i := 0; k := 0; n := N;
q := n div p[0];
r := n mod p[0];
do r = 0 ∧ q > p[k] →
    if r = 0 → i, f[i + 1] := i + 1, p[k]; n := q
    [] r ≠ 0 → k := k + 1
    fi;
    q := n div p[k];
    r := n mod p[k]
od;
if n ≠ 1 then i, f[i + 1] := i + 1, n fi
```

In this implementation the array p[0 . .] is assumed to contain an adequate list of primes necessary to complete the factorization of N, and the array f is used to store all the prime factors.

In attempting to provide an alternative implementation that matches the implicit structure in N we will make the same assumptions and attempt to produce a similar factor array f. In searching for a better implementation we are interested in identifying structural components that involve changing the least number of variables while still allowing progress towards establishing the postcondition. Pursuing this line of attack we find that it would be possible to completely factor a number without changing k, the index that allows the prime number variable to change. This would happen when N consisted of a single number raised to a power (e.g., $N = 2^{23}$)

Generalizing this perception, N may be thought of as having the form:

$$N = p_0^{e0} \times p_1^{e1} \times p_2^{e2} \times \ldots$$

where p_0, p_1, p_2, ... represent the primes' sequence and e0, e1 and e2, ... are their respective powers. This suggests that a major structural component of the implementation should be a mechanism that handles a *single* prime raised to a power. In fact, if such a mechanism is placed in a loop we end up with the following prime factorization algorithm which matches the implicit structure in the data. Note here the primes 2, 3, 5, ... are stored in p[1 . .]

Structured solution

```
i := 0; k := 0; n := N;
repeat
  k := k + 1;
  q := n div p[k];
  r := n mod p[k];
  do r = 0 →
    i, f[i + 1] := i + 1, p[k];
    n := q;
    q := n div p[k];
    r := n mod p[k]
  od
until q ≤ p[k];
if n > 1 then i, f[i + 1] := i + 1, n fi
```

In comparing the two implementations the following observations may be made

- The inner loop in the structured solution avoids changing k, and therefore does not change the prime number variable.

- In the flat solution the guard r=0 is tested twice with each iteration. This is not the case with the structured solution.
- The structured solution also avoids testing q ≤ p[k] while the power-multiplicity for a given prime is being determined. This can produce another gain in efficiency for the structured solution over the flat solution.

The structured solution can be made simpler be removing the variables r and q as they can result in some unnecessary assignments. When this is done we get the following implementation:

```
i := 0; k := 0; n := N;
repeat
  k := k + 1;
  do (n mod p[k]) = 0 →
    i, n, f[i + 1] := i + 1, n div p[k], p[k]
  od
until (n div p[k]) ≤ p[k];
if n > 1 then i, f[i + 1] := i + 1, n fi
```

EXAMPLE 2   Maximum finding

In solving the problem of finding the maximum in an array A[1..N] it is possible to take advantage of implicit structure in the data. The well-known conventional implementation for finding the maximum in an array has the following form:

Flat solution

```
max := A[1]; i := 1;
do i < N →
  if A[i+1] ≤ max → i := i + 1
  [] A[i+1] > max → i, max := i + 1, A[i + 1]
  fi
od
```

Now comes the question of what is the implicit structure in an array of N arbitrary numbers, and how can we take advantage of it? Knuth, in his analysis of this problem, makes the observation that on average for random data the maximum only gets updated $O(\log(N))$ times. What are the consequences of this? Our flat solution contains a loop that can change both the variables max and i. Knuth's analysis would seem to suggest that it might be better to have a structural component that only changes the variable i, since max will only need to be changed rarely by comparison. This comes back again to the suggestion that we saw earlier − the simplest way to establish a postcondition is often to try to confirm it. A mechanism that could confirm the postcondition would be one that selected one of the array elements and then tried to confirm that it was the maximum. A possibility for this would be

```
max := A[i]; i := 1;
do A[i+1] < max → i := i + 1 od
```

provided max was initialized and there was a way of preventing the loop running off the end of the array. A sentinel can be used for this purpose. The resulting implementation that matches the implicit structure in the data then assumes the following form:

Structured solution
```
i := 0;
do i < N →
   i, max, A[N + 1] := i + 1, A[i + 1], A[i + 1];
   do A[i + 1] < max → i := i + 1 od
od
```

The efficiency of the two implementations was compared by doing a 'statements executed' count using the Berkeley Pascal compiler for random data and N = 1000. It was found that on average 3010 statements were executed for the flat solution while the structured solution executed only 2023 statements on average. It is interesting to note that the structured solution was discovered by applying the rule of always trying to construct implementations that change minimum subsets of variables. Of course, as mentioned earlier, we do not in general recommend the use of sentinels.

EXAMPLE 3   Greatest common divisor_____
The greatest common divisor (gcd) problem is another example where it is possible to take advantage of implicit structure in data. For this problem it is required to find the gcd of two fixed natural numbers X and Y. An obvious implementation that follows from the rules:

$$x > y \Rightarrow \gcd(x, y) = \gcd(y, x - y)$$
$$y > x \Rightarrow \gcd(x, y) = \gcd(x, y - x)$$
$$x = y \Rightarrow x = y = \gcd(x, y)$$

is as follows.

Flat solution
```
x := X; y := Y;
do x ≠ y →
   if x > y → x := x − y
   [] y > x → y := y − x
   fi
od
```

This loop changes both x and y. Potentially x could be a multiple of y or vice versa. This suggests the possibility of having a loop that changes just x and another loop that changes just y. Incorporating these refinements we get the following structured implementation:

Structured solution 1

```
x := X; y := Y;
do x ≠ y
    do x > y → x := x − y od;
    do y > x → y := y − x od
od
```

This solution makes better use of situations like

$$x = p * y \quad \text{or} \quad y = p * x \quad \text{where } p > 1$$

whenever they arise in a computation. Consequently on average the guard x ≠ y will be tested fewer times by the structured solution than by the flat solution.

There is still some residual inefficiency in the structured solution. We find that *after* the first iteration of the main loop it is unnecessary to test the guard

$$x > y$$

directly upon entering the main loop. The test is unnecessary because in the previous iteration of the main loop it must have terminated with the condition

$$x ≥ y$$

true. The subsequent truth of the main loop guard x ≠ y can then only mean that x > y holds on entry into the main loop. Hence it is unnecessary to test it as soon as the main loop is entered. To remove this test, a repeat loop is needed. This must be accompanied by an iterative initialization to ensure that x ≥ y holds at the commencement of the very first iteration. We then get

Structured solution 2

```
x := X; y := Y;
do y > x → y := y − x od;        { iterative initialization }
do x ≠ y →
    repeat x := x − y until x ≤ y;
    do y > x → y := y − x od
od
```

This second somewhat controversial structured solution contains no unnecessary guard testing. On average it provides the best match with the structure of the data. The underlying form of the second structured solution is as follows:

```
A;
do x ≠ y →
   B;
   A
od
```

where A represents the **do** loop and B represents the **repeat** loop. There are many examples where a loop structure of this form is needed to match either implicit or explicit data structure. Data that exhibits the structure

ABABABA ... BA

or, using EBNF,

A{BA}

is said to possess a **parenthetic** structure. A very explicit example of data that has this form is a line of text with leading and trailing spaces, for example

{spaces} word {spaces}⁺ word {spaces}⁺ ... word {spaces}

A loop structure that matches the data structure in this case is

```
getspaces;
do while not end of line
   getword;
   getspaces
od
```

Three important variations on the parenthetic structure are:

(1)   the first A component is missing (i.e. we have BABA ... BA);

(2)   the last A component is missing (i.e. we have ABABA ... BAB);

(3)   the first and last A components are missing (i.e. we have BABA ... BAB).

For many applications the matched control structure needs to accommodate all three parenthetic variations, that is a line of text may have no leading and no trailing blanks, etc.

EXAMPLE 4   Partitioning problem_____

Partitioning (see Chapter 8) provides another example of the need to process parenthetically structured data. Suppose we are required to partition a fixed sequence of elements $(A_1, A_2, \ldots, A_N)$ using an array a[1..N] such that the first i elements are all less than or equal to X, and the remaining elements are greater than or equal to X. The postcondition and a flat solution for this problem are as follows:

$$R_D: (\forall p : 0 < p \leqslant i : a_p \leqslant X) \wedge (\forall q : j \leqslant q < N + 1 : a_q \geqslant X) \wedge i = j - 1$$
$$\wedge \, \text{perm}(a, A)$$

Flat solution

```
i := 0; j := N + 1;
do i ≠ j − 1 →
    if aᵢ₊₁ ≤ X → i := i + 1
    [] aᵢ₊₁ ≥ X → j := j − 1
    [] aᵢ₊₁ > X ∧ aⱼ₋₁ < X → swap(aᵢ₊₁, aⱼ₋₁); i := i + 1; j := j − 1
    fi
od
```

The primary application of partitioning is in the implementation of Quicksort (the sorting algorithm with the best average case performance). In implementations of Quicksort, the above partitioning algorithm is not used because it does not attempt to match or take advantage of implicit structure in the data. Typically the structure of the data is such that there are sequences or runs of adjacent elements that are respectively less than X and runs of values that are greater than X.

This suggests we should use a component like

```
do aᵢ₊₁ < X → i := i + 1 od
```

to increase i and a component like

```
do aⱼ₋₁ > X → j := j − 1 od
```

to decrease j. These partition-extension components will allow the implementation to take advantage of array runs in the data and consequently reduce the testing of the outer loop guard. A common implementation of partitioning that does this is as follows.

Structured solution 1

```
i := 0; j := N + 1;
do i < j − 1 →
    do aᵢ₊₁ < X → i := i + 1 od;
    do aⱼ₋₁ > X → j := j − 1 od;
    if i < j − 1 then swap(aᵢ₊₁,aⱼ₋₁); i := i + 1; j := j − 1 fi
od
```

In the flat solution we had a single loop that changed three variables i, j and a. By contrast the structured solution has been factored into three components.

- one component responsible for advancing i as far as it can go;
- a second component responsible for decreasing j as far as it can go;
- and a third component that changes i, j and a when necessary.

The swap command must be guarded by $i < j - 1$ to avoid swapping in the case where the i and j loops in combination have established the postcondition. This guard on the swap is relevant only on the very last iteration that the outer loop makes, as it is only then that we may need to block a swap. Notice also that the guard on the swap is the same as the guard on the outer loop. By restructuring the loop and thereby making a better match with the parenthetic structure of the data we can effectively eliminate the guard on the swap. The basic control structure we need is

```
A
do i < j - 1 →
  B;
  A
od
```

which translates directly to the following implementation needed to match the parenthetic structure of the data:

```
i := 0; j := N + 1;
do a_{i+1} < X → i := i + 1 od;
do a_{j-1} > X → j := j - 1 od;
do i < j - 1 →
  swap(a_{i+1}, a_{j-1}); i := i + 1; j := j - 1;
  do a_{i+1} < X → i := i + 1 od;
  do a_{j-1} > X → j := j - 1 od
od
```

EXAMPLE 5   Heapsort

Heapsort provides another interesting example of the effects of appropriate structuring. The sift operation as it is usually constructed in conventional heapsort implementations (see Wirth, 1976) is seemingly the most appropriate for dealing with heaps. In the sift operation for the sort, the heap is re-adjusted so that the element at the top of the heap is inserted into the heap to restore the heap property and consequently force the smallest element in the heap into the root position. This 'smallest element' is the next available 'sorted' element. The body of Wirth's implementation (in Pascal) for the sift operation takes the following form where the heap with root at a[1] is stored in the array segment a[1..r].

Implementation 1

```
i := 1; j := 2 * i; x := a[i];
while j ≤ r do begin
    if j < r then if a[j] > a[j + 1] then j := j + 1;
    if x ≤ a[j] then goto 13;
    a[i] := a[j]; i := j; j := ≤ * i
end;
13: a[i] := x
```

This implementation treats the tasks of finding the next 'sorted' element and inserting x, the element at the root of the heap, as a composite task. If these two tasks are treated separately a significantly more efficient implementation given below is obtained. This strategy for implementing heapsort has also been suggested by Floyd (see Knuth, 1973).

Implementation 2

```
i := 1; j := 2 * i; x := a[i];
while j ≤ r do begin
    if j ≤ r then if a[j] > a[j + 1] then j := j + 1;
    a[i] := a[j]; i := j; j := 2 * i
end;
j := i div 2;
while a[j] > x do begin
    a[i] := a[j]; i := j; j := j div 2
end;
a[i] := x
```

When this second sifting implementation is used in a heapsort it will on average use approximately the same number of array-element comparisons as Quicksort for random data. It is a pity this more efficient version of heapsort is not more widely known, because it is more competitive with Quicksort. In contrast when a conventional sift (as in implementation 1) is used heapsort makes nearly twice as many comparisons as Quicksort.

There is another improvement that we can make to the sift operation that avoids applying the guard j < r directly after the guard j ≤ r. Instead we may use the following loop:

```
while j < r do begin
    if a[j] > a[j + 1] then j := j + 1;
    a[i] := a[j]; i := j; j := 2 * i
end
```

It is then necessary to include a finalization mechanism *after* this loop to handle the very infrequent case where j = r occurs.

12.6 Lookahead Implementation

Lookahead is a very important programming technique that can ease the processing of data that must be accessed sequentially. In the processing of sequential data each element in the stream of data passes through an *access window*. See Figure 12.3.

At any stage of the processing the 'next' element to be consumed is usually of interest. The actions of a program on a given piece of data are often highly dependent on that data. For example the response of a program to the next character being a digit might be quite different to its response when the next character is alphabetic. We may have two mechanisms:

    alphaprocess   processes only alphabetic characters
    numberprocess   processes only numeric characters

Our programming strategy in this context may be to 'peek ahead' at the next character, and if it is alphabetic, then invoke alphaprocess; otherwise if it is a digit invoke numberprocess, that is

    if nextcharacter in alphabetic → alphaprocess
    [] nextcharacter in digit → numberprocess
    [] nextcharacter in other → otherprocess
    fi

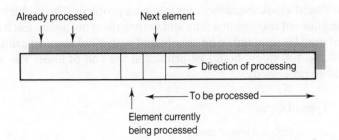

Figure 12.3   Schematic view of access window for the sequential processing of data

What is often important in this context is that the mechanism that controls the invocation of alphaprocess, etc., *does not consume* nextcharacter from the input stream. To achieve the best separation of concerns we may want to enforce the processing discipline that alphaprocess consumes *all* alphabetic characters, numberprocess consumes all digits, and so on. If this processing discipline is not enforced we may end up with a complicated mechanism to take special account of the *first* member in the stream of a given class. Some languages make this sort of processing easy (e.g. Pascal) while other languages do not (e.g. Modula-2).

If we were to tackle the above problem in Pascal we could take advantage of its buffered input and lookahead to write

```
if input↑ in alphabetic then alphaprocess ...
else if input↑ in digit then numberprocess
else ...
```

In this context input↑ achieves lookahead because it does not consume the next character in the input stream. Consumption of the next character is done by the invocation of a separate procedure called get. This facility allows us to achieve one-character lookahead when using Pascal. Pascal's successor, Modula-2, does not provide for this model of lookahead in the standard input/output modules that are usually provided. When using languages like Modula-2 it often makes our programming job easier if we write a set of routines that simulate one-character lookahead.

Of course, there are other programming problems that are best handled by a more general and extensive lookahead capability. For example, we may wish to look ahead a whole variable-length English text word. Such a capability is rarely provided by programming languages.

It is therefore instructive to examine how this more generalized lookahead can be simulated. We will start this discussion by examining the use of Pascal's lookahead facilities to solve a problem. The problem involves reading lines of text one at a time and writing them out again. Each input line of text may be assumed to be terminated with a full stop. In producing the output, no full stops should be printed at the end of lines. The whole file should be processed.

Typical input

```
This is a line of text.
And another line of text.
And a third line of text.
```

Required output

This is a line of text
And another line of text
And a third line of text

To solve this problem we will use a mechanism that processes a *single* line of text, and apply this mechanism iteratively until an end-of-file is encountered.

The Pascal program is

```
program readlines(input, output);
const EOF=true; ELN = true; FULLSTOP = '.';
var ch : char;
  i, j, n : boolean;
begin
  i := eof(input);
  while i <> EOF do begin
  j := eoln (input); n := ELN;
    while j <> n do begin
    if input↑ <> FULLSTOP then begin
      ch := input↑; get(input); write(ch); j := eoln (input)
      end
    else
      n := j
    end;
  read(ch);                    {skip full stop}
  readln; i := eof(input);     {move to new line}
  writeln
  end
end
```

In the Pascal implementation the Boolean systems function eof returns the end-of-file status whenever it is called and the function eoln returns the end-of-line status whenever it is called. The construct input↑ allows us to reference the next character in the input stream without advancing the position in the stream. The position in the stream is advanced one character by a call to get or read. The procedure readln advances the input to the next line.

It is now required to examine a problem that is solved by looking ahead one complete variable-length text word. To solve the problem a model is used that effectively allows us to look ahead a complete text word. Our solution is like Pascal's one-character lookahead facility.

The problem requires reading lines of text in the format:

Input

NEWGROUP/WORD1/WORD2/... /WORDN/
...............WORD/NEWGROUP/WORD1 ... .
...

The text consists of groups of words each prefixed by the string 'NEWGROUP'. These words are to be written out one per line. When a new group is detected a line is to be left before writing out the new group of words with the heading NEWGROUP.

Output

```
NEWGROUP

WORD1
WORD2
 .
 .
 .
WORDN

NEWGROUP

WORD1
WORD2
 .
 .
 .
```

Our program to complete the task is

```
i := eof(input); j := eoln(input); M := true; N := true;
inputword(word,w);
do i ≠ M →
   if j ≠ N → writeln; writeword(word,w); writeln; getword(j)
   [] j = N → readln; j := eoln(input)
   fi;
   n := N;
   do j ≠ n →
      inputword(word, w);
      if word ≠ 'NEWGROUP' → writeword(word, w); getword(j)
      [] word = 'NEWGROUP' → n := j
      fi
   od;
   i := eof (input)
od
```

In this implementation, the input/output facilities from Pascal have been borrowed. Effective one-word lookahead is achieved using the procedures inputword, getword, and the variable j. To appreciate how the lookahead functions consider the situation where the last word on a line is

```
... /NEWGROUP/
```

When inputword reads 'NEWGROUP/' it advances in the text to the end of the line. However, in this case, because we want to exploit lookahead we do not want to signal to the program's control structure that the end of a line has been reached. Instead we want to invoke the appropriate output formatting for the start of a new group. The fact that the end-of-line has been reached is hidden from the control structure because j, which controls the end-of-line status is *not* changed by inputword.† The status of j is controlled by the procedure getword. The body of the procedure getword consists only of the statement

    j := eoln(input)

which updates j to the current end-of-line status. The lookahead control structure used allows us to examine a word and process it if it does not indicate a new group. When the start of a new group is detected we can smoothly switch control to do the start-up processing.

To reinforce this technique we will consider a variation on the problem that provides a somewhat more concrete illustration of lookahead. Suppose in this new problem that the data is stored in an M × N array and that all the words are the same length and their lengths including separators '/' are a multiple of N. All other requirements are the same as for the previous problem. In this case our implementation has the form

```
i := 0; j := 0;
inputword(word, w);
do i ≠ M →
    if j ≠ N → writeln; writeword(word, w); writeln; getword(w, j)
    [] j = N → i := i + 1; j := 0
    fi;
    n := N;
    do j ≠ n →
        inputword(word, w);
        if word ≠ 'NEWGROUP' → writeword(word, w); getword(w, j)
        [] word = 'NEWGROUP' → n := j
        fi
    od
od
```

The body of procedure getword is:

    j := j + w

Again inputword does not change j because it is 'looking ahead'. The change in j is controlled by getword. Lookahead in this case allows us to achieve a simpler more efficient control structure than is otherwise possible.

In the section on forced synchronization we will see how simulated lookahead allows us to use a simple control structure for an otherwise difficult problem.

† The procedure inputword returns a word of length w.

12.7   Forced Synchronization of Loops

Often input and output of information are not synchronized. This results in structure clashes.

> **Structure clash**
> A structure clash is defined as an incompatibility between two or more data structures involved in a transfer of information.

A situation where data must be read in blocks of one size and written in blocks of another size is typical of such problems. That is, the input and output of blocks is not synchronized. If such problems are not carefully and systematically dealt with they can lead to clumsy, complex and potentially error-prone programs when implemented in conventional programming languages.

To handle problems of this type systematically some languages provide process-handling mechanisms called coroutines. When these facilities are not available there are two practical ways to handle such structure clashes. We can either use the program-inversion technique suggested by Jackson or we can use a prototyping technique called *forced synchronization*. Both approaches to such problems will be considered, but with the main focus on forced synchronization. The following structuring principle guides the latter approach.

> **Principle of structural simplification**
> For any problem for which there is a structure clash there is a correspondingly simpler problem for which there is no structure clash.

This principle can be used to identify an appropriate structure for a program which must resolve a structure clash. What we are suggesting is that the basic structure used in solving the problem where there is no structure clash should be preserved in solving the problem where there is a structure clash.

This is quite different to that of using program inversion where first two programs are written:

- one dealing with input of data that ignores the structure clash,
- and a second dealing with output of data that again ignores the structure clash.

Program inversion is then carried out by making one of the programs a procedure of the other. Inversion requires that loops are replaced by if statements that employ the same guards as the original loops. In effect, inversion reduces a loop structure to a guarded single-iteration mechanism. The technique will be demonstrated later in this section for the multiple copy problem. In adopting this approach, the structure of one of the two programs is preserved while the structure of the other is destroyed.

This structural bias can have two side effects:

- it can result in a combined program structure that is considerably more complex than the original programs;
- it can result in a program structure that is more difficult to maintain particularly should it be necessary to make changes to those parts of the program structure that originally belonged to the program that has been inverted.

Several very simple examples will now be considered to allow us to explore the fundamental nature of structure clashes and their resolution.

12.7.1   The copy problem

The simplest of all problems where the possibility of a structure clash can arise is that where it is necessary to copy information from one fixed storage area to another fixed storage area. In considering this problem, and the others in this section, arrays will be used as the main prototype storage medium. This choice has been made purely on the grounds of keeping the discussion as simple as possible. In practice, structure clash problems arise more commonly in dealing with different storage media.

The basic copying problem that we wish to consider is that of copying data from an array in[1 .. M] to another array out[1 .. N]. For this problem there are two possibilities:

(1) $M = N \rightarrow$ no structure clash

(2) $M \neq N \rightarrow$ a structure clash

Consider first the solution to (1), the unconditional copy:

Prototype copy $(M = N)$

```
i := 0, j := 0;
do i ≠ M →
    out_{j+1} := in_{i+1}; i := i + 1; j := j + 1
od
```

When it comes to dealing with a copy where it is possible that $M \neq N$, the copy process must cease either on exhausting the input or upon filling the output storage area. We call this a **fixed structure clash**. Our prototype copy is structured to cease on exhausting its input. To enable it to handle the situation where the output storage area is filled *before* the input is exhausted, the copy to the output will need to be made *conditional*.

One possible implementation of a conditional copy is:

Conditional copy: (M ≠ N) – fixed structure clash

```
i := 0; j := 0; m := M;
do i ≠ m →
    if j < N → out_{j+1} := in_{i+1}; i := i + 1; j := j + 1
    [] j = N → m := i
    fi
od
```

In this implementation we have used forced termination to stop the copy if the output buffer is filled before the input is exhausted. The structure of this implementation is exactly what one obtains when the program over the output is inverted. At this level at least there is no difference between making a conditional copy and applying program inversion. In practice, if it were necessary to copy between two arrays, a much simpler and more efficient conditional copy would be used, as follows.

Conditional copy (2)

```
i := 0; j := 0; m := min(M, N);
do i ≠ m →
    out_{j+1} := in_{i+1}; i := i + 1; j := j + 1
od
```

This technique of making the copy unconditional can be used only if the input and output bounds M and N are both available. This is not the case if the input is a file, i.e.

Conditional copy (3)

```
i := eof(in); j := 0; m := M;       {where M = true}
do i ≠ m →
    if j < N → out_{j+1} := in↑; get(in); i := eof(in); j := j+1
    [] j = N → m := i
    fi
od
```

12.7.2   The multiple copy problem

The next level of difficulty in copying arises where the input is consumed for output or processing by making a multiple number of copies of segments of fixed size. The refinement steps in developing this algorithm by our stepwise refinement method are

- one input segment, one output segment;
- one input segment, more than one output segment.

Here the prototype copy corresponds to the situation where the size of the input segment is an integral multiple of the size of the output segments. In the implementation for this problem we will assume an input in[1 . . M] and an output out[1 . . N] and a mechanism process which handles each segment:

Prototype multiple copy
```
i := 0;
do i ≠ M →
  j := 0;
  do j ≠ N →
    out_{j+1} := in_{i+1}; i := i + 1; j := j + 1
  od;
  process(out, N)
od
```

To handle the corresponding structure clash where the output is not a multiple of the input the copy to the output must be conditional on there being input available.

Conditional multiple copy (1)
```
i := 0;
do i ≠ M →
  j := 0; n := N;
  do j ≠ n →
    if i < M → out_{j+1} := in_{i+1}; i := i + 1; j := j + 1
    [] i = M → n := j
    fi
  od;
  process(out, n)
od
```

As with the simple copy the multiple copy can be made unconditional if the bounds are known in advance, that is

Conditional multiple copy (2)
```
i := 0;
do i ≠ M →                                        | loop
  j := 0; m := min(N, M − i);                      | over
  do j ≠ n →                        | loop over   | input
    out_{j+1} := in_{i+1}; i := i + 1; j := j + 1  | output  |
  od;                               |             |
  process(out,n)                    |             |
od
```

The conditional multiple copy solutions maintain the control structure of the original prototype multiple copy.

It is instructive to compare these solutions with the solution obtained by program inversion (the program will be inverted for output). The original 'output' program is:

Original output program

```
j := 0;
do j ≠ N →
    out_{j+1} := "consume input"
od;
process (out, N)
```

Inverted output program

```
if j < N → out_{j+1} := "consume input"
[] j = N → process(out, N); j := 0
fi
```

The inverted output program can be placed in the input program to yield the following complete program:

Multiple copy by program inversion (3)

```
i := 0; j := 0;
do i ≠ M →
    if j < N → out_{j+1} := in_{i+1}; i := i + 1; j := j + 1
    [] j = N → process (out, N); j := 0
    fi
od;
process (out, j)
```

At a first glance, this most recent solution is simpler, as it requires only a single loop rather than two loops. What the inversion has done, however, is destroy the match between the program structure and the data structure. The structural relationship between input and output is no longer readily apparent in the program text. A good way to describe this program structure is to say that it has a **hidden loop**. Hidden loops make programs harder to understand and modify.

To justify this claim consider what happens when it is necessary to modify such programs. We are not advocating that programs should be modified, but human nature tells us that all but the most idealistic will opt to modify an existing program rather than design and implement another program that incorporates the new requirements. We must therefore try to design programs that are robust enough, and simple enough, to withstand modification.

Program modifications are usually concerned with changes of boundary conditions. Such changes almost invariably affect either an initialization or a finalization mechanism somewhere in the program. The structural impact of such changes on the program developed by inversion is shown below, where BEFORE indicates a change impacting initialization for output and AFTER indicates a change impacting finalization for output.

```
i := 0; j := 0; BEFORE*;
do i ≠ M →
   if j < N → out_{j+1} := in_{i+1}; i := i + 1; j := j + 1
   [] j = N → process(out, N); AFTER ; j := 0; BEFORE
   fi
od;
process(out, N);
AFTER*
```

Here BEFORE and AFTER are additional sets of steps that must be applied respectively before and after processing *each* segment that is processed. The program segments marked with an asterisk must be guarded to prevent their application when an empty segment follows or precedes their application.

Before discussing the impact of these modifications let us examine how the same changes are made to our earlier solution.

Modified conditional multiple copy (5)

```
i := 0;
do i ≠ M →
   j := 0, n := min(N,M − i); BEFORE ;
   do j ≠ n →
      out_{j+1} := in_{i+1}; i := i + 1; j := j + 1
   od;
   process (out,n);
   AFTER
od
```

Comparing the two modified solutions (4) and (5), we see that both a BEFORE and an AFTER change require alterations in only one structural part of the program (5) whereas in (4) changes are required in *two* structural regions of the program. This can get particularly complex if BEFORE and AFTER modifications coalesce as they do when j = N applies as in solution (4). A second important structural difference between (4) and (5) is that in (5) the need to guard the extreme BEFORE and AFTER is avoided as they are already protected by the loop guards.

12.7.3 A mismatched copy (floating structure clash)

In the previous example, although the input was consumed in segments, after each segment was consumed, output took place. Then input of the next segment followed directly. A more interesting and challenging structure clash occurs when the input of a segment and the output of a segment are no longer directly synchronized, matched or coupled. That is, output of a segment may be required without the need for a new input segment, and vice versa. This is called a **floating structure clash**. Schematically segmentation of the input in and output out might be

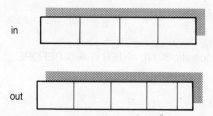

So far we have only considered copying problems where there is one input operation (i.e. one call to inbuff). We now want to consider cases where there are potentially multiple calls to both inbuff and outbuff and the two buffers M and N are of different sizes.

The prototype problem corresponds to the situation where *each* input buffer provided by a call to inbuff is copied to out and processed by a call to outbuff before there is a need for a new call to inbuff, i.e. we have

Prototype structure

```
k := 0;
do k ≠ N →
   inbuff (in,m,M); i := 0; j := 0;
   do i ≠ m →
      out_{j+1} := in_{i+1}; i := i + 1; j := j + 1; k := k + 1
   od;
   outbuff (out, m)
od
```

Ordinarily we will not know the value of N so processing will need to continue until the input is exhausted. This is signalled by inbuff returning $m = 0$ (note $0 \leq m \leq M$). Also m will be equal to M until the last iteration of the outer loop. A slightly more realistic prototype based on processing until the input is exhausted has the form given below:

Prototype structure

```
i := 0;
j := 0;
repeat
   inbuff(in,m,M);                          { Input }
   do i ≠ m →
      out_{j+1} := in_{i+1}; i := i + 1; j := j + 1;   { Process (in this case just a
   od;                                                   copy) }
   i := 0;
   outbuff(out, m); j := 0;                 { Output }
until m = 0;
```

With this particular type of problem, as soon as we admit the possibility that the input buffer in[1..M] and the output buffer out[1..N] may be different in length (i.e. M ≠ N) there is no longer any synchronization between the calls to inbuff and outbuff. This creates a loop structuring problem where more than one call to either inbuff or outbuff, or both, is needed.

In our introduction we suggested that a good strategy for handling problems of this type was to exploit the structure of the prototype solution that had no structure clash in constructing a solution that handles the structure clash.

Examining the structure of our prototype solution to the problem we see that it has the basic form

```
repeat
    (1)  input data
    (2)  process while not requiring input or output
    (3)  output the processed data
until termination condition
```

All that is required to handle input and output buffers of different size is to make the input of data and the output of data *conditional*. We only input data *when it is required*, and we only output data *when it is required*. This proposal preserves the prototype or natural *control* structure in the solution of the more complex problem.

We then have the augmented or synchronized structure:

```
repeat
    (1)  if require input then input data
    (2)  process while not requiring input or output
    (3)  if require output then output the processed data
until termination condition
```

With this new structure, because of the conditional input and conditional output, there is either input or output with each iteration of the outermost loop. When the input and output buffers are the same length (i.e. M = N) there will be input *and* output with each iteration because the two processes are synchronized. We say that this structure with conditional input and output implements the **forced synchronization** of the input and the output. The component of the structure that implements processing while there is no demand for either input or output is referred to as a **pipe**. The pipe controls the flow of information from the input to the output, intermittently suspending the flow when either the sink (output) is full or the source (input) is empty. Termination of the information flow through the pipe is achieved using the forced termination technique discussed in detail earlier in this chapter.

Surprisingly, these very simple guidelines can lead to the straightforward solution of a wide range of problems – including the present example. When forced synchronization is applied to our present problem we end up with the following implementation:

Mismatched copy

```
i := 0;                                      {Input initialization}
j := 0;                                      {Output initialization}
repeat
    if i = 0 then inbuff(in, m, M) fi;       {Conditional input initialization}
    p := m;
    do i ≠ p →
        if j ≠ N → out_{j+1} := in_{i+1}; i := i + 1;    {Process while not requiring
                   j := j + 1;                            input or output}
        [] j = N → p := i
        fi
    od
    if i = M then i := 0 fi;                  {Conditional input finalization}
    if j = N then outbuff (out, j); j := 0 fi;    {Conditional output finalization}
until m = 0;
if j ≠ N then outbuff (out, j) fi            {Final output finalization}
```

The advantage of the forced synchronization solution is that it retains the structure of the prototype problem. This means that input, processing, and output remain well separated. Hence, should it subsequently become necessary to make changes to one of these phases the separation will make the changes straightforward.

12.7.4   A structure clash

As a slightly more complicated example, suppose we have a file of student records (each record consisting of a course descriptor, student name, and mark) which are sorted by course. For example:

```
CS1    Name1     40
CS1    Name2     66
 .       .        .
 .       .        .
CS2    Name1'    75
CS2    Name2'    53
```

To process this data it is required to produce a report that is split into pages, with a heading on each page. The file is to be read and student names and marks are to be listed together with the total class count at the end of each course. In this problem there is an arbitrary relationship between course and page. For example,

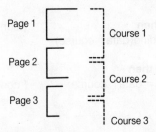

The prototype problem in this case is one where each course fits exactly on a page. It may take the following form.

Prototype solution†

```
M := TRUE;
get(data); i := eof(data);                    {input initialization}
do i ≠ M →
    WritePageHeading(data↑ .course);          {page output initialization}
    currentcourse := data↑ .course;           {course output initialization}
    classcount := 0;
    m := M;
    do i ≠ m →
        if data↑course = currentcourse →       {process while there is more
            write(data↑ .name); write(data      data, and it is the same
            ↑ .mark);                           course}
            get(data); i := eof(data) ; classcount
            := classcount + 1
        [] data↑course ≠ currentcourse → m := i
        fi
    od;
    write(classcount);                         {course output finalization}
    write(PAGEBREAK)                           {page output finalization}
od;
```

To handle the case where course and page boundaries do not correspond we need to conditionalize the initialization and finalization mechanisms for input and output and force termination of the inner course-processing loop when a new page is needed (that is when linecount=PAGEQUOTA). In this case there is *no* structure clash with the input, and it remains unconditional.

† Pascal's I/O has been borrowed and used here.

Forced synchronization solution

```
M := TRUE;
linecount := 0;                                    { page initialization }
classcount := 0;                                   { course initialization }
get(data); i := eof(data);                         { input initialization }

    do i ≠ M →
        if linecount = 0 then                      { conditional page init. }
            WritePageHeading(data↑ .course)
        fi;
        if classcount = 0 then
            currentcourse := data↑ .course         { conditional course init. }
        fi;
        m := M;
        do i ≠ m →
            if data↑ .course = currentcourse ∧ linecount ≠ PAGEQUOTA →
                write(data↑ .name); write(data↑ .mark); linecount := linecount + 1;
                get(data); i := eof(data); classcount := classcount + 1
            [] data↑ .course ≠ currentcourse ∨ linecount = PAGEQUOTA → m := i
            fi
        od;
        if data↑ .course ≠ currentcourse then
            write(classcount); classcount := 0        { conditional course
        fi;                                             finalization }
        if linecount = PAGEQUOTA then
            write(PAGEBREAK) ; linecount := 0         {conditional page
        fi                                              finalization}
    od;

    if classcount ≠ 0 then write(classcount) fi;   { course output finalization }
    if linecount ≠ 0 then write(PAGEBREAK) fi      { course page finalization }
```

12.7.5   Multiple input structure clash

The same basic prototyping strategy can easily be extended to handle more than one input and output. Suppose we extend our original buffering problem to a stream-addition problem where there are *two* inputs and one output – all of which may have different buffer sizes.

Stream	Buffer	
Input_A	A[1. .M]	
Input_B	B[1. .N]	{ where M ≠ N ≠ P }
Output	Out[1. .P]	

In the prototype solution we assume that the sizes of the buffers are the same (i.e. M = N = P).

Prototype solution

```
i := 0;                                          { Input_A initialization }
j := 0;                                          { Input_B initialization }
k := 0;                                          { Output initialization }
repeat
   inbuff(A, M, m);                              { Input_A initialization }
   inbuff(B, N, n);                              { Input_B initialization }
   do k ≠ P →
      out_{k+1} := A_{i+1} + B_{j+1};            { Process loop }
      i := i + 1; j := j + 1; k := k + 1
   od;
   i := 0; j := 0;                               { Input finalizations }
   outbuff(out,k); k := 0                        { Output finalization }
until m = 0 ∨ n = 0
```

To resolve the structure clash both the inputs and the output need to be conditionalized and the processing loop must be forced to terminate when either of its inputs are exhausted as well as when the output buffer is filled. Making these refinements we get the following:

Forced synchronization solution

```
      i := 0; j := 0; k := 0;                        {Input and output initializations}
      repeat
†        if i = 0 then inbuff(A, M, m) fi;           {Input_A conditional initialization}
†        if j = 0 then inbuff(B, N, n) fi;           {Input_B conditional initialization}
         p := P;
         do k ≠ p →                                  {Information transfer conditional
            if i ≠ m ∧ j ≠ n →                        on availability of inputs}
               out_{k+1} := A_{i+1} + B_{j+1};
               i := i + 1; j := j + 1; k := k + 1
                                                     {Processing }
            [] i = m ∨ j = n → p := k
            fi
         od;
††       if i = M then i := 0 fi;                    {Input_A conditional finalization}
††       if j = N then j := 0 fi;                    {Input_B conditional finalization}
         if k = P then outbuff(out, k); k := 0 {Conditional output finalization}
         fi
      until m = 0 ∨ n = 0;
      if k ≠ 0 then outbuff(out, k)  fi              {Terminal finalization}
```

---

† Note m and n are zero when there is no more input data.
†† Also note that the conditional finalizations and the conditional initializations may be combined if the same guard is employed. Here, the same condition would be used to signal that all the input has been processed as well as the need to (re)fill the input buffer. The corresponding initialization would indicate that all input has been processed. There are two views of the conditions. Firstly, there is the *transitional* view – where only one guard is required: the condition signals movement from one task to the next. Then there is a more *discrete* view – where there are two distinct guards: one condition signalling the start of a task and another signalling the end of a task.

12.7.6   Text formatting problem

The next problem that we wish to consider may be stated informally as follows:

> *Read lines of text until the input is exhausted. Eliminate redundant blanks between words, and print the text with a maximum of* L *characters to a line without breaking words between lines. It is also required that leading and trailing blanks should be removed and there should be the maximum number of words possible on each line.*

In attempting to design a solution to this problem we will first try to construct a solution for the prototype problem involving no structure clashes. We will then try to modify it using forced synchronization to handle the structure clash.

In the prototype solution a line of words is read, leading and trailing spaces are removed, and multiple spaces between words are discarded. The reformatted line is written out as it is built, one word at a time.

The prototype implementation to handle lines of text containing *one or more* words may take the form:

Prototype text formatter

```
M := true;
i := eof(input) ;
do i ≠ M →
    getspaces(j);                                    { input initialization }
    getword(word, w, j); getspaces(j);
    writeword(word, w); l := w;                      { output initialization }
    do j ≠ ENDLINE →
        getword(word, w, j); getspaces(j);           { input process }
        write(SPACE); writeword(word, w); l := l + w + 1; { output process }
    od;
    readln ; j := STARTLINE;                          { input finalization }
    writeln;                                          { output finalization }
    i := eof(input);
od
```

To proceed from the prototype solution to handle the structure clash we need to make the initialization for output conditional. We also need to make the finalization mechanisms for input and output conditional. The flow of information through the pipe must be suspended when the *next* word to be printed exceeds the output line length limit L. In our implementation we use the variable l to hold the current length of the output line and w to hold the length of the next word to be processed. The implementation of the formatter for handling text with non-empty lines takes the following form.

Text formatter

```
M := true;
l := 0 ; w := 0;                                    { output initialization }
j := STARTLINE;                                      { input initialization }
i := eof(input) ;
do i ≠ M →
   if j = STARTLINE then getspaces(j) fi;            { start of input line }
   if l = 0 ∧ w = 0 then getword(word, w, j);
                    getspaces(j) fi;
   if l = 0 ∧ w ≠ 0 then writeword(word, w);         { start of output line }
                    l := w; w := 0 fi;
   n := ENDLINE;
   do j ≠ n →
      getword(word, w, j); getspaces(j);
      if l + w + 1 ≤ L → write(SPACE); writeword(word, w);
                    l := l + w + 1; w := 0
      [] l + w + 1 > L → n := j
      fi
   od;
   if j = ENDLINE then readln; j := STARTLINE; i := eof(input) fi;
   if l + w + 1 > L then writeln; l := 0 fi             { end of output line }
od;
if l = 0 ∧ w ≠ 0 then writeword(word, w);            { output finalization }
               l := w; w := 0 fi;
if l ≠ 0 then writeln fi
```

Some additional comments about this implementation are in order. With each iteration of the outermost loop there may be initialization for the *output* of a new line of text. Furthermore, with each iteration of the outermost loop, there may be invocation of a finalization mechanism to terminate either the current output line or the current input line.

It is interesting to study the effects of complicating the present problem further by introducing another structure clash. For this we may consider a structure clash resulting from the requirement that there should be at most P characters on a page. A page is a sequence of the previously described lines of text. In addition, there should be the maximum number of words on a page.

To accommodate this new structure clash in our most recent implementation, we need to add a conditional initialization for new pages and a conditional finalization mechanism for a new page. The only other requirement is to add a condition that suspends information flow through the pipe when it is necessary to move to a new page. Augmenting our previous implementation with these modifications we obtain a paged-line text formatter.

Paged-line text formatter

```
M := true;
l := 0 ; w := 0;                          { line output initialization }
p := 0 ;                                  { page output initialization }
j := STARTLINE;                           { input initialization }
i := eof(input) ;
do i ≠ M →
    if j = STARTLINE then getspaces(j) fi;            { start of input line }
    if l=0 ∧ w=0 then getword(word, w, j); getspaces(j) fi;
                                                      { start of output line }
    if l = 0 ∧ w ≠ 0 then writeword(word, w); l := w; p := p+w; w := 0 fi;
    n := ENDLINE;
    do j ≠ n →
        getword(word, w, j); getspaces(j);
        if l + w + 1 ≤ L ∧ p + w + 1 ≤ P → write(SPACE); writeword(word, w);
                                l := l + w + 1; p := p + w + 1; w := 0
        [] l+w+1 > L ∨ p+w+1 > P → n := j
        fi
    od;
    if j = ENDLINE then readln; j := STARTLINE; i := eof(input) fi;
    if l + w + 1 > L ∨ p + w + 1 > P then writeln; l := 0 fi;
                                                      { end of output line }
    if p + w + 1 > P then write(PAGEBREAK); p := 0 fi
                                                      {conditional page
                                                       finalization }
od;
if l = 0 ∧ w ≠ 0 then writeword(word, w); l := w; p := p + w; w := 0 fi;
                                                      { output finalization }
if l ≠ 0 then writeln fi;
if p ≠ 0 then write(PAGEBREAK) fi  { write the final pagebreak if needed }
```

A comparison of this implementation with the previous one suggests that the changes needed to accommodate an additional structure clash are relatively minor provided we conform to the guidelines for conditional initialization and finalization. What is somewhat surprising about the last two implementations is that they both retain the same underlying structure that was used for the prototype problem. Furthermore the extra effort to handle the additional structure clash is small. It is in this domain where forced synchronization offers considerable advantages over program inversion.

SUMMARY

- Conventions, programming style, consistency and systematic methods add an important and useful dimension to programs that have been derived from formal specifications.

- Important style conventions are layout conventions, commenting conventions, naming conventions, and input/output conventions.

- Initializations for loops are important particularly because they must establish loop invariants initially. There are a number of defects that can be made in initializing loops. These include under-initialization, over-initialization, backstep initialization and premature initialization.

- Termination of loops is one of the most vulnerable aspects of program implementation. Forced termination is a useful technique for stopping loops early.

- A useful way of structuring loops is to ensure that the control structure for the loops matches the structure of the data being processed.

- Lookahead is a useful strategy for processing complex sequential data.

- To handle data that involves structure clashes it is useful to employ a strategy for implementing first a solution to the corresponding problem where there is no structure clash. This provides a framework for resolving the structure clash.

■ *EXERCISE 12   Program implementation problems*

1.   The basic input/output facilities provided with Modula-2 usually do not allow one-character lookahead. Write a set of procedures input, get, eoln, and eof to simulate the one-character lookahead of Pascal.

2.   Use the procedures developed in the previous example to solve the following problem. Given are lines of characters of the form

        /CAB ... ... XU
        ... ... AD/CF ... YQ

Each group of characters is preceded by a '/'. It is required to process the groups so that each group in the output appears on a *single* line. In the input a group may spread across one or more lines.

3.   Implement solutions to the digit/alphabet processing problem discussed at the start of this section using

(a) Pascal's lookahead facilities;

(b) Modula-2 with simulated one character lookahead.

4.   Provide a solution to the M × N array processing problem that does not use simulated lookahead.

Bibliography

Alagic, S. and M., Arbib (1978), *The Design of Well-structured and Correct Programs,* Springer-Verlag, New York.

Bentley, J.L. (1984), Algorithm design techniques, *Comm. ACM,* **27**(9), 865–9.

Codd, E.F. (1972), *Further normalization of the data base relational model,* Vol. 6, Courant Computer Science Symposia Series, Prentice-Hall, Englewood Cliffs, N.J.

Dijkstra, E.W. (1976), *A Discipline of Programming,* Prentice-Hall, Englewood Cliffs, N.J.

Dromey, R.G. (1988), Systematic program development, *IEEE Trans. on Soft. Eng.* **14**(1), 12–29.

Dromey, R.G. (1985), Forced termination of loops, *Software : Practice & Experience,* **15**(1), 30–40

Floyd, R.W. (1978), Paradigms of programming, *Comm. ACM.,* **22**(8), 455–60.

Feuer, A.R. and N.H. Gehani (1982), A comparison of the programming languages C and Pascal, *Comp. Surv.* **14,** 73–92.

Gries, D. (1981), *The Science of Programming,* Springer-Verlag, N.Y.

Jackson, M. (1976), *Principles of Program Design,* Academic Press.

Jackson, M. (1983), *Systems Development,* Prentice-Hall, London.

Knuth, D.E. (1969), *Art of Computer Programming,* Vol. 1, *Fundamental Algorithms,* (Section 1.2.10), Addison-Wesley, Reading, Mass.

Knuth, D.E. (1973), *Art of Computer Programming,* Vol. 3, *Sorting and Searching* (Section 5.2.3, problem [18]), Addison-Wesley, Reading, Mass.

Mayer, A. (1877), *Geschichte des Prinzips der kleinsten Action,* Leipzig.

Wirth, N. (1976), *Algorithms + Data Structures = Programs,* Prentice-Hall, Englewood Cliffs, N.J.

Whitehead, A.N. (1949), *The Aims of Education,* Mentor, N.Y.

Index

abort, semantics of 270
abs 135
absolute complement, of sets 99
absorption, law of 44
absurdity, law of 45
addition 53
   law of 44
adjunction 53
Alagic, S. 588
Algol-60 145
alphabet 146, 173
alternative command 268
analytic propositions 44
analytic transformations 43
AND 33
antecedent 35, 36
antisymmetry 119
Arbib, M. 588
arc 120
arguments, validity of 51
array relations 87
array specifications 241
array summation 210, 347, 548
ASCII 479
assignment 255
   multiple 158, 267
   weakest precondition for 255
assignment statement 150
associative 132
associative laws 44
asymmetry 119
asymptotic complexity 130
atomic expression 60
atomic formula 60, 61
auxiliary problem 328, 329, 333,
   435
   generation of 333
axiom of extensionality 93, 95, 104

axiom of specification 95 (fn)

back-step initialization 562
Backus-Naur Form BNF 145, 146
bag 139-144, 183
bag cardinality 141
bag deletion 143
bag difference 143
bag insertion 143
bag intersection 142
bag membership 139
bag operations 142
bag representation 139,145
bag sum 142
bag theory 139
bag union 142
base invariant 285, 304
   construction of 304
Berglund, G. 510
Bernouilli inequality 77
biconditional proposition 38
biconditional simplification 53
bijection 129
bijective 182
bijective function 126
binary relation 112, 114-116
   properties of 114-116
binary search 192, 438
   derivation of 402
binary tree 122, 164, 174, 175
bipartite graph 119-20, 128
Boolean expression 265, 268
bottom-up 203
bottom-up design 311
bound extension 303
bound function 188, 219
bound variable 62
bounds for variables 190

Boyer-Moore algorithm   475
Brooks, F.P.   423
bubble sort, derivation of   454
buffer copy   614

C   148
cand   39, 149, 576, 578
cardinality   174
    of bags   141
    of sets   97
Cartesian product   105-8, 115, 117, 119,
        178, 248
characteristic function   127
classes of sorting algorithms   451
closure   173
co-domain   115
    of function   123, 181
Codd, E.F.   581
command identification   261, 320
comments   150
comment skipping   491
common element search, derivation of
        411
commutative laws   44
comparison, design methods   311
complement, of sets   100
complement extension   302
complementation   99
completeness   7
complexity   130
composition, of functions   130
composition rules   309
comprehensive specification, principle of
        95, 104
computation of weakest preconditions
        254
conclusion   51
conditional connectives   39
conditional initialization   615
conditional proof   54
    rule of   52
conditional proposition   35
conditional sentences   36
confirming a postcondition   294, 331
conjunction   34, 108, 111
    law of   252
    preconditions and postconditions
        336
    truth table   35
conjunctive normal form   46
conjunctive resolution rule   49
conjunctive simplification   53
connectives   33
    conditional   39

elimination of   45
    logical   108
    propositional   108
consequent   36
consistency   7(fn), 532
constant   56
constant function   127
constant replacement   297, 313
constants   551
constructive postcondition   283
constructive problems   200, 201
constructive proof   31, 81, 193
contradiction   41(fn), 50, 111
contradiction law   44
contradictory propositions   43
contraposition   44
convention, for documentation   532
convention, for specifications   64
coordinate   105
copy problem   603
cor   39, 149
coroutines   602
correctness   3
    of loops   277
    proof of   5
correspondence principle   307, 581
counting operator   145
counting specifier   68
    empty range   68
currying, of functions   135
cycle   291

data structure match   506
data structure-control structure match
        294
data structures   294
    matching of   307
data variables   247
de Morgan   66
de Morgan's laws   46, 48, 100
debugging   4
declarative sentence   33
decomposition   9, 11, 12, 214, 262, 312,
        325-6, 328, 569
    by calculation   332
decomposition rules   306-9
deduction   76
deletion from text   486
delimiters   149
denials   73
derivation   6
    array summation   347
    binary search   402
    bubble sort   454

common element search   411
exponentiation   355
exchange   358
factorial   350
fast exponentiation   371
fast multiplication   372
fast quotient remainder   379
Fermat's algorithm   383
gcd algorithm   389
generating squares and cubes   361
heapsort   455
indirect selection sort   461
insertion sort   292
integer square root   366
linear search   400
majority element   498
matrix multiplication   374
multiplication by addition   359
pair-maximum   341
pair-relation   342
quicksort   465
quotient-remainder   353
Rubin's problem   414
rules of   50-51
saddleback search   418
selection sort   451
sequential file update   513
stores movement   506
string searching   472
telegrams analysis   520
two-dimensional search   407
two-squares sum   386
two-way merge   511
using tautologies   45
variant function   225
derivative invariant   286
derived inference rules   73
design   7, 9
    of loop   217, 348
design strategy   12
detachment, law of   45
development process, cycle in   291
difference of bags   143
    of sets   99, 107, 109
Dijkstra, E.W.   64, 65, 148, 197, 255, 265,
    365, 383, 389, 438, 469, 485, 565,
    576
direct proofs   76
direct selection sort   449, 452
direct insertion sort   450
    derivation   460
directed graph   119
disjoint sets   99
disjunction   35, 109, 111

law of   253
    truth table   35
disjunctive, normal form   46
disjunctive resolution rule   49
disjunctive simplification   53
disjunctive syllogism   53
distributive laws   44
DO statement   152
documentation conventions   533
dom   115, 124, 137, 180
domain   115
    of function   123
domain restriction operator   136
domain subtraction operator   137
double negation   53
double negation law   44
Dutch national flag   438
EBNF   144, 145, 148, 149, 152, 182, 469,
    485
editing text   483
elementary formula   60
elementary propositional expression   40
elimination
    of connectives   45
    of quantifier   69
empty bag   140
empty range   68
    counting specifier   68
    product   67
    quantification   65
    summation   67
empty set   96
encapsulation   550
entity   56
entity-property relation   56
equality relation   116
equivalence   38-39, 110
    logical   74
    truth table   39
equivalence classes   118
equivalence condition   284
equivalence relation   116, 118
equivalence transformations   6, 340
equivalent problem solution   339
errors   4-5
Euclid   79
exchange derivation   343
excluded middle law   44
excluded miracle, law of   251
existence proof   81
existential generalization   72, 81
existential quantification   59
existential quantifiers   59

existential specification   71
exists   59
explicit data structure   294, 583
explicitivity   326
exponentiation   355
    derivation of   355
EXPORT   550
exportation, law of   45
expression   56
    atomic   60
expression replacement   298
extensionality, axiom of   95
extensionality, principle of   75, 284, 297

factorial   261(fn)
    derivation of   350
fast exponentiation, derivation of   371
fast multiplication, derivation of   372
fast quotient-remainder   379
Fermat's algorithm   389
    derivation of   383
Feuer, A.R.   576
Fibonacci numbers   80
    sequence   169, 555
field   115
final states   8
finalization   597
finding the maximum   555
finding the median   435
finding the minimum   450
first coordinate   105
fixed free variable   63
fixed free variables   283
Floyd, R.   596
Floyd, R.W.   245
for all   58
for some   59
forced synchronization   602
forced synchronization of loops   602
forced termination   192, 575
forced termination of loops   573
formal specification   8-9, 202, 203, 238
formation rules   61
    propositions   39
formatting text   484
formula, atomic   60
formulae   61
free variable   62, 134
    fixed   63, 283
    non-fixed   63
functions   56, 103, 122-139, 181
    classes of   126-130
    classification of   126

inductively defined   133, 173
    inverse of   131
    lambda notation   133
    operators on   135
    partial   125, 135
    total   125, 139
function concept   122
functional composition   130-131
functional modularity   550
functional override   138

Gauss' formula   78(fn)
    proof of   162
gcd   190, 197, 198, 225, 275, 340, 389, 540, 591
gcd specification   296
Gehani, N.H.   576
generating auxiliary problems   332
generating squares and cubes, derivation of   361
generating sub-problems   330
goal   225
Goethe   27
grammar notation   148
graph relation   119
graph
    bipartite   119
    directed   119
    undirected   122
greatest common divisor   see gcd
Gries, D.   197, 340, 418, 565, 569
guard identification   259
guarded command   19, 148, 151, 153
    notation   154
    semantics of   265
guarded commands syntax   149
guarded loop   275
guidelines for postconditions   194

Hadamard, J.   91
Hamming's problem   565
heap   201
heap-insertion   458
heapsort   449, 595, 596
    derivation of   455
hidden loop   606
hierarchical modularity   544
Hoare, C.A.R.   325, 399
horn clauses   48
hypothetical syllogism   53

idempotent laws   44
identifier   110, 149

definition of   152
identity   74, 75, 92
identity element   67
   for multiplication   67
   for summation   66
identity function   127
identity of indiscernibles, law of   75
identity law   44, 75
identity relation   116
identity transformation   301
IF statement   150
   semantics of   272
image   123
   image extension   301
implementation   555
implication   35, 48, 110
   truth table   36
implication-simplification   44
implicit data structure   294, 583
implicit specification   194
IMPORT   550
importation, law of   45
inclusion   94, 110, 141
   of sets   96
incondition   277
in-degree   119, 121
indirect insertion sort   450
indirect proof   79
indirect selection sort   449, 453
indirect selection sort derivation   461
induction   77, 158-76, 184
   structural   174
   principle of   174
inductive proofs   171
inductive specification, of sets   172
inductively defined function   173
inference   48, 51, 75
   theory of   52
inference rule, identity   76
inference rules   52
   derived   74
   quantifiers   69
infinite loop   572
initial states   8, 250
initialization   313
   conditional   615
   of loops   554
   of postcondition   322
initialization sub-problem   331
injective   182
injective function   126
input   8
input assertion   188
input data   63, 191

input/output conventions   539
input variables   247, 248
insertion in text   483
insertion sort   23
   derivation of   282, 292, 460
integer square root   364, 366
   problem   201
interpretation of relations   88
intersection   108
   of arrays   102
   of bags   145
   of sets   98, 107
interval partitioning   431, 451, 465
introduction, of quantifier   72
invariant, *see also* loop invariant   17, 18,
   188, 206, 401
inverse function   128
inverse relation   116
inverse of programs   602
iteration   153, 265
iterative command   274

Jackson, M.   294, 307, 581, 583, 602
Jackson's method   510

Kettering, C.   187
Kleene closure   173
Knuth, D.E.   590
Kth largest element   435

lambda abstraction   134
lambda conversion   134
lambda notation   133, 135, 182
Langer, S.   30
Langer, S.K.   445
law of
   absorption   44, 45
   absurdity   45
   addition   44
   conjunction   252
   detachment   45
   disjunction   253
   excluded miracle   251
   exportation   45
   identity   75
   monotonicity   253
   separation of concerns   576
   simplification   45
laws of equivalence   84
laws of sets   101
layout conventions   533
leaf node   121
least action, principle of   286, 294
least fixed-point method   281

Leibnitz's Law   75
limited top-down design   311
Lin, S.T.   100
linear search   201, 574, 577
    derivation of   400
    tail recursion   155
linked list   579
logic   29
logic specifications   29
logical connectives   108
logical equivalence   50, 73
logical identity   75
logical inference   87
lookahead   581, 597
loop
    hidden   613
    proof rules   278
loop correctness, requirement for   277
loop design   345
loop finalization   575
loop guards   571
loop inhomogenity   214
loop invariant   206, 207, 208, 277
    homogenous   215
    interpretation of   231
    properties of   214
    in specification   207
    strength of   211
    use of   206
loop invariant-postcondition relationship
        216, 218
loop progress   213
loop statement   276
loop structure   213
loop structuring   581
loop termination   277, 571
loops
    forced synchronization   602
    forced termination of   573
    initialization of   554

majority-element problem   498
mapping   123
marriage relation   115
matching data structure   588
matching strings   474
mathematical induction   77, 158-78
    first principle   158-60
    generalized first principle   166-68
    second principle   168
matrix multiplication   202
    derivation of   375
matrix row-sum   511
MAX   228, 590

maximizing specifier   68
maximum   208
    specification for   191
maximum finding   538, 590
maximum sum-section problem   501
McDonald's problem   510
median finding   435
member   94
membership
    of bag   139
    of sets   92
merging   515
MIN   228
minimizing specifier   69
minimum finding   450
Modula-2   148, 152, 153, 544, 550, 567,
        568
modularization   544
mod   66
modus ponendo ponens   52
modus tollendo ponens   53
modus tollendo tollens   53
monotonicity, law of   253
monus function   144
multiple assignment   267
multiple copy problem   604
multiplication by addition, derivation of
        359-61
multiply occurring   203
multisets   139, *see also* bags
mutually exclusive sets   99

n-tuple   105, 113, 118
naming conventions   537
natural language   37, 81, 112, 114
natural language specifications   28
natural numbers   132, 141
natural termination   575
negation   34, 73, 109
    truth table   34
nested loops   312, 368, 569
node   119
non-constructive proof   81
nondeterminism   268
non-fixed free variable   63, 283
normal forms   46
normalization   581

O-notation   130
one-to-one correspondence function   126
one-to-one function   126
onto function   126
operations
    on bags   142

on sets   97, 107, 108
operators   33, 149
operators on functions   135
OR   33
or-simplification   44
ORD   480
order   145
order notation   129
order relation   113
ordered n-tuple   105, 113, 118
ordered pairs   104-5, 110, 113, 115, 141,
      144
ordered permutation   103
ordered triple   105, 106
ordering   446
      partial   119
ordering relations   119
ordering rule   104
outof function   144
out-degree   119, 121
output   8, 63
output variables   247
over-initialization   563
over-iteration   571
override operator   138

pair-maximum derivation   341
pair-relation derivation   342
pairing   104
      principle of   103
pairs
      ordered   110, 115, 141, 144
      unordered   103, 104
parameter passing   546
parameters   154, 282
parent-domain   115, 123
parentheses, use of   62
parentheses rule   40
parenthetic data structure   593
partial function   125, 144
partial ordering   119
partition   117-18
      interval   431, 451, 465
      pivot   428, 451, 489
      simple pivot   424
      straight pivot   426
partitioning algorithms   462, 464
partitioning problems   223, 442
partitioning program   223
Pascal   55, 148, 152, 275, 568, 569, 576
Pascal comments   491
Pascal I/O   540
pattern matching   470

pattern searching   472
permutation   103, 202
permutation function   129
Pick   19
pipe   609
pivot partitioning   see partitioning
plan   10
Polya, G.   11, 340
positional specifications   229
positive closure   173
positive integers   141(fn), 160
postcondition   8, 32, 193, 194, 201, 202,
      277
      confirmation of   22, 294, 331
      constructive form   283
      guidelines for   194
      initialization of   322
      strengthening of   335, 508
      stronger   431
      weakening of   333, 365
      weaker   431
postcondition-loop invariant relationship
      219
postcondition specifications   195
postcondition types   199
postfix refinement   309
power relation   115-16
powersets   96, 97, 115, 164, 179
pre-image   125
precedence rule   40
precondition   8, 32, 187, 193, 277
      strengthening of   333
precondition-postcondition conjunction
      336
predicate   30, 56, 57, 60, 81, 91, 103, 151
      relational   57
      strength of   111, 242
      strongest   111
      two place   57
      weakest   111
predicate calculus   54, 63, 81, 97
predicate transformer   31
predicates for state definition   110, 249
prefix refinement   309
premature initialization   569
premise   51
premises, rule of   52
primary decomposition rule   308
primary specification   188
prime factorization   588
prime factors   141
prime numbers   66, 95, 171
principle of
      abstraction   118

comprehensive specification 95, 104
extensionality 75, 284, 297
least action 286, 295
structural induction 174
structural simplification 602
weak induction 158(fn)
problem decomposition strategy 12, 328
problem specification 20
problem size 189
problem-solving 328
problem-solving strategies 325
procedure parameters 282
procedures 154, 549
product, identity 67
product specifier 67
production rules 146
program 149
binary search 192
gcd 190, 197
linear search 201
maximum 208
partitioning 223
quotient/remainder 190
summing an array 210
symmetric binary search 193
program correctness 4
program defects 5
program derivation 6, 16, 20, 23, 202, 325,
395, 531
an example 282
model for 293
nested loops 369
and specification strength 293
strategy for 245-6
program design 6
program development 520
program errors 24
program implementation 6
program inversion 602
program semantics 31, 250
program specification 6, 187
program structuring 569, 582
program variables 247
programming style 532
projection 108
Prolog 48
proof 6, 51, 54, 72, 87
constructive 81
of correctness 16
example of 278
of loop correctness 278
non-constructive 81
of a program 171

proof by contradiction 79
proof methods 76
proofs 69
direct 76
indirect 79
inductive 173
proper subset 94
property 56
proposition 33, 81
propositional calculus 32-33, 54, 81
propositional expression 39
rules for 40
propositional logic 70
propositional simplification 84
propositional variables 39
propositions
analytic 43
contradictory 43
elementary 39
synthetic 43
prototyping 602

quantification 58, 89
over empty range 65
equivalence relation 65
existential 59, 65, 65
over ranges 64
relationship 66
specifications 90
universal 58, 65, 197, 204
quantifier 58
quantifier elimination 69
quantifier inference rules 69
quantifier insertion 69
quantifier introduction 72
quantifier scope 61-2
quantifiers
use of 90, 206
quicksort 331, 596
derivation of 463, 465
quotes 247
quotient-remainder problem 16, 190, 224,
353

ran 115, 124, 125, 180
random-number generation 550
range 115, 216
of function 123
range extension 303
range restriction operator 136
range specifications 83
range subtraction operator 138
ranges 64

real numbers   136, 149
recursive composition   280
recursive refinement   311
reductio ad absurdum   79(fn)
refinement   11
 infix   311
 initial states   296
 iterative rule   311
 postfix   309
 prefix   309
 rule context for   308
 stages in   284
 strategy   286
refinement composition rules   309
refinement invariant   294
refinement process   294
reflexive   95
reflexive relation   114
Reichenbach, H.   30
relation   103, 112-22, 180
 binary   112, 114-16
 of equality   119
 equivalence   116, 118
 on graphs   119
 identity   116
 inverse of   116
 marriage   115
 power   115-16
 reflexive   114
 splitting of   463
 symmetric   114
 ternary   113
 transitive   114
 on trees   119
 universal   118
relational predicate   51
relations
 on arrays   87
 interpretation   88
relative complement   101
replacement   50
 rule of   51
replacement in text   484
resolution, simplification rules   49
resolution principle   49
root   121
row sums of matrix   311(fn)
row-sums problem   587
Rubin, F.   414
Rubin's problem, derivation of   414
rule of conditional proof   52
rule for interchanging quantifiers   73
rule of ordering   104
rule of premises   52

rule of replacement   51
rule of specialization   70
rule of substitution   50
rule of tautological implication   52
rule of universal specification   70
rule of variable restriction   63
rules
 for decomposition   308
 of derivation
  existential specification   71
  rules for formulae   61
  rules of inference   52-5, 69
  rules of simplification   49
Russell's paradox   100

saddleback search, derivation of   418
schema   53, 70
scope, of quantifier   61
scope rule   62
Scott   281
screen interaction   540
search problems   200
search specification   196, 229
searching   573
second coordinate   105
secondary decomposition rule   307
secondary specification   188, 206
selection   265
selection sort   449, 550
 derivation of   451
selective composition   268
semantics, of programs   250
sentence   149
sentential connectives   33
sentinel   192-3
sequence   105, 144, 265
sequence specification   158
sequential composition   265
sequential file update   151, 513
sequential problems   527
set   30
 empty   96
set cardinality   97
set difference   99, 178, 180
set equality   105, 178
set inclusion   178
sets, inductive specification   172
set intersection   98, 107, 178
set laws   101
set membership   93, 178
set operations   97, 102, 107, 108
 specification of   104
set of ordered pairs   115
set representation   93

set specification   179
set of states   110
set theory   92
set transformations   101
set union   97, 107, 178
sift   595
simple loops   345
simple pattern match   470
simple pattern search   472
simple pivot partitioning   424
simplicity   19
simplification, law of   45
simplification rules   49-50
sort   153
sort-check   572
sorting   21, 282
sorting algorithms, classes of   451
sorting by insertion   450
sorting by partitioning   450
sorting by selection   449
sorting specification   20, 195
specification   27, 64, 86, 89, 91, 116, 129,
        146
    array properties   241
    completion of   238
    convention   64
    explicitivity of   329
    extensional   95
    of gcd   190
    interpretation of   227
    linear search   201
    loop invariants   207
    for maximum   191
    methods   27
    of permutation   132
    positional   229
    of postconditions   195
    precision of   194
    of programs   187
    of quotient/remainder   190
    search   196, 229
    sequence maximum   64
    of set operations   102
    of sets   97, 179
    sorting   195
    strength of   293, 326
    stronger   196, 326
    top-down description   200
    transformation   30, 508
        complement extension   302
        comprehensive   95
        constant replacement   297
        expression replacement   298
        image extension   300

    splitting a variable   299
    transformations   446, 451
    using EBNF   184
    using normal language   28
    using programming language constructs
        28
    using quantifiers   240
specifier
    counting   68
    index maximization   68
    index minimization   68
    maximising   68
    minimizing   69
    product   67
    summation   66
specifier notation   66
specifiers   66
splitting a relation   463
splitting a variable   299
state   110
    defining predicate of   249
state model   8, 247
state-space   111, 248, 250, 283, 302
state-space extension   296, 297, 312
statements   33, 150
states, sets of   110
stepwise refinement   12, 15, 311, 317, 493
stores-movement problem   506, 583
Strachey   281
straight pivot partitioning   426
strategies for problem-solving   325
strength of loop invariant   210
strength of predicates   111, 242
strength of specifications   326
strengthening a postcondition   335
strengthening a precondition   333
string   150
string comparison   468
string searching   472
stronger postcondition   435
strongest precondition   14
strongest predicate   111
structural induction   174
    principle of   174
structural simplification, principle of   602
structure clashes   602, 610
style   532
sub-goal   314, 321, 498
sub-goal identification   262
sub-problem
    identification   328
    initialization   331
sub-problems, generation of   330

subbags   141
subset   94, 117
substitution, rule of   50
subtractive variants   221
successor function   132
sum, of bags   142
summation   77-78
    over empty range   65
    identity   66
    specifier   66
summing an array   210
    proof of   279
summing array elements   548
superset   94, 100
Suppes, P.   92
surjective   182
surjective function   126
swap   151, 248, 549, 595
    semantics of   266
syllogism   53
symbolization, of logic formulae   60
symmetric   94, 122
symmetric difference   103
    of sets   99
symmetric relation   114
synchronization, of loops   602
syntactic category   146
syntax   145, 149
    of well-formed formulae   61
synthetic propositions   43
systematic decomposition   312

tail recursion   155, 464
tautological equivalence   42
tautological implication   42, 52
tautologies, table of   44
tautology   41, 111
TDSD   155, 507
telegrams analysis problem   520
term   55, 56
terminal symbols   146
termination   277
    forced   192
termination condition   225
termination of loops   571
ternary relation   113
tertiary decomposition rule   308
text
    deletion from   483
    insertion in   483
    replacement in   484
text editing   483
text formatting   484, 614
textual substitution   255

theory of bags   139
theory of inference   52, 81
there exists   59
top-down   203
top-down design   294, 311, 325
total functions   125, 139
transaction processing   513
transactions   155
transformation   30, 508
    complement extension   303
    constant replacement   298
    expression replacement   299
    image extension   302
    range extension   304
    of specifications   328
    splitting a variable   299
transformation for insertion   450
transformation for partitioning   450
transformation for selection   449
transformations   302, 446
    on sets   101
transitive inclusion   94
transitive laws   44
transitive relation   114
tree, binary   122, 164, 174, 175
tree relations   119
tri-partitioning   442
truth table   34
    conjunction   35
    disjunction   35
    equivalence   39
    implication   39
    negation   34
    rows in   42
Turski, W.   554
two-dimensional search
    derivation of   407
two-place predicate   57
two-squares sum   386
two-way merge   511
type   116

under-initialization   554
under-iteration   572
undirected graph   122
union   109
    of bags   145
    of sets   97, 102, 107
universal generalization   72
universal instantiation   70
universal quantification   58, 197, 203
    definition   65
universal quantifier   58
universal relation   118

universal specification   69-70
universe   190
unordered pairs   103, 104

validity of arguments   51
value   110
variable   55, 56, 60, 211, 549, 551
    bound   62
    bounds   190
    free   62
variable restriction rule   63
variant
    additive   224
    subtractive   221
variant condition   226
variant function   188, 219, 220, 225
    derivation of   219
Venn diagram   97, 108
vertex   119

weakening a postcondition   333, 365
weaker postcondition   431
weaker sub-goal   498
weakest precondition   12, 18, 24, 32, 148,
    250-265, 312
    for assignment   255
    calculation of   259, 260

calculations   6, 12, 19, 320, 464
command identification   262
computation of   254
concept   319
definition of   251
dependent   257
empty   257
geometric interpretation   255
guard identification   260
for initialization   303
properties of   251
semantics of   256
sequential composition   265
sub-goals   262
weakest predicate   111
well-formed formula   60, 70, 95
    rules for   61
well-formed formula syntax   61
WHILE loop   153
Whitehead, A.N.   19, 531, 532
Wirth, N.   497, 595, 596
Wirth-Dijkstra strategy   317
wp(DO, R)   276
wp(IF, R)   272

XOR   103